American Criminal Courts

American Criminal Courts

Legal Process and Social Context

Casey Welch

Department of Social Sciences,
Flager College

and

John Randolph Fuller

Department of Criminology,
University of West Georgia

AMSTERDAM • BOSTON • HEIDELBERG • LONDON
NEW YORK • OXFORD • PARIS • SAN DIEGO
SAN FRANCISCO • SINGAPORE • SYDNEY • TOKYO
Anderson Publishing is an imprint of Elsevier

Acquiring Editor: Shirley Decker-Lucke
Development Editor: Gregory Chalson
Project Manager: Julia Haynes
Designer: Russell Purdy

Anderson Publishing is an imprint of Elsevier
225 Wyman Street, Waltham, MA 02451, USA

Library of Congress Cataloging-in-Publication Data
A catalogue record for this book is available from the Library of Congress

British Library Cataloguing-in-Publication Data
A catalogue record for this book is available from the British Library

ISBN: 978-1-4557-2599-1

Printed in Canada

14 15 16   10 9 8 7 6 5 4 3 2 1

Contents

Part 1 Formal Social Control

Acknowledgments and Dedications

Casey Welch

I dedicate this book to my wife Laurel Lee Welch, who has always been supportive of large undertakings, and our friend Glenn Coffey, who as a former prosecutor, a long-time Sociology and Criminology Professor, and a former department colleague, has debated with me the finer points of law and has greatly sharpened my analysis of the legal system. I doubt this project would have even gotten started without the two of them blowing wind into my sails. I would also like to acknowledge two professors and friends who have shaped my criminological outlook, Dr. David Bordua and Dr. Lonn Lanza-Kaduce, as well as the insights of M. Casey Condon, Judge Richard Poland, and Walter Eugene White. I extend my gratitude to several students who provided research assistance on the early chapters, including Kenneth Roach, Michelle Lewis, Chemal Cruz, Tristan Joynt, and Michael Nezbeth. My work on this book was partially supported by the Kahler Grant from Flagler College. Finally, I am in deep appreciation of the frank and thorough feedback from the many reviewers, including Sara Jane Phillips, Glenn S. Coffey, and Jacqueline Ward Talevi.

John Randolph Fuller

I wish to dedicate this book to Amy Hembree. Without her support, hard work, and keen insights this book would not have been possible. I am grateful for the support of my colleagues David Jenks, Catherine Jenks, Juyoung Song, Mike Johnson, Kelly Christopher, Laura Lutgen, and Richard Lemke. Additionally, Dean N. Jane McCandless has been a constant source of support for over 20 years. I am grateful for the confidence and patience afforded to us by the good people at Anderson Publishing. Shirley Decker-Lucke, Gregory Carlson, and Mickey and Susan Braswell are each appreciated for their support and contributions in making this book better.

Preface

Students hear about court cases from every facet of media. Famous actors getting convicted for driving under the influence (DUI), defendants being sentenced to years in prison for seemingly minor offenses, and guilty-looking defendants getting released because of procedural rules. With years of experience working in the justice system and teaching and researching it, we decided to team up in order to help people understand the formal structure of the criminal courts as well as the actual operations and decision-making within courts. Using a clear writing style that avoids unnecessary jargon or cultural references that readers may not know, this book introduces the reader to the structure of U.S. courts, the social context that shapes the courts, and the real humans who make legal decisions every day in criminal courts.

Students often, and quite reasonably, complain that textbooks jump from one topic to the next. To correct this common problem, we organize our book around three themes, which allows each chapter to be connected and build toward the later chapters:

1. courts have stable principles but are dynamic and adaptive to societal changes;
2. the framework of courts is a balance between crime control and due process mandates;
3. decision-making is influenced by an array of internal and external pressures, from rules of legal reasoning to media coverage and elections.

The book provides a condensed description of the European and U.S. history out of which modern courts emerged. This illustrates the wide array of social-control mechanisms and helps the reader understand why nations have developed unique families of law and comparative court systems. The historical foundation also provides an explanation of the ideals of justice embodied in the courts, particularly those of crime control and due process. Rather than present these as opposites that one must favor, we show that they are both involved in every stage of the court process.

By the time the reader gets to the chapters that detail the pretrial and trial stages, he or she already has an understanding of the historical context and legal principles of the court and is familiar with empirical research on legal decision-making. They'll know why the attorneys and judges do what they do, and the court process will actually make some sense rather than be a mysterious maze. They'll understand, for instance, that judges appoint attorneys to indigent defendants because of the legal principle embodied in the Sixth Amendment. They'll understand the structure of legal reasoning and the process of case assessment. For instance, when a prosecutor dismisses a case or pleas it down, they'll understand that caseload, quality of evidence, and other cues that led to that decision. This book brings to life how lawyers and judges go about making the many decisions required of them everyday. They'll not only know the basic legal rules and stages but also know the decisions that carry cases from one stage to the next. We want the students to not only learn about the court system but also feel what it's like to work in the U.S. courts and to handle criminal cases.

In the process of learning about the stages of the criminal court process and the decision-making involved, the reader will also learn other essential elements of the courts, such as:

- the many facets of jurisdiction, including state and federal, civil and criminal, and original and appellate;
- the elements of a crime;
- the growing diversity of courts, including diversion to alternative courts and other types of specialized courts.

This book can be used in online and brick-and-mortar courses, and in various departments, including criminal justice and criminology, political science, sociology, and pre-law. It assumes the reader has no prior coursework or experience with the court system. We provide concise explanations of the overall criminal justice system and criminal law, which serve as an introduction to the novice and a brief review for those who have completed foundational courses. The extensive supplements also add to the versatility of this book.

FEATURES AND SUPPLEMENTS

Every chapter enhances its coverage of content with the use of various discussion boxes. These include the following types of boxes:

- Focus on Discretion
- Landmark Due-Process Cases
- Courts in the Media
- Court Procedures
- Careers in the Court

Supplements for the students and professors include:

- Instructor's Resource CD
  - PowerPoint for each chapter
  - Test bank
  - Additional Supreme Court summaries and contemporary criminal cases
  - Biographies of famous jurists
  - Discussion questions
  - Class projects and assignments
- Student companion Web site
  - Learning objectives
  - Chapter summaries
  - Key terms
  - Study guides
  - Self-quizzes
  - Web-based exercises
  - Links to court decisions
  - Related links for research
- Online video that accompanies each chapter, which offers a summary of the chapter and a discussion of a controversial issue related to the chapter.

Online Instructor and Student Resources

Thank you for selecting Anderson Publishing's *American Criminal Courts: Legal Process and Social Context*. To complement the learning experience, we have provided a number of online tools to accompany this edition. Two distinct packages of interactive resources are available: one for instructors and one for students.

Please consult your local sales representative with any additional questions. You may also e-mail the Academic Sales Team at textbook@elsevier.com.

For the Instructor

Qualified adopters and instructors can access valuable material for free by registering at: http://textbooks.elsevier.com/web/manuals.aspx?isbn = 9781455725991.

- **Test Bank** Compose, customize, and deliver exams using an online assessment package in a free Windows-based authoring tool that makes it easy to build tests using the unique multiple choice and true or false questions created for *American Criminal Courts: Legal Process and Social Context*. What's more, this authoring tool allows you to export customized exams directly to Blackboard, WebCT, eCollege, Angel, and other leading systems. All test bank files are also conveniently offered in Word format.
- **PowerPoint Lecture Slides** Reinforce key topics with focused PowerPoints, which provide a perfect visual outline with which to augment your lecture. Each individual book chapter has its own dedicated slideshow.
- **Lesson Plans** Design your course around customized lesson plans. Each individual lesson plan acts as separate syllabi containing content synopses, key terms, directions to supplementary Web sites, and more open-ended critical thinking questions designed to spur class discussion. These lesson plans also delineate and connect chapter-based learning objectives to specific teaching resources, making it easy to catalog the resources at your disposal.

For the Student

Students can access all the resources below by simply following this link: http://www.elsevierdirect.com/v2/companion.jsp?ISBN = 9781455725991.

- **Introductory Videos** Each chapter is equipped with its own video in which the authors discuss key points and objectives.
- **Self-Assessment Question Bank** Enhance review and study sessions with the help of this online self-quizzing asset. Each question is presented in an interactive format that allows for immediate feedback.
- **Case Studies** Apply what is on the page to the world beyond with the help of topic-specific case studies, each designed to turn theory into practice and followed by three interactive scenario-based questions that allow for immediate feedback.

The United States has many laws to limit government abuse of power. Even though the criminal justice process is difficult, there is some effort to protect an individual's constitutional rights.

CHAPTER 1

Principles and Decision-Making in U.S. Criminal Courts

KEY TERMS

agents of the state
bureaucracies
courtroom workgroup
criminal procedure
due process
due-process provisions
executive orders

external ecology
internal ecology
judicial review
judiciary
jurisdiction
justiciability
legal merits

legal principles
legal procedures
legal reality
legal reasoning
legal rules
mandatory minimum
  laws

CONTENTS

Learning Objectives

After reading this chapter, you should be able to:

1. Discuss rule of law.
2. Tell why the study of criminal courts is important.
3. Define legal principles.
4. Explain how and why courts change over time.
5. Explain the two goals of the criminal courts.
6. Explain the crime control goal of the courts.
7. Define due process.
8. Explain legal reasoning and how it relates to legal principles.
9. Define internal ecology and tell why it is important.
10. Define external ecology and tell why it is important.

Imagine that you and a friend are leaving a movie theater in Boston, Massachusetts. It is summer, so you decide to go for an evening walk. Four blocks later you are stopped by two police officers who question you about a pipe bomb found in a trash can. You deny all knowledge of the incident. But

3

because you are walking down an empty street at night less than a block from the scene, because neither of you live in the city, and because you have a cell phone in your pocket that looks suspicious because it is damaged and does not work, they arrest both of you and put you in separate police cars. Before questioning you further, one of the officers informs you that you have certain rights, including the right to stop talking and the right to a defense attorney.

After the police book you the next day, the prosecutor reviews the police work and evidence and decides the case has some merit. You insist on an attorney. After they establish that you are impoverished, one is assigned to your case. With the attorney at your side, you go through several court stages. At the initial appearance, you hear the preliminary charges against you, and the judge agrees with the prosecutor that there is enough evidence, or probable cause, to detain you and continue the case. Later that week you have a bail hearing, and because the case is a potential domestic terrorism case, the prosecutor asks the judge to deny you bail. The judge agrees with the prosecutor and rules that you must remain in jail. The grand jury agrees with the prosecutor and issues an indictment, and the formal charges against you are read at the arraignment.

The prosecutor continues to gather evidence as well as testimonies at discovery depositions. Through a successful motion for discovery, your attorney gets copies of evidence from the prosecutor. She files a motion for a direct verdict to dismiss the case because of inadequate evidence and a motion to suppress the cell phone evidence arguing that the police had no right to search your jacket. The judge denies both. Several times over weeks of pretrial hearings, the prosecutor asks you to plead guilty to a lesser charge, illegal use of explosives, rather than face the more serious charge of conspiracy to commit terrorism. You maintain your innocence and refuse this negotiated plea offer.

Your case moves to trial after a couple of months. The judge and prosecutor call a pretrial settlement conference to reoffer the negotiated plea. You refuse. The attorneys participate in *voir dire* to select the jurors. At trial, the attorneys give their opening statements, question and cross-examine witnesses, present evidence, present more motions to the court, then give final arguments. The jury, a group of ordinary citizens with no special training in law, deliberate on the evidence. They return a not guilty verdict, the same verdict your friend received a couple of days earlier.

THE RULE OF LAW

Courts are essential to maintaining the rule of law that governs people and organizations fairly and equally. No individuals or groups should be subject to arbitrary government power, and no person is above the law.

[handwritten margin note: courts are always guided by the idea of innocence unless proven]

Courts hold a pivotal position in democratic governments: they monitor the government to ensure that it adheres to constitutional rules, respects the principles of justice, and protects the rights of people within its borders. Courts also convict and sentence people for breaking the criminal law. These are the due process and crime control goals of the court, and courts pursue both every day.

Courts adapt to changing social conditions, but they do not change at the whim of a president or governor. They are instead grounded by a set of enduring legal principles such as the presumption of innocence. When attorneys and judges apply the law to people accused of crime, their decisions are shaped by those goals and legal principles. A lawyer or judge cannot choose to be a "crime control" gal or "due process" guy, because their decisions are shaped by both mandates. Nor can they prosecute a case or sentence someone however they see fit. They are constrained by legal procedures and influenced by the internal operations of the court and external pressures, such as elections and the media.

Recall the opening scenario. Even though you suffered during the court process, your case was reviewed many times, and there was some effort to protect your constitutional rights. The attorneys and judges reviewed the police work; your defense attorney reviewed and challenged the prosecutor's work; and the grand jury and trial jury reviewed the work of the police and prosecutor. Your case could have been filtered out of the justice system at any time, from the police deciding there was not enough evidence to the judge dismissing the case. Now imagine two people leaving a theater in Iran. One of them is Kouhyar Goudarzi, an active member for the Committee of Human Rights in Iran. He is arrested but not informed of any rights. He is not provided an attorney, and his family does not know where he is taken. His fate is left to the whims of the government [1].

The difference in these two cases hinges largely on the power of the court systems to review the other branches of government. Iran's courts are too weak to constrain the rest of the government. The United States has many laws to limit government abuse of power. The laws alone, however, are not enough to deter abuses by police and prosecutors or to correct abuses once they occur. It is the court system that continuously reviews the government's work to ensure that the police and prosecutor do not violate the laws of procedure, and it is the court system that often throws out cases that are weak or involve abuse.

What distinguishes the U.S. legal system is not the people, resources, or hierarchy of courts. These are common across the world. Rather, it is the legal principles such as due process and the rules derived from them, the adversarial process that enforces these rules, judicial oversight and review, and the tendency of other branches to respect the courts' rulings. All these rules and court stages may seem cumbersome, but they serve as a barrier between individual rights and arbitrary government power [2]. As Harvard Law Professor Mary Glendon wrote in 1994, "Procedure implies structures and rules that endure beyond the controversies of the moment, that permit men and women to make reliable plans, that keep arbitrary discretion at bay" [3].

IMPORTANCE OF STUDYING CRIMINAL COURTS

The criminal courts are a cornerstone of the U.S. criminal justice system. Criminologists, political scientists, and legal philosophers study them. Thousands of lawyers deal with them every day. They influence everyone working in the criminal justice field, from police officers to paralegals to correctional officers. They affect millions of victims and suspects every year. The courts have **judicial lawmaking powers**, which are decisions that interpret statutes and the Constitution, establish legal principles, and influence later cases. Understanding the criminal courts is essential to understanding government power and succeeding in any occupation within the criminal justice system.

Most people have some knowledge of the court system from television, movies, or personal experience, and people reading a book about the criminal courts probably already have an even better understanding than the general public. Nonetheless, let's take measure of our starting knowledge.

Essay Quote →

At any given moment, the criminal court system may appear to operate like a predictable factory assembly line, handling every case in the same manner with no changes in procedure. In fact, however, the court system deals with peculiar situations daily, adapts to changing social conditions, and is shaped by legal actors who are motivated by many factors. This does not mean the courts are capricious and change dramatically depending on the mood of the lawyers and judges. Reality lies between the rigid factory model and the arbitrary justice model. Three themes in the study of courts illuminate this complex relationship between predictability and change.

First, U.S. law is based on steady principles, such as **precedent** (a legal decision that is cited as a rule to resolve similar legal questions in later cases), yet changes along with society. U.S. law is dynamic, not static. Second, the legal principles and procedures emerge within a tension between state power and individual rights, or what is commonly characterized as crime control and due process. Third, the day-to-day enforcement of law in the criminal courts is performed by thousands of individuals who simultaneously conform to patterns of behavior and vary in their actions. Many social structures—from procedural laws to organizational resources to political pressures—influence their decisions. Before explaining each theme, let's situate the courts within the larger criminal justice system.

OVERVIEW OF THE CRIMINAL JUSTICE SYSTEM

The criminal justice system is composed of four components—law, police, courts, and corrections—each one being a system within itself. A system refers to multiple parts that work toward some goal or task and are interdependent. In the case of the criminal justice system, this system is instrumental, meaning that it is designed to achieve clearly specified goals, namely the enforcement of **substantive laws** that prohibit certain activities (such as burglary or fraud) while adhering to **procedural laws** which constrain and direct the conduct of the agents of the state when they are processing a case.

As you look over the components in Focus on Discretion, keep in mind your evening in Boston. In that hypothetical case, you were subjected to all four components of the criminal justice system, and therefore all three branches of the government. The legislative branch wrote the laws that criminalized bomb-use by civilians. The executive branch, which controls the police, enforced the law and arrested you. You were detained in a correctional facility operated by the executive branch. And, fortunately for you, a separate branch of government, the judicial branch, operates the courts and determined that the police and prosecutor did not gather enough evidence to establish that you were guilty beyond a reasonable doubt.

[handwritten margin notes:]
Substantive
— Laws against
crime

Procedural
— Law shapening
the conduct
of agents

FOCUS ON DISCRETION

Relationship and Duties of the Four Components of the Criminal Justice System

None of the four components of the criminal justice system—law, courts, police, and corrections—could operate without the others (see Figure 1a). The U.S. legal system operates under the principle of *nullum crimen sine lege* ("no crime without law"). Even though law is developed in state capitols and Washington, D.C., far from the streets where most arrests are made, law is both the foundation of the criminal justice system and the boundary around it. It defines certain behaviors as crime. Criminal justice workers are not supposed to take action against a person unless that person is suspected of violating a criminal statute. Merely being immoral or offensive should not lead to an arrest, conviction, or punishment in the United States.

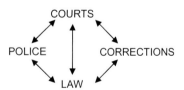

FIGURE 1A

The four subcomponents also reflect the checks-and-balances laid out in the U.S. Constitution. Checks-and-balances refer to the government structure where power is divided between three branches of government: the legislative, executive, and judicial. Congress writes the laws. The police, who work under the president or a governor, enforce the laws. The courts review the actions of the other two branches and determine if the suspects are guilty. This separation of powers inhibits any part of the government from getting too strong and thus prevents the government from abusing the rights of individuals.

THEME 1: STEADY PRINCIPLES AND CONTEXTUALIZED CHANGES

Analysis of the court system, or **judiciary**, does not end with identifying it as one of the four components of the larger criminal justice system. We must also understand how the judiciary behaves. On an institutional level, courts are stable, yet adaptive. Legal principles and criminal justice system goals provide a steady framework. The courts do not change with every new president or governor. On the contrary, some of the principles that hold the court together are centuries old. Yet the courts are a social construction, meaning their structure is not inevitable or immutable but rather was created over the course of history. This means the court system also adapts and changes as the large social context of values, technology, and priorities change. As legal scholar Roscoe Pound said, "The law must be stable, but it must not stand still."

Legal Principles as a Source of Stability

Since the ratification of the Constitution in 1788 and the creation of an independent court system in every state, the criminal courts have enjoyed a stability not seen in the judiciary of most other nations. The foundations of the court do not change with new presidents, wars, disasters, or economic turbulence. Change in courts is generally gradual and always narrow in scope [4]. In the economic market, a company like Wal-Mart can begin in 1972 and within 30 years radically alter the grocery store industry and systems of production and trade that supply them. The big box store is new, but already common. In jurisprudence, however, it took nearly a century to get from the end of the Civil War and the passage of Fourteenth Amendment, which granted due process to everyone, to the Supreme Court ruling in the *Brown* case that segregation in schools was a violation of the Fourteenth Amendment [5]. But even that change did not alter the overall operations of the courts. It profoundly, but narrowly, changed the way courts treat race discrimination cases.

This internal framework of legal principles guides and constrains criminal justice system procedures. Some of these principles and practices are codified in the Constitution, whereas others are established in statutes and court rulings. **Legal principles**, or general principles of law, are the ideals and imperatives that serve as the basis for legal thinking and guide legal decision-making. These principles are so widely revered that they are considered truths or axioms that do not need to be proved or defended in court [6]. For instance, no one in the court would argue against the principle of "innocent until proven guilty" or feel the need to defend the ideal of due process (even if they have to argue about its specifics).

Principles also serve as the logic and limits for the development of other laws. The principle of personal privacy, for instance, was why the Supreme Court struck down a federal effort to give police the power to monitor suspects using a GPS device without a warrant [7]. Certain legal principles, such as due process and precedent, encompass the entire judiciary and thus apply to all courts. Other principles are more relevant for particular types of courts. For instance, *parens patriae* (the principle that the government has the duty to act as guardian of people who cannot effectively take care of themselves) is much more influential in juvenile court than in criminal court [8]. Legislatures and courts create **legal rules**, or the specific laws and procedures derived from foundational legal principles. **Legal procedures** refer to rules that specify how lawyers and judges are to proceed when enforcing substantive criminal law. Court procedures define the basic principles within the judiciary that are always in force, regardless of who is president and what party controls Congress.

COURT PROCEDURES

Ideals that Constrain and Guide the U.S. Criminal Court System

Court Structure
Constitutional system
Article VI, section 2 establishes that the Constitution is the "supreme law of the land." No laws or government actions are allowed to violate the Federal constitution.

Federalism
As created by Article III and Amendment X of the U.S. Constitution, the federal and state governments have separate lawmaking powers, police, and courts.

Jurisdiction and hierarchy of courts
Courts specialize in certain types of cases. The type of case will determine which court hears it. This includes courts for different geographic regions, for criminal trials versus civil trials, and for appeals versus trials.

Court Duties
Judicial independence and judicial review
The judiciary is an independent branch of government and is therefore empowered with judicial review, which is when the courts evaluate the constitutionality of executive branch actions and legislative branch actions [9].

Judicial restraint
Judges enforce only written laws, usually avoid overturning laws or earlier decisions, and minimize allowing personal views to affect rulings.

Court Procedure
Adversary system
The prosecutor and defense attorney have competing, or adversarial, goals. The prosecutor exerts state power by trying to prove that the defendant is guilty. The defense works to acquit the

defendant, which constrains arbitrary government power by forcing the prosecutor to present a strong case before depriving someone of liberties.

Elements of a crime
In most cases, prosecutors must establish that the defendant intended to break the law and actually committed the act that caused harm.

Due process
Individuals have a right to be treated fairly by the government, and the government must adhere to rules while prosecuting a case. Specific rights under this broad principle include being informed of the charges, having the right to a defense, having a public jury trial, and receiving proportional punishment if convicted.

Presumption of innocence
A fundamental due-process right that requires that a suspect be treated as though innocent until convicted.

Burden of proof and reasonable doubt
For the government to convict the defendant, the prosecutor must present such good evidence as to override the presumption of innocence and prove guilt beyond a reasonable doubt. Mere accusations or weak evidence are not adequate proof to overcome reasonable doubt. Police are bound by lower burdens of proof, such as having "probable cause" to get a warrant.

Appeals
If rights were allegedly violated, a defendant can ask a higher court to review the case.

Precedent
Rulings in a current case must conform to rulings in similar previous cases.

The pillars of the court system stand in stark contrast with ancient legal systems because the stability of the principles allows for some predictability and fairness in the proceedings. In the past, as well in some nations today, trials were held in secret; people were charged with vague offenses such as heresy; and suspects were not allowed to speak in their own defense. For example, during New England's Salem witch trials of the 1690s, "...all of the executions relied heavily on standards of evidence and trial procedures that were controversial even at the time," such as hearsay and unreliable accusations. "The effects of the Salem Village witch trials were devastating: 141 people imprisoned, 19 people executed, and two more died from other causes directly related to the investigations" [10]. The combined effect of these principles is to reduce the chances of miscarriages of justice seen in the witch trials, totalitarian nations around the world, and even today in some U.S. courts.

Changes in the Courts
Steady principles do not create a fossilized judiciary. The court system is dynamic, meaning it changes over time as culture changes and varies when comparing one jurisdiction to another.

Change happens on institutional and organizational levels. **Institutional change, which is also called systemic or structural change, occurs when a change pervades the entire legal system** [11]. This involves a shift in the legal principles and legal norms throughout the court system. An example is the expansion of due-process rights. The constitutional principle of due process originally applied only to the federal courts, but because of the Fourteenth Amendment and court interpretations of it, due process now constrains every court in the nation. For instance, an impoverished suspect is entitled to an attorney in a felony trial no matter what state an offense occurs in. Another example of institutional change is the 1899 establishment of juvenile justice courts which resulted in special legal rules and procedures for young suspects [12].

Perhaps the most striking examples of institutional change are when the Supreme Court reverses its own decision. For instance, in *Brown v. Board of Education of Topeka Kansas*, the Court ruled that having separate facilities for different racial groups was unequal and therefore a violation of the Constitution [13]. This case was ruled in the 1950s, at a time when people were pushing for more equality. However, to come to this ruling, the Court had to reject its 1896 ruling in *Plessy v. Ferguson* which set forth that separate facilities do not violate the constitution as long as the facilities were similar [14]. *Plessy* was decided during a period of Jim Crow segregation, when laws in many states, especially southern states, were used to exclude black citizens and other minorities from facilities used by whites.

Other institutional changes include the introduction of new laws and changes in existing laws. Over the past couple of decades, for example, states and the federal government have created new laws regarding drugs, rape, and child abuse, and have made the penalties more severe. Thirteen states have passed laws regulating *salvia divinorum*, a plant that can be used to make a hallucinatory drug [15]. Florida and Louisiana have also banned "bath salts," which create an intense high and are sold under names such as "Vanilla Sky," "Ivory Wave," and "White Rush" [16]. Other states are moving toward controlling these drugs. Changes in rape and child abuse laws occurred because cultural attitudes changed. Women's rights were advanced from the 1960s to 1980s; researchers published articles and books on the extent and long-term harm of child abuse; and organizations mobilized the public and political leaders to address these social problems. Sometimes laws change because new technologies create new problems, such as "cyberbullying" [17].

Organizational change occurs within the operations of a specific court system or courthouse and involves changes in resources, personnel, fees, rules for handling cases, and so on. For instance, in November 2008, Matt Shirk was elected to run the public defender's office in Florida's Fourth Judicial Circuit. Endorsed by the Fraternal Order of Police and the district attorney,

Shirk's first action when taking office was to fire the 10 criminal defense attorneys and three administrators with the most legal experience. This weakened the public defender's office ability to defend suspects and therefore altered the operations of criminal courts in that area [18]. We will look at other examples and effects of organizational change in Chapter 5.

Variation in law and court operations occurs not only over time but also when comparing one **jurisdiction**—the legal authority of a court to hear and rule on a particular case—to another. For instance, if someone burglarizes a house in California and is caught in California, the case will not be tried in a Nevada courtroom. This is important because the laws in each state vary. For example, after the Supreme Court knocked down the Jim Crow laws of southern states, those states introduced punitive sentences in juvenile law that disproportionately impacted Blacks. In other words, states with an inclination toward segregation have been able to use the criminal law as a way to suppress and segregate a minority population [19]. Therefore, the conduct that leads to an arrest and the cases that go to trial will depend on the state a person is in.

THEME 2: STATE POWER AND INDIVIDUAL RIGHTS

In all U.S. courts, two connected goals shape the criminal law and courtroom activities: exertion of state power and protection of individual rights. One of the goals of state power is supposed to be the reduction of crime. In short, the government has the job of crime control and to accomplish that it must exert its power over the people [20]. The federal and state governments enact laws, hire police, fund courts, and build jails and prisons with the goal of deterring crime and apprehending and punishing offenders.

However, the nation's government is a democracy, not a dictatorship, and that democracy is founded on principles of equality and fairness. To ensure that the government does not expand its powers too much and to ensure that the law is fair, the government itself put into the Constitution and continues to enact provisions that limit the government. These are called the **due-process provisions**, the legal principles, laws, and criminal justice system rules that protect the rights of individuals who are being processed by the government and that constrain arbitrary or excessive government power.

Crime control and due process are not competing goals but two objectives that together form the framework of the criminal court system (Figure 1.1). They have a dialectical relationship, meaning they exist in a constant state of tension but cannot exist without both being present. If a government pursued crime control with all its power but had no due-process provisions that limited its power, it would be a dictatorship. Of course, if all the government did was protect individual rights, it would fail in its goal to reduce crime.

These two goals sometimes contradict each other and often lead to courtroom procedures that confuse and aggravate observers of the court. However, both goals are necessary in a democratic society. Take, for instance, your arrest in the opening scene. The officer, who works for the government, exerted state power over you in order to solve a criminal offense. At the same time, though, she questioned you without torturing you; she wore a badge that indicated her name so you could identify her; she informed you of some of your rights when arresting you; and she took you to the police station where your case was reviewed by someone else. All of these are due-process constraints, and most of the time criminal justice workers conform to these while working to control people.

But imagine if the officer had no constraints on her crime-solving efforts. She could beat a confession out of you and threaten to harm your family, search your apartment without a warrant, refuse to let you speak to an attorney, or lock you up in a jail without ever telling you why. This is not a justice system many Americans would support. In fact, most people in the United States support due-process rights even for terrorists [21]. The people of this nation value a balance between security and individual rights.

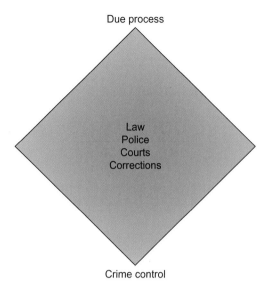

FIGURE 1.1

Crime control and due process serve as the boundaries of all four components of the criminal justice system.

Crime Control: The Exertion of State Power

Crime control involves any efforts by the government to reduce crime, including the state and federal governments passing more criminal laws, hiring more police, expanding court houses, building more prisons, offering reentry programs, and manipulating public attitudes. These are all public policies or government actions aimed at achieving specific goals [22]. Public policies are created and carried out by lawmakers, police, judges, and correctional officers, all of whom are **agents of the state**, meaning simply that they work for the state and exert the state's power when enforcing the law. Taken together, **public policy**—government efforts to achieve social goals—and agents of the state enable the government to control more people. This is not to say the government is an evil monster taking over our lives. On the contrary, most Americans support crime control policies, although the policies and level of support shift over time [23].

Examples of expanding crime control laws abound, such as those concerning child pornography, drugs, and other activities. Until relatively recently, no federal laws criminalized child pornography, but now these have been added to the already-existing state laws that prohibit it [24]. The same type of expansion of federal criminal law was seen earlier in the twentieth century as the federal government began to criminalize drug use, possession, manufacturing, and sales [25]. Other examples of behaviors that only recently have been criminalized on the federal or state level include driving while intoxicated, failure to wear a seatbelt, sending money to an organization that the government labels a terrorist group, and, in a growing number of states, watching or videotaping the police as they question a person or make an arrest. Over the past 70 years, the United States has seen a tremendous increase in the number of behaviors prohibited by law. These laws greatly expand the array of lawful reasons for which police can arrest someone. That is, they increase the number of people subject to arrest.

At other times, the government amends existing laws. This happens often when legislatures increase the penalty for criminal offenses. **Three-strikes laws**—which mandate a lengthy sentence on the third offense—and **mandatory minimum** laws—which mandate sentence lengths based on the type of offense—were popularized in the 1980s as get-tough on crime policies. Until recent years, these enhanced sentences were supported by most voters, and many politicians won elections in part because they advocated these [26]. A similar tough-on-crime policy has been the elimination of **parole**, which allows an inmate to be released early for good behavior or a demonstration of rehabilitative success [27]. In addition to more and harsher laws, the number of police in the United States continuously increases. The United States currently has approximately 900,000 state police officers [28]. With a single law in 1994, President Clinton dedicated over 8 billion dollars to hire 100,000 new police officers [29] .

As a result of more behaviors being criminalized, more police officers being hired, prosecutors' offices being expanded, judges being forced to issue long prison sentences, and states reducing or eliminating parole, the adult jail and prison population in 2009 (the most recent data available) is over 2.28 million [30]. This is approximately a 400 percent increase in the incarcerated population since 1980. The United States has the largest incarcerated population in the world and the highest incarceration rate. In addition to this prison population, more than 5 million people are serving **probation** (a sentence in which a convicted person stays in the community as long as he or she follows court-ordered conditions) and parole, plus millions more are in court-supervised diversionary programs, such as drug rehabilitation. Since 1980, correctional budgets have nearly quadrupled, and the overall criminal justice budget has increased by 270 percent [30] (Photo 1.1).

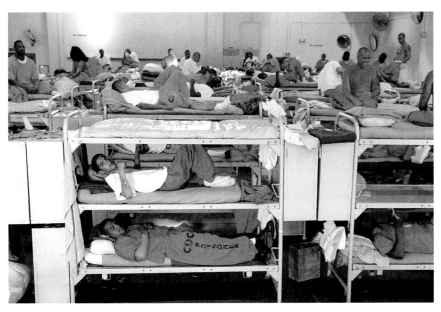

PHOTO 1.1
The U.S. incarcerated population has increased about 400 percent since 1980. Here, inmates live in crowded conditions at California State Prison in Los Angeles. Nearly 30 percent of the inmates are third-strike offenders.

Each crime control policy is an expansion of state power. Yet as scholar Vanessa Barker points out, public opinion over the past 40 years has indicated general support for this increase in police forces and incarceration rates [23]. Although public attitude is starting to shift toward supporting alternatives to incarceration such as rehabilitation, there is still a high rate of fear of crime and strong condemnation of behaviors such as drug use [31]. Fear of crime influences many policies, including such things as where to locate rehabilitation facilities. In southwest Atlanta, for instance, residents filed complaints with the city when a transitional home opened in their neighborhood [32].

Crime control efforts, however, are not solely arresting more people and incarcerating them for longer periods. **Rehabilitation and reentry programs**— plans that aim to improve offenders and prepare them for self-sufficient and law-abiding lives—are also effective ways to control crime. A growing body of research indicates that rehabilitation and reentry programs decrease reoffending and that the public increasingly supports these programs [33]. This support is particularly apparent when surveys ask people about particular offenses and offenders rather than about crime in general [31]. When asked about crime in general, people tend to support harsher sentences than when asked about particular situations, such as "What sentence should a 17-year-old male receive for stealing a bicycle?"

In addition to the crime control policies of arrest, punish, and rehabilitate, the government utilizes propaganda techniques to shift public attitudes. **Social engineering**, or government efforts to change the beliefs, attitudes, and behavioral patterns of a section of the population, uses media, speeches, and public outreach programs to deter people by warning them of the consequences of crime, to persuade people to condemn or fear certain activities, such as drug use, and to convince them to support government policies, such as the expansion and privatization of prisons. In each case, the government is casting its net of social control over more people.

Due Process: Individual Rights and Constraint of Arbitrary State Power

The exertion and expansion of state power, however, has limits created by due-process provisions, which are specified in constitutions, statutes, organizational policies, and court rulings. **Due process** serves as the central legal principle in the U.S. court system. Broadly speaking, it means two things, that a person's rights must be protected during government proceedings and that arbitrary and excessive government power must be inhibited.

There is no single point in history when due process was developed or defined [34]. Early empires and monarchies did not have this principle, so rulers had no logic for constraining their own power. But over the past 900 years, due process emerged as the principle in government charters or constitutions that limited the power of governments over their own people. Rather than be constrained by outside force, due process effectively meant that governments must constrain themselves in order to protect individual rights. Because the government is the most powerful entity (controlling the treasury, military, and police), if it does not control itself, it is unlikely that any other people or organizations would be powerful enough to counter its power. As societies gradually moved away from individualized treatment of offenses and tyrannical rule toward systematic and fair procedures, the due-process ideal generated many particular principles and rules that advance fairness and freedom from government oppression.

This internal control and protection of rights is clearly present in the Constitution and state constitutions, each of which has provisions that instruct the government on what they cannot do and what they must do. In the Constitution, this regulates how laws are written, how the government can conduct criminal investigations and trials, and what types of punishment are unacceptable. For instance, the Sixth Amendment prohibits the government from holding a secret trial. This constrains the power of the government, because it is more difficult for it to convict a suspect when the public, the defendant's family, and the media monitor the proceedings and expose or challenge violations of rights, such as torturing the defendant, using hearsay evidence, or denying a defendant the right to a defense attorney. See Table 1.1 for a list of many constitutional rights that constrain government power and protect individuals.

Table 1.1 How the Constitution Limits the Power of the Government. These Due-Process Provisions Are Common in Criminal Court Cases

Constraints on Lawmaking and Exertion of Power

Location in the Constitution	Constraint on Government
Article I, Section 10	Government cannot criminalize behaviors that have already occurred (no *ex post facto* laws).
First Amendment	Congress cannot censor the press nor endorse a religion, which means it will be monitored by an independent press and its power over personal activities is reduced.
Fifth Amendment	Prosecutors must get permission from a panel of citizens (a grand jury) before prosecuting someone for a felony.

Rights Granted to Individuals

Amendment	Constraint on the Government
First	Congress cannot criminalize religious practices, speech, or citizen protests without what the courts consider a compelling state interest. This protects basic freedoms from government suppression.
Fourth	Police must have a warrant for a search, which protects people from arbitrary searches.
Fifth	Courts cannot harass a person with multiple trials for the same offense (protection against double jeopardy).
Fifth	Police and prosecutors cannot torture people into confessions or force people to testify against themselves (protection against compelled self-incrimination).
Fifth and Fourteenth	Government cannot impose punishment without following transparent rules and must provide equal protection of the law (due process of law).
Sixth	Courts must inform the defendants of the specific charges against them, which inhibits arbitrary prosecution.
Sixth	Courts must provide a speedy, public trial in the area where the alleged offense occurred, which prevents the government from detaining someone without a conviction, from convicting people in secret trials, and from moving the trials far from where witnesses live.
Sixth	Courts must ask an impartial panel of citizens (a jury) to convict a defendant.
Sixth	Courts must let defendants build a defense by confronting witnesses against them (no hearsay), obtaining their own witnesses to counter the charges, and having a defense attorney to counter the government's attorney.
Eighth	Courts must allow defendants to remain free until proven guilty and cannot demand excessive bail.
Eighth	No one in the government can apply what the courts consider cruel or unusual punishment.

Due-process principles often do not specify exactly what the government can and cannot do. Specific due-process rules are articulated in **statutes** (laws written by the legislature), rules governing police departments and local courts, and judicial rulings. Consider the right to defend yourself. How could this be put into practice if you were arrested by a police officer who used excessive force? One way is to have your attorney question the officer about her or his actions. But that is possible only if you are able to identify the officer. That is why some states have laws that require police to wear clear identification, even when in riot gear. So the abstract principle of having the right to defend yourself against government accusations is the basis for the specific due-process provision that police must identify themselves.

Some of the most far-reaching due-process provisions come from court rulings. Appellate and supreme courts establish new due-process principles and rules every year. In *Griswold v. Connecticut* (1965), the U.S. Supreme Court established for the first time that Americans have a "right to privacy" even though the Constitution does not explicitly identify that right [35]. The justices argued that the right to privacy is implied throughout the Constitution. Even though that case protects a married couple's right to have contraceptives, this new right to privacy has influenced many cases since then and has become part of our popular understanding of rights.

A more recent example of a due-process ruling was *Graham v. Florida* (2011), in which the Court ruled that to sentence a juvenile to a life sentence without parole is cruel and unusual punishment and therefore a violation of due process and unconstitutional [36]. Usually the courts will develop new rights based on principles enumerated in the Constitution, but U.S. courts have also adopted due-process rights present in the English common law system or attributed to English jurisprudence, such as the principle of innocent until proven guilty [37].

Taken together, due-process provisions simultaneously protect the rights of individuals and define the nature of government. They require that laws do not violate the Constitution. They push the government to follow established and transparent rules when enforcing the laws, which allows for equality before the law. Due process also entails our right to challenge criminal justice actions such as police investigations and court decisions (known as procedural due-process challenges) and the constitutionality of laws themselves (known as substantive due-process challenges). These challenges happen in the courts, which means the courts have the power of **judicial review**, whereby they determine if procedures or laws violate due-process provisions or rights. These protections of rights bring stability and predictability to the government and its relationship with the citizens. As frightening or frustrating as it is to be arrested and go to court, imagine how much worse it would be if you were not told of the charges against you, could not have an attorney, and did not even know the possible punishments you were facing.

Due process, however, is not merely a list of isolated rights. The totality of rights and rules is what protects us from unjust abuses of power and protects our liberties. To understand this, consider Nazi Germany. During World War II, the Germans sent Jews to ghettos and concentration camps and then systematically killed millions of them. In other words, the Nazis treated all Jews equally, but the government had no mechanism to challenge the legitimacy of the laws, and there was no limit on the cruelty of the punishments.

Due process, then, is not merely about defendants' rights. Nor does it mean being "soft on crime" or favoring rehabilitation or being anti-police [38]. Such complaints ignore the facts that since the expansion of due-process protections in the 1960s, the nation greatly increased the number of behaviors defined as criminal offenses, the criminal justice system grew by nearly three-fold, and the prison population grew approximately 400 percent [39]. Rather, the due-process provisions assure that the government overall limits its arbitrary and abusive power over individuals. Court enforcement of the provisions actually deters the government from abusing our rights in the first place. Due process manages government authority but does not render the government powerless. Indeed, the presence of meaningful due-process restraints gives the government legitimate authority [40]. Citing the influential political and economic philosopher Friedrich Hayek, Steve Selinger argues that government's coercive powers are accepted by the people when the law is seen as legitimate and the coercion as minimal [41]. Due process is the bedrock of the criminal court, but the provisions are also specified in statutes, administrative rules, and executive orders.

Due Process and the Three Branches of Government

All three branches of the government advance the ideal of due process and are constrained by it. The judicial branches are the most pivotal in establishing due-process provisions and protecting individual rights. First, they have their own procedural rules—often in the form of judicial codes or judicial rules—for how lawyers must conduct themselves, when they must file certain paperwork, and so on. Courts also interpret state and federal laws, and in doing so set standards for government action of all branches.

Consider the Eighth Amendment's prohibition of "cruel and unusual punishment." The legislatures and courts are always struggling with the question of what constitutes cruel and unusual punishment. They do this by referring to past court rulings to illuminate "evolving standards of decency," "fundamental notions of human dignity," the harm of the offense, the types of punishments for other offenses in other jurisdictions, the intention of the framers of the

Constitution, and whether the punishment "shocks the conscience" [42]. When the Court ruled, for instance, that a person could be sentenced to life for a first-time drug offense or subjected to the electric chair twice (after he failed to die the first time), the state and federal legislatures were able to more confidently expand life sentences and executions [43]. However, rulings such as the *Graham* decision mentioned above, or rulings concerning beating a handcuffed inmate or chaining an inmate outside in the sun for an extended period of time reverberate through the criminal justice system because it sets limits on actions [44]. Often, however, a questionable law does not reach the Supreme Court, such as Louisiana's law to forcefully administer "chemical castration" drugs to some sex offenders, and the line between acceptable and unacceptable remains unclear.

Other examples of the judiciary addressing criminal-court due-process issues include interpretations of the Fourth, Fifth, and Sixth Amendments. The Fourth Amendment requires that the police get a warrant before searching someone's property, but what about the trash out by the curb? The Supreme Court has ruled that such a search does not violate the Fourth Amendment. The Sixth Amendment has seven due-process provisions, one of which states that "the accused shall have the Assistance of Counsel for his defense." The Supreme Court has ruled that this right to a defense attorney is meaningless if the defendant cannot afford an attorney, and that trial courts must provide a defense attorney if a defendant cannot afford one [45]. In another famous case, *Miranda v. Arizona* (1966), the Court ruled that police must inform suspects of some of their constitutional rights before taking them into custody and interrogating them [46].

When writing substantive laws, the legislature is constrained by these and other provisions and almost always conforms to them, which necessarily limits the power of the laws. A legislature, for instance, will not bother writing a law that criminalizes the practice of Islam because that would violate the First Amendment. Nor will members of Congress pass a law that criminalizes pornography because the Supreme Court has ruled that it is protected free speech.

The legislative branch is not only constrained by court rulings but also issues its own limits on state power. In particular, it has enacted thousands of procedural laws. State legislatures pass laws, for instance, that regulate police activity. In states such as Maryland, North Carolina, and Texas, legislative statutes require police to record interrogations in specific types of cases, usually murder cases [47]. The New York legislature has passed a bill that, if signed into law, will require "that all interrogations of suspects in police custody be recorded in their entirety" [48]. Congresses also pass laws that regulate court proceedings, such as the admissibility of evidence. For instance, rape shield laws prevent mentioning a rape victim's sexual history as evidence and sometimes limit questioning of rape victims in court.

The third branch of government, the executive branch, also has many rules that reflect due-process provisions. In addition to the many court and legislative procedural laws, police departments have enacted their own procedural rules. These regulate the officers' treatment and interrogation of suspects, collection of evidence, filing of reports, and testimonies in court. For instance, Maine's Chiefs of Police Association issued an order in 2005 that directed police to record custodial interrogations in serious offenses [49]. Every police department has a set of procedural rules that limit and direct police conduct.

The top executive branch officer—the president on the federal level and governors on the state level—can also issue **executive orders**, or rules declared by the executive branch that have the force of law. Some of these—such as orders from Presidents Bush and Obama to detain people indefinitely without notifying them of what they are being charged with and President Franklin Roosevelt's order that forced 120,000 U.S. citizens of Japanese ancestry into internment camps—reduce due-process protections. Less notable, and likely far less common, are executive orders that reflect the ideal of due process or expand due-process rights. In 2009, for instance, President Obama issued an order that ended the torture of terrorism suspects.

One of the most profound due-process executive orders in recent years was Illinois Governor George Ryan's commutation of all people on the state's death row. The president and governors have constitutional authority to issue clemency. Clemency includes pardons (vacated convictions), commutations (reduced sentences), and the restoration of rights or property [50]. After the work of Cardozo Law School's Innocence Project and Northwestern University School of Law's Center on Wrongful Convictions led to the exoneration of 13 men on Illinois's death row, Governor Ryan commuted all 167 people on death row to life in prison because of violations of rights and procedural laws, which included torture and coerced confessions, incompetent counsel, and unreliable evidence. He stated that the criminal court system was "haunted by the demon of error" and that "because the Illinois death penalty system is arbitrary and capricious—and therefore immoral—I no longer shall tinker with the machinery of death" [51].

Procedural Laws and Codes of Criminal Procedure

Criminal procedure is the process by which a case is handled, and includes police work, pretrial decisions, adjudication, sentencing, and appeals and post-conviction reviews of guilty verdicts. Each stage in this process is guided and constrained by "rules and legal principles that regulate the administration of criminal justice..." [52]. The laws that constrain and direct the conduct of the agents of the state when they process a case are called procedural laws. They affect when a police officer can arrest or question a suspect, what cases a prosecutor can take to court, what type of evidence will be heard in a trial, what type of sentences a judge can issue, and when an appeal can be filed.

This expansive set of procedural laws is set forth in constitutions, but specified in judicial rulings, legislative statutes, executive orders, and administrative rules. Most of these rules and laws are in turn compiled into books called codes of procedure such as the Federal Rules of Criminal Procedure, Code of Federal Regulations Index, and a separate code or rule book for each state's criminal court system [53].

Balancing Crime Control and Individual Rights

Sometimes crime control and due process are considered to be competing goals, but that is a false dichotomy, meaning that we cannot choose only one or the other. It is true that the debate over whether to increase crime control efforts, such as hiring more police or building more prisons, or increase procedural protections, such as recording interrogations, greatly affects public policy and expenditures. It is also true that police and courts sometimes abuse rights and that "due process hurdles," "cumbersome rights," and "legal obstacles" make police work harder and stymie some court cases [54].

Yet, tension was exactly the intent in designing this government. Government needs power to accomplish goals, but that power must be constrained to ensure liberties [55]. Police, prosecutors, judges, and correctional officers represent the power of the state, and due process is the mechanism to impede state power. It is the buffer between the most powerful entity in the nation, the government, and the weakest entity, the individual. Justice involves punishing those that cause social harm, but doing so with fair procedures [56]. As Supreme Court Justice Anthony Kennedy said, "Law and freedom [are] the meaning of the United States" [57].

Courts, and the criminal justice system in general, must constantly balance these two goals. They strive to convict people who violate the law, yet they review government policies and actions to be sure that government power is not arbitrary or excessive. Yes, the government says, we make the rules, we enforce the rules, and we punish the rule breakers, but we agree to follow principles of fairness and transparency at every turn in order to not let our power go unrestrained. The balance between them is both necessary and manageable, and together they create the organizing frame of the U.S. court system.

THEME 3: MOTIVATIONS, DECISIONS, AND ACTIONS OF THE COURTROOM WORKERS

The criminal courts are complex systems. They operate according to stable principles yet continually change to accommodate society's needs and demands. The courts also pursue two distinct but intertwined goals: crime control and protection of individual rights.

Added to this complexity are the workers themselves, the individuals doing their jobs every day in courtrooms across the nation. Many factors push and pull them. Understanding legal action entails taking into account many variables, including the legal principles and goals described in the first two themes and the sociological variables that occur within the courthouse and outside of it. We organize this wide array of influences into three categories.

- Most significantly, decision-making in courthouses and outcomes of court cases are shaped by the legal frame of the court, or the principles, procedures, and rulings that provide the limits and organizing logic of the judiciary. The principles and goals we have discussed not only shape the court system as a branch of government but also influence the people working in it.
- Second, the actions of lawyers and judges are also shaped by variables particular to a courthouse, or what we call the "internal ecology of the court."
- Finally, many factors that influence courtroom action come from outside sources, or what's called the "external ecology of the court."

Chapter 5 is dedicated to this theme, and each of these categories will be explained more thoroughly there.

Patterns and Variance

In order to situate the categories of influence within a courthouse, let's begin by illustrating how decision-making in courts both conforms to patterns and varies in predictable ways. Often, legal principles and internal and external ecologies prompt members of the courtroom workgroup to conform to what others around them are doing. Pressures to conform emanate from the ideal of justice (legal principles) they learned in law school; formal oversight and their informal work patterns (internal ecology); and political pressures (external ecology). For instance, procedural laws mandate that prosecutors share evidence with defense attorneys. They may also file the same paperwork as other attorneys, make predictable motions, and make similar compromises during negotiated pleas because they often work with the same judges and opposing attorneys every week over many years. This conformity in decisions and actions creates observable patterns within a courtroom.

In spite of the tendency toward predictability, lawyers and judges are not robots pressing out identical decisions [58]. The workers have different motivations and make different decisions, even when handling similar cases. One prosecutor may charge one third-time offender with habitual offender charges but another with a lesser violation. One defense attorney may encourage the defendant to plead guilty, and another may insist on going to trial. One judge may sentence drug-addicted defendants to prison, whereas another may send many to outpatient rehabilitation. Why is that? What makes two lawyers or judges, both trained in law school, treat nearly identical cases differently? The influences fall into the same three categories, and specific pressures may include the cohesion they have with their coworkers, availability of resources, direct and indirect pressures from partisan politics, and the performance of the police in gathering evidence.

Let's return to your arrest in Boston. At every point, the police, lawyers, and judges were enforcing laws and displaying the logic of the justice system as well as their own departments. They all adhered to the proper protocol and therefore conducted themselves in predictable manners in some respects. The police read you the Miranda rights and followed procedure when taking you into custody; the prosecutor filed the appropriate motions and scheduled hearings in a predictable manner; and the judge reviewed the law and facts of the case as one would expect. However, at any given point, the discretion of the actors could have led to a different outcome (Figure 1.2).

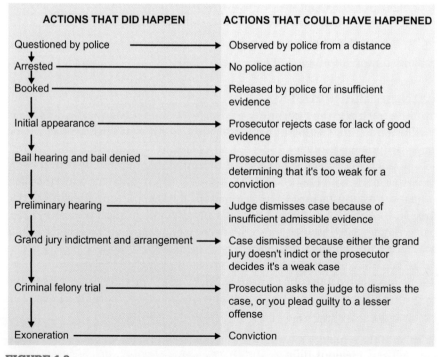

ACTIONS THAT DID HAPPEN	ACTIONS THAT COULD HAVE HAPPENED
Questioned by police	Observed by police from a distance
Arrested	No police action
Booked	Released by police for insufficient evidence
Initial appearance	Prosecutor rejects case for lack of good evidence
Bail hearing and bail denied	Prosecutor dismisses case after determining that it's too weak for a conviction
Preliminary hearing	Judge dismisses case because of insufficient admissible evidence
Grand jury indictment and arrangement	Case dismissed because either the grand jury doesn't indict or the prosecutor decides it's a weak case
Criminal felony trial	Prosecution asks the judge to dismiss the case, or you plead guilty to a lesser offense
Exoneration	Conviction

FIGURE 1.2
Your path through the Boston criminal justice system.

You could have been filtered out of the system earlier if the arresting officers had decided there was not enough evidence to arrest the two of you after questioning you or if the prosecutor had dismissed the case because he or she determined there was not enough evidence to establish your guilt. However, you could have ended up in prison. Your defense attorney could have convinced you to plead guilty to lesser felony charges rather than risk being convicted of the greater charge, or the judge or jury may have ruled that you were guilty. At the same time the principles and ecologies render practitioners' actions predictable, they allow for a range of options that open up every case to elements of unpredictability.

Legal Frame: Principles, Duties of the Court, Procedure, and Reasoning

The courts are framed by historic sets of principles, practices, and law, but legal principles do not just provide stability to the court system. They guide and constrain the legal action of every lawyer and judge. Sometimes people think of "law on the books" as distinct from "law in action," as though laws are written in one section of the nation, but criminal justice practitioners actually do whatever they want. In fact, legal action in the nation's court-houses cannot be understood without knowledge of the legal context. By looking at legal decision-making in light of these principles, rules, and laws, we find that the decisions and actions of attorneys and judges are tightly tied to the legal framework.

An owner of a construction company can have her or his workers do thousands of tasks. The same person can be instructed to sweep floors, file papers, pour concrete, direct traffic, and so on. The duties of courtroom workers are not as elastic. The chief prosecutor can assign an attorney to a drug case or a domestic abuse case, but the attorney is still obligated to prosecute criminal offenses and cannot go far beyond that. In short, courts are limited to enforcing the law of the land, or the actual codified laws established by the legislature and earlier court rulings. This single doctrine has many ramifications that can be grouped under the principle of **justicia-bility** (ju STISH ee a bil a tee), or whether or not a case can be heard by a court. Lawyers and judges must exercise restraint and not bring or hear a case if no law was violated, if there was no injury, if the case is outside of the court's jurisdiction, if the offense has not yet occurred, or if too much time has elapsed since it occurred [59].

This creates a narrow channel that lawyers and judges must navigate as they carry out their duties. Prosecutors and judges are not free to enforce their own norms, morality, or prejudices. Lawyers must argue cases in terms of the law and previous rulings, and judges will make their ruling based on the same knowledge. They are confined to these **legal merits** of the case—that is, the facts of the case, substantive law, and precedent that serve as the legal basis of attorney decision-making and judicial rulings.

The constraint imposed by principles and laws manifests also in the large and specific set of procedures that attorneys and judges conform to as they carry out their duties. These procedural laws largely steer legal decision-making. During the whole proceeding, the lawyers and judges follow preestablished patterns for when to file motions, when to speak, whom to address, and so on. Prosecutors, for instance, are not free to include in trial any information they want. If a person is charged with burglary, the prosecutor cannot mention that the defendant is a drug addict, a Muslim, or a vegetarian; she cannot bring up the defendant's relationship with his parents or his wife, or the fact that he has been rude to his neighbor. Procedural law mandates that prosecutor present only facts that are directly relevant to establishing that the defendant violated a burglary statute. Similarly, procedural law does not allow judges to deny a defendant an attorney or issue any sentence they want, no matter how repugnant he or she finds the defendant.

Another way to see the connection between principles and procedures is through the court's symbolic rituals. The defendant and defense attorney, for instance, sit at the same type of desk that the prosecution sits at, symbolizing equality between parties and the presumption of innocence. Such a simple practice may appear natural, until it is compared to the social construction of courtrooms in other countries. In Egypt, for instance, the defendant is brought into court in a cage. This symbolizes a presumption of guilt. This even happened to the former ruler of the country, Hosni Mubarak [60]. Judges in both courts, however, sit higher than everyone else and must be shown respect because he or she rules on matters of law and thus embodies the rule of law.

These scripted duties and procedures trickle down into the minds of lawyers and judges. They tend to understand and approach legal questions in a similar manner that is distinct from the general public but is based on a well-known legal reasoning. Unlike our typical day-to-day reasoning, **legal reasoning** is the logic, evidence, laws, principles, language, and strategies lawyers and judges use in deciding if the facts of the case match the law. It consists of ideas that follow confining dictates that prioritize what parts of reality are relevant. This involves establishing the facts of the case only as they relate to the substantive and procedural laws. During the appeal, it involves comparing the present case to past similar cases and adopting the rulings of the past cases [61].

When looking at the facts of an alleged offense, lawyers and judges assume that somebody is at fault. They are concerned overwhelmingly with whether or not the defendant committed the act, not remote causation, or conditions such as poverty and low intelligence that may have led the defendant to commit the act. They ask, did the defendant perform the illegal act through negligence or did he or she intend to produce the harm? Also, evidence must be legally obtained, and the court system strongly prefers direct and empirical evidence. This elevates eye witnesses, physical evidence, and forensic evidence and generally excludes hearsay, intuition, and speculation.

At the same time the courts present and evaluate particular types of evidence, they also adhere to the myriad legal principles, such as establishing a guilt beyond a reasonable doubt. People not trained in law often find legal reasoning frustrating because they want to include evidence that was obtained without a warrant, highlight that the defendant is an overall mean-spirited person or an otherwise nice kid who got caught up in peer pressure, or include rumors and hunches. And all that information is relevant among the general public, but in the court of law it is not.

Internal Ecology: Organization, Processes, and Relationships Within a Court

Notwithstanding the institutional framework of stable principles, general guidelines for procedure, and the prominence of legal reasoning, legal decision-making is greatly influenced by the internal ecology of each particular courthouse and courtroom. **Internal ecology** refers to the characteristics within the court and frames decisions, actions, and motivations of the individuals participating in it [62]. This explains local and regional patterns that vary significantly from one courthouse to another.

To begin, the United States has the federal court system, and each state has its own court system. Both systems generally divide their systems in two ways, by types of cases and by geographical location. Throughout the nation are courts that specialize in civil and criminal matters. Civil courts include traffic offenses, contracts, divorce and custody, torts (or damages), tax, probate (inheritance and estates), small claims, copyright, and bankruptcy. On the criminal side, a court may handle felonies, misdemeanors, juveniles, drug offenders, domestic abuse cases, appeals, or other specialized categories. Geographically, courts range from the town and municipal courts to county courts to districts and circuits to courts of last resort (usually called the supreme court of the state or nation). This incredible array means the United States has thousands of courthouses that operate largely independently of other courts.

Given these many specialized courts and geographic jurisdictions, and given that the United States has more than 14,000 state courts alone, it would be an overwhelming task to learn the activities within every courthouse and courtroom. However, every court's internal ecology has the same basic components. It encompasses:

1. The formal management and organization, such as official tasks, hierarchies within and between the various offices, and the indigent defense system.
2. Characteristics of cases, such as types of offenses that come to court and quality of evidence.
3. Informal norms and characteristics of the court workers, such as the political affiliation of lawyers and judges, informal procedures for handling regular cases and for dealing with unusual ones, and local legal culture.
4. The physical and spatial layout and the distribution of material resources.

Courts are formal organizations and most are **bureaucracies**, which means they have specific goals, an explicit hierarchy of authority, specialization, and standardization of many tasks [63]. No matter what part of the nation or size of the courthouse, each one has an official organizational structure and jurisdiction over particular cases. Yet, large variations can be seen across regions, such as rural courthouses versus urban ones and when comparing small court systems to large ones, but variations also exist between similarly situated courthouses. Courthouses vary in their workload, defense system for low-income defendants, pay, job assignments, official priorities, number of special units, availability of assistants and investigators, opportunities for promotion, oversight and discipline, and the rate of turnover among the courtroom workgroup [64].

No matter which court we examine, the workers still have to deal with the cases before them, and every case has unique characteristics that make handling them daunting. Even though the courts are explicitly designed to be adversarial, with each side competing to win each case, in many respects, the attorneys actually cooperate. This is why in their seminal research, James Eisenstein and Herbert Jacob refer to the prosecutors, defense attorneys, and judges in a court collectively as the **courtroom workgroup**, that is, the judge, attorneys, police officers, bail-bond agents, and others who do the work of the court [65]. They generally work together to dispose of cases as quickly as possible because of a heavy workload.

Attorneys group cases into categories so that they can be treated as routine cases, and the important merits of the case can be more readily assessed. Their routine handling of cases structures the court process into ritualized stages [66]. Their grouping of cases depends on the type of offenses that occur most commonly in the community, the priorities set by their offices, and the division the workers are in. For instance, if there is an increase in reported rapes, and the chief prosecutor instructs the office to vigorously prosecute those cases, rape becomes a particular category and receives greater resources, especially by the division that handles sex crimes or violent crimes.

The groupings also depend on the informal norms, such as an unofficial agreement that certain types of cases are less serious than others and can be plea-bargained quickly to a lesser charge. These routines emerge as the workers negotiate the court's formal rules and consult each other to solve problems [67]. This negotiated order creates informal patterns of behavior within the court's formal structure, which helps workers compartmentalize the real demands of their jobs in a way not established by the official protocol. This arrangement is then enforced through group expectations and pressures. Negotiated order structures the rate of pleas versus the rate of trials, speed of disposition, approaches to handling particular types of victims, offenders, and offenses, and the interpretation of law [68].

Because the negotiated order of the courtroom workgroup is informal, its form is influenced by unofficial variables. This can include sociological characteristics of the participants, such as their political affiliation, religion, and ideologies; their attitudes toward race, sex, and other social issues; the extent and quality of their legal education; and their duration of employment [69]. Informal patterns are also influenced by group dynamics, such as how long the participants work together and how often they meet outside of the courtroom or in the judge's chambers to discuss how to resolve a case without a trial. For instance, research indicates that courtroom workgroups that tend to be more adversarial than cooperative have a higher turnover, more young attorneys, a heavy workload, less informal negotiation, less predictability, and lower cohesion [65].

An **officer of the court** is any court worker who has an obligation to promote justice and effective operation of the judicial system. People generally expect them to adhere to the letter of the law in order to mete out justice fairly. As it turns out, following the letter of the law does not have a single outcome. The officers of the court exercise discretion, negotiate informal rules within the courtroom workgroup, and often process cases in a routine fashion.

Every ecological system, whether in nature or society, interacts with the physical environment. For courts, Eisenstein and Jacob refer to the physical surroundings as the "task environment," which captures the importance of it because the architecture structures interactions and how jobs are performed. For example, if the attorneys do not have a room to meet in, then they must meet in hallways, unused jury rooms, or jail cells. Attorneys are less likely to have an office to meet in if their office building is separated from the courthouse [70]. The availability of technology will affect how information is communicated and evidence presented. All of these affect how attorneys decide to handle a case.

External Ecology: Characteristics of Community

The courts, of course, exist in larger social contexts that impinge on the court procedures [71].

External ecology refers to the pressures on the courts from cultures, people, and organizations outside the court. The external ecology of courts includes community attitudes, politics that surround the election and appointment of court workers, the laws and funding from the legislature, police practices, and influences from media, research, activist groups, and law schools. Although these operate primarily outside of the courts, they have a profound effect on the courts' internal operations.

Courtroom workers often come from the same community they work in, and they generally live there, too. Local public opinion influences the decisions of court lawyers [72]. Local economic conditions and levels of inequality, racial homogeneity and dominant attitudes toward race, the religious affiliation of the community, rates of immigration and migration, average educational level, voter politics, and the size of the community all have been shown to affect actions within courthouses [73]. Courts, in short, are part of the local community culture.

Overlapping these local conditions is the election of judges, which occurs fully or partially (such as retention election) in 38 states. This process is becoming increasingly partisan and attracting more campaign contributions. From the 1990s to the 2000s, judicial campaign spending alone increased by 148 percent [74]. This influx of money and other incentives is to increase a person or group's influence over policy: if your group can get one or two judges elected, you can uphold or invalidate laws that are appealed, and buying those one or two votes is a lot cheaper than trying to buy a majority in the legislature. Groups can support candidates based on criteria such as whether they support the death penalty or whether they are lenient on corporate offenses. Similar trends are happening in jurisdictions that elect chief prosecutors and defense attorneys [75]. Even when judges and prosecutors are appointed, as on the federal level and some states, the process is still engulfed in political debate. We discuss this in more detail in Chapter 15.

Being part of a three-branch government, courts are also affected by the legislative and executive branches. Congress and state legislatures write the substantive laws courts enforce, many of the procedural laws, and the laws regarding elections of court workers, and they delineate the jurisdiction of each court. Legislatures provide the courts with their budgets, which affects the quality of the physical facilities, staff size, pay, and so on, and set up offender programs that affect courts, such as job training and drug rehabilitation. All of these legislative actions affect the work environment and decisions of the courtroom workgroup. For instance, in the absence of community-based rehabilitation facilities, a judge may be more likely to sentence people to prison or more likely to release them outright. In the federal government and many states, the legislature approves court appointees and retains the power to fire or impeach them. The executive branch, however, enforces the laws via the police and punishes the convicted through the correctional system.

Finally, a wide array of outside organizations and groups affect the courts. For instance, courts are increasingly relying on forensics, which means that science and even pseudo-science are influencing case outcomes [76]. Science also affects the courts through research on sentences and programs that best reduce crime, working conditions in courts, and unequal outcomes of the courts [77]. Media, both news and fiction, affect how the public perceives courts and arguably how courtroom actors behave. Citizen-based social movements and industry groups, which often utilize the media, pressure the courts through election campaigns, ridicule, statements submitted to the courts, and lawsuits.

Law schools and professional legal organizations have a significant and direct influence on courts. Law schools promote a legal subculture through their standardized curriculum that trains lawyers in the logic of law [78]. Professional law associations, such as the American Bar Association and its state bar affiliates, certify law schools, endorse or recommend candidates, submit *amici* (uh MEE kee) briefs that recommend a particular ruling on a case, and lobby Congress. Every occupation within the courts has its own national association, such as the Federal Judicial Center, National Center for State Courts, and the National Association of Criminal Defense Lawyers.

LEGAL REALITY

Courts are dynamic institutions. They are shaped by many forces, and they vary significantly in their operations. At the same time, courts collectively create a social reality that is distinct from other areas of society and can be understood as **legal reality**, which are the priorities, social relationships, hierarchies, values, and processes that are established and maintained by the legal system. Legal reality can be explained and understood only by looking at the internal operations of the courts, and it often differs from values and preferences held by the general public. For instance, the legal system has defined the relationship between victims and offenders, in which victims cannot extract punishment directly but rather are converted into mere evidence that the state uses against defendants. Some other examples of legal reality embodied in and created by the court system include:

- prioritizing the protection of individual rights and constraint of the state's power over stopping all crime;

- prioritizing the letter of the law rather than morality;
- prioritizing the legal merits of the case over all other types of logic and evidence;
- prioritizing certain types of offenses, evidence, and offenders;
- requiring access to a defense attorney and communication between defense and the prosecutor;
- using a unique vocabulary that many people outside of law do not understand;
- giving greater organizational power to the prosecutor than the defense;
- giving unique powers to the judge;
- valuing victory in a case more than the pursuit of truth;
- valuing abstract legal principles and precedent;
- following elaborate sets of ritualized procedures and rules that lead to outcomes that often baffle and anger people outside of the courts, such as suppression of convincing evidence, rough cross-examination of witnesses, dismissal of cases because of a prosecutorial error, and severe sentencing of youths and very low-IQ defendants.

This legal reality was not constructed in one effort, like the writing of a book or the starting of a new company. It emerged over time, was reinforced over time, and changed over time. Written laws and the practices of the courtroom workgroup reproduce and reshape it every day. Is legal reality a good thing? Is, for instance, legal reasoning superior to other styles of reasoning? Nearly every attorney and judge would probably say yes, but it is better to understand it as a simple fact of the legal and judicial system, regardless of whether it is superior to other forms of social organization or harmful to society. It is, for better or worse, what shapes the decision-making of the people in the courts and the operations of the courts across the United States.

SUMMARY

1. Discuss rule of law.
   - The rule of law governs people and organizations fairly and equally. No individuals or groups are subject to arbitrary government power, and no person is above the law.
2. Tell why the study of criminal courts is important.
   - The criminal courts are a cornerstone of the U.S. criminal justice system. It influences everyone working in the criminal justice field and affects millions of victims and suspects every year. The courts have judicial lawmaking powers, establish legal principles, and

influence cases. Understanding the criminal courts is essential to understanding government power and succeeding in any criminal justice system occupation.

3. Define legal principles.
   - Legal principles are the ideals and imperatives that serve as the basis for legal thinking and guide legal decision-making.

4. Explain how and why courts change over time.
   - Change happens on institutional and organizational levels. Institutional change occurs when a change pervades the entire legal system and involves a shift in the court system's legal principles and legal norms.
   - Organizational change occurs within the operations of a specific court system or courthouse and involves changes in areas such as resources, personnel, fees, and rules for handling cases.

5. Explain the two goals of the criminal courts.
   - Two connected goals shape the criminal law and courtroom activities: exertion of state power and protection of individual rights.
   - One goal of state power is crime control. The government does the job of crime control by exerting power over the people. The federal and state governments enact laws, hire police, fund courts, and build jails and prisons with the goal of deterring crime and apprehending and punishing offenders.
   - The government has enacted due-process provisions to protect individual rights. Due-process provisions are the legal principles, laws, and criminal justice system rules that protect the rights of individuals who are being processed by the government and that constrain arbitrary or excessive government power.

6. Explain the crime control goal of the courts.
   - Crime control involves government efforts to reduce crime, including passing more criminal laws, hiring more police, expanding court houses, building more prisons, offering reentry programs, and manipulating public attitudes.

7. Define due process.
   - Due process is the central legal principle in the court system. It means two things: (1) that a person's rights must be protected during government proceedings and (2) that arbitrary and excessive government power must be inhibited.

8. Explain legal reasoning and how it relates to legal principles.
   - Legal reasoning involves establishing the facts of the case only as they relate to substantive and procedural laws. During appeal, legal reasoning involves comparing the present case to past similar cases and adopting the rulings of the past cases.

9. Define internal ecology and tell why it is important.
   - Internal ecology refers to the characteristics within the court. It frames the decisions, actions, and motivations of the individuals participating in the court. The internal ecology of each particular courthouse and courtroom influences legal decision-making.
10. Define external ecology and tell why it is important.
    - External ecology refers to the political pressures on the courts. The external ecology of courts includes community attitudes; politics that surround the election and appointment of court workers; the laws and funding from the legislature; police practices; and influences from media, research, activist groups, and law schools.

Questions

1. What is the rule of law?
2. Why is the study of criminal courts important?
3. What are legal principles?
4. Why do courts change over time?
5. What are the two goals of the criminal courts?
6. What is the crime control goal of the courts?
7. What is due process?
8. What is legal reasoning? How does it relate to legal principles?
9. What is internal ecology? Why is it important in the courts?
10. What is external ecology? Why is it important in the courts?

REFERENCES

[1] Dehghan SK. Iranian activist missing after arrest, Guardian, <www.guardian.co.uk/world/2011/aug/26/iran-activist-arrest-kouhyar-goudarzi>; August 26, 2011 [accessed August, 2012].

[2] Eisenstein J, Jacob H. Felony justice: an organizational analysis of criminal courts. Boston, MA: Little, Brown; 1977. p. 19–20.

[3] Glendon MA. A nation under lawyers. New York, NY: Farrar, Straus, and Giroux; 1994. p. 247. Fogel D. We are the living proof: the justice model for corrections. 2nd ed. New York, NY: Anderson Publishing; 1979. p. 184. [Fogel describes the criminal justice process as the "superordinate goal" of all components of the criminal justice system.]

[4] Mensch E. The history of mainstream legal thought. In: Kairy D, editor. The politics of law: a progressive critique. New York, NY: Pantheon Books; 1990.

[5] *Brown v Board of Education of Topeka, Kansas*, 347 U.S. 483(1954).

[6] Tanner N. Disputing and the genesis of legal principles: examples from minangkabau. Southwestern J Anthropol 1970;26(4):375. [The general assumption is that legal principles are based on consensus and some natural morality humans share. This assumption has been challenged by many thinkers over the years, including Karl Marx and Max Weber. Tanner presents an excellent alternative to the consensus model, arguing that legal principles derive from "process conflict" and that the consensus rhetoric is merely a rationalization of the conflict.]

[7] *United States v. Jones,* 615 F. 3d 544(2011).

[8] Sanborn JB, Salerno AW. The juvenile justice system. Los Angeles, CA: Roxbury Publishing Company; 2005. p. 19−20. Platt AM. The child savers: the invention of delinquency. Chicago, IL: University of Chicago; 1969.

[9] Lowi T, Ginsberg B. American government: freedom and power. 3rd ed. New York, NY: W.W. Norton; 1994. p. 189−196.

[10] Callis M. The aftermath of the Salem witch trials in colonial America. Historical J Massachusetts 2005;33(2):187−213. Friedman LM. American law in the 20th century. New Haven, CT: Yale University Press; 2002;111−14. Foucault M. [Sheridan A, Trans.1975; reprint] Discipline and punish: the birth of the prison. New York, NY: Vintage Books; 1995.

[11] Halal WE. The collaborative enterprise: a stakeholder model uniting profitability and responsibility. J Corporate Citizenship 2001;1(2):27−42. For a shorter summary, see Halal at <home.gwu.edu/∼halal/Articles/IC.pdf>. For a summary of definitions and theories of institutional change see Kingston C, Caballero G. Comparing theories of institutional change. J Institutional Econ 2009;5(2):151−80.

[12] Sanborn JB, Salerno AW. The juvenile justice system. Los Angeles, CA: Roxbury Publishing Company; 2005.

[13] *Brown v Board of Education of Topeka Kansas,* 347 U.S. 483(1954).

[14] *Plessy v Ferguson,* 163 U.S. 537(1896).

[15] The states are California, Delaware, Florida, Illinois, Kansas, Louisiana, Maine, Mississippi, Missouri, North Dakota, Oklahoma, Tennessee, and Virginia. U.S. Drug Enforcement Administration, *Salvia divinorum,* <www.justice.gov/dea/concern/salvia_divinorum.html> [accessed August, 2012].

[16] Allen G. Florida bans cocaine-like 'bath salts' sold in stores, NPR, <www.npr.org/2011/02/08/133399834/florida-bans-cocaine-like-bath-salts-sold-in-stores>; February 8, 2011 [accessed August, 2012].

[17] National Conference of State Legislatures, Cyberbullying, <www.ncsl.org/issues-research/educ/cyberbullying.aspx> [accessed August, 2012].

[18] Grumet BH, Schwarb AW. July rise in court fees passes cost to users. St. Petersburg Times [Florida] June 26, 2004:1.

[19] Feld BC. The politics of race and juvenile justice: the 'due process revolution' and the conservative reaction. Justice Quarterly 2003;20(4):765−800.

[20] Packer HL. The limits of the criminal sanction. Stanford, CA: Stanford University Press; 1968.

[21] World Public Opinion. American support due-process rights for terrorism suspects. Washington, DC: Program on International Policy attitudes; 2006, <www.worldpublicopinion.org/pipa/pdf/jul06/TerrSuspect_Jul06_rpt.pdf>.

[22] Dye TR. Understanding public policy. 8th ed. Englewood Cliffs, NJ: Prentice Hall; 1992.

[23] Barker V. The politics of imprisonment: how the democratic process shapes the way America punishes offenders. New York, NY: Oxford University Press; 2009.

[24] Department of Justice, "Citizen's Guide to United States Federal Child Exploitation Laws," Retrieved <www.justice.gov/criminal/ceos/citizensguide/citizensguide.html> [accessed August, 2012].

[25] Walker S. Taming the system: the control of discretion in criminal justice, 1950−1990. New York, NY: Oxford University Press; 1993. Duster TS. The legislation of morality: law, drugs, and moral judgment. New York, NY: Free Press; 1970.

[26] Barker, The politics of imprisonment: how the democratic process shapes the way America punishes offenders.

[27] Kuziemko I. Going off parole: how the elimination of discretionary prison release affects the social cost of crime. National Bureau of Economic Research; 2007, <www.nber.org/papers/w13380.pdf>, Hoffman PB. History of the federal parole system. Washington, DC: United States Department of Justice; 2003, <www.justice.gov/uspc/history.pdf>, Herald Tribune. Herald Tribune (Sarasota, Florida), Review Florida's parole policies: legislation aimed at inmates convicted as juveniles is a start; September 1, 2009, <www.heraldtribune.com/article/20090901/OPINION/909011036>. The Florida Supreme Court upheld life without parole in *Darrick Terrell Adaway vs. State of Florida*; 2005.

[28] Bureau of Labor Statistics, Occupational outlook handbook, police and detectives, March, 2012, <www.bls.gov/oco/ocos160.htm> [accessed August, 2012].

[29] The White House, The Clinton Presidency: A Historic Era of Progress and Prosperity, <clinton5.nara.gov/WH/Accomplishments/eightyears-01.html> [accessed August, 2012].

[30] Bureau of Justice Statistics, Key Facts at a Glance: Direct Expenditures by Criminal Justice Function; 1982–2007, <bjs.ojp.usdoj.gov/content/glance/tables/exptyptab.cfm> [accessed August, 2012].

[31] Pratt T. Addicted to incarceration: corrections policy and the politics of misinformation in the United States. Los Angeles, CA: Sage; 2009. p. 48–57. PollingReport.com, Pew Research Center for the People and the Press Survey; 2001. Princeton Survey Research Associates. CNN/Opinion Research Corporation Poll 2011. Newsweek Poll; 2010, <www.pollingreport.com/drugs.htm> [accessed August, 2012].

[32] Jones T. Halfway house gets cease and desist order from city, WSB TV; October 11, 2011, <www.wsbtv.com/news/news/halfway-house-gets-cease-and-desist-order-city/nFFWD/> [accessed August, 2012].

[33] Ward T, Maruna S. Rehabilitation. London: Routledge; 2008. Smith E, Hattery A. Prison reentry and social capital: the long road to reintegration. Lanham, MD: Lexington Books; 2010. Currie E. Crime and punishment in America: why the solutions to America's most stubborn social crisis have not worked—and what will. New York, NY: Metropolitan Books; 1998. For a critique of unproven rehabilitation programs, see: Marlowe DB. When "what works" never did: dodging the "scarlet M" in correctional rehabilitation. Criminology Public Policy 2006;5(2):339–46. Piquero AR, Steinberg L. Public preferences for rehabilitation versus incarceration of juvenile offenders. J Criminal Justice 2010;38(1):1–6. ABC News/Washington Post Poll; 2010, <www.pollingreport.com/drugs.htm> [accessed August, 2012]. Nagin DS, et al. Public preferences for rehabilitation versus incarceration of juvenile offenders: evidence from a contingent valuation survey. Criminology Public Policy 2006;5(4):627–52.

[34] Orth JV. Due process of law: a brief history. Lawrence, KS: University Press of Kansas; 2003.

[35] *Griswold v. Connecticut* 381 U.S. 479; 1965.

[36] *Graham v. Florida*, 130 S. Ct. (2011).

[37] *Coffin v. U.S.*, 156 U.S. 432 (1895).

[38] Jackall R. Response to: police, prosecutors, and discretion in investigation. In: Kleinig J, editor. Handled with discretion: ethical issues in police decision making. Lanham, MD: Rowman and Littlefield Publishers; 1996. p. 181.

[39] Bureau of Justice Statistics, Key Facts at a Glance, <bjs.ojp.usdoj.gov/content/glance/incrt.cfm> [accessed 2 October 2012]. Kyckelhahn T. Bureau of justice statistics, justice expenditure and employment extracts, 2008—Final, <bjs.ojp.usdoj.gov/index.cfm?ty = pbdetail&iid = 4333> [accessed May 30, 2012].

[40] Weber M. Economy and society [1922; reprint] In: Roth G, Wittich C, editors. Berkeley, CA: University of California Press; 1978.

[41] Selinger S. The case against civil *ex post facto* laws. Cato J: An Interdis J Pub Pol Anal 1995–6;15(2/3):191–214.

[42] *Harmelin v. Michigan*, 501 U.S. 957 (1991). *Trop v. Dulles*, 356 U.S. 86 (1958). *In re Lynch* (1972) 8 Cal. 3d 410, 424. *People v. Almodovar* (1987) 190 Cal. App. 3d 732, 739–740. *Rochin v. California*, 342 U.S. 165 (1952).

[43] *Harmelin v. Michigan*, 501 U.S. 957 (1991). *Francis v. Resweber*, 329 U.S. 459 (1947).

[44] *Hudson v. McMillian*, 503 U.S. 1 (1992). *Hope v. Pelzer*, 536 U.S. 730, 734 (2002).

[45] *Gideon v. Wainwright*, 372 U.S. 335 (1963). *Powell v. Alabama*, 287 U.S. 45 (1932).

[46] *Miranda v. Arizona*, 384 U.S. 436.

[47] National Association of Criminal Defense Lawyers, <www.nacdl.org/sl_docs.nsf/freeform/MERI_resources?opendocument#laws> [accessed August, 2012].

[48] New York Senate, S1377-2011: Requires all interrogations to be ideotaped, <m.nysenate.gov/legislation/bill/S1377-2011> [accessed August, 2012].

[49] National Association of Criminal Defense Lawyers, <www.nacdl.org> [accessed August, 2012].

[50] Reinhart C. Pardon statistics from other states, OLR research report; 2005, <www.cga.ct.gov/2005/rpt/2005-R-0065.htm> [accessed August, 2012].

[51] BBC News. Governor clears Illinois death row <news.bbc.co.uk/2/hi/2649125.stm> [accessed January 11, 2011]. Ibid. For additional details, see Ryan G, Executive Order No. 4: The Creation of the Capital Punishment Commission <www2.illinois.gov/Government/ExecOrders/Documents/2000/execorder2000-04.pdf> [accessed 2000]. Amicis AP. Capital punishment and DNA testing final report, University of Pittsburgh, Graduate School of Public and International Affairs; 2003. Chicago Sun-Times. Illinois' death row officially shuts down; July 2, 2011, <www.suntimes.com/news/6282680-418/illinois-death-row-officially-shuts-down.html> [accessed August, 2012].

[52] Acker JR, Brody DC. Criminal procedure: a contemporary perspective. Gaithersburg, MD: Aspen Publishers; 1999. p. 1.

[53] Cornell University Law School, Legal Information Institute, <www.law.cornell.edu/rules/frcrmp/>. Procedure formulated in "Field Codes," named after David Dudley Field, who advocated codification of procedures in the nineteenth century.

[54] Posner R. Not a suicide pact: the constitution in a time of national emergency. New York, NY: Oxford University Press; 2006. Criminal Justice Legal Foundation, <cjlf.org>.

[55] Russell B. Power: the role of man's will to power in the world's economic and political affairs. New York, NY: W.W. Norton and Company; 1966 [1938; reprint, p. 12].

[56] Ibid., 179–180.

[57] Kennedy A. Commencement Address at Stanford University, YouTube, <www.youtube.com/user/StanfordUniversity#p/search/0/Ogemwplyl4s>; 2009 [accessed August, 2012].

[58] Blau P. The dynamics of bureaucracy. Chicago, IL: University of Chicago Press; 1963. Meyer JW, Rowan B. Institutionalized organizations: formal structure as myth and ceremony. Am J Soc 1977;83(22):340–63. Eisenstein J, Jacob H. Felony justice: an organizational analysis of criminal courts. Boston, MA: Little, Brown, and Company; 1977.

[59] Stidham R, Carp RA. Trial courts' responses to Supreme Court policy changes: three case studies. Law Policy Quarterly 1982;4:215–35. Abraham HJ. The judiciary: the Supreme Court in the governmental process. 6th ed. Boston, MA: Allyn and Bacon; 1983. *Flast v. Cohen*, 392 U.S. 83 (1968).

[60] CNN. Ailing Mubarak wheeled into courtroom cage for trial; August 3, 2011, <articles.cnn.com/2011-08-03/world/egypt.mubarak.trial_1_hosni-mubarak-habib-el-adly-egyptian-people> [accessed August, 2012].

[61] Levi E. An introduction to legal reasoning. Chicago, IL: The University of Chicago Press; 1949.

[62] Duncan OD, Schnore LF, Rossi P. Cultural, behavioral, and ecological perspectives in the study of social organization. Am J Soc 1959;65(2):132−53. Quinn JA. Human ecology. New York, NY: Prentice-Hall; 1950. Hawley AH. Ecology and human ecology. Social Forces 1944;22(4):398−405.

[63] Weber M. Bureaucracy. In: Mills CW, editor. *Max Weber: essays in sociology*, [Gerth H, Trans. 1922; reprint]. New York, NY: Oxford University Press; 1958.

[64] Carp, Stidham. Trial courts' responses to supreme court policy changes: three case studies.

[65] Eisenstein, Jacob. Felony justice: an organizational analysis of criminal courts, p. 67−97.

[66] Brown M. Working the streets: police discretion and the dilemmas of reform. New York, NY: Russell Sage Foundation; 1981. Jones TM. Ethical decision making by individuals in organizations: an issue-contingent model. Academy Manage Rev 1991;16(2):366−95.

[67] Blau. The dynamics of bureaucracy. Meyer, Rowan. Institutionalized organizations: formal structure as myth and ceremony.

[68] Klinger DA. Negotiating order in patrol work: an ecological theory of police response to deviance. Criminology 1997;35:277−306. Blumer H. Symbolic interactionism: perspective and method. Englewood Cliffs, NJ: Prentice Hall; 1969. Fine GA. Negotiated orders and organizational cultures. Ann Rev Soc 1984;10:239−62. Strauss A. Negotiations: varieties, contexts, processes and social order. San Francisco, CA: Jossey-Bass; 1978. Strauss A. Continual permutations of action. New York, NY: DeGruyter; 1993. Maines DR. The negotiated order. Beverly Hills, CA: Sage; 1982217. Basu O, Dirsmith M, Gupta P. The coupling of the symbolic and the technical in an institutionalized context: the negotiated order of the GAO's audit reporting process. Am Sociological Rev. 1999;64(4):506−26. Altheide DL. Mediating cutbacks in human services: a case study in the negotiated order. Sociological Quart 1988;29(3):339−55. Peters AW. Trafficking in meaning: law, victims, and the state, Ph.D. dissertation, Columbia University <www.ncjrs.gov/pdffiles1/nij/grants/231589.pdf>; 2010.

[69] Carp RA, Stidham R. Judicial Process Am. 2nd ed. Washington, DC: Congressional Quarterly Press; 1993. p. 283−314. Hagen J. Extra-legal attributes and criminal sentencing: an assessment of a sociological viewpoint. Law Soc Rev 1974;8:557−83. Hogarth J. Sentencing as a human process. Toronto: University Press; 1971. Redding RE, Repucci ND. Effects of lawyers' socio-political attitudes on their judgments of social science in legal decision making. The first 20 years of law and human behavior. New York, NY: Springer Publishing; 1999. p. 31−54.

[70] Eisenstein, Jacob. Felony justice: an organizational analysis of criminal courts, 41. Charles Derber, the pursuit of attention. New York, NY: Oxford University Press; 2000.

[71] Grana SJ, Ollenburger JC. The social context of law. Upper Saddle River, NJ: Prentice Hall; 1999. p. 3−20. Ehrlich E. 1936. Fundamental principles of the sociology of law. Cambridge, MA: Harvard University Press; 1912. Pound R. Sociology of law and sociological jurisprudence. University Toronto Law J 1943;5(1):1−20.

[72] Cook BB. Public opinion and federal judicial policy. Am J Political Sci 1977;21:576−600. Epstein L, Knight J. Walter F. Murphy: The interactive nature of judicial decision making. In: Maveety N, editor. The pioneers of judicial behavior. Ann Arbor, MI: University of Michigan Press; 2002. p. 178. Eisenstein J, Flemming R, Nardulli P. The contours of justice: communities and their courts. Boston, MA: Little, Brown; 1988.

[73] Sampson RJ, Laub JH. Crime, class, and community: an emerging paradigm. Law Soc Rev 1993;27:255−359. Alexes H, Evans H, Beckett K. Courtesy stigma and monetary sanctions: toward a socio-cultural theory of punishment. Am Sociological Rev 2011;76(2):234−64. Johnson BD, Dipietro SM. The power of diversion: intermediate sanctions and sentencing disparity under presumptive guidelines. Criminology 2012;50(3):811−50. Fearn NE. A multilevel analysis of community effects on criminal sentencing. Justice Quarterly 2005;22 (4):452−87. Ulmer JT, Bader C, Gault M. Do moral communities play a role in criminal sentencing? Evidence from Pennsylvania. Sociological Quarterly 2008;49(4):737−68. Daw R, Solomon A. Assisted suicide and identifying the public interest in the decision to prosecute. Criminal Law Rev 2010;10:737. Helms R, Jacobs D. The political context of sentencing: an analysis of community and individual determinants. Social Forces 2002; 81(2):577−604. Ulmer JT. Social worlds of sentencing: court communities under sentencing guidelines. Albany, NY: State University of New York Press; 1997. Ulmer JT, Kramer JH. Court communities under sentencing guidelines: dilemmas of formal rationality and sentencing disparity. Criminology 1996;34(3):383−408. Ulmer JT. Trial judges in a rural court community: contexts, organizational relations, and interaction strategies. J Contemporary Ethnography 1994;23(1):79−108. Clarke RV, Felson M, editors. Routine activity and rational choice: advances in criminological theory. New Brunswick, NJ: Transaction Books; 1993. Sommer U, Li Q. Judicial decision making in times of financial crises. Judicature 2011;95 (2):68−77. Stidham, Carp. Trial courts' responses to Supreme Court policy changes: three case studies. In: Heydebrand W, Seron C, editors. Rationalizing justice: the political economy of federal district courts. Albany, NY: State University of New York Press; 1990. Albonetti CA. Decision making and juvenile justice: an analysis of bias in case processing. Am J Sociology 2003;109(1):253−5.

[74] Sample J, et al. The new politics of judicial elections 2000−2009: decade of change. Washington, DC: Brennan Center for Justice at New York University School of Law, National Institute on Money in State Politics, Justice at Stake; 2010, <brennan.3cdn.net/ d091dc911bd67ff73b_09m6yvpgv.pdf>, p. 8−12.

[75] Wright RF. How prosecutor elections fail US. Ohio State J Criminal Law 2009;6 (2):581−610. Worrall JL. Prosecution in America: a historical and comparative account. In: Worrall JL, Nugent-Borakove ME, editors. The changing role of the American prosecutor. Albany, NY: SUNY Press; 2008. p. 3−27.

[76] Committee on Identifying the Needs of the Forensic Sciences Community. Strengthening forensic science in the United States: a path forward. Washington, DC: National Academy of Sciences, National Research Council; 2009.

[77] See for example <www.jrsa.org/resources/justicelink.htm;bjs.ojp.usdoj.gov>; and <www .courtstatistics.org>.

[78] Carp and Stidham. Judicial Process Am; 277−82.

PART **1**

Formal Social Control

OVERVIEW

Part 1 places courts within the larger historical context of social control and provides an overview of the criminal justice system, courts, and lawmaking. Modern criminal courts emerged from a long history of human efforts to achieve social order through the control of other humans. The exact structure of a court system, however, varies from one society to the next. Based on the Constitution, the United States developed a system that integrates British common law and more modern civil law. A unique feature of the U.S. system is that the federal government and each state have an independent court system. Yet each of these 51 courts systems has the twin goals of enforcing criminal laws and protecting the due-process rights of individuals in the process.

Not until the rise of empires did we start to see formal, written laws and the systems to enforce them. For example, the Egyptian empire established an elaborate system of formal social controls, such as the regulation of religious worship, taxation, legal rights for women, and local governors to enforce laws.

CHAPTER 2

Social Control, Comparative Courts, and the Development of the U.S. Judicial System

KEY TERMS

adjudication system
age of empires
Age of Enlightenment
Article III
Article IV
Bill of Rights
bureaucratization
case law
Case or Controversy
    clause
checks and balances
civil law
common law
constitution
constitutional courts
crime control
dual sovereignty

due-process revolution
Equal Protection clause
Establishment clause
Extradition Clause
federalist system
formal social control
Full Faith and Credit
    clause
informal social control
Jim Crow laws
judicial law
legal-rational authority
Magna Carta
net-widening
norms
organizational scripts
primitive legal systems

Privileges and
    Immunities clause
procedural justice
professionalization
religion-based court
    systems
Shari'a
social engineering
social order
Supremacy clause
test cases
transitional legal
    systems
trial by ordeal
tribal courts
urbanization

CONTENTS

American Criminal Courts.

Learning Objectives

After reading this chapter, you should be able to:

1. Explain social order and social control in simple societies.
2. Link norms and informal social controls to informal sanctions.
3. Discuss how empires changed the nature of social control.
4. Talk about how nation-states changed the nature of social control.
5. Summarize four families of legal and court systems.
6. Discuss how early U.S. politicians achieved social order while balancing the pursuit of justice and protection of rights with maintaining social control.
7. Understand the constitutional provisions that created the judiciary.
8. Explain why the Industrial Revolution led to significant changes in the U.S. courts.
9. Analyze bureaucratization and professionalization and explain how they altered the U.S. courts.
10. Explain what is meant by the due-process revolution and describe some of the changes that occurred.

The history of society is, in large part, a history of how people have expanded the range of social control. The modern U.S. criminal courts are part of this large spectrum of social control, and to better understand it, we must understand our history.

When people first started to form small hunting-and-gathering societies 50,000 years ago, they had no written language, no codified laws, and no government. Yet, they still needed rules to maintain their societies. Their only forms of social control were informal, such as giving gifts and other incentives or physically punishing and ostracizing those who did not follow the rules. That system of social control lasted around 45,000 years [1]. Not until the rise of empires about 5000 years ago did we start to see formal, written laws and the systems to enforce them, such as the Code of Hammurabi, Roman law, the laws of the Chinese Han empire, and the Napoleonic Codes.

Overlapping the end of empires was the Enlightenment, a period that began about 500 years ago in which people began to systematically analyze social control. These intellectuals challenged the prevailing logic of punishment and modes of adjudication, proposing instead new notions of justice, such as trials that follow rules of fairness and punishment that helps the community or changes the offender. They argued that governments should assert their power, but do so in a just manner. Courts were a crucial part of this new form of social control.

SOCIAL ORDER AND SOCIAL CONTROL

All societies must create and maintain solidarity or **social order**, which is a society's ability to operate in predictable patterns [2]. That simple definition captures the essence of people coming together in the formation of social groups. This is true even if the social order benefits some people and harms others. One requirement of societies is that social order must be maintained, whether in a hunting-and-gathering tribe, a densely populated city like Chicago, a capitalist economy, a socialist economy, a democracy, or a monarchy. Social order also exists in gangs, families, classrooms, and any other human group.

Social order depends on a second requirement of all societies, the control of the people within the population. Order cannot be achieved without limiting some behaviors and expecting other behaviors. **Social control** is any concerted effort or social process that constrains and directs the conduct of people by inducing conformity and preventing nonconformity. The term "social control" often conjures images of brutal repression. Although social control sometimes involves physical force, it also includes all the daily social mechanisms that encourage us to engage in particular behaviors while preventing us from engaging in other behaviors. This includes a wide range of inducements—the incentives that draw us toward certain conduct, such as being praised or receiving a raise—and compulsions, the application of negative sanctions to discourage certain conduct.

For the study of courts, compulsions are more important. Examples of social control via compulsions include dressing in popular fashions and avoiding clothes that may prompt people to laugh at you; sitting in the "student section" in class and raising your hand before talking to avoid being disciplined by the teacher or scorned by the classmates; and driving the speed limit to avoid a ticket. All these pushes and constraints on our behavior create boundaries between acceptable and unacceptable behavior [3].

All forms of social control entail two elements: rules and enforcement [4]. Rules can take the form of **norms** (cultural rules that constrain our behavior and guide us toward particular behavior), organizational policies like the student code of conduct or a company dress code, and laws. Rules, however, do not enforce themselves [5]. Enforcement of rules comes from subtle social exchanges like disapproving looks or praise for doing a job well to violent responses like vigilante lynchings and state-sponsored executions. No matter the form, social control is a mechanism for preserving social order.

Together, rules and sanctions create patterns in human behavior. Everyone does not behave in exactly the same way all the time, but our behaviors tend to be similar to the dominant patterns of behaviors around us. When people do not conform, we have mechanisms that respond to that deviation. Social life is structured, and does not consist of individuals doing whatever they want. Social structure refers to predictable and established patterns of behavior and social relationships.

The development of society can be studied as the development of social control. Simple societies relied entirely on **informal social control**, or efforts by people with no specific government authority acting unofficially to enforce norms and local customs. They had no government, police, courts, or prisons. As more complex empires developed, people began to write laws [6]. In the modern nation-state, which is the geographic and political organization of people into a formal governing union, we have added to all our informal social controls a vast array of government-orchestrated controls, from police to zoning to licensing. The criminal justice system, though perhaps the most recognizable system of government control, is just one part of an array of **formal social controls**, or efforts by official agencies, acting in their designated capacity, to constrain and direct the conduct of people.

SOCIAL ORDER IN SIMPLE SOCIETIES

Starting about 50,000 years ago, humans began to gather into small groups known as hunting-and-gathering societies, or what sociologists sometimes call *Gemeinschaft* societies, or small tribes in which everyone shares the same ethnicity and culture [7]. In these societies everyone eats the same food, lives in the same type of dwellings, has similar notions of the supernatural, and speaks the same language. They were homogenous, or culturally similar. This is the longest epoch of human history, composing about 45,000 years of our existence [8]. Some hunting-and-gathering societies still exist, such as the Kung San of the Kalahari Desert in Southern Africa, whom anthropologists have studied for the past 150 years.

These societies are sometimes called "primitive" or "archaic cultures" because they had no written language and had what are known as primitive legal systems [9]. **Primitive legal systems** are systems of control in simple societies that have no codified laws but rely exclusively on tradition, custom, and informal social controls to achieve social order within the community [10].

"Informal" does not mean the controls were weak and that people were free to do whatever they wanted. Instead, "informal" means that traditions, public shaming, and immediate physical punishment were used to bring people into conformity rather than arrest, conviction, and incarceration. No one had the sole job of enforcing the rules. For instance, the modern Ifugao tribe on Luzon Island in the Philippines has no central authority, maintains collective responsibility for the group's well-being, and relies on kinship groups to act as the judicial body [11]. Max Weber (VAY-bur) referred to societies that have no standalone government to write and enforce rules as "traditional authority" because the rules and leaders were respected and followed as a matter of the culture and traditions, not because they were elected or hired to do the work [12].

Traditional authority and informal social control preserve norms through informal sanctions, or responses to a violation of a norm by people with no particular legal authority to regulate that behavior. Although we still have informal sanctioning, in simple societies all sanctions are informal because there is no formal government. Informal social control is still a large part of our lives, but all modern societies have added formal social control to the older systems of informal control.

TRANSITIONAL HISTORY: EMPIRES AND THE BIRTH OF LAW AND COURTS

About 5000 years ago, a turning point in systems of social control occurred with the emergence of empires, which are societies that use military dominance to gain economic and political control over other societies. Empires started to take shape as far back as the Akkadian (or Babylonian–Assyrian) Empire in the fourth millennium B.C.E. in Mesopotamia. However, the **age of empires**, when most people around the world were controlled by empires, began around 1000 B.C.E. and continued up to the 19th century C.E.

During this epoch, empires, such as the Roman Empire, flourished on five continents [13]. Empires introduced written laws, formal social control, and formal sanctions. Formal social control depends on "formal sanctions", or responses to a violation of a codified rule by an agent of an official organization designated to enforce that rule. In short, this was the beginning of social order achieved through state power. A central authority, or early form of government, would, for instance, set and collect taxes and write and enforce laws about harming others.

These new forms of social control were necessary to deal with heterogeneous, or increasingly diverse, societies. People were concentrating in agricultural communities rather than foraging and hunting for food. Advances in technology, such as metalworking and transportation increased migration and trade, decreased mortality, increased inequality, and ultimately increased the size and diversity of empires [14]. Large and heterogeneous societies, called *Gesellschafts*, are complex societies compared to simple hunting-and-gathering communities [15]. The people within the Byzantine Empire, for example, spoke many languages, practiced diverse religions, had various diets, and formed unique family structures.

The informal social controls that worked for thousands of years were not adequate to control such societies because there were too many behaviors to control [16]. Systems of formal social control allowed rulers to centralize and standardize their rule making and rule enforcing. This enabled the conquering government to "transport" their rules to areas that were geographically distant from the central city [17]. These forms of central control may be considered inconsistent or weak by today's standards, but they marked a significant change for human society by providing the foundation for the further centralization and standardization of power.

Jonathan Turner [18] identifies these early legal systems as **transitional legal systems** because in these early stages of law, the central government lacked many of the features that we consider essential to a modern government. Transitional legal systems are systems of control in empires and early societies that had some codified laws and local courts but lacked a clear system of writing and enforcing laws. The rulers did not control all areas; they could not communicate messages rapidly and widely; travel was slow; the boundaries of the empires were not clearly demarcated; there was a high rate of illiteracy; local leaders opposed, ignored, or altered the laws; and lawmaking and law enforcement had not been professionalized.

Given all this, plus the fact that "law" was something new that many people had not heard of, informal social control remained in force at the same time rational law was developing. In short, the legal transition from informal to formal controls, as with all transitions, was fitful and inconsistent [19]. The schematic timeline below shows the tumult with which empires and legal codes developed:

- Early Mesopotamian civilizations, such as Uruk, Sumeria, the Akkadian Empire, and the Dynasty of Ur occupied the middle east beginning nearly 6000 years ago and made advances in architecture, writing, and law, including written law that predated the Code of Hammurabi [20].
- The Egyptian empire, which emerged about 5000 years ago, established an elaborate system of formal social controls, such as the regulation of religious worship, taxation, legal rights for women, and local governors to enforce laws.
- The Babylonian Empire emerged around 4000 years ago. One of its rulers, Hammurabi, produced the Code of Hammurabi. Although the code was actually a summary of decisions he made about issues, many consider it to be the first official legal code known [21].
- The Israelite kingdom, which existed about 3000 years ago in and around the modern nation of Israel, drafted religion-based transcendent rules, which were rules that the leaders had to adhere and that persisted from one ruler to the next [22].
- The Roman Empire began around 750 B.C.E., lasted a 1000 years, and produced a legal system that included the Twelve Tables of Rome

(450 B.C.E.) and the Justinian Code, which influences courts to this day [23]. Classical Greece, which flourished at the same time, produced Draco's harsh code of laws in 621 B.C.E., which is where the word "draconian" comes from. The laws of Solon, which replaced all of Draco's laws except those pertaining to murder, also regulated many details of family life.

- The Chinese dynasties emerged around 2000 B.C.E. The Han Dynasty in modern China 2000 years ago was matched in size only by the Roman Empire.
- The Byzantine Empire began in the 4th century C.E. as the eastern part of the Roman Empire and ruled what is now modern eastern Europe for a 1000 years.
- The Inca and Aztec Empires flourished about 700 years ago in western South America and Central America, respectively. The Aztecs, in particular, had an elaborate legal system for commerce and other aspects of life.
- The Mali Empire of West Africa ruled Western Africa during the same period as the Incas and Aztecs.
- The Napoleon, British, Ottoman, and Prussian Empires spanned centuries up to the 20th century, and provided much of the law and court structure still in use today.

Although profoundly diverse in their social structure, these societies collectively contributed to several changes that laid the early foundation of modern courts. First, they developed a written language that was then employed to create codified laws. When the leader died, the laws were often replaced, but many of the empires moved, at least with some legal codes, toward laws that persisted regardless of who was in power. This served as a springboard for the later development of laws based on constitutions. Such a shift may have increased the public's acceptance of law and therefore given it greater potency in controlling the people.

Second, the domain of laws expanded, from basic religious instructions to the regulation of family, money, taxation, land-use, and an assortment of behaviors that would later become known as crime [24]. Third, enforcement of the law became more consistent and far-reaching. For instance, in 1215, English barons forced King John to sign the **Magna Carta**, a charter that, for the first time, limited the king's power by making him follow written rules and protected the rights and liberties of people under his rule. In particular, Chapter 39 protects individuals against judgments that do not adhere to "the law of the land," which was translated in 1354 from Latin to read "by due process of the law" [25]. By the time civilization got to the last centuries of the age of empire, these developments had made way for the modern nation-state.

THE MODERN NATION-STATE AND THE EXPANSION OF COURTS

In 1648, a set of treaties known as the Peace of Westphalia ended the Thirty Years War in Europe, and Europe's governments agreed to recognize the legitimacy of other governments and honor the boundaries separating sovereign states. This event did not mark the beginning of sovereign nations or formal law, but it did usher in a modern system of governance. These modern states, less encumbered by outside threat (even though European nations continued fighting among themselves for centuries more), were more readily able to articulate their goals in the form of laws. Thus, legal systems became even more elaborate. More rules were written, and punishments became less capricious as courts had to follow the rules. People began to move away from settling disputes using tradition, conscience, prayer, and their own sense of fairness, mercy, and justice and toward relying on the content and technicalities of the written law.

What makes the modern nation-state important for our discussion of court systems is the degree to which law regulated the conduct of both the people and the governments. Every new law increased the number of justifications for the government to punish someone, and the legal system increasingly became an apparatus of power and domination [26]. At the same time western European governments were enacting laws in a quantity as never before, political philosophers such as Montesquieu, Jeremy Bentham, John Locke, and others were mapping strategies to use government power and structure to constrain government power itself [27]. As stated in Article VI of France's 1789 *Declaration of the Rights of Man*, "The law must serve everyone, those it protects as well as those it punishes" [28].

This tension between expanding government power and efforts to constrain it certainly was not a harmonious path of progress. European societies, and later the United States, saw countless incidents of governments abusing powers and people disregarding the law to exact punishment themselves, such as with the thousands of lynchings in the United States, mostly of black people in the post-Civil War south. Nonetheless, a new understanding of law and punishment was emerging.

The era of nation-states, which produced the United States and other nations, developed along with what is often called the Age of Enlightenment. The **Age of Enlightenment** is the 18th-century era during which intellectuals advanced science and reason as ways to improve the human condition, increase human knowledge, and advance the ideals of individual rights and justice, which included fair adjudication procedures. During this period, intellectuals systematically developed new ways of thinking and understanding the world, such as the political theory of separation of powers alluded to above and the liberal ideas of reason, rights, and tolerance. These Enlightenment principles profoundly affected U.S. courts in three fundamental ways: advancing the notion of rights and justice, demanding methods for protecting rights and fairly adjudicating accusations, and applying reason to the adjudication process.

Scholars of the day knew people needed to be controlled, but they believed the control could be exerted in a way that protected the rights of all people, was humane and predictable, and improved the human condition. The question then became, "What type of social control is good and just?" The first step in answering this was to address the law itself. Law must serve the purpose of community good. It must protect the people and change people for the better. Second, law must be independent of the rulers, which means there must be clear procedures for enacting or revoking it, and the rulers must be subject to it such that it constrains the government. This is often described as law being valid, legitimate, or rational [29]. Finally, the law must protect the rights of the people, such as their liberty to speak about controversial issues and practice no religion or a religion of their choice.

The creation of just laws, however, tended to precede their fair application. Early court judges were hired, fired, and sometimes punished at the will of the king or other ruler (a structure that still exists in many nations, such as Russia). In nations such as France, court positions were sold, and courts often enforced a combination of central laws and local tradition, which created an administration of justice that was "slow, arbitrary, and unfair [and] an insult to reason" [30]. This situation created corrupt courts and nations that had rights granted in laws and constitutions but not actually enjoyed by the citizens.

To correct this, progressive leaders argued for an **adjudication system**, or a system for reviewing and applying laws, that was both independent of the ruler or ruling party and constrained through checks and balances, procedural rules, and a process of appeals [31]. This required a robust court system, an "authority of the legally organized community" that could review, apply, and uphold the law [32]. Independent courts created a new form of dispute resolution in which an impartial outsider would resolve conflict nonviolently among individuals and between individuals and the state. Such a system would create an environment that clearly defines rights, duties, and prohibitions, provides equal access to the protection of those rights, and allows everyone to practice their acceptable freedoms [33]. For justice to be achieved, adjudication, not just legislation, was essential [34]. Legislation, or the enactment of law, pursues justice by achieving some specific social end. This is a utilitarian form of justice. These courts would pursue a new notion of justice, the justice of fairness achieved by following procedural steps in the application of law and protection of rights.

One particular court-process issue was the question of ascertaining truth, or how to go about establishing what happened and affixing blame. Ancient methods of establishing guilt or innocence included trial by battle in which two opponents would fight each other until submission or death, with the winner being declared the legal victor; trial by ordeal, in which the accused would be physically tortured with the belief that an innocent person would be delivered from the ordeal by divine intervention; and trial by compurgation in which a defendant would establish innocence by asking or paying others to testify to the accused's innocence. In contrast, the Enlightenment brought about the ideas of reason and the scientific method, a technique of investigation. Truth was most closely approximated by clear logic and the use of evidence [35]. This is why the courts of England, and later the United States, relied on evidence presented in the adversarial method: two advocates compete to find the best evidence and logic to win the case. Focus on Discretion illustrates how citizens still pressure the courts to change how cases are processed and truth is ascertained.

FOCUS ON DISCRETION

Citizen Oversight of Laws, Court Procedures, and Legal Decision-Making

Because the United States has a history of protesting government power and has protected that right in the First Amendment, people often form organizations that push back against abusive government power manifest in the courts. Read the examples described below, then consider how these tactics could be applied to other issues in the legal system.

■ In 2006, the American Civil Liberties Union filed a lawsuit against the National Security Agency over its wiretapping program, stating that domestic eavesdropping is unconstitutional and that President George W. Bush exceeded his authority by authorizing it [36].

■ Television cameras are usually allowed in courtrooms. However, in pretrial hearings in the case against Dr. Conrad Murray, who was eventually convicted of involuntary manslaughter in pop star Michael Jackson's death, Los Angeles County Superior Court Judge Michael Pastor blocked all television cameras from the courtroom. Is it important for citizen oversight to allow trials to be recorded and broadcast? [37]

■ The National Association for the Advancement of Colored People (NAACP) uses **test cases** to challenge the constitutionality of laws. Test cases are strategies that involve having someone violate a law, be convicted in a trial, and then appeal the case on the grounds that the law is unconstitutional. The organization has done this with "racial covenant" laws that prohibit black people from moving into white neighborhoods, laws allowing segregated schools, and other cases of racial segregation [38].

■ Organizations and individuals often submit *amici* briefs, which are legal arguments given to the court by people not involved in the case to influence the court. Such briefs were submitted in the *Furman v. Georgia* (1972) case that put a four-year moratorium on executions in that state [39].

■ The Innocence Project challenges convictions by reviewing shaky cases and using DNA evidence to exonerate the wrongfully convicted [40].

■ In states that elect judges, prosecutors, and defense attorneys, people may campaign against those they do not like. In states that appoint these court workers, individuals and organizations can lobby the governor and legislature to appoint their preferred candidate.

COMPARATIVE LEGAL AND COURT SYSTEMS

Not all nations took the same path out of the Enlightenment, so there are several types of law around the world [41]. These families of law include, among others, common law, civil law, religion-based law, and American Indian courts.

Common law, or law that emanates from judicial rulings, began in English courts and is still partially practiced in many of Britain's former colonies, including the United States and Canada. The distinguishing elements of common-law courts are judicial law and precedent. **Judicial law** or **case law** is a judgment that becomes a law for all cases. The judge interprets the facts of a case and makes a judgment that becomes a law common for all people. When making judgments, courts should as much as possible follow earlier court rulings, a practice known as precedent. Some common-law nations do not have a constitution that anchors the courts. Instead, they rely on precedent.

Civil law is law based on codes written by governing bodies, such as Congress. In civil-law systems, courts should remain true to the civil laws. Civil-law courts, which are sometimes called Napoleonic courts and are the most common type of court, eliminate, or at least try to minimize, both the power of the courts to make law and the requirement that they follow precedent.

In practice today, most nations blend elements of both civil law and common law. Common-law courts must still enforce statutes written by the legislature, and civil-law courts generally respect the idea of precedent and try to remain consistent with past rulings. The United States is an example of a hybrid court system, with precedent and limited judicial law firmly established and an elaborate system of statutes that determine the rulings in most trial courts.

Religion-based court systems have elements of common-law precedent and civil-law statutes, but add a religious component to their proceedings and are thus considered theocratic systems. During the Roman Empire and early nation-state eras, most nation-states had strong religious influences, and courts were bound by those tenets. However, over the past three centuries, most courts have become more secular because religious texts cannot address society's growing diversity and complexities. Today, official religious courts exist only in some predominantly Muslim nations, Israel, and Vatican City, all of which have a dual court system of civil law and religious law. In Muslim nations **Shari'a**, which is law derived from the Koran, is set up as a separate court system for handling specific issues like divorce and child custody under the auspices of religious Islamic teachings [42]. These courts do not have civil laws; instead, a religious leader makes each ruling based on his interpretation of how the religious tenets apply to the case. For instance, a Saudi woman was recently executed by such a court for practicing magic [43]. Some of these nations, such as Saudi Arabia, do not have a constitution. Court Procedures examine the efforts of many Americans to create Christian religious courts in the United States.

Tribal courts are courts operated by American Indian tribes and Alaska Native Nations to handle wrongs that occur on land controlled by the respective tribe. They vary considerably in style and scope, from handling civil issues to handling some criminal matters. However, they have increased considerably since the tribal sovereignty movement of the 1970s. Like courts of religion-based laws, these courts mix law with tradition. Historically, American Indians had no written law, so they rely on oral traditions. Generally, these courts aim toward peacemaking by trying to mediate reconciliation between the offender and the injured [44].

The court procedures of different nations are amazingly unique, even within each family. Some use juries; some give victims a prominent role; some require judges to wear wigs; and some have no defense attorneys or plea bargaining. Nonetheless, there is a general movement toward some similar characteristics. All nations now rely on codified civil law; all nations have a court system; and nearly all nations have a constitution. Most nations now have specialized courts, such as for business contracts or serious crimes; alternative courts and dispositions, such as community courts; and a hierarchy of courts. Most nations, with the United States being a notable exception, have shifted to a nationally unified court system in order to eliminate the confusions of multiple local courts. Also, all nations' courts ascertain truth, to a greater or lesser degree, through the presentation of evidence and legal argument, even if the style of presentation and admissibility rules vary. Over 40 percent of nations have formalized judicial review and therefore allow courts to rule on the legitimacy of a law [45]. (Dictatorships, of course, will probably never have an independent judiciary or judicial review.)

This increased similarity of courts, as well as the growing number of international courts, may be a function of greater global connections. In order to live or do business in another nation, individuals must be familiar and comfortable with the legal system [46].

COURT PROCEDURES

Should the Courts Become Religion-based Courts?

The First Amendment includes the **Establishment clause**, which prohibits the government from favoring or endorsing one religion over another. Nonetheless, many Americans believe that the courts should explicitly incorporate religious values.

- For several decades powerful fundamentalist leaders like Pat Robertson have successfully lobbied for the appointment of devout Christians to the federal bench [47].
- More than 40 members of Congress submitted a brief arguing that the nation was created under the will of God and should acknowledge that [48].
- Many have argued, including prominent political figures like Newt Gingrich, that the courts should strike down laws that permit abortion and access to birth control because such behaviors supposedly violate the the the law of God.
- Several authors advocate the infusion of Christian practices into the U.S. legal system. Author Tim Ballard states that, "God explicitly participated in and oversaw the manifestation of the U.S." and that "America needs to "invoke God at the highest levels of government" [49].
- When running for the Republican presidential nomination in 2011, Rick Santorum stated, "God gave us rights [and] the laws of this country should comport with that moral vision" [50].
- Cities and states have tried since 2001 to ban the practice of Islam, and some judges have prohibited displays of Islam from their courts [51].
- Judges in some courthouses have erected displays of the Christian Ten Commandments, even after the Supreme Court ruled such conduct unconstitutional [52].

It is unclear how such theocratic courts would be structured, but most advocates say the United States should retain a constitution, civil law, and courts with the power of judicial review [53]. Even with a constitution, if the United States were to move in the direction of Saudi Arabia and Iran and build one religion into the structure of the nation's laws, constitutional rights and the legal principles that guide courts would have to change.

Questions

Should the United States abolish the Establishment clause and create religion-based laws and courts?
What would be positive and negative outcomes of such a shift?

THE CREATION AND ADAPTATION OF U.S. COURTS

The roots of the U.S. legal system and courts lie within English law and the ideals of Enlightenment. When these intertwined with the American Revolution against Britain, the world witnessed what is sometimes called the "great democratic experiment," an attempt to build a lasting constitutional democracy in a large and diverse nation. Such a government is what Bertrand Russell describes as an "identity of interests," that is, matching the interests of those who rule (the government) with the interests of those who are governed (the subjects) [54]. The government is put in place and removed by those whom it rules and therefore cannot be indifferent to the people.

This idea that the government will both rule the people and take account of the people's interests to the point of structurally constraining itself is common for us, perhaps, but it was a bold idea. The first U.S. politicians had to achieve social order within this new balance of pursuing justice and protecting rights, on the one hand, and controlling the people on the other. They turned to the courts as the branch to strike this balance. Courts not only adjudicated accusations of wrongdoing and issued punishments for people who violated laws, but also forced the agents of the state to follow procedural rules.

Prior to independence from Britain, each North American colony had a colonial court system, which was designed within the political and cultural conditions of the colony but were always subject to the colonizing government, such as England, Spain, or France. Some colonial courts, called the royal courts, were more closely tied to the king of the colonizing government. Others, often called proprietary courts, had more independence. In both cases, these were clearly defined courts that enforced the rule of law in civil and criminal matters [55].

However, the people living in these colonies did not all believe that King George III of Great Britain respected this rule of law. In the Declaration of Independence, signed on July 4, 1776, the delegates listed 26 accusations against the king to explain why they were revolting. According to Thomas Jefferson, this "long train of abuses and usurpations" included:

- The King not following the rule of law himself ("He has refused his Assent to Laws")
- The King refusing to allow judicial independence ("He has made Judges dependent on his Will alone")
- The King denying basic due process of law, such as "depriving us in many cases of the benefits of Trial by Jury"

The Declaration was the beginning of the American Revolutionary War. During the war, the 13 former colonies declared their independence and became states, but they needed a new government to unify them, so they ratified the Articles of Confederation and Perpetual Union in 1781 to serve as their constitution. Although this founding document created a rule of law (freedom of speech, for instance), it was considered by many as too weak because it did not give the federal government enough lawmaking and law-enforcement powers, and it did not allow the government to adapt to changes in society. In fact, its only provision for a federal court system was the Court of Appeals in Cases of Captures. Most judicial power was left to state courts [56]. Just 3 years after the Treaty of Paris formally ended the American Revolutionary War in 1784, representatives of the states convened to write the Constitution of the United States, which went into effect in 1789 and is still in force today.

The Federal Constitution

A **constitution** is created to describe the structure of a government and delegate authority among its branches. It designates relative power of each core unit of government [57]. In the United States, the Constitution serves the additional function of being a compact among the states and the federal government. As James Madison, one of the draftsmen of the Constitution, wrote,

> If men were angels, no government would be necessary. If angels were to govern men, neither external nor internal controls on government would be necessary. In framing a government which is to be administered by men over men, the great difficulty lies in this: you must first enable the government to control the governed: and in the next place oblige it to control itself [58].

A National Judiciary

The Constitution not only created federal **constitutional courts**—courts that create the core of the federal judiciary and hear federal criminal trials and appeals—but also allowed the states to create their own court systems. The U.S. court system, however, was not laid out in detail in the Constitution, or in any of the writings of the Founding Fathers. The structure and role of the courts was established after the nation was formed. This "organic" nature of the court allows for it to continue to adapt and change to this day. It is actually amazing that the massive U.S. court system is grounded in four short constitutional provisions: Article III, Article IV, Article VI, and the Tenth Amendment.

The first three articles of the Constitution establish the national government, which includes three branches that are supposed to check the power of the other branches. This system is called **checks and balances**, which is the right of each branch of a government to amend or void acts of another that fall within its purview. Articles I and II created the legislative and executive branches respectively, and gave Congress the power to write laws and the presidency the power to enforce those laws. **Article III**, which is a mere 369 words, created the federal courts as an independent branch of the government and broadly outlined their jurisdiction and limitations. Section 1 of Article III states:

> The judicial power of the United States, shall be vested in one Supreme Court, and in such inferior courts as the Congress may from time to time ordain and establish. The judges, both of the supreme and inferior courts, shall hold their offices during good behaviour, and shall, at stated times, receive for their services, a compensation, which shall not be diminished during their continuance in office.

In outlining the court's authority, Section 2 states that the "judicial power" shall cover cases arising from laws. This created an important limit on the courts, known as the **Case or Controversy clause**, the constitutional requirement that a court cannot exercise its jurisdictional authority unless one party brings a lawsuit against another party. Courts, for the most part, only review and resolve legal disputes, such as one person suing another for violating a contract or the state charging a person with breaking the law. They rarely, on the other hand, create public policy or offer advisory opinions. They do not sit at the table with Congress and help write laws. They do not decide how much funding public schools get or how much college tuition costs. They do not proactively advise the executive branch on the best policy practices. Their principal job is reactive, which means they handle problems or injuries that arise out of existing laws and policies. Section 2 goes on to require the use of juries and to require criminal trials be held in the state where the offense occurred.

> The trial of all crimes, except in cases of impeachment, shall be by jury; and such trial shall be held in the state where the said crimes shall have been committed . . .

This is why every state now has at least one federal district, so that if the federal government is going to prosecute someone, it will do so in the state where the offense occurred rather than transport the defendant to a more distant location. Article IV, Article VI, and the Tenth Amendment gave powers to states and described their relationship with the federal government, thereby laying the groundwork for the federalist system.

The Federalist System

The Constitution explicitly creates the federal government and judiciary, but it does not directly map out state powers. Rather, state power is implied throughout the document [59]. What this means is that the very document that created the federal government limited the federal government by balancing its own power with states' powers. A system of government in which the national government shares power with each of the states is called a **federalist system** or **dual sovereignty**.

Article IV is perhaps the clearest place in which states are given independent power to handle affairs within their borders. It describes in general terms the mutual relationship between the states, sometimes called horizontal federalism. Three clauses are of particular importance to each state's criminal courts.

- The **Privileges and Immunities clause** requires that states treat the state residents and residents of other states equally. It does not specify basic rights, but it does mean that if a Texas resident commits an offense

PHOTO 2.1

Constitutional congress members Benjamin Franklin, Alexander Hamilton, and others talk about the framing of the U.S. Constitution at a gathering in Philadelphia in 1787. Much of the discussion about the Constitution occurred at informal meetings such as these.

in Arizona, he or she will still receive the same type of trial that an Arizona resident would receive.

■ The **Full Faith and Credit clause** requires that states respect other states' laws. For instance, you do not need a Virginia driver's license to drive there from your home in North Carolina, nor does a couple have to get remarried every time they move to a new state.

■ The **Interstate Rendition clause**, which is often called the **Extradition clause**, requires that a state return a criminal suspect to the state in which the offense occurred if that state makes a request and pays the expenses.

Article VI contains what is known as the **Supremacy clause**, which is the constitutional requirement that contradictions between state and federal law shall be resolved in favor of the federal law. All judges, federal and state, must uphold the Constitution and federal law.

This Constitution, and the laws of the United States ... shall be the supreme law of the land; and the judges in every state shall be bound thereby, anything in the Constitution or laws of any State to the contrary notwithstanding.

This clause has not been interpreted to mean that all judges have jurisdiction over federal law. A court in Iowa cannot convict someone for violating the federal law prohibiting giving aid or money to an organization on the federal list of organizations labeled terrorist. However, if a state law contradicts federal law—such as a state law declaring all charitable donations as lawful—then a judge either should not enforce the state law or, if the judge does, an appellate court should declare the state law unconstitutional. Most likely, in fact, the local prosecutor would not charge the defendant (and the local judge would therefore never hear the case) but would give it to a federal court and prosecutor to begin with.

Within 2 years of the Constitution going into effect, the **Bill of Rights**, or the first 10 amendments, were ratified and added to the Constitution. The Tenth Amendment further addresses the separation of federal and state powers, this time giving more power to the states by pointing out that if the federal government does not have constitutional authority over a matter (such as most criminal offenses), then the states have the authority to regulate it. According to the Tenth Amendment, the U.S. government does not have what is called inherent powers, or power over whatever it so chooses. Rather, its power must be specified by the Constitution.

> The powers not delegated to the United States by the Constitution, nor prohibited by it to the States, are reserved to the States respectively, or to the people.

The balance of power in Articles IV and VI and the Tenth Amendment has been important for criminal courts, sometimes giving powers to the state over federal efforts and sometimes ruling that the federal law preempts the state law. The Supreme Court ruled in 2011, for instance, that the states are allowed to punish employers who hire illegal immigrants, even though the federal government controls most immigration issues [60]. In an earlier case, the Court used the same logic and ruled that the federal government cannot create "gun free zones" within states; that is the jurisdiction of state courts [61].

Federal supremacy, however, prevails over state law and courts if a state passes a law that either violates the Constitution or is federal jurisdiction [62]. The Supreme Court has ruled, for instance, that states cannot decriminalize marijuana because federal law legitimately criminalizes it [63]. The Court, however, will probably rule on this issue again. The Court has also struck down as unconstitutional state laws that enforced racial segregation (part of what were called **Jim Crow laws**), criminalized all abortions and homosexuality, and criminalized burning the U.S. flag [64]. The federal courts can also rule on state criminal justice system procedures, such as requiring that they provide public defenders and prohibiting police from arresting without a warrant immigrants suspected of committing a criminal offense [65].

With these four short provisions, the early representatives of the nation compromised between having a strong federal government and a weak one. Although the balance between state sovereignty and national supremacy has been disputed in many cases, these provisions did create a unique system of governance in which the national government shares power with each of the states [66]. This means that the government and courts are simultaneously centralized and regional. It also means federal and state power is sometimes independent and sometimes overlapping, which creates jurisdiction problems that must be figured out every day. As researchers have pointed out, this dual court system is "one of the most important, most interesting, and most confusing features of the judiciary in the United States..." [67].

Dialectics of Due Process and Crime Control

The men who laid out the framework of the U.S. court system drew on both due process and crime control. Due process is the central legal principle in the court system that states that a person's rights must be protected during government proceedings and that arbitrary and excessive government power must be inhibited. Crime control is the use of government power to reduce behavior prohibited by criminal law. The federal and state governments have the power to write and enforce their laws and to convict and punish law-breakers. This enables the government to exert its power over the people in order to reduce crime and maintain social order. However, this power is not limitless. Government officials themselves must adhere to laws, particularly procedural laws, that limit their authority. This is why legal philosopher Martin Golding refers to due process as **procedural justice**: it is the expectation of fairness in legal proceedings [68].

The founders established the federalist system without providing details for the structure or operation of the federal court system or the state court systems. There was no mention, for instance, of prosecutors, juvenile justice courts, or drug courts. The Constitution created neither public defenders offices, nor a victims' bill of rights. The number or size of federal districts was not specified. The state courts themselves were not described. The precedent of dismissing a confession because the police did not read the *Miranda* rights did not exist. All these types of courts and procedures emerged over the next 200 years in each of the states and at the federal level.

The push and pull between government power and individual rights is the basis of the thousands of changes to the U.S. courts over the past two centuries. Shifts in legal principles and procedures began to occur within a year of the ratification of the Constitution [69]. The new Congress established a federal court system based on Article III provisions, which offered few specifics on how the courts should be structured. The Judiciary Act of 1789 created a

Supreme Court with six justices (it was increased to nine in 1869) and a system of federal district courts, and it specified the duties of each court. This stabilized the power of the federal judiciary and its relationship with state courts, namely, by establishing the dual court system [70]. In particular, it gave the Supreme Court the power to review state laws and nullify them if they violated the Constitution. This greatly expanded federal power.

However, the Bill of Rights enumerated many of the rights people in U.S. courts have and many of the cornerstone procedures of the federal criminal courts, both of which constrained the power of the federal government. Seventy years later, just after the U.S. Civil War, Congress passed and the states ratified three Civil War Amendments, which, in addition to eliminating slavery and giving black males the right to vote, required in the Fourteenth Amendment that state courts follow due process of law just as the federal courts did. In each case, there is a tension and rebalancing between government exerting its own power and the government protecting some rights of individuals.

Between the end of the Revolutionary War in 1784 and 1800, the Articles of Confederation were replaced by the nation's current Constitution, and 16 states had been established. Each new state ratified its own constitution and created its own court system, often based on the legal principles established in English common law and modeled after the federal government structure. Over the next two centuries, the fundamental principles and hierarchical structure of the courts has persisted, but the number of state courts more than tripled and the internal organization of the courts changed considerably.

Modern Changes in the Criminal Courts

U.S. law is part of what is called **legal-rational authority**, meaning that its creation and enforcement is based on stable principles and rules [71]. This, however, does not mean that law and the courts are static. In fact, they change, or are dynamic. Within the nation's first 100 years, the U.S. courts had firmly established its foundation. It was a viable branch of the "checks and balance" government; it was a federalist system that required federal and state courts; and it had a tiered judiciary that created different courts for different issues, such as a trial versus an appeal of a trial.

In that first century, however, the state and federal court systems were decentralized, and each courtroom operated with a great deal of independence [72]. This was largely the result of relatively weak central governments, geographic separation of many small courthouses, less advanced communication technology, and nonstandardized training. The Civil War amendments, especially the Fourteenth Amendment, greatly strengthened federal control over state courts. Since the Civil War, the nation has gone through monumental changes in society, government, and courts. Several of these larger cultural shifts have tremendously altered the courts' structure, as well as the duties and procedures of the people who work in them.

Industrial Revolution, Immigration, and Urbanization

The Industrial Revolution of the late 19th century shifted the United States economy from agriculture to predominately manufacturing. This economic movement required more workers and a greater concentration of workers to operate the factories. Thus, the nation accepted a large influx of immigrants, and more people moved from rural areas to urban areas, a process called **urbanization**. The pressure these changes placed on urban criminal courts generated growth in both urban state courts and federal courts. For example, New York City in 1900 could not rely on a rotation of volunteer constables or a small rural courthouse. Such systems were adequate in *Gemeinschaft* societies, but not in *Gesellschaft* societies. The criminal justice system had to expand if it was to continue as a component of social control.

Bureaucracies and Professional Training

Overlapping these economic and population shifts were changes in academic knowledge and operations of organizations. The new school of scientific positivism argued that an issue could be better understood if it is broken down into its smallest components. For instance, Frederick Taylor and Henry Ford developed what became known as "scientific management," in which they aimed to improve productivity by assigning each worker a single task within the factory line or work team.

This shift in thinking aided the move toward the professionalization and **bureaucratization**—the process of a system becoming more bureaucratic—of the criminal justice system [73]. As societies became more complex with greater population numbers and density, more technology, more occupations, and greater diversity, governments had to develop more complex systems of control. The bureaucracy became the fundamental system of social organization for the criminal justice system [74]. Police departments, courts, and correctional systems began to add to their local and informal systems rationally designed procedures to complete tasks efficiently. This includes having a clear, top-down chain of command, written rules, and division of labor in which each person has a job title and specializes in completing a specific number of tasks.

Police work, for instance, first relied on the conscription of male citizens whose service was mandatory and often unpaid. Now it is done by officers who go to college and police academies and often make police work a lifelong career [75]. To maintain this standardization, bureaucracies rely on

professionalization, or the professional training and certification of workers. Professionalization of the courts eventually eliminated lawyers and judges self-taught in law, as was the case for the first century of the nation. Judges and attorneys today must earn law degrees from accredited law schools and pass the state bar exam.

Receiving professional training and working within a bureaucracy creates greater standardization in decision-making and legal actions. In law school, students perform roughly the same course work; they are taught the same writing styles; and they learn the habits of legal reasoning. When they work in the courts, particularly the criminal courts, they must follow the numerous procedures that everyone else follows. This process of channeling the way people think about and deal with a task is often called "bracketing". Brackets induce the workers to accept standard frames for assessing acceptable and unacceptable conditions, prioritizing tasks, and solving problems [76]. Careers in the Court describes some of the training a courtroom worker receives and how this brackets her or his thinking and behaviors.

CAREERS IN THE COURT

The Professional Training of a State Prosecutor

By the time a prosecutor reviews a case, negotiates with a defense attorney, or stands before a judge, he or she has been thoroughly versed on the standard principles of law, trained in the formal organizational scripts for that courthouse, and immersed in the informal culture of the court workers. **Organizational scripts** are patterns of thought which are created by the organization in which one operates, that lead people to selectively perceive information and filter out other considerations, and allow people in the organization to make decisions quickly without giving much thought to alternatives. To become and remain a state prosecutor, a person must:

- complete college
- take the national standardized Law School Admission Test (LSAT)
- complete law school
- pass the bar exam
- complete training for special divisions, such as the "Investigation and Prosecution of Child Abuse," "Prosecuting Drug Cases," and "Forensic Evidence" [77]
- regularly attend conferences such as the Conference on Domestic Violence or Missouri's "Prosecutor Bootcamp"

Public Policy and Social Engineering

The increasing bureaucratization and professionalization of courts has not been neutral. It has actually led to an increase in state power. The nation has not lost law as the cornerstone of its justice system, but with bureaucracies and professional organizations, the state can much more effectively use public policy to achieve goals of **social engineering**, which is an intentional effort by the government to change a population's beliefs, attitudes, and behavioral patterns. Social engineering is not peculiar to modern governments. Since the days of early societies, governments have tried to persuade or force the masses to revere the rulers, but modern social-engineering efforts are more precise and pervasive.

One recent example of social engineering has been the governments' successful campaign to persuade most Americans to condemn or even fear particular drugs, such as marijuana or crack cocaine, while accepting others, such as alcohol, caffeine, and prescription painkillers [78]. Another example is the increase in the rate of drivers and passengers wearing seatbelts. This was the result of a gradual campaign, first in the 1980s encouraging seatbelt-wearing, then ticketing drivers pulled over for another offense for not wearing their seatbelts, and finally today proactively pulling over drivers if anyone in the car is not wearing a seatbelt. Nationally, over 75 percent of drivers wear a seatbelt on a regular basis, but in the absence of seatbelt laws, under 20 percent of drivers wore them [79]. In these examples, we can see that governments use bureaucracies to enforce their policies and achieve social-engineering goals. Courts are one of these bureaucracies.

Professional Organizations

Professional organizations—bureaucracies that train and certify people for particular occupations, continually regulate the activities of the participants, and lobby on their behalf—have made professionalization possible. These exist in many industries. For example, police and correctional officers have associations and unions. Courts have powerful associations that regulate many of the courtroom actors, including court reporters, paralegals, and investigators. Attorneys and judges are subject to the most certification and oversight.

Two types of professional organizations bear on the courts, ones that deal directly with field of law and ones that are not focused principally on the law but nonetheless affect it. The American Bar Association is the nation's largest legal organization. Along with the state bars, it has effectively gained control over law-school education, certification of attorneys, discipline of attorneys, and representation of attorneys when lobbying lawmakers. All federal judges and nearly all state judges were trained in law and therefore subject to the Bar. Whether the effect has been positive or negative is another question. What is clear is that these affiliated organizations have shaped the courts perhaps more than any other force in the 20th century. Two other organizations that have influenced the court are the American Psychological Association and the American Psychiatric Association.

In the 19th century, early psychological notions gave rise to such judicial changes as the insanity defense, rehabilitation, and a separate justice system for juveniles. These are part of what is often called the criminal justice system's "progressive era." However, psychology and psychiatry also became a vehicle for the state to exert more control over populations by labeling some people incompetent, supposedly treating them in custodial asylums, and justifying an increasingly powerful probation system [80]. Historian Michel Foucault describes the effect of psychology as creating "gigantic moral imprisonment" [81]. Courts in the Media describes how the media has portrayed the effects of psychology.

COURTS IN THE MEDIA

Psychiatry's Effect on the Courts

Fiction

Ken Kesey, a Stanford graduate student who worked in a mental health facility, wrote the novel *One Flew Over the Cuckoo's Nest* in 1962, which was adapted into a film in 1975. The book and film are still considered among the best portrayals of the problems inherent in institutional psychiatry and the application of psychiatry in the criminal justice system.

Set in an Oregon psychiatric hospital, the story demonstrates subtle and brutal methods of controlling people who are labeled mentally ill, from therapy sessions based on behaviorism to electric shock therapy. In the story, Randle Patrick McMurphy, the main character, faked mental illness to get out of prison. Once in the mental hospital, McMurphy realizes his release depends on the diagnosis of the doctors and nurses. If they do not like him, he could spend the rest of his life in the psychiatric ward. Similar findings have been reported in many nonfiction research projects, such as Erving Goffman's *Asylum* and David L. Rosenhan's study "On Being Sane in Insane Places."

Nonfiction

Thin Blue Line, a documentary film directed by Errol Morris, analyzes the conviction of Randall Adams, who was sentenced to death for the murder of a police officer. Through interviews with witnesses, lawyers, police officers, and others, Morris depicts a court process that convicted an innocent man.

The conviction was based primarily on a witness who had only a brief view of the offender, possibly just enough to identify the color of the perpetrator's hair, and three other drivers who said they saw the defendant near the crime scene when they drove past it. The death-penalty sentence hinged on the testimony of Dr. James Grigson, a psychiatrist who stated that Randall Adams would commit violent acts in the future if released. Grigson's conclusions were based on interpreting drawings by Adams. Grigson, who has earned the nickname Dr. Death, has given the same testimony in hundreds of capital cases—that the defendant will kill again if given the chance—often making this diagnosis without having met the defendant [82]. In Adams's case, he testified that the only way to stop Adams from killing again was to execute him.

After the film compelled the courts to review this case, it was revealed that the prosecution used witnesses who lied on the stand; the prosecution did not give evidence to the defense as required by law; and the judge gave contradictory jury instructions. After 12 years in prison, Randall Adams was released [83].

Question

Many critics argue that psychology, psychiatry, and to a lesser extent, sociology and criminology, have been co-opted by the government, courts, and prisons, and are now used as instruments of oppression more than research-based fields that can improve people's lives. How can the criminal justice system utilize academic and research fields without harming people subject to them and without diminishing the integrity of research?

Other academic and professional disciplines, such as political science, which offers some justifications of expanding state power, and sociology, which has provided research used to justify **net-widening** policies (activities undertaken by a legal system to increase the numbers of people involved in the system and to increase the involvement of those already in the system) such as early intervention and probation, have also altered the administration of justice in positive and negative ways.

Due-Process Revolution

As always, the expansion of state power exists alongside the protection of individual rights. The United States, on the whole, has expanded rights over its 200 years, such as rights for black people, women, American Indians, people who engage in homosexual activity, and members of diverse religions. From the 1950s to the early 1970s, the **due-process revolution** rapidly expanded due-process protection for protesters, criminal defendants, minorities, and others. In most of these cases, individual rights were protected from the state's power.

Brown v. Board of Education (1954), though not a criminal case, is often identified as the beginning of that era. In that case, the court greatly limited the states' power to discriminate against people based on race. It ruled that separate facilities, such as schools, are inherently unequal and therefore a violation of the Fourteenth Amendment's **Equal Protection clause** which prohibits states from denying any person within their jurisdictions equal protection of the law [84].

SUMMARY

1. Explain social order and social control in simple societies.
   - All societies must create and maintain solidarity or social order, which is a society's ability to operate in predictable patterns. Social order depends on the control of the population.
   - Social control is any concerted effort or social process that constrains and directs the conduct of people by inducing conformity and preventing nonconformity.
2. Link norms and informal social controls to informal sanctions.
   - Norms are cultural rules that constrain our behavior and guide us toward particular behavior. Primitive societies relied entirely on informal social control and had no government, police, courts, or prisons.
   - Traditional authority and informal social control preserve norms through informal sanctions, or responses to a violation of a norm by people with no particular legal authority to regulate that behavior.

3. Discuss how empires changed the nature of social control.
   - Empires introduced written laws, formal social control, and formal sanctions. Formal social control depends on formal sanctions, or responses to a violation of a codified rule by an agent of an official organization designated to enforce that rule. This was the beginning of social order achieved through state power.
4. Talk about how nation-states changed the nature of social control.
   - The modern nation-state is important to the development of the court system because of the degree to which law regulated the conduct of people and governments. New laws increased the number of justifications for the government to punish. The legal system of the nation-state increasingly became an apparatus of power and domination.
5. Summarize four families of legal and court systems.
   - Common law emanates from judicial rulings and began in England. It is still partially practiced in many of England's former colonies. The distinguishing elements of common-law courts are judicial law and precedent.
   - Civil-law systems remain true to laws based on codes written by governing bodies.
   - Religion-based court systems add a religious component to the elements of common-law precedent and civil-law statutes.
   - American Indian tribal courts rely on oral traditions. These courts try to mediate reconciliation between offenders and victims.
6. Discuss how early U.S. politicians achieved social order while balancing the pursuit of justice and protection of rights with maintaining social control.
   - Early U.S. politicians turned to the courts to balance the protection of rights and maintenance of social control. Courts not only adjudicated accusations of wrongdoing and issued punishments for people who violated laws, but also forced the agents of the state to follow procedural rules.
7. Understand the constitutional provisions that created the judiciary.
   - The U.S. court system is grounded in four constitutional provisions: Article III, Article IV, Article VI, and the Tenth Amendment.
   - Article III created the federal courts as an independent branch of the government and broadly outlined their jurisdiction and limitations. Article IV, Article VI, and the Tenth Amendment gave powers to states and described their relationship with the federal government.
8. Explain why the Industrial Revolution led to significant changes in the U.S. courts.
   - The Industrial Revolution shifted the United States from agriculture to manufacturing. This economic shift required more workers and

a greater concentration of workers to operate the factories. The pressure these changes placed on urban criminal courts generated growth in urban state courts and federal courts.

9. Analyze bureaucratization and professionalization and explain how they altered the U.S. courts.

- The bureaucracy, an organization designed for efficiency, became the fundamental system of social organization for the criminal justice system. Bureaucratization is the process of a system becoming more bureaucratic. To maintain this standardization, bureaucracies rely on professionalization, or the professional training and certification of workers.
- Professionalization nearly eliminated self-taught lawyers and judges. Receiving professional training and working within a bureaucracy creates greater standardization in decision-making and legal actions.

10. Explain what is meant by the due-process revolution and describe some of the changes that occurred.

- The due-process revolution from the 1950s to the early 1970s rapidly expanded due-process protection for protestors, criminal defendants, minorities, and others. In most cases, individual rights were protected from the state's power.

Questions

1. What is social order and social control in simple societies?
2. How do norms and informal social controls relate to informal sanctions?
3. How did empires change the nature of social control?
4. How did nation-states change the nature of social control?
5. What are four families of legal and court systems?
6. How did early U.S. politicians achieved social order while balancing the protection of rights with the maintenance of social control?
7. What constitutional provisions created the judiciary?
8. How did the Industrial Revolution significantly change the U.S. courts?
9. What are bureaucratization and professionalization? How did they alter the U.S. courts?
10. What is the due-process revolution? What did it change?

REFERENCES

[1] Parsons T. Societies: evolutionary and comparative perspectives. Englewood Cliffs, NJ: Prentice Hall; 1966.

[2] Durkheim E. [Lewis A. Coser, Trans. 1893; reprint] The division of labor in society. New York, NY: Free Press; 1997.

[3] Black DJ. The social structure of right and wrong. San Diego, CA: Academic Press; 1998. p. 161.

[4] Becker HS. Outsiders: studies in the sociology of deviance. New York, NY: The Free Press; 1963. p. 147−164.

[5] Durkheim E. The normal and the pathological [George E. Catlin, Trans. 1895; reprint]. In: Sarah A, Soloway, Mueller JH, editors. The rules of sociological method. New York, NY: Macmillan Publishing; 1966. p. 65−73.

[6] Morgan LH. [1877; reprint, S.I.] Ancient society. General Books; 2009.

[7] Pfeiffer J. The emergence of society: a prehistory of the establishment. New York, NY: McGraw-Hill; 1977. Tönnies F, Loomis CP. Community & society: (Gemeinschaft und Gesellschaft). New York, NY: Harper & Row; 1963. [This book provides a fascinating and comprehensive overview of the history of societies. Chapters 2 and 3 examine hunting-and-gathering and early agricultural societies.]

[8] Mumford L. The myth of the machine. New York, NY: Harcourt, Brace & World; 1967.

[9] Mumford L. The transformation of man, 24. New York, NY: Harper & Row; 1956. p. 38. Turner J. Patterns of social organization: a survey of social institutions. New York, NY: McGraw-Hill; 1971. p. 216−218. Turner JH. Human institutions: a theory of societal evolution. Lanham, MD: Rowman & Littlefield; 2003.

[10] Sumner WG, Keller AG. Folkways: a study of the sociological importance of usages, manners, customs, mores, and morals. Boston, MA: Ginn and Co; 1940.

[11] Lowie RH. Primitive society. New York, NY: Liveright; 1947. p. 397−380.

[12] Weber M. from Max Weber: Essays in Sociology, [C. Wright Mills, Trans.] In: Hans Gerth, editor. The three types of legitimate rule. New York, NY: Oxford University Press; 1958.

[13] Drapkin I. Crime and punishment in the ancient world. Lexington, MA: Lexington Books; 1989.

[14] McNeill WH. Human migration: a historical overview. In: Friedenfels R, editor. Social change: an anthology. Dix Hills, NY: General Hall; 1998. Caldwell JC. The role of mortality decline in theories of social and demographic transition. In: Friedenfels R, editor. Social change: an anthology. Dix Hills, NY: General Hall; 1998. Pfeiffer J. The emergence of society: a prehistory of the establishment, New York, NY: McGraw-Hill; 1977. p. 21-25, 459−462.

[15] Tönnies Ferdinand. Community and Society. New York: Harper; 1963 (1887).

[16] Maine HS. Ancient law: its connection with the early history of society and its relation to modern ideas. Boston, MA: Beacon Press; 1963.

[17] Turner J. American society: problems of structure. New York, NY: Harper & Row; 1972. p. 222.

[18] Ibid.

[19] Parsons T. Societies: evolutionary and comparative perspectives. Englewood Cliffs, NJ: Prentice Hall; 1966.

[20] Coffin JG, Stacey RC, Burns EM. Western civilizations: their history & their culture. New York, NY: W.W. Norton; 2008.

[21] Davies WW. Codes of Hammurabi and Moses. Whitefish, MT: Kessinger Publisher; 2003. Chambliss R. Social thought, from Hammurabi to Comte. Fort Worth, TX: Harcourt College Publishers; 1981.

[22] Parsons T. Societies: evolutionary and comparative perspectives. Englewood Cliffs, NJ: Prentice Hall; 1966.

[23] Jenks E. Edward plantagenet: the English Justinian or the making of common law. North Stratford, NH: Ayer Company Publishers; 1989. Berry P. History of Rome: from the earliest record (753 BC) to the code of Justinian (AD 534). Lewiston, NY: Edwin Mellen Press; 2006.

[24] Mumford. The transformation of man, 41−42.

[25] Grilliot HJ. Introduction to law and the legal system. Boston, MA: Houghton Mifflin; 1975. p. 33.

[26] Wrong DH. Power, its forms, bases, and uses: with a new preface. Chicago, IL: University of Chicago Press; 1988. p. 21−36. This book traces the types of power imbued in law. See also Weber M. Law in Economy and Society, Trans. Shils EA, Rheinstein M, editors. Max Rheinstein [1914; reprint], Cambridge, MA: Harvard University Press; 1954. Russell B. [1938; reprint] Power: the role of man's will to power in the world's economic and political affairs. New York, NY: W.W. Norton; 1966. Marcuse H. One-dimensional man: studies in the ideology of advanced indus-trial society. Boston, MA: Beacon Press; 1964.

[27] de Secondat Montesquieu C. [1748; reprint] The spirit of the laws. New York, NY: Hafner; 1949.. Russell Bertrand. Power: The Role of Man's Will to Power in the World's Economic and Political Affairs. NY: W.W. Norton and Company; 1966 (1938).

[28] Fogel D. We are the living proof: the justice model for corrections. 2nd ed. New York, NY: Anderson Publishing; 1979.

[29] Weber. Law in economy and society. Fuller LL. Empirical natural law, human nature, science. Pleasantville, NY: Pace University; 1994.

[30] Perry M, et al. Western civilization: ideas, politics & society, Boston, MA: Houghton Mifflin; 2000. p. 470, 496.

[31] Gould M. Islam, the law, and the sovereignty of God. Policy Rev 2008;149: Online at <www.hoover.org/publications/policy-review/article/5693>.

[32] Barker E. The purpose of the state and the idea of justice. In: Fisk M, editor. Justice. Atlantic Highlands, NJ: Humanities Press; 1993. p. 106−11.

[33] Maine Henry S. Ancient law: its connection with the early history of society, and its rela-tions to modern ideas. New York: Beacon; 1963 (1861).

[34] Dworkin R. Integrity. In: Fisk M, editor. Justice. Atlantic Highlands, NJ: Humanities Press; 1993. p. 137−65.

[35] White LA. The science of culture, a study of man and civilization, New York, NY: Farrar, Straus; 1949. p. 69, 111.

[36] CNN. Two groups sue over NSA wiretap program, <www.cnn.com/2006/LAW/01/17/aclu.nsa>.

[37] Duke A. Judge warns Conrad Murray to keep quiet about his rulings. CNN <articles.cnn.com/2011-09-06/justice/california.conrad.murray.hearing_1_pretrial-hearings-casey-anthony-murder-trial-conrad-murray> [accessed September 6, 2011]. Duke A. Conrad Murray sentenced to four years behind bars. CNN <www.cnn.com/2011/11/29/justice/california-conrad-murray-sentencing/index.html> [accessed November 30, 2011].

[38] Power G. *Meade v. Dennistone*: the NAACP's test case to '…Sue Jim Crow out of Maryland with the Fourteenth Amendment'. Maryland Law Rev 2004;63(4):773−810. *Briggs et al. v. Elliott et al.*, 342 U.S. 350(1952) and *Brown v Board of Education of Topeka Kansas*, 347 U.S. 483(1954).

[39] O'Connor K, Epstein L. Amicus curiae participation in U.S. supreme court litigation: an appraisal of 'Hakman's folklore'. Law Soc Rev 1981;16(4):311−20: Online at <epstein.usc.edu/research/Hakman.html>. *Furman v. Georgia*, 408 U.S. 238, 240(1972).

[40] Available from: <http://www.innocenceproject.org/>.

[41] Fairchild E, Dammer HR. Comparative criminal justice systems. 2nd ed. Belmont, CA: Wadsworth-Thomson Learning; 2001.

[42] Elliott J. This is what imposition of religious law looks like: Israeli lawmakers push for the use of traditional Jewish laws in courts, <Salon.com> [accessed August 4, 2011], <www.salon.com/2011/08/04/creeping_halakha>.

[43] Saudi Arabia executes woman convicted of 'sorcery, Associated Press; <news.yahoo.com/saudi-arabia-executes-woman-convicted-sorcery-132159048.html> [accessed December 12, 2011].

[44] Friedrichs DO. Law in our lives. New York, NY: Oxford University Press; 2012. p. 157–61.

[45] Fairchild E, Dammer HR. Comparative Criminal Justice Systems. 2nd ed. Belmont, CA: Wadsworth-Thomson Learning; 2001.

[46] Shelton D. Normative hierarchy in international law. Am J Int Law 2006;100(2):291–323.

[47] Berg TC. Order in the court: how judges should think. Christian Century 2003;120 (26):26–31.

[48] The American Center for Law and Justice, Brief Amici Curiae for *Newdow v. Congress* of the United States of America, 2006. Case No. 06-16344.

[49] Hallowell B. What does author Tim Ballard say Americans must do to 'save this nation'? Blaze <www.theblaze.com/stories/what-does-author-tim-ballard-says-americans-must-do-to-save-this-nation> [accessed May 18, 2012].

[50] Saletan W. Rule of Lord. Slate <www.slate.com/articles/news_and_politics/human_nature/2011/11/christian_theocracy_how_newt_gingrich_and_the_gop_would_abolish_courts_and_legislate_morality_.html>2011, [accessed November 21, 2011].

[51] Murphy K. Kansas governor, Sam Brownback, signs anti-sharia bill, effectively banning Islamic law. Reuters <www.reuters.com/article/2012/05/12/us-usa-sharia-kansas-idUSBRE84B0AW20120512.>2012, [accessed May 12, 2012].

[52] Fox News. Supreme court bars commandments from courthouses, <www.foxnews.com/story/0,2933,160781,00.html> [accessed June 28, 2005].

[53] Hirschl R. Holy glocalization. Harvard Int Rev 2010;32(2):38–42.

[54] Russell Bertrand. Power: the role of man's will to power in the world's economic and political affairs. New York, NY: W.W. Norton and Company; 1966 (1938).

[55] White GE. Law in American history: from the colonial years through the civil war, vol. 1. New York, NY: Oxford University Press; 2012.

[56] Joseph F. Zimmerman, contemporary American federalism: the growth of national power. Westport, CT: Praeger; 1992; 82–102. Klein F. Federal and state court systems: a guide. Cambridge, MA: Ballinger Publishing Company; 1977.

[57] Dodd WE. Expansion and conflict. Boston, MA: Houghton Mifflin; 1915.

[58] J. Madison. The federalist no. 51: the structure of the government must furnish the proper checks and balances between the different departments, Ind J February 6, 1788: Online at <www.constitution.org/fed/federa51.htm>.

[59] Printz. Sheriff/Coroner, Ravalli County, *Montana v. United States*, 521 U.S. 898(1997).

[60] *Chamber of Commerce of the United States of America v. Whiting*, 558F. 3d 856(2011).

[61] *United States v. Alfonso Lopez, Jr.*, 514 U.S. 549(1995).

[62] *Arizona v. United States*, 641F. 3d 339(2012).

[63] *Gonzales v. Raich* (previously *Ashcroft v. Raich*), 545 U.S. 1 (2005). See also *United States v. Oakland Cannabis Buyers' Cooperative*, 532 U.S. 483(2001).

[64] *Roe v. Wade*, 410 U.S. 113 (1973). *Heart of Atlanta Motel Inc. v. United States*, 379 U.S. 241 (1964). *Loving v. Virginia*, 388 U.S. 1 (1967). *Lawrence v. Texas*, 539 U.S. 558 (2003). *Texas v. Johnson*, 491 US 397(1989).

[65] *Gideon v. Wainwright*, 372 U.S. 335 (1963). *Arizona v. United States*, 641F. 3d 339(2012).

[66] Brownell H. Dual sovereignty under the constitution, prepared for delivery before the Fordham Law Alumni Association, February 11, 1956.

[67] Carp RA, Stidham R. Judicial process in America. 2nd ed. Washington, DC: Congressional Quarterly Press; 1993, p. 19.

[68] Golding MP. Philosophy of law. Englewood Cliffs, NJ: Prentice Hall; 1975. p. 118−25.

[69] Semmes R. [1922; reprint, Reprint Series] Crime and punishment in early Maryland. Montclair, NJ: Patterson Smith; 1970. Lowi T, Ginsberg B. American government: freedom and power. 3rd ed. New York, NY: W.W. Norton; 1994.

[70] Klein. Federal and state court systems: a guide, 5.

[71] Weber Max. The three types of legitimate rule. In: Edited and translated by Hans Gerth, C. Wright Mills. From Max Weber: Essays in Sociology. New York City, NY: Oxford University Press; 1958.

[72] Carp, Stidham. Judicial Process Am 65−8.

[73] Ibid. Fish PG. The politics of federal judicial administration. Princeton, NJ: Princeton University Press; 1973.

[74] Weber M. Economy and society [1922; reprint] In: Roth G, Wittich C, editors. Berkeley, CA: University of California Press; 1978.

[75] Williams K. Our enemies in blue: police and power in America. New York, NY: Soft Skull Press; 2004.

[76] Haney-Lopez IF. Racism on trial: the Chicano fight for justice. Cambridge, MA: Harvard University Press; 2003. Gioia DA. Why I didn't recognize pinto fire hazards: how organizational scripts channel managers' thoughts and actions. In: Ermann MD, Lundman RJ, editors. Corporate and governmental deviance: problems of organizational behavior in contemporary society. 5th ed. New York, NY: Oxford University Press; 1996. p. 139−57. Cooley CH. Social organization. New York, NY: Charles Scribner's Sons; 1937. Gerth HH, Mills CW. Character and social structure: the psychology of social institutions. New York, NY: Harcourt, Brace; 1953. Zajonc RB. Social facilitation. Science 1965;149:269−74. Shibutani T. Reference groups as perspectives. Am J Soc 1955;60(6):562−9. Mills CW. White collar: the American middle classes. New York, NY: Oxford University Press; 1951. See p. xii, where Mills refers to workers in bureaucracies as "cheerful robots.". Mills CW. Situated actions and vocabularies of motive. Am Sociological Rev 1940;5:904−13. Bales RF. Interaction process analysis: a method for the study of small groups. Cambridge, MA: Addison-Wesley Press; 1950. Roethlisberger FJ, Dickson WJ. Industrial social psychology: the Hawthorne experiment. In: Sahakian WS, editor. Social psychology: experimentation, theory, research. Scranton, PA: Intext Educational Publishers; 1972. p. 319−30. Hochschild AR. The managed heart: commercialization of human feeling. Berkeley, CA: University of California Press; 1983. Milgram S. Obedience. University Park, PA: Pennsylvania State University; 1969. Asch SE. Social psychology. New York, NY: Prentice Hall; 1952. Couch CJ. Social processes and relationships: a formal approach. Dix Hills, NY: General Hall; 1989. Hollander EP. Competence and conformity in the acceptance of influence. J Abnormal Soc Psychol 1960;61:365−9.

[77] National District Attorneys Association, 2012.

[78] Duster TS. The legislation of morality: law, drugs, and moral judgment. New York, NY: Free Press; 1970.

[79] Hakes JK, Viscusi WK. Automobile seatbelt usage and the value of statistical life. South Econ J 2007;73(3):659−77. U.S. Federal News Service, "Gov. Vilsack Announces Iowa's Seat Belt Compliance Rate of 90 Percent," November 29, 2006, Washington, D.C.: U.S. Federal News Service. U.S. Federal News Service, "Study Shows Benefits of 'Primary

Enforcement' of Seatbelt Laws," Washington, D.C.: U.S. Federal News Service, June 1, 2007. U.S. Federal News Service, "Primary Enforcement Law and Educational Campaign Are Needed to Increase Seatbelt Use Among Missouri Teens," Washington, D.C.: U.S. Federal News Service, May 22, 2007.

[80] Goffman E. Asylums: essays on the social situation of mental patients and other inmates. Garden City, NY: Anchor Books; 1961. Foucault M. The birth of the clinic: an archaeology of medical perception. New York, NY: Pantheon Books; 1973. Szasz TS. The myth of mental illness. Am Psychol 1960;15:113−8. Starr P. The social transformation of American medicine: the rise of a sovereign profession and the making of a vast industry. New York, NY: Basic Books; 1982. Rosenhan DL. On being sane in insane places. Science 1973;179:250−8.

[81] Foucault M. [Sheridan Smith A.M., Trans.] The archaeology of knowledge. New York, NY: Pantheon Books; 1972.

[82] Tolson M. Doctor's effect on justice lingers. Houston: Chronicle; June 17, 2004, <www .chron.com/CDA/archives/archive.mpl/2004_3773186/doctor-s-effect-on-justice-lingers-testified-in-ma.html>.

[83] Adams RD. Filmmaker helped free innocent man, northwestern law center on wrongful convictions, <www.law.northwestern.edu/CWC/exonerations/txAdamsSummary.html> [accessed June, 2011]. Radelet ML, Bedau HA, Putnam CE. In spite of innocence: erroneous convictions in capital cases. Boston, MA: Northeastern University Press; 1992. For more information on this case and film, see < www.errolmorris.com > and < www.journeyof-hope.org/pages/randall_dale_adams.htm > .

[84] *Brown v. Board of Education of Topeka Kansas*, 347 U.S. 483(1954).

The members of the U.S. Supreme Court as of 2012. Seated, from left, are Associate Justices Clarence Thomas and Antonin Scalia, Chief Justice John Roberts, and Associate Justices Anthony M. Kennedy and Ruth Bader Ginsburg. Standing, from left, are Associate Justices Sonia Sotomayor, Stephen Breyer, Samuel Alito Jr., and Elena Kagan.

CHAPTER 3

The Structure of Federal and State Courts

KEY TERMS

Assimilative Crimes Act

appellate jurisdiction

civil courts

docket

extradite

finder of fact

general jurisdiction

geographic jurisdiction

habeas corpus

hierarchical jurisdiction

higher courts

hung jury

intermediate courts of appeals

justiciable

justiciability doctrines

petition

limited jurisdiction

original jurisdiction

remand

subject-matter jurisdiction

trier of law

writ of *certiorari*

CONTENTS

Learning Objectives

After reading this chapter, you should be able to:

1. List and discuss the court's two general roles.
2. Define jurisdiction. Explain subject-matter jurisdiction, geographic jurisdiction, and hierarchical jurisdiction.
3. Describe the duties of original jurisdiction courts, appellate courts, and high courts.
4. Differentiate constitutional courts and legislative courts.
5. Discuss the purpose and functions of U.S. Magistrate Courts.
6. Talk about the requirement for U.S. District Court cases and what that court's work involves.
7. Examine the work of U.S. Circuit Courts of Appeals.
8. Describe the jurisdiction of the U.S. Supreme Court.
9. Compare and contrast state courts with federal courts.
10. Analyze potential advantages and problems of state court unification.
11. List and discuss common features of specialized state courts.

U.S. courts process over 20 million criminal cases annually: 21.4 million state criminal cases and about 80,000 federal criminal cases [1]. This mammoth undertaking is possible because the courts have a defined and narrow set of duties and because the nation has a clear jurisdictional structure that allows most cases to be assigned quickly to the appropriate court. This structure includes separate courts for the federal and state governments, geographical regions within both systems, a separation of civil and criminal cases, and a separation of serious felonies from other offenses. Still, however, the court system is criticized for issues such as a lack of oversight of small local courts, inadequate attention given to the circumstances of offenders, and efforts to change the courts to address these problems. This chapter will cover the role of the criminal courts and the functions of the different types of criminal courts.

THE ROLE OF CRIMINAL COURTS: LIMITATIONS AND DUTIES

The main limitations on the courts are based on the **justiciability doctrines**. These legal principles, which include standing, ripeness and mootness, advisory opinions, political questions, and judicial restraint, identify what issues can and cannot be heard in a court of law [2]. As Court Procedures demonstrates, courts will hear only identifiable cases with clear violations of law or harms. These doctrines prevent a prosecutor from filing charges against someone who is a jerk but has not harmed the community and limit appeals to hearing cases in which there is an actual injury and controversy.

COURT PROCEDURES

Limits on the Court: Judicial Restraint and Doctrines of Justiciability

Courts cannot hear any case they want or even any case that is important. Lawyers and judges must exercise restraint and hear only appropriate cases. To be heard in court, a case must be **justiciable**, which means that the case must be within the domain of judicial powers. Justiciability is based on interpretations of the Case or Controversy clause of Article III, which specifies that the court's role is simply to review and rule in a lawful manner on disputes that come before it. Here are four main doctrines of justiciability:

- Prosecutor (or plaintiff in civil cases) must have standing. "Standing" means that someone can lawfully bring a case. By limiting who has standing, courts increase judicial efficiency by limiting the number of cases it must hear. To do that, the following conditions should be met: (1) There must be distinct injury to the community or a person, which excludes frivolous claims of injury, "merely" unethical or immoral behavior, and injury may occur in the future. (2) The party bringing the case must be the party injured, which means that if an offense occurs in Virginia, the person cannot be prosecuted in Pennsylvania because that community was not harmed by crime. (3) The injury has to have been caused (at least allegedly) by the accused/defendant, which usually excludes bringing charges against people who legally sell guns that are later used in criminal offenses and people who watch an offense occur. (4) The court can do something about it, which means there has to be an actual defendant who can be punished, not just evidence that a criminal offense occurred.

- The case must be ripe. "Ripeness" means the controversy is ready to be heard by the courts. Similar to the doctrine concerning standing, ripeness requires that a controversy exists and that the court can meaningfully adjudicate it.
- The case cannot be moot. "Mootness" means that a case is missing an important component and is therefore either not yet ripe or no longer ripe. For instance, if the suspect dies or pleads guilty, the case is moot—there is no longer an actual legal controversy—and cannot be taken to trial.
- The court will issue no advisory opinions and will not address political questions. Courts will not issue nonbinding opinions that merely assesses a legal question, such as "Should an action be criminalized?" When the debate revolves around a hypothetical legal question, there is no actual dispute or harm. Thus, no one has standing, the case is not ripe, and a ruling will not affect people's lives. With no dispute to hear or sentence to issue, courts will not get involved. In criminal courts, the state must prosecute an actual suspect. Similarly, appellate courts will not hear a case in which someone alleges that a law may someday violate constitutional rights. Injury must occur before the courts can be invoked.

Questions

What are the justiciability doctrines based on?

What happens if the suspect in a murder case dies? Does the case still go to trial?

Even with the justiciability limitations, courts have a wide range of roles to fulfill. Among the four components of the criminal justice system, lawmaking by the legislature serves as the foundation and framework of the entire justice system. Federal and state criminal and appeal courts, however, have a wider range of roles than the other components. They connect written laws, the actions of the police, and corrections. In a broad sense, the courts' roles are to exert the power of the state through its crime-control efforts and protect due-process rights by evaluating the actions of the criminal justice system. The court's specific roles include:

- Crime control powers, such as: issuing search warrants to police, charging people with criminal offenses, obtaining convictions through plea bargains and trials, conducting trials, issuing sentences or sanctions, and enforcing some judicial decisions, especially sentences of probation.
- Creation and maintenance of due-process provisions, such as: monitoring the court process and assuring that police and court officers follow procedural laws, hearing appeals, evaluating the constitutionality of laws (judicial review), and establishing precedent (judicial law).

Most criminal cases are settled at the trial court level. They are dismissed; a guilty plea is negotiated; or it is resolved in trial. The tension between due process and crime control shapes the contours of each of these paths. The prosecution and defense are engaged in a contest of interpretation, in which they present evidence and argument according to procedural rules in order to convince the judge or jury that their position is the better one. During the trial, either the judge or jury acts as the **finder of fact**, a task that largely corresponds with the crime-control role of the courts: they apply substantive law to the charges and evidence presented against the defendant, or the facts of the case. The critical finder-of-fact question is, "Did the defendant commit the crime and did he intend to do it, or does the prosecution fail to prove that beyond a reasonable doubt?" Judges and juries tend to look favorably on the prosecution and try to find reasons to agree with the charges.

At the same time, the judge has the role of **trier of law**, which is an obligation to assure due process of law and protect the rights of the accused. The critical trier-of-law question is, "Were the proper procedures followed by the police, attorneys, and other criminal justice system practitioners?" As a trier of law, a judge may dismiss a case, rule on motions, suppress evidence, enforce deadlines, strike trial statements from the record, remove immaterial witnesses, rule on objections, give jury instructions, and punish misconduct in the courtroom. Many of these actions confuse people who do not understand legal reasoning and lead to criticisms that the courts are "pro-defendant" or "letting criminals loose" on technicalities. Such criticisms misunderstand the dual role of courts, one of which is to restrain the government to better protect everyone's liberties.

Cases sometimes go beyond the trial and into appeals. At this level, the main two roles of the court are to review alleged violations of rights at the trial level and, less frequently, to review the constitutionality of law. This is not a retrial but a review of particular issues of law that arose out of the trial. Perhaps the most common criminal trial appeal involves the legality of evidence. Defendants convicted at trial may appeal that the police conducted the search without a warrant, were too suggestive during the identification stage by showing the same photo repeatedly, or were too brutal during interrogation *and* the trial judge failed to suppress that particular evidence. See Landmark Cases for an example of how a Supreme Court ruling has changed police work. Appeals are covered extensively in Chapter 11.

LANDMARK CASES

Chimel v. California (1969)

A police officer may conduct a search pursuant to an arrest without a search warrant but may only search in areas that the arrestee can readily access.

Police officers suspected Ted Chimel of stealing some rare coins and acquired a warrant for his arrest. The officers were admitted into Ted Chimel's home by his wife. When Chimel came home, the officers served him with the arrest warrant. He denied the officers' request to "look around," but they searched the house anyway "on the basis of the lawful arrest," despite not having a search warrant. The police found some

of the coins, and Chimel was tried for burglary. At his trial, the coins were admitted over the objection that they had been seized unconstitutionally. California appellate courts affirmed Chimel's conviction, holding that the arrest was lawful and that the search was justified as incident to a lawful arrest.

The U.S. Supreme Court later held that even though the arrest was lawful the warrantless search of the house was unconstitutional under the Fourth and Fourteenth Amendments and could not be constitutionally justified as incident to that arrest. The Court set forth that searches "incident to arrest" are limited to the area within the suspect's immediate control.

Few people criticize the power of judicial review, primarily because it is created in Article III and many Supreme Court rulings, and the Constitution employs abstract concepts like "due process" and "freedom of speech" that must be interpreted. In short, the judicial branch is supposed to test the constitutionality of law. Nonetheless, people attack appellate courts when the judges overturn laws that they favor. Indeed, when the court uses its power to abolish, change, or create law, it is often criticized for "judicial activism," "judicial excess," "judicial gloss," "acting as the imperial judiciary," "legislating from the bench," and "judicial policy-making" [3]. Such criticisms are usually partisan accusations made when one side of the political spectrum is not happy with a ruling. This issue is covered more extensively in Chapter 15. For now, however, it is important to remember that the judiciary does nullify, change, and make law.

DIFFERENT COURTS FOR DIFFERENT DISPUTES

The U.S. criminal court system is diverse and dynamic. In order to disentangle the distinct structures, we will describe issues of the judiciary that are common to most courts, review the structure of the federal court system, then look at issues that are common among the state criminal courts. This section summarizes what happens in each particular court. (Figure 3.1 maps out the dual court system in the United States.) Later chapters will fully explain the trial and appeal court processes.

Issues Common to Federal and State Courts

Federal and state courts have many distinctions. However, they are all bound to honor the Constitution, they share many organizational and procedural features, and they are built upon many of the same legal principles. In both systems, the trial procedure is the same, with opening statements, evidence and witnesses, closing statements, verdict, and sentencing for the convicted. Also, both systems adhere to principles such as due process, precedent, judicial review, and judicial restraint. One structural feature shared by the state and federal court systems are various aspects of jurisdiction, including having separate procedures and courts for civil and criminal cases, arranging the judiciary from a high court to the lower courts, and allowing defendants in some cases to appeal from lower courts to the high court.

Jurisdiction

Jurisdiction is perhaps the most important principle in understanding the structure of U.S. courts because it has allowed our courts to become specialized and hierarchical [4]. Each court has a specialized jurisdiction, which means a case cannot be put in any courtroom but must be heard by the court

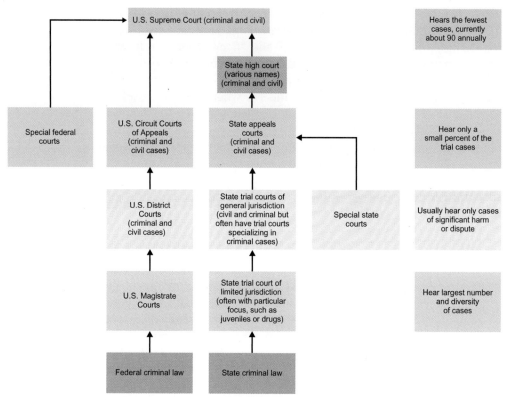

FIGURE 3.1
Overview of the U.S. federalist court system.

with jurisdiction over that issue. Jurisdiction also creates a hierarchy of courts, which allows higher courts to correct mistakes made in lower courts. The advantages of following rules of jurisdiction include the orderly handling of an immense caseload, a predictable court system, and having judges who can become experts in focused areas of law. The principal question for criminal courts is that of **subject-matter jurisdiction**, which refers to the type of cases a court can hear. Subject-matter jurisdiction encompasses:

1. the type of offense
2. the location of the offense
3. the aspect of the case being reviewed

The type of offense is usually straightforward. A crime is designated by statute as a felony, misdemeanor, or some lesser offense such as traffic or city ordinance violations. Most courts hear only one type of criminal case, and most criminal courts do not hear noncriminal issues such as bankruptcy. Most criminal courts have **limited jurisdiction**, which means they are usually limited to handling misdemeanors and less serious felonies, as well as a wide array of other judicial duties such as preliminary hearings, warrants, and bail hearings. Criminal courts that deal with serious felonies have **general jurisdiction**.

Location issue is often called **geographic jurisdiction**, which refers to a court's authority to hear a case as determined by the location of the offense. It includes federal jurisdiction, state boundaries, and district or county boundaries. Usually the location of the offense dictates which court hears the case, as mandated by Article III and the Sixth Amendment. Therefore, if a suspect is caught in Wisconsin for an alleged crime in Indiana, Indiana will hear the case, not Wisconsin. Indiana will have to **extradite** (the official process in which one state surrenders a criminal suspect or offender to another state) the suspect, or the suspect will be released by Wisconsin.

The "aspect of the case" question is more complicated because it involves different types of trial and appellate courts. The central question is, where on the judicial hierarchy of courts will the case be heard. The answer to that question can be understood in terms of what is called **hierarchical jurisdiction**, or a court's authority to hear a case as determined by the court's function. Most cases are heard by a trial court. **Original jurisdiction** is the power of a court to hear the case first and rule on the **facts of the case**. These "trial" courts are the courts most often depicted on television and in movies. This court decides if the accused is guilty or not guilty based on the evidence, or facts of the case.

Limited and general jurisdiction courts both have original jurisdiction. They are considered lower courts in judicial hierarchy. The **higher courts**, however, are the appeals courts. These courts do not hear trials but instead have **appellate jurisdiction**, which means the aspect of the case they review are alleged errors of the lower court. Appellate courts therefore have the power to review lower court decisions and correct perceived errors. Within the judicial hierarchy, an intermediate appeals court can correct a trial court, and the highest court (or supreme court) can correct an intermediate appeals court.

Taken together, these dimensions of jurisdiction create an efficient and predictable system for sorting out the millions of cases processed annually in the United States. In nearly all cases, anyone trained in law can glance at the dispute and know which courthouse will hear a case. If someone steals a car in Tempe, AZ, and is caught in Arizona, the case will not be tried in a divorce court or misdemeanor court; it will not be tried in a Colorado courtroom; and it will not be heard by an appellate court until after the trial court hears it. As soon as you hear the facts of the case, you know that almost certainly it will be heard in the Maricopa County district court of Arizona.

Civil Courts

If your roommate violates the lease by not paying rent, if the neighbors break your windows while practicing golf, if you slip on an unmarked wet floor in Wal-Mart, or if your doctor accidently amputates your leg, you can sue the other party in a state or federal civil court, depending on which has jurisdiction. **Civil courts** have subject-matter jurisdiction over noncriminal cases involving one party suing another for damages or injunctions. This is generally referred to as "private law," as opposed to the public law that is composed of criminal statutes and criminal courts. Even though these courts are not part of the criminal court system, it's useful to understand them because they are the largest part of the U.S. judicial system, and it will clarify the subject-matter limits of criminal courts and the principles and procedures unique to criminal courts.

Civil courts are older than criminal courts. They emerged about a 1000 years ago as a way for one citizen to sue another citizen for damages or injury, and for the dispute to be heard by a third party (a judge) who would rule on the case. This type of dispute resolution was less bloody than violent feuds, and these early cases included harms that today would be handled in a criminal court. In the case of murder, for instance, the victim's relative would sue the suspect, and the judge would decide the case based on their presentations. Today, of course, we have separate courts for criminal matters, but we still have a robust civil system whose caseload at the state level has actually grown 28 percent since 2000 and is currently at over 75 million filed cases [5].

Original jurisdiction civil courts are similar to criminal courts in that they both follow rigid procedural rules, lawyers filter out weak or frivolous cases by refusing to carry them forward, the trial process follows roughly the same steps, and both have the option of jury trials. Nonetheless, civil courts have seven characteristics that distinguish them from criminal courts.

- Injury or harm. In a criminal court, the defendant is accused of injuring the entire community. In a civil court, the harms are much more specific and include violation of contract, damages to property, premise liability (slipping and falling in the store), medical malpractice, automobile accidents, slander/libel, and other types of torts, or civil wrongs.
- Standing and initiation of the case. In a civil court, one party (the plaintiff) sues another party (the defendant) over an injury, such as a tort or contract violation. No prosecutor is involved.
- Role of the court. In civil courts, the government is usually not involved as a party, nor does it provide anyone a lawyer. The government merely provides a forum in which citizens can resolve disputes. The judge maintains the rules of conduct and procedural laws, and either the judge or jury will act as finder of fact and issue a ruling. If the plaintiff

wins, the judge will usually order the defendant to pay for the harm done to the plaintiff.

- Level of evidence necessary to establish culpability (and to win the case). In a civil trial, the plaintiff must present a preponderance of the evidence, or clear and convincing evidence, that the defendant created the harm. This means that more than 50 percent of the evidence must indicate that the defendant is at fault.
- Possible rulings on culpability. The civil court will find for either the plaintiff or the defendant, meaning that the respective party won the case.
- Possible rulings on behalf of the plaintiff. In a modern civil trial, a defendant who loses the trial is not "sentenced" and does not risk execution or incarceration (with few exceptions, such as contempt of court, or defying a court order). However, the judge or jury can levy a wide range of sanctions against the defeated defendant. Damages, or money that goes to the plaintiff, could be nominal (a small amount intended to symbolically represent wrongdoing), compensatory (the amount necessary to restore the harmed person to the pre-injury condition), or punitive (damages above compensation in order to punish the defendant). Damages may be paid with cash, liens on property, garnishing of wages, and so on. The median compensatory and punitive final awards for plaintiff winners in recent years is $28,000. Specific performance and other injunctions either instruct the defendant to abide by the contract or cease particular conduct. Revocation of contract is when the court revokes a contract and orders the parties to return assets to the level prior to the contract.
- Effect on one's criminal record. Even if the defendant loses a civil trial, he or she will not have an arrest or conviction record.

Original Jurisdiction: Criminal Trial Courts

The federal government and all states have trial courts set up to hear cases involving alleged criminal offenses. On the federal level, this happens in district courts (with assistance from the magistrate courts), and on the state level it happens in courts with various names, such as circuit court, superior court, and supreme court (in New York). Even though these are considered lower courts within the judicial hierarchy, they include all limited and general jurisdiction courts and therefore handle most of the criminal cases from start to finish.

In these courts, the prosecutor brings the case forward, because in legal reality it is assumed that the entire community, not just the victim, is "harmed" by the crime, and the prosecution represents the community and therefore has standing. Thus, in criminal cases the court (or government) is active and instrumental. The court not only maintains rules of procedure, but the

Table 3.1 Comparing Civil and Criminal Original Jurisdiction Courts

	Civil Courts	Criminal Courts
Type of law violated	Civil or common law	Substantive criminal statute
Injuries reviewed by the court	Civil wrongs (such as damage from an auto accident) and contract violation	Violation of criminal laws, which are considered injuries to the entire community
Party with standing	Plaintiff: Individual(s) or organization harmed by the defendant's alleged act	Prosecutor (as a representative of the "injured" community)
Party who pays to bring the case	Plaintiff	State
Role of the court during the trial	Maintain rules of conduct and procedural laws, rule on the case, and award damages	Prosecute case, provide defense counsel for indigents, maintain rules of conduct and procedural laws, rule on the case, and declare a sentence
Level of evidence necessary to establish culpability	Preponderance of the evidence, or clear and convincing evidence	Proof beyond a reasonable doubt
Party that has the burden of presenting evidence	Plaintiff	State/prosecutor
Possible decision or verdict	Find for the plaintiff or find for the defendant	Not guilty (acquitted), guilty (convicted), or special verdict (such as suspended sentence or guilty but not culpable)
Judgments or sentences	Judgments: monetary damages, injunction that specifies what the defendant must do or must refrain from doing, or other awards	Sentences: monetary penalties (such as fines or restitution to the victim), community service or probation, incarceration, loss of life
Criminal record if defendant loses the case	No record	Criminal record if convicted

government is also the one bringing the case and having to establish culpability, or proof beyond a reasonable doubt. Table 3.1 compares many of the differences between civil and criminal courts.

These courts handle all the pretrial stages that lead up to trials, like having bail hearings and ruling on motions. Most cases in original jurisdiction courts never make it to trial but are either dismissed or resolved with a negotiated guilty plea. Of those cases that go to trial, most are resolved definitively at the end of the trial. However, sometimes an original jurisdiction court will have a second trial for a case. This happens if there is a **hung jury** (a jury that cannot agree on a verdict of guilty or not guilty), and the prosecutor's office decides to try a second time with a whole new trial. A second trial will also take place if an appeal court **remands** a case (sends it back to the trial court for further action), and the trial court decides to hold a whole new trial. If a conviction is established through either a plea or a trial, the original jurisdiction court will impose the sentence (and often oversee people on probation).

One duty that courts share with other agencies is the investigation. Lawyers and judges usually do not go out and gather evidence and interrogate suspects. This is left mostly to the police, but public defenders offices and private defense attorneys will often conduct their own investigations in order to counter or compensate for the police investigation.

Appellate Jurisdiction: Intermediate Appellate Courts

In the judicial hierarchy, intermediate appeal (or appellate) courts are between original jurisdiction trial courts and the highest court. On the federal level these courts are called Circuit Courts of Appeals, and most states also use the name "court of appeals" or "circuit court."

Appeals courts do not conduct retrials. They usually do not reconsider the facts of the case or hear new facts, hear from trial witnesses, or use juries. They do not declare a person guilty or not guilty. Their primary function is that of review. They have jurisdiction over disputes of law that arise from trials. Most often, they review the evidence or procedures in a criminal trial court that led to its verdict or the final judgment. This power of review is sometimes called the error-correcting function of the appellate courts because they review the trial court proceedings and sometimes correct perceived errors.

Nearly all criminal appeals are filed by defense. A defendant who lost a criminal trial may submit a written request or **petition** in an appeals court to review a particular aspect of the trial. If a prosecution were to appeal a not-guilty verdict, the person could be forced into a second trial, which the courts have ruled is a violation of the Fifth Amendment prohibition of double jeopardy. The trial and final judgment, then, "attach jeopardy" to the defendant. (In the civil court system, however, either the defendant or plaintiff can appeal.) The petition must argue that the defendant's rights were violated during the trial, and the petitioner's goal is to have the trial ruling overturned (or dismissed), or at least some aspect of the trial case reconsidered (such as a retrial with a competent attorney instead of drunk one or a retrial with the confession that was the result of abuse suppressed).

The existence of appellate jurisdiction provides the court system an internal self-correcting procedure whereby judges can review alleged errors of other judges and attempt to correct them. However, this jurisdiction is much more limited than trial court jurisdiction. There is no universal right to appeal. Usually the criminal petitioner must convince the appeals court that it actually does have jurisdiction over some legal dispute about rights. Without a convincing allegation of a violation of rights, a defendant cannot appeal the trial verdict or sentence. Because most trials do not have a substantial error that legal reality considers a threat to due-process rights, most do not lead to appeal. In short, the defendant cannot appeal if he or she had lost in a fair trial, or at least what the appellate court considers a fair trial. Also, in most cases, the defendant cannot appeal if he or she pleads guilty, which represents over 90 percent of the convictions.

Less often, appeal courts will review the constitutionality of a law or part of a law. This is the process of judicial review discussed above. These cases are also initiated by the criminal trial defendant. However, instead of arguing that the procedures violated rights, the petitioner argues that he or she was harmed by an unconstitutional law. The appeal court will evaluate the constitutionality of the law, which involves determining if it violates a provision in the state or federal constitutions. If the appeal court agrees with the petitioner, it will strike down or alter the law or policy. This is the lawmaking function of the appellate courts, and it demonstrates how the courts are independent of the other branches of government.

The High Court

The high court of every state and the federal Supreme Court are actually appeals courts. They do not hold criminal trials (except in very narrow cases, such as treason), and they have little original jurisdiction. They mostly review disputes that began at the trial stage and went through the intermediate court of appeals. The party that lost at the appellate stage can petition the high court to review the ruling of the appellate court. Thus, this high court is often called the court of last resort or superior court and has authority over all inferior courts, which include intermediate appeals courts and lower courts.

The legal principles—judicial review, precedent, judicial restraint, and so on—and jurisdictional questions are the same as for the intermediate appellate courts. The main difference is that the superior court can rule on errors that happened in the intermediate court of appeals as well as in the trial court. The effect of the rulings is also different. Intermediate courts of appeals set precedents for themselves and the lower courts. Decisions made in the high court set precedent for itself in all inferior courts, which allows for greater uniformity within the entire court system. Table 3.2 compares the three levels of courts.

Jurisdiction and Structure of Federal Constitutional Courts

Because the United States has a federalist form of government, the federal government and each of the state governments have distinct political jurisdictions and therefore their own court systems. Most of the federal courts fall into one of two categories: constitutional courts and legislative courts [6].

Table 3.2 Trial Courts and Appellate Courts: Jurisdiction, Role of the Judge, and Outcomes

	Jurisdiction	Primary Role of Judge	Outcomes
High Court (Superior appellate court)	Appellate	Trier of law	• Affirm lower court • Correct errors in intermediate court • Correct errors in trial court • Judicial review • Create policy • Establish precedent
Intermediate Courts of Appeals (ICA)	Appellate	Trier of law	• Affirm lower court • Correct errors in trial court • Judicial review • Create policy • Establish precedent
Trial Courts	Original (either limited or general)	Finder of fact (either by a jury or judge) and trier of law	• Issue verdict • Issue sentence if verdict is guilty

Constitutional courts, or Article III courts, derive their power from Article III of the Constitution, and the judges serve lifetime appointments. These include U.S. District Courts, U.S. Circuit Courts of Appeals, and the U.S. Supreme Court.

Legislative courts, which include most other federal courts, are created by Congress under Article I powers [7]. These include:

1. U.S. Magistrate Courts;
2. bankruptcy courts;
3. the U.S. Court of Military Appeals;
4. the U.S. Tax Court;
5. the U.S. Court of Veterans' Appeals.

The jurisdiction of these courts is more limited than constitutional courts, and their rulings can be appealed to constitutional courts. The judges generally serve for a limited time, often 8 years. Only the first of these, U.S. Magistrate Courts, deals with civilian crime. Other courts exist at the federal level, such as Tribal Courts, but are beyond the scope of this book.

As the nation has grown over the past two centuries so has its court system. Part of the growth has been the growth in population and urbanization, but part of it has been an increase in federal subject-matter jurisdiction. The Constitution gives the federal courts jurisdiction over constitutional matters, disputes between states, federal crimes, and so on. The Constitution defines only treason and counterfeiting as crimes, and in the first century of the nation, there were only a few federal criminal statutes, such as laws against kidnapping that crossed state lines and bank robbery, so these courts did not hear many criminal cases.

However, as the federal government has given itself power over more conduct by enacting federal criminal statutes, the federal court's jurisdiction has necessarily expanded to include those. The Mann Act of 1910, which criminalizes prostitution that crosses state lines, is often considered a turning point in the growth of federal criminal statutes. Since then, and especially since the 1980s, the federal government has added hundreds of criminal statutes regarding drugs, pornography, street gang activity, racketeering, firearms, and so on. Over 3000 acts are now defined as federal crimes.

Even beyond this expansion in federal criminal statutes, federal courts prosecute behaviors covered by the **Assimilative Crimes Act**, a federal statute that allows state law to apply to non-federal criminal offenses committed on property that has been reserved or acquired by the federal government [8]. For instance, there is no federal law against assault, but if someone were to threaten a person in a post office in Chicago, which is federal property, the federal court will "assimilate" the state law criminalizing assault and will prosecute the defendant for assault in federal criminal court. The United States also participates in international criminal courts.

The effect of this growth in the federal courts can be seen at the beginning and end of the court process. Currently around 1 million cases are filed annually in federal courts, of which only about 10 percent are criminal cases (70 percent are bankruptcy cases) [9]. Most are settled before trial, but the court is still involved in the settlement process. Regarding the effect on prisons, from the 12-month period ending in June 2005, the federal system accounted for over 25 percent of the nation's prison population growth, adding over 5000 inmates. The 10-year trend from 1995 to 2005 is even more significant, with the federal prison population increasing at an annual average of 7.4 percent, and the state prison system increasing at an average of 2.5 percent annually [10]. With this growth in population, jurisdiction, and criminal cases, the federal judiciary now has 1700 judgeships [11]. Many of these judges handle criminal cases in the following courts:

- Supreme Court;
- 13 Circuit Courts of Appeals;
- 94 District Courts (with original jurisdiction). Various numbers of magistrate judges are attached to and assist each district court.

Table 3.3 Executive Branch Agencies That Perform Federal Criminal Investigations

Justice Department

- Federal Bureau of Investigation (FBI)
- Drug Enforcement Agency (DEA) and National Drug Intelligence Center
- Bureau of Alcohol, Tobacco, Firearms, and Explosives (BATF, partially under Treasury Department)
- U.S. Marshals Service
- Office of Tribal Justice
- Office on Violence Against Women
- National Central Bureau of INTERPOL

Department of Homeland Security (DHS)

- Secret Service (partially under Treasury Department)
- Office of Civil Rights and Civil Liberties
- U.S. Coast Guard
- U.S. Immigration and Customs Enforcement (ICE)

Other Federal Agencies That Perform Criminal Investigations

- Financial Crimes Enforcement Network
- Postal Inspector (U.S. Postal Service)
- Environmental Protection Agency (EPA) (independent agency)
- Other interagency task forces that enable local law enforcement to share information with and assist federal agencies

The Article III judges are all appointed by the president and confirmed by the Senate, and hold a life-tenured position. The magistrate judges are appointed by district judges and serve 8-year terms. Even with this significant workforce, the courts do not have the capacity to do their own investigations. Rather, they rely on other agencies from the executive branch [12]. See Table 3.3 for some of those agencies and the departments they are under.

U.S. Magistrate Courts

Congress created the U.S. Magistrate Courts in 1968 in order to help district courts carry out their duties [13]. District judges not only appoint magistrate judges but also supervise them and assign them judicial tasks. Magistrates thus have limited jurisdiction, which means their authority within original jurisdiction cases is granted to them by district courts and can be overridden by district judges. Their authority is "limited" compared to the authority of district judges. For instance, district judges assign criminal trials to magistrate judges for non-felony cases (and smaller civil cases), if both parties in the case consent. In such misdemeanor trials, magistrates also have the authority to impose sentences.

The bulk of their criminal trial work, however, comes from handling most of the pretrial stages for the district judges. They issue search warrants, preside at initial appearances and preliminary hearings, appoint counsel to indigent defendants, set bail and rule on detention hearings, rule on motions including suppression of evidence, and negotiate pleas. For the 12-month period ending September 30, 2010, magistrate judges conducted 2,369 misdemeanor trials but handled 554,494 felony pretrial duties (in addition to 353,847 judicial duties in civil cases) [14].

In the preliminary proceedings alone, magistrate judges disposed of 116,983 cases through, for instance, case dismissals or guilty pleas. This work greatly lightens the load of the district judges. However, in a felony case where no plea is reached, the district judge will take over and hear the actual criminal trial. Even in these cases, the magistrate judges often recommend sentences. Their work continues in the post-conviction stages, such as hearing and filing recommendations in prisoner *habeas corpus* appeals and civil rights cases. As of 2011, 527 full-time and 41 part-time U.S. magistrate judge positions were authorized [15].

U.S. District Courts

The federal capacity to hear trials changed and grew significantly in the nation's first 100 years [16]. With the Judiciary Act of 1789, Congress divided the nation into 13 federal judicial districts and established what were called circuit courts to hear most trials and appeals in each district. These were called "circuit" courts because some of the justices actually had to "ride the circuit" from one courthouse to another. The panel in these circuits consisted of one Supreme Court judge and a judge from the respective district. These courts were altered by the Judiciary Acts of 1801 and 1802, and by additional laws in 1855, 1863, 1867, and 1869. In 1891, Congress separated the appellate jurisdiction from these courts by creating the U.S. Circuit Courts of Appeals. Finally, the Judicial Code of 1911 abolished these circuit courts of original jurisdiction and gave U.S. District Courts sole authority over original jurisdiction trials in the federal judiciary. District courts are now where federal civil and criminal cases begin.

Today, the United States has 94 District Courts. Every state has at least one federal district court, and more populous states, such as California, have as many as four. Because they are Article III courts, the judges are nominated by the president, confirmed by the Senate, and have lifetime appointments. A district may have as many as 28 judges. These courts have general jurisdiction because they have the authority to hear all aspects of most original jurisdiction cases, even though they assign many of these duties to Magistrate Courts and usually focus on felony trials or significant civil trials. When a jury is used, it reviews the evidence and rules guilty or not guilty, and the judge monitors issues of law, such as proper procedure. When a jury is not present, the judge performs both the finder of fact and trier of law roles.

District court cases must have a federal question, which means the federal government has jurisdiction over the dispute. This includes, for instance, violation of congressional statute or assimilated criminal acts, in which an alleged violation of a state law occurs on federal land and is therefore prosecuted in federal court; or civil suits by people from different states; or citizens disputing with a party outside of the United States. The majority of their work involves civil cases. Of the nearly 375,000 cases filed with federal district courts in 2011, 21 percent (around 80,000) were criminal cases. Those cases involved over 100,000 defendants. Of those criminal cases, 80 percent were felonies, and around 25 percent were drug cases. These figures do not account for the more than 350,000 cases that were carried over from the previous year [17].

U.S. Circuit Courts of Appeals

In the Judiciary Act of 1891 (also called the Evarts Act), Congress divided the United States into nine appellate circuits and created Circuit Courts of Appeals. These **intermediate courts of appeals** (ICA) allow district courts to focus on original jurisdiction cases and relieve the U.S. Supreme Court's appellate load. In fact, they hear nearly all appeals from district courts. Today, there are 13 federal appellate courts with 179 judgeships. Each is called the "U.S. Court of Appeals for the [1st, 2nd,...13th] Circuit." In recent years, Congress has debated whether to divide some of the existing circuits and create new ones. The Ninth Circuit (see Photo 3.1) may soon be divided into two courts [18].

Because these Article III courts have appellate jurisdiction, they review district trial cases for mistakes in law. They rarely review the facts of the case, hear witnesses, or gather new evidence. When reviewing a case on appeal, the court will usually have three of the appellate judges sit as a panel. These three will then vote on the outcome, and the majority will become the ruling and will write the opinion (if one is written at all). In more serious cases, the court will sit *en banc*, which means all of the judges in that circuit will hear and rule on the case. From March 2010 to March 2011, over 55,000 cases were filed with the U.S. Appeals Courts, and nearly 45,000 were pending, or carried over, from the previous year [19].

PHOTO 3.1
Judges of the 9th U.S. Circuit Court of Appeals listen to oral arguments in San Francisco.

U.S. Supreme Court

The Supreme Court is known as the "highest court in the land," "the final arbiter," and the "court of last resort." Congress can sometimes override a Supreme Court ruling, but no other court in the nation has the authority to review its decisions. Except in limited cases such as treaties, the Supreme Court has appellate jurisdiction and hears cases coming from U.S. circuit courts or state high courts. This means that it does not hear criminal trials but instead reviews accusations that the intermediate court of appeals or state high court erred, often in its supposed failure to correct a substantial trial court error.

The U.S. Supreme Court is the only court created explicitly in the Constitution. Article III places the judicial power of the federal government in "one supreme Court, and in such inferior Courts" that Congress may establish. Congress also has the authority over the Court's composition. In the Judiciary Act of 1789, it designated that the Court shall be composed of six **justices**, or judges: one chief justice and five associate justices. The number of justices fluctuated up and down between 1807 and 1869, when Congress increased it to nine justices, where it remains today [20]. As with all Article III courts, the president nominates the justices and the Senate approves or refuses to approve them. If confirmed, they hold a lifetime appointment; if not confirmed, the president must nominate someone else and go through the whole confirmation process again.

At first, the Supreme Court had to hear most cases that were appealed, but over the years it gained more discretionary power over its **docket**, or the schedule of cases it has to hear. In 1988, Congress granted the Supreme Court almost total control over its own docket [21]. In recent years, the Supreme Court agrees to hear only about 1 percent of the cases that are filed with it, which amounts to about 100 cases per year.

To have a case reviewed by the Supreme Court, the petitioner (the party who lost in the inferior court) files a petition for a writ of *certiorari* (sur-shee-uh-RAIR-ee), which asks the Court to review an alleged error in the inferior court that is a question of federal law. According to the Rule of Four, four justices must agree to hear the case for the case to be heard. When the Court does agree to hear a case, it usually issues a **writ of *certiorari*** (or grants cert.), which is an order to the intermediate court of appeals, district court, special federal court, and/or state high court to send their trial or appeal transcripts to the Supreme Court for review. If, however, the Court refuses to hear the case, then the decision in the inferior court stands, or remains in force. Because the Supreme Court hears so few cases, the intermediate court of appeals is, in effect, the court of last resort for most federal cases.

All Supreme Court cases are heard in Washington, DC, where the Court sits. When the Court does grant *certiorari* it usually affirms the ruling of the inferior court but can also reverse its ruling or remand the case. An additional power of the Supreme Court is to create binding precedent, which means all courts must follow the decision. This is why, for instance, local, state, and federal police all read a suspect the *Miranda* rights before interrogation. If they do not, it would be a violation of the judicial law set in the Supreme Court case *Miranda v. Arizona* (1966), and all courts would be required to suppress information, including confessions, that came out of the interrogation.

A particular type of case that the Supreme Court has Constitutional authority to hear is a **habeas corpus** petition, or an order to bring a party before the court. *Habeas corpus* is Latin for "you have the body," and the Supreme Court may issue a writ of *habeas corpus* ordering that an inmate or other detainee be brought to the Court so that it can determine if the incarceration is lawful. This is called the "great writ" because it is a judicial check on executive power. It requires that if the federal or state government is going to deprive a person of his or her liberties, it must do so within the powers of the law and not arbitrarily or unjustly. If the government cannot provide a lawful justification for the incarceration, then the person shall be released. As the Supreme Court wrote in 1969, the writ is "the fundamental instrument for safeguarding individual freedom against arbitrary and lawless state action" [22]. After the Civil War, Congress expanded this power to review cases of state inmates and to grant relief if federal law was violated. More recently, lower federal courts have been given authority to review some of these petitions.

An application for a writ of *habeas corpus* is often handwritten from the inmates themselves, such as Clarence Earl Gideon, whose petition eventually led to the landmark *Gideon v. Wainwright* (1963) decision that requires states to provide counsel in all felony trials. When a court does grant *cert.* it may appoint counsel if the applicant is indigent.

As important as *habeas corpus* is to due-process liberties, it is not easy to have one reviewed by the High Court or to succeed in winning relief. First, the Court is not required to review any particular one. It is discretionary. Thousands are filed annually, but only a few are reviewed. In the 2011 session, the Court reviewed only nine *habeas corpus* petitions [23]. Second, due to the principle of judicial restraint, the Court tends to rule in favor of state authority and uphold the trial court sentence. Third, even though every inmate has a right to file an application, it must show that the error was "substantial and injurious." Because most writs fail to meet this evidentiary threshold, they are dismissed without comment. Fourth, Congress and the Supreme Court itself have constrained the *habeas corpus* right in recent years through stringent dead-lines, limiting the number of petitions, and other restrictive mechanisms.

State Courts

The Constitution does not describe the structure of state courts. In fact, they are not even mentioned. Given the Constitution's content, it is actually possi-ble for a state to have no court system at all if it chose not to put one in its own constitution. Each state is free to structure its government in whatever way it sees fit, as long as it does not violate the federal constitution or federal law. As it turns out, however, every state has created three branches of gov-ernment and an independent judiciary in much the same way as the federal government [24].

All states also follow the same legal principles, such as due process, adversar-ial trials, and precedent. (Louisiana formally does not obligate judges to follow precedent but, in practice, precedent is cited in trials and influences outcomes because it is a mechanism for consistency.) In each state, the pros-ecutor, or state, has the burden of proof; the judge is the trier of law; rules of discovery are in place; and trial stages are the same. The structure and jurisdiction of state courts are similar. Each one has trial courts of original jurisdiction and a process for judicial appeals. Some cases in each state system can be appealed to the federal court system, such as cases involving alleged violation of constitutional rights. The dual sovereignty of the United States has thus led to a federal court system and 50 state court system that overlap and are similar in many ways. Nonetheless, there are significant differences between the federal and state judiciaries, such as their caseload, jurisdiction, selection of judges, and the types of specialized courts.

State Court Caseload and Jurisdiction

State courts handle a greater variety of cases and many more cases than the federal judiciary. Federal courts have a larger geographic jurisdiction (the entire nation) but hear only cases with a federal question, such as disputes between states, copyright cases, or violation of federal law. States have jurisdiction over all other trials and appeals because they write most of the laws. Nearly all lawsuits are resolved in state courts, and 94 percent of criminal trials are held in state courts [25]. Nearly 50 million non-traffic cases are filed annually in the states and are heard by over 30,000 judges [26]. On average, a general-jurisdiction court judge hears 1,800 new cases annually [27].

From 1987 to 2004, case filings (at least those not related to traffic) in state appellate and trial courts increased by almost 45 percent, even though the rate of criminal cases per 100,000 people has decreased 1 percent in the past decade [28]. Up through the mid-2000s, only six states had no increase in judicial staffing, and 26 had over a 10 percent increase [29]. Even though many states have made cuts since the 2008 recession, their caseload continues to rise. That states carry the heaviest judicial load was arguably the intent of the framers of the Constitution, as they prevented federal courts from becoming common-law courts that hear every sort of case. States hear cases regarding criminal offenses or civil disputes that occur within their borders and that the federal government does not have jurisdiction over. To avoid the risk of every state having a legal system that became entirely disconnected from other states, the Full Faith and Credit clause (which we discussed in Chapter 2) obligates each state to recognize many of the policies, records, and judicial proceedings of other states [30].

Subject-matter jurisdiction is much more complex than geographic jurisdiction. Many states have a separate court for various categories of cases, such as courts for juvenile delinquency, traffic, family matters, and so on. Assigning a case to a particular court is often a complex process, such as deciding if a case should be heard in juvenile or adult court. Here are some of the types of criminal and civil cases that state courts have the authority to hear. Many of these cases, such as traffic offenses, juvenile delinquency, or divorce cases, are almost never heard in federal courts.

- criminal offenses
- delinquency and status offenses (cases involving juveniles who violate laws that apply only to juveniles)

- traffic offenses and other infractions
- personal harm cases and contract disputes
- family law
- cases involving wills and estates
- business and commerce law

Structure of State Courts: Original and Appellate Jurisdiction

Unlike the federal courts, state court systems generally handle far more criminal cases than civil cases, but how they handle these criminal cases varies widely. No two states have identical judicial systems. To confuse matters more, states use different names for the same level of courts. For instance, in California, the high court is the Supreme Court, but in New York "supreme courts" refers to trial courts. Nonetheless, most states have the same hierarchical structure as the federal system. These include:

- Trial courts of limited original jurisdiction. These handle a great number of "smaller" cases such as misdemeanors, traffic, small claims, probate, family disputes, and so on at the municipal, county, and state levels. These usually have no jury, often specialize in a particular area of law (such as misdemeanors, juveniles, traffic offenses, probate, family disputes, and small claims), and, in more sparsely populated counties, have a single judge running the courthouse. These are sometimes called common plea courts, municipal courts, justice courts, or township courts. These courts hear 66 percent of the state cases, of which 43 percent are traffic cases, and 14 percent are criminal cases [31].
- Trial courts of general original jurisdiction. These courts hear more serious cases, such as felonies and civil disputes over large amounts of money, and often involve a jury. These courts also hear some appeals from the limited-jurisdiction courts. States have different names for these courts, including district courts, circuit courts, courts of common pleas, and (in New York) supreme courts.
- Intermediate courts of appeals (ICAs) hear disputes of law regarding trials and review the legality of the trial procedures. A few states, such as Delaware and Nevada, do not have an intermediate court of appeals. Various names are used for these courts, including appellate court, superior court, and court of special appeals.
- High courts act as the final arbiter in the state system. Like the U.S. Supreme Court, these courts have discretion as to whether to hear some cases, are obligated to hear some cases, and have original jurisdiction in a narrow range of cases. They also have the authority to review the constitutionality of state law and create precedent within the state court system. Most states call their high court the state supreme court, but others refer to it as the court of appeals.

The states differ significantly, however, on how they divide the state into judicial regions. All states have multiple districts for trials, but in some areas trials are heard on the county level, and in other areas they are heard on multi-county level. Some states also grant cities, towns, and villages the authority to operate their own trial courts. These municipal courts hear many minor cases involving violation of municipal ordinances, such as public intoxication. As for appellate circuits, some states, like California and Louisiana, have several appellate circuits, whereas states with lower populations may have none or only one, such as Alaska.

States use various methods for selecting judges. These methods are discussed in greater detail in Chapters 5 and 15.

Budgets and Unification of State Courts

State courts are funded by state appropriations and local appropriations, but the respective amounts vary widely. State funding of court operations varies from 11 to 100 percent. States where the courts do not receive all their operating costs from the capitol, counties, and sometimes cities have to pay some or all of the court costs, which leads to considerable variation of court budgets within a single state [32].

To deal with inconsistencies in funding and operations within states, some states are moving toward state court unification. This entails centralization of the judicial system at the state level, which can involve centralizing the entire state court structure or centralizing only its administration [33]. This usually happens with the trial courts because the appellate courts already operate at the state, not local, level. States enact consolidation in different ways and to different degrees, but it generally includes centralization of administration and rule-making powers, unified (versus local) funding and budgeting, and trial court consolidation [34]. The federal government consolidated its courts throughout the 20th century, but states have been doing it more recently and less consistently.

Unification, according to its advocates, simplifies the court structure by reducing the number and types of courts, the funding sources, and the rules. Ideally, unification increases professionalism among court workers and the quality of justice [35]. Advocates of unification argue that allowing each county to operate its own judicial system, which is known as "decentralized courts," creates a fractured system with too much variation and serious miscarriages of justice. Local courts do not always follow state judicial rules, sometimes issue frivolous warrants, have too many cases in which the defendant has no attorney, and violate due-process rights, depending on what county court hears it.

Opponents of unification argue that centralization will likely bureaucratize the local courthouses, increase their operating costs, and reduce "judicial independence by making judges subservient to the courts superior to their own" [36]. Yet oversight of the courts is difficult, inconsistent, and sometimes nonexistent [37]. Funding from taxes and fees varies tremendously from county to county, and some have specialized courts for issues like drug and mental health cases, but others have no specialized courts. Courthouse operations vary even within one state, which makes it difficult for attorneys to learn the different procedures for each county and difficult for the state to maintain statewide records and audits. The decentralized system may respond to local needs but is seen by many as fragmented and inefficient. Ultimately, it leads to inconsistent justice because similar cases are handled differently. Focus on Discretion illustrates some problems of decentralization.

FOCUS ON DISCRETION

Village Courts: Local Justice or Abuse?
The 12,50 town and village courts in New York have been in place since the region was a colony of Great Britain. Smaller than county and city courts, they hear traffic offenses, ordinance violations, and misdemeanors, as well as issue search warrants, impose fines and incarceration up to 2 years, and issue restraining orders [38].

The nearly 2,000 judges in these courts, who still carry the colonial name of "justices of the peace," comprise two-thirds of New York's judges and hear 300,000 criminal cases annually. Yet only one in four are lawyers. Their legal education consists of:

> "...training [that] is six days of state-administered classes, followed by a true-or-false test so rudimentary that the official who runs it said only one candidate since 1999 had failed. A sample question for the justices: 'Town and village justices must maintain dignity, order and decorum in their courtrooms' — true or false?...[New York] demands more schooling for licensed manicurists and hair stylists" [39].

As a result of some of these judges' ignorance of the law, due-process rights are often abused and procedural rules ignored. People are incarcerated without being convicted; the public is excluded from hearings; recordings or transcripts of the hearings are inconsistently kept, which makes appealing cases difficult; judges communicate with parties in private before trials; and judges express racial and sexual bigotry. According to the *New York Times*, "One justice freed a rape suspect on bail as a favor to a friend. Another sentenced a welfare recipient to 89 days in jail after she failed to pay a $1.50 cab fare. One failed to appoint a lawyer for a 19-year-old mentally retarded alcoholic."

About 30 states still use justices of the peace, but many states, including Delaware and California, have substantially modernized or abolished them. Advocates of the New York system, especially the politically powerful organization of the justices, the State Magistrates Association, argue that hometown justice allows for common-sense solutions and costs much less than modern courts.

Every attempt to abolish or fundamentally reform these courts by staffing them with more lawyers and instituting more oversight have failed. There is still almost no supervision from the State Commission on Judicial Conduct, no audit of their budget or fines they collect, and no clear count of the cases they hear or incidents of abuse. One New York justice of the peace, who has served for 13 years, said, "I just follow my own common sense. And the hell with the law" [40].

Question
Is it worth reducing due-process provisions and oversight in order to keep justice informal and local? Should states update or shut down these village courts?

Specialized State Courts

Another area in which state courts have much greater variety than federal courts is in their creation and implementation of specialized courts. Courts and congresses introduce these alternative courts in order to handle particular types of cases in a new manner. Juvenile justice courts, for instance, were introduced more than a century ago to handle youthful offenders in a non-adversarial and non-public manner. The principal goals of these alternative courts is to reduce crime by treating offenders, reduce the caseload in trial courts so they have more capacity to handle serious felony cases, and reduce incarceration. However, these legal innovations also tend to expand government power by blurring lines between criminal and non-criminal jurisdiction, which creates ambiguous quasi-judicial systems that reduce due-process protections and disguise state coercion as social welfare [41].

These courts are, first and foremost, judicial diversionary options. They allow the court to remove a case from the traditional criminal trial track while maintaining control over the offender. They are often called therapeutic jurisprudence, problem-solving court-based programs, and problem-solving courts because they experiment with new ways to deal with crime and some problems that plague offenders [42]. Their structure and operations vary considerably, but common features include:

- Use of suspended or deferred sentences in which the judge agrees to erase the sentence (and sometimes the conviction) if the defendant completes community service hours, drug counseling, or an other program.
- Adherence to principles of treatment, which views crime as a "symptom" of underlying problems, such as addiction or low education, that can be changed through rehabilitation programs.
- Expanded judicial discretion, which enables judges to assess the offender's situation more carefully than is done in the typical criminal court and offer graduated sanctions and rewards.
- Extended involvement of the courts, in which courts intervene immediately with offenders and monitor them for a longer time.
- Use of non-adversarial proceedings and multidisciplinary teams, which often exclude defense attorneys and the recording of proceedings and involve counseling, direct apologies to the victim or community, and participation from community organizations such as schools and homeless shelters [43].

Sometimes these courts are stand-alone judicial organizations. Other times, they are branches of other courts. For instance, a truancy court may be operated by the state or county family court. After World War II, alternative courts began to proliferate at a greater rate than before, largely because of greater social scientific knowledge such as sociology and psychology, and also because of growing populations and growing prison populations. Their creation and use has rapidly increased in the past couple of decades [29]. Table 3.4 lists specialized courts that operate in many states.

Table 3.4 Specialized State Courts That Deal with Criminal Offenses

Type of Court	Court Features
Juvenile justice courts	• Began in 1899 in Cook County, IL and now in every state • Handle delinquency and status-offense cases • Generally these now abide by clear procedural rules
Drug courts	• Began in 1989, rapidly expanded, but now suffering budget cuts • Over 2500 drug courts for adults and juveniles
Community courts and community prosecution programs	• Began in New York 1993 by Center for Court Innovation • Try to reduce crime and incarceration by engaging community members, improving communities, and helping the offenders reintegrate into law-abiding society • "Judges" are community members; process is less costly and quicker than regular courts; offender stays in the community
Gun courts	• Work to reduce possession and use of firearms • Adult gun courts do not aim to be therapeutic, but rather work to process cases quickly and issue long prison sentences for offenders • Juvenile gun courts are more in line with the treatment principles: early intervention, education about consequences, reduction of recidivism rates, and increase in youth involvement in community programs
Domestic violence courts	• Began in the 1970s; separate courts emerged in the 1990s; over 200 operate in the United States • Attempt to reduce domestic violence through rehabilitation rather than merely more aggressive policing and harsher sentences
Mental health courts	• Began in 1997 in Florida; now over 150 in the United States • Treat mental illness first, and view criminal offending as a by-product of that
Teen courts	• Began in the 1940s, expanded rapidly in 1990s, now over 800 in the United States • An attorney or judge serves as judge, but teens (often ex-offenders) serve as prosecution, defense, bailiff, and jurors, and the teens issue punishments such as community service, counseling, and apologies • Offense removed from offender's record • Focus on minor, usually first-time, offenders
Re-entry courts	• Began in 1990s and modeled after drug courts • Promote law-abiding behavior among parolees in order to reduce the rate of return to prison
Veteran courts	• Began in New York in 2008 • Over 75 in operation in the United States • Instead of jail time, get military veterans counseling and treatment for depression, stress, and substance abuse
Other courts	• Hear cases that may include criminal offending • Traffic courts, truancy courts, family courts, family treatment courts, tribal courts, administrative courts to handle regulation cases, and quasi-court programs such as victim-offender mediation and arbitration

These legal innovations may lower court costs, help many offenders, reduce stigma, and reduce rates of recidivism, but they entail many complications and potential problems [44]. The funding and logistics can be daunting. Funding for an experimental program must be secured, criteria for inclusion in the program must be established, and a means of assessing its success must (or at least should) be implemented. The program must also be balanced with other organizations in order to both avoid duplicating efforts and to assure that necessary services are in place (such as the availability of treatment facilities for low-income people).

A more fundamental concern is that the expansion of government powers that is created by these programs reduces the protection of rights and oversight of the operations [45]. These powers:

- Reduce suspects' rights by compelling them to incriminate themselves and confess guilt in order to avoid trial or participate in the more lenient and positive program, lowering the standards of proof (allowing evidence that would not be permissible in a trial); denying the rights to be innocent until proven guilty and reasonable doubt by punishing suspects without a conviction; and sometimes denying the rights of defense counsel and public hearings [46].
- Violate due process by handling similar cases differently, so that, for instance, a veteran who commits burglary will receive treatment and no incarceration, but a non-veteran who commits the same offense receives a prison sentence without treatment.
- Reduce procedural rules by emphasizing immediate intervention over procedural laws, by involving people who are not judges or even trained in law in the loss-of-liberties and other punishment decisions, and by sometimes providing no transcripts of the hearings and making appeal difficult.
- Expand judicial discretion by allowing judges to use religious principles, prejudices, intuition, and other nonlegal factors in making decisions [47].
- Create potential conflicts of interest because the community members making the disciplinary decisions may know the offender personally, and worse, treatment agencies involved in decisions may financially profit from forcing more people to attend their rehabilitation center in order to avoid incarceration.
- Extend the responsibility of the defendants and their punishments beyond the harm of the offense.
- Reduce oversight from judicial commissions.
- Widen the net of social control by allowing the courts to control people that otherwise would have been released or never even taken to court [48].

SUMMARY

1. List and discuss the court's two general roles.
   - The court's two specific roles include crime control and maintaining and creating due-process provisions. Crime control includes issuing search warrants to police, charging people with criminal offenses, obtaining convictions through plea bargains and trials, conducting trials, issuing sentences or sanctions, and enforcing some judicial decisions, especially sentences of probation. Maintaining and creating due-process provisions includes monitoring the court process and assuring that police and court officers follow procedural laws, hearing appeals, evaluating the constitutionality of laws, and establishing precedent.

2. Define jurisdiction. Explain subject-matter jurisdiction, geographic jurisdiction, and hierarchical jurisdiction.
   - Jurisdiction is the legal power or authority of a court to hear particular types of cases, adjudicate on such cases, and issue orders.
   - Subject-matter jurisdiction refers to a court's authority to hear a case as determined by the type of offense. Subject-matter jurisdiction encompasses the type of offense, the location of the offense, and the aspect of the case being reviewed.
   - Geographic jurisdiction refers to a court's authority to hear a case as determined by the location of the offense. It includes federal jurisdiction, state boundaries, and district or county boundaries.
   - Hierarchical jurisdiction is a subcategory of subject-matter jurisdiction and refers to a court's authority to hear either original jurisdiction trials or appellate hearings. Most cases are heard by a trial court.

3. Describe the duties of original jurisdiction courts, appellate courts, and high courts.
   - Original jurisdiction courts are lower courts within the judicial hierarchy. They make up most courts and handle most of the criminal cases from start to finish.
   - Appellate courts are between original jurisdiction trial courts and the highest court. Their primary function is that of review, and they have jurisdiction over disputes of law that arise from trials. Most often, they review the evidence or procedures in a criminal trial court that led to its guilty verdict.
   - High courts are appeals courts. They do not hold criminal trials and have little original jurisdiction. They mostly review disputes that

began at the trial stage and went through the intermediate court of appeals. The high court is often called the court of last resort or superior court and has authority over all inferior courts, which include intermediate appeals courts and lower courts.

4. Differentiate constitutional courts and legislative courts.
   - Constitutional courts include U.S. District Courts, U.S. Circuit Courts of Appeals, and the U.S. Supreme Court. These courts create the core of the federal judiciary and hear federal criminal trials and appeals. These courts derive their power from Article III of the Constitution. The judges serve lifetime appointments.
   - Legislative courts, which include most other federal courts, are created by Congress under Article I. These include U.S. Magistrate Courts, bankruptcy courts, the U.S. Court of Military Appeals, the U.S. Tax Court, Tribal Courts, and the U.S. Court of Veterans' Appeals. These courts' jurisdiction is more limited than constitutional courts, and their rulings can be appealed to constitutional courts. The judges serve for a limited time.

5. Discuss the purpose and functions of U.S. Magistrate Courts.
   - Congress created the U.S. Magistrate Courts to help U.S. District Courts carry out their duties. District judges appoint magistrate judges, supervise them, and assign them judicial tasks. Magistrates have limited jurisdiction. Much of their criminal trial work comes from handling most of the pretrial stages for District judges.

6. Talk about the requirement for U.S. District Court cases and what most of that court's work involves.
   - District courts are where federal civil and criminal cases begin. District court cases must have a federal question, which means the federal government has jurisdiction over the dispute. Most of the court's work involves civil cases.

7. Examine the work of U.S. Circuit Courts of Appeals.
   - U.S. Circuit Courts of Appeals have appellate jurisdiction. When reviewing a case on appeal, the court will usually have three of the appellate judges sit as a panel. These three will vote on the outcome, and the majority will become the ruling and will write any opinion. In serious cases, all of the judges in that circuit will hear and rule on the case.

8. Describe the jurisdiction of the U.S. Supreme Court.
   - The Supreme Court is known as the "highest court in the land," "the final arbiter," and the "court of last resort." No other U.S. court may review its decisions. The Supreme Court has appellate

jurisdiction and hears cases coming from U.S. Circuit Courts or state high courts. It does not hear criminal trials *per-se*.

9. Compare and contrast state courts with federal courts.
    - State courts handle a greater variety of cases and more cases than the federal judiciary. Federal courts have a larger geographic jurisdiction but hear only cases with a federal question. States have jurisdiction over all other trials and appeals. Nearly all cases are resolved in state courts. Most state systems have the same hierarchical structure as the federal system, including trial courts of limited original jurisdiction, trial courts of general original jurisdiction, intermediate appellate courts, and high courts.

10. Analyze the potential advantages and problems of state court unification.
    - Unification simplifies court structure by reducing the number and types of courts, the funding sources, and the rules. Unification increases professionalism among court workers and the quality of justice. A decentralized system has too much variation. Local courts do not always follow state judicial rules, sometimes issue frivolous warrants, have too many cases in which the defendant has no attorney, and violate due-process rights.
    - Unification may bureaucratize local courthouses, increase their operating costs, and reduce judicial independence. The decentralized system responds to local needs.

11. List and discuss common features of specialized state courts.
    - Specialized state courts use suspended or deferred sentences, adhere to principles of treatment, allow for expanded judicial discretion, extend involvement of the courts, and use of non-adversarial proceedings and multidisciplinary teams.

Questions

1. What are the court's two general roles?
2. What is jurisdiction? What are the different types?
3. Describe the duties of original jurisdiction courts, appellate courts, and high courts.
4. What is the difference between constitutional courts and legislative courts?
5. What are the purpose and functions of U.S. Magistrate Courts?
6. What is the requirement for U.S. District Court cases? What does that court's work involve?
7. What does the U.S. Circuit Courts of Appeals do?
8. What is the jurisdiction of the U.S. Supreme Court?
9. How do state courts like federal courts? How are they different?

10. What are potential advantages and problems of state court unification?
11. What are common features of specialized state courts?

REFERENCES

[1] Kyckelhahn T. Bureau of Justice Statistics. Justice expenditure and employment extracts, 2008 - Final. <http://bjs.ojp.usdoj.gov/index.cfm?ty=pbdetail&iid=4333> [accessed May 30, 2012]. Administrative office of the United States Courts. 2011 Annual Report of the Director: Judicial Business of the United States Courts. Washington, DC: United States Courts, 2012, <http://www.uscourts.gov/Statistics/JudicialBusiness.aspx>. Court Statistics Project, "Examining the work of state courts: an analysis of 2009 state court caseloads, 2011, <www.courtstatistics.org/Criminal.aspx>. United States Courts, Federal District Court workload increases in fiscal year 2011. 2012 Administrative office of U.S. Courts.

[2] Siegel JR. A theory of justiciability. Tex Law Rev 2007;86(73):74−139.

[3] Nagel RF. Unrestrained: judicial excess and the mind of the American lawyer. New Brunswick, NJ: Transaction Publishers; 2008.

[4] An excellent source for legal definitions and explanations is Cornell University Law School's Legal Information Institute at <www.law.cornell.edu/wex/>.

[5] Court Statistics Project, Civil caseloads level off after three years of growth, <www.courtstatistics.org/Civil/CivilGrowth.aspx>; 2012 [accessed October 6, 2012].

[6] Abraham HJ. The judiciary: the supreme court in the governmental process. 6th ed. Boston, MA: Allyn and Bacon; 1983.

[7] Carp RA, Stidham R. 2nd ed. Judicial process in America. Washington, DC: Congressional Quarterly Press; 1993. p. 47.

[8] Assimilative Crimes Act, 18 § 13.

[9] Federal Judicial Center, <www.fjc.gov/federal/courts.nsf/autoframe?OpenForm&nav=menu2e&page=/federal/courts.nsf/page/5DD5E0A65BA87BCA8525682400517BA5>; 2012 [accessed September 15, 2012].

[10] Harrison PM, Beck AJ. Prison and jail inmates at midyear 2005. Washington, DC: Bureau of Justice Statistics Bulletin, U.S. Department of Justice; 2006, p. 2−3: Online at <bjs.ojp.usdoj.gov/content/pub/pdf/pjim05.pdf>.

[11] Federal Judiciary Center, <www.fjc.gov/federal/courts.nsf/autoframe?OpenForm&nav=menu2e&page=/federal/courts.nsf/page/5DD5E0A65BA87BCA8525682400517BA5>; 2012 [accessed September 15, 2012].

[12] USA.gov, Federal Executive Branch, <www.usa.gov/Agencies/Federal/Executive.shtml>. Louisiana State University Libraries, Federal Agency Directory, <http://www.lib.lsu.edu/gov/index.html>; 2011 [accessed July 5, 2011].

[13] USC 28, Part III, Chapter 43, § 631, <www.law.cornell.edu/uscode/28/631.html>; 2012 [accessed September 15, 2012].

[14] Federal Magistrate Judges Association, <www.fedjudge.org>; 2012 [accessed September 15, 2012].

[15] Ibid.

[16] Federal Judicial Center, history of the federal judiciary: the U.S. Circuit Courts and the Federal Judiciary, <www.fjc.gov/history/home.nsf/page/courts_circuit.html>; 2012 [accessed September 15, 2012].

[17] United States Courts, Caseload Statistics 2011, <www.uscourts.gov/Statistics/FederalJudicialCaseloadStatistics/FederalJudicialCaseloadStatistics2011.aspx>.

[18] Federal Judicial Center, history of the federal judiciary: the U.S. Circuit Courts and the Federal Judiciary, <www.fjc.gov/history/home.nsf/page/courts_circuit.html>; 2012 [accessed September 15, 2012].

[19] United States Courts, Caseload Statistics 2011, <www.uscourts.gov/Statistics/FederalJudicialCaseloadStatistics/FederalJudicialCaseloadStatistics2011.aspx>.

[20] Federal Judicial Center, history of the federal judiciary: the Supreme Court of the United States and the Federal Judiciary, <www.fjc.gov/history/home.nsf/page/courts_supreme.html>;. 2012 [accessed September 15, 2012].

[21] Ibid.

[22] *Harris v. Nelson*, 94 U.S. (1969);286:290−1.

[23] Kirshbaum J. Supreme court cases—current term, Habeas Corpus Blog. <habeascorpusblog.typepad.com/habeas_corpus_blog/pending-supreme-court-cases.html>; 2012 [accessed September, 15, 2012].

[24] Frase RS. State sentencing guidelines: diversity, consensus, and unresolved policy issues. Columbia Law Rev 2005;105(4):1190−232.

[25] Vail J. State courts do the work federal courts can't—and shouldn't. Trial 2004;40 (1):68−71. U.S. advisory commission on intergovernmental relations. Guide to the criminal justice system for general government elected officials. Washington, D.C.: U.S. Advisory Commission on Intergovernmental Relations; 1993.

[26] Langton L, Cohen TH. State court organization, 1987−2004. Washington, DC: U.S. Department of Justice Office of Justice Programs Bureau of Justice Statistics; 2007: Online at <bjs.ojp.usdoj.gov/content/pub/pdf/sco8704.pdf>.

[27] LaFountain RC, et al. Examining the work of state courts: an analysis of 2009 state court caseloads. Arlington, VA: National Center for State Courts; 2011, 5: Online at <www.courtstatistics.org/FlashMicrosites/CSP/images/CSP2009.pdf>.

[28] Langton, Cohen. State court organization, 1987−2004. LaFountain, et al. Examining the work of state courts: an analysis of 2009 state court caseloads, 20.

[29] Langton, Cohen, State court organization, 1987−2004.

[30] 18 USC § 2265 (Title18 of the U.S. Code covers Crimes and Criminal Procedures. Section 2265 of 18 USC mandates Full Faith and Credit to Protective Orders).

[31] LaFountain, et al. Examining the work of state courts: an analysis of 2009 state court caseloads.

[32] U.S. Advisory Commission on Intergovernmental Relations. Guide to the criminal justice system for general government elected officials, 24.

[33] Rottman, David B. and William E. Hewitt. 1996. Trial Court Structure and Performance: A Contemporary Reappraisal. National Center for State Courts. #R-183. Berkson L. 1980. "Why Probate Judges Fear Unified Courts - Most of Them Claim They Won't Work - But Others Say They Are Wrong." Judges' Journal (published by the National Institute of Justice). Volume 19 Issue 2 P.16−21. Lawson HO. State court system unification. Am Univ Law Rev 1982;31:273−89.

[34] Renee Cobb. Justice and public safety reference manual: a practical guide to justice and public safety agencies and their information systems. Arlington, VA: Cobb JPS Consulting; 2006.

[35] Langton, Cohen. State court organization, 1987−2004. Rosenbaum J, Berkson L, Carbon S. Implementing court unification—a map for reform. Duquesne Law Rev 1979;17:419−71.

[36] Berkson, Why probate judges fear unified courts.

[37] Glaberson W In tiny courts of New York, abuses of law and power The New York Times September 26, 2006, (A1).

[38] Ibid.

[39] Ibid.

[40] Ibid.

[41] Freiberg A, O'Malley P. State intervention and the civil offense. Law Soc Rev 1984;18 (3):373−94.

[42] Lahey MA, Christenson BA, Rossi RJ. Analysis of trial court unification in California final report. American Institutes for Research <www.courts.ca.gov/documents/928rept.pdf>. Rottman D, et al. State court organization, 1998. Washington, DC: U.S. Department of Justice Office of Justice Programs Bureau of Justice Statistics; 2000: Online at <bjs.ojp. usdoj.gov/content/pub/pdf/sco98.pdf>. Rottman D. Does effective therapeutic jurisprudence require specialized courts (and do specialized courts imply specialist judges)? Court Rev 2000; Spring:22−7. Rottman, David B. and William E. Hewitt. 1996. Trial Court Structure and Performance: A Contemporary Reappraisal. National Center for State Courts. #R-183.

[43] Freiberg, O'Malley. State intervention and the civil offense.

[44] Hirschi T. Causes of delinquency. Berkeley, CA: University of California Press; 1969, Coleman JS. Social capital in the creation of human capital. AJS Suppl: Organ Inst: Sociol Econc Approaches Anal Soc Struct 1988;94:S95−120. Matza D. Delinquency and drift. New York, NY: John Wiley & Sons; 1964.

[45] Freiberg, O'Malley. State intervention and the civil offense.

[46] Minnesota Judicial Branch, Truancy courts, <www.mncourts.gov/?page=1718>. For an example of letter sent to parents threatening formal court proceedings if they do not participate, see model truancy prevention programs at American Bar Association, <www.american-bar.org>.

[47] Goffman E. Asylums: essays on the social situation of mental patients and other inmates. Garden City, NY: Anchor Books; 1961.

[48] Konanova Y, Truancy courts violate the law, threaten parents and children, American Civil Liberties Union, 2010, <www.aclu.org/blog/racial-justice/truancy-courts-violate-law-threaten-parents-and-children>.

George Washington's annotated copy of the Constitution and Bill of Rights.

CHAPTER 4

Criminal Law, Crime, and the Criminal Court Process

KEY TERMS

actus reus

administrative laws

arraignment

bench trial

bill of indictment

burden of production

burden of proof

charge

civil law

common law

complaint

concurrence

constitutional law

corpus delicti

crime

criminal law

discovery

deposition

felony

grand jury

indictment

information

initial appearance

law

misdemeanor

mens rea

motions

nolle prosequi

procedural due process

public law

statutory law

substantive due
  process

Learning Objectives

After reading this chapter, you should be able to:

1. Define law.
2. Define constitutional, statutory, administrative, and common law and identify the source of each.
3. Explain the difference between substantive criminal law and procedural law.
4. Define crime and explain how it serves as the boundary of the criminal justice system.
5. Explain what is meant by "the elements of a crime" and define *actus reus, corpus delicti, mens rea*, and concurrence.
6. List and define the types of criminal offenses.
7. Explain the difference between a misdemeanor and a felony.
8. Explain how legal reasoning relates to the court process.

111

9. List and explain the felony pretrial stages.
10. Explain how legal principles, due process, and crime control inform the structure of the criminal court process.

Principles, law, and procedures reign supreme in the U.S. courts: checks-and-balances, due process, reasonable doubt, precedent, jurisdiction, pretrial stages, and so on. The procedures run the length of the system, from rules on writing laws to rules on executing people. In all of this, the criminal courts supposedly have the noble goals of finding truth and delivering justice. That is one of the main reasons that nations around the world have created massive systems of formal social control.

In reality, though, truth is muddled by weak and uncertain evidence, procedural requirements, and the competing goals of the prosecution and defense. The courts themselves have competing goals of exerting the state's power and constraining that power. To balance this tension between different notions of justice—finding and punishing offenders and protecting people from arbitrary and excessive government power—the courts have found a third path, treating justice as a process. Justice is the idea of being subject to properly enacted laws. Justice is receiving a fair trial, in which the proceedings are public, the accused can present a defense, and the stages and rules are predictable and transparent. Justice is having procedural laws that curtail unlawful police and prosecutorial power. Justice is having a right to appeal.

None of this guarantees truth. None of it will make everyone happy or satisfy everyone's sense of justice, but the assumption is that at least the process was fair. This chapter will summarize the types of law, giving special attention to criminal statutes, and explain the steps a prosecutor must take simply to apply the elements of a crime to a suspect. The chapter will then introduce the court process, providing an overview of the pretrial stages and the main aspects of the criminal trial. This will give you a better sense of how process is valued in the legal reality of the United States.

LAW AS THE FOUNDATION OF STATE POWER AND INDIVIDUAL RIGHTS

The United States, like most nations today, is a constitutional government. This means its powers are described in a constitution, not created by whatever king, religious leader, or dictator happens to be in power. As District Judge Anna Diggs Taylor stated, "There are no hereditary Kings in America and no powers not created by the Constitution. So all 'inherent powers' must derive from that Constitution" [1]. In these types of political systems, the government has the power to write laws to achieve its goals as long as the laws do not violate the constitution or basic rights.

Law is the cornerstone of the U.S. justice system: it is not only the engine of formal social control but also the harness on government power. The legislation of law specifies what people in the United States are prohibited from doing, when the police may arrest someone, and when the courts may punish someone [2]. Yet the adjudication of law specifies the procedures those police officers and all other agents of the state must follow when creating and enforcing the law. This constitutional principle of government restraint applies to all three branches of the government, not just the courts [3].

Definition of Law

What exactly is "law?" This short and commonly used word has caused much debate and controversy over the centuries, and it has hundreds of definitions. Some focus on the process of lawmaking, the principles underlying lawmaking, the intent of lawmakers, the interpretation of judges, the effects of law, or a critique of law [4,5]. At a basic level, we refer to "codified" and "positive" law when we discuss law in the criminal justice system. "Codified" means written, and "positive" means created by humans. Laws that U.S. courts enforce are written by humans; they are explicit and can be read by any literate person [6]. This is different from unwritten customs or religious sentiment, which are sometimes referred to as "natural laws." For one of these written rules to be a law, it must be enacted by the sovereign state power. In other words, it must be written by the government. Because the creation and enforcement of laws is more complicated than informal social controls, Roscoe Pound, former Dean of the Harvard Law School, identified law as "a highly specialized form of social control" [7].

Given this foundation, we define **law** as codified rules of conduct that are established by the government, that the people within the jurisdiction must follow, and that agents of the government can enforce with the use or threat of punishment [8]. Three important realities stem from this definition of law.

- First, modern laws are impersonal. They are written and interpreted by professionals who follow clear procedures; they are uniform, predictable, and rational; they narrowly focus on regulating particular activities; and even though they are subject to change, they are, for the most part, stable on a day-to-day basis. None of this could be expected from rules of conduct established informally within a group [9].
- Second, no matter how fair and widely accepted a law may be, it is still backed by government power [10]. It is, in other words, a "command of the sovereign" [11]. This is why sociologist Max Weber, one of the first people to systematically study legal systems, called law "coercive" and a form of "domination" [12].

■   Third, the government employs workers to carry out this power. Weber refers to these as "staff(s) of people" given authority by the government to enforce compliance [13].

The law in most modern nations follows four principles of legality or, which are often referred to as the "rule of law."

■   First, the legislature must write clear laws and clearly specify punishments. Laws cannot punish behaviors that happened in the past; such laws would be called "*ex post facto*" laws [14]. The collective rules of writing legitimate laws are sometimes referred to as the "morality of law" [15].
■   Second, the courts must interpret the law in a way that respects the intention of the legislature and the constitution, but that favors the defendant's rights when the law or evidence is unclear.
■   Third, the government cannot punish someone unless a law exists proscribing, or prohibiting, that behavior. This is captured in the phrase, "no crime or punishment without law." In other words, you cannot be arrested and taken to court just for being bad or disliked. The government must already have enacted a law prohibiting whatever you did.
■   Fourth, no person is superior to the law [16]. This means that the law transcends all people. No matter how rich or powerful a person is, he or she must follow the law.

Types and Sources of Law

The United States is often described as a nation of laws. This generally means it is a constitutional government that abides by the principles of legality. But it can also refer to the fact that the United States has tens of millions of laws that touch nearly every aspect of social life. There are laws that regulate procreation (statutory rape and marriage laws) and birth (certifications for midwives and hospitals); death (mortuary regulations); and nearly everything between (consumer products, education, work, drug use, and, of course, crime). Figure 4.1 displays the main categories of law and the respective branch of government that enacts them.

Constitutional Law

The foundation of U.S. law is **constitutional law**, or obligations and powers specified in the government's charter. According to its own Article IV, the Constitution, which was written by federal lawmakers and ratified by the state legislatures, is the "supreme Law of the Land." "Judges in every State shall be bound thereby" and no other laws can contradict the Constitution. If any law is ruled by the courts to contradict the Constitution, that law is unconstitutional and therefore unenforceable. The Constitution is actually rather short—it is 7,818 words, including the 27 Amendments. To put this in perspective, the

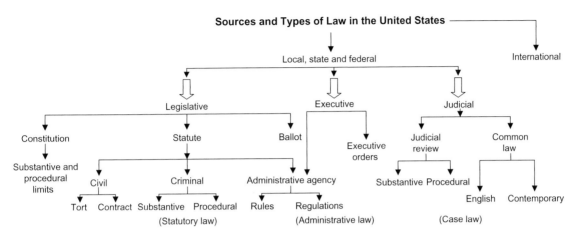

FIGURE 4.1
Sources and types of law in the United States.

USA Patriot Act, which was passed by Congress after the terrorist attacks on the World Trade Center and Pentagon on September 11, 2001, is 57,896 words, and that's one law among millions.

Each state also has its own constitution which was written by the state legislature and ratified either by that body or by popular vote. Amendments are added in the same manner. These are the supreme laws within the states.

Statutory Law: Private and Public

Most of the laws that regulate our daily lives are **statutory laws** that are enacted by national and state legislatures and **administrative laws** written and enforced by executive branch agencies (such as the DEA and IRS) [17]. Some states also grant municipalities and counties limited lawmaking power. The United States has over a hundred lawmaking bodies and hundreds more regulatory and policy-setting entities (from school boards to the U.S. Postal Service).

Criminal laws are statutory public law, and the overwhelming majority are enacted at the state level [18]. **Civil law** defines and regulates obligations between private parties (individual and organizations), and disputes arising from these laws are heard in civil court. This includes business arrangements, property issues, contracts, torts, copyright, and so on. **Public law** defines and regulates the relationship that individuals and organizations have with the state [19]. **Criminal law**, which falls within this category, defines certain behaviors as harms against the community, rather than harms against the victim alone, and authorizes the government to prosecute offenders and punish them with fines, limits on behavior (such as community service hours), and/or incarceration. This is why they are also called "penal law." Criminal laws create the category of behavior known as crime. A behavior is a criminal offense only if it is identified as such in a criminal law. As irresponsible and immoral as some may consider such behavior, a 22-year-old getting drunk at home and sleeping through work the next day is not a crime, but drinking one beer while driving is. The difference is in how they are defined by law, not the morality of the acts.

Federal supremacy requires that if a state law conflicts with a federal law, the federal law shall prevail, and the state law must be changed, abolished, or overridden by federal enforcement [20]. State laws that prohibited black people, Hispanics, Asians, and American Indians from marrying white people were abolished by federal law, as were state laws that racially segregated schools. A recent debate over state rights and federal supremacy can be seen in the area of medical marijuana and marijuana legalization (see Focus on Discretion 4.1).

FOCUS ON DISCRETION 4.1

Should States Be Allowed to Legalize and Regulate Marijuana?

Although people have used marijuana for thousands of years, many nations have classified it as an illegal drug. The U.S. government continues to enforce federal laws prohibiting marijuana, even in states with some form of legalization. A House of Representatives committee report asserts that state legalization runs counter to the Supremacy Clause, which allows federal law to trump state law when they contradict.

Over the past two decades, there has been a growing movement to legalize marijuana, for medical as well as personal uses. The governors of Washington state and Rhode Island have asked the federal government to reclassify marijuana as a drug with accepted medical uses so states can regulate it without risking federal prosecution. Colorado and Washington, which had already legalized medical marijuana, has legalized possession of small amounts for personal use.

Currently, 20–30 million people in the United States use marijuana, and about half of Americans, depending on the poll, support its legalization. According to some researchers, the "war on drugs" appears to have accomplished little

more than high incarceration rates and has cost taxpayers $1 trillion in the last 40 years. It has also stimulated uncontrolled drug-gang violence in Afghanistan, Mexico, and other struggling nations. During Prohibition in the United States, the nation witnessed the creation of a violent criminal underworld that became wealthy and powerful by ensuring that anyone who wanted alcohol could buy it. By 1933, Prohibition was appealed.

Ethan Nadelman, the founder and executive director of the Drug Policy Alliance, and Doug Fine, author *Too High to Fail: Cannabis and the New Green Economic Revolution*, argue that states should be allowed to legalize marijuana. Yet some legal scholars, including the Supreme Court majority opinions in *United States v. Oakland Cannabis Buyers' Cooperative* and *Gonzales v. Raich*, argue that states cannot decriminalize it as long as the federal government criminalizes it.

Question

Should states be allowed to write their own marijuana laws, even if the federal law criminalizes marijuana? Or should the states abide by the federal statute and Supreme Court rulings?

Judicial Law

Civil law actually has a second definition: all laws written by a lawmaking branch of government, the legislature. This usage is to distinguish legislative law from judicial law. The United States has a hybrid lawmaking system, with civil law created by the legislative branch and common law created by the judicial branch. Common law has two sources. Some U.S. common law was adopted from the English common law system. This category of law was much more prominent during the nation's early years. More often today, common law refers to the rulings of state and federal judges, especially in appellate courts, that create precedent on how the law is to be understood and applied. For this reason, judicial law is also called "case law" and "precedential law." The advantage of allowing common law and precedent is that the legislative branch does not have to enact specific statutes that apply to every scenario. Courts will interpret and apply the law to new and peculiar situations. Focus on Discretion 4.2 illustrates how common law affects discretionary choices in the criminal justice system.

FOCUS ON DISCRETION 4.2

Creating and Applying Precedent

Statutory law does not specify every situation in which a police officer can or cannot search a vehicle without a warrant. Rather, the Supreme Court has established broad legal guidelines in a series of rulings, including the recent *Arizona v. Gant* (2009). In that case, the Court agreed with precedent that a police officer under some circumstances can search at least part of a car without a warrant, such as to secure evidence or weapons that may be in reach of an uncuffed suspect. However, the Court limited this warrantless search power by ruling that a police officer can search a car without a warrant only if he or she reasonably believes the car contains evidence related to the alleged offense that prompted the arrest.

Rodney Gant was arrested, handcuffed, and placed in the back seat of a police car for driving with a suspended license. Police searched Gant's car and found cocaine in the back seat. The court ruled that because Gant could not reach the back seat of his car while sitting cuffed in the police cruiser and because no evidence in the back seat of Gant's car could possibly relate to why he was arrested (they already had all the evidence they needed to arrest him for driving with a suspended license). The Court ruled:

> Police may search a vehicle incident to a recent occupant's arrest only if the arrestee is within reaching distance of the passenger compartment at the time of the search or it is reasonable to believe the vehicle contains evidence of the offense of arrest. When these justifications are absent, a search of an arrestee's vehicle will be unreasonable unless police obtain a warrant or show that another exception to the warrant requirement applies.

Police, in other words, cannot search a car merely for having pulled someone over for a traffic violation or for an arrest unrelated to the content of the car. Through legal reasoning, attorneys may transpose the principle of privacy in this ruling onto other vehicles without any new statutes having to be written. If, for instance, a police officer searches a motorcycle after an arrest for hiring a street prostitute and finds counterfeited money in the saddle bag, the defense may argue that the search was illegal because there was no reasonable expectation that evidence related to hiring a prostitute would be in the saddle bag. If successful, the counterfeit evidence would be suppressed.

Questions

How did the Supreme Court limit the warrantless search power of the police?

Create an example in which the principle of privacy in *Arizona v. Gant* is transposed onto other vehicles.

Law created in all three branches can vary significantly across jurisdictions and cover a wide array of issues. Of all these laws, two types are particularly central to U.S. courts: substantive criminal laws and procedural laws.

Substantive Criminal Laws: Criminal Justice System Powers and Boundaries

Substantive criminal laws define particular acts as crime and specify the punishment an offender will receive. These are the laws that tell everyone what they cannot do and what the state will do to someone caught doing it. In the United States, substantive criminal laws are public statutory law: congresses enact them, and they regulate our relationship with the government.

These are the laws talked about most often. They include a wide range of violent and property offenses, such as assault, murder, burglary, auto theft, and fraud. Clearly, these laws are intended to constrain the behavior of the public and give power to the state. Once something is prohibited by substantive law, the police and courts can enforce it. Conversely, however, substantive laws constrain the power of the state by drawing a boundary around the criminal justice system: police, prosecutors, and courts can round up and punish only people who violate a substantive criminal law, but not people who are simply rude, immoral, unethical, or mean. In order to "activate" the criminal justice system, a person or organization must pierce that boundary by committing, or being accused of committing, a crime.

Procedural Laws: Rules for Enforcing Rules

Even when a substantive law is being violated, police and courts do not have the freedom to enforce it in any way they see fit. On the contrary, the United States has rules about enforcing rules. These procedural laws tell criminal justice system practitioners what they can do, what they cannot do, and what they must do when they write substantive law, enforce substantive law, process a defendant, and execute a punishment. Due process of law—giving instructions and limits on the exertion of power—holds in check the abuse of power and is therefore essential in a fair court system. Formalized procedural laws allow the nation to constrain criminal justice conduct prior to a violation of rights and provide mechanisms for remedying violations that occur.

Created by constitutional law, statutory law, administrative rules, and case law, this elaborate system of laws harness and restrain lawmaking, police conduct, attorneys, witnesses, judges, correctional officers, and everyone else in the criminal justice system. In other words, these are the navigators of the court process. There are rules on the types of laws that can be written; how police can gather physical evidence and interrogate people; when attorneys must file paperwork and the types of witnesses they can call; and what judges must communicate to jurors and what evidence they must suppress.

If an agent of the state fails to follow established procedure, it may result in the suppression of evidence or the release of an arrested suspect before the completion of a trial or after an appeal.

Procedural laws, which reflect the ideal of due process, have two forms: procedural due process and substantive due process. **Procedural due process** means that government agents must adhere to lawful procedures when they are processing a case and trying to deprive someone of freedom and rights. In other words, they must follow the due process of law. This well-established constitutional law is evident in the Fifth and Sixth Amendments, which specify what police and courts must do and cannot do when processing a criminal case. **Substantive due process** refers to the constitutional principle that people have basic rights, such as privacy and freedom of speech, that the government cannot violate without clear justification. In other words, the substance of the law must not trample on fundamental rights, some of which are stated in the Constitution and some of which are considered fundamental rights implied by the Constitution or articulated elsewhere, such as the right to privacy or education [21]. This has been a more recent interpretation of the due-process clause, and although controversial because it expands the judiciary's review powers and weakens the legislatures' power to write laws, it is widely accepted. After all, following proper procedures while enforcing a cruel or unjust law cannot lead to any form of justice.

Judicial review entails applying both sides of due process. Procedural due process is a bit easier to understand. If police gather evidence without a warrant, that is a violation of a constitutionally mandated procedure and the evidence may be suppressed. However, what if a law states that same-sex people cannot engage in sexual intercourse in the privacy of their own home, and the police enter the home with a lawful warrant? Is the ensuing arrest and conviction lawful? If the courts enforced only procedural due process, then yes, it is lawful because the proper procedures were followed in writing the law and enforcing it, regardless of the law's content.

Because the courts ruled that people in the United States have a right to privacy in their home, the law itself violates a basic, or substantive, right, and therefore violates the due process of law, contradicts the Constitution, and is nonenforceable [22]. Similar issues have come before the Supreme Court for 200 years. Can a state force black people to go to a separate school if it follows proper procedure when enforcing the segregationist law? Can a state prohibit women from working in a factory or attending school? Can a state lawfully arrest someone for burning a U.S. flag? In each case, the appellate courts have eventually ruled that even if proper procedure was followed in enforcing the laws, each law was itself unconstitutional. As advocates of this power of judicial review have argued, the government cannot follow just procedure if the law being enforced is unjust. Whether at a trial or during an appellate courts review, adherence to procedural law depends on transparency. Careers in the Court describes the court reporter's role in that essential task.

CAREERS IN THE COURT

Court Reporters and Transparency

The court reporter, who is sometimes called the stenographer, produces a record of court proceedings that is essential to assure that procedural laws are followed. Court reporters transcribe verbatim, usually on a stenotype machine connected to a computer, witness testimonies in depositions and trials, opening and closing statements by attorneys, jury instructions by judges, and other legal utterances and events in the courtroom. These records are often required for legal correspondences, motions, and appeals and judicial reviews by a higher court.

This recording of the trial creates transparency and prevents secret trials. The transcripts are available to the public, including the media, and are how we learn about what happens in a courtroom without actually going to a hearing or trial. Depending on the local customs within a courtroom, court reporters often have other duties, such as assisting attorneys and judges search official records and explaining court procedures to people new to that particular court. They also often operate closed captioning for people with poor hearing and translations for people not fluent in English.

THE DEFINITION OF CRIME: LEGAL REALITY AND THE CRIMINAL JUSTICE SYSTEM BOUNDARY

Crime is an intentional act or omission committed without justification or defense which is in violation of criminal law and punishable by the state. This requires that, in most cases, a person must actually intentionally do something prohibited by criminal law. It also means that only the state can punish someone for breaking the criminal law, which is intended to make punishment more humane, transparent, and dispassionate than personal vengeance and to avoid feuds that could erupt out of vigilantism. Criminal law, and therefore criminal offenses, form the boundary around the criminal justice system. It is therefore important to understand clearly what is meant by the word "crime."

"Crime" is used in many nonlegal ways, such as saying, "It's a crime that gas companies raise prices in the summer." There are also misuses of the legal definition of crime, with many people defining it as violations of norms, natural law, or divine law. In precise legal terms, these do not correctly define crime. Sometimes what is legally defined as a crime overlaps with what many

PHOTO 4.1

For a prosecutor to succeed in convicting a defendant of a criminal offense, he or she must establish that particular elements of the crime exist. The elements of crime include an act, intent, and concurrence.

people consider a violation of norms or religious teachings. Most people think murder is morally wrong. Murder is also a crime. So it is true that ethics, morals, and norms often serve as the impetus behind the creation of law.

However, the line between unethical, offensive, and immoral behavior and crime is of extreme importance. Some people in the United States, for instance, probably consider it a violation of norms for a man to wear a dress or for people to eat bugs, but in neither case will a person be arrested. Coming from the other direction, fewer and fewer people consider smoking marijuana a violation of norms, but the federal government and most states still criminalize it and punish its manufacture, distribution, possession, and use. Some pacifists consider all killing, even in war, to be a sin, but soldiers who lawfully kill in war are not arrested and convicted for murder.

Norms and religious sentiment are often unspecific and are always debated. They are generally vague standards of conduct. We can debate for weeks, for instance, whether or not it is deviant for a man to wear a dress. In the United States, however, criminal offenses are a specific category of behaviors defined as such by codified statutes. They are explicit, not ambiguous. Only if a behavior is defined by law as a crime is it a crime. All other behaviors are noncriminal. Once the court establishes the facts, it declares a clear designation: this person committed a crime, or this person did not commit a crime. Is it fair that laws fail to address all of our moral inclinations, that what some think is immoral is legal and what others think is acceptable is criminalized? Perhaps not, but it is part of legal reality. Crime is a product of the legal system, and that is what becomes the behavioral domain of the criminal justice system. What is defined as crime can be regulated by the criminal justice system, and what is not, generally cannot be.

Elements of a Crime

The definition of crime actually contains significant legal principles that guide legal reasoning and decision-making. For a prosecutor to succeed in having someone convicted, he or she must establish that particular elements of the crime exist. These include the following:

- An act. An act prohibited by criminal statute actually occurred, and the accused did it.
- Intent. The accused intended to commit the act or cause the harm or at least should have known harm could arise.
- **Concurrence**. The intention to produce harm occurred at the same time as the criminal act and harm.

Most criminal statutes involve only these three elements. They define particular intended acts as a crime, regardless of the harm produced. For instance, burglary statutes often criminalize illegal entrance of a property (*actus reus*) with the intent of committing a felony (*mens rea*). Even if the offender flees before stealing anything, it is still a burglary because the person committed the act with the criminal intent, and the intent and act occurred at the same time (concurrence). These laws effectively assume that the act itself is harmful to society. The elements can be visualized as intent + act + concurrence = crime.

Some criminal statutes have the additional element that a particular harm must result from the act. For instance, for an aggravated battery to occur, the act usually must cause great bodily harm. If someone punches someone else, but it results only in a swollen lip, the offense most likely will be charged as a simple battery. Similarly, unless someone actually dies, a suspect will not be charged with murder or manslaughter. The elements for these types of "harm" crimes are intent + act + concurrence + causation and harm = crime of harm.

Consider the scenarios in the following example and see if you can figure out which have all the elements for a criminal charge. You go to a party and see someone you have always hated on the other side of the room talking to your friends and laughing. You have a gut feeling your nemesis is making fun of you and that everyone is laughing at you. So you decide to kill her. Consider each of these scenarios and ask yourself if all the elements of a crime are met.

> A: You tell some friends that you want to kill your nemesis but leave without approaching her.
> B: You tell two people that you want to kill your nemesis. You get a shotgun and bring it into the party, but you get nervous and lean it against the wall. It falls over, goes off, and kills someone other than your nemesis.
> C: You do not tell anyone that you want to kill your nemesis, but you go get a gun and shoot her dead in front of everyone.
> D: You tell three friends your desire to kill your nemesis. You get in your car to go get a gun, put on your seat belt, turn on the lights and windshield wipers, back out of the parking spot, and hit your nemesis who is bicycling on the sidewalk behind you with no lights or reflectors and wearing black pants and shirt. She falls, hits her head, and dies.

Have you committed a criminal offense in any of these situations? In each situation there are clearly some components, but others are not there or unclear. Let's start with the easiest.

- In Scenario A, you expressed your intention, but there was no act that produced harm, so it is unlikely the court would prosecute you for anything.
- In Scenario B, you probably will not be charged with intentional murder because even though your action harmed someone, that harm does not correspond with your intention. Nonetheless, you may be charged with negligent manslaughter, and because the crime involved a firearm, some states will add that as an extra charge. However, the state may decide it was an accident and charge you with nothing.
- In Scenario C, you killed someone. Had you clearly announced your intention, then you would probably be convicted of murder. However, because you did not, the state will have to argue that intention was implied in the action, and you will have to argue that you were trying to shoot a squirrel that got into the house.
- Scenario D is the most interesting. Your intention is clearly on record, and the harm was ultimately produced (a dead nemesis), but did your action (driving) correspond with your intent? No. You were driving sober and responsibly with the intention of leaving the party. It was a coincidence that your nemesis was behind you. You may be charged with murder, but conviction is unlikely because of a lack of correspondence. Most likely, this one gets chalked up as an accident.

Actus Reus, Corpus Delicti, *Harm, and Causation*

Actus reus (AK-tes RAY-es), or "reality of the act," refers to a voluntary act that causes legally prohibited harm. This is one of the main burden-of-proof hurdles for the prosecution. Because of its importance in U.S. jurisprudence, the act-harm requirement has two to four steps, depending on the type of statute.

The first step in establishing whether or not someone committed a prohibited act is to establish that a crime actually occurred. A person usually cannot be convicted for a confession of a crime if the prosecution does not present evidence that the crime actually occurred. This is the *corpus delicti* (KOR-pes di-LIK-tie) rule, which means "body of the crime" and refers to the evidence of the offense. It may sound simple and obvious, but it is actually important in the protection of individual rights. This prevents someone with a mental illness, for instance, from confessing to fabricated offenses, and prevents people from being coerced into a confession. If someone confesses to selling a hundred kilograms of cocaine or to murdering a prostitute, but no other evidence of the crime is presented to the court, then the *actus reus* has not been established, and the *corpus delicti* rule prohibits a conviction [23].

The second step of *actus reus* is to establish that the accused actually did something that contributed to the criminal act. This is a core principle in U.S. jurisprudence: there usually must be a physical act for something to be defined as a crime in criminal law and for someone to be punished by the criminal justice system. The government cannot punish people for (1) thoughts alone, such as mentally envisioning a crime, believing in a particular religion, harboring anti-government ideas, or having evil thoughts; (2) a supposed propensity to commit crime or for something they may do in the future; or (3) being in a particular state or category, such as being a drug addict. For instance, in *Robinson v. California* (1962), the Supreme Court ruled that the state cannot convict someone for the offense of being "addicted to the use of narcotics." The California court did not convict Lawrence Robinson for doing anything but for being something. The U.S. Supreme Court ruled that the lower court ruling violated constitutional law [24].

Establishing criminal activity sometimes also entails proving necessary attendant circumstances, or simply "attendant circumstances." For instance, to be convicted of the federal crime of transporting child pornography, a person must perform particular actions (transport, receive, or distribute the items across state or national borders) and possess the attendant circumstance of knowing that the media depicted minors engaged in sex.

There are, however, types of offenses that have expanded the boundaries of what is now considered an act within legal reality and therefore satisfies the *actus reus* requirement. These include conspiracy, possession, accessory, and obstruction. In each case, a person is charged not with carrying out an offense but of assisting in the preparation or execution of an offense. "Conspiracy" is when someone engages in a series of actions that build toward a crime, even if each of those individual actions (such as buying a gun and ski mask, renting a car, and observing a bank's opening and closing routine) are legal. "Possession" is merely being in control of illegal substances or stolen goods without the intent to distribute it. "Accessory" is assisting or facilitating the commission of a crime, such as being the lookout. "Obstruction" is interfering with a law-enforcement investigation. In each case, the person does not commit the act at the center of the statute, such as murder or robbery, but is nonetheless charged with one of the other offenses above. See Court Procedures for another expansion of *actus reus*.

COURT PROCEDURES

Is Doing Nothing a Crime?

In general, common law and U.S. courts abide by the "no duty to act" rule: a person has no legal obligation to prevent harm. Some exceptions include the requirement to aid your own child or spouse, to aid those under your care at work (such as at a nursing home or hospital), to aid those who are harmed by your actions (such as someone who falls from ladder you left leaning against your house), and to aid those whom you witness being victimized in a criminal offense. This last category is known as the Good Samaritan criminal laws. They require you to render aid in some situations (such as calling the police when you witness a rape) or risk criminal conviction if you do not.

These "positive duty" or "duty to assist" laws were prompted by several cases, including the 1964 Kitty Genovese case in which Genovese was murdered outside a New York City apartment building by Winston Moseley, who followed her home one night from work. The case was controversial because although many residents lived in the building, Moseley was able to complete the murder and get away. Initial reports stated that "38 people" witnessed the murder and did almost nothing to help. Although the situation was actually more complicated—no one saw the struggle in its entirety; one neighbor went to Genovese's side as she was dying; and some neighbors called the police—the resulting controversy about what was perceived to be the uncaring nature of modern life began a national discussion about the "duty to assist" [25]. Later influential cases include the 1984 New Bedford, MA, incident in which patrons of Big Dan's Bar did nothing to intervene as Cheryl Ann Araujo was raped by at least four men; and the 1997 Primm, Nevada, case in which David Cash, Jr., watched his friend Jeremy Strohmeyer rape and strangle 7-year-old Sherrice Iverson in a casino bathroom [26].

In all three cases, the people who witnessed the offenses and did nothing were not prosecuted because there was no criminal law requiring action. Although most states have laws protecting those who render assistance from liabilities for injuries occurring during the course of assistance, only four states—Minnesota, Rhode Island, Vermont, and Wisconsin— require bystanders to provide assistance [27].

Proponents argue that the social contract, the implicit agreement to follow society's rules in order to enjoy the security it offers, requires that we act to make the community a safer and better place. Opponents do not argue that we should not help others, but rather that requiring to do so by criminal law runs counter to the centuries-old legal principle of *actus reus* and may compel people to enter dangerous situations.

Question

Should a person be charged with a criminal offense for failing to help another person who is being victimized in a criminal offense? What types of actions, if any, should be required?

For "harm crimes," the third and fourth step of *actus reus* are that harm resulted from the action and the action directly caused the harm. Most offenses, like drunk driving, burglary, drug use, and threatening someone with violence, are considered harmful in themselves or harmful to the community and are therefore criminal offenses, even if no person or property is actually harmed. However, imagine, for instance, that a person cuts the brake lines of car, which is clearly an action, but the driver had a heart attack and died in the driveway before ever getting into the car, which is a harm. The court will probably not be able to establish that the action caused the harm. Something else, a heart attack, brought about the driver's death. Harm can also elevate an act from a comparatively simple crime to a serious one. For instance, drunk driving can result in fines and some jail time. If you kill someone while drunk driving, however, that could become vehicular manslaughter, and you may spend years in prison.

Does this mean that if you are driving down the road lawfully (an act), and you hit and kill a child who runs in front of your car (harm and causation), that you can be charged with murder? Probably not, because you did not intend to produce the harm, nor were you reckless or negligent. Let's take a look at this element of intent.

Mens Rea *and Levels of Intent*

Mens rea (menz RAY a), or "reality of the mind," is the intent of the accused to commit the offense and, for some laws, produce the resultant harm. It is the legal principle that allows most modern courts to distinguish accidents, such as hitting a child with a car while driving legally, from crime. The term is actually shorthand for criminal *mens rea*. Sometimes the term *scienter*, which means "knowingly," is used instead. To establish *mens rea* means to prove that the defendant intended to commit the offense or failed to take reasonable precautions.

Recall the previous scenario. You did not intend to harm anyone when you leaned the gun against the wall. What do the courts do with harms that are directly caused by someone's actions but were not intended? Sometimes these are just accidents, such as when you hit the child who ran in front of your car. Other incidents, such as killing someone while driving drunk, the law considers more than simple accidents and attaches culpability.

In most jurisdictions, criminal courts rely on four levels of intent which allow the court to assess a defendant's blameworthiness or culpability. In decreasing order of culpability, they are:

1. intentionally/purposely/willfully;
2. knowingly;
3. recklessly;
4. negligently/carelessly.

The distinction between each level is murky and part of the legal reality of a case that is determined in the courts. In other words, the lawyers will argue for higher (prosecution) or lower (defense) levels of intent, and the judge or jury will decide. A different courtroom may come to a different conclusion with the same case.

A person is said to intend a crime and the harm if he or she has the conscious objective of purposely committing the act or knows the harmful outcome is almost certain. The prosecution will often meet this level by establishing that the accused had motivation, necessary skills and resources, and opportunity [28]. This would likely be the level of intent when you announced your intention to shoot your rival.

However, the state has expanded intent to include harms that result from lesser actions, even if the person did not actually intend to produce the harm. When a person "acts with knowledge" or knowingly commits a crime, he or she does not consciously set out to produce the harm. Still, the person is either aware that the actions could result in the harm or deliberately ignores important facts. Playing with a gun may fall into this line of reasoning because a reasonable person should know such behavior can likely injure or kill someone. Recklessness and negligence both involve gross disregard for reasonable care. In reckless cases, the defendant is accused of being aware of the "substantial and unjustifiable" risk but choosing to disregard it. Negligence is a step down the culpability ladder. The defendant is not accused of ignoring risk but of not seeing risks that a reasonable person would have seen and therefore not taking reasonable precautions [29]. Leaning a loaded gun against the wall at a party and without putting on the safety switch would possibly fall into one of these last two levels.

As muddled as the line is between each level of intent—and people often disagree with a court's determination of intent—they have a profound effect on a case. The difference between being convicted of intentional homicide and negligent homicide could be the difference between a death sentence and a couple of years in prison.

Mens rea generally has to be proved by the state, but it is often difficult to establish. For that reason, states have begun to eliminate the *mens rea* element from some statutes. Strict liability laws require only *actus reus*. This means that the prosecution only has to prove that the defendant did the illegal action, but not that he or she did it knowingly or with intent. Offenses that are commonly drafted as strict liability include sex with a minor, selling alcohol to a minor, and traffic offenses. However, state legislatures are trying to expand strict liability statutes because they shift more power to the government.

A Florida drug statute, for instance, has eliminated the element that the defendant "knowingly" possessed or distributed an illegal substance. As a result, defendants have been convicted for possessing drugs when someone else put the drugs in the defendant's backpack or purse or hid them in the defendant's car. A federal judge ruled in 2011 that the removal of intent is "repugnant" to U.S. common law and the rule of law, and she struck down the law, but a year later the Florida Supreme Court ruled that the law is constitutional. Currently, the case is headed to the federal Circuit Court of Appeals, where legal reality in this matter will be more clearly established [30]. Nonetheless, nearly all criminal statutes still specify both *actus reus* and *mens rea* components, as well as concurrence.

Concurrence

The final element of a criminal offense is concurrence. The action and intention must occur at the same time. Let's return to the last scenario at the party in which you run over your nemesis with your car. Even though real harm was done, the act did not correspond, or concur, with the actual intent of shooting the person. This would probably not be charged as murder.

Types of Criminal Offenses and Offenders

U.S. criminal courts handle a wide variety of offenses and offenders, but there are definite biases within the process. Crimes are generally placed in one or more of the following categories. Crimes against property involve damaging or stealing someone else's possessions, such as burglary and theft. Crimes against the body refer to violent crimes against a person, such as rape, murder, or unsafe working conditions. Victimless, or consensual, crimes are a bit unusual because everyone involved agrees to be involved, so there is no clear harm or victim. These are generally considered moral or public-order crimes, and include things like the sale and purchase of drugs or sex. Street crimes include violent crimes like murder, property crimes like larceny, or consensual crimes like drug sales. White-collar and corporate crimes are committed by people or organizations in positions of power and run a wide gamut of actions that violate criminal and regulatory law. These can harm property or body, such as economic crimes (fraud, unsafe working conditions, or price fixing) and environmental crimes (illegal dumping or use of prohibited chemicals). Also, they can threaten the integrity of our government when they involve political crimes like bribery.

These offenses can fall under state or federal jurisdiction as a felony, misdemeanor, or delinquent act. **Felonies** are considered the more serious offenses and usually carry a possible sentence ranging from over a year incarceration in prison to execution. Many felony convictions do not lead to any incarceration but instead to probation or a diversionary program; nonetheless, the conviction is still for a felony. **Misdemeanors** occur at a much higher rate than felonies but are considered a lesser offense. Usually the maximum sentence in this category is 1 year incarceration in a county jail, but the majority of these convictions lead to a fine, community service, probation, and other forms of community corrections. If a minor violates a felony or misdemeanor law, it will usually be considered a delinquent act. If a minor violates a law that applies only to minors—like running away, truancy, and drinking alcohol—it is a status offense.

Criminal law focuses overwhelmingly on the individual. This can be seen with the definitions of crime, which focus on observable action, intent, and direct consequences. These elements are difficult to affix to organizations or to people involved in complex white-collar crimes. So before a police officer even walks onto the street, the criminal justice system is already prejudiced against individuals and in favor of organizations like corporations. There is also a class bias. Low-income people receive greater police scrutiny, conduct more activities outdoors (where they can be seen by police and witnesses), are more likely to commit a street crime (which generally has the most severe penalties) than white-collar crime, make bail less often, and more often have no attorney for misdemeanors and rely more on public defenders for felonies. As fair as a police department or court system strives to be, police suppression in the United States falls more heavily on the impoverished than on the wealthy, and prisons are built primarily to house the impoverished, not all people who harm society.

INTRODUCTION TO THE COURT PROCESS

Let's now turn our attention to how a suspect is processed through the criminal courts. This chapter will provide an overview of the entire system. Later chapters will cover each stage in greater detail and will explain how the process can vary at each stage.

As we have described, the criminal justice system has rather clear boundaries around it. It generally does not deal with noncriminal behaviors, is not

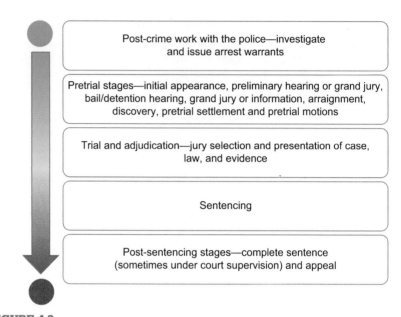

FIGURE 4.2
Five broad stages of the criminal court process.

involved in events or social conditions that exist prior to a crime occurring, and generally does not deal with people once they are released from court and correctional supervision. The system's limited role is to process criminal cases from detection of a crime to punishment. The five broad stages involved in processing misdemeanor and felony criminal cases are depicted in Figure 4.2.

Once a behavior is defined by law as a crime, its commission "punctures" the boundary of the criminal justice system and justifies police action. The police investigate the allegation, arrest suspects, book suspects, and file a **complaint**, or a sworn accusation of wrongdoing given to prosecutors office. After that, the court system takes over the case.

Legal Reasoning: Due Process and the Assessment of Cases

When attorneys receive complaints, they must analyze them in legal terms to decide how to proceed. Although morals, political ideology, and religious or non-religious affiliation do influence attorneys, they overwhelmingly adhere to legal reasoning. In short, when assessing a case they "think like a lawyer." They must sort through the facts to verify that harmful behavior occurred, called the "issue," and de-emphasize generally unlawful evidence, such as hearsay or intuition.

Next, they must identify the specific law (the "rule") the behavior violated. Occasionally a case is thrown out because the prosecutor identified the wrong criminal statute. Using linguistic analysis, they match the facts with the wording of the law. Especially in appeals, analysis will also involve reasoning by analogy, which means to find similar cases that were ruled on in the past. After presenting the facts and issue, the law, and the analysis, the attorney concludes the case, or argues how the court should rule [31]. This process, covered more in the next two chapters, is often called the IRAC (issue, rule, analysis, and conclusion) method.

Attorneys employ legal reasoning more to win cases than to pursue truth, but legal reasoning also constrains them through due process. Prosecution works to establish culpability if the evidence of the case warrants that. The defense works to challenge the state's case and show its weaknesses. Though truth is not the central pursuit, this orderly process of assessing cases helps attorneys resolve them within the adversarial system while also requiring that the government is justified in the application of punishment. Legal reasoning thus reflects the larger themes of the court system, including stable legal principles and due-process restraints on government power. It forces attorneys to adhere to the rule of law and elevates constitutional, case, and statutory law above the emotional pleas of victims or community members. Similarly, the principles of presumption of innocence and reasonable doubt force them to prioritize evidence over moral or religious reasoning. It is sometimes said that "evidence is king."

Misdemeanor Court Process

In terms of police work, there is not too much official difference between misdemeanor and felony cases. Police are supposed to enforce all criminal statutes. In practice, however, some police departments and divisions, such as rape or drug-enforcement divisions, give more or exclusive attention to felonies, and it is reasonable to assume that police direct more of their investigation energy toward felonies.

The court system, on the other hand, has a two-tiered system by design. If the defendant is charged with a misdemeanor, the case will be disposed of and sentenced in a court of limited jurisdiction, such as the Magistrate Court. The court process is generally a truncated version of the felony process described below. This often amounts to a police officer filing a complaint, a prosecutor taking the case, and a local judge, such as a county magistrate, ruling on it and sentencing the offender [32].

Often this is done the first time a defendant appears in front of a judge, which is called the **initial appearance**. The defendant pleads guilty, is sentenced, and gets a criminal record: no bail hearing, no witnesses, and no opportunity to appeal. The Supreme Court's *Gideon v. Wainwright* (1963) and *Argersinger v. Hamlin* (1972) rulings do not require that states provide public defense for most people charged with misdemeanors, so defendants must provide their own [33]. Because the overwhelming majority of suspects brought into the criminal justice system are impoverished, few misdemeanor hearings have a defense attorney present to counter the prosecution. For those that do not plead guilty at that initial stage, bail is often set at the same hearing.

As you read about the more elaborate felony process, keep in mind that several of these stages are not available for misdemeanor cases. In addition to lacking a defense attorney in most cases and little police investigation, which could find exculpatory evidence, misdemeanor cases have no preliminary hearing, grand jury, or arraignment, and have no right to a jury trial unless the statute authorizes more than six months of incarceration [34].

Felony Pretrial Stages

Courtrooms vary considerably in how they process felony cases, but the main stages tend to be:

1. Initial appearance
2. Preliminary hearing or grand jury presentation
3. Bail/detention hearing
4. Grand jury or Information
5. Arraignment
6. Discovery
7. Pretrial settlement and pretrial motions

Several issues concerning the diversity of pretrial stages are important to keep in mind. Although these are the pretrial stages for felony cases, they are often heard in the courts of limited jurisdiction, the same ones that hear misdemeanor cases. These courts do not have jurisdiction over felony trials, but they may hold hearings leading up to the guilty plea or trial. As described below, if the person is indicted, the case will be transferred, or bound over, to felony court. Second, not every stage is covered in every case. Some courts combine two or more stages, like the preliminary hearing and bail, into one hearing, and some courts have additional stages, such as a witness conference prior to trials. Also, most cases filed with a felony prosecutor do not even make it to the end of the pretrial stages. Most are dismissed, plead out, or diverted before getting to trial. Nearly 60 percent are released conditionally or unconditionally prior to adjudication [35]. Therefore, each hearing along the pretrial path handles progressively fewer cases.

The prosecutor is the primary impetus in moving a case along these pretrial stages. He or she decides whether or not to charge and what to charge, or whether to dismiss. Only if he or she makes the initial decision to pursue charges and a conviction are a judge and defense attorney brought into the case. If the prosecutor dismisses the complaint, the judge and defense attorney will likely never hear about it. Nonetheless, the prosecutor does not have unfettered power. They are tethered to the rule of law by having to move a case through many stages before ever getting to trial. Each stage should serve as a filter before trial. That is, each stage filters out weak cases and reduces government abuse of power by testing the quality of the case and the legality of the process.

In some courts, the prosecutor may dismiss a case even before the initial appearance (which is sometimes called a first appearance). In others, this is the first time a prosecutor sees a case. In fact, in some jurisdictions, the police, not the prosecutor, handle the initial appearance even if the prosecutor reviews it. Regardless of the method used, this is the defendant's first hearing after arrest, and it is often held the same day the defendant is arrested. Pretrial hearings may be brief, but much happens in them.

- The charges are explained to the defendant.
- The defendant is told her or his rights.
- The defendant is permitted to obtain an attorney or is assigned a public defender.
- The judge (or magistrate if held in a lower court) decides if probable cause exists to detain the defendant.
- The judge may dismiss the case if it lacks adequate evidence.
- The prosecutor may drop the charges, which is called *nolle prosequi* (NOL ee PROS-i-kwie).
- The case may be diverted out of the standard court system and into a specialized court or pretrial intervention, in which a prosecutor suspends prosecution of a case pending the fulfillment of special conditions by the defendant, such as community service or drug rehabilitation.
- Sometimes bail is set if the court decides the defendant can be safely released.
- A date is set for the preliminary hearing.
- Although defendants usually cannot plead guilty hear because the limited-jurisdiction court does not have jurisdiction, the lawyers can start to lay the foundation for negotiation.

Bail and detention hearings are moved around in the court system. Bail, which refers to both the pretrial release and the process of deciding the conditions of pretrial release, is often compressed into other hearings. Sometimes there will be a bail hearing to determine the bond amount, or the money the defendant has to leave with the court as a security that he or she will return for the next stage. If, however, the prosecution is requesting that the defendant be denied bail and kept in custody until the trial, then there will be a separate detention hearing. In order to deny someone the Eighth Amendment right to bail, the prosecution must convince the judge that preventive detention, or keeping the defendant incarcerated even though he or she is still legally innocent, is necessary to keep the public safe, protect evidence, or assure that the defendant does not flee [36]. Combining those who cannot come up with the bond (generally low-income defendants) and those under preventive detention, the majority of violent felon suspects are detained from arrest to dismissal or conviction.

The preliminary hearing starts to bring the case into focus. The prosecutor has had time to look over the case and write revised charges against the defendant. A **charge** specifies the alleged criminal offense and the *corpus delicti* of the crime, the elements of the offense that match the criminal statute, the person(s) alleged to have committed it, her or his intention, and the date, time, and location of the offense. Both defense and prosecution are present, and the hearing is open to the public. Evidence is presented, and sometimes witnesses are subpoenaed to testify, but if so, it is usually just a police officer. The prosecutor does not have to establish guilt, but he or she does have the burden to establish probable cause that the defendant has committed the offense charged.

The preliminary hearing involves either moving a case to a grand jury or testing an information. If a grand jury is to be used, the judge decides at the preliminary hearing if the evidence is adequate for the case to move forward to the grand jury hearing. If no grand jury is to be used, the prosecutor drafts the formal accusation in what is called an **information**, that is, a criminal charge brought by the prosecutor without a grand jury indictment. The information is submitted to the court in a process known as "testing the information," which involves evaluating the charges in terms of their legal merits. If the judge finds that the information provides enough evidence, the case is bound over to the felony court for arraignment. Whether headed for the grand jury or testing of the information, if the judge finds the evidence weak, he or she should dismiss the case. Also, the prosecution can request a *nolle prosequi* at this stage if he or she decides not to pursue the case. If the prosecution reduces the charges to a misdemeanor, the defendant can plead guilty, and the judge can issue a sentence.

If an information is not used, the case goes before a **grand jury**, in what is called the "grand jury presentment." This is a panel of citizens who are convened to review the prosecutor's **bill of indictment**, which is similar to the information in that it specifies the charges against the defendant. Witnesses and evidence may be presented, but the defense and public are excluded, and in some states, the grand jury can conduct its own investigation and subpoena its own witnesses.

In some cases, testimony given at this stage can be presented in trial. If the grand jury agrees that there is probable cause to justify carrying forward the prosecution, it endorses the prosecutor by issuing a true bill of indictment, which is sometimes called a "true bill" but most often called an **indictment**. They are effectively stating that they think the defendant probably committed the crime. The judge then sends the case to the felony court for arraignment. If the grand jury finds the case weak, it "returns a no true bill" and effectively stops the case. In this instance, there is no indictment and no prosecution. The case is dismissed, and the accused is usually released if detained.

The case is then bound over to **arraignment**, the hearing designed to inform defendants of the formal charges against them and allow them to enter their first plea. (In misdemeanor cases in which the defendant does not plead guilty, there is no grand jury or preliminary hearing, and the case generally goes straight from the initial appearance to the arraignment, where the prosecution presents the information.) This stage shares some elements with the initial appearance but is more formal. The judge informs the defendant of the formal charges in the information or indictment and reviews her or his rights. The defendant pleads guilty or not guilty. A guilty plea may be the result of negotiation in which the prosecution offers to lower the charges or divert the case and defer prosecution. If he or she pleads guilty, the case goes directly to sentencing. If the defendant pleads not guilty, bail and detention may be reviewed; the prosecution may request a *nolle prosequi* and dismiss the case; the prosecution may reduce the charge to a misdemeanor and send the case back to the lower court; and/or a trial date will be set.

After arraignment, lawyers will continue the discovery and pretrial motions, may engage in a pretrial settlement conference, and will conduct a jury selection if the case is headed for a jury trial. **Discovery** (the process accessing the opposing party's documents, **depositions** (sworn statements), testimonies, evidence, evaluation of the mental and physical health of people in the case, and interrogatories (answers to written questions about the evidence) that relate to the case), was likely started prior to arraignment but will go into full swing now that a trial date is set.

Discovery is more important for the defense than the prosecution because the prosecution almost always has more resources and the cooperation of police and therefore unequal opportunity to build a sound case. For everyone preparing for a trial, this process reduces "surprises" at trial, so the outcome is more a matter of facts than the tactical strategies of attorneys. **Motions** also may have begun prior to arraignment but pick up after it. These are requests for the judge to rule on aspects of the case, such as requests to suppress evidence, compel discovery, delay the start of the trial (continuance), or change the location (venue) of the trial.

Just before trial, final negotiations and jury selection occur. Some courts hold pretrial settlement conferences with the attorneys, judge, and defendant to try to negotiate a plea prior to the more expensive and accountable public trial. These meetings operate under the unofficial presumption of guilt and are designed to compel defendants to plead guilty. Jury selection is the process of the attorneys, and sometimes the judge, questioning a panel of prospective jurors and choosing a trial jury from that panel. Now all the pieces are in place for a trial: explicit charges against the defendant, evidence gathered and shared, pretrial issues settled, a jury selected, and a defendant who refuses to plead guilty.

Trial Procedure

Trials, unlike the pretrial stages, follow a more standardized script. U.S. courts follow the procedure inherited from England's common law system. The prosecution and defense have an adversarial relationship, and the judge acts as a neutral party who should assure that the proceedings are fair. The typical trial process follows these steps in order.

1. Indictment or information read
2. Defendant enters a plea
3. Jury instructions (if a jury used)
4. Prosecution opening
5. Defense opening
6. Prosecution presents the state's case—witness and evidence presented, and witnesses and experts questioned by prosecution, crossed by defense, impeached by defense (where credibility is challenged), redirected by prosecution, and recrossed by defense
7. Defense presents counter argument (optional)—same process for evidence and witnesses
8. Defense closing
9. Prosecution closing
10. Judge instructs jurors about procedures and verdicts
11. Final verdict
12. Defendant acquitted (found not guilty) and released or convicted (found guilty) and sentenced

Each of these trial stages are detailed in Chapters 8 through 10, but pointing out a few important issues—the prosecution's burdens, defense obligations and strategies, and the roles of the judge and jury—will help you understand both the structural design of the system and decision-making that go into processing a case. The state or federal prosecutor does have the advantage of more resources, police cooperation, and the goodwill of the judges, but they also have the obligation to overcome the presumption of innocence and prove the defendant's guilt. There are two parts to this obligation. First, the prosecution has the **burden of production**, that is the task of producing the *corpus delicti* to establish that an act occurred that violated a criminal statute. Second, the prosecution has to prove guilt beyond all reasonable doubt. This is called the **burden of proof**, which refers to the prosecutor's task of convincing a finder of fact that of all the elements of the crime. The prosecution has these burdens because, as an agent of the state, he or she is trying to deprive people of liberties and must do so cautiously and with restraint.

The defense will challenge charges levied by the prosecution as well as the government's power to deprive the defendant of liberty. Two main strategies are a "negating defense" and an "affirmative defense." Negating defenses try to establish a mistake of fact, that is, that the prosecution has failed to prove some element of the crime. This defense generally aims to undermine the prosecution's evidence, witnesses, and experts by pointing out weaknesses within the evidence, such as a witness with bad eyesight or vindictiveness toward the defendant, shoddy fingerprints, experts with little formal scientific training, a lack of evidence to establish *mens rea*, and so on. In affirmative defenses, the defense must persuade the court to accept an alternative explanation of what happened. The defense must therefore present evidence that reduces, excuses, or voids the defendant's culpability, such as establishing an alibi or self-defense. But the defense can also use a procedural defense, arguing that the state violated procedural law, such as laws requiring a speedy trial.

Standing outside this adversarial presentation and refutation of evidence is the judge and jury. A **bench trial** occurs when the judge decides the case, and there is no jury. In this case, the judge issues the guilty or not-guilty ruling. When a jury is present, it is the "finder of fact," which means that it decides if the defendant committed the offense as charged. A typical trial jury is called a "petit jury" to distinguish it from a grand jury. Whether the trial is a jury trial or bench trial, the judge is the trier of law. He or she monitors the procedures, rules on motions and objections by attorneys, gives jury instructions, and maintains proper behavior in the courtroom. See Courts in the Media for a look at media portrayal of problems that have occurred in the court process.

COURTS IN THE MEDIA

Injustice in the Criminal Courts

Nearly all criminal cases are open to the public. It is a great idea to look up a court's docket and go watch a few hearings and trials to see the court system up close, but there are also great descriptions of the trial process in nonfiction books and film.

- John Grisham's nonfiction book, *The Innocent Man: Murder and Injustice in a Small Town* describes several wrongful convictions in an Oklahoma court. In 1982, a cocktail waitress named Debra Sue Carter, 21, was raped and murdered in Ada, OK. For 5 years, the police could not solve the crime, but suspected two men,

Ron Williamson and his friend Dennis Fritz. Police arrested the men in 1987 and charged them with capital murder. Having no physical evidence, the prosecution built its case on the testimony of jail and prison inmates, junk science, and contrived dream confessions. A jury found both men guilty. Fritz was sentenced to life in prison, and Williamson was sent to death row.

- *After Innocence* is a documentary about erroneous convictions, the exonerations based on DNA and the work of the Innocence Project, and the struggles of those released from prison to reintegrate into society. The film focuses on seven men who were wrongly convicted and served time in prison and on death row, and their efforts to rebuild their lives.

- *Murder on a Sunday Morning* documents the case of Brenton Butler, a 15-year-old black teenager who was wrongly accused of a murder in Jacksonville, FL, in 2000. The prosecution had no physical evidence linking Butler to the shooting, and the case relied on an identification made by the victim's husband and on Butler's coerced confession, which he made without a lawyer present.

Question

Discuss a book or film that you think portrays the court process particularly well.

Appeal

If before or during the trial, one of the parties objects to an error of law that will likely alter the outcome of the case, such as the judge suppressing evidence that the prosecutor believes should not be suppressed, then they can appeal at that time. Also, people who have been convicted and incarcerated can submit a *habeas corpus* appeal that argues that their incarceration is illegal. Both of these are relatively rare. Most appeals in the criminal process come from defendants who lost at trial and are appealing an issue of law. They do not appeal the whole case, or even the verdict. Rather, they appeal a particular part of the trial that they argue violated due process and substantially altered the outcome of the case. For instance, if the defense argued that the confession was coerced by brutal police tactics, but the judge chose not to suppress the confession as evidence, the defense can appeal if the defendant is convicted at the end of the trial. Appeals are discussed in detail in Chapter 11. Figure 4.3 illustrates the court process.

DISCUSSION OF THE CRIMINAL COURT PROCESS

Viewing the criminal trial process through the three themes introduced in Chapter 1 brings courts into sharper focus. The steady legal principles, the crime-control mandate, and the due process restraints together help to make sense of the structure of the court process. The state hires the prosecutor to exert its crime-control powers and establish a case that justifies the

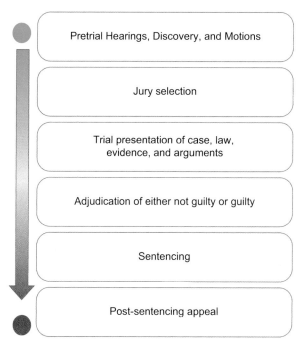

FIGURE 4.3
A review of the court process.

punishment of people accused of crime. The judge has the task of issuing sentences for the same reason. If the nation pays these people to control crime, why have all these extra stages that are just obstacles to getting to trial and a conviction? Because they are designed to be obstacles. They are in place to assure allegiance to the legal principles of legality and presumption of innocence, and, above all, due process. The court process is, in short, oriented toward process more than quick punishment.

You may have noticed also that the victim plays only minor role in the court process. This aggravates many people, but again, it makes sense given the legal reality of U.S. courts. The courts are designed in part to deprive people of liberty. The core of due process is the protection of individual liberties against government power. It is the offender, not the victim, who is at risk of losing liberties to the government. For this reason, the offender and state are moved to the center stage, and victims are deprioritized. No well-established stage involves helping the victim or even including the victim. Victims are, in terms of the court process, just another witness or piece of evidence. You will read in later chapters about the victims' rights movement, but unless the very foundation of U.S. jurisprudence is changed, the main focus will remain on the defendant and state.

In the next two chapters we develop the third theme—that multiple factors affect the decision-making of the lawyers and judges—and situate those explanations of legal action into the court process. Why, for instance, does a prosecutor pursue some cases but dismiss others? The chapters following that will detail the decisions that go into each of the pretrial and trial stages.

SUMMARY

1. Define law.
    - Law is "codified rules of conduct that are established by the government, that the people within the jurisdiction must follow, and that agents of the government can enforce with the use or threat of punishment."
2. Define constitutional, statutory, administrative, and common law, and identify the source of each.
    - Constitutional law is the obligations and powers specified in the government's charter and forms the foundations of U.S. law.
    - Statutory laws represent most of the laws that regulate our daily lives and are enacted by national and state legislatures.
    - Administrative laws are written and enforced by executive branch agencies.
    - Common law is judge-made law and has two sources. Common law refers to the rulings of U.S. state and federal judges that creates precedent on how the law is to be understood and applied. Some U.S. common law were adopted from the English common law system.
3. Explain the difference between substantive criminal law and procedural law.
    - Substantive criminal laws define particular acts as crime and specify punishment. Procedural laws tell criminal justice system practitioners what they can do, what they cannot do, and what they must do when they are writing substantive law, enforcing substantive law, processing a defendant, and executing a punishment.
4. Define crime and explain how it serves as the boundary of the criminal justice system.
    - Crime is an intentional act or omission committed without justification or defense which is in violation of criminal law and punishable by the state. Substantive laws constrain the power of

the state by drawing a boundary around the criminal justice system. Police, prosecutors, and courts can round up and punish only people who violate a substantive criminal law. To "activate" the criminal justice system, a person or organization must pierce that substantive-law boundary by committing, or being accused of committing, a crime.

5. Explain what is meant by "the elements of a crime" and define *actus reus, corpus delicti, mens rea,* and concurrence.

   - The elements of the crime include the following: an act, intent, and concurrence.
   - *Actus reus* means "reality of the act" and refers to a voluntary act that causes legally prohibited harm.
   - *Mens rea*, or "reality of the mind," means that the accused intended to commit the offense and produce the resultant harm.
   - *Corpus delicti* means "body of the crime" and refers to the evidence of the offense.
   - Concurrence is the final element of a criminal offense. It means that the action and intention occur at the same time.

6. List and define the types of criminal offenses.

   - Crimes against property involve damaging or stealing someone else's possessions, such as burglary and identity theft.
   - Crimes against the body refer to violent crimes against a person, such as rape or unsafe working conditions.
   - In victimless, or consensual, offenses everyone involved agrees to be involved, so there is no clear harm or victim. These are generally considered moral or public-order crimes.
   - Street crimes may include violent crimes like murder, property crimes, or consensual crimes.
   - White-collar and corporate crimes are committed by people or organizations in positions of power who use their position to violate criminal and regulatory law.

7. Explain the difference between a misdemeanor and a felony.

   - Felonies are considered serious offenses and usually carry a possible sentence ranging from over a year incarceration in prison to execution. Many felony convictions do not lead to incarceration but instead to probation or a diversionary program.
   - Misdemeanors are considered lesser offenses than felonies. Usually the maximum sentence is 1 year incarceration in jail, but must convictions lead to a fine, community service hours, probation, and other forms of community corrections.

8. Explain how legal reasoning relates to the court process.

   - Legal reasoning is the logic, evidence, laws, principles, language, and strategies lawyers and judges use in deciding if the facts of the case match the law. Attorneys must sort through the evidence to establish a case.

9. List and explain the felony pretrial stages.
   - The main felony pretrial stages tend to be initial appearance, preliminary hearing and information or grand jury presentation, bail/detention hearing, arraignment, discovery, and pretrial settlement and motions.
   - The charges are explained to the defendant, the defendant is told her or his rights, the defendant is permitted to obtain an attorney or is assigned a public defender, the judge decides if probable cause exists to detain the suspect, the judge may dismiss the case if it lacks adequate evidence, the prosecutor may drop the charges, the case may be diverted into a specialized court or pretrial intervention, bail may be set, a date is set for the preliminary hearing, and the attorneys can start to lay the foundation for trial and negotiation.

10. Explain how legal principles, due process, and crime control inform the structure of the criminal court process.
    - Legal principles, the crime-control mandate, and due process restraints help to make sense of the structure of the court process. Due process provisions are designed to be obstacles; they are in place to assure allegiance to the legal principles of legality and presumption of innocence, and, above all, due process. The court process is oriented toward process more than quick punishment.

Questions

1. What is law?
2. What is constitutional, statutory, administrative, and common law? What is the source of each?
3. What is the difference between substantive criminal law and procedural law?
4. What is crime? How does it serve as the boundary of the criminal justice system?
5. What is meant by "the elements of a crime?" What is *actus reus, corpus delicti, mens rea*, and concurrence?
6. What are the types of criminal offenses?
7. What is the difference between a misdemeanor and a felony?
8. What is legal reasoning? How does it relate to the court process?
9. What are the felony pretrial stages?
10. How do legal principles, due process, and crime control inform the structure of the criminal court process?

REFERENCES

[1] *ACLU v. NSA*, 438F. Supp. 2d 754, 782 (E.D. Mich. 2006).

[2] Dworkin R. Law's empire. Cambridge, MA: Belknap Press; 1986.

[3] Ibid.

[4] Fuller LL. The morality of law. New Haven, CT: Yale University Press; 1969.

[5] Holmes OW. The path of the law. Harvard Law Rev 1897;(8):457−78. Cardozo BN. The growth of the law. New Haven, CT: Yale University Press; 1924. Kantorowicz H. The definition of law. Cambridge, UK: University Press; 1958.

[6] Fuller. The morality of law.

[7] Pound R. Social control through law: the Powell lectures. Hamden, CT: Archon Books; 1968. p. 41.

[8] Weber M. Law in economy and society, Shils EA, Rheinstein M. editors [Rheinstein M., Trans. 1914; reprint] Cambridge, MA: Harvard University Press; 1954.

[9] Vago S. Law and society. 7th ed. Upper Saddle River, NJ: Prentice Hall; 2003. p. 37. Berman HJ, Greiner WR. The nature and functions of law. Mineola, NY: Foundation Press; 1980. p. 28.

[10] Grilliot HJ, Schubert FA. Introduction to law and the legal system. 5th ed. Boston, MA: Houghton Mifflin Harcourt; 1991. p. 1.

[11] Fogel D. We are the living proof: the justice model for corrections. 2nd ed. New York, NY: Anderson Publishing; 1979. p. 183.

[12] Weber M. [1922; reprint] In: Roth G, Wittich C, editors. Economy and society. Berkeley, CA: University of California Press; 1978. p. 212. See also Black D. The behavior of law. New York, NY: Academic Press; 1976. p. 2. Golding MP. Philosophy of law. Englewood Cliffs, NJ: Prentice Hall; 1975. p. 46. Hart HLA. The concept of law. Oxford: Clarendon Press; 1961.

[13] Weber M. Economy and society. In: Hoebel EA, editor. The law of primitive man: a study of comparative legal dynamics. Cambridge, MA: Harvard University Press; 1974. p. 276.

[14] *United States v. Wiltberger* (1820).

[15] Fuller. The morality of law.

[16] Hallevy G. A modern treatise on the principle of legality in criminal law. Berlin: Springer; 2010.

[17] Davies J. Legislative law and process in a nutshell. St. Paul, MN: West; 1975.

[18] Carp RA, Stidham R. Judicial process in America. 2nd ed. Washington, DC: Congressional Quarterly Press; 1993. p. 2.

[19] Judicial process in America, 6. Vago S. Law and society. 5th ed. Upper Saddle River, NJ: Prentice Hall; 1997. p. 36.

[20] Zimmerman JF. Contemporary American federalism: the growth of national power. Westport, CT: Praeger; 1992. p. 87.

[21] *Griswold v. Connecticut*, 381 U.S. 479 (1965).

[22] *Lawrence v. Texas*, 539 U.S. 558 (2003).

[23] Moran DA. In defense of the corpus delicti rule. Ohio Law Rev 2003;64:817−54: Online at <moritzlaw.osu.edu/students/groups/oslj/files/2012/03/64.3.moran_.pdf> [accessed March, 2012].

[24] *Robinson v. California*, 370 U.S. 660 (1962).

[25] On the media, the witnesses that didn't: transcript, <www.onthemedia.org/2009/mar/27/the-witnesses-that-didnt/transcript> [accessed March 27, 2009]. C.A.Rentschler An urban physiognomy of the 1964 Kitty Genovese murderSpace Culture 14 2011 310 329 J.

Sexton Reviving Kitty Genovese case, and its passions The New York Times, <www
.nytimes.com/1995/07/25/nyregion/reviving-kitty-genovese-case-and-its-passions.html>
[accessed July 25 1995].

[26] Pateakos J. Brothers break silence in Big Dan's rape case Herald News, <www.heraldnews
.com/news/x665149028/After-26-years-brothers-break-silence> [accessed October 26, 2009]
Tribune News Services, Man's inaction over girl's killing angers 20,000, Chicago Tribune,
<articles.chicagotribune.com/1998-08-26/news/9808260077_1_sherrice-iverson-jeremy-
strohmeyer-david-cash> [accessed August 26, 1998].

[27] Hayden A. Imposing criminal and civil penalties for failing to help another: are "good
samaritan" laws good ideas?" New England Int Comp Law Annu, Spring 2000; <www.nesl
.edu/userfiles/file/nejicl/vol6/hayden.pdf>.

[28] Sheley JF. Critical elements of criminal behavior explanation. Sociol Quart, 1983;24
(4):509−25.

[29] Kaplan J, Skolnick JH, Feeley MM. Criminal justice: introductory cases and material.
Westbury, NY: The Foundation Press; 1991.

[30] National Association of Criminal Defense Lawyers, 2012.

[31] Levi EH. An introduction to legal reasoning. Chicago, IL: University of Chicago Press; 1949.
Porto BL. The craft of legal reasoning. Fort Worth, TX: Harcourt Brace; 1998.

[32] Littrell WB. Bureaucratic justice: police, prosecutors, and plea bargaining. Beverly Hills, CA:
Sage; 1979. p. 33−4.

[33] *Argersinger v. Hamlin*, 407 U.S. 25 (1972).

[34] *Baldwin v. New York*, 399 U.S. 117 (1970).

[35] Bureau of Justice Statistics. State court processing statistics: felony defendants in large urban
counties, 2006, U.S. Department of Justice Office of Justice Programs, 2010.

[36] *United States v. Salerno*, 481 U.S. 739 (1987).

Negotiating Discretion, Making Decisions

OVERVIEW

Part 2 examines the workers within the courts and the factors that influence their decisions. These workers have a great deal of discretion, yet they must negotiate many pressures in order to establish some predictable patterns in their jobs. The first set of these influences is the legal principles that bind together all courts. These include ideals such as due process and the rule of law, and more specific principles such as giving each court a specific range of power (jurisdiction) and requiring that courts generally follow the rulings of earlier courts (precedent). The second set of influences includes the many factors within the courthouse, such as the process of providing defense attorneys to low-income defendants, types of crimes that police most often bring to the court, and informal culture among the court workers. The third set of influences encompasses the world outside the courthouse. This includes the legislature, which writes all the criminal laws, as well as judicial elections, the media, and the law schools. These influences shape legal decision-making from the moment a case lands on a prosecutor's desk. Before a case makes it to trial or a plea bargain, it goes through the process of assessment. This involves the prosecutor and defense attorney evaluating the strength of the case based on legal and non-legal cues, such as the quality of the evidence, the believability of the victim, and the race of the defendant. The prosecutor must then decide whether to dismiss a case or charge the defendant with a crime, and if the decision is to charge, the prosecutor must decide what to charge the defendant with.

Court workers make decisions in millions of cases every year.

CHAPTER 5

The Reality of Legal Action: Principles, Organizations, and Public Pressure

KEY TERMS

adversarial system
compartmentalized prosecution
conforming cases
cues
discretion
exceptional cases
external ecology of courts

IRAC method
internal ecology of courts
legal imperatives
legal logic
legal principles
negotiated order
principle of legality
ripe

socialization
sociological variables
stare decisis
systemic agency
systemic imperatives
venue
vertical prosecution

CONTENTS

Learning Objectives

After reading this chapter, you should be able to:

1. Understand that decision-making and actions vary from one court to another.
2. Explain what negotiated order is and how it helps to explain variation across courtrooms.
3. Define legal principles and explain how they influence legal decision-making.
4. Explain the process of legal reasoning and how it guides and constrains legal decision-making.
5. Discuss the internal and external ecologies of the courts.
6. Tell why the structure and decision-making patterns vary from court to court.
7. Describe how factors outside the court also affect the administration of justice.
8. Describe non-legal factors that influence decision-making.

The U.S. judiciary is a non-majoritarian branch of government. Even though some judges and court attorneys are elected in some states, for the most part, our court systems are operated by judges and attorneys who were not elected.

This poses a legitimacy problem for the courts. Think about how the other two branches of government get and keep their power. The public gives the president, governors, and legislators their official power by voting them into office. If the public is not satisfied with the legislative or executive branches, they can vote them out of office. The power of those branches is generally considered legitimate because they are voted in and kept in by the electorate. Courts do not get that stamp of approval from the voting public every 4 or 6 years. So how do they gain respect from a public that does not vote them into office? In part, it is by staying out of most of the nasty mudslinging campaigns and political battles. In part, it is through the formal rituals of the courtroom and the distinguished building and chambers of most courthouses. In large part, though, it is by maintaining an idealized image of justice, or the "myth of legal reasoning" [1].

Inside the court system and among the general public, there is a belief that laws are clear and neutral; facts and truth are discovered in the courts through the evidence-based application of law; and legal reasoning is objective and outcomes predictable. Certainly, many principles permeate the court system. Yet, when we look behind this image of rational law, we see that patterns within courts and the handling of particular cases are greatly shaped by varying interpretations of legal principles, resources, and relationships within the courts, as well as pressures from external forces such as the media and social science research. Looking at courts from these angles will help us better understand why lawyers and judges do what they do.

LEGAL ACTION: MOTIVATIONS, DECISIONS, AND ACTIONS OF THE COURTROOM WORKERS

The massive U.S. court system draws together many positions: lawmakers and judges; defense attorneys and prosecutors; police and police detectives; attorney staff, clerks, bailiffs, and probation officers; and many others. The United States has 7,917 state and federal legislators, 461,000 sworn local police officers, over a million law enforcement employees, about 800,000 attorneys, over 60,000 judges (all but about a thousand in state courts), and nearly 100,000 probation officers [2]. Just the lawyers and judges represent about 860,000 actors.

These workers make decisions in millions of cases every year—whether to charge or dismiss a case, what evidence to present or motions to file, whether to rule guilty or not guilty—that affect the defendant's liberty [3]. Yet the people making these decisions are not robots who crank out identical rulings. We cannot predict their behavior by looking at a single variable, such as religious affiliation. Rather, many factors influence them, so we must explain their actions in relationship to the structure, process, and cultural context of the court system in which they work. Even withholding from consideration corrupt and incompetent decisions, they still have many legitimate options at nearly every turn. What motivates them to make one decision over another?

Considering the hundreds of research efforts that have addressed this question over the past 50 years, the answer is complicated. Many variables—such as the type of offense and suspect, victim characteristics, quality of police investigations, availability of assistants, directives from bosses, elections and budgets—influence legal decision-making. Some of these variables are at the macro-level, which includes large-scale phenomena such as institutional principles, and state and federal budgets. Others concern such things as individual attitudes or small group interactions in the courthouse and are therefore micro-level. Some variables occur within the courthouse, and others come from outside.

To organize this large array of influences, we can arrange the variables into three categories.

- Legal principles explain how the U.S. court system, though decentralized, is arranged according to old principles, such as due process, the adversarial system, and exclusive jurisdictions. This is the foundation of legal reasoning.
- Internal ecology refers to variables that arise within the courthouse, from official procedures to aspects of the case to informal rules among the attorneys.
- External ecology is the large array of societal pressures that affect the people working in the courts, including community attitudes and partisan elections, the other branches of government, and activist organizations (See Figure 5.1 for an illustration of how these three categories frame legal decision-making.).

Patterns and Limited Variance

This comprehensive framework of legal action illuminates the social structure of courts, or the established and predictable patterns of behaviors and social relationships. Court workers often behave in the same way as those around them, and even when their behaviors are not identical, they are usually within a range of options that are considered acceptable and normal. We thus need to explain both patterns in behavior and patterns in predictable (or limited) variance: people

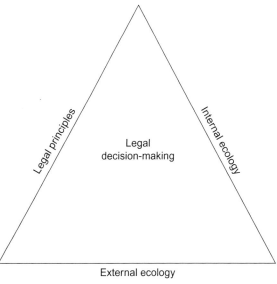

FIGURE 5.1

Variables that influence the decision-making of lawyers and judges can be grouped into three categories.

performing the same action in the same way and people choosing from the same range of accepted options.

Legal decisions are often described as discretionary decision-making. This does not mean that lawyers and judges have the freedom to do whatever they want. Rather, they must decide how to handle each particular case but make those decisions within a range of options narrowed by principles, policies, laws, and norms that frame their thinking and motivation. If, for instance, the district attorney instructs everyone in the office to pursue vigorously all offenses involving firearms, the individual prosecutors will have less discretion to negotiate such cases with the defense. They will have to seek the maximum punishment. Similarly, state laws that increase penalties for illegal drugs and Supreme Court rulings that require prosecutors to share evidence with the defense have altered the range of acceptable decisions. **Discretion**, then, is having the capacity to choose from a range of permissible options that exist within the organizational and institutional constraints [4].

Negotiated Order

Standing between all these legal and non-legal pressures on patterns of action within courts are the lawyers and judges [5]. They must negotiate among themselves how best to handle all the requirements and social pressures. Research shows that non-legal variables, such as religious affiliation and the amount of oversight, affect legal action; that patterns emerge over time from a complex set of lower-level patterns (such as funding); and that the actual practice of law entails the "craft" of applying identifiable techniques in creative ways [6].

In order to learn how workers juggle legal rules, non-legal influences, the craftwork of justice, and emerging patterns, sociologist Anselm Strauss conducted over 20 years of research on organizations. While observing the routines in various businesses and agencies, Strauss found that in order to understand the operations of organizations, such as a courtroom, we must study the motivations, actions, and social relationships of the people working in them [7]. Workers must know which rules must be followed, which are to be ignored, and which can be modified; they must know when deference to authority is necessary and when they can make their own decisions; and they must know how to work with their coworkers. They have to balance the official structures such as administrative rules with daily demands of their job and coworkers [8]. In the process of negotiating all these variables, the workers develop knowledge about how to perform the job within the existing formal structure [9].

The **negotiated order**, then, is the patterns or routines among the workers that emerge over time as the workers interact with the institutional frame, each other, and external organizations and conditions [10]. Neither the formal nor the informal rules alone create routines in a workplace. Workers conform to both, and this is what creates internal regularity and predictability.

The institutional frame includes the legal principles such as the right to counsel; official rules, goals, and mandates of the organization such as deadlines to file motions; and the work that must be done and the clients or customers who must be dealt with [11]. This formal system sets boundaries around worker conduct [12]. For instance, a prosecutor cannot take someone to trial for being rude to homeless people, even if he or she finds it immoral to insult those who are disadvantaged. The institution of law does not permit them to prosecute someone for immoral acts, but only for alleged violations of criminal statutes [13].

Yet workers do not merely obey all the rules of the institutional frame. They ponder, discuss, and interpret these rules [14]. In the process, they develop unofficial local norms, which includes shared interpretations of the law and formal rules, informal or unofficial rules, commonly held priorities, and routines to accomplish tasks [15]. Once a social structure is established, the workers conform to the norms and expect their coworkers to conform [16]. Sometimes they do so strategically, such as in an effort to get along with coworkers, but other times the conformity is unconscious or part of their tacit knowledge [17]. For instance, if the local norms of a district attorney's office define driving under the influence (DUI) cases as more serious than drug-possession cases, the prosecutors will probably pursue DUI cases more aggressively.

Workers must also negotiate external forces, such as the media and crime rates [18]. In one study, a researcher found that in high-crime areas police tend to view crime as normal, consider the victims less deserving of assistance, have less time to devote to all offenses, and therefore investigate most offenses less vigorously [19].

The influence of the institutional frame on the workers' negotiations is called "coupling" (which means the connecting of two things). In some organizations, the formal rules and informal arrangements of the workers may be loosely coupled, meaning that the workers respond to the official frame but retain their distinct practices [20]. Over time, the workers negotiate with the weak institutional frame and each other and gradually form patterns of behavior that may diverge from, or even contradict, the official policies and goals.

For instance, police have a high degree of autonomy from administrative control and therefore may develop a subculture and patterns of behavior that are different from the official expectations [21]. This can be seen when groups of officers create a crime syndicate, such as the Los Angeles Police

Department Rampart scandal of the late 1990s, in which 70 officers were implicated in misconduct from stealing drugs to committing drive-by shootings [22]. Other research has found similar loose coupling in prisons, in which the guards design their own rules of acceptable and unacceptable behavior while still following the formal rules enough to appear as though they are complying with them [23].

Courts, however, are more tightly coupled than police, prisons, and most other organizations because courts must maintain "an internally consistent set of rules" that conform to firmly established legal principles [24]. Nonetheless, the reality of their day-to-day work involves non-regular tasks, unpredictable situations, and inconsistent clients, all of which require considerable judgment. Therefore, for the sake of efficiency, they must be flexible and negotiate with the official rules and coordinate with their colleagues to establish patterns that allow them to handle the many cases that come into the court system while abiding by the formidable array of legal principles and organizational rules [25].

LEGAL FRAME: PRINCIPLES THAT CONSTRAIN AND GUIDE LEGAL ACTION WITHIN U.S. CRIMINAL COURTS

Similar to workers in all industries, judges and lawyers have job descriptions, schedules, and tasks. Unlike most other professions, however, their work is circumscribed by centuries of legal principles and procedures. For over 200 years, the U.S. court system has retained and embellished a set of principles that frames activities within it. The motivations, decisions, and actions of courtroom actors are tightly coupled to principles, rules, reasoning, and practices that are peculiar to the practice of law. As Supreme Court Justice Stephen Breyer said at a Yale University lecture, the legal logic of the courts entails "principles that do not change applied to circumstances that do" [26].

Legal logic refers to the capacity to understand and engage power, disputes, and resolutions in terms of legal principles and rules. This logic establishes an array of constraints and directives that are described in general terms as systemic imperatives, but more specifically as legal imperatives. **Systemic imperatives** refer to what a person or organization must do in order to survive and flourish within a system. For instance, to succeed as a student, you must adhere to education mandates: attend class, complete assignments, take exams, and be somewhat courteous to professors. In courts, the legal principles, rules, and procedures form a strong set of **legal imperatives**, which are also called legal norms. Prosecutors must work to control crime, file charges, disclose evidence to the defense, and prosecute. Defense attorneys must file motions, cross-examine, defend the accused, and assure that the government follows due-process principles and rules. Judges must rule on motions and objections, suppress or allow evidence, and often declare a defendant guilty or not guilty. These are imperatives imposed on the workers not by a single boss but by the legal system itself, and therefore are referred to as **systemic agency**. The agency of these principles establishes what some scholars call a "legal subculture," which guides and constrains lawyers and judges in the following ways:

- dictate the system of law in the United States
- define the duties of practitioners
- frame legal reasoning
- outline procedures in every court [27]

Legal Principles and the U.S. System of Law

Legal principles are standards used to formulate the law. The U.S. legal system exists within the shifting balance between crime control and due process. Its **adversarial system**—a framework in which the prosecutor and defense attorney have competing goals of conviction and exoneration—allows the courts to pursue both goals [28]. This relationship is continually invoked as courts process over 21 million criminal cases a year: 21.4 million state criminal cases and about 80,000 federal criminal cases, out of over 100 million total cases filed in state courts and nearly 2 million federal cases [29]. This "nonaccountable partisanship" requires tight court rules to maintain ethical conduct [30].

Due process and legality, then, are the bedrock of U.S. courts: they dictate the type of court system in the United States and frame the actions of legal workers. The principle of due process, in general terms, means individuals should be protected against excessive and arbitrary government power, and, in more specific terms, means the government must follow the principles of fairness such as transparent proceedings. The **principle of legality**, which is also called the rule of law, is closely related to due process. It mandates:

- that the courts enforce only positive laws, or the law of the land
- that the laws apply equally to all members of the society
- that lawmaking itself adhere to corollary principles, such as no *ex post facto* or secret laws

These principles encompass the other principles, such as reasonable doubt, right to counsel and confrontation, and judicial review. Victorian jurist A.V. Dicey argued that this principle of legality was the defining characteristic of civilized democracies because it subjected everyone, even the most powerful, to the democratically derived laws [31]. Echoing this sentiment, U.S. District

Court Judge Anna Taylor wrote in a 2006 opinion, "There are no hereditary Kings in America and no powers not created by the Constitution. All 'inherent powers' must derive from that Constitution"[32]. As John Adams said, the United States is a government of laws and not of men.

Due process and legality together have two profound effects. On the national level, they inhibit government power and thereby protect the rights of all people within the nation. In each courtroom, however, they serve as the rope that tethers the agents of the state. Prosecutors cannot prosecute their political enemies or people whom they do not like, and judges cannot incarcerate disagreeable political dissenters. Most of the time, these and other courtroom actors will act within this framework of the courts: they will enforce only positive laws and adhere to procedural laws.

Principles and the Duties of Courts

In the process of upholding the rule of law, lawyers and judges are constrained and directed by additional principles of justiciability, jurisdiction, and judicial independence. The first principle, justiciability requires that certain criteria be met before the courtroom actors will even take up a case. The state must have standing, and the case must be **ripe**, that is, the facts of a case must allow the courts to hear it and make a useful decision. In short, if a case is not justiciable, a prosecutor will rarely bother with it, and the judge must dismiss it [33]. This translates into prosecutorial restraint and judicial restraint.

The second principle is jurisdiction. Even if the case is something which a criminal court should prosecute, the lawyers must be sure it is assigned to the right court. Because courts have the legal authority to hear and rule only on some types of cases, the courtroom workers are effectively prohibited from doing anything with cases outside of that domain. **Venue** is the particular court that hears the case. A misdemeanor court cannot rule on a felony case; a prosecutor in Illinois cannot take a criminal case that occurred in Minnesota; cases involving minors will usually be heard in a separate juvenile system and are subject to different rules; and a trial court usually will not hear an appeal [34]. Jurisdiction clearly demarcates which cases a lawyer or judge can and cannot handle.

The third principle that circumscribes the decision-making and actions of courtroom actors are judicial independence and judicial review. Prior to the establishment of these filters, courts did the bidding of whatever ruling group was in power, as their pay, jobs, and lives could be jeopardized if they did not. This is why the Declaration of Independence condemned King George III for tying the colonial courts too closely to the Crown and laid the groundwork for separation of powers. As an independent branch, courts must apply the substantive laws but do so while abiding by procedural laws and remaining at least somewhat detached from the other branches. In trial courts, lawyers and judges apply criminal statutes to defendants and review the actions of the police. In appellate courts they review the procedures of the lower courts and in some cases review the constitutionality of the laws themselves. Judicial independence allows for "free and fearless judging" when reviewing cases [35].

Principles and Legal Reasoning

Once a case is handed to a prosecutor and a defense attorney, how do they analyze it in order to move it from the criminal event to a conviction or exoneration? Legal reasoning is the *evaluative process* that lawyers and judges use to determine the legal relevance of a case and the *strategic process* of preparing a case for trial. It involves examining the facts of a case in light of the principles, laws, and rules; identifying the most relevant legal facts; and then building the case from there. Legal reasoning thus narrows their view of what is relevant, binds the practitioners to a logic that is historical and internal to the U.S. system of law and justice, and prioritizes specific aspects of reality over other aspects [36].

There is actually much debate about legal reasoning in the world of legal scholarship, with some following jurist Oliver Wendell Holmes, Jr. [37] and arguing that there are no binding rules, only the judges' preferences, and some arguing that legal reasoning has rules but that those rules are the same we all use in everyday life. Most scholars, however, propose a particular framework of legal reasoning [38]. Although it is true that personal preferences and external ecologies do affect how people handle cases (as we will discuss later), the actual handling of cases is tightly coupled to the institutional frame of courts. The only way for courts to limit prejudicial treatment of cases and deal coherently with a stream of unique cases is to have a common process for extracting the essential legal characteristics from each case and focusing on them almost exclusively [39]. Legal reasoning allows for coherence within the case and across cases.

As the "rule of decisions" used by lawyers and judges, legal reasoning distinguishes what is relevant and included in legal arguments from what is excluded [40]. The victim's siblings, spouse, parents, and neighbors may want to talk about how the crime changed them and their community, and the defendant's family and pastor may want to describe how the defendant is actually a good-hearted person. However, none of that is relevant for the legal reasoning used in processing the case. Rather, legal reasoning in the U.S. courts entails understanding the offense in legal terms, not in personal, moral, or social terms. It requires weighting some aspects of the case more than others, such as giving more weight to properly obtained evidence than to illegally obtained evidence, regardless of which one is closer to truth [41]. The priorities, limitations, and conclusions arrived at in court can only be explained and understood by looking at the internal logic of the courts.

To more clearly understand the importance of legal reasoning and the coherence it creates, imagine a court system in which the judges do not feel bound by law, legal principles, or past decisions. Decisions would be based on personal preferences; decisions would not be explained; and prejudice and incompetence would go unchecked. This is exactly what happens in nations with dictatorships and no independent judiciary, and sometimes in the village courts of New York (described in Chapter 3) [42].

The Stages of Legal Reasoning

Even though it baffles many people, legal reasoning is a rather orderly process by which lawyers argue and judges decide actual cases. At its core, legal reasoning is interpretation and coherence [43]. A lawyer must interpret the evidence and the facts of the case, the substantive statutes, and the procedural laws, and then make a coherent recommendation based on links between the facts and the law. The goal is to establish, refute, or judge a case.

The lawyers must first assess the facts to determine what type of case they have. Gathering and interpreting the facts is an iterative process, meaning that the lawyer will gather some facts from the case, compare it to several laws and draw a tentative interpretation, gather more facts, refine the interpretation, and so on. The objective of the prosecution is to figure out which law or laws may have been violated and to establish the elements of crime. The objective of the defense is to refute the elements of the crime. Facts are the essential components of a strong case. In simple cases, lawyers can skim the arrest report and be finished quickly with this stage; more complicated cases may require months to evaluate. Once facts and law are fairly well settled on, the lawyers analyze and summarize the case using what is often called the IRAC (issue, rule, analysis, and conclusion) method, described in Court Procedures 5.1. The **IRAC method** is a common model of legal reasoning that encourages attorneys and judges to analyze cases in terms of legally relevant facts and laws.

COURT PROCEDURES

Using Legal Reasoning and IRAC: Do the Facts of the Case Match the Prohibited Behavior Described in the Statute?

Imagine that you are a prosecutor in San Diego, California, and an alleged burglary case lands on your desk. You look over the police report a few times and maybe even talk to the police to be sure that this is probably a burglary and not a trespass or robbery. It looks like a burglary. Now you have to see if you can pin it on the suspect. So you review the facts and law using the IRAC method you learned in law school and refined on the job.

- Issue: You state the alleged crime. "Did the defendant violate the California statute prohibiting burglary? Yes, as the state will show, she did."
- Rule (or the law): You specify the statute that the defendant allegedly violated and each legal component of it. "Penal Code 459 states that burglary is 'entering a structure with the intent to commit a felony (or a petty theft) once inside.'"
- Analysis: Now you draw a clear line from each component of the statute to the material facts of the case. "The facts establish each of the following: (1) the defendant entered; (2) a building, apartment, vehicle, vessel, cargo container, or mobile home; (3) with the intent to commit petty theft, grand theft, or any other felony. Witnesses saw the defendant enter the victim's apartment, and upon arrest just outside of the apartment, police found on the defendant checkbooks that belonged to the victim and that the defendant stole from the apartment."
- Conclusion: You tie these threads together and recommend conviction. "Given that the evidence confirms that the defendant did enter the apartment with the intent to steal the checkbooks, she did in fact violate California statute 459. Therefore the court should find her guilty."

You are going to tell this to the defendant and defense attorney to try to pressure them to negotiate a guilty plea in exchange for recommending to the court leniency. If that does not work, you are going to make this same argument in trial.

However, keep in mind that you are not the only driver on the road. The defense attorney will try to pick your case apart, finding every weakness and ungrounded assumption in it: the incident happened in the dark of evening; the witnesses had been drinking; the defendant found the checkbooks on the stairs, and so on, and therefore the court should find the defendant not guilty.

Question
Create a similar criminal offense and apply the IRAC method.

This is a complex dance that requires adherence to strict and often peculiar rules and also the ability to finesse details in unique ways. Systemic agency is bearing down on the attorneys—they must use a special language, and they must push everything that is not legally relevant out of the analysis. As retired judge Richard Poland [44] states, legal reasoning is essential in the operations of our courts, but it is "not easily mastered, even by those of us who think that we use this process on a daily basis."

Legal Reasoning in Appellate Cases Versus Trials
Discussion of legal reasoning is sometimes a bit confounding because some parts of legal reasoning are common in all court proceedings, whereas others are much more common in a particular type of proceeding, such as a criminal trial or appellate case. Legal reasoning in all court proceedings requires that the practitioners interpret the case within the framework of law. Criminal

hearings and trials, however, rest more heavily on material facts and matching the facts of the crime to the language of the substantive statutes. Most of these cases are decided based on the facts and the statute, and with adherence to procedural laws. Appellate cases, however, involve reviewing the facts of the criminal trial procedure or the constitutionality of the law. These are generally considered disputes over law instead of disputes over facts. These cases do not ignore statutes or the facts of the crime, but they do discount them in favor of a more explicit reliance on legal principles articulated in previous rulings.

As a result of earlier rulings having a prominent role in appeals, three aspects of legal reasoning are much more common in appellate cases: precedent, analogy, and deduction. Precedent both specifies an earlier ruling that creates a rule and involves a court following an earlier appellate court decision because the cases are the same in some important legal respect. This is also called the doctrine of *stare decisis et non quieta movere* (or **stare decisis** for short): "to stand by decisions and not disturb settled points." In general, a lower court is bound by the rulings in higher courts (intermediate and high court). The connection between the case at hand and the precedent is identified through analogy and deduction. The lawyer will identify some legally relevant similarity or analogy between cases, even if it is only one set of facts that are similar, and then deduce that the earlier decision should be followed in the present case because of the similarity [45]. Appellate court legal reasoning will be explained further in Chapter 11.

Principles and Procedures

Procedural law, which is also called procedural rules and rules of practice, have a direct and daily effect on the decision-making of lawyers and judges. They specify what they can, cannot, and must do when processing a case. As Table 5.1 shows, the procedures are rooted in legal principles and span the entire court process.

Being derived from well-established legal principles, these legal procedures create what distinguished Northwestern University Professor Herbert Jacob [46] describes as a "... ritualism that is unmatched in American government." There are rules on what must or should be said, rules on what not to say, and patterns of interactions [47]. Moreover, there are specific people who are allowed to utter particular parts of the trial, which excludes others from voicing their thoughts [48]. The clearest example of this is that it is the prosecutor who presents the case, not the victim or the victim's family. In fact, the prosecutor will sometimes not call any of them to the witness stand, in which case they have no voice in the trial.

Table 5.1 The Foundation of Procedural Laws in Legal Principles

Criminal court procedure is grounded in the principles that frame the legal system. This list—which is by no means exhaustive—shows some of the procedures that are based on older principles

Legal Principles	Procedures
Presumption of innocence and reasonable doubt	Prosecution opens the trial with the accusation.
	Prosecutor has the burden of proof, to establish proof beyond a reasonable doubt of the defendant's guilt.
	Defendant is provided counsel if unable to afford it.
	Prosecution must participate in discovery.
	Line-ups and other means of identification must be objective and not suggestive.
	Defense may file motions challenging evidence and actions of the prosecution.
	Suspect has the right to bail.
No double jeopardy	Only the defense can appeal in most situations.
	Defendant cannot be tried in both juvenile court and adult court.
No compelled confession	Court will suppress confessions in which the suspect was not Mirandized or the interrogation failed to follow other rules.
Public trial and jury trial	The public (in audience and jury) and media are permitted to attend hearings and trials.
Right to bail	The court must hold a bail hearing.
	Pretrial detention must be justified.
No cruel and unusual punishment	The convicted may not be tortured or mutilated.
Due process	The suspect must be informed of charges.
	The Speedy Trial Act caps the length of the court process.
	Courts must follow precedent.
	Judges must adhere to sentencing guidelines or justify divergence.

ECOLOGICAL PERSPECTIVE

Principles and laws are essential for understanding courts, but these alone cannot explain legal action [49]. We must also account for the social context of court workers. To do this, we turn to the idea of human ecology. Human ecology is the interdisciplinary study of human behavior that explains human behavior in terms of our social and physical environment [50]. It explains patterns of human behavior and variation in those patterns as collective adaptations to our complex environments. These include:

- Social structure: formal and informal organization of activities, resources, and social interactions, patterns in social problems, and the cultural symbols and values.

- ■ Population characteristics: migration, immigration, growth or decline in populations, educational and employment level of population, and so on.
- ■ Physical environment and technology: natural environment such as weather patterns, built environment such as homes and office space, and human inventions such as communication technology and computers [51].

The social context of courts includes the world inside the courthouse, as well as the influences from outside. A court's internal ecology includes its organizational structure and job duties, types of cases and protocol for handling them, buildings and technology, and the interactions of the workers themselves. The external ecology includes the other branches of government, elections, law schools, and a wide array of social pressures such as local community attitudes, citizen activists, interest groups, and media.

INTERNAL ECOLOGY OF U.S. CRIMINAL COURTS

All courtroom workers must adjust their behaviors to the legal principles, substantive laws, and legal procedures that permeate the entire nation's legal system. Yet research has also found that the structure and decision-making patterns vary from court to court, even when they are enforcing the same laws and bound by the same rules of procedure [52]. This is true within states, between states, and among federal courts [53].

The organizational context of courtroom action, that is, the formal bureaucratic structure and the informal practices and characteristics, in large part explains the different patterns of decision-making [54]. The working conditions, in other words, affect the choices the courtroom workers make. Internal ecology refers to the social attributes within a particular courthouse or local court system where, for the most part, the same people work on thousands of cases together [55].

Given that the United States has over 14,000 courts, it would be an overwhelming task to learn the unique activities within every courthouse and courtroom. To help in the study of courts, the internal ecology of any criminal court can be organized with the following categories:

- ■ formal organizational structure
- ■ crime patterns and case characteristics
- ■ physical environment and technology
- ■ informal culture among workers

Together, these variables serve as a framework and internal stimuli for legal action [56]. Courtroom actors learn these patterns of behavior and how to respond to stimuli through **socialization**, or the process of learning a group's norms and habits. Lawyers and judges are socialized by media, their families, religion, college, and law school before even entering the profession. They are socialized formally while in the profession of law—receiving job training and explicit instructions from their supervisors—and informally, by observing and interacting with their peers. Sometimes the socialization process is direct, such as being rewarded or punished for doing something. Other times it is subtle, such as learning what is expected by observing what others are doing. Through these multiple pressures and influences, a worker's "legal mind" tends to align with the attitudes and behavioral patterns of the courtroom workgroup [57].

Formal Organizational Frame: Bureaucratic Structure, Jurisdiction, and Size

The best way to structure the courts has been debated in the United States since its founding, and there are still debates over the most efficient size and structure of courts [58]. This explains why there is so much variance across the nation in the formal organizational frame of courts. Regardless of the structure, however, every court is a complex organization that influences the actions of those who work in it [59].

Courts are not as clearly hierarchical and specialized as other formal organizations like factories, but they do have mandates, goals, and procedures that exist independently of the workers and that limit discretion and variance [60]. In his famous analysis, criminologist Abraham Blumberg [61] described courts as bureaucracies with explicit organizational mandates, hierarchy of authority, standardized training, specific administrative tasks divided among the specialists, interrelated offices, written rules, and the goal of efficiency. Blumberg [62] found that this bureaucratic structure actually eclipses other sources of motivation: the court includes "pragmatic values, bureaucratic priorities, and administrative instruments" that prompt defense attorneys, for instance, to abandon their "professional commitments to the accused client in the service of these higher claims of the court organization." Research on other criminal justice organizations has found similar influence of the formal organization [63].

Inside this bureaucratic structure, we find that courts have unique tasks and procedures. Beyond jurisdiction and the number of lawyers and judges in the court, the formal court system has five important components:

- indigent defense system and specialized units
- style and structure of management
- availability and quality of assistants and experts
- official procedures for handling cases
- specialized duties

Let's explore these further.

Indigent Defense Systems and Special Prosecutor Units

Lawyers vary not only in their quantity but also in their organization and funding. This is true for defense attorneys and prosecutors. A defendant can hire a private defense attorney. Low-income defendants, however, receive services from one of the following indigent defense systems:

1. a public defender's office where lawyers specialize in criminal defense
2. assigned counsel in which the judge orders a local attorney to defend the accused
3. contract attorneys who defend indigents for a fee paid by the court
4. community defender organizations that provide a range of services, including criminal defense [64]

Public defenders are often experienced, but many of the other defense attorneys have no specialized training, and all have few resources [65]. The type of defense attorney may therefore greatly affect the decisions attorneys make and how the case is processed, such as whether to negotiate a plea deal or push for a dismissal by filing motions and pursuing a trial [66]. With only 22 states funding public defender offices in parts of the state, it is clear that there is no consensus on the best way to provide counsel to low-income defendants.

Prosecutor offices are more established within the court system, most of them being full-time employees, but there is still a wide variety of structures. They vary in their specialized units, such as having attorneys for juvenile, rape, murder, domestic abuse, habitual offenders, and other particular types of cases. An increasing number have also started to offer victim services and community prosecution.

Management, Coordination, and Oversight of Court Offices

Management structure and goals, level of coordination among offices, and systems of oversight all significantly affect worker decisions and actions [67]. A prosecutor's job, for instance, will be affected by the amount of discretion or directives that come from the top down. Interaction among offices will also affect the workers. The police department, prosecutor's office, public defender system, clerk's office, sheriff, and judicial office all have separate budgets, separate regulations, and their own goals, and all send agents to be part of the court process. They are therefore both autonomous and interdependent. How they manage this complexity influences their jobs.

For instance, in some jurisdictions the prosecutor's office has a collaborative relationship with the police department, and therefore receives assistance on securing good evidence. Other jurisdictions have distrust between the two offices, which makes the prosecutors' jobs more difficult [68]. The same variability exists in the relationship between prosecution and defense offices.

Ultimately, every organization has a system of quality control, but those systems vary. The quantity and style of oversight, discipline, and promotion will influence motivation and decisions on whether to conform and deviate from expectations. Less oversight means less accountability and less likelihood of being disciplined for deviation or even misconduct, such as malicious prosecution, in which the prosecutor knows the defendant is innocent [69].

Political scientist Peter G. Fish [70], in his groundbreaking analysis of the judicial system as a political system, argues that judicial independence and decentralization has fostered individualism and low accountability. Efforts over the twentieth century—such as professionalization and bureaucratization—have attempted to curtail some of this individualized expression of justice. Increasingly supervisory goals are embedded into the structure of the offices, so, in some jurisdictions for instance, a prosecutor's decision on how to handle a case is always reviewed by others. Each of the three main offices now has codes of conduct. For instance, the Judicial Code of Conduct regulates conflict of interest for lower federal courts. A lack of incentives for good work has also been a problem for courts; therefore many now attach raises and promotions to explicit goals, such as expeditious handling of cases and increasing the integrity of the office [71]. Insofar as the lawyers are rational actors, they will be motivated to earn the rewards, and the oversight and incentives will alter their decisions.

Assistants and Experts

Lawyers and judges could not do their job without the involvement of many auxiliary workers. Of course, courts are not equal, and some courts and offices have access to more assistants and experts than others. This unequal availability of human resources has a significant effect on the administration of justice. A defense attorney who is not provided with her or his own investigator must rely on evidence provided by the police and prosecutor, which will weaken the opportunity to build the best defense.

Greater access to translators, victim and witness assistance coordinators, paralegals, secretaries, and forensic and psychology experts generally strengthens a lawyer's case. A court will be able to handle its caseload better if it has in place probation, arbitration and mediation, and social services. The availability and skills of these support workers affect both caseload and overall workload. An office can process more cases efficiently and fairly if it has sufficient staff.

Official Procedures for Handling Cases

A courthouse's official protocol for processing cases is tightly coupled to the system-wide legal principles and rules. All cases must include things like informing the defendant of the charges and providing the defendant with bail or a bail hearing, but the style of moving cases from one stage to the next is largely a local, internal decision [72].

The U.S. criminal court process has been compared to a factory assembly line in which cases are moved along toward conviction as rapidly as possible, with little attention to treatment or due process [73]. However, this metaphor glosses over two important realities of criminal courts. First, a great variety of methods are used in processing cases, from prioritizing certain offenses for prosecution to use of diversionary programs. Second, each case receives at least some "individualized treatment" [74]. See Court Procedures 5.2 for more about these methods.

COURT PROCEDURES

Dealing with the Flow of Cases: Issues and Strategies in U.S. Criminal Courts

The number of criminal statutes, police, arrests, and suspects all grow faster than the court resources and personnel. At the same time, pressure to be more professional has increased, which has, in turn, increased the number of cases and the transparency required to handle each case.

Courts have implemented several strategies to deal with case-flow and the demands of justice. These strategies include using forms of case management to place cases on case-type tracks, increasing cooperation across offices, and reducing the backlog of cases to process cases faster. In Philadelphia, these methods reduced case-processing time by 25 percent and saved hundreds of thousands of dollars [75].

A particular example of changes in case processing has been some courts' adoption of vertical prosecution instead of compartmentalized prosecution. **Vertical prosecution** means that a single attorney (or a small team of attorneys in complex cases) handles a case from the initial screening all the way to dismissal, acquittal, or sentencing. In vertical prosecution, cases will often be assigned to an attorney with expertise in that area. In **compartmentalized prosecution**, a case is handled by a different attorney at each stage—one attorney handles the first appearance, another the preliminary hearings, and yet another the trial.

Question

If you were a prosecutor, which type of prosecution system would you prefer? Do you have other suggestions on how to handle the flow of cases?

"It's Our Job": Division of Labor, Specialization, and Scripted Behaviors

A court's official structure is not merely words on paper. It dictates to a large extent how millions of people across the United States do their jobs every-day. The courts divide the task of processing cases into niches, and people specialize in one specific section of the court process. This includes police who bring in cases and victim services and social welfare workers who help people in need. An attorney does the initial screening of the case and starts to work with investigators, witness coordinators, paralegals, and office staff. With evidence, witnesses, and experts in tow, the prosecuting attorney goes before, usually, several judges at several hearings: initial, preliminary, bail or detention, arraignment, motions, and negotiated pleas. At the same time, the defense counsel meets with the defendant, witnesses, experts, the judges, and the prosecutor, as well as the office staff, county clerk, and judicial staff. Then many of these people meet in the court for trial.

The three prominent niches are the judge, the defense attorney, and the prosecutor. Given the cumulative effect of the legal imperatives, legal reasoning, jurisdictional duties, formal organization of their particular courthouse, and specialized job, the behaviors of the courtroom workers are, to a considerable extent, scripted and bracketed. Although they have discretionary powers, how they think about, describe, and handle cases are largely mapped out, or scripted, for them by the rationalized bureaucracy. The choices they make are actually delimited, or bracketed, by their official duties. Given these scripts, the court actors end up with a narrow view of what is relevant and a narrow range of acceptable options. In short, the organization structures how lawyers and judges deal with victims and offenders, each other, and the tasks before them [76].

Crimes and Cases

Caseload significantly influences decision-making by lawyers and judges: how many cases do they have to handle and what type of cases? Some courts have many misdemeanors and public disturbances and others a few. Some have many drug offenders, and others mostly property-crime defendants, and so on. This is a product of crime patterns in the jurisdiction and patterns of police enforcement.

At the heart of the court system are the cases themselves. Each case has attributes that influence how lawyers and judges handle it. These include:

- legal merits of the case
- legal attributes of the case other than its evidentiary merits
- sociological aspects of a case
- typical versus unusual cases

Members of the trial court cannot carefully review every fact, law, and background issue in every case. To handle the caseload and reduce uncertainty, they rely on salient signs, or cues, to frame the case [77]. **Cues** are legal and non-legal attributes of a case that tend to trigger a particular response from lawyers or judges, such as to dismiss, plea, or vigorously prosecute a case. They serve as shortcuts that allow the actors to make decisions on how to handle a case without having to do a thorough analysis of it [78]. "Long rap sheet" may be a cue to treat the defendant as a "habitual offender."

PHOTO 5.1
Cues are attributes of a case that tend to trigger a particular response from lawyers or judges "Long rap sheet" may be a cue to treat the defendant as a "habitual offender."

"Has job" may be a cue to reduce charges. Some researchers have attempted to find single cues, or stimuli, that have the most influence, but it is more useful to look at cues as a collection of signals that lawyers and judges must combine and weigh in totality [79].

The legal merits of a case are the elements of the case that are relevant to the statute. This includes the type of alleged offense and the available evidence to establish the elements of the crime and culpability. This also includes other issues, such as ripeness and the defendant's criminal history if a habitual offender statute applies. Cues related to the legal merits, arguably, are the most important cues because they are tied directly to the outcome of most cases.

Legal issues tied to the case but not part of the material facts or merits may also serve as cues. Cruelty during the offense, the defendant's lack of remorse, the defendant's prior record, and pretrial detention, which are not in most statutes or relevant for conviction, may cue a prosecutor to push for harsh punishment. But if a drug-sales case has a mandatory minimum of 36 months for a first-time offender, the prosecutor may be cued to reduce the charges or divert the case. An uncooperative victim, which is common in rape and domestic abuse cases, may cue a prosecutor to dismiss or plea down a case [80]. A cue at sentencing may be the mode of conviction. Pleading guilty instead of going to trial may reduce sentence severity because a guilty plea is often interpreted as sign of remorse [81].

The third set of cues is even further away from the letter of the law. **Sociological variables** refer to attributes that place people into social categories, such as race, social class, sex, and employment status [82]. Even though the United States does not have separate laws for these groups, a growing body of research, though inconsistent in its findings, is establishing that race, sex, social class, education, victim–offender relationship, perceived dangerousness, rehabilitation potential, and the likely effect of a sentence do affect some cases, though usually less than the legal merits of the case [83]. It seems that the goal of including these nonlegal variables in legal decision-making is to predict the defendants' future behaviors and the most appropriate sentence [84].

There is no evidence that decisions based on limited sociological information are accurate, but the practice nonetheless appears common. What does seem more clear is that having low social capital—low income, low education, marginal employment, and being a minority male—not only confers disadvantage throughout life but also may disadvantage people in court [85].

Racial inequality demonstrates the influence of sociological variables as cues for legal decision-making. It is uncontested that the court system falls hardest on minority groups, especially blacks, Hispanics, and American Indians [86]. They are convicted and sentenced to incarceration at far higher rates than other racial or ethnic groups. It is difficult to determine if race affects courts because nearly any given legal decision can be justified without mentioning race, but the macro-level patterns reveal bias. Here are some examples:

- When the Supreme Court placed a moratorium on executions, it was in large part because of the patterns of racial inequality and arbitrariness of its use [87].
- Minority and male offenders are less likely to receive alternative sentences in lieu of incarceration [88].
- Public defenders representing black defendants tend to settle for harsher negotiated sentences than when representing white defendants [89].
- Defense attorneys representing Spanish-speaking clients may less often investigate the defendant's mental illnesses with a "competent to stand trial" evaluation, which means mentally-ill minority defendants are more likely to face trial [90].
- A study of 300 homicide cases found that black offenders are more likely to be sentenced to death, especially when the victim was white [91]. Though this research has been challenged, other research has produced similar results [92].

- In terms of race leading to leniency, two researchers found that judges are more likely to depart from sentencing guidelines in favor of whites who were just convicted. The net effect is that blacks are more likely to be sentenced to incarceration [93].

The race effect on any one case is probably much smaller than the influence of type of offense, evidence, and prior record, but it still contributes to adverse patterns that affect black and Hispanic defendants, their families, and their communities. The cumulative effect of these "minor" patterns over the course of a person's life and multiple generations creates an onerous and unjust burden on the people and their communities. This is discussed more in the final section.

Other sociological variables of a case include attributes such as the perceived deservedness of the victim. Research has found that in cases in which the victim and offender know each other, prosecutors are more likely to dismiss the case if the victim has a criminal record [94]. It may be that some victims are considered either more deserving or more believable [95].

The fourth set of cues involve whether a case is conforming or exceptional. When handling many cases, lawyers and judges develop patterns in interpreting cues and see some cases as typical or normal cases. These **conforming cases** are the type the court handles most regularly. Based on courthouse prioritization, worker assumptions, and legal reasoning, these cases tend to lead to particular decision-making. Designating some types of cases as normal or conforming is a product of negotiated order: criminal court lawyers develop informal routines within the framework of formal rules that treat "normal" offenses less stringently and reduce charges against those defendants through plea bargaining [96]. Sociologist Jeffrey Ulmer cites judges who describe how they dispose of familiar cases in a routine fashion:

> With an eye to knowing how overburdened everybody is, I might call up the lawyers and say, "Hey, what's the problem with this case? It looks like a garden variety burglary," or whatever. Then I'll signal a sentence that I think is appropriate and everybody knows what's going to happen, and it'll be a plea.

According to another judge:

> I say, "make it an open guilty plea." They can just trust that I will do what the guidelines require, or else go below them. I keep telling people—I told one defense attorney today that I did three felony thefts last week and all of them got probation. Hint, hint, hint—do an open plea ... Now I don't do that on homicides or rapes, but some of these cases are really nonsense, and I don't want to hear it [97].

Cases that do not conform to definitions of a normal case are called **exceptional cases**. Lawyers and judges cannot rely on the informal routines of the court and therefore probe these unusual cases more deeply to find an appropriate strategy. This leads them to tap into other sources of interpretation, such as stereotypes about the non-criminal status of the defendant, partisan affiliation, likely outcome of various rulings, scientific evidence, and policy analysis [98]. The strategies of assessing a case are detailed in Chapter 6.

Physical Environment of a Court: Buildings and Technology

Most discussion about courts covers social and historical aspects, such as legal principles and the formal organization. However, lawyers and judges "operate in a common task environment, which provides common resources and imposes common constraints on their actions" [99]. The task environment— or the material, physical setting in which courts operate—influences legal decision-making, and the distribution of these resources is not equal, which explains some of the variation in how courts process cases [100].

The buildings are the most salient part of the built environment. Architecture structures interaction. In many courthouses, for instance, attorneys do not have a chamber attached to the courtroom and therefore must meet with their clients, witnesses, experts, and other attorneys in unused jury rooms, the lockup, the bailiff's room, break rooms, or even hallways or bathrooms. Sometimes their offices are blocks away from the court. Some of these office spaces provide meeting rooms for interviews and discussions, whereas others are small and provide little opportunity to discuss sensitive matters in private. Each situation affects the amount of attention the attorney can give to that part of the case and the decisions they make [101].

A particular aspect of the physical environment is technology, which affects evidence, internal case processing, and communications. At the basic level, technologies include vehicles available for the attorneys to do investigations, cell phones, and closed-circuit television that can reduce the need to transfer defendants from the jail to initial appearances and preliminary hearings. Forensics, discussed more below, often involves technology in the analysis of fingerprints, semen, bullets, blood, hairs, DNA, hand writing, shoe prints, paint, teeth, toxins, psychology, intelligence, witness identification, computers, cell phones, and so on [102].

Computers and network systems include basic functions but are increasingly used for critical functions, such as serving legal documents. Increased levels of automation allow for case tracking; monitoring caseload and disposition outcomes; docket scheduling; information sharing among law enforcement, prosecutors, courts, probation/parole, and corrections; and the

Integration of research to inform sentencing [103]. Automatic notifications and reminders reduce non-appearances at hearings and trials, which even in minor cases will lead to an arrest warrant, and therefore warrants and jail costs [104].

The Local Legal Culture of Courtroom Workgroups

An essential aspect of negotiated order and ecological studies is the local legal culture of a court, or "the practitioner attitudes and norms governing case handling and participant behavior in a criminal court" [105]. When court workers negotiate the formal rules, official job duties, tasks of other workers, actual cases, and physical environment, they are not left with personal codes of conduct. They generally develop standard, local procedures that help them collectively manage the uncertainty of the work and create predictability in the case outcomes [106].

In their groundbreaking research, political scientists James Eisenstein and Herbert Jacob describe the workers as forming courtroom workgroups. These courtroom workgroups provide stability and familiarity within the ecology of the court system [107]. In these groups, workers learn and follow routines, communicate informally, do each other favors, and sanction those who do not cooperate. No two courtroom workgroups are alike. However, they all have, to a greater or lesser degree, a common task environment, a network of relationships and communication, and processes of socialization.

Lawyer and judges handle their tasks as a group activity that depends on constant communication. They share caseloads, cases, and all the stages of the cases; the formal tasks of processing the case while protecting rights; records and evidence; and decision-making regarding the cases [108]. The workers must continuously communicate within networks of relationships to carry out these decision-making tasks.

Some communication is unilateral, and some is adversarial, but mostly their communication seems to be negotiation and cooperation [109]. Their tasks are interdependent, so they tend to employ reciprocal accommodations—in which individuals provide assistance to one another to accomplish work-related objectives—and develop bonds of reciprocity. Their common focal concerns—or the limited features of the case they think are important—enable them to quickly assess, rank, and dispose of cases [110]. Research varies, but some focal concerns that probably influence decision-making include perceived dangerousness of the defendant, blameworthiness of the defendant, use of a weapon, pretrial release or detention, race of the defendant, and deservedness of the victim [111].

An example of cooperative decision-making is the principle of limited methods, in which they work together to come up with least harsh sentence necessary to achieve the goals of punishment. Minor cases, for instance, may quickly have charges reduced or dropped because of the shared attitude that the process of getting arrested and being prosecuted was an adequate punishment [112]. Sometimes the courtroom workgroup will even undermine a legislative effort in order to maintain their mutual interpretations and patterns, such as changing charges to avoid mandatory minimums, departing from sentencing guidelines, or narrowly applying laws such as the Trafficking Victims Protection Act of 2000, which attempts to increase penalties for forced prostitution [113].

Through processes of on-the-job socialization, workers learn the attitudes, behavioral patterns, and local norms of the court they work in. The group norms, tacit knowledge, and negotiated order is maintained by group and personal expectations [114]. Given the similar tasks, task environments, networks, and socialization, courtroom workgroups tend to process similar cases in a similar fashion, even when multiple prosecutors and multiple defense attorneys work on the same case [115].

Socialization occurs in each courthouse, and the process is tightly coupled because the formal structure powerfully shapes informal socialization. Yet, each courtroom workgroup varies in its degree of cohesiveness. Courts with high worker turnover, more rotation of workers between offices, more young attorneys, and higher rates of privately retained defense attorneys tend to have lower cohesion among the workers. These courthouses tend to have less consensus on how to handle cases, lower rates of mutual accommodations, and less negotiation. They tend to be more adversarial, have more trials, and have more "break downs" of the docket because the unpredictability of trials makes it hard to stay with the schedule. One study found that the prosecutors who have less than 5 years of experience spend 35 percent less time in the initial screening of cases but end up spending nearly twice as much time bringing cases to disposition, largely because they decide to take more cases to trial [116].

High-cohesion courtroom workgroups, however, generally have worked together for longer and tend to work out resolutions cooperatively prior to going before the judges, which reduces the average time from initial appearance to case disposal. This avoids the "risk" of formal, public, lengthy, unpredictable, and recorded trials and settles conforming cases with guilty pleas [117]. These workers tend to share attitudes of cues and focal concerns, normal cases, and appropriate punishments and treatments.

A courtroom workgroup, even a cohesive one, is not deterministic of behaviors: not everyone in the group will adhere all the time to the same informal rules [118]. The attorneys may not agree on the strength of a case or an appropriate plea, and judges often vary in their rulings on similar cases [119]. Research has found that workers hold different notions of justice and that they vary on measures of values and attitudes, including:

- attitudes toward crime
- law-and-order attitudes (Female judges may sentence slightly more harshly, especially repeat offenders, and especially black repeat offenders.)
- policy preferences
- attitudes toward social science research as good evidence;
- conceptions of one's role (e.g., crime fighter or upholder of all laws, including procedural laws) and their self-esteem
- inclination toward "cause lawyering," that is, "lawyers who use the law as a means of creating social change in addition to a means of helping individual clients"
- attitudes toward particular populations, such as American Indians
- attitudes toward diversity (such that female attorneys and judges receive less respect) [120]

EXTERNAL ECOLOGY: THE WORLD OUTSIDE THE COURTS

As demonstrated above, legal decision-making draws from the legal frame of U.S. courts as well as organizational features within the courthouse. Factors outside of the court, however, also affect the administration of justice [121]. This external ecology of legal action is the social context of the court system that is not controlled by the court system or its actors and includes:

- social conditions and attitudes at the national and community levels
- election and appointment process for judges and court lawyers
- legislative branch policies
- executive branch policies
- research and science (both legitimate science and folk science)
- media and advocacy organizations
- law school and professional legal organizations

Some scholars call these "linkages" between influences outside the courtroom and decision-making inside the courtroom [122]. It is impossible to understand the operations of U.S. criminal courts without understanding these linkages along with the influences of legal principles, legal reasoning, and the internal ecology of courts [123].

Courts and Society

Legal philosopher Eugen Ehrlich [124] described courts as part of "living law": legal norms emerge out of an interaction between social conditions and formal laws. In Chapter 2, we saw how macro-level social conditions, such as the ideas of the Enlightenment and the rise of professionalism, shaped U.S. courts. Courts, in other words, are not legalistic machines or insular subcultures. Popular values temper legalism and courtroom norms [125].

On the national level, the U.S. courts have changed as a result of wars, public fear, technology, and shifting notions of equality. The amorphous "war on terrorism" has expanded police powers domestically, such as enhancing the government's ability to spy on citizens, and weakened the courts' ability to review those actions. Increases in public fear have also lead to changes in laws and courts. Beginning in the 1960s, the fear of illegal drugs increased, which led to the panoply of drug laws that are collectively called the War on Drugs, which led to a historically unmatched number of cases coming into criminal courts [126]. Courtroom workgroups responded and sent millions of Americans to prison [127].

As technology changes, courts often create new precedent, such as ruling on wiretapping and monitoring Internet use [128]. As artificial intelligence advances, the courts may have to address the issues of intent and culpability of robots. As Americans have shifted from more prejudicial attitudes toward attitudes of greater equality, the courts have generally been in line. When the Supreme Court ruled in 1896 that the separation of the races in public facilities was acceptable and constitutional, the dominant ideology was that blacks were inferior. The dominant ideology after World War II started to shift more toward equality, and in 1954 the Court ruled against the state of Kansas, stating that separate educational facilities are inherently unequal [129]. Similar shifts in ideology and court rulings can be seen in other areas, such as equality of the sexes [130]. Not only has there been a move toward social equality in the appellate rulings, but the courts have also become more aware of rape cases and less likely to blame the victim [131].

The social structure of individual communities, of course, varies, and courts are part of these local cultures [132]. Research on local culture and public opinion finds that both have a partial influence on judicial decision-making [133]. Court workers often grew up in the same region, read the same news as their neighbors, socialize with people in the community, and are often elected. As a New Orleans judge who had to rule on a school integration case told researchers, "[We] live in a white, middle-class suburb and my neighbors feel pretty strongly against busing [as a means of integrating public school students] and I have to be careful not to express my thoughts on the matter in front of them. My wife gets this kind of 'static' from the neighbors all the time" [134]. It is unreasonable to assume that this type of social experience will not influence the decision-making of the courtroom workgroup. Local community characteristics affect the cases that come to court, decisions to charge, sentencing outcomes, and court structure [135].

Research on court workers' decisions indicates that the punitiveness of local courtroom actors increases, especially toward minorities and men, as the following increases:

- political conservatism
- racism
- rate of evangelical Christian residents
- the dominance of one Christian denomination
- economic inequality [136]

The same tendency toward punitiveness is found in suburban and rural courts when compared to urban courts [137]. A similar influence is that prosecutors seem to be less likely to prosecute cases of assisted suicide or marijuana production in communities with strong support for these activities [138].

Local communities do not just set up the cultural context of state courts but also usually fund them, at least partially. If tax revenue declines, chances are good that there will be a reduction in the criminal justice system and services that reduce crime [139]. Unemployment and depressed wages could also affect how judges rule in cases, such as offering more leniency to certain types of economic offenses or supporting more economic regulations [140].

Election, Appointment, and Post-Government Employment of Judges, Prosecutors, and Defense Attorneys

There are several ways to become a judge or attorney. All are political and therefore may affect decision-making [141]. Most frontline prosecutors and public defenders are hired as salaried or contract workers. However, judges and chief prosecutors and defense attorneys are appointed or elected [142]. Appointments are made by other political branches, such as governors appointing state judges. Most states, however, have some form of judicial election [143]. Many argue that elections cost so much money that they reduce the independence and integrity of the judiciary [144]. Others argue that elections make courtroom workers accountable to the public [145]. This controversy is explored in Chapter 15. Similar to the influence of elections, favors such as lucrative contracts and promises of post-government employment may influence decision-making. This influence may be subtle but is nonetheless significant [146].

Legislature: Statutes, Jurisdiction, Funding, and Oversight

Congress is supreme in legislative matters, and it is legislation that sets the boundaries of judicial authority [147]. Changes that occur regularly in statutes and codes have an immediate effect on prosecutorial workload and court dockets. The main areas in which legislative actions can alter court actions are:

- passing criminal statutes, which alter prosecutorial decisions to charge, plea bargain and trial rates, rate of juveniles automatically transferred to adult courts, aggravating circumstances attached to crimes, and rates and predictability of certain types of sentences
- passing procedural laws, which can change the use of grand juries, require the inclusion of victims, and add more paperwork to each case
- changing jurisdictional boundaries and establishing specialized courts, which will change the types of cases the courtroom workgroup has to handle
- deciding appropriations, which will affect funding for indigent defense, assistants and experts, physical resources, and so on [148]

As a couple of examples, consider the criminalization of some behaviors and court budgets. The power to write substantive law is one of the greatest powers of a democratic government, and use of the power has pushed court workers into particular actions. Southern courts, for instance, would convict and punish a black person for looking a white person in the eye, known as "reckless eyeballing" [149], because that was prohibited by law. In terms of budgets, courts may deal with ideals like due process, but they still need buildings, staff, and other resources, and those are getting scarcer. Since the recession of 2008, the state court budgets have shrunk in nearly all states [150]. The American Bar Association (ABA) estimates the overall cuts to be between 10 percent and 15 percent, with some jurisdictions like San Francisco and Atlanta cutting around 40 percent of the court budget [151].

Prosecutor and defense attorney offices in many jurisdictions have lost assistants, investigators, and even attorneys. Case backlogs are growing and defendants are being released before a plea is even reached; some prosecutor offices are ignoring nearly all misdemeanors or nonviolent crimes and using less forensic evidence; civil cases are being delayed even more; and indigent defense is shrinking at a greater rate [152]. Supreme Court Chief Justice John Roberts calls the current situation a "constitutional crisis" because judges are leaving the bench for higher paying jobs and competent attorneys may be less attracted to court jobs.

Executive Branch: Appointments, Enforcement of Laws, Detention, and Punishment of the Convicted

Within the operations of the criminal justice system, the executive branch bookends the courts: it operates the police and the most of correctional system. Police are the frontline law enforcers, and the quality and style of their work affects the decisions of courtroom actors. Focus on Discretion illustrates the relationship between the police and prosecutors.

FOCUS ON DISCRETION

Police Action and Prosecutors' Decisions

Police department strategies during arrests, investigations, and bookings, as well as department resources and priorities, affect the quality of the evidence and strength of a case for the prosecution. Consider the following police actions and prosecutor reactions.

The Police...	The Prosecutor...
Search without a warrant	Throws out the case after initial appearance
Have a bad relationship with the community	Pleas a case down because witnesses will not cooperate
Write reports in a sloppy or overly honest manner	Dismisses or pleas the case down

The Police...	The Prosecutor...
Store evidence in a disorganized or contaminated manner	Excludes critical evidence from trial
Interview witnesses, especially children, inappropriately [153]	Spends time re-interviewing witnesses
Provide few patrols in remote areas	Dismisses cases for lack of evidence [154]
Focus on arresting more drug users	Prosecutes more drug dealers [155]

Question

Explain why the activities of the police affect the actions of the prosecutor. For example, why would the prosecutor have trouble with witnesses if the police have a bad relationship with the community?

In addition to police, the state executive branches operate most jails, which hold defendants awaiting hearings and trials and incarcerate people sentenced to less than 1 year and prisons, which generally incarcerate people sentenced to a year or more. Alternatives to incarceration and availability of jail or prison beds may influence sentence recommendations and prosecutors' decisions to charge more than the legal aspects of the case [156]. For instance, a prosecutor is probably not going to spend time on cases that lead to county jail sentences if the jail is over capacity and already giving early release to all non-violent misdemeanor inmates.

Finally, we must remember that prosecutors are fundamentally law enforcers and typically employed by the executive branch. This means they carry out the directives or preferences of the chief executive leader, whether it is to focus more on white-collar crime or to focus more on domestic violence [157].

Research, Science, and Pseudoscience

Research is part of the social structure of courts and can be seen in jury selection, the use of DNA evidence, and rehabilitation programs. This includes good science and research, such as DNA evidence. However, it also includes information that uses scientific rhetoric but is not verified using the scientific method. The National Academy of Sciences has found that most forensic sciences—such as fingerprints, ballistics, arson analysis, and bite marks—are plagued with an absence of scientific verification; unprofessional testing and presentation; and structural bias when the laboratory is housed in the police department. Psychology and psychiatry in courts suffer from similar flaws. This means that defendants have been sentenced to years in prison or death based on unscientific forensic evidence. Research indicates that unscientific evidence leads to about 20,000 wrongful felony convictions annually in the United States [172]. Illinois Governor George Ryan was motivated by similar research when he commuted all inmates on death row to life in prison.

Media, Citizen Groups, and Industry Pressures

Other external influences on legal action come from media and organizations that push for court change. The media not only have the constitutionally protected right to monitor courts but also influence legal decision-making. Selective media coverage frames how people understand the courts and what courtroom actors must take that into account when pursuing cases and preparing for elections. Media attention, especially television cameras, is also likely to compel judges and lawyers to change their behaviors during trials and may contaminate juries by giving them information that would not be admitted into the trial *per se* [158].

The "CSI effect" is a term commonly used to indicate that jurors may expect more extensive "crime scene investigation" forensic evidence than is available in most real trials. Research is not clear on the effect on jurors, but attorneys may nonetheless feel compelled to include it as often as possible. The media's heavy and selective reporting can also create moral panics, or increased fear of particular offenses, which can lead to more people contacting the police and more cases ending up on the prosecutor's desk.

Judges must also decide when to suppress the media. The Supreme Court has given trial and appellate judges conditional authority to limit media access to hearings, relocate hearings to another jurisdiction with less media coverage, prohibit lawyers and others from communicating with the media, and isolating jurors from the media [159]. Courts in the Media considers what level of media access is appropriate.

COURTS IN THE MEDIA

Television and the Courts

The press is considered the "fourth estate" or fourth branch of government because of its critical role in keeping the government transparent. It is the only industry explicitly protected in the Constitution. This is why members of the press are allowed to attend hearings and trials, and even to televise them. But in the *Estes v. Texas* (1965) and *Sheppard v. Maxwell* (1966) cases, the Supreme Court ruled that excessive media coverage at pretrial hearings or during a trial can prejudice a jury enough as to deny a defendant a fair trial.

Question

Should cameras be allowed in all courtrooms in order to keep an eye on the courts? Should they be prohibited because they turn the courts into a circus and expose innocent people to public condemnation? Is there a compromise between these two positions?

Overlapping with the media are citizen and industry groups that advocate for change in the law and courts. Social movements are citizen-based efforts to bring about change. Sometimes these groups can be short-lived when citizens organize quickly to protest a case, often demanding increased charges or reduced or dismissed charges [160]. Other social movements involve established activist organizations, such as the NAACP's Legal Defense Fund, Project Innocence, the National Organization of Women, the American Indian Movement, and the Megan Nicole Kanka Foundation. These groups persist over time and take up multiple legal issues. They submit *amici* briefs, organize rallies, lobby lawmakers, provide *pro bono* counsel, and use test cases [161].

Such groups have succeeded in agenda setting, or changing court behaviors by amplifying one topic of reform, such as victims' rights, over others [162]. In other cases, industry organizations, such as the National Rifle Association and American Petroleum Institute, will use similar tactics to change decisions on a case or to change the context in which those decisions are made [163]. Such groups can also fund judicial campaigns and alter court actions indirectly by pressuring the legislature to change the laws [164].

Judicial Apparatuses: Law School, the Bar, and Other Professional Associations

The final, but no less relevant, source of external pressures on legal decision-making are law schools and professional legal organizations. The professionalization of courts a century ago gave rise to both these entities: law schools are accredited by the ABA and provide a largely standardized curriculum to all law students. As discussed earlier, this frames students' decision-making with similar legal principles and legal reasoning. As Harvard law Professor Duncan Kennedy writes, "students act affirmatively within the channels cut for them."

Law school teaches the ideology, hierarchy, and ultimately the logic of law, and students adopt that as a form of common sense thinking [165]. This system constantly filters out those who cannot or will not conduct themselves according to the legal imperatives (such as a prosecutor or judge who refuses to enforce drug laws) and retains and promotes those who conform. Therefore, those within the courts almost universally structure their decisions to align with the mandates of law and legal reasoning, even if conformity perpetuates problems such as inequality [166].

Legal organizations also shape the post-law school work environment. The ABA and the state bar associations also enforce codes of ethic, such as rules regarding recusal and punishment for violations of ethics. The threat of being dismissed or suspended from the bar and prohibited from practicing law has a deterrent effect on legal decision-making. The ABA and other organizations, such as the National Center for State Courts, American Judicature Society, National District Attorneys Association, the National Association of Criminal Defense Lawyers, National Legal Aid and Defender Association, and the American Judges Association, also affect courts by lobbying Congress, recommending appointees, and providing research.

THE SOCIAL SELECTION OF DISCRIMINATION: RACE AND THE COURTS

Since the signing of the Civil Rights Act of 1964, much progress has been made, particularly with the abolition of laws that explicitly treated minorities more harshly. Nonetheless, given that the principle of the U.S. courts is equality before the law, it is important to take measure of persistent inequality. Efforts have been made to eliminate prejudice through the rationalization of procedures such as sentencing guidelines, but non-legal factors still influence decision-making, even if less intensely than in the past. Judicial morality, victim involvement, and attitudes among the voting public all allow for prejudice and bias to enter the actions of courtroom actors [167].

The research on race and courts has shown that the merits of a case have the largest effect on case outcomes but that race will often have a slight influence on decisions above and beyond the material facts. This race effect is the result of the election of law-and-order judges whose harsh sentences tend to fall more heavily on minority men; the reduction of state funding for public defenders in jurisdictions with a greater fear of a "minority threat"; public defenders representing black clients slightly less vigorously; minorities receiving less favorable bail and greater rates of preventive detention; minorities receiving harsher sentences, including execution, for particular types of crimes; minorities less often receiving intermediate sentences; and whites receiving slightly more leniency in sentencing [168]. This does not even account for racial disparities in policing, arrests, probation assignment and revocation, treatment in prison, and parole decisions.

If we view the cumulative effect of these patterns through the logic of natural selection, we can identify the social selection of discrimination in which small discriminatory practices and outcomes will have a profound multiplier effect over time on the individual, community, and nation. Consider the approximately 1 million annual felony convictions, of which approximately 40 percent are of defendants who are black. That is approximately 400,000 minority convictions every year (excluding Hispanics, who are sometimes counted as white and other minority groups) [169]. If there is only a 1 percent total race effect in convictions and sentencing—which is lower than the research indicates and actually excludes the race effect at multiple stages—that means every year nearly 4,000 black people receive a criminal record or harsher court-ordered punishment because of their race [170].

Over a 20-year period, or one generation, then, the justice system disadvantages an additional 80,000 black people, weakening their families and neighborhoods. Approximately 80 percent, or 64,000, are black males [171]. Consider the fallout this has for individuals, families, and communities: more time in prison, difficulty finding housing after release, difficulty finding employment, exclusion from some jobs, decrease in income, denial of welfare assistance, damaged credit, loss of rights like voting and gun ownership, increased police surveillance and questioning, family discord, mental and physical health problems, decreased self-esteem and self-efficacy, stigmatization of children, greater rates of poverty, reduced influence of positive role models, increased delinquency, and increased prejudicial attitudes and fear of a minority threat. Even more troubling is that the race effect is likely larger than 1 percent.

SUMMARY

1. Understand that decision-making and actions vary from one court to another.
   - The variables that influence legal decision-making can be arranged into three categories. (1) Legal principles explain how the U.S. court system is arranged according to old principles, such as due process, the adversarial system, and exclusive jurisdictions. (2) Internal ecology refers to variables that arise within the courthouse. (3) External ecology is the large array of societal pressures that affect the people working in the courts.

2. Explain what negotiated order is and how it helps explain variation across courtrooms.
   - Negotiated order is the patterns or routines among the workers that emerge over time as the workers interact with the institutional frame, each other, and external organizations and conditions.

3. Define legal principles and explain how they influence legal decision-making.
   - Legal principles are standards used to formulate the law. Due process and legality dictate the type of court system in the United States and frame the actions of legal workers. These principles encompass the other principles, such as reasonable doubt, right to counsel and confrontation, and judicial review.

4. Explain the process of legal reasoning and how it guides and constrains legal decision-making.
   - Legal reasoning is the evaluative process that lawyers and judges use to determine the legal relevance of a case and the strategic process of preparing a case for trial. It involves examining the facts of a case in light of the principles, laws, and rules; identifying the most relevant legal facts; and then building the case. Legal reasoning narrows the view of what is relevant, binds the practitioners to a logic that is historical and internal to the U.S. system of law and justice, and prioritizes specific aspects of reality over other aspects.

5. Discuss ecological perspectives of the courts.
   - A court's internal ecology includes its organizational structure and job duties, types of cases and protocol for handling them, buildings and technology, and the interactions of the workers themselves. The external ecology includes the other branches of government, elections, law schools, and social pressures such as local community attitudes, citizen activists, interest groups, and media.

6. Tell why the structure and decision-making patterns vary from court to court.
   - Working conditions affect the choices the courtroom workers make. Internal ecology refers to the social attributes within a particular courthouse or local court system where, for the most part, the same people work on thousands of cases together.

7. Describe how factors outside the court also affect the administration of justice.
   - The external ecology of legal action is the social context of the court system that is not controlled by the court system or its actors. It includes: social conditions and attitudes at the national and community levels; election and appointment process for judges and court lawyers; legislative branch policies; executive branch policies;

research and science; media and advocacy organizations; and law school and professional legal organizations.

8. Describe non-legal factors that influence decision-making.

- Judicial morality, victim involvement, and attitudes among the voting public all allow for prejudice and bias to enter the actions of courtroom actors. The merits of a case have the largest effect on case outcomes, but race will often have a slight influence on decisions above and beyond the material facts.

Questions

1. How do decision-making and actions vary from one court to another?
2. What is negotiated order? How does it help to explain variation across courtrooms?
3. What are legal principles? Explain how they influence legal decision-making.
4. What is the process of legal reasoning? How does it guide and constrain legal decision-making?
5. What are the ecological perspectives of the courts?
6. How do structure and decision-making patterns vary from court to court?
7. How do factors outside the court affect the administration of justice?
8. How do nonlegal factors influence decision-making?

REFERENCES

[1] Kairys D. The politics of law: a progressive critique. New York, NY: Pantheon Books; 1990. p. 2–8. See also Milovanovic D. A primer in the sociology of law. New York, NY: Harrow and Heston; 1988. [In Chapter 6, Milovanovic describes the "mystification" of law, including a unique language and arcane rituals.]

[2] National Conference of State Legislatures. Legislator data and services, <www.ncsl.org/legislatures-elections/legisdata/legislator-data-and-services-overview.aspx>; 2009. Bureau of Justice Statistics. Local police, <bjs.ojp.usdoj.gov/index.cfm?ty=tp&tid=71>; 2012. Federal Bureau of Investigation. Crime in the United States: police employee data, <www2.fbi.gov/ucr/cius2009/police/index.html>; 2012. Bureau of Labor Statistics, Occupational outlook handbook, police and detectives, <www.bls.gov/oco/ocos160.htm>; March, 2012. Bureau of Labor Statistics, Occupational outlook handbook. Lawyers, <www.bls.gov/ooh/Legal/Lawyers.htm>; April, 2012. Statistics Division Office of Judges Programs, U.S. courts. Judicial business of the United States courts. Washington, DC: U.S. Government Printing Office; 2010: Online at <www.uscourts.gov/uscourts/Statistics/JudicialBusiness/2009/JudicialBusinespdfversion.pdf>. Bureau of Labor Statistics, Occupational outlook handbook: probation officers and correctional treatment specialists, <www.bls.gov/ooh/community-and-social-service/probation-officers-and-correctional-treatment-specialists.htm>; 2012. Statistics Division Office of Judges Programs, U.S. courts. Judicial business of the United States courts. Washington, DC: U.S. Government Printing Office; 2010: Online at <www.uscourts.gov/uscourts/Statistics/JudicialBusiness/2009/JudicialBusinespdfversion.pdf>.

[3] Kleinig J. The ethics of policing. Cambridge, UK: Cambridge University Press; 1996. [1. Kleinig cites American Bar Foundation research from 1956.]

[4] Dworkin R. Taking rights seriously. Cambridge, MA: Harvard University Press; 1977. p. 31. Dworkin describes making choices within the "belt of restrictions".

[5] Loevinger L. An introduction to legal logic. Indiana Law J 1952;27(4):471−522.

[6] Langevoort DC. Behavioral theories of judgment and decision-making in legal scholarship: a literature review. Vanderbilt Law Rev 1998;51(6):1499−540. Frank J. Law and the modern mind. New York, NY: Coward-McCann; 1949. McGloin JM, Sullivan CJ, Kennedy LW. When crime appears: the role of emergence. New York, NY: Routledge; 2012. Kritzer HM. Are court decisions consistent with public preferences? Judicature 2008;92(2):84−5.

[7] Wellman B. Network analysis: some basic principles. Sociol Theory 1983;1:155−200.

[8] Littrell WB. Bureaucratic justice: police, prosecutors, and plea bargaining. Beverly Hills, CA: Sage Publications; 1979. p. 51−6.

[9] Svensson R. The interplay between doctors and nurses—a negotiated order perspective. Sociol Health Illn 1996;18(3):379−98.

[10] There is no firmly established use of "organization" and "institution." In this book, we use the latter to refer to large systems that stretch across many places (like legal principles) and the former to categorize local systems in which people operate (like a courthouse). In some of the negotiated order literature, "institution" is used to refer to both the larger systemic frame and a single local company or building, like a hospital. In this section, we adhere to that usage, but elsewhere in the book, we use our distinction between the two.

[11] Basu O, Dirsmith M, Gupta P. The coupling of the symbolic and the technical in an institutionalized context: the negotiated order of the GAO's audit reporting process. Am Sociol Rev 1999;64(4):506−26.

[12] Strauss A. Negotiations: varieties, contexts, processes and social order. San Francisco, CA: Jossey-Bass; 1978.

[13] For a contrary view that rejects the influence of formal goals, structure, and training on workers' behavior, see Meyer JW, Rowan B. Institutionalized organizations: formal structure as myth and ceremony. Am J Sociol 1977;83(2):340−63.

[14] Hallett T. Between deference and distinction: interaction ritual through symbolic power in an educational institution. Soc Psychol Q 2007;70(2):148−71.

[15] Strauss A, et al. The hospital and its negotiated order. In: Freidson E, editor. The hospital in modern society. New York, NY: Free Press; 1963. See also Strauss A. Continual permutations of action. New York, NY: De Gruyter; 1993. Blumer H. Symbolic interactionism: perspective and method. Englewood Cliffs, NJ: Prentice Hall; 1969. Fine GA. Negotiated orders and organizational cultures. Annu Rev Sociol 1984;10:239−62. Fine GA. The sad demise, mysterious disappearance, and glorious triumph of symbolic interactionism. Annu Rev Sociol 1993;19:61−87. Maines D. In search of mesostructure. Urban Life 1982;11(3):267−79. Nisim S, Benjamin O. The speech of services procurement: the negotiated order of commodification and dehumanization of cleaning employees. Hum Organ 2010;69(3):221−32. Altheide DL. Mediating cutbacks in human services: a case study in the negotiated order. Sociol Q 1988;29(3):339−55.

[16] Bourdieu P, Accardo A, Ferguson PP. The weight of the world: social suffering in contemporary society. Stanford, CA: Stanford University Press; 1999.

[17] Garfinkel H. [1967; reprint] Studies in ethnomethodology. Malden, MA: Polity Press; 1991. Atkinson P. Ethnomethodology: a critical review. Annu Rev Sociol 1988;14:441−65. Giddens A. The constitution of society: outline of the theory of structuration. Berkeley, CA: University of California Press; 1984. calls this "practical consciousness." For a critique of tacit knowledge, see. Turner SP, Factor RA. Max Weber: the lawyer as social thinker. London: Routledge; 1994.

[18] Altheide. Mediating cutbacks in human services. Hall P, Spencer-Hall DA. The social conditions of the negotiated order. Urban Life 1982;11(3):328−49.

[19] Klinger DA. Negotiating order in patrol work: an ecological theory of police response to deviance. Criminology 1997;35:277−306. Brown M. Working the streets: police discretion and the dilemmas of reform. New York, NY: Russell Sage Foundation; 1981.

[20] Orton DJ, Weick KE. Loosely coupled systems: a reconceptualization. Acad Manage Rev 1990;15(2):203−23.

[21] Manning PK. Police work: the social organization of policing. Cambridge, MA: MIT Press; 1977. Klinger DA. Negotiating order in patrol work: an ecological theory police response to deviance. Criminology 1997;35:277−306. Manning's work on police is insightful research on how police and police dispatchers create their own rules of communication and behavior within the frame of the official rules. See Manning PK. Producing drama: symbolic communication and the police. Symbolic Interact 1982;5:223−41. Manning PK. Symbolic communication, signifying calls and the police response. Cambridge, MA: MIT Press; 1988. See also Meehan AJ. I do not prevent crime, I prevent calls: policing as a negotiated order. Symbolic Interact 1992;15(4):455−80.

[22] Frontline. 2012. "LAPD Blues." < http://www.pbs.org/wgbh/pages/frontline/shows/lapd/scandal/cron.html > (accessed August 9, 2012)

[23] Thomas J. Some aspects of negotiated order, loose coupling and mesostructure in maximum security prisons. Symbolic Interact 1984;7(2):13−31.

[24] Parhankangas A, et al. Negotiated order and network form organizations. Syst Res Behav Sci 2005;22(5):431−52.

[25] Ibid.

[26] Kammen M. A machine that would go of itself: the constitution in American culture. New York, NY: Alfred A. Knopf, 1987. Supreme Court Justice Stephen Breyer, YouTube, Future: will the people follow the court? <www.youtube.com/watch?v=RxyXPd0f18Q&lr=1>; History: challenges the court has faced, <www.youtube.com/watch?v=-bKLXQzZXLk&lr=1>.

[27] Carp RA, Stidham R, editors. Judicial process in America. 2nd ed. Washington, DC: Congressional Quarterly Press; 1993.

[28] Louisiana has elements of the French system, which is more inquisitorial and cooperative.

[29] Court statistics project. Examining the work of state courts: an analysis of 2009 state court caseloads, <www.courtstatistics.org/Criminal.aspx>; 2011. United States courts. Caseload statistics, <www.uscourts.gov/Statistics/FederalJudicialCaseloadStatistics/FederalJudicialCaseloadStatistics2011.aspx>; 2011, 2012. Bureau of justice statistics, local police. Administrative office of the United States courts, 2011 Annual report of the director: judicial business of the United States courts. Washington, DC: United States Courts, 2012.

[30] Nagorcka F, Stanton M, Wilson MJ. Stranded between artisanship and the truth? A comparative analysis of legal ethics in the adversarial and inquisitorial systems of justice. Melb Univ Law Rev 2005;29(2):448.

[31] Dicey AV, Wade ECS. Introduction to the study of the law of the constitution. London: Macmillan; 1961.

[32] Goodman A, Gonzales J. Judge rules NSA warrantless spy program unconstitutional. Democracy Now; <www.democracynow.org/2006/8/18/there_are_no_hereditary_kings_in>; August 18 2006.

[33] Siegel JR. A theory of justiciability. Tex Law Rev 2007;86(73):74−139.

[34] Rubin S. Law of juvenile justice, with a new model juvenile court act. Dobbs Ferry, NY: Oceana Publications; 1976. Scalia J. Juvenile delinquents in the federal criminal justice system. U.S. Department of Justice, Office of Justice Programs, Bureau of Justice Statistics; 1997. <http://www.bjs.gov/content/pub/pdf/Jdfcjs.pdf>.

[35] Slapper G. How the law works. London: Collins; 2007.

[36] Stelmach J, Brozek B. Methods of legal reasoning. Dordrecht, The Netherlands: Springer; 2006.

[37] Holmes OW. The path of the law. Harv Law Rev 1897;10(8):457−78. Alexander L, Sherwin E. Demystifying legal reasoning. Cambridge, UK: Cambridge University Press; 2008.

[38] Levi EH. An introduction to legal reasoning. Chicago, IL: University of Chicago Press; 1949. Porto BL. The craft of legal reasoning. Fort Worth, TX: Harcourt Brace; 1998. Levi and Porto are two of the more prominent scholars of legal reasoning. See also Wasserstrom RA. The judicial decision: toward a theory of legal justification. Stanford, CA: Stanford University Press; 1961, for a more philosophical interpretation of legal reasoning.

[39] Wrong DH. The oversocialized conception of man in modern sociology. Am Sociol Rev 1961;26(2):183−93. This article presents a useful description on avoiding the "oversocialized" or deterministic view of humans Weber M. [1922; reprint]. In: Roth G, Wittich C, editors. Economy and society. Berkeley, CA: University of California Press; 1978 [Wasserstrom. The judicial decision: toward a theory of legal justification. See Chapter 4].

[40] Wasserstrom. The judicial decision: toward a theory of legal justification, p. 6, 25.

[41] Porto, The craft of legal reasoning, p. 2.

[42] Glaberson W. This is not America: in tiny courts of New York, abuses of law and power. The New York Times, <www.nytimes.com/2006/09/25/nyregion/25courts.html>; September 25, 2006.

[43] Dickson J. Interpretation and coherence in legal reasoning, Stanford encyclopedia of philosophy, Zalta E N, editor, 2010. <plato.stanford.edu/entries/legal-reas-interpret>.

[44] Poland R. Pre-law handbook for undergraduates. St. Augustine, FL: Flagler College; 2012.

[45] Lamond G. Precedent and analogy in legal reasoning, the Stanford encyclopedia of philosophy. E N Zalta, editor. <plato.stanford.edu/entries/legal-reas-prec>.

[46] Jacob H. Using published data: errors and remedies, 10. Beverly Hills, CA: Sage Publications; 1984.

[47] Penman RA. Comprehensible insurance documents: plain English isn't good enough. Canberra: Communication Research Institute of Australia; 1990.

[48] Wagner A, Cheng L. Exploring courtroom discourse: the language of power and control. London: Ashgate; 2011. Milovanovic D. A primer in the sociology of law. New York, NY: Harrow and Heston; 1988.

[49] Dixon J. The organizational context of criminal sentencing. Am J Sociol 1995;100(5):1157−98. Pound R. The law and the people. Chicago, IL: University of Chicago Press; 1910.

[50] Hawley AH. Ecol Hum Ecol 1944 n.p.; 403−40.

[51] Duncan OD, Schnore LF, Rossi P. Cultural, behavioral, and ecological perspectives in the study of social organization. Am J Sociol 1959;65(2):132−53. Foley RA. Another unique species: patterns in human evolutionary ecology. Harlow, Essex, UK: Longman Scientific & Technical; 1987. Hawley AH. Human ecology: a theoretical essay. Chicago, IL: University of Chicago Press; 1986.

[52] Jansen S, Hood R. A framework for high performance prosecutorial services. Washington, DC: Association of Prosecuting Attorneys; 2011. [See p. 11 for a description of courthouses as "communities," which illuminates the uniqueness of each one.]

[53] Ulmer JT. Localized uses of federal sentencing guidelines in four U.S. district courts: evidence of processual order. Symbolic Interact 2005;28(2):255−79.

[54] Dixon. The organizational context of criminal sentencing.Kautt PM. Location, location, location: interdistrict and intercircuit variation in sentencing outcomes for federal drug-trafficking offenses. Justice Q 2002;19(4):633−71.

[55] Duncan, Schnore, Rossi. Cultural, behavioral, and ecological perspectives in the study of social organization. In: Quinn JA, editor. Human ecology. New York, NY: Prentice Hall; 1950.

[56] Jones TM. Ethical decision making by individuals in organizations: an issue-contingent model. Acad Manage Rev 1991;16(2):366−95.

[57] Beverly B. Cook, the socialization of new federal judges: impact on district court business. Wash Univ Law Q 1971;253−79. Murphy WF, Tanenhaus J. The study of public law. New York, NY: Random House; 1972. Kastellec JP. Panel composition and judicial compliance on the U.S. courts of appeals. J Law Econ Organ 2007;23(2):421−41. Srivastava SB, Banaji MR. Culture, cognition, and collaborative networks in organizations. Am Sociol Rev 2011;76(2):207−33.

[58] Noam EM. Resource allocation and access to criminal courts: an economic model. Windsor Yearb Access Justice 1982;2:208−23. Lawson HO, Gletne BJ. Planning in the court environment: perceptions and prospects. Washington, DC: Adjudication Technical Assistance Project, Bureau of Justice Assistance; 1987.

[59] Ermann MD, Lundman RJ, editors. Corporate and governmental deviance: problems of organizational behavior in contemporary society. 5th ed. New York, NY: Oxford University Press; 1996. Pugh DS, editor. Organization theory: selected readings. 3rd ed. New York, NY: Penguin Books; 1990. Watkins-Hayes C. The new welfare bureaucrats: entanglements of race, class, and policy reform. Chicago, IL, 2009.

[60] Hagan J. Parameters of criminal prosecution: an application of path analysis to a problem of criminal justice. J Crim Law Criminol 1974;65(4):536−44. Walker S. Taming the system: the control of discretion in criminal justice, 1950−1990. New York, NY: Oxford University Press; 1993.

[61] Blumberg AS. The practice of law as confidence game: organizational cooptation of a profession. Law Soc Rev 1967;1(2):15−40. Littrell WB. Bureaucratic justice: police, prosecutors, and plea bargaining. Beverly Hills, CA: Sage Publications; 1979. Weber M. Bureaucracy. From Max Weber: essays in sociology, [C. Wright Mills, Trans] Hans Gerth, editor. New York, NY: Oxford University Press; 1958.

[62] Blumberg AS. The practice of law as confidence game: organizational cooptation of a profession. Law Soc Rev 1967;1(2):15−40.

[63] Brown MK. Working the street: police discretion and the dilemmas of reform. New York, NY: Russell Sage Foundation; 1981.

[64] Bureau of Justice Statistics, Indigent defense systems. <bjs.ojp.usdoj.gov/index.cfm?ty=tp&tid=28>; 2012 [accessed October 10, 2012].

[65] Bright SB. Counsel for the poor: the death sentence not for the worst crime but the worst lawyer. Yale Law J 1994;103(7):1835−83.

[66] Nardulli PF. Insider' justice: defense attorneys and the handling of felony cases. J Crim Law Criminol 1986;77(2):379−417. Emmelman DS. Justice for the poor: a study of criminal defense work. In: Sarat A, editor. Law, Justice and Power. London: Ashgate; 2003. Regarding capital cases, see White WS. Litigating in the shadow of death: defense attorneys in capital cases. Ann Arbor, MI: The University of Michigan Press; 2006. Grisham J. The innocent man: murder and injustice in a small town. New York, NY: Bantam Dell; 2006. Laceky T. Fellow inmates in montana adopt freemen legal tactics. Oregonian 1997;26:A30.

[67] Perrow C. Complex organizations: a critical essay. 3rd ed. New York, NY: McGraw-Hill; 1986.

[68] Eisenstein J, Jacob H. Felony justice: an organizational analysis of criminal courts. Boston, MA: Little, Brown and Company; 1977.

[69] Duncan MJ. The (so-called) liability of criminal defense attorneys: a system in need of reform. Brigh Young Univ Law Rev 2002;1(2002):1−52.

[70] Fish PG. The politics of federal judicial administration. Princeton, NJ: Princeton University Press; 1973.

[71] Nugent-Borakove ME, Budzilowicz LM. Do lower conviction rates mean prosecutors' offices are performing poorly? Alexandria, VA: National District Attorneys Association, American Prosecutors Research Institute, Prosecution Performance Measurement Project; 2007.

[72] National Workload Assessment Project. How many cases should a prosecutor handle? Alexandria, VA: American Prosecutors Research Institute, Office of Research & Evaluation; 2002. p. 7.

[73] Smith A, Madden S. Three-minute justice: haste and waste in Florida's misdemeanor courts. Washington, DC: National Association of Criminal Defense Lawyers; 2011.

[74] Eisenstein, Jacob. Felony justice: an organizational analysis of criminal courts, p. 9.

[75] Jacoby JE, Ratledge EC, Gramckow HP. Expedited drug case management programs: issues for program development. Washington, DC: Jefferson Institute for Justice Studies; 1992.

[76] Gioia DA. Why I didn't recognize pinto fire hazards: how organizational scripts channel managers' thoughts and actions. In: Ermann MDavid, Lundman RJ, editors. Corporate and governmental deviance: problems of organizational behavior in contemporary society. 5th ed. New York, NY: Oxford University Press; 1996. p. 139−57. See also Haney-Lopez IF. Racism on trial: the chicano fight for justice. Cambridge, MA: Harvard University Press; 2003. For a discussion of scripts as ostensible "common sense" and Kuhn TS. The structure of scientific revolutions. 2nd ed. Chicago, IL: University of Chicago Press; 1970. For a discussion of "paradigms" as a dominating mode of thought.

[77] Bushway SD, Apel R. Overview of: "a signaling perspective on employment-based reentry programming: training completion as a desistance signal". Criminol Public Policy 2012;11 (1):17−20. [Bushway and Apel use this term to identify successful re-entry programs, but it is useful to apply here.]

[78] Carp, Stidham. Judicial process in America, p. 322−24.

[79] Baum L. Policy goals in judicial gatekeeping: a proximity model of discretionary jurisdiction. Am J Pol Sci 1977;21(1):13−35. Songer DR. Concern for policy outputs as a cue for supreme court decisions on certiorari. J Polit 1979;41(4):1185−94. Pritchett CH. Divisions of opinion among justices of the U.S. supreme court. Am Polit Sci Rev 1941;35:890−8. Murphy WF, Tanenhaus J. The study of public law. New York, NY: Random House; 1972. Provine DM. Case selection in the United States supreme court, 174. Chicago, IL: University of Chicago Press; 1980. Perry HW. Deciding to decide: agenda setting in the United States supreme court. Cambridge, MA: Harvard University Press; 1994. p. 116−25.

[80] Ford DA. Wife battery and criminal justice: a study of victim decision-making. Minneapolis, MN: National Council on Family Relations; 1983.

[81] Johnson BD. Racial and ethnic disparities in sentencing departures across modes of conviction. Criminology 2003;41(2):449−89. Farrell RA, Holmes MD. The social and cognitive structure of legal decision-making. Sociol Q 1991;32(4):529−42.

[82] It is important to note that "race" is a notion invented by humans about 500 years ago. There are no genetically distinct racial groups. Racial categories are social creations, but they still have real effects on people's lives, and criminology uses these categories in its research.

[83] Albonetti CA. Decision making and juvenile justice: an analysis of bias in case processing. Am J Sociol 2003;109(1):253−5. Black DJ. Sociological justice. New York, NY: Oxford

University Press; 1989. Ulmer JT. Social worlds of sentencing: court communities under sentencing guidelines. Albany, NY: State University of New York Press; 1997. Ulmer JT, Kramer JH. Court communities under sentencing guidelines: dilemmas of formal rationality and sentencing disparity. Criminology 1996;34(3):383−408. Steffensmeier D, Demuth S. Ethnicity and sentencing outcomes in U.S. federal courts: who is punished more harshly? Am Sociol Rev 2000;65(5):705−29. Steffensmeier D, Demuth S. Ethnicity and judges' sentencing decisions: Hispanic-black-white comparisons. Criminology 2001;39(1):145−78. Cohen LE, Kluegel JR. Detention decision: a study of the impact of social characteristics and legal factors in two metropolitan juvenile courts. Soc Forces 1979;58(1):146−61.

[84] Albonetti. Decision making and juvenile justice: an analysis of bias in case processing.

[85] Bourdieu P, Wacquant L. An invitation to reflexive sociology. Chicago, IL: University of Chicago Press; 1992.

[86] Steffensmeier, Demuth. Ethnicity and judges' sentencing decisions: Hispanic-black-white comparisons.Ulmer JT, Kurlychek MC, Kramer JH. Prosecutorial discretion and the imposition of mandatory minimum sentences. J Res Crime Delinq 2007;44(4):427−58.

[87] *Furman v. Georgia*, 408 U.S. 238, 240 (1972).

[88] Johnson BD, Dipietro SM. The power of diversion: intermediate sanctions and sentencing disparity under presumptive guidelines. Criminology 2012;50(3):811−50.

[89] Edkins VA. Defense attorney plea recommendations and client race: does zealous representation apply equally to all? Law Hum Behav 2011;35(5):413−25.

[90] Varela JG, et al. Do defense attorney referrals for competence to stand trial evaluations depend on whether the client speaks English or Spanish? Law Hum Behav 2011;35(6):501−11.

[91] Paternoster R. Prosecutorial discretion in requesting the death penalty: a case of victim-based racial discrimination. Law Soc Rev 1984;18(3):437−78.

[92] Ben Cohen G, Smith RJ. The racial geography of the federal death penalty. Wash Law Rev 2010;85(3):425−92. Paternoster R, Brame R. Reassessing race disparities in Maryland capital cases. Criminology 2008;46(4):971−1008. Eberhardt JL, et al. Research report. Psychol Sci 2006;17(5):383−6.

[93] Kramer J, Steffensmeir D. Race and imprisonment decisions. Sociol Q 1993;34(2):357−76.

[94] Beichner D, Spohn C. Modeling the effects of victim behavior and moral character on prosecutors' charging decisions in sexual assault cases. Violence Vict 2012;27(1):3−24.

[95] Erez E, Tontodonato P. The effect of victim participation in sentencing on sentence outcome. Criminology 1990;28(3):451−74.

[96] Sudnow D. Normal crimes: sociological features of the penal code in a public defender office. Soc Probl 1965;12:255−76. Similar patterns are exhibited by the police, see Waegel WB. Case routinization in investigative police work. Soc Probl 1981;28:263−75, and Waegel WB. How police justify the use of deadly force. Soc Probl 1984;32:144−55.

[97] Ulmer, Kramer. Court communities under sentencing guidelines: dilemmas of formal rationality and sentencing disparity, p. 390.

[98] Farrell RA, Holmes MD. The social and cognitive structure of legal decision-making. Sociol Q 1991;32(4):529−42. Carp RA, Rowland CK. Policymaking and politics in the federal district courts. Knoxville, TN: University of Tennessee Press; 1983. Carp, Stidham. Judicial process in America, p. 310−11.

[99] Eisenstein, Jacob. Felony justice: an organizational analysis of criminal courts, p. 10.

[100] Eisenstein, Jacob. Felony justice: an organizational analysis of criminal courts, p. 40−63.

[101] Derber C. The pursuit of attention. New York, NY: Oxford University Press; 2000.

[102] Lissitzyn CB. Forensic evidence in court: a case study approach. Durham, NC: Carolina Academic Press; 2008.

[103] National Workload Assessment Project. How many cases should a prosecutor handle?

[104] U.S. Advisory Commission on Intergovernmental Relations. Guide to the criminal justice system for general government elected officials. Washington, DC: U.S. Advisory Commission on Intergovernmental Relations; 1993.

[105] Church T. Examining local legal culture: practitioner attitudes in four criminal courts. Washington, DC: National Institute of Justice; 1982. See also George Cole's summary of Church's work in performance measures for the criminal justice system. Washington, DC: U.S. Department of Justice, 1993.

[106] Blau P. The dynamics of bureaucracy. Chicago, IL: University of Chicago Press; 1963. Meyer JW, Rowan B. Institutionalized organizations: formal structure as myth and ceremony. Am J Sociol 1977;83(22):340−63. Albonetti CA. An integration of theories to explain judicial discretion. Soc Probl 1991;38(2):247−66.

[107] Eisenstein, Jacob. Felony justice: an organizational analysis of criminal courts, p. 20, 40−64. Eisenstein J, Flemming RB, Nardulli PF. The contours of justice: communities and their courts. Boston, MA: Little, Brown and Company; 1988.

[108] Lowi T, Ginsberg B. American government: freedom and power. 3rd ed. New York, NY: W. W. Norton & Co.; 1994.

[109] Eisenstein, Jacob. Felony justice: an organizational analysis of criminal courts, p. 30−32.

[110] Srivastava, Banaji. Culture, cognition, and collaborative networks in organizations.Fearn NE. A multilevel analysis of community effects on criminal sentencing. Justice Q 2005;22 (4):452−87. Gainey RR, Steen S, Engen RL. Exercising options: an assessment of the use of alternative sanctions for drug offenders. Justice Q 2005;22(4):488−520.

[111] Albonetti. An integration of theories to explain judicial discretion. Fearn. A multilevel analysis of community effects on criminal sentencing. Gainey, Steen, Engen. Exercising options: an assessment of the use of alternative sanctions for drug offenders.

[112] Feeley MM. The process is the punishment. New York, NY: Russell Sage Foundation; 1992.

[113] Ulmer. Social worlds of sentencing: court communities under sentencing guidelines. Ulmer, Kramer. Court communities under sentencing guidelines: dilemmas of formal rationality and sentencing disparity.Harris J, Jesilow P. It's not the same old ball game: three strikes and the courtroom workgroup. Justice Q 2000;17(1):185−203. Ulmer JT. Localized uses of federal sentencing guidelines in four U.S. district courts: evidence of processual order. Symbolic Interact 2005;28(2):255−79. Peters AW. Trafficking in meaning: law, victims, and the state. Res Rep Dig 3. 2011.

[114] Bourdieu P. Outline of a theory of practice. Cambridge, UK: Cambridge University Press; 1977. Coleman JS. Social capital in the creation of human capital. Am J Sociol 1988;94:95−120. See Coleman for an analysis of how personal rational calculations are embedded in a social context Thaler RH, Sunstein CR. Nudge: improving decisions about health, wealth, and happiness. New York, NY: Penguin Books; 2009.

[115] Eisenstein, Jacob. Felony justice: an organizational analysis of criminal courts, p. 72−73.

[116] National Workload Assessment Project, How many cases should a prosecutor handle? p. 6, 28.

[117] Eisenstein, Jacob. Felony justice: an organizational analysis of criminal courts, p. 67−97. Heumann M. Plea bargaining: the experiences of prosecutors, judges, and defense attorneys. Chicago, IL: University of Chicago Press; 1978.

[118] Maynard DW. Defendant attributes in plea bargaining: notes on the modeling of sentencing decisions. Soc Prob 1982;29(4):347−60.

[119] Maveety N, editor. The pioneers of judicial behavior. Ann Arbor, MI: University of Michigan Press; 2002.

[120] Podgorecki A. Law and society. Boston, MA: Routledge; 1974. p. 235−36. Holmes. The path of the law. frank, law and the modern mind. Rawls. J. A Theory of Justice. Cambridge, MA: The Belknap Press of Harvard University Press; 1971. For a classic political science view on this model of judicial decision-making, see Pritchett, "Divisions of Opinion Among Justices of the U.S. Supreme Court." Segal JA, Spaeth HJ. The supreme court and the attitudinal model revisited Cambridge, MA: Cambridge University Press; 2002. p. 86−98. Hettinger VA, Lindquist SA, Martinek WL. Comparing attitudinal and strategic accounts dissenting behavior on the U.S. courts of appeals. Am J Pol Sci 2004;48(1):123−37. Schubert G. The judicial mind. Evanston, IL: Northwestern University Press; 1965, Frank J. Courts on trial. Princeton, NJ: Princeton University Press; 1950. Epstein L, Knight. J. Walter F. Murphy: the interactive nature of judicial decision making. In: Maveety N, editor. The pioneers of judicial behavior. Ann Arbor, MI: University of Michigan Press; 2002. p. 172−92. Hagan J. Extra-legal attributes and criminal sentencing: an assessment of a sociological viewpoint. Law Soc Rev 1974;8:557−83. Hogarth J. Sentencing as a human process. Toronto: University of Toronto Press; 1971. Hagan J. Law, order and sentencing: a study of attitude in action. Sociometry 1975;38(3):374−84. Steffensmeier D, Hebert Chris. Women and men policymakers: does the judge's gender affect the sentencing of criminal defendants? Soc Forces 1999;77 (3):1163−96. Johnson SW, Songer DR. The influence of presidential versus home state senatorial preferences on the policy output of judges on the United States district courts. Law Soc Rev 2002;36(3):658. Redding RE, Repucci ND. Effects of lawyers' socio-political attitudes on their judgments of social science in legal decision making. Law Soc Rev 1999;23(1):31−54. Carp, Stidham. Judicial process in America, p. 313−14. Siemsen C. Emotional trials: the moral dilemmas of women criminal defense attorneys. Boston, MA: Northeastern University Press; 2004. See Siemsen for a description of female defense attorneys. Gibson JL. Personality and elite political behavior: the influence of self esteem on judicial decision making. J Polit 1981;43(1):104−25. Etienne M. The ethics of cause lawyering: an empirical examination of criminal defense lawyers as cause lawyers. J Crim Law Criminol 2005;95(4):1195−260. Hermann JR. American Indian interests and supreme court agenda setting: 1969−1992, October terms. Am Polit Res 1997;25(2):241−60. Bogoch B. Courtroom discourse and the gendered construction of professional identity. Law Soc Inq 1999;24(2):329−75.

[121] Cole GF, Gertz MG, Bunger A. The criminal justice system: politics and policies. 9th ed. Belmont, CA: Wadsworth; 2004. [This text provides a good collection of articles on the relationship between politics and courts.]

[122] Kritzer HM. Are court decisions consistent with public preferences? Judicature 2008;92 (2):84−5.

[123] Brace Paul, Melinda GH. Haves' versus "have nots" in state supreme courts: allocating docket space and wins in power asymmetric cases. Law Soc Rev 2001;35(2):393−413. [They argue that the external variables are the most influential. We find that they provide a necessary but only a partial explanation of legal action.]

[124] Ehrlich E. Fundamental principles of the sociology of law. Cambridge, MA: Harvard University Press; 1936.

[125] Carp, Stidham. Judicial process in America, p. 285.

[126] Barker V. The politics of imprisonment: how the democratic process shapes the way America punishes offenders. New York, NY: Oxford University Press; 2009. Gordon. DR. The justice juggernaut: fighting street crime, controlling citizens. New Brunswick, NJ: Rutgers

University Press; 1991. Garland D. Punishment and modern society: a study in social theory. Chicago, IL: University of Chicago Press; 1990. Garland D. The culture of control: crime and social order in contemporary society. Chicago, IL: University of Chicago Press; 2001.

[127] Garland. Punishment and modern society: a study in social theory. Garland. The culture of control: crime and social order in contemporary society.

[128] Rembar C. The law of the land: the evolution of our legal system, 36. New York, NY: Simon & Schuster; 1980.

[129] *Plessy v. Ferguson*, 163 U.S. 537 (1896); *Brown v. Board of Education of Topeka* (1954).

[130] Baer JA, editor. Women in American law: the struggle toward equality from the new deal to the present. 3rd ed. New York, NY: Holmes & Meier Publishers; 2002. [Similar patterns have been observed internationally. See Hung-En Liu, "Mother or Father: Who Received Custody"? The Best Interests of the Child Standard and Judges Custody Decisions in Taiwan, International J of Law, Policy and the Family 2001; 15(2):185−85. For example, the following cases illustrates the rather recent transition in court rulings and dominant ideology: *Bradwell v. State of Illinois*, 83 U.S. 130 (1873) (allowed states to prohibit women from entering law school); *Goesaert v. Cleary*, 335 U.S. 464 (1948) (allowed states to prohibit women from certain occupations); *Hoyt v. Florida*, 368 U.S. 57 (1961) (allowed states to effectively exclude most women from juries); *Roe v. Wade*, 410 U.S. 113 (1973) (prohibited states from criminalizing all abortions); *United Auto Workers v. Johnson Controls, Inc.*, 499 U.S. 187 (1991) (prohibited companies from discriminating against women); and *United States v. Virginia*, 518 U.S. 515 (1996) (prohibited schools receiving public money from excluding female students).]

[131] Tyson D. Sex, culpability, and the defence of provocation. New York, NY: Routledge; 2012.

[132] Eisenstein F, Nardulli. The contours of justice: communities and their courts. In: Sarat A, Silbey SS, editors. Studies in law, politics, and society: a research annual, 11. Greenwich, CT: JAI Press; 1991. Fearn, A multilevel analysis of community effects on criminal sentencing. Calvin B, Collins PM, Eshbaugh-Soha M. On the relationship between public opinion and decision making in the U.S. courts of appeals. Polit Res Q 2011;64 (4):736−48.

[133] Cook BB. Public opinion and federal judicial policy. Am J Pol Sci 1977;21:576−600. Epstein, Knight. Walter F. Murphy: The interactive nature of judicial decision making, p. 178. Flemming E, Nardulli. The contours of justice: communities and their courts.

[134] Carp, Stidham. Judicial process in America. p. 301. See also their discussion of localism, regionalism, and temporalism, p. 285−300.

[135] Heydebrand W, Seron C. Rationalizing justice: the political economy of federal district courts. Albany, NY: State University of New York Press; 1990.

[136] Sampson RJ, Laub JH. Crime, class, and community: an emerging paradigm. Law Soc Rev 1993;27:255−359. Alexes H, Evans H, Beckett K. Courtesy stigma and monetary sanctions: toward a socio-cultural theory of punishment. Am Sociol Rev 2011;76(2):234−64. Johnson, Dipietro. The power of diversion: intermediate sanctions and sentencing disparity under presumptive guidelines. Fearn. A multilevel analysis of community effects on criminal sentencing.Ulmer JT, Bader C, Gault M. Do moral communities play a role in criminal sentencing? Evidence from Pennsylvania. Sociol Q 2008;49(4):737−68. Helms R, Jacobs D. The political context of sentencing: an analysis of community and individual determinants. Soc Forces 2002;81(2):577−604.

[137] Ulmer. Social worlds of sentencing: court communities under sentencing guidelines. Ulmer, Kramer. Court communities under sentencing guidelines: dilemmas of formal rationality and sentencing disparity. Ulmer JT. Trial judges in a rural court community:

contexts, organizational relations, and interaction strategies. J Contemp Ethnogr 1994;23 (1):79–108. Carp, Stidham. Judicial process in America, p. 297–98.

[138] Daw R, Solomon A. Assisted suicide and identifying the public interest in the decision to prosecute. Crim Law Rev 2010;10:737.

[139] Johnson, Dipietro. The power of diversion: intermediate sanctions and sentencing disparity under presumptive guidelines.

[140] Sommer U, Li Q. Judicial decision making in times of financial crises. Judicature 2011;95 (2):68–77. Stidham R, Carp RA. Trial courts' responses to supreme court policy changes: three case studies. Law Policy Q 1982;4:215–35.

[141] Johnson SW, Songer DR. The influence of presidential versus home state senatorial preferences on the policy output of judges on the United States district courts. Law Soc Rev 2002;36(3):657–75. See also Carp, Stidham. Judicial process in America. p. 340–43. Jacobs H, editor. Justice in America: courts, lawyers, and the judicial process. 4th ed. Boston, MA: Little, Brown and Company; 1984.

[142] Garcia PA. Judicial selection: the process of choosing judges. Chicago, IL: American Bar Association; 1998. Rottman DB. State court organization, 2004. Washington, DC: Bureau of Justice Statistics; 2006.

[143] Hurwitz MS, Lanier DN. Diversity in state and federal appellate courts: change and continuity across 20 years. Justice Syst J 2008;29(1):47–70. For a state by state description, see <www.judicialselection.us>, <www.ncsc.org, and http://ajs.org/selection/index.asp>.

[144] Carrington PD, Long A. Selecting Pennsylvania judges in the twenty-first century. Dickinson Law Rev 2002;106(4):747–53. Goodman SJ, Marks LA. Lessons from an unusual retention election. Court Rev 2006;42:6–14.

[145] Choose your judges, <www.chooseyourjudges.org/choosejudge>; 2012 [accessed October 22, 2012]. *Republican Party of Minnesota et al. v. White, Chairperson, Minnesota Board of Judicial Standards, et al.*, 536 U.S. 765 (2002). Bright SB. Political attacks on the judiciary: can justice be done amid efforts to intimidate and remove judges from office for unpopular decisions? N Y Univ Law Rev 1997;72(2):308–36. Hasen RL, Lithwick D. Slate. Evil men in black robes. <http://www.slate.com/articles/news_and_politics/politics/2010/10/evil_men_in_black_robes.html>; 2010 [accessed October 26, 2010]. Bandyopadhyay S, McCannon BC. The effect of the election of prosecutors on criminal trials. Soc Sci Res Netw 2010; dx.doi.org/10.2139/ssrn.1641345. Cann Damon. Beyond accountability and independence: judicial selection and state court performance. Judicature 2007;90(5):226–32. Champagne A. Interest groups and judicial elections. Loyola Los Angel Law Rev 2001;34:1391–409. Champagne A. Political parties and judicial elections. Loyola Los Angel Law Rev 2001;34:1411–27. Champagne A. The politics of judicial selection. Policy Stud J 2003;31(3):413–9. Witold B. Judicial elections: changes and challenges. Court Rev J Am Judges 2006;42(3):. Keith, Rollin E. Agenda setting in an elected supreme court: the case of Ohio. Justice Syst J 2006;27(2):160–79. *Caperton v. A. T. Massey Coal Co.*, 129 S. Ct. 2252 (2009). *Citizens United v. Federal Election Commission*, 558 U.S. 50 (2010). Sample J, et al. The new politics of judicial elections 2000–2009: decade of change. Washington, DC: Brennan Center for Justice at New York University School of Law, National Institute on Money in State Politics, Justice at Stake; 2010, <brennan.3cdn.net/d091dc911bd67ff73b_09m6yvpgv.pdf>. For other state examples, see <www.ajs.org/cji/cji_fire.asp>. Danos CP. Fostering judicial independence in state and federal courts. Williamsburg, VA: National Center for State Courts; 1998. Escovitz SS, Kurland F, Gold N. Judicial selection and tenure. Washington, DC: American Judicature Society; 1975. Geyh CG. Why judicial elections stink. Ohio State Law J 2003;64:43–79.

[146] Boylan RT. What do prosecutors maximize? Evidence from the careers of U.S. attorneys. Am Law Econ Rev 2005;7(2):379–402.

[147] Beckett K, Sasson T. The politics of injustice: crime and punishment in America. 2nd ed. Thousand Oaks, CA: Sage Publications; 2004.

[148] Savelsberg J. Law that does not fit society: sentencing guidelines as a neoclassical reaction to the dilemmas of substantivized law. Am J Sociol 1992;97:1346−81. Frase RS. State sentencing guidelines: diversity, consensus, and unresolved policy issues. Columbia Law Rev 2005;105(4):1190−232. Stith K. The arc of the pendulum: judges, prosecutors, and the exercise of discretion. Yale Law J 2008;117(7):1420−97. Tonry MH. Sentencing reform impacts. Washington, DC: U.S. Department of Justice, National Institute of Justice; 1987. Parent D, et al. Key legislative issues in criminal justice: mandatory sentencing. Washington, DC: U.S. Department of Justice, National Institute of Justice; 1997. Tonry. Sentencing reform impacts. Parent et al. Key legislative issues in criminal justice: mandatory sentencing.Nugent ME, Miller ML. Basic factors in determining prosecutor workload. Prosecutor 2002;36(4): Online at <www.ndaa.org/prosecutor_basic_factors_v36no4. html>. Johnson C, Webster B, Connors E. Prosecuting gangs: a national assessment. Washington, DC: U.S. Department of Justice, National Institute of Justice; 1995. Tonry MH. Sentencing matters. New York, NY: Oxford University Press; 1996. Harris, Jesilow. It's not the same old ball game: three strikes and the courtroom workgroup. National Workload Assessment Project. How many cases should a prosecutor handle?? p. 4.

[149] Berry MF, Blassingame JW. Long memory: the black experience in America. New York, NY: Oxford University Press; 1982.

[150] National Center for State Courts. State activities map, <www.ncsc.org/information-and-resources/budget-resource-center/states-activities-map.aspx>; 2012 [accessed October 2, 2012].

[151] Bluestein G. State budget cuts clog criminal justice system. Associated Press; 2011.

[152] Farole Jr. DJ, Langton L. A national assessment of public defender office caseloads. Judicature 2010;94(2):87−90. Phillips S. Legal disparities in the capital of capital punishment. J Crim Law Criminol 2009;99(3):717−55. Ogletree Jr. CJ. Beyond justifications: seeking motivations to sustain public defenders. Harv Law Rev 1993;106(6):1239−94. [For a series of articles on court budgets, see <www.statebudgetsolutions.org/issues/view/breaking-news/7/courts-corrections>.].

[153] Wood JM, Garven S. How sexual abuse interviews go astray: implications for prosecutors, police, and child protection services. Child Maltreat 2000;5(2):109.

[154] TePas K, et al. Police presence, isolation, and sexual assault prosecution. Crim Justice Policy Rev 2011;22(3):330−49.

[155] Nugent H, McEwen JT. Prosecutors' national assessment of needs. Washington, DC: U.S. Department of Justice, National Institute of Justice; 1988.

[156] Rainville G. An analysis of factors related to prosecutor sentencing preferences. Crim Justice Policy Rev 2001;12(4):295−310.

[157] Barak G. On the rhetoric and reality of fighting financial fraud on wall street. Criminologist 2012;37(4):1−7.

[158] *Chandler v. Florida*, 449 U.S. 560 (1981); *New York Times Co. v. Sullivan*, 376 U.S. 254 (1964). Chiasson LE, editor. The press on trial: crimes and trials as media events. Westport, CT: Greenwood Publishing; 1997. Welch M, Fenwick M, Roberts M. Primary definitions of crime and moral panic: a content analysis of experts' quotes in feature newspaper articles on crime. J Res Crime Delinq 1997;34(4):474−94. Vining RL, et al. Patterns of newspaper reporting on state supreme courts. Justice Syst J 2010;31(3):273−89: Online at <ncsc.contentdm.oclc.org/cgi-bin/showfile.exe?CISOROOT = /ctmedia&CISOPTR = 24>. *Estes v. Texas*, 381 U.S. 532 (1965); *Sheppard v. Maxwell*, 384 U.S. 333 (1966).

[159] Ibid.

[160] Jones RG. Louisiana protest echoes the civil rights era. The New York Times September 21, 2007.

[161] Haines H. Flawed executions, the anti-death penalty movement, and the politics of capital punishment. Soc Probl 1992;39(2):125–38. Epstein L. Courts and interest groups. In: Gates John, Johnson Charles, editors. The American courts: a critical assessment. Washington, DC: CQ Press; 1991. p. 335–71. O'Connor K, Epstein L. Amicus curiae participation in U.S. Supreme Court litigation: an appraisal of Hakman's folklore. Law Soc Rev 1981;16(4):311–20.

[162] Iyengar S, Peters MD, Kinder DR. Experimental demonstrations of the not-so-minimal consequences of television news programs. Am Polit Sci Rev 1982;76(4):848–58. Peters CS. Getting attention: the effect of legal mobilization on the U.S. Supreme Courts attention to issues. Polit Res Q 2007;60(3):561–70. O'Connor, Epstein. Amicus curiae participation in U.S. Supreme Court litigation: an appraisal of Hakman's folklore.

[163] Murphy WF, et al. Courts, judges and politics: an introduction to the judicial process. 6th ed. New York, NY: McGraw-Hill; 2006.

[164] Palmer J. Abolishing plea bargaining: an end to the same old song and dance. Am J Crim Law 1999;26(3):505.

[165] Kennedy D. Legal education as training for Hierarchy. In: Kairy D, editor. The politics of law: a progressive critique, 38. New York, NY: Pantheon Books; 1990. Haney-Lopez. Racism on trial: the chicano fight for justice.

[166] Williams PJ. The alchemy of race and rights. Cambridge, MA: Harvard University Press; 1991. Bennett W. The lawyer's myth: reviving ideals in the legal profession. Chicago, IL: University of Chicago Press; 2001. Milovanovic D. A primer in the sociology of law. New York, NY: Harrow and Heston; 1988.

[167] Gottfredson MR, Gottfredson DM. Decision making in criminal justice: toward the rational exercise of discretion. 2nd ed. New York, NY: Plenum Press; 1988. Devlin P. The enforcement of morals. Can Philos Rev, 2. 1968, p. 321–23. Posner RA. How judges think. Cambridge, MA: Harvard University Press; 2008. Karstedt S. Emotions and criminal justice. Theor Criminol 2002;6(3):299–317. Bandes SA, editor. The passions of law. New York, NY: New York University Press; 1999. [See Bandes for an argument in favor of the emotionalization of law.]

[168] Sampson, Laub. Crime, class, and community: an emerging paradigm. Ulmer, Bader, Gault. Do moral communities play a role in criminal sentencing? Davies ALB, Worden AP. State politics and the right to counsel: a comparative analysis. Law Soc Rev 2009;43 (1):187–219. Edkins. Defense attorney plea recommendations and client race: does zealous representation apply equally to all? Varela et al. Do defense attorney referrals for competence to stand trial evaluations depend on whether the client speaks English or Spanish? Bridges GS, Steen S. Racial disparities in official assessments of juvenile offenders: attributional stereotypes as mediating mechanisms. Am Sociol Rev 1998;63 (4):554–70. Alexes, Evans, Beckett. Courtesy stigma and monetary sanctions: toward a socio-cultural theory of punishment. Paternoster. Prosecutorial discretion in requesting the death penalty: a case of victim-based racial discrimination. Cohen, Smith. The racial geography of the federal death penalty. Paternoster, Brame R. Reassessing race disparities in Maryland capital cases. Eberhardt et al. Research report. Johnson, Dipietro. The power of diversion: intermediate sanctions and sentencing disparity under presumptive guidelines. Kramer, Steffensmeier. Race and imprisonment decisions.

[169] Durose MR, Langan PA. Felony sentences in state courts, 2004. Washington, DC: U.S. Department of Justice, Office of Justice Programs, Bureau of Justice Statistics; 2007: Online at <bjs.ojp.usdoj.gov/content/pub/pdf/fssc04.pdf>.

[170] Stuntz WJ. The collapse of American justice. Cambridge, MA: The Belknap Press of Harvard University Press; 2011. [These calculations are simple estimates that set aside many complicating factors, which could reduce the quantity (particularly through an incapacitation effect or demographic shift in which there are fewer people in the high-crime age bracket of 16–22) but, more likely, would increase it (bias in arrest and parole, multiplier effects, parole and probation violation effect, amplification of children's criminality, trends in juvenile courts, and so on)].

[171] Ibid.

[172] Koppl, Roger. 2010. Forensic Science and Criminal Law: That Not How It Works on TV. Institute for Forensic Science Administration. <www.fdu.edu/ifsa>. Lecture available at < http://www.youtube.com/watch?v=nEJgx0hokl8&feature=related > [accessed August 15, 2012.]

Prosecutors in the United States dismiss approximately half of all felony arrests before they even get past the lower court pretrial stages.

CHAPTER 6

Case Assessment, Case Attrition, and Decision to Charge

KEY TERMS

affirmative defense
alibi defense
bind over
Brady rule
burden of persuasion
case assessment
case attrition
case-initiation decision
case mobilization
case theory
charge
circumstantial
   evidence
complaint
declination
defer prosecution

demonstrative
   evidence
direct evidence
dismissal
enhancers
exclusionary rule
exhibit
factual defense
final charges
initial charges
material
motion
motion for continuance
motion for severance of
   defendants or
   offenses

motion to dismiss
motion to suppress
   evidence
objection
pre-charge disposition
presumptions
procedural defense
prosecutorial discretion
rape shield laws
real evidence
relevant
rules of evidence
testimony

Learning Objectives

After reading this chapter, you should be able to:

1. Define case mobilization and case assessment.
2. Explain how case assessment involves both exerting state power and protecting due process rights.
3. Describe how legal reasoning and precedent affect case assessment.
4. Discuss how ecological features, such as courthouse procedures and focal concerns, affect assessment.

5. Explain prosecutorial discretion and briefly discuss why it is controversial.
6. List the main questions that influence the prosecutor's assessment.
7. Tell what "overcharging" is and why prosecutors do it.
8. Give reasons a prosecutor may decide to drop a case.
9. Give reasons that defense attorneys are at a disadvantage compared to prosecutors.
10. Define motions and objections and explain why they are advantageous for the defense.

When a case moves from booking to the courts, a prosecutor will evaluate the strength and legality of the evidence and decide to dismiss the case or charge the defendant based primarily on that assessment. The power to make this decision has a tremendous effect on the flow of cases through the courts and the lives of people accused of crime [1]. There is little oversight from the judge or anyone else outside of the prosecutor's office [2]. The prosecutor continues the assessment as charges are specified and changed, which explains why charges will often change between initial appearance and arraignment. Based on prosecutorial assessment, the defendant may be denied bail and kept in pretrial detention. The prosecutor also retains the power of dismissal as the case moves through the pretrial stages, which explains why cases are dismissed sometimes as late as the beginning of the trial. Evidence will be reviewed repeatedly, substantive laws read, witnesses interviewed, the case vetted with other attorneys, experts and judges consulted, and hearings held.

All of this is happening as the case is moving from one pretrial stage to the next, and at each stage, the prosecutor has to decide what to do at the next stage. The prosecutor's power, however, is not uninhibited. It is hemmed in by the principle of legality, procedural rules, the judge, and the opposing attorney. After the filing of initial charges a defense attorney takes up the case and begins assessing it with an eye on protecting the rights of the accused.

FILTERING CASES: TEMPERING STATE POWER WITH DUE PROCESS

Case mobilization and case assessment are two processes that cannot be pinned down to a single stage or single decision, with a lawyer sitting in a room, reviewing a file once, and making a definitive decision at that time of whether or not to go to trial. It is a process. **Case mobilization** is the movement of a case from police booking through the preliminary hearings to trial or another disposition. Case assessment is the continual evaluation that overlaps this movement of the case. It is arguably the most important set of decisions in the court process because of its effect on the caseload and people's lives.

Prosecutors in the United States dismiss approximately half of all felony arrests before they even get past the lower court pretrial stages [3]. This occurs because of a dialectical relationship between prosecutorial and defense case assessment. **Case assessment** involves legal reasoning (examining the facts of the case and the law), categorization of cases as conforming or exceptional, prioritization of cases, and consideration of the extralegal factors (such as the believability of the witnesses and the capacity of the jail to hold the defendant) in order to decide if the case should proceed toward trial and how to best prepare it in the event that it does.

Prosecutors assess cases with the objective of increasing their confidence that a crime occurred, that the accused committed the crime and had culpability (intended to produce the harm or was negligent), and that the case could be won in trial. Defense works with the objective of casting doubt on the prosecutors' cases. The tension between competing assessments reveals the strength and weaknesses of cases before they get to trial. Most cases with weak evidence are culled from the caseload. Thus, case assessment is as much about filtering cases as mobilizing them [4]. An illegal search, a strong alibi, a victim's contradictory statement, a police interrogation that did not follow proper procedure, and the lack of physical evidence all will greatly weaken a case.

Sometimes the defendant can still be pressured into pleading guilty, and sometimes the prosecutor may go to trial anyway, but often the prosecutor will just toss out the case. This filtering of cases happens only because the attorneys are engaged in counterbalancing assessments. The prosecutor must filter the assessment through the screen of due process, and the defense must filter the assessment through the law of the land. Prosecution without defense would be totalitarian; defense without prosecution would be lawless.

CASE ASSESSMENT FOR PROSECUTORS AND DEFENSE

Though they have competing objectives in their assessment, the prosecution and defense are both officers of the court and adhere to the same principles and many of the same rules of assessment [5]. First, both interpret the facts of the case and the law. Facts do not exist in a static form, readily visible to everyone. Lawyers must render or even construct facts from the case. The process of interpreting the meaning and relevance of evidence, then arguing these interpretations in court, is called the "linguistic analysis" of legal reasoning [6]. Second, both adhere to the array of institutional constraints, most importantly due process and legal reasoning. For both, the cases and facts before them are their principal stimuli. In short, their jobs are framed by the same legal reality.

The assessment of evidence is not only legally complex and subject to multiple interpretations but also colored by organizational, sociological, and political variables. Heavy caseloads, a dearth of assistants, informal focal concerns and routine, media attention, pressure to include the victim more, and concerns about promotion or re-election all influence assessment and decisions [7]. Because these factors vary, there is no single solution, procedure, or set of priorities for charging, dismissing, negotiating, or arguing cases. They all hinge on the contextualized assessment.

Early-stage case assessment is almost exclusively the work of the prosecutors. This is when they make a **case-initiation decision**, which is the decision of the prosecutor to dismiss a case or assign it a case number and schedule it for a hearing. Should the case be assigned a case number and taken past initial appearance, or should it be dismissed immediately? [8] It is, in effect, part of the prosecutors' case-management duties: they must deal with scheduling interviews, hearings, trials, and so on. Getting rid of cases quickly helps them and the entire courtroom workgroup.

If the case moves toward preliminary hearing, a private attorney will be hired or a court-appointed attorney will be provided. (In this chapter, we will discuss only felony trial cases that involve a defense attorney, except in a few places where noted.) The competing attorneys both engage in case assessment as they confer with witnesses and each other, go through discovery and multiple hearings, and prepare for trial. For both sides, this is the work that is done mostly outside the courtroom and involves bureaucratic paperwork and meetings behind closed doors [9]. Case assessment is a function of job duties, legal principles and presumptions, internal ecology characteristics, and external ecology pressures and influences, all of which overlap and together structure the handling of cases.

Legal Reasoning and Case Assessment

Legal influences, in the narrowest of terms, refer to aspects of the case and substantive law and the evidentiary link between the two. When assessing a case and preparing for trial, both prosecution and defense are bound by the substantive law written by the legislature, and they must establish or refute that the evidence from the crime satisfies each element of the law: *corpus delicti*, *actus reus*, *mens rea*, and concurrence between the act and the intent.

Gathering and organizing evidence is, to a large extent, a process of exclusion, namely, excluding from the assessment the large amount of evidence that cannot be included in the hearings or trial. For evidence to be legally admissible, it usually must be the following:

- relevant—related to the present case and proves a "governing" or important fact of the case (not an incidental fact)
- material—important enough to affect the case

- legally obtained
- not prejudicial—does not unduly sway the jury beyond the effect of the legal facts, such a graphic photos
- not hearsay—not presented by a third party such that the person with the original knowledge cannot be challenged in court
- disclosed in discovery
- statutorily permitted

Legal reasoning frames how to assess evidence and prepare a case for trial, which makes for a rather complex set of rules to determine what can and what cannot be included. It requires that the lawyers evaluate the culpability of the defendant in terms of statutes and the alleged crime itself, not morality or sociological conditions. It requires that they establish and enunciate specifically what law was supposedly violated and what defense is being asserted, and that they clearly identify which facts are **relevant**, that is, legally permissible in trial because it is presented to prove or disprove an assertion of fact or to counter evidence the opposing attorney presented [10]. It requires that they follow the rules of procedure, such as participation in discovery and the **rules of evidence**—legal rules used to determine whether evidence is admissible in a trial—many of which are established in precedent.

Precedent and Case Assessment

Appellate and high court rulings shape legal reasoning in criminal trial courts primarily by establishing rules of what evidence is and is not admissible. When the court assigns meaning to, for example, "privacy expectation" or "conspiracy," those meanings enter linguistic circulation and attorneys must use that new meaning in order to do their jobs properly [11]. When assessing a case, attorneys on both sides must look through this precedent frame and try to determine what evidence is probably admissible and what might get suppressed.

For instance, the 1963 Supreme Court case *Brady v. Maryland* introduced the **Brady rule**, which requires that a prosecutor participate in discovery and disclose to the defense all exculpatory evidence, or evidence that indicates the innocence of the defendant [12]. So if the evidence is not disclosed prior to trial, there is a good chance it will be objected to and suppressed. In *Daubert v. Merrell Dow Pharmaceuticals* (1993), the Supreme Court tried to establish what type of science is good enough for trial courts, deciding that the judge will determine if the testimony is based on scientifically valid reasoning or methods and thus admissible [13]. Because of the Daubert ruling, when assessing evidence, attorneys must predict what the judge will consider a good science. Another ruling that led to some confusion was the more recent case *United States v. Booker* (2005), in which the court effectively ruled that federal sentencing guidelines in federal courts are advisory, not mandatory. This alters how attorneys negotiate cases because they are less certain of what the outcome would be if the defendant is convicted in trial [14].

Not all evidence is allowed in court. The admissibility of evidence hinges on the legality of the methods used to procure it. The courts know people who possess evidence of crime. Their role, though, is not to strategize about how to obtain it but to assure that all people feel some level of security against government intrusion. What is considered a legal method, however, changes with the tides of court rulings and procedural statutes. The legality of police searches is one example.

In *Weeks v. United States* (1914) (see Landmark Cases) and *Nardone v. United States* (1939), the Supreme Court ruled that evidence gathered by federal authorities without a search warrant was tainted—or "fruit from a poisoned tree"—and could be excluded. This **exclusionary rule**—a court rule stating that evidence secured by illegal means cannot be introduced in a criminal trial—serves two goals: to deter future police violation of the Fourth Amendment and to provide a remedy for those whose rights have been violated.

The exclusionary rule was incorporated (or applied to state courts) in *Mapp v. Ohio* (1961) (see Landmark Cases). Since then, the Court established the "expectation of privacy" doctrine in *Katz v. United States* (1967), which states that people in the United States have an expectation of privacy wherever they are. For example, the Court has specified that the thermal imaging of a house and the use of a tracking device on a car violate the expectation of privacy and therefore require search warrants [15].

Yet overlapping these cases, and expanding in recent years, have been cases that weaken the exclusionary doctrine by providing exceptions to the warrant requirement [16]. Evidence obtained without a proper search warrant can still be used if:

- the search was incident to a lawful arrest
- it was a pat-down frisk to search for weapons (known as a Terry frisk)
- it is used during grand jury questioning instead of a trial
- the police would have found it anyway (inevitable discovery exception)
- it is used to impeach (discredit) a defendant who is testifying on his own behalf
- the police search an open field
- the evidence was in plain view and the officer had a right to be looking into the otherwise private space
- the evidence was obtained from garbage at the curbside
- they search a student at school

- the search was performed by a nongovernment agent and the government later obtained the evidence ("private person search" exception)
- the police received consent to perform the search [17]

The Court will certainly continue to adjust the lines of what is legal evidence, such as whether police can data-mine a cell phone without a warrant.

LANDMARK CASES

Weeks v. United States (1913)

Evidence gathered by authorities without a search warrant cannot be used against a defendant at trial.

Police officers went to the home of Fremont Weeks and, without a search warrant, entered the house with the help of a neighbor who told them the location of the key. They searched Weeks's room and took some papers, which they turned over to the United States Marshal. Later the same day, the police returned with the marshal, who, still without a warrant, wanted to look for additional evidence. They were let in by someone living in the house. The marshal searched Weeks's room and took letters and envelopes from a drawer. Police arrested Weeks at his place of employment in Kansas City, Missouri.

Weeks was charged with using the mail for transporting lottery tickets. Before the trial, Weeks petitioned for the return of his possessions, which included lottery tickets. The court denied his petition, and the papers were used as evidence at trial. Weeks was convicted and received a sentence of a fine and imprisonment.

In a unanimous decision, the U.S. Supreme Court held that the seizure of items from Weeks's residence violated his constitutional rights and that the government's refusal to return his possessions violated the Fourth Amendment. In the first application of the exclusionary rule, the Court reasoned that to allow private possessions to be seized and used as evidence against defendants would mean that the Fourth Amendment right to be secure against such searches and seizures would be useless.

Mapp v. Ohio (1961)

Evidence obtained by searches and seizures that violate the U.S. Constitution is inadmissible in a criminal trial in a state court.

In May 1957, three police officers went to the Cleveland, Ohio, home of Dollree Mapp on information that a person wanted in connection with a recent bombing was hiding there and that the evidence related to the bombing was kept there. When officers arrived at the house, they knocked on the door and demanded entrance. Mapp, who had phoned her attorney, refused to let them in without a search warrant.

Three hours later, additional officers arrived, and the group again tried to enter the house. Mapp did not answer the door immediately. The officers forced open one of the doors to the house and went inside. Mapp's attorney arrived, but the officers did not permit him to see Mapp or enter the house. Mapp demanded that the officers produce the search warrant. One of the officers held up a piece of paper and said it was the warrant. Mapp grabbed the paper and placed it inside her clothing. After a struggle, the officers recovered the paper and handcuffed Mapp. Mapp was then forced upstairs to her bedroom where the officers searched through the furniture, some suitcases, a photo album, and Mapp's personal papers. They also searched Mapp's daughter's bedroom, the living room, the kitchen, and the basement. In a trunk kept in the basement, the officers found some materials considered to be obscene.

Mapp was convicted of possession of the materials. She appealed the conviction on the basis of the Fourth Amendment requirement that the government obtain a search warrant prior to a search. The U.S. Supreme Court ruled in favor of Ms. Weeks stating that "all evidence obtained by searches and seizures in violation of the Federal Constitution is inadmissible in a criminal trial in a state court."

Extralegal Influences on Case Assessment

Variation in case assessment does not rest solely on the legal interpretations of partisan attorneys. Although the lawyers are trained in case evaluation and legal reasoning, there are still distinctions between the "law on the books" and the "law in their minds" [18]. All of the ecological variables discussed in Chapter 5—local legal culture of the courtroom workgroup, statutes, organizational priorities, number of assistants, elections, media, and so on—affect case assessment to some degree [19]. The negotiated order of courts manages all these legal and non-legal influences and creates patterns in the rate of trials and guilty pleas, the work techniques, the speed to disposition, severity of sentences, and caseloads.

Of particular importance to case assessment is that the negotiated order also establishes focal concerns and weights some of them as important cues. These touch on the types of crime, the strength of evidence, and the sociological variables of the defendant and victim [20]. If the courtroom workgroup, for instance, does not consider bicycle theft as a serious enough problem to warrant much attention, then a prosecutor may have a higher evidentiary standard in order to dismiss more of those cases quickly and **charge**, or specify an alleged criminal offense, only in those that can be disposed easily. The primary cues seem to be legal aspects of the case, but extralegal aspects of a case also influence how they strategize framing the case. Perceived believability and appearance, race, social class, sex, criminal record, and pretrial detention may all affect assessment decisions even though none are relevant to the criminal statutes [21]. Use of focal concerns enables attorneys to process a large number of diverse cases more expeditiously by categorizing them as "conforming" or "exceptional," and then prioritizing them [22].

As Oliver Wendell Holmes, Jr., and other legal realists pointed out, there is no essence or pure objectivity to legal reasoning. It does involve an effort to be objective and to adhere to the letter of the law. It also entails many factors not related to the case or law—resources, focal concerns, consideration of the effect on the defendant—that frame the assessment [23].

Strategies of Case Assessment

Many case assessment strategies are common to prosecution and defense. Both must assess the case amidst the swirl of influences. Justice and victory are at the heart of assessment. Prosecution represents the notion that social control and protection of the community is justice; defense represents the notion that individual rights and restraint of government power is justice. The goal of each is to pursue their respective legal mandate by winning cases. This is done by building strength in one's own position and finding weakness or opportunities to weaken the opponent's position.

Strategies of assessing a case necessarily depend on legal reasoning. It involves looking directly at the case and looking at each choice in terms of what the opposing attorney or the judge may do. Attorneys will often frame or visualize the case immediately as though it is at trial [24]. Looking at a case through the lens of trial allows the attorneys to anticipate outcomes and develop, ideally, a clear and sturdy **case theory**, that is, an attorney's strategy for assessing, organizing, preparing, and arguing a case. At the core, this involves establishing and connecting the facts of the case: harm, action, and intent. Though called "facts," these are actually the elements of the crime that are alleged, such as "the defendant deliberately punched the victim on Tuesday, September 11, 2012 at approximately 9:30 p.m." The prosecution will try to establish these alleged facts, and the defense will try to show that at least one of the facts is not true, or at least not convincingly proven. The narrow logic of legal reasoning may not standardize case processing to the point of uniformity but it compels the attorneys to handle case assessment in relatively consistent manner: try to lawfully prove or disprove the elements of the crime in court [25].

Evidence and Interpretation of Statutes

Proving each element of a crime relies on the interpretation of evidence and statutes. Evidence is information intended to convince people of the truth or falsity of a fact of the case. Though the ultimate goal is to convince the jury or trial judge to believe the alleged facts or to reject them, in the pretrial process, the attorneys will try to demonstrate the strength of their evidence in order to get the opponent to capitulate and plead guilty or get the judge to dismiss the case. The presence and quality of evidence is therefore a primary cue because strong evidence increases the likelihood of winning a trial.

Evidence seems to be a simple notion, but there are actually several ways to categorize evidence. **Direct evidence** proves a fact without the finder of fact having to infer anything, for instance, a witness stating, "I saw the defendant punch the victim." **Circumstantial evidence** requires that the judge or jury draw a logical conclusion regarding the fact in dispute, for instance, a witness saying, "The two were arguing in the back room, and when the victim came out he had a bloody nose." This implies that the defendant punched the victim. Circumstantial evidence is generally considered to be weaker because the finder of fact has to assess its credibility, then draw an inference regarding the fact of the crime.

Evidence is also separated based on its form, testimonial or real. **Testimony** is information that a witness or expert states under oath. Witness testimony can be direct or circumstantial. A witness to the crime (which is particularly strong evidence) or a police officer restating a confession is direct testimonial evidence [26]. Expert testimony, usually based on an examination and interpretation of physical evidence, is usually circumstantial. **Real evidence** encompasses all objects presented in trial (weapons, bloody shirts, computer hard drives, documents, and so on). Real evidence is usually presented as an **exhibit** and includes physical evidence from the alleged crime or **demonstrative evidence**, or evidence that is intended to represent some feature of the crime and clarify a testimony, such as photos or maps. Demonstrative evidence can clarify either direct or circumstantial testimony. Sometimes, in order to move a trial along, the judge will instruct the jury to accept something as a fact even though the attorneys do not present either testimony or real evidence. This occurs with stipulations (in which the attorneys agree that a fact exists), judicial notice (when the judge assumes the issue is a commonly known fact), and presumptions (in which the judge instructs the jury that because basic facts have been established they should assume others to be true as well).

Four dominant areas of evidence include:

1. search and seizure of physical evidence
2. interrogations and confessions
3. identification of defendants, often in lineups
4. witnesses (both expert and non-expert)

For each of these, there are two filters, quality and admissibility. First, the attorneys will consider the quality of the evidence, that is, its capacity to establish the guilt of the defendant or the errors in the prosecution's case. They must decide what is weak evidence that should be ignored or what is potentially strong and should be developed. This will include authenticating the evidence and anticipating how persuasive it is, especially with regards to witnesses. Perceived reliability of eyewitnesses and believability or cooperation of the victim strongly affect attorneys' assessments [27].

Second, the attorneys must consider the admissibility of the evidence, or the rules of evidence. Strict rules limit what can be properly admitted as evidence, but dozens of exceptions often mean that creative attorneys find a way to introduce such testimony or other items into evidence. Admissible evidence generally must be:

- obtained legally
- permitted in trial
- legally relevant
- material

To test whether it was legally obtained, the attorneys must compare the police and investigation procedures with procedural statutes, Supreme Court and appellate court rulings, and court policies. Evidence that does not follow procedural law may be suppressed. Regarding permissible evidence, many rules of evidence simply prohibit some types of evidence. For instance, past criminal behavior usually cannot be used to establish the intent to commit the offense currently being tried.

To be legally relevant in a criminal trial, the evidence must be presented to prove or disprove an assertion of fact (substantive evidence) or to counter the evidence the opposing attorney presented (such as to impeach a witness). Substantive evidence that is strong is said to have probative value. Even evidence that relates to the facts and has probative value cannot prejudice the jury. If someone is accused of burglary, people may be inclined to identify all the faults of the person—that he or she stole something years earlier, that he or she has a bad temper, that he or she is a creep who runs with a bad crowd, and that he or she is known to do drugs. In most criminal trials, this information will not be admissible because it does not directly connect the facts of the case to the law, that is, it is prejudicial and not relevant. However, bringing in a witness to describe how the defendant threatened the victim will likely be admissible because it helps to prove intent and is therefore probative. What the prosecution must prove is that the defendant entered a private property and removed belongings and intended to do so. Everything else about the defendant is irrelevant. Materiality overlaps relevance. For evidence to be **material**, it must potentially make a difference to the outcome of the case. It may then be legally permissible in trial. For instance, the fact that the defendant had a bologna and ketchup sandwich before the alleged crime is immaterial if that information, though legally obtained, will not have any bearing on culpability. Combining the two filters we have: quality of evidence + admissibility of evidence = strength of case.

Legal relevance of evidence often will rely on interpretation of a statute. If a burglary statute refers to "dwelling," does that include a car that someone is living in? The prosecutor may push that interpretation in order to have the person convicted of burglary instead of mere larceny theft. He or she then must present evidence that proves the defendant committed each element of the crime. The defense, however, may argue that the fact that the defendant stole from a car is legally irrelevant because that does not constitute a dwelling.

The process of gathering evidence and interpreting statutes, as described in Chapter 5, is an iterative process of legal reasoning. Lawyers get evidence from police, opposing attorneys, and their own investigations [28]. They review police reports, interview victims and witnesses, and conduct legal research. They filter the stories of defendants and witnesses by disregarding what they consider irrelevant information and asking questions to direct the story to relevant information. They try to reconstruct past events that are not conclusive, often while dealing with people who are concealing or fabricating information. This is further convoluted by poor quality of physical evidence, bad science, bad cops, conjecture on the part of the police and witnesses, contradictions among the witnesses, changes in testimony among victims and witnesses, witnesses afraid to testify, witnesses with a personal vendetta against the accused, and other variables [29].

Trying to establish or disprove *mens rea* and *actus reus*, needless to say, is often not a straightforward effort. As an attorney sifts through all these variables—assessing the blameworthiness of the defendant, establishing the facts of the case and legal guilt or innocence, and dealing with shifting notions of the defendant's action and intent—he or she will often change how they frame the case [30]. They will modify how they interpret the case; they will change the charges or defense strategies; and they will reconsider the relative value of many pieces of evidence. In many ways, building a case is a process of elimination, trying to find the best evidence to match to one of many criminal statutes or trying ways to weaken such an alleged link.

Case Theory

After filtering the alleged criminal offense through legal reasoning, due process, rules of evidence, and ecological influences, many attorneys will organize their assessment and strategy into a case theory, often specified as a "prosecutor theory" or "defense theory" [31]. Legal reasoning breaks an incident into component parts. A case theory enables an attorney to bring the relevant facts of the case back into a cogent story intended to persuade the jury and judge. This is often considered the storytelling or narrative aspect of trials because it draws on emotions as well as law and facts. The attorneys must be prepared to stand in front of a jury and convince them that their interpretation of the case is the best. The evidence may be good, but is it believable in court? [32] The two goals of the case theory are to bring a clear focus to one's own case so that during pretrial and trial the attorney will be prepared and convincing, and to look at the case through the opposing attorney's lens in order to prepare for likely opposition, as well as surprises.

There is no official way of doing this, but it involves writing down key evidence, a chronology of events, interpretations of laws and events, decisions on how to handle likely events in the case, and a frame for telling the story. Attorneys will often start one of these files or notebooks at the beginning of the assessment process and modify it as the assessment continues. They will continually ask themselves, "What needs to be cut because its unconvincing or likely to be suppressed? What's going to survive to trial?" These files allow them to order the objective and subjective parts of the case and their decisions regarding each. Objective parts include the charges and facts that are clearly established. Subjective elements include chosen strategies, such as ways to make the defendant appear malicious or forgivable, to make a witness appear more believable or dishonest, likely motions to make pretrial and objections to make during the trial, evidence to contest, and ways to tap into the jury's fears and prejudices. On both the objective and subjective sides, the attorney must identify the weaknesses and strengths of her or his position and decide what to include, exclude, highlight, and diminish.

The prosecution, in general, wants to create the appearance of certainty in the allegations. The defense generally wants to use witnesses, evidence, and logic to create reasonable doubt. As prosecutors will sometimes say, "The enemy is reasonable doubt." Both want to prepare a case that is interesting, understandable, and convincing to the layperson and can be succinctly summarized.

The case theory is often designed with a jury trial in mind, but it guides the attorneys as they work at the pretrial stages. It will influence interviews with witnesses, questions during depositions, and arguments made during the preliminary hearing. It will suggest to attorneys what to request during discovery and what motions they will consider filing, such as motions to suppress. Also, it will give them a strategy for asking potential jurors questions during *voir dire* and deciding whom to exclude from the jury.

PROSECUTORIAL CASE ASSESSMENT

The modern U.S. public prosecutor's office started to take shape in the late nineteenth century. In the early years, the "jury of public opinion" did not demand neutrality and fairness but swift punishment of the accused because of widespread fear of social disorder [33]. Today more than 2300 state prosecutor offices that handle felony cases are bound by elaborate principles and rules [34]. (This chapter focuses on felony cases because they subsume misdemeanor stages.) [35].

This does not mean that prosecutorial decisions are formalistic or uniform. Scientific research beginning 40 years ago has consistently shown that prosecutors exercise a large amount of discretionary power within the legal framework [36]. **Prosecutorial discretion** is the capacity to make choices regarding a case, including to charge or dismiss a case, divert a case (screen it for alternative courts), change charges, plea bargain, develop a case theory, argue a case as he or she sees fit, and recommend leniency or the maximum sentence [37]. Some observers and court members argue that prosecutors need more discretion to control crime effectively. Others argue that the large degree of

PHOTO 6.1
During the early years of the public prosecutor's office, the public demanded swift punishment of the accused because of fear of social disorder. Here, inmates of the South Cell House Penitentiary, Menard, Illinois, stand outside their cells, *circa* 1900.

prosecutorial discretion already weakens the rule of law and allows for abuse of government power and inequality [38]. That debate, though interesting, is beyond the scope of this book. We will simply describe the main aspects of discretion during assessment. In assessing a case, the prosecutor asks:

- "Could this case be prosecuted?" This is the legal sufficiency question.
    - Is there evidence of factual guilt?
- "Could this case be won in trial?" These are the trial sufficiency or trial-outcome questions.

- Is a conviction by a jury or judge likely?
- Are there factors, like gaps in evidence or strong defense evidence, that make the case unpredictable?
- How cooperative and believable are law enforcement agents, victims, and witnesses?
- Are there resources for investigations and forensic analysis?
- What is the quality of the defense counsel?

- "Should this case be prosecuted?" These are the social good and justice, system efficiency, and aspiration questions.
  - What is the nature of the offense? Was it heinous and malicious?
  - What are the defendant's criminal history and sociological traits?
  - Is the defendant dangerous?
  - How complex is the case and how much time and resources will it demand?
  - Will the punishment match the effort put into the case?
  - Will the sentence be fair and just? [39]
  - How will a win or loss be portrayed by media and affect public opinion?
  - Will this win or loss affect promotion or reelection?

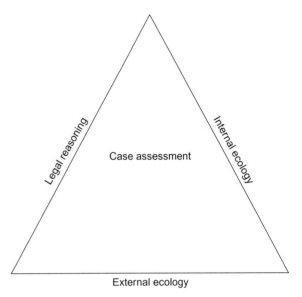

FIGURE 6.1

A prosecutor's assessment of each case can be complex and is affected by pressures from within and outside the courts.

Prosecutorial discretion and assessment have a profound effect on the court system. Some research indicates that from the mid-1970s to the mid-1990s (the years of an unmatched increase in prison populations), prosecution and sentencing accounted for 60 percent of the increase in incarceration rates. Population growth and arrest rates, however, each accounted for less than 10 percent of the prison population growth, and reported crimes accounted for just under 20 percent [40]. "The prosecutor's office is the key to how many people will be in the criminal justice system, where, for how long, at what level of security and, therefore, at what cost" [41]. Figure 6.1 shows how these decisions are shaped by the three sets of influences.

Prosecutorial Options on Case Disposition

So many aspects of the court process depend on what the prosecutor decides. After a **complaint** (a formal accusation of crime) is signed by a law enforcement officer or prosecutor, an arrest is made, and the defendant booked the prosecutor will do the initial assessment, or screening of the case, just before, during, or shortly after the initial appearance [42]. (In some jurisdictions the police handle the initial appearance; in others, the prosecutor does.)

This first decision to dismiss or file **initial charges**—the first charges filed by either police or prosecution and presented in a complaint or arrest warrant or at booking or initial appearance—alters thousands cases in the criminal courts every year. **Dismissal**, or disposition of a case prior to conviction or trial, may happen when the case is first presented to the prosecutor before initial appearance (called a **pre-charge disposition**) or shortly after the initial charges are filed. Prosecutors may also send a case back to the police for further investigation or to charge as an ordinance violation. If the case makes it past this initial stage, the prosecutor can still dismiss the case before the preliminary hearing or at it by motioning for a *nolle prosequi* (sometimes shortened to "*nol. pros.*"), in which the prosecutor states that no further action will be taken and asks the judge to allow the case to be dismissed. Even after this, the prosecutor alone can dismiss cases up through arraignment and to the beginning of the trial.

If the prosecutor does not dismiss, he or she will "file the complaint" and has discretion over the charges. A **charge** specifies an alleged crime; the elements of the alleged crime; the person(s) alleged to have committed it; her or his intention; and the date, time, and location of the alleged crime. Initial charges, usually filed within 72 hours of arrest, are stated in a complaint, arrest warrant, booking, and/or an initial appearance. **Final charges**, or charges presented in the indictment or information, can restate or change the initial charge and are potentially based on much more in-depth assessment. These can be "on-the-nose charges," in which the charges match the act, reduced charges from the complaint (often from a felony to misdemeanor), or inflated charges [43]. The prosecutor can also decide to suspend or **defer prosecution**, which means the charge is dismissed if the defendant completes terms of some program picked by the prosecution, such as drug rehabilitation or anger management. If he or she fails to complete the program, the defendant is prosecuted for the original charges [44].

If felony charges are filed, the court will **bind over** an adult case from the lower court (limited jurisdiction) to the felony trial court (general jurisdiction). ("Bind over" is a court directive to appear in court, particularly to transfer a case from one court to another.) For a juvenile, the prosecutor usually decides whether to process the case in the juvenile system or bind it over to the criminal court. (We cover juvenile case processing in more detail in Chapter 12.) The prosecutor may also unilaterally reject a plea and force a trial. In cases that go to trial, the prosecutor decides whether to bundle multiple charges or multiple defendants for a single trial or to have separate trials for each. However, he or she can choose to negotiate with defense, and either accept a guilty plea with the filed charges or accept a guilty plea to lesser charges. Each of these decisions depends on the case assessment, the legal merits or strength of the case, as well as the ecological factors that impinge the assessment.

This is not a simple factory line because there is often considerable variation across cases, and many of these decisions overlap others. Bail will be decided at different stages; charges are filed and changed on the same day that they are being dropped; diversion is sometimes used and sometimes not; some of the pretrial stages will happen in the lower court, and sometimes some of them are handled in the court of general jurisdiction. The prosecutor intertwines assessing the case, building a case theory, and assembling participants, much of which happens behind the scenes. Research in one state found that over 60 percent of the time spent on a case was out of court (excluding all hearings and trial stages) – reviewing the case, reviewing law, meeting with witnesses, and so on. This corresponds with all studies conducted by the American Prosecutors Research Institute [45]. While this effort to dispose of cases is going on, the prosecutor is also keeping records, controlling defendants, and scheduling cases. Moreover, the prosecutor is being pushed by legal mandates, such as providing a speedy trial.

The dismiss-charge decisions are the areas where prosecutorial power is clearest. As one legal scholar wrote, "No government official has as much unreviewable power or discretion as the prosecutor. Few regulations bind or even guide prosecutorial discretion, and fewer still work well" [46]. This discretionary power is greater in the United States than in most other nations [47]. They have the power to dismiss or charge, and the power to designate what to charge, which can greatly affect the defendant's potential sentence [48]. This "sovereign power of prosecutors" allows them to choose when to apply the law, when not to, whom to show leniency, and whom to show harshness [49]. There are proposals and efforts to curtail this power—such as increasing oversight; offering incentives for outcomes other than conviction rates; publishing data on dismissals, convictions, plea bargains, and sentences; and separating the power to file charges from the power to accept pleas—but as it stands now, prosecutors wield the greatest power in the assessment and mobilization of cases [50].

Influences and Strategies of Prosecutorial Assessment

Some strategies and influences are particular to prosecutors or most prominent for them. Their strategy is focused primarily on assessing the blameworthiness of people often assumed to be lawbreakers [51]. This leads to a distinct framing of the case: prosecutors tend to search for evidence to establish guilt.

Prosecutors also have the burden of proof, which can be separated into two parts. First, the prosecution has the burden of production, which means the obligation to present evidence that proves the elements of the crime: that a crime occurred (*corpus delicti*), that the defendant did it (*actus reus*), and that the defendant intended the harm or was negligent (*mens rea*). This is also called the "burden of going forward with evidence." Evidence may be king, but it is not very elegant on its own. Second, the prosecutor also has to present a case theory or story that convinces the finder of fact beyond any reasonable doubt of the defendant's culpability. This is called the **burden of persuasion**. The defendant can, and actually sometimes does, say nothing. The Supreme Court ruled in *Griffin v. California* (1965) that the prosecutor and judge are not allowed to mention the defendant's silence or imply that it is an admission of guilt [52]. The entire burden of proof falls on the state, not on the individual.

The presumption of innocence and these prosecutorial burdens are a cornerstone of U.S. jurisprudence. More than protecting the defendant, as some complain, they constrain the overwhelming might of the government. As stated in *In re Winship* (1970), "a society that values the good name and freedom of every individual should not condemn a man for commission of a crime when there is reasonable doubt about his guilt" [53]. The benefit that befalls a defendant is a by-product of efforts to constrain abusive government power.

In "making the case" the prosecutor is influenced by more than just the objective evidence and law, which explains why there is variation when handling similar cases [54]. The victim preference and credibility, witness reliability, and police weigh heavily on these decisions of whether or not to charge [55]. Privately hired defense attorneys or competent public defenders may induce prosecutors to more readily dismiss cases. The office priorities on the types of cases to win and benchmarks for conviction rates will prompt them to charge particular crimes and dismiss cases that do not have a good chance of winning [56].

The mental category of "conforming cases" allows prosecutors to focus on only a few characteristics of the case and therefore process it quickly and with less uncertainty, whether with dismissal, diversion, or pursuit of conviction. Exceptional cases may also be dismissed or prosecuted through trial, but they are unusual and therefore require more assessment and preparation. The **enhancers**, or attributes that make cases more complicated and time intensive, that may ultimately weaken the case include:

- victim or witness under age 10
- victim or witness over age 65 and with frailty
- victim or witness with a disability
- victim or witness from out of state

- uncooperative victim or witness
- language barrier and cultural diversity
- complex evidence and investigation—scientific evidence, financial records, or computer evidence involved
- family offense
- capital offense, in which the prosecutor files a notice of intent to pursue the death penalty
- insanity defense or diminished capacity
- difficult defense attorney
- multiple defense attorneys
- media attention [57]

Research has found that overall these enhancers can increase attorney case-processing time by 55 percent, investigator time by 24 percent, and victim/witness assistance coordinator time by 21 percent. Child victims/witnesses, capital offenses, and complex evidence have the greatest effects on case-processing time [58].

When a prosecutor considers a case straightforward or complex, and when he or she decides to dismiss or pursue it, the assessment is often based partially on typification of the victim, in which they typecast alleged victims as credible and deserving of state protection or as having precipitated the crime herself or himself (such as in rape cases) [59]. Cases with victims who are considered credible and deserving (older, white, and employed) get charged more often, even if the evidence is otherwise equal [60]. However, rape cases in which the victim does not show up for interviews with the prosecutor, changes her or his story, or is otherwise uncooperative are more likely to be dismissed [61].

The research also found that rapes by strangers are more likely to be dismissed [62]. In sexual assault cases involving people who know each other, however, the prosecutors are more likely to consider the victim's character and behavior preceding the alleged crime, which are non-legal focal concerns. This can include any criminal record of the victim or if the victim had been drinking alcohol prior to the alleged assault [63]. This means legally sufficient rape cases are dismissed because of the negative moral and/or strategic judgment of the victim's behavior. To reduce the effect of prejudicial attitudes toward rape victims, some states have altered prosecutorial (and defense attorney) assessment with **rape shield laws**. These prohibit irrelevant evidence about a victim's sexual history, reputation, or past conduct.

Other extralegal variables that affect initial assessment and later assessment include priority prosecution policies, prosecution case assignment and diversion policies, available DNA and other lesser forensics, criminal record of the suspect, media, industry influence, attitudes of local politicians and the public, jail overcrowding, victim and witness services, and the amount of time assigned to other tasks like community outreach and attending meetings [64]. An interesting influence that is technically extralegal but arguably at the heart of the courts is "doing justice." The Supreme Court focused on this issue in *Berger v. United States* (1935), stating that "The United States Attorney is the representative not of an ordinary party to a controversy, but of a sovereignty whose obligation to govern impartially is as compelling as its obligation to govern at all; and whose interest, therefore, in a criminal prosecution is not that it shall win a case, but that justice shall be done." Prosecutors should not lie, manipulate witnesses, mischaracterize evidence, or otherwise behave unprofessionally, and should also pursue justice.

The prosecutor is hired to enforce the law. However, is justice served if for the first-time offense of selling two 5-gram bags of marijuana, a young college student is sentenced to 2 years in prison, gets expelled from school, and will forever have difficulty finding employment? Some prosecutors may find such an outcome unjust and offensive to the principle of limited methods. They may reduce the charges not because of weak evidence but for the social good. Similarly, if a defendant is cooperative and remorseful, a prosecutor may reduce the charges. Research has indicated that prosecutors do this type of charge reduction particularly with crimes that have mandatory-minimum sentences [65].

Prosecutor's Assessment of Evidence

Although factors such as office logistics and judgments of victim's deservedness certainly influence cases, if evidence indicates blameworthiness of the defendant and will likely garner a conviction, the prosecutor is much more likely to pursue a case [66]. The central goal of prosecution is to build a strong case that is likely to win in trial or result in a guilty plea without significant concessions from the prosecutor. This structures how they prioritize cases and deal with evidence. Missing, ambiguous, inconsistent, or suppressible evidence makes a weak case. Weak cases are generally filtered out by being dismissed and pled down. Even if the case is won, it still faces appeal. Strong evidence is relevant, admissible, and convincing [67]. Prosecutors must deal with all the areas and types of evidence but have particular interest in, and problems with, testimony from witnesses. Table 6.1 illustrates the decision-making process with two matrices.

Decision to Charge and Case Attrition: Predicting Outcomes

Case assessment is one of the great engines that turn the wheels of justice. It entails countless decisions driven by a wide range of motivations and influences. It affects the work of the courtroom workgroups across the nation and

Table 6.1 Prosecutorial Assessment of Evidence

	Admissible Evidence	Suppressible Evidence
Convincing Evidence	Strong case	Weak case
Ambiguous Evidence	Weak case	Very weak case–usually dismissed

	High Quality of Evidence (likely to convince the finder of fact of the defendant's guilt)	Admissibility of Evidence (likely to withstand a motion to suppress)
Search and Seizure	Establishes *corpus delicti*, *actus reus*, and *mens rea*	Police had proper search warrant or legitimate exception to warrant requirement
Confession/Interrogation	Establishes *actus reus* and *mens rea*	Suspect Mirandized Suspect gave information knowingly and voluntarily Police followed proper protocol (e.g. recording the interrogation if required)
Identification (line up, photo ID, etc.)	Establishes *actus reus*	No undue prejudicing of witness Defense attorney present
Witnesses	Cooperates with prosecution[1] Believable[2] Establishes *corpus delicti*, *actus reus*, and *mens rea*	Willing to testify Consistent Competent

The prosecutor must ask, "Is the evidence good enough to convince a jury that it proves guilt beyond a reasonable doubt? If so, is it admissible or suppressible?" the prosecutor wants high-quality, admissible evidence. We can visualize the decision-making process with the above two tables.
[1]*Spohn, Cassia, Dawn Beichner and Erika Davis-Frenzel. 2001.*
[2]*Spohn, Cassia, Dawn Beichner and Erika Davis-Frenzel. 2001.*

the millions of people arrested each year. Early-stage decisions to charge vary across courthouses, and include police arrest warrants, citizen or prosecutor complaints, arrests pursuant to a crime, and initial appearances. These begin courtroom negotiations, but can sometimes be rushed and given little review. (See Courts in the Media for an incident in which case assessment went awry.)

The second filing of charges, via an information or indictment, is usually based on a more thorough assessment. It may take a few weeks from the first filing to the second, but usually takes a couple of months, and sometimes a couple of years, depending on the complexity of the case and workload. This formal charge gets the case on the docket and is what the plea negotiations will be based on. This also means the prosecutor has decided to invest time and resources into one case, which necessarily means less time for other cases and tasks. Time per case varies. One study found that the average prosecutor time for a homicide case was just over 2,100 hours, but for rape, the offense demanding the next highest number of hours, it was 75 hours per case. Others, such as misdemeanors in general, burglary, felony drugs, and juvenile delinquency cases, all required under 10 hours per case on average [70].

Prosecutors regularly position themselves for plea bargaining by charging the maximum criminal offense the elements of the crime will justify, which is often called overcharging, and include the lesser offenses that are also justified by the evidence. If the highest charge does not lead to a conviction, perhaps one of the lower ones will. Also, and more regularly, the maximum charge induces defendants to file a vertical plea, that is, waive their right to a trial and plead guilty to one of the lesser crime.

Some critics say this effectively coerces confessions and have called it "structural coercion," which undermines the voluntariness of confessions and constrains the judge's ability to review the process. It imposes costs on defendants who exert their constitutional right to the presumption of innocence and a trial [71]. Nonetheless, the Supreme Court has ruled that tactics including threats and overcharges are constitutionally permissible [72]. Because of its efficiency, this method generates over 90 percent of the convictions in the United States.

Many of the cases handed to prosecutors do not end up with a conviction. **Case attrition** is when a case is removed from the court process after arrest but before a plea or trial. It most clearly refers to pre-trial decisions of:

1. refusal to charge (called a **declination** or "an entry made on the record") before or at the initial appearance; and
2. dismissal at any other pre-trial stage by a judge or by a *nolle prosequi* motion [78].

COURTS IN THE MEDIA

Tulia, Texas: When the Court Fails

Early on the morning of July 23, 1999 in Tulia, Texas, local police and state troopers dressed in para-military SWAT uniforms roused 47 men and women from their homes, took them in front of news cameras, and charged them with dealing drugs [73]. The evidence consisted of the testimony of one witness, undercover officer Tom Coleman. No real evidence, such as videos, pictures, voice recordings, or even drugs, was presented, and no witnesses were able to corroborate the accusations. Although those arrested were charged with selling expensive powder cocaine, there was no evidence that any of them were wealthy enough to buy the drug.

Some initial defendants pled guilty because of the threat of harsher charges. In these cases, Swisher County District Attorney Terry McEachern won sentences up to 90 years, even for defendants with no criminal records [74]. Seven

black defendants asked for jury trials. The elected judge refused to allow the defense to impeach the single witness, Coleman, even though his sworn testimonies were contradictory, he had a criminal record, and he was a former member of the Ku Klux Klan. All seven were convicted and given sentences from 20 to 361 years.

The thirty remaining defendants agreed to plead guilty in exchange for relative leniency. Sixteen received probation, deferment, or a fine. The rest received prison sentences ranging from 1 to 18 years. In all, 38 Tulia residents were convicted, leaving behind children, jobs, and homes [75]. Coleman was designated "Officer of the Year" in 2000 by Texas Attorney General (later U.S. Senator) John Cornyn [76].

Racism permeated this scandal. Tulia had 400 black residents out of a population of 5000, but 40 of the 47 arrestees were black, and 34 of the 38 convicted were black [77]. One white defendant was sentenced to prison for 10 years.

All of the defendants had low income and could not afford private counsel. Two local citizens started Friends for Justice, which got the attention of the local media and local defense attorneys. Eventually, the national media noticed the case, and the NAACP Legal Defense Fund became involved.

The first four convictions to be heard on appeal were confirmed, even though the prosecutor illegally withheld information during discovery, and the witness committed perjury. The next four were remanded and exonerated on retrial by a new judge. In 2003, Texas Governor Rick Perry pardoned all who were convicted.

A few years later, the wrongfully convicted won a civil suit and each person received about $80,000 for each year spent in prison. Coleman was later convicted of perjury but never spent a day in jail or paid any fines.

Question

   Why did case assessment fail to filter out these weak cases?

Because of a lack of national measurements and ambiguities (such as whether diverted cases or acquittal at trial are counted as attrition), the exact number is not certain, but research from the 1920s onward have found that about half the cases are dropped after arrest and before plea or trial [79].

Some consider case attrition as the "loss" or "deterioration" of cases and push for a reduction in attrition rates [80]. In fact, though, it is an essential part of the criminal justice funnel, in which weak cases get sifted out. Attrition is the outcome of assessment and prosecutorial discretion. The prosecutor may decide to drop the case if:

- the evidence does not meet the elements requirement
- a conviction at trial is uncertain
- witnesses are not cooperating or credible or cannot be located
- the defendant is wealthy or the defense attorney is tough
- the defendant is not considered a threat to the community
- the defendant has favorable cues
- the law has not been enforced for a long time
- office priorities are directing resources to other cases
- the voting public opposes the trial [81]

Weak or missing evidence, especially as a result of arrest policies, is likely the largest reason for attrition. One attorney, explaining the problem of weak evidence said, "A three-legged dog can still get around, but not well" [82]. This relates to what is called the "production ethic" and the "expeditious pursuit of justice": maximize productive output (convictions) by the efficient allocation of resources [83]. Case attrition does not undermine justice, and dismissal is not surrender or failure by the prosecution. The state exerted its power by arrest and initial charges—which itself has a deterrent effect—and then restrained its power on further consideration [84].

DEFENSE ATTORNEY ASSESSMENT

The defense attorney not only represents individual rights and the restraint of abusive government power, but is also responsible for the life, liberty, and financial well-being of an individual accused by the government, as well as the defendant's family and community. The principal strength of defense assessment is not to direct the flow of cases but to counter prosecutorial power, to weaken or refute the allegations. So although the defense's legal reasoning is the same as the prosecution, the objective is the opposite. (Defense duties are discussed in depth in Chapter 9. In this section we will focus only on assessment and preparation of cases.)

Defense assessment hinges on the prosecutor's decisions. If the prosecution declines a case, a defense attorney may likely never see it. If the prosecution dismisses the case, the defense's job is over: no appeals can be filed, and nothing else can be done by defense. If the prosecution offers a plea deal that the defendant wants to accept, the defendant waives rights to a trial and appeal, and the defense attorney is done after the sentencing. If the prosecutor wants to go to trial, and the defendant will not plead guilty to the highest charges, the defense attorney is legally bound to represent the defendant in trial. There are limited exceptions to each of these scenarios, but by and large, they describe how the prosecutor circumscribes the work of defense attorneys.

Defense attorneys are at a marked disadvantage compared to prosecutors. Private defense attorneys can be hired even prior to arrest if a suspect knows an arrest is impending, and many private attorneys are hired immediately after arrest. Indigent defense attorneys, however, come onto a case much later, sometimes between initial appearance and preliminary hearing, but often not until the arraignment. This reduces the capacity of defense attorneys to assess cases and build a case theory. Other obstacles for defense attorneys' assessment and case preparation include the following:

- The prosecutor files the charges, and the defense must react to those and assess their veracity.
- The police tend to be less cooperative with defense.
- Many in the criminal justice system operate with a presumption of guilt of those charged with a criminal offense.
- The prosecutor may not disclose all relevant information during discovery.
- The defense attorney may be given cases they have no experience or interest in.
- The defense attorneys have less money and resources than police and prosecutors. "Compared to total expenditure for criminal justice,

government money spent on criminal defense is negligible. ... The American system operates to the disadvantage of the poor ...". This reduces their capacity to hire expert witnesses and assistants, or even adequate attorneys.

- Many of their clients are difficult to work with because of illiteracy, distrust of government workers, addictions, mental illness, humiliation and anger, fear, and other issues.

Whether in a strong position or not, the defense attorney has to assess cases with the mindset of developing a case theory and strategies that weaken the prosecutor's case [85]. For the most part, factual guilt or innocence is not a significant concern for the defense. The framing effort is to refute evidence of the alleged action, intent, or harm.

Defense and Preliminary Hearing

The preliminary hearing provides an often dramatic shift in defense case assessment. The prosecutor must present evidence to the court that establishes probable cause to justify the continuation of the case, or otherwise risk the judge dismissing the case for insufficient evidence. This gives the defense a chance to see some of the evidence and assess its strength and gaps. The defense attorney can also cross-examine the witnesses politely to find out how believable they will be in trial or aggressively to rattle them and expose contradictions. The defense can also choose to waive the preliminary hearing to keep damaging evidence out of the official record. A defense attorney is usually using this stage to re-assess the case. If the prosecutor's case is weak but the court still finds for it (approves it), the defense may be able to convince the prosecutor to dismiss the case or accept a plea to a reduced charge, often even a misdemeanor. If the prosecutor has a solid case, the defense may encourage her or his client to plead guilty.

If the defendant refuses to plead guilty, the defense can use what is learned in the hearing to prepare for the next pretrial stage and the trial itself. In some jurisdictions, the two attorneys can also agree to "submit the case on the record," which asks the judge to rule on guilt or innocence based on the preliminary hearing transcript. This is generally done when it is rather clear who would win in trial, and it therefore speeds up the process and gets to a conviction (and possible appeal) or exoneration more quickly.

Defense and Trial Preparation

The defense attorney, as with the prosecutor, usually has an eye on the possibility of going to trial. The defense assessment therefore also entails preparing for motions, objections, and defense strategies. A **motion** is a request that the judge make a legal ruling on a limited legal issue in the case without a ruling on the case-in-chief, that is, without ruling on the general issue of guilt or innocence. An **objection** also challenges the legality of an aspect of the opponent's case but is presented during the trial proceedings in direct response to something the other attorney presents.

Motions and objections are presented by either defense or prosecution. Motions and objections, however, are particularly important for the defense to prepare for because:

1. unless evidence is opposed, the court will generally treat it as legal; and
2. they "preserve" legal arguments for appeal, which means that unless they submitted a motion or objections during the trial court process, they generally cannot bring the issue up on appeal.

It is also possible that the defense carries a slight advantage on motions and objections precisely because judges and prosecutors generally want to avoid one of their cases being appealed and may therefore be inclined to grant defense motions and objections.

Motions in particular are generally considered more advantageous for the defense. The goal is either to undermine the opponent's case (suppress evidence) or to clear up ambiguous matters. Most of them happen before trial, but some occur during trial. Motions are made in writing in some jurisdictions but presented orally in others. Although some are standard and routine in many jurisdictions, such as a motion that a court reporter record jury *voir dire*, crucial ones must be customized to the case. Motions are extra work and not only increase the amount of time attorneys on both sides spend on a case, which could be a stalling tactic but also may resolve problems more expeditiously than could be done in front of a jury and may facilitate a plea negotiation [86].

A few common motions include:

- **Motion to dismiss**. Motion by the defense that asks the court to dismiss the case because it does not prove the elements of the crime or there is some other defect in the indictment or information. (A motion for *nolle prosequi* is effectively seeking the same outcome, dismissal, but comes from the prosecution.)
- **Motion for continuance**. A request to postpone the next hearing or trial, usually to afford more time to assess the facts and gather witnesses.
- **Motion for severance of defendants or offenses**. A request to have a separate trial for each defendant or charge, usually to allow for a fair trial.
- **Motion to suppress evidence or statements**. A request, usually by defense, to exclude from trial real or witness evidence, usually because the legality of evidence is in question. The other party, then, has the burden of justifying the inclusion of the evidence. (Defense probably uses this more often with defendants who have a criminal record or were otherwise engaged in illegal behavior [87].)

Of course, the assessment, case theory, and pretrial motions are for the preparation of a trial. Even though most cases do not go to trial, the defense attorney will usually have at least a rough sense, based on the assessment, of how to challenge the government's accusations. When assessing a case, defense attorneys may find that one type of defense is better than others. The options include factual or negating defense, procedural defense, or affirmative or positive defense.

Factual defenses—defense strategies aimed at showing that the prosecution's evidence is weak, invalid, or inconclusive—are probably the most common. They include various efforts to point out that the prosecutor's evidence fails to prove that a crime occurred, that the defendant did it, or that the defendant intended to do it. The defense has no evidentiary obligation to prove innocence. The defendant is presumed to be innocent, and the prosecutor must prove guilt. Perhaps too often, defense attorneys will literally do almost nothing. However, through cross-examination and the presentation of contrary evidence, they will usually challenge the validity and sufficiency of the prosecution's evidence.

Sometimes a factual defense is strong and direct, other times circumstantial. An **alibi defense** is when the attorney takes an active role to prove the "accused was somewhere other than at the scene of the crime at the time it occurred" [88]. "Yes," the defense says, "a crime occurred but the witness and credit card record show that the defendant was at a restaurant during the crime and therefore could not have committed it." If the defense has a good alibi, the case is usually dismissed before trial. In the absence of a good alibi, the defense attorney has to cast less direct uncertainty onto the evidence. The core of this factual defense is, "Yes, a crime did occur, but when we look at the evidence, we just cannot be sure what happened." The O.J. Simpson and Casey Anthony trials both relied on this type of defense. Yes, there was a victim in each case, and no, neither had a good alibi, but the evidence left too much doubt about the defendant's *actus reus* and *mens rea*.

Imagine if you are on a jury and a woman is charged with marijuana possession. The fact that she had marijuana in her purse is not in question. However, the defense is challenging the intent and points out that the purse is like an open bag with no zipper, that the defendant rents two rooms to boarders, that the purse was unattended in the break room at work, and that she was reading while waiting for the bus and others were milling around. Someone could have easily put it in her purse. Is that enough doubt to establish reasonable doubt and rule her not guilty?

A **procedural defense** casts doubt on evidence, tries to have of the evidence suppressed and excluded from the trial, or argues that the case should be dismissed for violation of rights. Common "defects" in the criminal prosecution include that too much time has passed and it is no longer a speedy trial; police gathered evidence in unethical or illegal ways such as entrapment or brutal interrogations; or the prosecutor has committed misconduct such as vindictive prosecution. The film discussed in Chapter 4, *Murder on Sunday Morning*, shows how defense attorneys can cast doubt on evidence by pointing out sloppy, incompetent, and possibly illegal police work that produced the evidence.

Affirmative defenses require a whole different assessment and framing. They acknowledge that the essential act and/or intent the prosecutor is charging as a crime is proved by the evidence but argue that the defendant is not culpable. When a defense attorney frames out such a case theory, he or she takes on the burden of proving that circumstances beyond the defendant's control caused the ostensibly criminal act to occur. These defenses entail presenting more evidence than normal, and generally are categorized as justifications (the act was justified by overwhelming circumstances) or excuses (the defendant had diminished control over her or his actions).

Perhaps the most popular in media is the insanity defense, in which the defense argues that the defendant has a defect of mind or mental illness such that he or she could not understand the nature of the actions [89]. This defense is rarely used and rarely successful when used. Other affirmative defenses include self-defense, in which defendants admit to hurting or killing someone but argue that it was to protect their own lives or family; and duress, in which defendants admit to committing the crime but argue that they did it only because someone else threatened to harm them if they did not. The core of all these affirmative defenses is unusual because the defense attorney admits to most elements of the crime and effectively says, "Yes, a crime occurred, and yes, clearly my client did it, but he lacked *criminal* intent. He did not freely choose to go out and commit a crime."

SUMMARY

1. Define case mobilization and case assessment.
   - Case assessment involves legal reasoning, categorization of cases as conforming or exceptional, prioritization of cases, and consideration of the extralegal factors in order to decide if the case should proceed toward trial and how to best prepare it in the event that it does.
   - Case mobilization is the movement of a case from police booking through the preliminary hearings to trial or another disposition.
2. Explain how case assessment involves both exerting state power and protecting due process rights.
   - Prosecutors assess cases with the objective of increasing their confidence that a crime occurred, that the accused committed the crime and had culpability, and that the case could be won in trial.

Defense works with the objective of casting doubt on the prosecutors' cases. The prosecutor filters the assessment through the screen of due process, and the defense must filter the assessment through the law of the land.

3. Describe how legal reasoning and precedent affect case assessment.
    - Legal reasoning frames how to assess evidence and prepare a case for trial. It requires that the lawyers evaluate the culpability of the defendant in terms of statutes and the alleged crime itself. It requires that they establish and enunciate specifically what law was supposedly violated and what defense is being asserted, and that they clearly identify which facts are relevant. It requires that they follow the rules of procedure, such as participation in discovery and the rules of evidence, many of which are established in precedent. Attorneys on both sides must look through this precedent frame and try to determine what evidence is probably admissible and what might get suppressed.

4. Discuss how ecological features, such as courthouse procedures and focal concerns, affect assessment.
    - Use of focal concerns enables attorneys to process a large number of diverse cases more expeditiously by categorizing them as "conforming" or "exceptional," then prioritizing them.
    - Official courthouse procedures directly influence how attorneys assess a case and prepare for each preliminary stage and the eventuality of trial. This includes case-screening protocols, deadlines, use of grand juries, jury selection, rules of evidence and motions, inclusion of victims, and availability of diversionary programs.

5. Explain prosecutorial discretion and briefly discuss why it is controversial.
    - Prosecutorial discretion is the capacity to make choices regarding a case, including to charge or dismiss a case, divert a case, change charges, plea bargain, develop a case theory, argue a case, and recommend leniency or the maximum sentence.
    - Some observers argue that prosecutors need more discretion to control crime effectively. Others argue that the large degree of prosecutorial discretion already weakens the rule of law and allows for abuse of government power and inequality.

6. List the main questions that influence the prosecutor's assessment.
    - In assessing a case, the prosecutor asks the legal sufficiency question: "Could this case be prosecuted?"
    - The trial sufficiency or trial-outcome questions include: "Could this case be won in trial?"
    - The system efficiency, social good and justice, and aspiration questions ask: "Should this case be prosecuted?"

7. Tell what "overcharging" is and why prosecutors do it.
   - Overcharging is when prosecutors position themselves for plea bargaining by charging the maximum criminal offense the elements of the crime will justify and include the lesser offenses justified by the evidence. If the highest charge does not lead to a conviction, perhaps one of the lower ones will. The maximum charge induces defendants to file a vertical plea.

8. Give reasons a prosecutor may decide to drop a case.
   - The evidence does not meet the elements requirement; a conviction at trial is uncertain; witnesses are not cooperating or credible or cannot be located; the defendant is wealthy or the defense attorney is tough; the defendant is not considered a threat to the community; the defendant has favorable cues; the law has not been enforced for a long time; office priorities are directing resources to other cases; the voting public opposes the trial.

9. Give reasons that defense attorneys are at a disadvantage compared to prosecutors.
   - Obstacles for defense attorneys' assessment and case preparation include the following: the prosecutor files the charges, and the defense must react to those and assess their veracity; the police tend to be less cooperative with defense; many in the criminal justice system operate with a presumption of guilt of those charged with a criminal offense; the prosecutor may not disclose all relevant information during discovery; the defense attorney may be given cases they have no experience or interest in; the defense attorneys have less money and resources than police and prosecutors.

10. Define motions and objections and explain why they are advantageous for the defense.
    - A motion is a request that the judge make a legal ruling on a limited legal issue in the case without a ruling on the case-in-chief. An objection challenges the legality of an aspect of the opponent's case but is presented during the trial proceedings in direct response to something the other attorney presents.
    - The defense may carry a slight advantage on motions and objections because judges and prosecutors generally want to avoid one of their cases being appealed and may therefore be inclined to grant defense motions and objections. Motions also may resolve problems more expeditiously than could be done in front of a jury and may facilitate a plea negotiation.

Questions

1. What is case mobilization? Case assessment?
2. How does case assessment involve both exerting state power and protecting due process rights?
3. How do legal reasoning and precedent affect case assessment?
4. How do ecological features, such as courthouse procedures and focal concerns, affect assessment?
5. What is prosecutorial discretion? Why is it controversial?
6. What main questions influence the prosecutor's assessment?
7. What is "overcharging"? Why do prosecutors do it?
8. Why may a prosecutor decide to drop a case?
9. Why are defense attorneys at a disadvantage compared to prosecutors?
10. What are motions and objections? Why are they advantageous for the defense?

REFERENCES

[1] Stuntz WJ. The collapse of American criminal justice. Cambridge, MA: The Belknap Press of Harvard University Press; 2011.

[2] Littrell WB. Bureaucratic justice: police, prosecutors, and plea bargaining. Beverly Hills, CA: Sage Publications; 1979. p. 36.

[3] Petersilia J, Abrahamse AF, Wilson JQ. Police performance and case attrition. Santa Monica, CA: Rand Corporation; 1987.

[4] Jacobs H. Justice in America: courts, lawyers, and the judicial process. 4th ed. Boston, MA: Little, Brown and Company; 1984. p. 180.

[5] Rembar C. The law of the land: the evolution of our legal system. New York, NY: Simon & Schuster; 1980. p. 38. Toutant C. Judge facing ethics charges seeks recusal of two high court justices. New Jersey Law J August 30, 2006.

[6] Porto BL. The craft of legal reasoning. Fort Worth, TX: Harcourt Brace College Pub.; 1998.

[7] Agency Directory. Office of the attorney general of state of Mississippi, <www.ago.state.ms.us> [accessed October 18, 2012].

[8] American Prosecutors Research Institute. Rhode Island department of the attorney general: workload assessment. Alexandria, VA: Office of Research & Evaluation, ND, 3: Online at <www.rijustice.state.ri.us/documents/reports/AG%20Caseload%20Final%20Report.pdf> [accessed October 18, 2012].

[9] Eisenstein J, Jacob H. Felony justice: an organizational analysis of criminal courts. Boston, MA: Little, Brown and Company; 1977. p. 19–20.

[10] Wasserstrom RA. The judicial decision: toward a theory of legal justification, 18–19. Stanford, CA: Stanford University Press; 1961. p. 35–9.

[11] Milovanovic D. A primer in the sociology of law. New York, NY: Harrow and Heston; 1988. p. 134–6.

[12] *Brady v. Maryland*, 373 U.S. 83 (1963).

[13] *Daubert v. Merrell Dow Pharmaceuticals*, 509 U.S. 579 (1993). Jurs AW. Science court; past proposals, current considerations, and a suggested structure. Virginia J Law Technol 2010;15 (1): Cunningham MD, Reidy TJ. Violence risk assessment at federal capital sentencing: individualization, generalization, relevance, and scientific standards. Criminal Justice Behav 2002;29(5):512−37.

[14] *United States v. Booker*, 543 U.S. 220 (2005). Jordan SD. Have we come full circle? Judicial sentencing discretion revived in Booker and Fanfan. Pepperdine Law Rev 2006;33(3): See also *Apprendi v. New Jersey*, 530 U.S. 466 (2000) and *Blakely v. Washington*, 542 U.S. 296 (2004).

[15] *Katz v. United States*, 389 U.S. 347 (1967). Alderman E, Kennedy C. The right to privacy. New York, NY: Vintage Books; 1997. *Kyllo v. United States*, 533 U.S. 27 (2001). See also *Washington State v. Young* 123 Wash. 2d 173, 867 P.2d 593 (1994). *UnitedStates v. Jones*, No. 10-1259 (2011).

[16] McInnis TN. *Nix v. Williams* and the inevitable discovery exception: creation of a legal safety net. Public Law Rev 2009;28(2):397−446.

[17] *Chimel v. California*, 395 U.S. 752 (1969). *Carroll v. United States*, 267 U.S. 132 (1925). *Terry v. Ohio*, 392 U.S. 1 (1968). *United States v. Calandra*, 414 U.S. 338 (1974). *Nix v. Williams*, 432 U.S. 1031 (1975). *United States v. Havens*, 446 U.S. 620 (1980). *Oliver v. United States*, 466 U.S. 170 (1984). *Coolidge v. New Hampshire*, 403 U.S. 443 (1971). *Horton v. California*, 496 U.S. 128 (1990). *Arizona v. Hicks*, 480 U.S. 321 (1987). *California v. Greenwood*, 486 U.S. 35 (1988). *New Jersey v. T.L.O.*, 469 U.S. 325 (1985). Holley B. Digitizing the Fourth Amendment: limiting the private search exception in computer investigations. Virginia Law Rev 2010;96(3):677−717 *Illinois v. Rodriguez*, 497 U.S. 177 (1990).

[18] Schuck PH. Law and the study of migration. In: Brettell C, Hollifield JF, editors: Migration theory: talking across disciplines. New York, NY: Routledge; 2000.

[19] Cole GF. Performance measures for the trial courts, prosecution, and public defense. Performance measures for the criminal justice system. Washington, DC: United States Department of Justice; 1993. p. 93. Church Jr. TW. Examining local legal culture. Law Soc Inq 1985;10(3):449−510. Littrell. Bureaucratic justice: police, prosecutors, and plea bargaining, p. 29. Cole GF. Performance measures for the trial courts, prosecution, and public defense. Performance measures for the criminal justice system. Washington, DC: United States Department of Justice; 1993. p. 93. Church Jr. TW. Examining local legal culture. Law Soc Inq 1985;10(3):449−510. Siegel AM. When prosecutors control criminal court dockets: dispatches on history and policy from a land time forgot. Am J Criminal Law 2005;32(3):325−79. Hanley JR, Schmidt WW, Robbins RK. Introduction to criminal evidence and court procedure. 4th ed. Berkeley, CA: McCutchan Publishing; 1999. p. 16. Carp RA, Stidham R. Judicial process in America. 2nd ed. Washington, DC: Congressional Quarterly Press; 1993, Chapter 11. Stickels JW, Mobley SJ. Texas criminal defense attorneys' perceptions of crime victim involvement in criminal prosecutions. J Police Criminal Psychol 2008;23(1):35−44.

[20] Sampson RJ, Laub JH. Crime, class, and community: an emerging paradigm. Law Soc Rev 1993;27:255−359. Ulmer JT, Bader C, Gault M. Do moral communities play a role in criminal sentencing? Evidence from Pennsylvania. Sociol Quart 2008;49(4):737−68. Davies ALB, Worden AP. State politics and the right to counsel: a comparative analysis. Law Soc Rev 2009;43(1):187−219. Edkins VA. Defense attorney plea recommendations and client race: does zealous representation apply equally to all? Law Human Behav 2011;35 (5):413−25. Varela JG, et al. Do defense attorney referrals for competence to stand trial evaluations depend on whether the client speaks English or Spanish? Law Human Behav 2011;35(6):501−11. Bridges GS, Steen S. Racial disparities in official assessments of juvenile offenders: attributional stereotypes as mediating mechanisms. Am Sociol Rev 1998;63 (4):554−70. Harris A, Evans H, Beckett K. Courtesy stigma and monetary sanctions: toward a socio-cultural theory of punishment. Am Sociol Rev 2011;76(2):234−64. Paternoster R. Prosecutorial discretion in requesting the death penalty: a case of victim-based racial discrimination. Law Soc Rev 1984;18(3):437−78. Cohen GB, Smith RJ. The racial geography

of the federal death penalty. Washington Law Rev 2010;85(3):425−92. Paternoster R, Brame R. Reassessing race disparities in Maryland capital cases. Criminology 2008;46 (4):971−1008. Eberhardt JL, et al. Research report. Psychol Sci 2006;17(5):383−6. Johnson BD, Dipietro SM. The power of diversion: intermediate sanctions and sentencing disparity under presumptive guidelines. Criminology 2012;50(3):811−50. Kramer J, Steffensmeier D. Race and imprisonment decisions. Sociol Quart 1993;34(2):357−76. Cooney M. Evidence as partisanship. Law Soc Rev 1994;28(4):833−58.

[21] Sigall H, Ostrove N. Beautiful but dangerous: effects of offender attractiveness and nature of the crime on juridic judgment. J Personality Soc Psychol 1975;31(3):410−4. Cohen LE, Kluegel JR. Detention decision: a study of the impact of social characteristics and legal factors in two metropolitan juvenile courts. Soc Forces 1979;58(1):146−61. Sampson, Laub. Crime, class, and community. [Paternoster. Prosecutorial discretion in requesting the death penalty. Paternoster, Brame. Reassessing race disparities in Maryland capital cases. Eberhardt, et al. Research report.]

[22] Steffensmeier D, Demuth S. Ethnicity and sentencing outcomes in U.S. federal courts: who is punished more harshly? Am Sociol Rev 2000;65(5):705−29. Farrell RA, Holmes MD. The social and cognitive structure of legal decision-making. Sociol Quart 1991;32(4):529−42.

[23] Menand L. American studies. New York, NY: Farrar, Straus and Giroux; 2002.

[24] Emmelman DS. Gauging the strength of evidence prior to plea bargaining: the interpretive procedures of court-appointed defense attorneys. Law Soc Inquiry 1997;22(4):927−55.

[25] Miller FW. Prosecution: the decision to charge a suspect with a crime. Boston, MA: Little, Brown and Company; 1969.

[26] McAllister HA. Effects of eyewitness evidence on plea-bargain decisions by prosecutors and defense attorneys. J Appl Soc Psychol 1990;20(18):1461−73.

[27] Ford DA. Wife battery and criminal justice: a study of victim decision-making. Minneapolis, MN: National Council on Family Relations; 1983.

[28] Hanley, Schmidt, Robbins. Introduction to criminal evidence and court procedure, p. 16, 17, 19, 58.

[29] Huber P. Galileo's revenge: junk science in the courtroom. New York, NY: Basic Books; 1993.

[30] Robinson PH. Rules of conduct and principles of adjudication. Univ Chicago Law Rev 1990;57(3):729−71.

[31] Ogilvie T. The theory of the case: what prosecutors can teach us about competitive intelligence. Competitive Intell Rev 1997;8(2):12−9.

[32] Devine DJ. Jury decision making: 45 years of empirical research on deliberating groups. Psychol Public Policy Law 2001;7(3):622−727.

[33] Ramsey CB. The discretionary power of "public" prosecutors in historical perspective. Am Criminal Law Rev 2002;39(4):1309−93.

[34] Perry SW. Prosecutors in state courts, 2005. Washington, DC: Bureau of Justice Statistics; 2006.

[35] Littrell. Bureaucratic justice: police, prosecutors, and plea bargaining, p. 33−34.

[36] Cole GF. The decision to prosecute. Law Soc Rev 1970;4(3):331−44. Weaver S. Decision to prosecute: organization and public policy in the antitrust division. Cambridge, MA: MIT Press; 1977.

[37] Belenko S, Fabrikant N, Wolff N. The long road to treatment: models of screening and admission into drug courts. Criminal Justice Behav 2011;38(12):1222−43.

[38] Allen FA. The habits of legality: criminal justice and the rule of law. New York, NY: Oxford University Press; 1996. Sarat A, Clarke C. Beyond discretion: prosecution, the logic of sovereignty, and the limits of law. Law Soc Inquiry 2008;33(2):387. Barkow RE. Separation of powers and the criminal law. Stanford Law Rev 2006;58(4):989−1054. Harris A. Diverting

and abdicating judicial discretion: cultural, political, and procedural dynamics in California juvenile justice. Law Soc Rev 2007;41(2):387–427.

[39] Jacoby JE. The prosecutor's charging decision: a policy perspective. Washington, DC: United States Department of Justice; 1977. p. 16–19.

[40] U.S. Advisory Commission on Intergovernmental Relations. Guide to the criminal justice system for general government elected officials. Washington, DC: U.S. Advisory Commission on Intergovernmental Relations; 1993. p. 10.

[41] Ibid., 18.

[42] American Prosecutors Research Institute. Prosecution in the 21st century: goals, objectives, and performance measures. Alexandria, VA: American Prosecutors Research Institute; 2004.

[43] Littrell. Bureaucratic justice: police, prosecutors, and plea bargaining, p. 131–33.

[44] Washington State Institute for Public Policy. Deferred prosecution of DUI cases in Washington state: evaluating the impact on recidivism. Olympia, WA: Washington State Institute for Public Policy; 2007: Online at <www.wsipp.wa.gov/rptfiles/07-08-1901.pdf>.

[45] American Prosecutors Research Institute. Rhode Island department of the attorney general: workload assessment, p. 9: Online at <www.rijustice.state.ri.us/documents/reports/AG%20 Caseload%20Final%20Report.pdf> [accessed October 18, 2012].

[46] Bibas S. Prosecutorial regulation versus prosecutorial accountability. Univ Pennsylvania Law Rev 2009;157(4):959–1016.

[47] Ma Y. Prosecutorial discretion and plea bargaining in the United States, France, Germany, and Italy: a comparative perspective. Int Criminal Justice Rev 2002;12:22–52.

[48] Bjerk D. Making the crime fit the penalty: the role of prosecutorial discretion under mandatory minimum sentencing. J Law Econom 2005;48(2):591. Wooldredge J, Griffin T. Displaced discretion under Ohio sentencing guidelines. J Criminal Justice 2005;33 (4):301–16. Miller JL, Sloan III JJ. A study of criminal justice discretion. J Criminal Justice 1994;22(2):107–23.

[49] Sarat, Clarke. Beyond discretion.Barkow. Separation of powers and the criminal law.

[50] Barkow RE. Institutional design and the policing of prosecutors: lessons from administrative law. Stanford Law Rev 2009;61(4):869–921.

[51] Robinson. Rules of conduct and principles of adjudication.

[52] *Griffin v. California*, 380 U.S. 609 (1965).

[53] *In re Winship*, 397 U.S. 358 (1970).

[54] Littrell. Bureaucratic justice: police, prosecutors, and plea bargaining, Chapter 3. Spohn C, Fornango R. U.S. attorneys and substantial assistance departures: testing for interprosecutor disparity. Criminology 2009;47(3):813–46.

[55] Hirschel D, Hutchison IW. The relative effects of offense, offender, and victim variables on the decision to prosecute domestic violence cases. Violence Against Women 2001;7(1):46–59. Kerstetter WA, Van Winkle B. Who decides? A study of the complainant's decision to prosecute in rape cases. Criminal Justice Behav 1990;17(3):268–83. Holleran D, Beichner D, Spohn C. Examining charging agreement between police and prosecutors in rape cases. Crime Delinquency 2010;56(3):385–413. [The authors found that victim credibility is an equal focal concern regardless of the style of prosecution.]

[56] Weaver. Decision to prosecute.

[57] American Prosecutors Research Institute. Rhode Island department of the attorney general: workload assessment, Appendix B.

[58] Nugent ME, Rainville G. Resource needs of Georgia district attorneys' and solicitors'. General offices: interim final report. Atlanta, GA: Prosecuting Attorneys Council of Georgia; 2000.

[59] Frohmann L. Discrediting victims' allegations of sexual assault: prosecutorial accounts of case rejections. Soc Probl 1991;38(2):213–26.

[60] Beichner D, Spohn C. Prosecutorial charging decisions in sexual assault cases: examining the impact of a specialized prosecution unit. Criminal Justice Policy Rev 2005;16 (4):461–98. Myers M, Hagan J. Private and public trouble: prosecutors and the allocation of court resources. Soc Problems 1979;26(4):439–51.

[61] Ford DA. Wife battery and criminal justice: a study of victim decision-making. Minneapolis, MN: National Council on Family Relations; 1983. Spohn C, Beichner D, Davis-Frenzel E. Prosecutorial justifications for sexual assault case rejection: guarding the "gateway to justice". Soc Probl 2001;48(2):206–35.

[62] Spohn, Beichner, and Davis-Frenzel. Prosecutorial justifications for sexual assault case rejection.

[63] Beichner D, Spohn C. Modeling the effects of victim behavior and moral character on prosecutors' charging decisions in sexual assault cases. Violence Victims 2012;27(1):3–24.

[64] Chaiken MR, Chaiken JM. Priority prosecution of high-rate dangerous offenders. In: Eskridge CW, editor. Criminal justice: concepts and issues. 3rd ed. Los Angeles, CA: Roxbury Publishing Company; 1999. p. 178–86. Jacoby. The prosecutor's charging decision, Perry SW, Banks D. Prosecutors in state courts, 2007—statistical tables. Washington, DC: Bureau of Justice Statistics; 2011. Carol J. DeFrances, prosecutors in state courts, 2001. Washington, DC: Bureau of Justice Statistics; 2002. Abramovsky A. An unholy alliance: perceptions of influence in insurance fraud prosecutions and the need for real safeguards. J Criminal Law Criminology 2008;98(2):363–427. Jansen S, Hood R. A framework for high performance prosecutorial services. Washington, DC: Association of Prosecuting Attorneys; 2011. p. 27. Jacoby. The prosecutor's charging decision, p. 1. Jansen, Hood. A framework for high performance prosecutorial services, p. 10.

[65] Bjerk. Making the crime fit the penalty. Wooldredge, Griffin. Displaced discretion under Ohio sentencing guidelines.

[66] Fearn. A multilevel analysis of community effects on criminal sentencing. Spohn, Beichner, Davis-Frenzel. Prosecutorial justifications for sexual assault case rejection.

[67] Myers, Hagan. Private and public trouble.

[68] Spohn C, Beichner, Davis-Frenzel, Prosecutorial justifications for sexual assault case rejection.

[69] Ibid.

[70] American Prosecutors Research Institute. Rhode Island department of the attorney general: workload assessment, p. 13.

[71] Littrell. Bureaucratic justice: police, prosecutors, and plea bargaining, p. 193.

[72] Ehrhard S. Plea bargaining and the death penalty: an exploratory study. Justice Syst J 2008;29(3):313–25. I Bordenkircher v. Hayes, 434 U.S. 357 (1978).

[73] Mosle S. "Tulia": the case of the lone star witness. The New York Times 2005 <www.nytimes.com/2005/10/30/books/review/30mosle.html> [accessed 30 October, 2005].

[74] Ibid.

[75] Rob Warden. Texas "Officer of the year," chalked up 38 wrongful convictions, Northwestern University School of Law center on wrongful convictions, <www.law.northwestern.edu/wrongfulconvictions/exonerations/txtuliasummary.html> [accessed October 15, 2012].

[76] Ibid.

[77] Blakeslee N. Tulia: race, cocaine, and corruption in a small Texas town. New York, NY: PublicAffairs; 2005. Northwestern Law Center on Wrongful Convictions, <www.law.northwestern.edu/wrongfulconvictions/exonerations/txtuliasummary.html> [accessed October 18, 2012].

[78] Eisenstein, Jacob. Felony justice: an organizational analysis of criminal courts.Feeney F, Dill F, Weir AW. Arrests without conviction: how often they occur and why. Washington, DC: United States Deptartment of Justice, National Institute of Justice; 1983. p. 32.

[79] Feeney, Dill, Weir. Arrests without conviction: how often they occur and why, p. 42.

[80] Feeney, Dill, Weir. Arrests without conviction: how often they occur and why.Petersilia, Abrahamse, Wilson. Police performance and case attrition. Garofalo J, Neuberger AR. Reducing avoidable felony case attrition through enhanced police-prosecutor coordination. Albany, NY: Hindelang Criminal Justice Research Center, State University of New York at Albany; 1987.

[81] Hagan J. Extra-legal attributes and criminal sentencing: an assessment of a sociological viewpoint. Law Soc Rev 1974;8:557–83. Jacoby. The prosecutor's charging decision, p. 6.

[82] Feeney, Dill, Weir. Arrests without conviction: how often they occur and why. Coffey G. 2012. Personal correspondence.

[83] Casper JD. American criminal justice: the defendant's perspective. Englewood, NJ: Prentice Hall; 1972. American Prosecutors Research Institute. Prosecution in the 21st century: goals, objectives, and performance measures, p. 6.

[84] Feeley MM. The process is the punishment. New York, NY: Russell Sage Foundation; 1992 Flemming RB. Punishment before trial. New York, NY: Longman; 1982.

[85] Bailey FL, Aronson H. The defense never rests. New York, NY: Stein and Day Publishers; 1972.

[86] National Workload Assessment Project. How many cases should a prosecutor handle? Alexandria, VA: American Prosecutors Research Institute, Office of Research & Evaluation; 2002, 10: Online at <www.ndaa.org/pdf/How%20Many%20Cases.pdf> .

[87] Laudan L, Allen RJ. The devastating impact of prior crimes evidence and other myths of the criminal justice process. J Criminal Law Criminology 2011;101(2):493–527.

[88] Cornell University Law School's Legal Information Institute (LII), Alibi, <www.law.cornell.edu/wex/alibi> [accessed September 19, 2010].

[89] King JD. Candor, zeal, and the substitution of judgment: ethics and the mentally ill criminal defendant. Am Univ Law Rev 2008;58(2):207.

3 PART

Decision-Making in the Pretrial and Trial Process

OVERVIEW

Part 3 offers a road map of the pretrial and trial process. The pretrial process, which includes preliminary hearings and arraignments, takes care of the vast majority of cases that make it past the police filter and the prosecutor's case assessment. In other words, most cases are dismissed or diverted to an alternative system or end with the defendant pleading guilty. When a case ends up in trial, the prosecutor has the distinct role of representing the power of the state. While negotiating the various internal and external pressures, he or she must pursue a conviction yet still adhere to the ideal of a just process. The defense attorney must also negotiate many pressures, but her or his job is to represent the accused and counter-balance the power of the state. The judges and juries review the arguments of the prosecutor and the defense and determine if the evidence clearly establishes guilt. The courtroom workers must balance state power and individual rights at all of these stages.

An arrest is the first step in the court process. Here, a New York City police officer escorts a man who was part of the Occupy Wall Street protests after his arrest in lower Manhattan.

The Pretrial Process

KEY TERMS

Alford plea	charging document	preliminary hearing
arraignment	diversion	pretrial motions
arrest	good-faith exception	release-on-recognizance
bail	horizontal plea bargain	rules of evidence
bail-bond agent	*nolo contendere*	vertical plea bargain
bond	petit jury	wergeld
culpability	plea bargain	

Learning Objectives

After reading this chapter, you should be able to:

1. Briefly describe the process of arrest and what happens afterward.
2. Understand the reasons for bail.
3. Discuss the advantages of diversion programs for defendants.
4. Compare and contrast the advantages and disadvantages of plea bargaining for prosecutors, defendants, and society.
5. Identify the functions of the preliminary hearing.
6. Explain why the grand jury is criticized as a tool of the prosecutor.
7. Tell what happens during an arraignment.
8. Explain why the pretrial process is an important part of the court system.

The popular concept of the U.S. court is centered on the criminal trial. Film, television programs, and novels often portray the fascinating and important work that is done in deciding the guilt or innocence of the accused [1]. Although this focus on the criminal trial is the truth and nothing but the truth, it is not the whole truth. Several processes that significantly affect what

239

happens in the courtroom precede the trial. Many of the pretrial processes have more to do with the actual disposition of justice than does the criminal trial. In this chapter, we will review the most important of the pretrial processes: the decision to divert the case from the criminal justice system; the arrangements for bail, plea bargaining, and preliminary functions such as the preliminary hearing; presentation to the grand jury and indictment; and the arraignment of the case before a judge.

These pretrial processes are important for the student to comprehend because not only do they soak up much of the court's time and resources but also they structure the pattern in which the courts dispose of cases. Without this appreciation of pretrial processes, the student is left with a skewed view of the activities of the court and the political and social demands that guide the disposition of justice in the United States.

ARREST

An **arrest** is the deprivation of the liberty of an individual by a legal authority. The pretrial process begins with the arrest of the accused. Once an individual is arrested and brought to the local jail, the responsibility for processing the case shifts from law enforcement to the courts. An intake officer at the jail decides whether the case is serious enough and if there is enough evidence to further detain the accused. At this point, the accused may be released for several reasons, including a clarification of what actually happened and officials' realization that the accused is innocent. Additionally, it may be determined that the accused is actually the victim of a criminal offense, not the perpetrator, or that no offense has been committed at all. However, these decisions are typically not made at this point but rather during further pretrial processes.

Once it is determined that there is enough evidence to detain the individual, he or she is booked into the jail. This entails developing a paper trail of the case that includes the exact criminal code that has been violated, fingerprinting, and the taking of a photograph or mug shot. Once this paper trail has been established, the discretion on the part of police and court officials is limited because of the requirements that the pretrial processes be documented. This documentation includes a **charging document** that specifies the law that has been broken and the date and location of the offense. This paper trail is necessary for an individual to be able to challenge the specific details of the alleged offense.

The paper trail also includes a complaint by the arresting officer or the victim alleging that the offense has been committed by the accused. In some jurisdictions, this complaint is replaced by an information arguing that there is sufficient information about the offense to initiate felony charges. This important gatekeeping function performed by the prosecutor determines which cases enter the criminal justice system.

It is important to understand that this charging decision represents one of the key points of discretion by an actor in the criminal justice system. Although our popular concept of justice is that anyone who breaks a law will be charged, the prosecutor may actually forgo charging individuals for many reasons [2]. These reasons might include lack of sufficient evidence; a determination that the alleged offense is not of sufficient seriousness to expend the limited resources available to the prosecutor's office and the courts; or, in selected cases, the prosecutor may determine that it is politically unwise to prosecute.

Considerable tension may exist between the police and the prosecutor over who controls the charging decision [3]. On the one hand, the arresting police officer is closer to the case, having dealt with the arrestee, the victim, and the aftermath of the offense. This officer is, in many ways, in the best position to determine the seriousness of the offense and its effects. On the other hand, the prosecutor has a more objective view of the case and can determine how the seriousness of the offense matches with other offenses committed in the jurisdiction. This gives the prosecutor a better control over the efficiency of the charging decision and ensures that there is an element of fairness in that minor cases to get treated in a similar fashion.

Another reason police officers may resist ceding the charging decision to the prosecutor is because it suggests that the police may have made a mistake if the prosecutor decides not to charge the accused. The prosecutor's discretion takes away discretion from police officers who believe they should be responsible for the charging decision. Jurisdictions can vary widely in who gets to make the charging decision, but we cannot overemphasize that this is a key discretionary point in the criminal justice system or one that can have a profound effect on which cases enter the criminal justice system. There may not be a perfect way to make this decision because, in many respects, it is a political decision in which prosecutors and law enforcement officers vie for power.

BAIL

Bail is the amount of money the court requires to secure the release of an accused person from jail. Once an arrestee is booked into jail, he or she will most likely be released before the case is concluded. Whether the case is plea-bargained or goes to trial, the chances of the accused remaining in jail depend on several factors, including seriousness of the offense. The Eighth Amendment prohibits "excessive bail" on the presumption that a person is innocent until proven guilty. Therefore, almost all defendants will be given an opportunity to post bail or participate in some other pretrial release procedure [4].

When the accused appears in court and follows all of the rules of the proceedings, the entire bail amount is refunded. The posting of bail serves as a guarantee that the accused will return for a future court date. If the accused does not appear in court, the bail is forfeited. There are a couple of arguments for the benefits of bail.

- Social costs. Keeping people in jail is expensive. Individuals must be guarded, fed, and provided a space to sleep. Although most of us would certainly want to keep dangerous people in jail even though they have not had their day in court, it is difficult to determine exactly who these dangerous people are. Without bail, we risk jailing minor offenders who pose no threat to society. Furthermore, one of the foundations of our justice system is that a person is "innocent until proven guilty." As long as we can ensure that the accused parties will appear for future court hearings, we wish to respect this presumption of innocence and allow them their freedom. Additionally, people in jail may lose their jobs, be unable to supervise their children, or pay taxes. It is in the society's best interest to detain only those who pose a threat to others or who are unlikely to meet their obligations to attend future court proceedings.
- Crowding. Jails in many, if not most, jurisdictions are severely crowded. Crowding challenges numerous regulations that govern the quality of conditions in the jail. Jails simply do not have the resources to detain one prior to the disposition of their cases, so bail performs a vital and necessary function in the criminal justice system [5].
- Incentive for the accused. Accused individuals have an incentive to be released on bail and return for court proceedings. Not only are liberty and autonomy greatly limited in jail but also jails are often dangerous [6].

One major criticism of bail is that it favors people with money and property. In essence, the wealthy can secure release while the impoverished remain in jail awaiting the disposition of their case. One way to compensate for this economic privilege is to allow someone else to use their promise of collateral to ensure that the accused will appear in court. In this case, the accused will purchase a **bond**, or promise to pay. **Bail-bond agents**, people who are hired to promise to pay the accused's bail if he or she does not show up for court, provide this function for a fee.

Typically, the bail-bond agent charges the accused 10 percent of the bond for guaranteeing that the accused will appear for future court hearings. For example, if bail is set at $10,000, the bail-bond agent promises the court that he or she will pay the full $10,000 should the accused failed to appear. In turn, the accused pays the agent $1000 for making a promise to the court. The $1000 is paid immediately to the bail-bond agent and is not refunded to the accused upon appearance in the court. The percentage of the bond is the price they receive for their service.

However, the bail-bond agent does not keep thousands of dollars lying around the office to pay the court when they post the bond. Rather, they arrange with an insurance company to produce the money if needed. This means that the bail-bond company must be right more often than wrong in judging whether an accused person will appear in court. Consequently, the business of the bail-bond company is to choose cases that are most likely to result in the accused keeping his or her word and appearing in future hearings. A bail-bond company could not afford to have too many cases fail to appear, because the insurance company would quickly drop their coverage.

Judges have a tremendous amount of discretion when setting bail. Although most cases will receive an expected amount of bail based upon the seriousness of the charge, the court also considers possibilities such as the chances that someone will flee the jurisdiction. In these cases, the court will set the bail at a much higher level in order to ensure the accused's cooperation. In some cases, the bail will be set so high that the accused will be unable to find a bail-bond agent who will take the risk. In capital cases in which the death penalty is possible, bail will not be set at all because the accused may have more incentive to flee rather than appear at future hearings [7].

The History of Bail

The word "bail" is from the Old French word *baille*, which means "to deliver." However, there are two ideas concerning the origin of the practice of bail. The first idea is that it is related to the ancient English practice of hostageship, in which a hostage was held until a promise was fulfilled by the opposing side. The second idea is that bail emerged from ancient English system of **wergeld**, traditionally the monetary value of a person's life paid as compensation by the family of an accused murderer to the family of the deceased in order to prevent a blood feud. The idea of wergeld evolved to one in which a person accused of committing a wrong or harming another had to promise to pay a sum of money to the accuser if the accused's guilt was proven [8]. The concept of crime being an offense against the state had not yet been established, so most offenses were considered to be private matters between accused and accuser, with payments of money being considered the most just way to settle the issue. People who were considered as a danger to the community were typically mutilated or executed, so bail did not apply in those situations [9].

The practice of bail became more formal from 1000 to 1300. In early practice, the accused would find a person, usually a friend or relative, willing to be responsible for payments to the victim and the king if the accused fled before the court date. These payments were equal to the amounts the offense required if the accused had been found guilty in court. So if the accused fled, the payments would still be made and the matter settled. Later, the system became more complicated. Although the practice of quick executions and mutilations ended, corporal punishment became a common penalty, and accused individuals spent more time behind bars waiting for justice [10]. The appearance of a traveling judge might be years apart, and the local sheriff became the one responsible for ensuring that the accused showed up at the time of trial. This system led to corruption as sheriffs could decide who received bail and who did not.

The first law governing bail, the first Statute of Westminster, was passed in 1275 [11]. This legislation established which offenses could receive bail and established penalties when proper procedures were not followed. The process of bail gradually shifted from the sheriff to the judge. Additionally, discretion was limited as the types of cases that were eligible for bail were based upon the accused's character and the risk of flight. Excessive bail was prohibited by the 1689 English Bill of Rights and was incorporated into the Eighth Amendment, which, although not guaranteeing bail, does state that "Excessive bail shall not be required." In 1951, the Supreme Court in *Stack v. Boyle* ruled that the presumption of innocence would lose its meaning if bail was excessive.

Who Gets Bail?

Not all accused individuals get their bail set at the same rate. For the most part, the setting of bail is routine, so cases with the same qualities tend to be treated in a similar fashion. Many jurisdictions have set up bail schedules that specify the amount of bail based upon the seriousness of the offense. Thus, the decision about the amount of bail is predictable in most cases. Several factors determine how bail schedules are created, and judges also consider these factors when considering an individual case for bail.

- Severity of offense. The more serious the offense, the higher the bail. The rationale behind this is that those who are accused of serious offenses are more likely to get more severe sentences if convicted. Therefore, those accused of serious offenses are at greater risk of not appearing for future court hearings because they are at greater risk of incarceration and of being incarcerated for a longer time than those accused of less serious offenses. By matching the bail amount to the seriousness of the offense, the courts pass on to the bail-bond agent the task of making the judgment as to whether the accused is likely to appear at future hearings or flee. Bail-bond agents are reluctant to back risky clients if the potential losses of the bail are high. Consequently, those accused of more serious offenses are less likely to get bail.

- Prior record. Those with criminal records are less likely to get bail than those who have never been in trouble with the law. Because prior record is often used as an indication of the possibilities of rehabilitation, courts look at the type of trouble the accused has been in before and whether he or she has successfully completed treatment programs. Those who have shown that they have been unsuccessful in taking advantage of treatment programs or have shown that being sanctioned by the criminal justice system has not stopped them from breaking the law are considered more likely not to appear because their sentences may be longer if convicted. There is a corollary to this idea, however. Some bail-bond agents continue to take chances on regular customers. They know these individuals well and are confident that they will be able to locate them and ensure their appearance before the judge.

- Defendant demeanor. In setting the bail, the judge may consider the accused's appearance and demeanor. The judge may ask questions to the accused to determine his or her honesty and uses information in deciding whether the accused is at good risk in setting bail. Those who are hostile, uncommunicative, or seem untrustworthy are likely to receive a higher bail or be denied bail. In some high-profile cases, the judge may require a higher bail than normal. For instance, an athlete or an entertainer who makes millions of dollars might be required to pay a higher bail than someone else because not only can they afford it but also because in the glare of publicity the judge may be motivated to appear tough on crime. Also, individuals with financial means have more opportunity to flee. Additionally, the judge may believe that the accused would continue to break the law while out on bail. This is especially true if the accused appears to be violent. If a husband in a domestic dispute has made threats against his wife, the judge may decide that releasing him would be risky. In another example, youths in a street gang may appear to pose a threat even though their offenses were minor.

- Victim statements. The judge may consider the statements of crime by the victims in setting bail. Individuals may be afraid of the accused and wish them to remain in detention. Victims can give a human face to crime and sway the judge in the bail decision even though the accused has not been convicted of any offense. Judges do not want to be accused of ignoring the wishes of victims, especially if those victims are further harmed by an accused person out on bail.

Bail-Bonds as a Business

The first for-profit bail-bond business in the United States is believed to have been started in the late nineteenth century in San Francisco by Peter and Thomas McDonough who began underwriting bonds as favors to the lawyers who frequented their father's bar. The brothers eventually began charging fees for the bonds and by 1891 had turned the bar into the McDonough Brothers firm [12]. A 1937 investigation branded the firm "a fountainhead of corruption," stating that not only did it have the entire police force in its pocket but also brothels and gambling establishments paid the firm thousands of dollars annually to insure them from arrest. The "Old Lady of Kearny Street," as the company was known, held on until 1941 when it was denied a license by the state licensing commission [13]. By this time, however, the bail-bond business was well underway in the United States [14].

The business of modern bail-bond agencies can be good if clients consistently appear for court hearings (see Focus on Discretion for criticism on the business of bail-bond agencies). The industry also has a political dimension. Bail-bond agents not only must work with local criminal justice officials, but also with state legislators to ensure that the industry thrives. Currently, four states, Illinois, Kentucky, Oregon, and Wisconsin, have outlawed commercial bail-bonds, and the District of Columbia, Maine, and Nebraska only rarely allow bail-bonds [15].

Bail-bond agents are also motivated to remain in the good graces of those in the local criminal justice system. Although they typically advertise, the best way to generate business is by word of mouth. Consequently, having good relationships with public defenders, judges, bailiffs, and those who work in the jail is essential. Bail-bond agents whose clients consistently fail to appear quickly gain a bad reputation around the courthouse. As part of the informal courtroom workgroup, the bail-bond agent's advice may be solicited when decisions about probation, work release, home confinement, and other alternative sentences are considered. The agent may better understand the reliability of individual offenders, and this expertise is often considered by prosecutors and judges in making sentencing decisions. Finally, the bail-bond agent must have a good reputation among offenders as these individuals may refer family and friends to the agent.

A fascinating secondary occupation to that of the bail-bond agent is that of the bail-enforcement agent or, as they are sometimes called, bounty hunters. Some bail-enforcement agents work with bail-bond agents, often on a contract basis, whereas some bail-bond agents do their own enforcement work. The profession of bail-enforcement agent is peculiar to the United States. The early recognition in the United States of bail as a right combined with the nation's size, not to mention the vastness of the American continent,

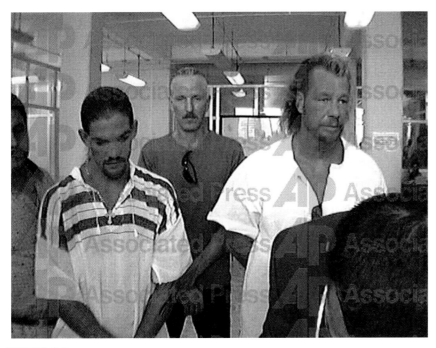

PHOTO 7.1

Notorious bounty hunter, Duane Lee "Dog" Chapman was arrested in 2003 in Mexico while attempting to capture Max Factor cosmetics heir and convicted rapist Andrew Luster. Here, Leland Chapman, left, Timothy Chapman, center, and Duane Chapman meet with a judge in a Puerto Vallarta, Mexico, courthouse. A Mexican court dismissed all criminal charges in 2007.

provided defendants not only with the opportunity to strike out for freedom but also with plenty of places to hide. Thus, the occupation of bounty hunter has evolved alongside those of the rest of the courtroom workgroup [16] (Photo 7.1).

FOCUS ON DISCRETION

Freedom for Sale

Bail-bonding is a business that must make a profit. A bail-bond agency is not required to take on every client that approaches it. A successful company chooses clients who pose the least risk and return the most profit. Critics of bail-bonding point to this as a serious flaw in a system that controls the freedom of everyone who enters it.

Bail-bond agents try to protect their businesses through political avenues by donating to and lobbying elected officials. This can affect the success of state and local pretrial release programs, which seek to get many accused individuals released on recognizance without posting bail. For example, in a report on a pretrial release program in Lubbock, Texas, the local official who runs the program says the city's bond agents lobby to keep the program small, underfunded, and ineffective. That way, no defendants who may purchase a bond slip out of jail for free under the program [17].

Requiring bail especially works against arrestees who believe they are innocent and want to contest their case. In this instance, the arrestee, either not wanting an offense on his or her record or simply believing in the justness of their cause, will refuse a plea bargain. If the arrestee is unable to afford bail or bond, he or she may remain in jail for weeks or months waiting for the case to come before a judge. In some cases, arrestees may remain in jail for nearly as long as they would have if they had accepted the plea bargain [18].

A final strike against bail-bonding, according to critics, is outright corruption and what could be considered as fee gouging. Often, bond agencies collect more than the typical 10 percent, and many tack on extra fees. In one Texas case, a woman purchased a bond for her son who had been arrested for fighting and given $750 bail. After the bonding company's fees, she owed the company more than half the cost of the bond, not just 10 percent. Prosecutors dropped the case, but weeks later she was still trying to repay the bond company. This lack of

regulation over bond companies extends to the freedom of their clients. A bond agent can revoke any client's bond, regardless of his or her behavior. For example, over a 4-month period in New York in 2010, one bond agent sent 89 clients back to jail, some of whom had not missed any court appearances.

Proponents of bail-bonding assert that the system not only works for most arrestees but also benefits the state financially. If a defendant skips bail, the bonding agency must either track down the person or pay the full bail amount. However, jurisdictions do not always collect. In Lubbock, Texas, bail-bond agents usually only pay 5 percent of the bond to the county when a client skips bail. As of 2011, California bond agents owed counties $150 million; New Jersey bond agents owed $250,000, and Erie, Pennsylvania, officials discovered that collecting from bond agencies was so difficult that they gave up [19].

Questions

In your opinion, should bail-bond companies be more tightly regulated?

Why is supporting pretrial release programs so difficult for politicians? Why are bail-bond companies opposed to such programs?

Bail Reform

The bail-bonds industry is constantly under attack [20]. Many believe that it is inherently skewed in favor of the wealthy. Those who are released have some advantages over those who remain incarcerated.

- Preparing a defense. Individuals released on bail are better able to help their attorneys prepare their defense. They can help find people who can support an *alibi* and generate money to pay for their defense.
- Presenting a better image in court. Those who are out on bail can show up for further hearings looking more respectable than those who are incarcerated. Well-dressed defendants make a better impression than those who show up in an orange jumpsuit with the county jail name stenciled on the back. Although the court should not consider appearances, those who come directly from the jail appear less reliable and more dangerous than those who are able to improve their appearance.

- Maintaining employment. Those who are out on bail are able to keep their jobs and demonstrate that they are a good prospect for probation because they are integrated into the community. Those who remain incarcerated are likely to lose their jobs and have a more difficult time convincing the court that they are good candidates for probation.

It is clear that being unable to obtain bail puts impoverished people at a distinct disadvantage when it comes to dealing with the criminal justice system. Critics of the bail system question the justice of paying what some consider to be a ransom. States that have outlawed the bail-bond system have had to come up with other ways of releasing individuals prior to their court hearings. The primary pretrial release mechanism that has been adopted by such jurisdictions is release-on-recognizance.

Release-on-Recognizance

Many courts have instituted policies that mirror the work of a bail-bond agent but do not require accused individuals to put up money or property to guarantee that they will appear at future hearings. The presumption of innocence suggests that even though individuals may have been charged with a criminal offense, they are still reliable citizens and should not be penalized until the court has considered their case. **Release-on-recognizance** is the release of a defendant without bail based on the defendant's promise to return to court.

Release-on-recognizance requires that intake officers or court officials determine the trustworthiness of the accused. Those who have ties to the community are most likely to appear at future hearings and thus can be awarded the trust of the court. The court considers several factors when deciding to grant release-on-recognizance [21].

- Residence in the community. If an accused person has lived in a community for a long time, he or she is likely to want to maintain their good reputation and will show up at future court hearings. Conversely, a college student on a spring break in Florida may decide to return to the northeast and not make another trip to Florida to appear at court hearings. This type of person is more likely to be required to post bail in order to secure release.
- Employment. Individuals employed in the community have an interest in ensuring that they meet the court's requirements to reappear because failure to do so could mean long-term incarceration. Employment signifies an investment in the community, and the court takes this into consideration.
- Family ties. Individuals with family members in the community have a support group to help them deal with the criminal justice system and are

considered more likely to appear at future court hearings. Having family in the community allows the court to have a greater number of contacts to reach the accused should he or she not appear at future court proceedings.

- Home or business ownership. Home and business owners are unlikely to desert those assets to flee the jurisdiction. Being financially invested in the community means that the accused has a greater motivation to maintain their good standing and are considered more likely to appear for future court proceedings.

These criteria are similar to those a bail-bond agent would consider. The key here is to determine the trustworthiness of the accused. For many people who are caught up in the criminal justice system, the alleged offense is an anomaly rather than a lifestyle, and the presumption of innocence and reappearance at future court hearings can be assumed. Other individuals might not be so reliable and therefore must either be kept in jail or have the bail posted for them.

The release-on-recognizance system allows trustworthy people to maintain their freedom before their court hearings, but does not penalize those without the financial means to post bail. However, it must be recognized that ties to the community, employment, owning a home or business, and other criteria the court considers in deciding release-on-recognizance will always favor those who have reached middle-class status. The homeless, the impoverished, youths without parental support, and other marginal people will not be deemed as trustworthy as those with community ties and may end up in jail or having to post bail [22].

DIVERSION

Diversion is the removal of a case from the courts to another form of legal dispensation. Many types of cases are better handled outside the court system for various reasons. These may be cases of first offenders, minor offenses, or offenses with special circumstances such as drug or alcohol use in which there are alternative mechanisms to more effectively handle these cases. These types of cases are often diverted from the formal court system and placed in programs or agencies that are presumed to better deal with concerns such as treatment.

Considerable discretion is vested in the judge or intake officers who decide to direct the case onto an alternative path. Typically, the case is diverted to some type of program and the charges held in abeyance, meaning that they are only dismissed if the accused successfully completes the program. If the accused is unsuccessful, he or she will come back before the judge or intake officer, and the case will proceed in the traditional manner. Diversion benefits many of the parties involved.

- The accused. Diverting a case from the formal criminal justice system greatly benefits the accused. Typically, diversion means the accused will be treated or rehabilitated rather than punished. For those with drug or alcohol problems, who are first offenders, or who have committed minor offenses, diversion may mean that no formal charge will be made. This has important ramifications for many activities the accused may pursue in the future, such as getting a job, applying for a loan, or getting into a university. Additionally, diversion to an alternative program may mean avoiding prison or even probation. However, in many respects, diversion is similar to probation in that the accused is expected to maintain good behavior and perform some activity such as going to school, engaging in community service, holding down a job, or completing a treatment program. Failure to meet the diversion program's requirements may mean a return to the traditional criminal justice system process [23].
- The criminal justice system. The first benefit to the criminal justice system is the reduction of caseload. The criminal justice system can formally handle only so many cases. As you may remember from our discussion of the criminal justice funnel, cases drop out of the system at many points, of which diversion is the first. In fact, short of simply releasing a person, diversion is one of the most common ways of getting rid of cases that still imposes some type of social control over the accused. In this way, diversion satisfies both the demands of the system to reduce the number of cases and the demands of society that "something happen" to those who break the law [24].
- Defense attorneys. Defense attorneys benefit from diversion because they can claim that they spared their clients the full brunt of the criminal law. The defense attorney or public defender can make clients happy by getting a reduced sanction and save them from the risk of a criminal conviction. This allows the defense attorney to dispose of the case quickly and move on to more pressing cases.
- Prosecutors. The prosecutor can agree to divert a case to a treatment program or a mild sanction and not have to spend time and resources prosecuting more serious charges. The major benefit to the prosecutor is that he or she can claim that they did not lose the case and that the accused is "paying" for the offense and not going completely free. Diversion allows prosecutors in jurisdictions where they are elected to amass an impressive record of disposing cases successfully.
- Society. Citizens benefit from diversion because they are spared the expense of processing a case through the traditional criminal justice

system. By diverting the case, the time and resources of the courtroom workgroup can be dedicated to other cases. Additionally, the case is presumably better served because treating or rehabilitating the accused may prevent him or her from being a problem in the future.

Some critics of the diversion process contend that it can be problematic. Specifically, scholars like Thomas Blomberg argue that unless diversion programs are carefully structured, they can engage in net-widening. Before diversion programs, many people were simply released because their cases were minor; the evidence against them was inadequate; or the court had too many other serious cases to deal with. With the advent of diversion programs, cases that would otherwise have been dismissed are now brought into the criminal justice system. One may argue that this is a good thing because it compensates for the lack of court resources and allows the court to handle cases that it otherwise would have been reluctant to dismiss. The danger, however, lies in increasing the scope of social control by requiring individuals to complete programs in order to escape the criminal justice system [25].

For example, consider a youth who is a minor juvenile delinquent. A diversion program might require him or her to engage in family counseling to address the problems of being incorrigible. Part of this requirement may be that the parents should participate. If the father refuses to participate in the youth's program, the youth returns to the juvenile justice system. At this point, the judge may look at the family and decide that because the father is unwilling to participate, the family's other children are in danger of being neglected or inadequately supervised. Therefore, the judge places the siblings in foster care.

The danger here, according to the critics of net-widening, is that because of one youth's minor delinquency and the parent's refusal to participate in family counseling, siblings who have done nothing wrong are brought into the juvenile justice system. Although some may argue that this is desirable, it is not the intent of diversion. The program has increased the power of the state over individuals based not upon their behavior, but on other life circumstances.

PLEA BARGAINING

Perhaps the most important and controversial aspect of the pretrial process is the negotiation of justice, or, as it is more commonly known, plea bargaining. A **plea bargain** is a negotiation between the defense and the prosecution, in which the defendant agrees to plead guilty or no contest to some offenses in return for reduction or dismissal of some charges or a reduced sentence.

Only a small fraction of cases actually go to trial because the prosecutor and the defense attorney are able to arrive at a compromise sentence that spares the court the expenditure of time and resources that a trial would entail. There is much dissatisfaction with plea bargaining because the public wants lawbreakers to pay for their offenses with severe penalties [26]. However, trials are not always necessary when the facts are clear; the accused realizes the evidence is stacked against him or her; and the sentence is routinely agreed upon by the judge, prosecutor, and defense attorney.

Without plea bargaining, courts would grind to a halt. If an accused person demanded a jury trial, the court docket would be hopelessly overcrowded and the serious cases in which guilt or innocence is truly in question would receive little or no attention. Furthermore, those detained in jail would have to wait an extremely long time for their trials. Prosecutors would be forced to drop cases because of the speedy-trial rule and many guilty people would go free while the innocent would languish in jail.

Even though the public demands an end to plea bargaining, it would create so many problems and expenses that eventually citizens would advocate for some method to expedite the movement of cases. Members of the courtroom workgroup also have interest in plea bargaining because it makes their jobs easier. Plea bargaining has the following benefits for all those concerned with the criminal justice system [27].

- Guilty defendants. The most obvious benefit of plea bargaining is for those defendants who are actually guilty. They make a deal with the prosecutor for a sentence that may be far less severe than what they would receive if their case went to trial and they received the full sentence available under the law. Depending upon the type of plea bargain, they may receive a shorter incarceration time, probation instead of incarceration, or escape the designation of an undesirable criminal status (such as sex offender). Many defendants are happy to plea bargain knowing that they can get a better deal from the prosecutor than from a judge after a trial.
- Innocent defendants. Plea bargaining shrinks the docket so much that those who are truly innocent can have their day in court and receive a trial in a timely manner. If plea bargaining were not available, such defendants could wait a long time before their cases could be heard.
- Prosecutors. Plea bargaining allows prosecutors to claim victory in a case because they were able to extract a guilty verdict without having to expend valuable court resources. Some prosecutors measure their legal expertise by their won–loss record, and engaging in extensive plea bargaining allows them to rack up a high percentage of victories.

- ▪ Defense attorneys and public defenders. With plea bargaining, defense attorneys and public defenders are able to spare their clients the full effects of the criminal law in sentencing, and can claim partial victory by citing the length of incarceration that their clients might have received. Aggressive bargaining on the part of defense attorneys can increase their reputations as effective lawyers and will attract future business from defendants.
- ▪ Taxpayers. Plea bargaining is often considered a good financial mechanism for reducing criminal justice system costs. Not only are salaries of judges, prosecutors, public defenders, bailiffs, court reporters, and other court workers greatly reduced, but plea bargaining also allows for more lenient sentences that save taxpayers the costs of incarceration. The criminal justice system can be an expensive institution, and plea bargaining is one way the cost of justice can be negotiated.

Although it is clear that plea bargaining has many advantages, critics contend that it must be carefully controlled and monitored to ensure that justice is consistent. One of the most persistent criticisms of plea bargaining is that it gives prosecutors too much leverage in extracting guilty pleas from defendants. In circumstances in which the prosecutor may not have a convincing case of guilt, he or she may dangle a plea bargain before a defendant to entice him or her to accept a lesser sentence rather than risk a longer sentence should the case go to trial [28]. Prosecutors are not required to fully disclose the quality of their case and so may manipulate defendants into accepting a plea bargain when, if the truth were known, the case would be dismissed [29].

Related to the practice of prosecutorial bluffing is the problem of overcharging. Here, the prosecutor may charge the defendant with an offense greater than the circumstances of the offense and that the evidence may actually justify. By charging a defendant with capital murder when in actuality the charge should be only manslaughter, the prosecutor can exact a plea for a manslaughter charge before the case is carefully examined by the defense attorney or the judge. This overcharging allows prosecutors increased leverage in plea bargaining and subverts justice by allowing the prosecutor to coerce defendants into pleas.

Another criticism of plea bargaining is that it often leaves victims dissatisfied. This is a serious issue because most victims believe that their case is serious and deserving of the full resources of the court and that the perpetrator or assailant should receive the maximum sentence possible. Court workers understand that victims often exaggerate the importance of the case and that routine plea bargains can appear fair to those in the courtroom workgroup but leaves victims unsatisfied. The problem is that both the victims and the public become dissatisfied with what they perceive to be the quality of justice.

Types of Plea Bargaining

All plea bargains are not the same. Let's consider four types of plea bargains: vertical, horizontal, reduced-sentence, and avoidance-of-stigma pleas.

- Vertical pleas. **Vertical pleas** are an agreement with the prosecutor in which a defendant pleads guilty or no contest to a charge less serious than the one with which he or she was originally charged. For instance, a first-degree felony can be pled down to a third-degree felony. The advantage to the defendant is the reduced penalty that comes with the lesser charge. Vertical plea bargains are the most common and most attractive to defendants. Prosecutors can still get a victory and ensure that the defendant experiences at least some of the force of the criminal law. Vertical pleas are most attractive to defendants when the conviction is reduced from a felony to a misdemeanor.
- Horizontal pleas. Defendants are often charged with several offenses. A **horizontal plea bargain** is an agreement with the prosecutor in which the prosecutor dismisses several charges in return for a guilty plea on one of them. For instance, if a defendant is charged with 10 cases of breaking-and-entering, he or she may plead guilty to one charge in exchange for the other nine being dismissed. Horizontal pleas are an attractive way for many cases to be cleared from the court docket and for many offenses to be cleared by the police for statistical purposes. Multiple charges for the same offense may result in concurrent sentences. Therefore, the horizontal plea means that the defendant accepts the maximum sentence for one of the charges.
- Reduced-sentence plea. Here, the plea is for a reduced sentence. If a sentence carries a maximum incarceration of 10 years, the reduced-charge plea may be for only 5 years, which allows the defendant to spend only half the time in prison. This type of plea has the advantage of saving taxpayers money by reducing the length of incarceration while also giving the prosecutor a victory.
- Avoidance-of-stigma plea. Some criminal charges expose the defendant to a stigma that goes far beyond the sentence imposed by the court. For instance, those charged with sex offenses may be labeled as sex offenders, which can have a deleterious effect on where the defendant (if convicted) can live, what type of job he or she may obtain, and may prevent them from having unsupervised interaction with their children [30]. Additionally, avoidance-of-stigma pleas are attractive to those who live in jurisdictions that have "three strikes" types of sentencing that can propel the defendant into a special status of "career criminal," which can result in mandatory sentences that limit the judge's discretion to impose lighter sanctions [31].

Plea Bargaining and Discretion

One way to limit plea bargaining would be to impose fixed mandatory sentences in which one who commits a certain type of offense ends up with the same punishment. This would limit the prosecutor's discretion to craft individual deals with defendants and presumably satisfy society's demands that similar cases are treated equally. Such a policy may be beneficial in some ways, but it would also be problematic. Discretion is inherent in the criminal justice system, and the debate should not be, and cannot be, whether to allow it or not, but rather where to invest the authority to exercise discretion [32].

Abolishing plea bargaining would limit the prosecutor's discretion but would not eliminate discretion itself. Abolishing plea bargaining would simply shift the discretion from court officials to the legislature. Lawmakers could decide mandatory sentences for each offense which would provide a semblance of equality of justice. However, this type of policy could hamper the criminal justice system's ability to effectively and efficiently administer its caseload.

A good example of this is the war on drugs. Since the 1980s, mandatory sentences were handed out for a vast number of drug-related cases until the prisons were filled with drug offenders who were not necessarily the type of violent offenders the legislatures intended when they passed the drug laws. Today, many prison systems have limited budgets, and prisons have been swelled with offenders who are there because of mandatory sentences, not because they are a danger to society. Limiting prosecutorial discretion would further exacerbate such problems because prosecutors would be motivated to under-charge cases they believed mandatory sentences would punish too severely.

Without plea bargaining, defense attorneys would take more cases to trial. With an "all or nothing" philosophy, the defense attorney has an incentive to force the criminal justice system to prove the guilt of his or her client because the sentence imposed will be the same whether the defendant pleads guilty or is found guilty. There is really no incentive not to go to trial if one is charged with a mandatory sentence, so any such attempt to reform plea bargaining by the legislature would result in courts being clogged with cases that could have been negotiated by plea bargaining. The question then becomes not whether to have plea bargaining, but rather, how to structure plea bargaining so that justice is served [33].

Plea bargaining can occur at any phase of the process. It usually happens before a trial, but the defense and prosecutor can agree on a disposition any time before the verdict. Once it is decided that a case is going to trial, each side makes several maneuvers in an effort to gain advantage in shaping the grounds upon which the trial is held. These steps and maneuvers are called pretrial motions.

PRELIMINARY HEARING

A **preliminary hearing** is a court proceeding to determine if a suspect charged with a felony should be tried based on probable cause that he or she committed the offense. An important stage in the pretrial process, preliminary hearings vary from jurisdiction to jurisdiction in form and substance but must be held shortly after the arraignment. In some places it is used relatively rarely; however, in other jurisdictions it plays a crucial gatekeeping function in determining whether a case moves forward.

The preliminary hearing is held at the magistrate court level and is used to determine whether the case will go to a higher court. The prosecution must present enough evidence that a criminal offense has been committed and that the accused committed it. The prosecution is not obliged at this stage to prove the suspect's guilt beyond a reasonable doubt, or even present a preponderance of evidence testifying to this allegation. The prosecutor only has to show probable cause, meaning that there is enough evidence to suggest that further investigation by the court is warranted.

The preliminary hearing can benefit both the prosecutor and the defense. The prosecutor gets to present some of the evidence to the judge and get a ruling on whether the case is strong enough to proceed. The defense attorney gets to see the core of the prosecutor's case and can challenge whether there is enough probable cause, as well as start preparing a strategy for the defense. Often, the defense attorney or the prosecutor may determine that calling the other's bluff is not a good strategy given the strength of the case revealed by the preliminary hearing. Consequently, the preliminary hearing can stimulate plea bargaining once each side sees what the prosecution presents and how the judge views it.

The prosecutor does not have to present all the evidence at the preliminary hearing. This is not an occasion for "discovery" in which the prosecution is required to present the defense with a list of witnesses, what they will testify to, the types of physical evidence to be used, and any other evidence the defense attorney has a right to know about in order to prepare an intelligent defense. Therefore, the prosecutor only has to present enough evidence to convince the court that there is probable cause rather than show all the cards to the defense.

In many jurisdictions, it is routine for the defense attorney to waive the preliminary hearing. Much of the work of determining probable cause occurs during discussions between the prosecutor and the defense attorney, and the preliminary hearing is considered redundant. The defense attorney may have other reasons to waive the hearing. In cases in which the suspect is a celebrity or the case is sensational, the defense attorney may decide that the publicity of a preliminary hearing will damage the quality of the defense or the suspect's reputation. For celebrity suspects, each courtroom appearance is an opportunity for journalists, photographers, and paparazzi to create publicity. One need to only look at the endless stream of celebrities accused of driving while intoxicated, shoplifting, domestic abuse, or drug use to see how the media feed on celebrity suspects. The hearing is held in open court which means the public and the press may attend. Waiving the preliminary hearing gives the defense an opportunity to deny at least one opportunity for such unwanted publicity.

Unlike grand jury proceedings, the preliminary hearing is adversarial. The defense can cross-examine adverse witnesses and present evidence in support of the suspect (such as an *alibi*). Most important, the suspect has a right to be present at the hearing. The preliminary hearing may also be an occasion for cases to be plea-bargained or dismissed. The judge may decide that there is not sufficient probable cause because a police officer made a procedural mistake; the prosecutor did not present sufficient cause; or because a witness did not show up or appeared unreliable or dishonest. Other reasons for dismissing the case at the preliminary stage may have to do with issues other than the quality of the evidence. For instance, in one case:

> The judge dismissed an armed robbery charge against an old man who had stumbled drunkenly around a liquor store demanding a bottle of whiskey and waving a toy pistol over his head. Clearly the evidence contained all the legal elements defining the crime of robbery. Nevertheless, the judge ordered the man released. The judge did not give explicit reasons for dismissing the charge, but he obviously did not consider the incident serious enough to justify the potential expense of a trial to the state and to the defendant. He was also impressed by the prosecutor's lack of enthusiasm, as well as by the complaining witnesses' apparent amusement now that the episode was over.
> In most courthouses, such cases are called "cheap"—a cheap robbery, a cheap burglary, and so on [34].

Dismissal of a case at the preliminary hearing stage does not necessarily mean the case is over. The prosecution may decide to present the case to the court again with additional evidence aimed at showing probable cause. The prosecution may also take the case to a grand jury to get an indictment. At first glance this seems like a case of double jeopardy, the constitutional safeguard against trying people twice for the same offense. A person who has been found not guilty by a jury or entered into a plea bargain with the prosecutor cannot be brought back to court for the same offense. The preliminary hearing is immune from double jeopardy because it does not result in a sentence with a punishment, but rather only a determination that there is probable cause to bind the case over to a higher court.

GRAND JURY AND INDICTMENT

A grand jury is a panel of citizens who hear the evidence in a criminal case and determine whether the accused should be charged with a criminal offense. Grand juries also investigate criminal offenses and the conduct of public affairs such as wrong-doing by public officials or inefficiencies in jurisdictional governments. The Fifth Amendment provides that "no person shall be held to answer for a capital, or otherwise infamous crime, unless on a presentment or indictment of a Grand Jury." The Supreme Court has held that the states are not bound by this section of the Fifth Amendment, so although all states have provisions for grand juries, only about half use them [35]. However, the Fifth Amendment requires a grand jury indictment for federal criminal charges, so all federal court districts use grand juries. (See Table 7.1 for a few other differences between federal grand juries and state grand juries.)

The number of people on a grand jury must be more than 12, but less than 24, with the number of jurors varying by jurisdiction. As with **petit juries**, the juries that sit on trials, grand jurors are selected from the general population and require no special skills or training. Grand juries only hear evidence on serious criminal cases and some types of civil matters, but the grand jury's work is not like a trial, and suspects do not have the same rights as in a criminal court. Since grand juries must only determine if there is probable cause that a suspect broke the law, they do not hear all the evidence in a case or even evidence that may exonerate a suspect. Only the prosecutor may bring evidence to a grand jury, and it is up to the prosecutor as to what evidence to bring (more on this later).

Table 7.1 Differences Between State and Grand Juries

State	Federal
Not bound by the Fifth Amendment grand jury requirement	Bound by the Fifth Amendment requirement that charges for all capital and serious offenses be brought by a grand jury
Composed of between 12 and 23 people	Composed of between 16 and 23 people; typically 23
Hears testimony from police officers	More likely to hear testimony from federal agents than police officers
At least 20 states allow nonprosecutorial counsel in the jury room	Witnesses, suspects, and investigative targets cannot be accompanied into the grand jury room by their attorney
Jurors serve for a term up to 24 months	Two types of jury: regular and special. Regular grand juries sit for 18 months, but that term can be extended up to 24 months. Special grand juries sit for 18 months, but that term can be extended to up to 36 months
Investigates civil as well as criminal matters	No investigation of civil matters

Grand jury sessions are secret. Generally, only jurors, witnesses, and the prosecutors are allowed in the grand jury room, and neither suspects nor witnesses have a right to counsel in the room. Those who have attorneys must step outside the room to speak with them. Although this may sound unfair to suspects, investigative targets, and witnesses, it is meant to help ensure that witnesses come forward; potential defendants do not flee; that the jury's deliberations and witnesses' testimony are open and honest; and that the public does not learn about the investigations of those who turn out to be innocent of any probable cause.

Still, the prosecutor's have nearly absolute control over what goes on in the grand jury room and suspects' and investigative targets' relative lack of rights continues to be sharply criticized. The adage, "A grand jury would indict a ham sandwich if the prosecutor asked it to" reflects the prosecutor's power. Depending on the state, the prosecutor does all or most of the following:

- make an opening statement
- examine witnesses
- introduce physical evidence
- prepare the draft indictment
- instruct the grand jury on how to conduct the investigation
- remain in the room while the grand jury deliberates.

Conversely, defense or witness attorneys play no part in the proceedings. The **rules of evidence**—the definitions of what constitutes evidence and how it is introduced in court—do not apply to grand jury proceedings, nor do suspects' or witnesses' rights to be secure from unreasonable searches and seizures, to confront opposing witnesses, or to testify in their own defense [36]. A witness may invoke the Fifth Amendment privilege against self-incrimination, but some prosecutors may subpoena witnesses whom they know will claim this privilege in an effort to intimidate or embarrass them. Prosecutors can even arrange for witnesses to be subpoenaed so quickly that they have no opportunity to retain or consult with a lawyer. These privileges have made the use of grand juries somewhat unpopular (recall that only half the states use them), and of the states that do use them, at least 20 have changed the conventions to allow witnesses' attorneys in the grand jury room [37].

The suspect's rights remain limited when it comes to grand jury investigations since such investigations are only a search for probable cause. For instance, there is no "double jeopardy" protection for suspects. Prosecutors may resubmit evidence to another grand jury (and any succeeding grand juries) if a prior grand jury failed to find probable cause. Also, grand juries do not have to reach a unanimous decision to indict a suspect: a typical indictment requires only 12 votes. The rights of witnesses called by grand juries are limited, too. Grand juries have broad authority to subpoena witnesses and evidence and may do so for as long as its investigation continues. Because witnesses have not been indicted, they have no constitutional right to a lawyer. However, witnesses who want an attorney and cannot afford one can ask the court to provide them with one. Witnesses who refuse to obey grand jury orders may be held in contempt and fined or incarcerated. Suspects may waive the right to be indicted by a grand jury. In that case, the prosecutor can make the charge using an information.

ARRAIGNMENT

An **arraignment** is a defendant's first appearance before a judge. The charges against the defendant are read; the defendant is provided with a written copy of the charges; a lawyer is appointed if the defendant cannot afford one; and the defendant's plea is entered. Typically, the defendant will respond to the charges, usually orally (more on this later). The judge will then set up a schedule for other courtroom procedures, such as a preliminary hearing, a hearing on pretrial motions, and the trial. The judge will also decide any unresolved bail matters, such as raising or lowering the bail amount or even releasing the defendant on recognizance.

In *Mallory v. United States* (1957), the U.S. Supreme Court ruled that arraignments should take place "as quickly as possible" after arrest. The quick arraignment requirement is for the benefit of suspects because it requires police to have evidence of a criminal offense at the time of arrest or at least shortly thereafter. If the period of time to an arraignment was not restricted, suspects could conceivably be left in jail until police found evidence of an offense days or weeks later. Usually, arraignments are held about 48 hours after arrest, although court holidays and weekends—days that are not counted toward the 48-hour period—can extend this duration. In some states, Mondays are considered court holidays. That means if a person is arrested on Friday, the arraignment may not take place until Tuesday or Wednesday.

As mentioned earlier, the defendant must enter a plea at the arraignment. The plea may be of four varieties: guilty, not guilty, Alford, or *nolo contendere*, a Latin term for "I will not contest" that is usually shortened to "no contest." Let's look at these pleas in a bit more detail:

- Guilty. Here, the defendant pleads guilty to the offense, usually for one of two reasons: the defendant is guilty of the offense and thinks it best to plead guilty or as part of a plea-bargain deal with the prosecutor. Before accepting a guilty plea, the judge must question the defendant as to whether he or she understands the charge and the penalty for conviction, that by pleading guilty the defendant waives the right to a jury trial, and if the defendant is satisfied with the defense lawyer. These questions not only protect the defendant, but also go on court record in case the defendant tries later to claim that he or she was forced to plead guilty.

- Not guilty. The defendant pleads not guilty to the offense. These pleas often lead to a trial, especially for serious offenses.

- **Nolo contendere** or no contest. This plea allows defendants to neither admit nor deny responsibility for the charges but still accept punishment. Why would a defendant want to enter such a plea? Pleading no contest prevents the plea from being used against the defendant in a civil case. So, by pleading no contest, a defendant in a drunk-driving case involving an accident with another automobile accepts the criminal punishment for the offense, but cannot have the plea used against him or her in a civil suit brought by the driver of the other car. However, in a criminal case, *nolo contendere* is treated as a guilty plea [38].

- Alford plea. An **Alford plea**, a plea of guilty in which a defendant does not admit guilt, is an unusual plea that is somewhat like a no-contest plea. In *North Carolina v. Alford* (1970), the defendant, Henry Alford, said he pleaded guilty to murder because if he did not, "they would gas me for it." That is, if the case went to trial and Alford was found guilty, the penalty would probably be death. Instead, Alford claimed innocence but admitted that, given the large amount of evidence against him, a jury would probably find him guilty. So, he pleaded guilty to second-degree murder, while insisting that he did not commit the murder, in order to avoid the death penalty. Some courts will not permit Alford pleas, whereas others consider them a way to relieve the system of lengthy, expensive jury trials [39].

PRETRIAL MOTIONS

Both defense attorneys and prosecutors use **pretrial motions**, which are arguments made before a trial about how the trial is to be conducted. The goal is to limit the types of evidence that the other side can use in presenting their case. Several motions are typically filed by the attorneys in order to get the judge to put on the record that an issue was considered. This is important because the case could be overturned on appeal if a motion was not filed for a controversial and case-deciding issue.

For example, if the defendant gave a confession to the police, the defense attorney would attempt to get the confession thrown out of court. If a pretrial motion was not filed to suppress the confession, an appeal could be brought by another attorney claiming that the defense erred. To many people, the long list of pretrial motions may seem like a waste of time and resources; however, they play a crucial role in ensuring that the case is processed in a professional manner.

The list of issues upon which pretrial motions can be filed is long and exhausting. For the purposes of this chapter, we will highlight some of the more common and critical motions and give examples to explain how they are an important part of preparing for a trial, or, in many cases, serve as a backdrop for plea negotiations. For instance, if a judge would rule in favor of the defense and suppress a piece of evidence, the prosecutor may determine that his or her case is too weak to go to trial successfully and may offer the defense a negotiated settlement. Now let's turn to the major pretrial motions.

Motions to Suppress Evidence

Motions to suppress evidence are important prior to criminal trials because they can affect whether there is enough evidence for the prosecution to plea bargain or go ahead with a formal trial. In motions to suppress evidence, the defense attorney claims the evidence gathered by police violates the established criminal procedure and affects the defendant's constitutional rights.

The basis for most motions to suppress hinge on the defendant's Fourth, Fifth, or Sixth Amendment rights. The types of evidence will usually consist of physical objects such as narcotics, weapons, stolen property, or a statement made by the defendant, testimony by witnesses, or the procedures used in identification, such as a police lineup. If any of these types of evidence were gathered improperly, they may be considered "fruits of the poisonous tree" meaning that even if they are true, accurate, and establish the **culpability** (sufficient responsibility for criminal offenses to be at fault and liable for the conduct) of the defendant, they should be inadmissible because they were gathered illegally [40].

The exclusionary rule prohibits introduction of tangible evidence, concessions, identifications, or knowledge obtained through constitutional violations [41]. Thus, an unlawful intrusion into a home in which contraband is found may result in exclusion of the contraband. Because the exclusion of evidence discovered as a direct result of unconstitutional police conduct may be insufficient to deter police from illegal searches, the rule also excludes secondary evidence that is a product of the illegal search [42]. For example, if police were to discover the address book with the names of a prostitute's clients while illegally searching her apartment for drugs, that address book would not be permissible evidence for a charge of prostitution against her or the clients.

Several exceptions to the exclusionary rule allow evidence gathered in the unlawful way to be considered by the court. One of these exceptions is the **good-faith exception** by which a police officer might search premises without a warrant if given permission by a third party who he or she believes has the authority to allow the search [43]. The facts of each case are subject to intense scrutiny by the courts and measured against not only the statutes, but also precedent from prior cases. Although several Supreme Court cases guide the admissibility of evidence, each state also has case law that affects how the court considers pretrial motions.

Search and Seizure

Another pretrial motion common to criminal cases is challenges to the laws of search and seizure. Search and seizure concerns are covered by the Fourth Amendment, which stipulates that individuals have a right to expect privacy: "The right of the people to be secure in their persons, houses, papers, and effects, against unreasonable searches and seizures, shall not be violated, and no warrants shall issue, but upon probable cause, supported by oath or affirmation, and particularly describing the place to be searched and the person or things to be seized."

Motions to suppress evidence based upon search or seizure rules will first look at the warrant issued by the court. The factual accuracy of the warrant will be examined to determine whether the police officer established probable cause, searched the right address, and a number of other factors that are necessary to make the warrant legal. If property was seized under a badly worded warrant, it can be excluded from the case, and the prosecution may be forced to plea bargain or dismiss the case entirely [44].

A condition of reasonableness can allow warrantless searches to be admissible in court. In arresting the occupant of a house under another charge, police officers may gather evidence that is in plain sight. For instance, if police are called to a domestic disturbance and find drugs and drug paraphernalia in plain sight, they may use this evidence to prosecute the home's occupants. Another example of a reasonable exception would be if the police impounded an automobile after an accident and found drugs in it during their inventory. Although the automobile owner may not have consented to a search of the car, it is considered reasonable on the part of police to search the car and inventory its contents as part of its accident investigation.

Confessions and Admissions

Another crucial pretrial motion that may be filed by the defense is a motion to exclude evidence in which the defendant admitted to or confessed to an offense. At issue is whether the defendant understood the ramifications of a confession [45]. Police officers often attempt to manipulate a confession out of a defendant under the pretense of promising a lighter sentence from the court [46]. Defendants are unlikely to get their own statements excluded from the trial except when those statements are gathered in inadmissible way by the prosecutor or the police. The court can hear numerous and complicated issues when considering pretrial motions. We will limit the discussion here to the major rules in order to alert students to the main types of concerns that the court could consider.

The McNabb–Mallory Rule

This rule states that arrestees are entitled to a prompt hearing to determine if there is probable cause for the arrest. If an unreasonable amount of time elapses between the arrest and the hearing, the defense can challenge any confession or admission to guilt. The issue is the possibility that a long delay may compel a suspect to confess or admit guilt just to get out of jail. This rule is often referred to as the "prompt appearance rule."

The Voluntariness Standard

The prosecutor must establish any confession or admission of guilt as having been given voluntarily. Torture of the suspect would obviously violate the standard. Voluntariness can be difficult to determine because each case is different. The court uses the "totality of circumstances" to determine if the admission of guilt was voluntary. The defense attorney cannot claim a violation of the voluntary standard just because the defendant is unaware or uninformed about the self-destructive nature of a confession. It must be shown that police officers or the prosecutor misled, tricked, or coerced the defendant into making a confession.

One issue the court considers is the defendant's sophistication [47]. Police will be given more latitude with defendants who are more matured, experienced, and tougher and less latitude with those who are less aware, vulnerable, and weaker. Circumstances such as the length and the number of interviews may be considered. Defendants who were deprived of food and beverages or denied restroom breaks for long periods of time may claim that their confession was coerced. When interrogators work in teams for long periods of time and hold the suspect in isolation, it is likely that the defense attorney will claim that the police overcame the suspect's free will and that the admission of guilt was coerced.

Another concern of the courts is whether the police promised more lenient treatment. The police may suggest that they can put in a good word with the prosecutor, but they are not authorized to engage in plea bargaining in order to secure a confession. The courts will look at whether these issues were simply discussed or whether the police actually made a promise.

Other circumstances that may make a confession involuntary are threats by police to physically harm the defendant or threats to arrest family members who are not involved in the case. However, it is important to note that a certain amount of deception on the part of police is permissible and is a standard technique used in police interrogations.

The *Miranda* *Doctrine*

The *Miranda* doctrine established what is popularly known as the "*Miranda* rights," which dictate conditions under which police may interrogate suspects [48]. It provides a layer of protection to suspects by dictating that all interrogation must cease once the defendant invokes the right to silence or the right to counsel.

Miranda law is complicated and, according to some scholars, is "so complex that it is no doubt beyond the comprehension of law enforcement officers" [49]. The central issues important for pretrial motions are the terms "custody" and "interrogate." Interrogation must occur while the suspect is in custody in order for a violation of *Miranda* rights to be considered by the court in its pretrial motions.

So what is custody? The clearest case is when the police officer arrests the suspect. This triggers the *Miranda* protections regardless of whether the arrestee is in the back of the squad car, standing on the street, or in the police interrogation room. Other determinations of custody under the *Miranda* language include the use of physical restraints, threats of force, and whether officers advised the subject that he or she was under arrest or free to leave. The concept of interrogation is similarly complicated. Once the suspects have been advised of their *Miranda* rights, it is still possible for them to legally incriminate themselves. For instance, if a suspect volunteers incriminating information, the police use this information and ask follow-up questions. The key here is whether the police initiated the conversation or whether the suspect volunteered it [50]. (See Landmark Cases for *Rhode Island v. Innis* (1980), in which the Supreme Court further defines the nature of interrogation of a suspect.)

LANDMARK CASES

Rhode Island v. Innis (1980)

The Supreme Court further defines the nature of interrogation of a suspect, differentiating conversation amongst police officers from the express interrogation of a suspect.

Police arrested Thomas J. Innis on suspicion of the robbery of a cab driver and the murder of another. Although Innis was unarmed when arrested, he was suspected of using a shotgun during the offenses. Innis, who was advised of his *Miranda* rights three times during the arrest, asked to speak with a lawyer. The officers had been instructed not to question Innis. In the police car on the way to the station, two officers discussed the shotgun and the possibility that if it had been discarded near a local school for handicapped children, one of the children might find it and harm themselves or others. Innis interrupted the conversation and asked the officers to direct the car to where the shotgun could be found. Before arriving at the scene, Innis was advised of his *Miranda* rights again, but waived those rights because he said he wanted the gun removed from the area of the school.

At trial, the court denied Innis's motion to suppress the shotgun and his instructions regarding its recovery, ruling that Innis had waived his *Miranda* rights. Innis was convicted. The state supreme court set aside the conviction, concluding that Innis was entitled to a new trial because he had invoked his *Miranda* rights to counsel and that all interrogation, including the conversation between the police officers, should have ceased because his lawyer was not present.

The U.S. Supreme Court held that the police officers' conversation constituted neither interrogation nor express questioning, and therefore did not violate Innis's *Miranda* rights. In such cases, the defense must establish that a suspect's incriminating words or actions are a response to the words or actions of police officers who are aware that they are reasonably likely to bring an incriminating response from the suspect.

In pretrial motions challenging the *Miranda* warning, the defense attorney may contend that the warning was not given in a clear and ascertainable manner. Police officers have developed a number of techniques to ensure that their *Miranda* warnings will pass the court's test. Because the pretrial motions may occur months after the arrest, police officers sometimes provide a written copy of the *Miranda* warnings to the suspects and have the suspects sign it.

Another technique is to videotape the *Miranda* warnings given to the suspect. However, the *Miranda* warning may be considered unnecessary by the court if a matter of public safety is an issue. When establishing the safety of themselves or others at the scene of an offense, the police are not required to read the suspect's *Miranda* rights. For instance, in one case, a police officer who was arresting a suspect found an empty shoulder holster and asked the suspect where the gun was. The suspect pointed out that the gun was nearby, and the officer retrieved it. This was all done before the suspect read any *Miranda* rights. The court found that this was permissible because public safety warranted the officer's action because of the obvious danger [51].

A number of other pretrial motions are important to the criminal court process. These are not as common as what we have discussed so far, but they still are important to be aware of (Table 7.2).

Table 7.2 The Most Common Types of Pretrial Motions

Motion	Purpose
Motions to suppress evidence	To disallow specific evidence in a trial because it would violate the defendant's constitutional rights
Search and seizure	Directed at the legality of the search of a defendant and/or seizure of evidence
Confessions and admissions	To suppress a defendant's confessions or admissions
Identification procedures	Directed at whether the identification of the defendant as a suspect was carried out in accordance with the law
Disco, competency, and related motions	Concerned with the defendant's ability to acquire information from the prosecution in order to present a defense
Motions to quash subpoenas	To prevent or modify subpoenas compelling witness, attendance, and testimony or the production of physical evidence such as documents or physical evidence
Pretrial detention	Motion by the government or the court to detain or continue to detain a defendant prior to the trial
Forfeiture of property	Motion by the government to order seizure of property
Joinder and severance of offenses or defendants	Joinder is the combining of several lawsuits with the same legal issues and the factual situations into one lawsuit. Severance is separation of trials for criminal defendants charged with the same offense
Motion *in limine*	A motion made at the beginning of a trial requesting that the judge rule that some evidence cannot be introduced
Change of venue	To move the trial from one location to another, usually to ensure the fair trial of a defendant or for the convenience of other parties or witnesses
Motions to exclude the public or press or seal the record	To keep information about a trial out of the media or the community, usually be a defendant concerned about public opinion becoming biased against the defendant
Disqualification of the trial judge	To disqualify a justice, judge, or magistrate from a trial; most commonly directed at trial judges
Withdrawal by or disqualification of counsel	A request for removal of defense counsel or prosecutor
Withdrawal of guilty pleas	A defendant may withdraw a guilty or *nolo contendere* plea prior to acceptance of the plea by the court for any reason. After the court accepts the plea, the defendant may withdraw it only if the court rejects the plea agreement or if the defendant can provide a fair and just reason
Motions for continuance	A request to postpone or delay the start of a trial or hearing to a later time

SUMMARY

1. Briefly describe the process of arrest and what happens afterward.
   - Arrest and booking are processes in which the suspect is taken into custody and formally charged with a criminal offense. Arrest and booking procedures ensure that suspects are treated in a systematic

way that allows the criminal justice system to track their progress through the pretrial process. Suspects are apprised of the offense they are being charged with and given an opportunity to understand their rights.

2. Understand the reasons for bail.

   - The Eighth Amendment prohibits "excessive bail" on the presumption that a person is innocent until proven guilty. Bail helps prevent jail overcrowding and reduces the expense of keeping people in jail. Bail helps suspects remain in the community, retain employment, and prepare for their cases. The Eighth Amendment does not guarantee bail, states that "Excessive bail shall not be required."

3. Discuss the advantages of diversion programs for defendants.

   - The diversion of a case may happen at many points along the criminal justice process, and it depends on the characteristics of each case. Cases are often diverted to treatment or rehabilitation programs to help suspects avoid the stigma of a criminal conviction and receive help in addressing the problems that brought them to court. Common diversion programs include drug and alcohol counseling, community service, and educational programs.

4. Compare and contrast the advantages and disadvantages of plea bargaining for prosecutors, defendants, and society.

   - Plea bargaining has the following benefits for all those concerned with the criminal justice system: guilty defendants may make deals for lighter sentences; the court docket is kept manageable so that innocent defendants can have trials; prosecutors may claim victory in cases without having to expend court resources; defense attorneys and public defenders are able to spare their clients the full effects of the law in sentencing; court costs are reduced for taxpayers.

   - A criticism of plea bargaining is that it gives prosecutors too much leverage in extracting guilty pleas from defendants. A prosecutor who does not have a convincing case may offer a plea bargain to a defendant to entice him or her to accept a lesser sentence rather than risk a longer sentence should the case go to trial. Prosecutors may also overcharge in order to plea the case down to a lesser charge. Plea bargaining also often leaves victims dissatisfied.

5. Identify the functions of the preliminary hearing.

   - The preliminary hearing allows the prosecutor to establish probable cause. This entails showing that a specific offense has been committed and that there is enough evidence to establish that the accused is the likely suspect. The preliminary hearing is an adversarial procedure in which the defense can challenge the evidence and cross-examine witnesses. The prosecution does not have to establish beyond a reasonable doubt that the defendant is guilty but only that there is enough evidence to claim probable cause.

6. Give some reasons why the grand jury is criticized as a tool of the prosecutor.

- The prosecutor exercises broad discretion in determining which cases are brought before the grand jury, and only the prosecutor presents evidence. The defense or witness attorneys play no part in the proceedings. The rules of evidence do not apply to grand jury proceedings, nor do suspects' or witnesses' rights to be secure from unreasonable searches and seizures, to confront opposing witnesses, or to testify in their own defense. Prosecutors may resubmit evidence to another grand jury. Prosecutors can even arrange for witnesses to be subpoenaed so quickly that they have no opportunity to retain or consult with a lawyer.

7. Tell what happens during an arraignment.

- An arraignment is a defendant's first appearance before a judge. The charges against the defendant are read; the defendant receives a written copy of the charges; a lawyer is appointed if the defendant cannot afford one; and the defendant's plea is entered. The defendant will respond to the charges. The judge will set a schedule for courtroom procedures such as a preliminary hearing, a hearing on pretrial motions, and the trial, as well as deciding any unresolved bail matters.

8. Explain why the pretrial process is an important part of the court system.

- Pretrial processes constitute a large part of the court's activities and, in many ways, are more important than the actual trial. Pretrial decisions concern arrests, booking, bail, release-on-recognizance, plea bargaining, and pretrial motions.
- Pretrial motions may significantly affect the structure of the trial. These motions include attempts to suppress evidence by claiming that it was gathered unlawfully by the police, defense claims of an illegal search or improperly gathered confession, and that the evidence gathered should not be admissible.

Questions

1. What happens in an arrest?
2. What are the reasons for bail?
3. What are the advantages of diversion programs for defendants?
4. What are the advantages and disadvantages of plea bargaining for prosecutors, defendants, and society?
5. What is the function of the preliminary hearing?
6. Why is the grand jury criticized as a tool of the prosecutor?

7. What happens during an arraignment?
8. Why is the pretrial process an important part of the court system?

REFERENCES

[1] Rafter N. American criminal trial films: an overview of their development, 1930–2000. J Law Soc 2001;28(1):9–24.

[2] Zlatic JM, Wilkerson DC, McAllister SM. Pretrial diversion: the overlooked pretrial services evidence-based practice. Fed Probat 2010;74(1):28–33.

[3] Buchanan J. Police-prosecutor teams: innovations in several jurisdictions. NIJ Rep 1989;214:2–8.

[4] Lee J, Ruiz JM. Investigating discriminative bail setting: multivariate analysis in Louisiana. J Ethn Crim Justice 2011;9(1):22.

[5] Hess J. Jail overcrowding. Am Jails 2008;22(5):4.

[6] Specter D. Everything revolves around overcrowding: the State of California's prisons. Fed Sentencing Rep 2010;22(3):194–9.

[7] Goldkamp JS, Gottfredson MR. Guidelines for bail: an experiment in court reform. Philadelphia, PA: Temple University Press; 1985.

[8] Schultz D. Encyclopedia of the United States constitution. Bail. New York: Facts on File, Inc.; 2009. p. 44.

[9] Schnacke TR, Jones MR, Brooker CMB. The history of bail and pretrial release. Washington, DC: Pretrial Justice Institute; 2010. p. 19, <www.pretrial.org/HistoryBailDocuments/History%20of%20Bail%20(2010).pdf/>.

[10] Ibid.

[11] Ibid.

[12] TIME. The old lady moves on, <www.time.com/time/magazine/article/0,9171,802159-1,00.html/> [accessed August 18, 1941].

[13] Ibid.

[14] Schnacke J, Brooker. The history of bail and pretrial release, p. 7.

[15] Ibid.

[16] Burns R, Kinkade P, Leone MC. Bounty hunters: a look behind the hype. Policing 2005;28(1):118.

[17] Sullivan L. Bail burden keeps U.S. jails stuffed with inmates. NPR, <www.npr.org/2010/01/21/122725771/Bail-Burden-Keeps-U-S-Jails-Stuffed-With-Inmates/> 2010, [accessed January 21, 2012].

[18] Sullivan L. Inmates who can't make bail face stark options. NPR, <www.npr.org/templates/story/story.php?storyId=122725819/> 2010, [accessed January 22, 2012].

[19] Sullivan L. Bail burden keeps U.S. jails stuffed with inmates.

[20] Goldkamp S. Danger and detention: a second generation of bail reform. J Crim Law Criminol 1985;76(1):1–74.

[21] Petee TA. Recommended for release on recognizance: factors affecting pretrial release recommendations. J Soc Psychol 1994;134(3):375–82.

[22] Demuth S. Racial and ethnic differences in pretrial release decisions and outcomes: a comparison of Hispanic, black and white felony arrestees. Criminology 2003;41(3):873–907.

[23] White MD, Hallett M. Revisiting anomalous data from the "Breaking the Cycle" program. J Offender Rehabil 2005;42(1):1−22.

[24] Buddress LAN. Federal probation and pretrial services—a cost-effective and successful community corrections. Fed Probat 1997;61(1):5−13.

[25] Blomberg TG. Diversion and accelerated social control. J Crim Law Criminol 1977;68(2):274−82.

[26] Rich RF, Sampson RJ. Public perceptions of criminal justice policy: does victimization make a difference? Violence Victims 1990;5(2):109−18.

[27] Guidorizzi DD. Should we really "Ban" plea bargaining? The core concerns of plea bargaining critics. Emory Law Rev 1998;47(2):753−83.

[28] Douglass JG. Fatal attraction? The uneasy courtship of Brady and plea bargaining. Emory Law Rev 2001;50(2):437−517.

[29] Eric Luna, Wade M. Prosecutors as judges. Washington Lee Law Rev 2010;67(4):1413−532.

[30] Bonnar-Kidd KK. Sexual offender laws and prevention of sexual violence or recidivism. Am J Public Health 2010;100(3):412−9.

[31] MacKenzie DL, Clear T. Three strikes. Criminol Public Policy 2002;1(3):351−2.

[32] Merritt N, Fain T, Turner S. Oregon's get tough sentencing reform: a lesson in justice system adaptation. Criminol Public Policy 2006;5(1):5−36.

[33] Langer M. Rethinking plea bargaining: the practice and reform of prosecutorial adjudication in American criminal procedure. Am J Crim Law 2006;33(3):223−99.

[34] Rossett A, Cressey DR. Justice by consent: plea bargains in the American courtroom. New York, NY: J.P. Lippincott; 1976. p. 18.

[35] Cases in which the Supreme Court decided that the states are not bound by the grand jury section of the Fifth Amendment: *Hurtado v. California*, 110 U.S. 516 (1884). *Palko v. Connecticut*, 302 U.S. 319, 323 (1937). *Alexander v. Louisiana*, 405 U.S. 625, 633 (1972). American Bar Association, FAQs about the Grand Jury System, <www.abanow.org/2010/03/faqs-about-the-grand-jury-system/> [accessed March, 2010].

[36] Cassidy RM. Toward a more independent grand jury: recasting and enforcing the prosecutor's duty to disclose exculpatory evidence. Georgetown J Legal Ethics 2000;13(3):361−404.

[37] Hall J. Grand jury reform. Fed Sentencing Rep 2008;20(5):334−6.

[38] Oberstein N. Nolo contendere: its use and effect. California Law Rev 1964;52(2):423.

[39] Gooch AD. Admitting guilt by professing innocence: when sentence enhancements based on Alford pleas are unconstitutional. Vanderbilt Law Rev 2010;63(6):1755−92.

[40] Adams JA, Blinka DD. Pretrial motions in criminal prosecutions. San Francisco, CA: LexisNexis; 2008. p. 3.

[41] Bradley CM. Reconceiving the Fourth Amendment and the exclusionary rule. Law Contemp Prob 2010;73(3):211−38.

[42] Adams, Blinka. Pretrial motions in criminal prosecutions, p. 29.

[43] North Dakota Supreme Court Review. Criminal law—search and seizure—good faith exception to the exclusionary law. North Dakota Law Rev 2009;85(2):532−6.

[44] Davis TY. The Supreme Court Giveth and the Supreme Court Taketh away: the century of Fourth Amendment search and seizure doctrine. J Crim Law Criminol 2010;100(3):933−1041.

[45] Deslauriers-Varin N, Lussier P, St-Yves M. Confessing their crime: factors influencing the offender's decision to confess to police. Justice Q 2011;28(1):113−45.

[46] Davis D, Leo RA, Follette WC. Selling confession: setting the state with the sympathetic detective with a limited time offer. J Contemp Crim Justice 2010;26(4):441−57.

[47] Scott Hayward C. Explaining juvenile false confessions: adolescent development and police interrogation. Psychol Rev 2007;31:53−76.

[48] Frantzen D. Interrogation strategies, evidence, and the need for *Miranda*: a study of police ideologies. Police Pract Res 2010;11(3):227−39.

[49] Adams JA, Blinka DD. Pretrial motions in criminal prosecutions. 4th ed. Cincinnati, Lexis Nexis; 2008. p. 476

[50] Leo RA. *Miranda*'s revenge: police interrogation as a confidence game. Law Soc Rev 1996;30(2):259−88.

[51] *New York v. Quarles*, 104 S. Ct. at 2632. See also Adams, Blinka. Pretrial motions in criminal prosecutions, p. 542−43.

The criminal trial process is often stressful for defendants and victims.

The Prosecutor and the Exertion of State Power

Learning Objectives

After reading this chapter, you should be able to:

1. Explain why the prosecutor acts primarily in the state's interest.
2. List and explain the factors that guide prosecutor discretion when representing the state.
3. Discuss the three main governmental levels at which prosecutors operate.
4. Define and discuss community prosecution.
5. Describe Christie's criticism of the role of the victim in the prosecution.
6. List and describe the forms of plea bargaining.
7. Explain why prosecutors are interested in good relationships with the courtroom workgroup and defense attorneys.
8. Define *voir dire.*

9. Tell what burden of proof is and the two concepts that comprise it.
10. Analyze the composition of the prosecution's case-in-chief.

The prosecutor plays a pivotal role in the U.S. court system. Because of the prosecutor's unique power, he or she is able to influence the management, the court caseload, as well as the quality of justice in a way that supersedes all other members of the courtroom workgroup, including the judge. According to one scholar:

> [Prosecutors] are armed with more and better weaponry than the adversary; they exercise an inordinate influence over the referee and score-keeper; and they can cheat without getting caught or suffering any penalty. And the prosecutor's cheating costs more than losing a game or a title; it may cost a person his liberty or his life [1].

Although the prosecutor is a member of the judicial branch of government, one of the roles the prosecutor performs is actually a function of the executive branch. That is, the prosecutor represents the state (both the government and the people) and acts as an advocate rather than a passive functionary of the court system [2].

In this chapter, we will highlight the prosecutor's various roles in the criminal court system. Our goal is to describe the prosecutor's various duties and to highlight the important discretionary decisions that are vested in the prosecutor's duties. Although it may seem an exaggeration to say the prosecutor is the most important person in the courtroom, it will become apparent that the power to make decisions concerns not only the defendants but also the entire operation of the criminal court. In order to properly understand the prosecutor's role, we must understand how the prosecutor represents not individuals but the state [3].

Because of the organization of the U.S. court system, each jurisdiction has its own courts, judges, and prosecutors. That means there are 50 state prosecution systems, as well as the federal system. Each state is also broken down into judicial circuits that have various levels of courts. Later in this chapter, we will look more closely at the hierarchy of courts and prosecutors, but here it is sufficient to note that there are many different types and levels of prosecutors, and we can speak of them only in the most general terms.

THE STATE AS VICTIM

In the eyes of the law, when an offense is committed against an individual, it is committed against all of us. We must all be protected from predatory offenders and it is the prosecutor's job to ensure that offenders receive a fair trial and are sentenced in a way that deters them from future crime, punishes them, or incapacitates them. Although indirectly performing these duties in the interest of the aggrieved victim, the law dictates that the prosecutor is primarily acting in the state's interest. Therefore, when an offender goes on trial, it is not the victim who is the aggrieved party, but society. In representing the state, the prosecutor also represents the victim, but the state's interests are the driving force behind the prosecutor's actions. This important distinction can stress and confuse crime victims when the prosecutor makes decisions in the interests of the state rather than the individual [4]. See Focus on Discretion for a look at how prosecutors must balance the interests of the state, the victim, and the defendant.

FOCUS ON DISCRETION

The Prosecutorial Balancing Act

In 2001, Marie Hess was sentenced to 30 years in prison for shooting her husband to death while he slept. At her sentencing hearing, the family of police officer James Hess had shown a professionally made video showing Hess's childhood and his high school graduation, his fishing trips, his puppy, and finally his grave. A decade later, in September 2011, Marie Hess was back in court to hear the New Jersey Supreme Court overturn her sentence in part because the video had prejudiced the court against her [5].

Has the push for victims' rights gone too far? In 2004, the federal Crime Victims' Rights Act gave victims in federal criminal proceedings extended rights, which several states incorporated into their own victims' rights legislation [6]. Victims' rights generally include the right to restitution; to be protected from the accused; and to be notified of, to be present, and to be heard at court proceedings [7]. Victim impact statements that include materials like the video at Marie Hess's sentencing hearing have also become common.

The prosecutor must balance consideration for the victim, the defendant, and the state [8]. Too much consideration for the victim affects the prosecutor's impartiality. Too much concern for the defendant may distress the victim and risk releasing a possibly dangerous defendant. Too much focus on the state may cause the prosecutor to slight both the defendant's and the victim's rights. A good prosecutor is neutral to all three demands [9].

In colonial times, victims were responsible for their own justice. They had to investigate the offense, arrest the suspect, file charges, and prosecute the defendant. Bringing a case to court was too expensive and difficult for many victims. The creation of the public prosecutor, then, served not only the social demands for deterrence, rehabilitation, and retribution, but also completed a new style of public criminal justice system that included professional law enforcement and prisons. This shift from private to public prosecution also meant the victim's needs became secondary to those of society [10].

Granting extended rights to victims remains controversial because the defendant is the only party in the criminal court process whose liberty (and possibly life) is at stake. Critics of victims' rights legislation are concerned with the prosecutor's ability to balance the concerns of the victim, the defendant, and the state, as well as the defendant's chance to get a fair decision from a jury who must decide the case using evidence rather than emotion [11].

Question

What is your opinion of victims having more rights in criminal trials? Does this hinder prosecutors in their duties? Why or why not?

In representing the state, the prosecutor must keep several factors in mind. These factors speak to a range of interests representing the various constituencies to which the prosecutor must answer. Therefore, it isn't easy to predict which case will receive the most attention because these demands originate from political pressures, social norms, organizational demands, and historical precedents. The complex factors that guide prosecutor discretion include the following concerns:

- Protection of society. The prosecutor has the sole responsibility in deciding, which cases are brought to trial. Given the excessive workload of the U.S. court system, the prosecutor's decisions are often criticized. One of citizens' foremost demands is that the most dangerous offenders be incarcerated and that the streets be made safe. Typically, the more severe the offense, the more likely the prosecutor will select it for attention and the more severe the penalty will be if a conviction is reached. Although the legislature specifies the system of penalties within laws, it is the prosecutor who decides what offense to charge someone with and whether to use court resources to prosecute the case. Prosecutors make their reputations—and depending on the type of jurisdiction—get re-elected by being "tough on crime."

- Deterrence of criminal offenders. Given that every case cannot be prosecuted to the fullest extent, decisions must be made as to what type of cases will receive the attention of the courts. These decisions involve value judgments made by the prosecutor that also has an influence on lawbreaking in the jurisdiction. For instance, if the prosecutor decided that illegal gambling was of low priority in the prosecutor's workload, then gamblers would be more likely to engage in their activities. Police who see that gambling arrests do not receive serious attention by prosecutors would be less likely to make gambling arrests. The result is gamblers will not be deterred by the likelihood of arrest and prosecution. Conversely, prosecutors who devote resources to the prosecution of sex offenders will find police officers investigating cases more rigorously and potential sex offenders more likely to be deterred from committing their offenses.

- Management of court resources. In representing the state, the prosecutor's office must make decisions on a variety of resources and financial issues that determine the efficiency of the court system. Depending on the jurisdiction, the chief prosecutor is responsible for issues such as jury management, victim and witness programs, diversion programs, and staffing of courts with prosecutors. Sometimes these responsibilities are under the auspices of a judge or a court administrator, but the prosecutor's office plays a vital role in ensuring that court resources are used in an effective and efficient manner. There are not enough resources for all the demands of the court, and the chief prosecutor must make management decisions for the court to function properly. In this way, the prosecutor's office is responsible to the state to maximize its effectiveness with limited resources.

- Representation of victims. Although the ultimate responsibility of the prosecutor is to the state, he or she also must keep crime victims in mind. Although victims have little say—so in how an offender is charged or whether the case is plea bargained—prosecutors make sincere efforts to ensure victims are satisfied with the outcome of the case. It is not possible to satisfy every victim because of the excessive caseload in most jurisdictions, but prosecutors are still responsible for ensuring that victims' interests are attended to. By listening to victims and keeping them informed about the case, prosecutors can manage victim expectations. In many jurisdictions, victim and witness programs help prosecutors ensure that victims believe their needs are being met [12].

JURISDICTIONS OF PROSECUTORS

Because of the decentralization of the U.S. criminal court system, prosecutors' offices are also decentralized. Prosecutors' offices vary in structure according to level of government (federal, state, or local). The structure of the prosecutor's office also varies depending on workload issues and resources. This section will focus on the differences between federal and state prosecutors, while recognizing that state jurisdictions can vary widely in the size and scope.

Prosecution at the Federal Level

The Department of Justice is responsible for federal prosecutions and is headed by the attorney general who is a member of the president's cabinet. The Department of Justice comprises more than 50 legal agencies that include the Drug Enforcement Agency, the Federal Bureau of Investigation, the U.S. Marshals Office, the Federal Bureau of Prisons, and the U.S. Parole Commission. The organizational chart of the U.S. Attorney's Office shows the range of agencies (Figure 8.1).

The mission statement of the Department of Justice reflects their broad mandate:

> To enforce the law and defend the interests of the United States according to the law; to ensure public safety against threats foreign and domestic; to provide federal leadership in preventing and controlling crime; to seek just punishment for those guilty of unlawful behavior; and to ensure fair and impartial administration of justice for all Americans [13].

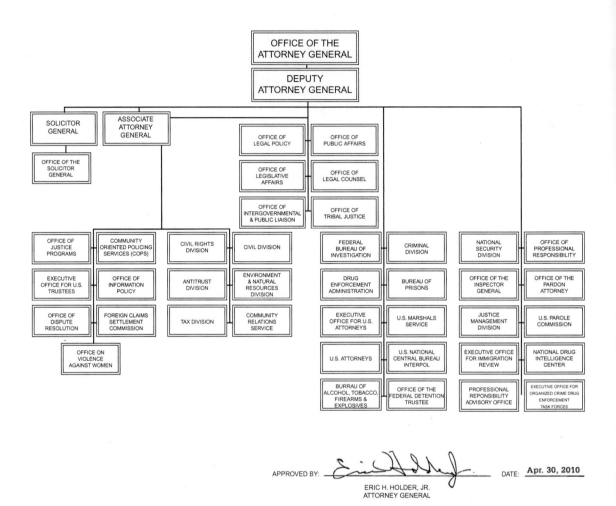

FIGURE 8.1

The U.S. Department of Justice, Department of Justice Agencies, www.justice.gov/agencies/index-org.html.

There are three types of prosecutors within the attorney general's office. Each of these types of prosecutors has different types of duties.

■ Solicitor general. The solicitor general is a ranking member of the attorney general's office. The solicitor general represents the government in cases that appear before the Supreme Court. Attorneys from the solicitor general's office perform a dual function in that they represent the interest of both the executive branch and the judiciary [14]. This office also determines which cases the United States government will appeal when the verdict goes against it. The office has an important gatekeeping function in that it decides which cases that the government will bring to the U.S. Supreme Court, which is especially important given that the government is involved in approximately two-thirds of the cases are heard there [15].

- Criminal Division of the Justice Department. The Criminal Division is responsible for overseeing more than 900 federal statutes. They also prosecute several nationally significant cases. They provide legal advice to federal agencies that oversee programs such as the national Witness Protection Program. Additionally, they have task forces related to dealing with gangs, organized crime, and fraud. Furthermore, the Criminal Division has initiatives that deal with child exploitation and obscenity, computer crime intellectual property, and human rights. Finally, this division develops and implements policy that affects the prosecutorial efforts of the Justice Department.
- U.S. Attorneys. The U.S. attorneys are the workhorses of the Justice Department's prosecution efforts. There are 94 U.S. attorneys assigned to geographical jurisdictions throughout the United States and its territories. Their statutory responsibilities are:
  1. The prosecution of criminal cases brought by the federal government.
  2. The prosecution and defense of civil cases in which the United States is a party.
  3. The collection of debts owed by the federal government that are administratively uncollectible [16].

There is a great deal of variation in the types of cases the U.S. attorneys prosecute in their jurisdictions for two reasons. First, certain parts of the nation have unique problems with issues such as gangs, immigration, drugs, or political corruption [17]. Second, because of their geographic dispersion, U.S. attorneys enjoy a certain amount of autonomy that those working in the nation's capital may not. Although these attorneys serve at the pleasure of the President, many are chosen because of their reputations as experienced lawyers and because they have the support of the congressman and senators in their jurisdictions. Politics is often part of the selection process for U.S. attorneys, and sometimes it takes a scandalous dimension and ends up in the media.

Prosecution at the State Level

The prosecutor's role is even more varied at the state level than at the national level. Because each state operates under its own constitution and has its own legislature, each handles the prosecution of criminal cases differently. Each state has a state attorney general who is similar to the U.S. attorney general. The state attorney general has duties that include representing the state in court when the state's actions are questioned. Additionally, the state attorney general investigates cases of fraud, consumer lawsuits, and, to a limited degree, criminal statutes. Their duties are primarily centered around representing the state in cases, in which the state sues corporations or individuals. State prosecutors rarely prosecute felony cases unless a statewide issue is being decided. For example, when there is a conflict of interest or an allegation of corruption concerning a county-level prosecutor, the state may step in and handle the case [18].

Prosecution at the County or City Level

The city- or county-level prosecutor is the next level in the state prosecutorial system. This individual represents the state in criminal cases. With the exception of four jurisdictions (Alaska, Connecticut, New Jersey, and the District of Columbia), this prosecutor is elected rather than appointed [19]. Each state may call its prosecutor by a different term. For instance, in some states, the chief prosecutor is called the "district attorney," while in other states the term may be "state's attorney." In Kentucky and Virginia, which are commonwealths, they are called the "commonwealth attorney." Regardless of the title, the chief prosecutor handles both misdemeanor and felony cases. Again, depending on the state, the jurisdiction may be divided along county lines or judicial circuits that encompass several counties [20]. Each state has its own organization based primarily on population and geography. The chief prosecutor is responsible for establishing the policies of the prosecution's office, but most of the cases are tried by assistant district attorneys or state attorneys depending on the jurisdiction.

Although the chief prosecutor may argue high profile cases, it is the assistant prosecutors who handle most of the court's business. The prosecutor's role is highly visible and can have a beneficial effect upon lawyers who successfully prosecute cases. Often, prosecutors will make a name for themselves and end up with a political career as an elected judge or legislator at the state or national level. Additionally, becoming a prosecutor is a good career move for someone who wants to become a partner in a successful law firm. The visibility as well as the courtroom experience makes prosecutors attractive to influential law firms. Most felonies and misdemeanors are handled at the county level, which becomes an excellent training ground for judges and attorneys in private law firms.

The organizational structure of prosecutor's offices is fairly consistent across jurisdictions [21]. The state attorney or district attorney is usually an elected official who is responsible for the administration of the office, establishing policies and priorities, and dealing with community groups, the media, and other government officials. The chief prosecutor is responsible for assigning prosecutors to specific courtrooms or judges, assigning cases, and overseeing the work of the prosecutors. Depending on the size of the office, prosecutors may be assigned to felony courts or misdemeanor courts. Small jurisdictions may have one part-time prosecutor, and large jurisdictions may have a couple of dozen. In large cities, a prosecutor's office may serve a population of over 1 million. Prosecutor's offices also employ administrative assistants. Other staff members in the office may include investigators (often former police officers) and victim–witness personnel, both of whom who assist prosecutors in dealing with victims or those who have knowledge of an offense and may be beneficial to its prosecution [22].

Because the prosecutor plays such a pivotal role, they often reach out to the community and involve law enforcement agencies, civic groups, and citizens in helping to improve the public safety and the quality of community life. Prosecutor's offices can enlist community members in helping to identify general crime patterns as well as specific offenders. In many ways, **community prosecution** is like **community policing**. It allows the prosecutor's office to enlist the aid of the community in preventing and addressing many types of crime. It is aimed at increasing quality of life by dealing with problems before they result in crime. The prosecutor's office can act as a central coordinating area for community projects that address the problems of delinquents and criminal offenders. These projects might include:

- Brooklyn Domestic Violence Court. Participation in this community court allows the prosecutor's office to work with other members of the courtroom workgroup and influential public agencies to deal with domestic violence in both traditional and innovative ways [23].
- The Harlem Community Justice Center. The center seeks to solve neighborhood problems—including youth crime, landlord–tenant disputes, and the challenges faced by parolees—in East and Central Harlem. As a multi-jurisdictional civil and family court, Harlem is unique among community courts. Among the many nontraditional services the Justice Center has assembled are: programs to help local landlords and tenants resolve conflicts and access financial support; programs for at-risk youth, including a youth court; and reentry programs for both juvenile and adult ex-offenders returning to the community [24].
- New York's Midtown Community Court. The Midtown Community Court targets quality-of-life offenses, such as prostitution, illegal vending, graffiti, shoplifting, farebeating, and vandalism. Typically in these cases, judges are forced to choose between a few days of jail time and nothing at all—sentences that fail to impress the victim, the community, and the defendants that these offenses are taken seriously. In contrast, the Midtown Community Court sentences low-level offenders to pay back the neighborhood through community service, while at the same time offering them help with problems that often underlie criminal behavior [25].

Like community policing, community prosecution is based on the idea that by having the prosecutor work closely with the local community, he or she will be better able to address crime and delinquency at an early stage. The rigorous prosecution of misdemeanors may head off more serious offenses. The theoretical perspective behind community prosecution is similar to Wilson and Kelling's broken windows theory, which basically states that a community that appears to be neglected invites more crime.

According to the National Center for Community Prosecution, community prosecution has four main principles:

1. Recognizing the community's role in public safety. Community prosecutors invite community members to talk about their safety concerns, identify community problems, create appropriate responses, and help the prosecutor's office prioritize problems.
2. Engaging in problem solving. Community prosecutors should not only focus on individual offenses but also try to understand the offenses within a context as part of a larger community problem or set of problems.
3. Establishing and maintaining partnerships. Community prosecutors should encourage greater communication, improved coordination, and stronger partnerships among criminal justice agencies.
4. Evaluating outcomes of activities. Community prosecutors should evaluate their activities and effect on neighborhoods and adapt to the community's needs [26].

Community prosecution programs are available in only a few jurisdictions as there are a couple of dynamics that work against the establishment of these programs. The first reason is that the skill set of prosecutors does not necessarily lend itself to working with community agencies to prevent crime. Many prosecutors do not see community prosecution as important or as serious as criminal prosecution. The second reason is the lack of resources. The prosecutor's office may not have the time and personnel to work with community court projects because of their high caseloads. They see community prosecution as not being central to the prosecutor's duties and, in an era of scarce resources, one that is expendable.

DUTIES OF THE PROSECUTOR

As we have learned, the prosecutor's office wears many hats. Foremost among the prosecutor's duties is the responsibility to represent the state in criminal cases. Individual victims may be part of the court proceedings, but the larger issue is that the fabric of society must be repaired.

Representing the State

Victims (or their families) can seek damages from their aggressor by going to civil court. If a defendant is found guilty in criminal court or has accepted a plea bargain, it is much easier for the victim to recoup damages in civil court. However, in criminal court, it is the prosecutor who determines what offense has been committed, what charge will be filed, and whether to engage in plea negotiations. Victims may be asked their opinion, but the prosecutor ultimately determines these issues (Photo 8.1).

In representing the state, the prosecutor takes away from the victim much of the righteous indignation of victimhood. Criminologist Nils Christie uses the phrase "conflicts as property" to illustrate this point. Christie argues that by taking victimhood away from the victim, the state prevents any reconciliation between victim and offender. A simple apology or private restitution is not possible, and the case takes on a much more formal quality that can further estrange the victim and offender.

PHOTO 8.1
The prosecutor represents the state, not the victims of a criminal offense. Here, a prosecutor shows jurors a photograph from an auto crash.

The Charging Decision as Social Control

Representing the state can be a perplexing problem for the prosecutor because the state has many interests that often conflict. For instance, people generally believe that offenders should pay for their offenses [27]. To this end, the prosecutor is expected to fairly evaluate a criminal offense and decide on the appropriate charges. If the evidence supports it, society desires a first-degree murder charge rather than a manslaughter charge. However, the prosecutor must make several crucial decisions in deciding the actual charge, which may involve factors other than the offense itself. For instance, the workload of the prosecutor's office often prevents it from charging each case with the maximum charges possible. In addition to the strength or weakness of the case, a number of other important cases, the availability of resources to hire expert witnesses, and the personality and proclivities of the presiding judge must be considered in deciding the eventual charge.

This decision enables the prosecutor to exercise a great deal of discretion that affects not only the rest of the criminal proceedings but also the entire criminal justice system. It is hard to overestimate how profoundly important the charging decision is. In representing the state, the prosecutor sets in motion a vast bureaucracy. Prosecutors who seek to establish justice in society or to simply make a name for themselves can use this charging decision to influence the case. For instance, defendants can be coerced into a plea bargain because of an aggressive charging position by the prosecutor [28]. The difference in the punishments in being charged with possession of drugs or as a drug dealer gives the prosecutor leverage in plea negotiations.

Plea Bargaining

In representing the state, the prosecutor also decides how, or if, the state will plea bargain. Realistically, plea bargaining begins with the charging decision by which the prosecutor can establish the parameters within which a plea may be negotiated [29]. Once the charges are decided, there is an incentive for the defendant to bargain for the best deal possible. Defendants who believe they are innocent may insist upon a trial, whereas defendants who know they are guilty will sometimes "roll the dice" if they think the prosecutor's case is weak. Most cases, however, result in some type of plea negotiation that allows the prosecutor to claim victory and the defendant to receive a more lenient disposition. Plea bargains work in several ways:

■ Vertical plea. The vertical plea is the most advantageous for defendants. It allows them to plead guilty or **no contest** to a lesser charge than the one for which they have been charged. For instance, a rape charge may turn into a sexual assault charge, or a homicide charge into a manslaughter charge. The penalties for each offense is set by the legislature, and by pleading to a lesser charge, the defendant enjoys a reduced range of penalties. In some states, a capital murder charge carries the potential of the death penalty, and defendants may be eager to negotiate a lesser charge in order to avoid exposure to capital punishment. The prosecutor may be motivated to use a vertical plea because of the weakness of the case. The prosecutor may decide that premeditation will not be easy to prove and that rather than to go to trial and risk losing the case, a plea of manslaughter would be more desirable [30].

- Horizontal plea. The horizontal plea allows the prosecutor to dismiss many or all of these charges in return for a guilty plea on one of them. Often, an offender might have committed multiple offenses by the time of capture. For instance, a burglar is arrested in someone's house, and the police link his fingerprints to a series of burglaries in the city. The prosecutor can then charge the defendant with multiple offenses. Each charge has its own potential for incarceration and, although an individual charge may carry a maximum of five years, by the time several of these charges add up, the defendant may be facing a long time behind bars. The benefits for the defendant are obvious: he serves a short sentence for one offense rather than a long sentence for all of them. The prosecutor also benefits. In addition to not having to go to trial, the prosecutor must keep in mind that prison space is limited and sending a burglar to prison for a long time is not the wisest use of state resources.

- Reduced-sentence plea. In a **reduced-sentence plea**, the prosecutor and the defense attorney reach an agreement in which the defendant agrees to serve less than the maximum sentence in exchange for a guilty plea. These pleas occur often because it gives the prosecutor a victory without having to go to trial, and it allows the defendant to receive a specific, but reduced, penalty.

- Avoidance-of-stigma plea. An **avoidance-of-stigma plea** allows a defendant to strike a deal in order to avoid a damaging label or status. For example, "career criminal" status may mean a defendant is exposed to additional punishments. In another example, in states with "three-strikes" laws, defendants find that even though the current offense is minor, he or she is now subject to a long incarceration because the current offense is number three. So in order to secure a plea bargain, prosecutors may waive the "three-strikes" law or "career criminal" status. A similar type of avoidance-of-stigma plea involves sex offenders. Being labeled a sex offender usually carries a host of requirements that may affect the quality of life. For instance, some states place sex offenders' names on a publicly accessible, statewide registry. An offender may accept a guilty plea to a lesser charge in order to avoid being labeled a sex offender.

The prosecutor has tremendous discretion in the plea bargaining negotiation, and the defendant has much more at stake than the prosecutor [31]. Plea bargaining is a routine part of the prosecutor's job, but it can decide whether a defendant is placed on probation or sent to prison. Although the judge must approve the plea bargain, it is the prosecutor who strikes a deal with the defense attorney. The prosecutor and defense attorney are both members of the courtroom workgroup, so both understand the deal to be made. Because so many cases are similar, a "going rate" develops in which certain types of cases are understood to have certain types of plea bargains, and the plea negotiations become somewhat predictable. If the defense attorney argues for a greatly reduced sentence compared to what other types of cases have settled for, the prosecutor is unlikely to agree [32].

Establishing the Defendant's Guilt

One of the core features of the prosecutor's job is to develop a case that establishes the defendant's guilt. Before we move on to matters of evidence, it is important to note that the prosecutor's behavior is a critical element of the prosecution. Prosecutors are expected to treat everyone in the courtroom, including those who take the stand, fairly and with respect. Prosecutors are expected to "serve justice, play by the rules, and not hit below the belt." This was established in the 1935 U.S. Supreme Court case *Berger v. United States*, in which a defendant won a new trial not only because the evidence against him was weak but also because the prosecutor conducted the case in an unprofessional fashion (see Landmark Cases 9.1).

As for evidence, the prosecutor must marshal enough to prove **beyond a reasonable doubt** that the person charged with the offense actually committed it. Most of this work is done by the police officers who conducted the arrest and investigation. Before a prosecutor makes a charge, he or she reviews the police's work to determine whether the evidence is sufficient to carry the case forward. There is a difference, however, between being convinced that the suspect committed the offense and being able to prove it in court [33]. The prosecutor uses several criteria in establishing whether there is enough evidence to prove a suspect committed an offense. These criteria include:

- Motive. Did the defendant have a reason to commit the offense? If someone was killed during a robbery, the motive would be money.

LANDMARK CASES 9.1

Berger v. United States (1935)

"It is as much the duty of the United States Attorney to refrain from improper methods calculated to produce a wrongful conviction as it is to use every legitimate means to bring about a just one."

Harry Berger was indicted in a federal district court for having conspired with seven other people, including Katz, Rice, and Jones, for possession of counterfeit bank notes and conspiracy to deal in counterfeit notes. Katz testified that Berger was involved in a transaction in which Katz gave Berger a few counterfeit notes that Berger then gave to Jones. Katz also stated that he gave notes to Rice and Jones, but Berger was not involved. Katz's testimony was unreliable, and the jury acquitted Berger of possessing counterfeit notes but convicted him of conspiracy. He was sentenced to a year and a day in the penitentiary.

Berger's appeal eventually went to U.S. Supreme Court. Part of his argument, aside from claiming innocence, was

that the prosecutor's misconduct was so egregious that it destroyed Berger's ability to prove his innocence. The prosecutor's strategy included insinuations that Berger was a liar; that he had made statements to the prosecutor that Berger claimed he had not said; insinuations that Berger had participated in immoral behavior; false and inflammatory claims about Berger's character; and attacks on Berger's lawyer.

The Court agreed that the evidence of Berger's involvement in the conspiracy was weak and condemned the prosecutor's behavior for its "evil influence upon the jury." The Court further stated that: "Moreover, we have not here a case where the misconduct of the prosecuting attorney was slight or confined to a single instance, but one where such misconduct was pronounced and persistent, with a probable cumulative effect upon the jury which cannot be disregarded as inconsequential." The judgment against Berger was reversed, and he received a new trial.

Other motives may include sexual gratification (rape and sexual abuse), revenge (assault or arson), or thrill-seeking (vandalism or motor vehicle theft).

- Opportunity. Did the defendant have the opportunity to commit the offense? For instance, when the bodies were discovered in the OJ Simpson murder case, Simpson was on a plane to Chicago [34]. The prosecution had to establish a timeline that showed that Simpson had enough time to commit the murders then board an airplane to demonstrate that he had the opportunity to commit the offense. Often, the defense is an *alibi* that illustrates that the defendant did not have the opportunity.
- Means. Did the defendant have the capabilities of committing the offense? If someone is accused of hacking into a bank computer network and committing embezzlement, the prosecution would be able to establish that the person had the computer skills to do so. Someone who did not own a computer and did not know how to use one could claim that they did not have the means necessary to engage in this criminal activity. Similarly, if a large man were found brutally beaten to death, the

prosecution may have a difficult time establishing that his 105-pound wife had the physical strength to do it.

These three pillars of culpability are not sufficient to prove guilt [35]. The prosecution must also show the accused acted upon these criteria. Typically, showing that someone committed an offense also involves some type of evidence such as eyewitness testimony or physical forensic evidence that augments the determination that the defendant had the means, motive, and opportunity. This requires that the prosecutor develop the evidence and present it to the court in a logical and understandable way [36]. To this end, the prosecutor often uses expert witnesses. An expert witness can be a great aid for the prosecutor, but may also have some drawbacks because the witness is always cross-examined by the defense.

The Expert Witness

Expert witnesses are chosen by the prosecution to give testimony because their education, training, or experience qualifies them to use their expertise to bolster the prosecution's case. The court requires expert testimony in many areas in order to interpret technical evidence. For instance, when dealing with the insanity defense, it is useful to have a psychiatrist or psychologist advise the court on whether the defendant meets the criteria necessary to claim insanity [37]. In cases involving firearms, experts can be called to provide analysis of their examination of rifle marks on bullets, caliber of bullets, and a number of other technical issues that can show that a bullet came from the defendant's weapon.

Handwriting experts can also be called into court to testify on cases of forgery or fraud, and experts dealing with issues of intellectual property can shed light on cases in which plagiarism or theft have occurred. The prosecution has the burden of proving the case and expert witnesses can provide the testimony that can convince a jury that the defendant is guilty [38].

One of the dangers for the prosecution in the use of expert witnesses is that the defense can provide their own experts. It is then up to the judge or the jury to decide, which side presented the most credible evidence. The prosecutor and the defense attorney may challenge the qualifications of each other's expert witnesses and closely examine their testimony to find contradictions and inaccuracies [39].

Where does the prosecutor find expert witnesses? They are everywhere. The real key for prosecutors is to find expert witnesses who are available, local, inexpensive, and convincing. Some individuals can make a living as an expert witness, while most only do it occasionally to supplement their income, provide a community service, or establish their expertise. Prosecutors will typically use expert witnesses they have used before and can rely upon to give the type of evidence they need to provide a convincing case [40].

WORKING WITH THE COURTROOM WORKGROUP

Although we typically imagine prosecutors working in an adversarial setting, they actually spend most of their time working within the courtroom workgroup to move cases through the court. This requires that the prosecutor spends more time cooperating with those he or she works with rather than battling them. The prosecutor is interested in having cordial and professional relations with defense attorneys rather than adversarial and competitive ones [41].

The prosecutor is the most important person in the courtroom workgroup because he or she is responsible for deciding which cases are entered into the system. This is an important gatekeeping function that has ramifications for not only the entire court system but also the correctional system. The discretion exercised by the prosecutor affects the other members of the courtroom workgroup in the following ways:

- Selecting cases for prosecution. It is the prosecutor who decides whether a case actually goes forward. Defense attorneys might try to convince the prosecutor to dismiss the case, but if there is sufficient evidence or the case is serious enough, the prosecutor will file charges over the pleadings of the defense attorney. Thus, the work of the prosecutor affects public defenders, bailiffs, court reporters, and judges.
- Plea bargaining. As mentioned earlier, the prosecutor represents the state in plea bargaining. It is the prosecutor's responsibility to drive a hard bargain on behalf of the state to ensure that the guilty are given appropriate punishments and that the court docket is efficiently handled. The prosecutor must ensure that plea bargains are attractive enough to defense attorneys and defendants that a large percentage of them are accepted. Otherwise, the court would grind to a halt should too many defendants insist upon their right to a trial.
- Diversion. The prosecutor has the authority to not only dismiss cases but also divert them from the normal processing of the criminal justice system to alternative dispositions. For instance, many jurisdictions have first-offender programs in which those accused of minor offenses and who do not have a criminal record may be diverted to a treatment program or community service where they demonstrate their trustworthiness and address their problems. Once the defendant has successfully completed the diversion program, the case can be dropped and the defendant would have no criminal record [42].

Although the prosecutor has a position of great responsibility in the courtroom workgroup, he or she is also subject to working within established norms in the courthouse. An overzealous prosecutor may find that other members of the courtroom workgroup resent the aggressive nature of the prosecutor. Defense attorneys may advise their clients not to accept plea bargains that deviate too far from what is customarily accepted as a reasonable deal. If too many defense attorneys advise their clients in such a way, the court docket slows, and the prosecutor will be unable to move cases efficiently through the system. On the other hand, the judge may advise that the plea-bargain deals being offered are too lenient and reject the sentencing recommendation.

Prosecutors choose cases for prosecution, engage in plea bargaining, and make sentencing decisions based upon their understanding of how the judge likes to run the courtroom. Having a judge complain to the chief district attorney can cause the assistant district attorney to be reassigned to another courtroom or even lose his or her job. Additionally, other assistant district attorneys may exert pressure on a prosecutor who is too lenient or too aggressive in prosecuting cases.

Funneling Cases

Many more cases are brought to the prosecutor's office than can be adequately handled given the resources of most jurisdictions. The prosecutor must decide to eliminate a large percentage of the cases. These decisions must be made within the bounds of the norms of the courtroom workgroup. Defense attorneys, especially public defenders, the judge, and even the bailiffs who bring the defendants into the courtroom are affected by these decisions and have an influence in how they are made. The types of questions that prosecutors must address in deciding which cases to funnel out of the system include:

1. Is the case serious? At a certain level, all cases that reach this stage are serious. However, some cases are more serious than others. The prosecutor must determine which ones to spend time and resources on. Serious personal injury cases such as murders and sexual assaults will be prosecuted more vigorously than larcenies in which only a small amount of money is at stake [43].

2. Is the case solid? Some cases have better evidence than others. In cases in which the police have done a good job and have touched all the bases necessary to prepare a solid case, the prosecutor is more likely to decide to carry the case forward. In cases in which the evidence is weak, the prosecutor may decide the court's resources will be better used on cases with a better chance of successful prosecution [44].

3. Is the case highly visible? Much of the work of the courts escapes the attention of the media and the public. However, when a celebrity or athlete is involved, people get interested, and these cases are more likely to be prosecuted because of the increased attention. Even when the case is minor, such as the Winona Ryder shoplifting case, it can be singled out for much more attention than is actually warranted. Cases involving missing children or serial murder are also targets of the media, and this puts more pressure on the prosecutor to pursue the case even if it is not particularly solid.

4. Is the case high priority? Occasionally, prosecutor's offices will direct increased attention at a type of offense. The prosecutor's office may be under political pressure to clean up the streets because **street crime** is damaging the tourist industry. The prosecutor's office, along with the police, will then focus on offenses such as mugging, vandalism, and street prostitution [45].

5. Does the case involve a powerless person? This controversial point addresses the idea that the criminal justice system is biased against people of color and the impoverished. Those who do not have the financial means to hire high-powered private attorneys are supposedly more likely to receive the attention of prosecutors than those who do [46]. We will address this issue in greater detail in other parts of the book.

Discovery

Once the prosecutor decides to pursue a case, the information upon which the decision was made must be shared with the defense. The defense attorney must have the opportunity to examine the evidence and prepare an adequate defense for the accused. The type of evidence that is required as part of the discovery portion of the case includes police reports, lists of witnesses, description of physical evidence, and transcripts of any confession the defendant may have given to the police. Additionally, the prosecutor is required to hand over any exculpatory evidence. If there were other suspects in the offense whom the police decided not to detain or if there were fingerprints that did not match the defendant's, then the prosecutor must make the defense attorney aware of this information. The prosecutor is not allowed to suppress evidence because it does not support the case [47].

The discovery portion of the proceedings is important because it allows the defense to determine the strength of the prosecution's case. If the case is strong, it could also help convince the defendant to enter into plea negotiations [48]. When seeing the array of evidence stacked against them, the defendant and defense attorney can calculate their chances of winning. Discovery is an important foundational principle of the U.S. justice system because it is linked to the protections of the Sixth Amendment, which states that the defendant is entitled "to have compulsory process for obtaining witnesses in his favor." Without discovery, the defendant would not know what evidence is stacked against him or her and would not be able to develop an adequate defense [49].

Voir Dire

Voir dire is a process in which the court questions potential jurors from the jury pool before selecting the 12 that will sit in judgment of a criminal trial. The term is French in origin and means "to see, to say." During *voir dire*, the prosecutor and defense attorney attempt to select jurors they believe will be sympathetic to their side of the case. Ideally, all jurors would be completely neutral, and any individual chosen from the jury pool would be as suitable as any other. However, by excluding or deselecting potentially hostile jurors, the prosecutor and defense attorney can increase the likelihood of winning the case [50].

This is done differently in federal courts and in state courts, but there is a general pattern. Basically, the judge, the prosecutor, and the defense attorney seek to screen potential jurors to ensure the resulting jury can give a fair decision. However, each of these individuals will have a different perspective as to what characteristics a juror should possess.

For the prosecutor, several criteria must be addressed. In selecting the jurors, the prosecutor wants to ascertain whether the candidate has any links or predisposition to favor the defendant. Obviously, such issues as whether the juror is related to the defendant is employed by the defendant or is a neighbor would make a potential juror undesirable. The prosecution will also delve into other concerns to get a sense of the potential juror's attitude [51]. These questions can cover issues such as the juror's occupation, spouse's occupation, membership in organizations, prior military service, exposure to the media, or someone who is a big fan of television crime programs and has unrealistic expectations about the criminal justice system's ability to gather evidence. For instance, a prosecutor dealing with a case of driving under the influence would want to know about a potential juror's involvement in Mothers Against Drunk Driving (MADD). Conversely, a potential juror who had been convicted of driving under the influence would signal the prosecutor that the juror may not be someone who would be sympathetic to the prosecution's case [52].

BURDEN OF PROOF

The burden of proof is the task of convincing a decision-maker that a given version of the facts is true. In a criminal trial, the burden of proving the defendant guilty is on the prosecution. The presumption of innocence granted to defendants is based on the "due process" clauses of the Fifth and Fourteenth Amendments. Because the defendant's liberty, or even life, is at stake, the government, in the form of the prosecutor, must prove the defendant guilty beyond a reasonable doubt, which is the highest standard of proof. Although the prosecutor must prove every element of the offense beyond a reasonable doubt, exactly what constitutes a "reasonable doubt" is not clear (more on this later).

However, the burden of proof is actually more complicated than this. Two concepts comprise the burden of proof: the **burden of producing evidence** (sometimes called the burden of production) and the burden of persuasion. Both burdens initially rest with the prosecutor in a criminal trial, but the burden of producing evidence may move back and forth depending on what is going on in the case. Let's look at these concepts a bit more closely.

The Burden of Producing Evidence

This is the responsibility of providing evidence that a fact exists. When the responsible party does not produce evidence, the fact does not go to the jury, and the case may receive a **directed verdict**. In a criminal trial, the prosecution is initially responsible for the burden of producing evidence. The defense only assumes this burden if mounting an **affirmative defense** or during some trial-related disputes. For example, the prosecution must produce evidence that a defendant should be detained prior to trial. Once detained, it is up to the defendant to produce evidence justifying reconsideration of his or her detention. The prosecutor's evidence must produce the evidence in a sufficient amount to make it possible to conclude that the fact in question exists (quantity), and it must be thorough enough to support the fact beyond a reasonable doubt (quality).

The Burden of Persuasion

This is the responsibility of persuading the judge or jury that the fact at issue is true. Throughout the trial, the burden of persuasion remains with the party that wishes to change the *status quo*: the prosecutor. The only time a defendant carries the burden of persuasion is when using an affirmative defense, such as the insanity defense. The prosecutor, however, must prove that the defendant committed every element of the offense charged. The prosecutor's standard of proof in the burden of persuasion is "beyond a reasonable doubt."

There are eight standards of proof in the law. These are in order from least restrictive to most restrictive: (1) no proof, (2) mere suspicion, (3) articulable reasonable suspicion, (4) **probable cause**, (5) **preponderance of the evidence**,

(6) **clear and convincing evidence**, (7) **beyond a reasonable doubt**, and finally, (8) beyond all doubt.

- The first and last, "no proof" and "beyond all doubt," are self-explanatory, and "beyond all doubt" is not required in any U.S. court.
- "Mere suspicion," "articulable reasonable suspicion," and "probable cause" are mainly for law enforcement. "Mere suspicion" is a hunch but will not stand up in the court. "Articulable reasonable suspicion" was established in *Terry v. Ohio* (1968), as reasonable to conduct a "stop and frisk." "Probable cause" is required to make an arrest, conduct a search, or seize evidence. Also, prosecutors must provide evidence to this standard during preliminary hearings (more on that later).
- Two remaining standards concern the prosecutor a bit more. "Preponderance of the evidence" is the standard of proof for plaintiffs in civil cases and the prosecutor's standard in establishing exceptions to the **exclusionary rule**. "Clear and convincing evidence" is a plaintiff's standard in some civil cases, as well as the state's standard for the **civil commitment** of a dangerous, mentally ill person.
- The standard that most concerns the prosecutor is "beyond a reasonable doubt." If the prosecutor fails to prove any element of an offense occurred beyond a reasonable doubt, then the defendant must be acquitted. Unfortunately, there is no commonly accepted definition of exactly what the reasonable doubt standard is. It is more than probable guilt, but less than mathematical certainty. Simply, the jury must be satisfied that the prosecutor has proven that all the charges are almost certainly true. So, if this standard is so confusing, why does it exist at all? Where did it come from? Legal scholar James Q. Whitman offers an explanation. The origins of the reasonable doubt standard are quite old and reach back through the centuries to when religion held more sway in society and English common law. The standard was not intended to protect defendants. It was supposed to protect the souls of those judging the defendant. In Christian tradition, judging a person was dangerous because convicting an innocent person was a mortal sin. Being a juror meant risking eternal damnation, especially if the punishment involved torture or execution (and they usually did). According to theology at the time, it was safest for a Christian not to do anything if doubt was present. So, if a jury doubted a defendant's guilt, inaction was safest for the jurors, *not* the defendant. As a response to hesitant juries, the reasonable doubt standard appeared during the late eighteenth century. This standard assured jurors that if they felt more than reasonable doubt that a person committed an

offense, they could convict, and their souls would be safe. Thus, one reason the standard causes so much consternation today is that it is being leveraged into a task it was never meant to do: protect the defendant [53].

Preliminary Hearing

A preliminary hearing is a proceeding at which the judge decides whether the prosecutor has produced enough evidence for the defendant to stand trial [54]. The judge uses the "probable cause" standard in making this determination. Both the prosecutor and defense may offer arguments at this hearing, and the prosecutor may call witnesses to testify. The defense may cross-examine these witnesses and question any of the evidence presented in an attempt to convince the judge that the evidence is too weak to proceed to trial and that the defendant should go free.

Not every state uses a preliminary hearing in every situation. In some states, a preliminary hearing is only held when the charge is a felony. Other states use a grand jury (see next section) to decide whether the case is sound enough to proceed to trial. Finally, the prosecutor and defense may resolve the issue with plea bargain prior to the hearing. Also, the prosecutor may charge the defendant with new counts of an offense.

Preliminary hearings carry no **double jeopardy** protections. Even if the charges are dismissed, the prosecutor may re-file them later. Each state has its own version of how the preliminary hearing should proceed. For instance, in the Maryland district court, within 30 days, the prosecutor must file a charging document in the circuit court, enter an "unwilling to proceed" or "a stay of proceedings" in the district court, or amend the charges so the defendant can be tried [55]. If the court finds probable cause to believe the defendant committed the offense, the defendant will go to trial. If not, which is relatively rare, the defendant is released.

Grand Jury

A grand jury is a group of people who, like trial (or petit) juries, work on cases. Depending on the state, grand jury duties include deciding whether a case has enough evidence to go to trial and investigating specified state, local, or jurisdictional issues [56]. Recall that we just discussed how the judge at the preliminary hearing decides if a case has enough evidence for a trial. What is the difference between a grand jury and a preliminary hearing?

The answer is that it depends on the state. Some states use grand juries; others use preliminary hearings. In fact, all states except Connecticut, Pennsylvania, and the District of Columbia use grand juries to begin criminal trials, although they may not use them in all cases. The District of Columbia and 23 states require grand jury indictments for very serious offenses. Grand jury indictments are optional in 25 states, and all the states and the District of Columbia use grand juries for investigations [57]. For example, many states use grand juries to review the operation and condition of jails and prisons and investigate the conduct of public officials, as well as other matters of public health and safety. The only state that does not use a grand jury composed of ordinary citizens is Connecticut, which uses an investigating grand jury of one to three judges [58].

Like trial jurors, grand jurors are selected and sworn in by the court, and are usually chosen from the same pool as trial jurors. State grand juries, which can have from 2 to 23 members, typically sit longer than trial juries. A grand jury may sit for a month, 6 months, or a year, depending on the state, but they do not convene every day. A state grand jury may convene as little as once a month or not unless requested by the prosecutor. In some states, prosecutors do not have to use grand juries. In that case, the prosecutor may bring the charges using an information. If the prosecutor decides to use the grand jury, he or she will draft an indictment. If the grand jury finds the indictment sufficient to prove probable cause, then they will vote to return the indictment or **true bill**, and the case proceeds. If the grand jury finds no probable cause, they will return a **no bill**, and there is no case at that time. A unanimous vote is not required for a true bill, only a majority vote will suffice.

Prosecutors have a special relationship with grand juries. In fact, for a grand jury, they are the most important member of the courtroom workgroup. Grand juries meet in private, and their proceedings are secret. No one is allowed to contact with a grand jury but the prosecutor and the witnesses the prosecutor allows. (Although a judge may have contact with a grand jury, this is not common since the normal rules of evidence do not apply here.) The prosecutor controls what evidence the grand jury sees and can compel witnesses to appear [59]. Witnesses' lawyers are not even allowed in the jury room, but must stand outside it if they want to be available for their clients. This secrecy and privacy is to protect witnesses, so that they may speak without fear of retaliation, and to protect the targets of investigation in case the grand jury does not issue an indictment. The target of an investigation may not even know that he or she is being investigated. However, this also means grand juries make their decisions without hearing both sides of the case. The grand jury is often criticized as being a "rubber stamp" for the prosecutor, and, actually, grand juries vote for a true bill most of the time [60].

Trial

If all attempts at plea bargaining fail, and the judge or grand jury find probable cause, the case goes to trial. There are two types of trial: bench trial and jury trial. A bench trial takes place before a judge, but without a jury. A jury trial requires a jury. Bench trials are more common in civil proceedings. In criminal proceedings, the defendant must waive his or her right to a jury trial.

Once the jury is selected, the trial begins. At the trial, the charges are read, and the prosecutor and the defense attorney present their opening statements. No arguments are made or evidence presented at this point. The prosecution begins by laying out the state's case; this is followed by the defense attorney's statement. This stage is important because it provides the jury with a scenario of what to expect.

Next, the prosecutor presents the state's case-in-chief (we will go into this in detail in the next section), in which he or she presents witnesses and evidence, and the defense cross-examines. Once the prosecution rests, the defense presents its case, which is typically a series of witnesses and possibly even the defendant. The defense then rests, and the prosecution conducts a rebuttal in which witnesses are called or evidence given to refute the defense.

Opening Statements and Closing Arguments

The prosecution's opening statements to the jury are simply to lay out the case. No arguments, evidence, or objections will be made, and neither the prosecutor nor the defendant is actually required to make a statement. The statement may be a brief rundown of the case and how the prosecution plans to prove the defendant guilty, or it may be more creative and involve weaving a storyline around the case that captures the jury's imagination. Often, the prosecutor will describe the evidence to the jury [61].

After all evidence has been presented and witnesses called, each side makes its closing arguments. Here the prosecution makes the first and the last arguments because the state bears the burden of proof. As in the opening statement, no evidence is presented, and the prosecution and defense can only discuss what was presented during the trial. The prosecution will open by summarizing the evidence, followed by the defense which typically claims that despite the prosecution's case, reasonable doubt remains. The prosecution then rebuts the defense's closing argument. See Figure 8.2 for the procedure of a criminal trial.

THE PROSECUTION'S CASE-IN-CHIEF

A **case-in-chief** is the main body of a case, not including rebuttals or opening statements. Both the prosecution and the defense have a case-in-chief. The

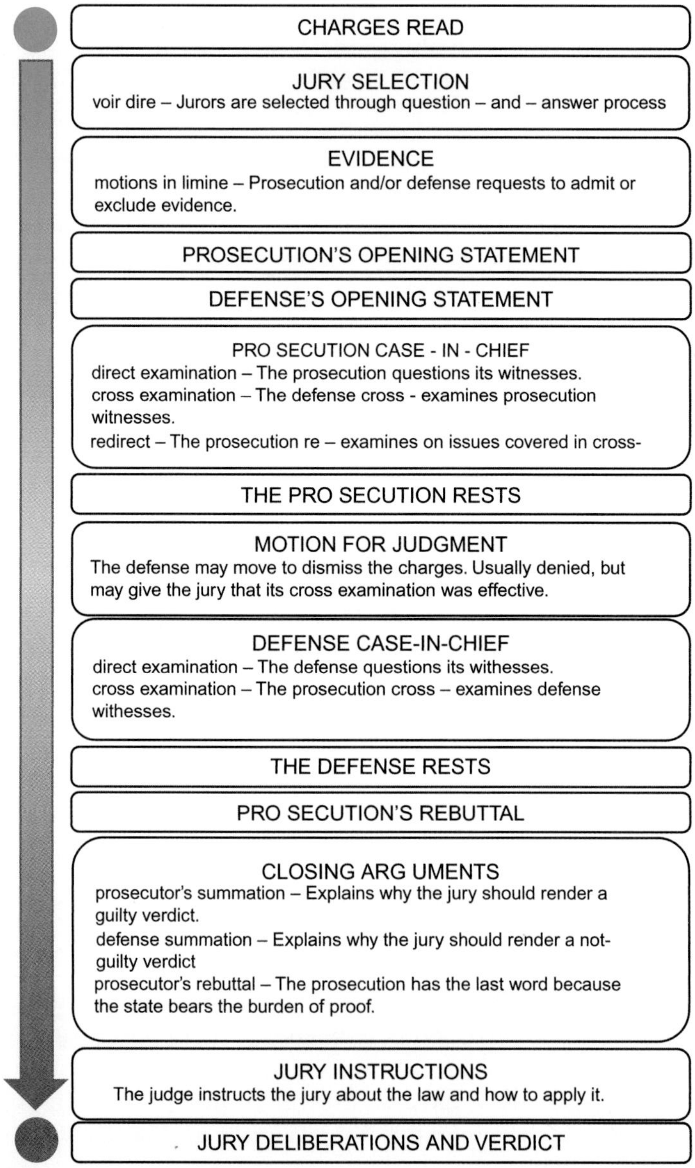

FIGURE 8.2
The Criminal Trial Process.

prosecution's case-in-chief is composed of the direct examination of the prosecution's witnesses, the defense's cross-examination of those witnesses, the prosecution's redirect examination, and, finally, the defense's re-cross-examination of the witnesses.

Evidence is composed of items or testimony presented for the purpose of proving or refuting an issue. The prosecutor uses evidence in court to try to prove the defendant is guilty of the charge or charges. The two main issues concerning evidence are the types of evidence and the rules of evidence.

Types of Evidence

The two groups of evidence are real/testimonial and direct/indirect. For example, evidence can be real and direct, but not both real and testimonial. Here is a breakdown of the four types:

- Real evidence. **Real evidence** is anything concrete linking the defendant to the charge: fingerprints, DNA, documents, photographs, clothing, hair, fibers, and so on.
- Testimonial evidence. **Testimonial evidence** heard from lay witnesses (people who testify based upon their personal knowledge and experiences of the offense), expert witnesses (people who testify based on their specific knowledge in a certain field), police officers, and the victim (if possible). Lay witnesses may only testify about what they experienced via their senses of sight, touch, taste, smell, and hearing. Unlike expert witnesses, they cannot express opinions or draw conclusions. Expert witnesses, on the other hand, can discuss anything within their field.
- Direct evidence. **Direct evidence** is evidence that, on its own, proves an issue at hand. Eyewitness and victim testimony and confessions are good examples of direct evidence.
- Indirect evidence. **Indirect evidence** (often called circumstantial evidence) is a weaker link between the defendant and the charge, serving as an intermediate step for the prosecutor in proving the case. For example, the defendant's fingerprints on a handgun help prove that the defendant touched the gun, but it does not prove that the defendant shot the victim.

Rules of Evidence

The **rules of evidence** define what constitutes evidence and how it is introduced in the court. In the United States, the Federal Rules of Evidence govern the introduction of evidence in federal, civil, and criminal proceedings. These rules were written to promote predictability and uniformity in the admission of evidence in the federal courts, but they do not anticipate every evidentiary problem that may occur. This means the rules are sometimes challenging to interpret and apply to real-life cases [62]. Forty-three states have based their evidence rules on the Federal Rules of Evidence typically borrowing most of the language and adapting specific rules to fit the state's needs [63].

The two most important qualities of evidence are relevance and competence. According to Rule 401 of the Federal Rules of Evidence, relevant evidence is that which makes "the existence of any fact that is of consequence to the determination of the action more probable or less probable than it would be without the evidence." For example, a security camera's recording of a liquor store robbery is relevant evidence. Evidence that the suspect had not paid his rent that month would not be relevant.

The other quality, competence, is the idea that a given piece of real evidence really is what it is stated to be or that the person giving testimonial evidence is competent to give it [64]. In the case of the liquor store robbery, if some bullets are presented as having come from the wall of the store where they lodged after being discharged during the robbery, then it must be established that they are actually that. A crime scene technician may testify to removing the bullets from the wall and what he or she did with them after removing them. Because the technician is also giving testimonial evidence, his or her credentials must be established so the jury knows he or she is competent to give the testimony.

Examinations

During the direct examination, the prosecutor will ask questions to help introduce the witnesses and allow them to testify about what they know about the case. The witnesses have already given this information in their depositions, but the jurors must hear it, too. Also, the prosecution and the witnesses have rehearsed the testimony to some degree so the witnesses will know what questions to expect and how to answer them, and the prosecutors know generally what the witnesses will say. **Leading questions**—or a question that suggests to the witness the preferred answer—are not allowed in direct examination. This is because the law assumes a connection between the witness and the questioner (in this case, the prosecutor). Therefore, if leading questions were permitted, the prosecutor would be able to speak for the witness through leading questions and control what was placed into evidence [65]. The exceptions to this rule are instances when asking leading questions prevents confusion and speeds up the trial process. The leading questions must lead as little as possible and only enough to spur the action. The general exceptions are as follows:

1. When facts are not in dispute. Some nondisputed evidence in the direct examination may be necessary to establish background for the disputed evidence.
2. When attention must be directed to subject matter. This is to speed up the process. Having to ask questions around a subject just so the witness's attention can be directed to it is time consuming. This is often

used when witnesses are testifying about conversations they had. Instead of a witness going over everything he or she said to his or her friend, which may include a lot of irrelevant subjects, the prosecutor may simply ask if anything was said about a recent assault.

3. When the witness cannot remember something. This allows the prosecutor to move the testimony forward.

4. Witnesses who make a mistake. Sometimes witnesses give the wrong testimony inadvertently. This is common in the recollection of dates or times. The prosecutor is allowed to ask a leading question to correct the inadvertent testimony.

5. Weak witnesses. Some witnesses have trouble focusing and their minds may wander. Such witnesses may include children, the very elderly, or people with mental disabilities. Leading questions to help such witnesses focus their attention are permissible, but the court must give permission.

6. Hostile witnesses. Some witnesses are clearly identified with one side and will be considered adversarial (or adverse) if called by the other. Family members and good friends fall into this category. The other category contains witnesses who change their testimony at the last minute and testify in a manner other than what is expected.

After the defense's cross-examination, the prosecution will use the redirect examination to try to repair any damage done by the cross-examination. During these subsequent examinations, neither side can continue asking the same questions or going over what was covered in prior examinations. The purpose of the cross- and re-examinations is so that each side can bring out or address new issues. For example, during the redirect examination, the prosecutor can only address new issues that came out during cross-examination [66].

SUMMARY

1. Explain why the prosecutor acts primarily in the state's interest.
   - In the eyes of the law, an offense committed against an individual is an offense committed against all of us. In a criminal trial, the society is the aggrieved party, not the victim. The prosecutor also represents the victim, but the state's interests are the driving force behind the prosecutor's actions.

2. List and explain the factors that guide prosecutor discretion when representing the state.
   - The factors that guide prosecutor discretion when representing the state are as follows: (1) the protection of society: one of citizens'

foremost demands is that the most dangerous offenders be incarcerated; (2) the deterrence of criminal offenders: the prosecutor's decisions have an influence on lawbreaking in the jurisdiction; (3) the management of court resources: the prosecutor's office must make decisions on a variety of resources and financial issues that determine the efficiency of the court system; and (4) the representation of victims: prosecutors make sincere efforts to ensure victims are satisfied with the outcome of the case.

3. Discuss the three main governmental levels at which prosecutors operate.
   - The three main governmental levels at which prosecutors operate are as follows: (1) the federal level: the Department of Justice is responsible for federal prosecutions and is headed by the attorney general; (2) the state level: state prosecutors' duties are focused on representing the state in cases in which the state sues corporations or individuals; and (3) the county or city level: this prosecutor represents the state in criminal cases.

4. Define and discuss community prosecution.
   - The prosecutor's office enlists the community in preventing and addressing many types of crime. Community prosecution is aimed at increasing quality of life by dealing with problems before they result in crime. The prosecutor's office can act as a central coordinating arena for community projects that address the problems of delinquents and criminal offenders.

5. Describe Christie's criticism of the role of the victim in the prosecution.
   - The victim has little role in a criminal prosecution. Christie argues that by taking victimhood away from the victim, the state prevents the reconciliation between victim and offender. A simple apology or private restitution is not possible, and the case takes on a much more formal quality that can further estrange the victim and the offender.

6. List and describe the forms of plea bargaining.
   - The vertical plea allows defendants to plead guilty or no contest to a lesser charge than the one for which they have been charged. The horizontal plea allows the prosecutor to dismiss many or all charges in return for a guilty plea on one of them. In a reduced-sentence plea, the prosecutor and the defense attorney reach an agreement in which the defendant agrees to serve less than the maximum sentence in exchange for a guilty plea.

An avoidance-of-stigma plea allows a defendant to avoid a damaging label or status.

7. Explain why prosecutors are interested in good relationships with the courtroom workgroup and defense attorneys.
   - Prosecutors spend most of their time working within the courtroom workgroup to move cases through the court. This requires that the prosecutor cooperate with the courtroom workgroup. Therefore, the prosecutor is interested in professional relations with defense attorneys rather than adversarial ones.

8. Define *voir dire.*
   - *Voir dire* is a process in which the court questions potential jurors from the jury pool before selecting those who will sit for a criminal trial. Also, the prosecutor and defense attorney will attempt to select jurors they believe will be sympathetic to their side of the case.

9. Tell what burden of proof is and the two concepts that comprise it.
   - The burden of proof is the task of convincing a decision-maker that a given version of the facts is true. The two concepts comprising the burden of proof are the burden of producing evidence and the burden of persuasion. Both burdens initially rest with the prosecutor, but the burden of producing evidence may also involve the defense later in the case.

10. Analyze the composition of the prosecution's case-in-chief.
    - A case-in-chief is the main body of a case, not including rebuttals or opening statements. The prosecution's case-in-chief is composed of the direct examination of the prosecution's witnesses, the defense's cross-examination of those witnesses, the prosecution's redirect examination, and the defense's re-cross-examination of the witnesses. After the defense's cross-examination, the prosecution will use the redirect to try to repair any damage. The purpose of the cross- and re-examinations is so each side can bring out or address new issues.

Questions

1. Why does the prosecutor act primarily in the state's interest?
2. What factors guide prosecutor discretion when representing the state?
3. At what three main governmental levels do prosecutors operate?
4. What is community prosecution? What idea is it based on?
5. According to Christie, what is the role of the victim in the prosecution?
6. What are the forms of plea bargaining?

7. Why are prosecutors interested in good relationships with the courtroom workgroup and defense attorneys?
8. What is *voir dire*?
9. What is burden of proof? What two concepts comprise it?
10. What is the prosecution's case-in-chief composed of?

REFERENCES

[1] Gershman BL. Hard strikes and foul blows: *Berger v. United States* 75 years after. Loyola Univ Chicago Law J 2010;42:177−206: Online at <www.luc.edu/law/activities/publications/lljdocs/vol42_no1/pdf/gershman_hard_strikes.pdf>.

[2] Miller RN. Balancing the duty to prosecute and the obligation to do justice. Litigation 2011;37(4):46−53.

[3] Sarat A, Clarke C. Beyond discretion: prosecution, the logic of sovereignty, and the limits of law. Law Social Inquiry 2008;33(2):387−416.

[4] Levine D. Public wrongs and private rights: limiting the victim's role in a system of public prosecution. Northwestern Univ Law Rev 2010;104(1):335−61.

[5] Camilli D. Hess returns to court in "99 killing of officer husband." Burlington County Times, <www.phillyburbs.com/news/local/burlington_county_times_news/hess-returns-to-court-in-killing-of-officer-husband/article_b450a2f1-6522-561f-87dc-8f766ea1bf55.html>. [accessed September 27, 2011]. Hefler J. New Jersey case is latest bid to balance victim impact, defendants' rights. Philadelphia Inquirer August 2, 2011:A02.

[6] Levine D. Public wrongs and private rights: limiting the victim's role in a system of public prosecution. 104 Northwestern Univ Law Rev 2010;335−62: Online at <www.law.northwestern.edu/lawreview/v104/n1/335/LR104n1Levine.pdf>.

[7] Gershman BL. Prosecutorial ethics and victims' rights: the prosecutor's duty of neutrality, Pace Law Faculty Publications; 2005. p. 559−579: Online at <digitalcommons.pace.edu/lawfaculty/122/>.

[8] Levine. Public wrongs and private rights.

[9] Gershman. Prosecutorial ethics and victims' rights.

[10] Levine. Public wrongs and private rights.

[11] Vanderpool T. Sympathy vs. Truth: defense attorneys say that some victims' rights laws go too far. Tucson Weekly, <www.tucsonweekly.com/tucson/sympathy-vs-truth/Content?oid=1945865> 2010, [accessed April 29, 2010].

[12] Lauren Bennett Cattaneo, et al. The victim-informed prosecution project: a quasi-experimental test of a collaborative model for cases of intimate partner violence. Violence Against Women 2009;15(10):1227−47.

[13] U.S. Department of Justice. Attorneys general of the United States, <www.justice.gov/02organizations/about.html> [accessed March, 2012].

[14] Chandler AD. The solicitor general of the United States: tenth justice or zealous advocate? Yale Law J 2011;121(3):725−37.

[15] U.S. Department of Justice. Office of the Solicitor General, <www.justice.gov/osg/about-osg.html> [accessed August, 2011].

[16] U.S. attorneys. United States attorneys' mission statement, December 2012, <www.justice.gov/usao/about/mission.html>.

[17] Lu LD. Prosecutorial discretion and racial disparities in federal sentencing: some views of former U.S. attorneys. Federal Sentencing Reporter 2007;19(3):192−201.

[18] Taylor Jr. AL, Troy AF, Smith KWT. State attorneys general: the robust use of previously ignored state powers. Urban Lawyer 2008;40(3):507−20.

[19] Perry SW. Prosecutors in state courts, 2005. Washington, DC: U.S. Department of Justice Office of Justice Programs; 2006: Online at <bjs.ojp.usdoj.gov/content/pub/pdf/psc05.pdf>.

[20] Perry S. State court prosecutors. In: Conference Papers—Law & Society (2006 Annual Meeting). p. 1.

[21] Barkow RE. Organizational guidelines for the prosecutor's office. Cardozo Law Rev 2010;31(6):2089−118.

[22] Roberts AR. Delivery of services to crime victims: a national survey. Am J Orthopsychiatry 1991;61(1):128.

[23] Center for court innovation. Brooklyn domestic violence court, <www.courtinnovation.org/project/brooklyn-domestic-violence-court> [accessed August, 2012].

[24] Center for court innovation. Harlem community justice center, <www.courtinnovation.org/project/harlem-community-justice-center> [accessed August, 2012].

[25] Center for court innovation. Midtown community court, <www.courtinnovation.org/project/midtown-community-court> [accessed August, 2012].

[26] National district attorneys association. National center for community prosecution, <www.ndaa.org/nccp_home.html> [accessed August, 2012].

[27] Holleran D, Beichner D, Spohn C. Examining charging agreement between police and prosecutors in rape cases. Crime Delinq 2010;56(3):385−413.

[28] Vorenberg J. Decent restraint of prosecutorial power. Harvard Law Rev 1981;94(7):1521.

[29] Savitsky D. Is plea bargaining a rational choice? Plea bargaining as an engine of racial stratification and overcrowding in the United States prison system. Rationality Soc 2012;24(2):131−67.

[30] Bowers J. Punishing the innocent. Univ Pennsylvania Law Rev 2008;156(5):1117−79.

[31] O'Keefe K. Two wrongs make a wrong: a challenge to plea bargaining and collateral consequence statutes through their integration. J Crim Law Criminol 2010;100(1):243−64.

[32] Kramer GM, Wolbransky M, Heilbrun K. Plea bargaining recommendations by criminal defense attorneys: evidence strength, potential sentence, and defendant preference. Behav Sci Law 2007;25(4):573−85.

[33] Urbas G. The golden thread of criminal law: what is "beyond reasonable doubt"? Legaldate 2008;20(3):4−5.

[34] People. *The People vs. Simpson*, October 10, 1994, <www.people.com/people/archive/article/0,,20104089,00.html>.

[35] Gold A. Criminal culpability and self-control: back to M'Naughton. Psychiatry Psychol Law 2011;18(4):525−36.

[36] Porter S, ten Brinke L, Gustaw C. Dangerous decisions: the impact of first impressions of trustworthiness on the evaluation of legal evidence and defendant culpability. Psychol Crime Law 2010;16(6):477−91.

[37] Bourg S, Connor EJ, Landis EE. The impact of expertise and sufficient information on psychologists' ability to detect malingering. Behav Sci Law 1995;13(4):505−15.

[38] Mnookin JL. Scripting expertise: the history of handwriting identification evidence and the judicial construction of reliability. Virginia Law Rev 2001;87(8):1723.

[39] Fulero SM. Admissibility of expert testimony based on the Grisso and Gudjonsson scales in disputed confession cases. J Psychiatry Law 2010;38(1–2):193–214.

[40] JurisPro expert witness directory, <www.jurispro.com> [accessed August, 2012].

[41] Haynes SH, Ruback B, Cusick GR. Courtroom workgroups and sentencing. Crime Delinq 2010;56(1):126–61.

[42] Cowell A, Broner N, DuPont R. The cost-effectiveness of criminal justice diversion programs for people with serious mental illness co-occurring with substance abuse. J Contemp Crim Justice 2004;20(3):292–315.

[43] Kwan P, et al. Perceived crime seriousness: consensus and disparity. J Crim Justice 2002;30(6):623–33.

[44] Holleran D, Beichner D, Spohn C. Examining charging agreement between police and prosecutors in rape cases. Crime Delinq 2010;56(3):385–413.

[45] Campbell M. Punishment and politics in Texas: an examination of how prosecutors shaped penal reform and the prison boom. In: Conference Papers—Law & Society (2010 Annual Meeting). p. 1.

[46] Franklin TW. The intersection of defendants' race, gender, and age in prosecutorial decision making. J Crim Justice 2010;38(2):185–92.

[47] Grubman SR. Bark with no bite: how the inevitable discovery rule is undermining the Supreme Court's decision in *Arizona v. Gant*. J Crim Law Criminol 2011;101(1):119–70.

[48] The justice project. Expanded discovery in criminal cases: a policy review, <www.pewtrusts.org/uploadedFiles/wwwpewtrustsorg/Reports/Death_penalty_reform/Expanded%20discovery%20policy%20brief.pdf>; 2007.

[49] Pafundi B. Public access to criminal discovery records: a look behind the curtain of the criminal justice system. Univ Florida J Law Public Policy 2010;21(2):227–71.

[50] Bennett JMW. Unraveling the Gordian knot of implicit bias in jury selection: the problems of judge-dominated *voir dire*, the failed promise of Batson, and proposed solutions. Harvard Law Policy Rev 2010;4(1):149–71.

[51] Ferrara ML. The psychology of voir dire. Jury Expert 2010;22(6):32–41.

[52] Scholtes J. Voir dire: the first brick in your trial foundation. Young Lawyer 2012;16(6):1–3.

[53] Whitman JQ. What are the origins of "reasonable doubt"? Yale Law School 2008; <www.law.yale.edu/news/6300.htm> [accessed February 25, 2008].

[54] Newman SH. Proving probable cause: allocating the burden of proof in false arrest claims under § 1983. Univ Chicago Law Rev 2006;73(1):347–76.

[55] District court of Maryland, arrested information, <www.courts.state.md.us/district/selfhelp/arrested.html> 2012, [accessed May 7, 2012].

[56] Newman SH. Proving probable cause: allocating the burden of proof in false arrest claims under § 1983. Univ Chicago Law Rev 2006;73(1):347–76.

[57] Superior court of California, County of Glenn, grand jury, 2011, <www.glenncourt.ca.gov/court_info/grand_jury.html>.

[58] Brenner S, Shaw L. Federal grand jury, grand jury functions, <campus.udayton.edu/~grandjur/stategj/funcsgj.htm> [accessed August, 2012].

[59] Brown E, Christine SD, Levin C, Allen AR. Preparing a grand jury witness: sweaty palms, racing heartbeat. Litigation 2011;37(4):28–31.

[60] Offit A. Ethical guidance for a grander jury. Georgetown J Legal Ethics 2011;24(3):761–81.

[61] Lopez DT. Getting the best results from opening statements. Trial Practice 2011;25(3):6–7.

[62] Scallen EA. Interpreting the federal rules of evidence: the use and abuse of the advisory committee notes. Loyola Los Angeles Law Rev 1995;28:1283–302: Online at <open .wmitchell.edu/facsch/124>.

[63] Lininger T. Should Oregon adopt the new federal rules of evidence? Oregon Law Rev 2011;89(4):89.

[64] Camson J. The federal rules of evidence: half a century in the making. Proof 2010;18(3):1–12.

[65] Sharman SJ, Powell MB. A comparison of adult witnesses' suggestibility across various types of leading questions. Appl Cognit Psychol 2012;26(1):48–53.

[66] Nolan KP. Cross-examination. Litigation 2011;37(2):63–6.

Defense attorneys must often take on controversial cases and defend suspects the public finds unsympathetic. Here, James Holmes, accused of killing 12 people in a 2012 shooting rampage in a Colorado movie theater, appears in court with his defense attorney

CHAPTER 9

The Defense and Constraint on State Power

double jeopardy

English common law

first appearance

hearsay evidence

Miranda rights

mistrial

presentence

investigation

CONTENTS

Learning Objectives

After reading this chapter, you should be able to:

1. List and explain the advantages and disadvantages of the position of defense attorney.
2. Discuss the obligations the defense attorney must fulfill to adequately represent a client.
3. Explain how the defense attorney acts as a check on state power.
4. Describe the defense attorney's role in ensuring that procedural rules are followed.
5. Understand the most basic responsibility of the defense attorney.
6. Compare and contrast private defense attorneys and public defenders.
7. List and explain the four primary indigent defense systems.
8. Discuss three points during the court process at which the defense attorney may influence the defendant's outcome.
9. Detail the differences between the two main types of defense arguments.

The work of the criminal defense attorney is quite different from how the media portrays it. The defense attorney is part of the courtroom workgroup, so they are constrained by several factors that take the romance out of the occupation [1]. Nevertheless, it is the one position in the courtroom workgroup that enjoys some of independence from the state. Defense attorneys, unless they are public defenders, are not paid by the government, so not only are they free from state constraints, but also they have an obligation to challenge the government. In some nations, the defense is part of the government and must work within a system that does not grant it total independence; however, in the United States the criminal defense attorney has an adversarial relationship with the prosecutor [2].

In this chapter, we will see how this relationship is subject to a great deal of variation depending on the case, the jurisdiction, and the norms of the particular courtroom workgroup. However, the defense attorney stands out among the courtroom workgroup as the one responsible for protecting the rights of the accused and contesting the power of the state to deprive an individual of liberty and possibly life.

THE PRICE OF INDEPENDENCE

Independence from the state not only allows a degree of freedom for the defense attorney but also entails some distinct disadvantages that make the occupation precarious. Let's look at some of the structural constraints on the defense attorney.

- The role of entrepreneur. The defense attorney is a private business person. Whether part of a large private law firm or a sole proprietor, the defense attorney must meet expenses in order to maintain the enterprise. Rent, utilities, insurance, salaries for staff and associates, and a profit must all be generated from the money clients pay to be defended against criminal charges. When one considers how many defendants are without these types of financial resources—which may be why they are in trouble in the first place—it is easy to see how the basic task of meeting payroll may be a difficult prospect for the law firm. Consequently, many lawyers do not specialize exclusively in criminal defense work. They also write wills, represent parties in divorces, and perform a host of other legal duties. Some large firms will devote the time and energy of a few attorneys to criminal defense work, while the rest labor in more lucrative fields of law [3].
- Bringing in clients and money. The attorney must have clients in order to maintain a private legal practice, and there is competition for clients who are able to pay for their representation. Some defendants do not have a history of paying their bills in a timely manner. Therefore, the defense attorney must cast a wide net for clients but carefully screen the ones that are most likely to afford their defense [4]. Sometimes, the most expensive representation is necessary for those who are least able to afford it. Sometimes, those who can best afford legal representation are those who are most likely guilty, such as the accused drug dealer who has happens to have thousands of dollars in cash [5]. It is because of legal expenses that almost all jurisdictions have a public defender.

- Image. Although the defense attorney has a romantic media image, in reality he or she may be looked down upon in the legal profession and by society [6]. Being a defense attorney often means having a client who is guilty, sometimes of a heinous offense. The defense attorney does not have to like the client or believe the client is innocent of the offense in order to provide legal counsel. The suspending of moral judgment is part of the professionalism of the occupation. This often comes at a price, however, in terms of standing in the community and the personal angst associated with helping someone "get away with murder" [7].

One of the reasons the criminal justice system seems so chaotic is that the defense attorney has a mandate to challenge the government's case and provide expert assistance to those accused of crimes. Although the prosecutor and the police may get it right most of the time, it is defense attorney's obligation to challenge the charges every time to ensure that individuals receive a fair consideration of their case. This tension between the state and the defense attorney is considered a healthy one in the pursuit of justice [8].

Duties of the Defense

The defense attorney must fulfill several obligations to the client in order to adequately represent him or her. These obligations can be summarized as the following:

1. Advise the defendant of his or her legal rights in the criminal prosecution.
2. Defend the client in court.
3. Examine the evidence against the client and contest its credibility.
4. Ensure the police follow due process in the arrest, search and seizure, and in the interrogation.
5. Make proper and timely motions and objections during the trial.
6. Present evidence (direct and/or circumstantial) alibis and witnesses to testify on the client's behalf.
7. Advise the client about the advantages and disadvantages of plea bargain offers.
8. Bargain with the prosecutor for reduced charges or sentences.
9. Prepare the case for appeal if the defendant is found guilty.

Defense attorneys must perform specific duties in the handling of criminal cases. These duties require expertise to perform and not every attorney is temperamentally suited to handle criminal trials. There is a self-selection process that channels some attorneys into criminal work and others into corporate, environmental, or labor law. Here, we will look at some of the background requirements and duties of criminal defense attorneys [9].

Becoming a Defense Attorney

Many students are influenced by the romantic notion of defense attorneys and desire to defend the innocent. Others drift into the profession because they like the prestige and status of being an attorney and believe the occupation can be lucrative. Regardless of the motivation, several steps must be taken in order to practice law [10]. Although the first requirement to become an attorney is to graduate from an accredited law school, this has not always been the case. President Abraham Lincoln, who had almost no formal education, learned law by reading law books.

Admission to law school requires an undergraduate degree, a high score on the Law School Application Test (LSAT), high moral character (despite the jokes about lawyers), and the means to pay for a legal education [11]. Law school typically takes 3 years of full-time study during which one often does internships at legal firms or clerks for a sitting judge [12]. After law school, prospective attorneys must pass their state's bar exam. Also, new attorneys typically join their local legal organization so they can network with other attorneys and judges. Attorneys who are well-connected in their local and state professional organizations can refer cases to one another or bring on other lawyers as co-counsel when their caseload gets too large or they need specific expertise for special cases. (See Careers in the Court for more about the criminal defense profession.)

CAREERS IN THE COURT

The Criminal Defense Attorney

The defense attorney is a key player in the U.S. court system. Although some private attorneys have enough cases to specialize in criminal defense work, many others must also practice other types of law. Typically these include civil cases such as bankruptcy, divorce, drawing up wills, and real estate law. Criminal defense work may be only a small portion of their overall workload. However, this diversification, especially in smaller communities, exposes defense attorneys to a wide range of potential clients for their criminal law endeavors. For example, the banker a defense attorney is working with on a real estate case may be accused of embezzlement. Although many large law firms will have at least one partner who specializes in white-collar crime, most defense lawyers are solo practitioners. They may share office space with other attorneys, but, for the most part, they are in business by themselves.

Many new defense attorneys cut their teeth in the public defender's or prosecutor's office. According to the Bureau of Labor Statistics, about 25 percent of attorneys are self-employed as partners either in law firms or in sole practices [13]. Self-employed attorneys may spend long hours dealing with their client's cases. Like many people in private business, they do not work a regular 8 a.m. to 5 p.m. workday and will often spend their own money and resources on cases with the expectation that if they win, they will be able to recoup their losses plus a profit. Top attorneys may charge anywhere from $350 to $500 an hour for their time in addition to expenses.

As a rule, criminal defense work is not the most lucrative. Other specializations command a lot more money because of the types of cases and the clients' financial circumstances. Attorneys who practice corporate law have a much larger financial upside than those who practice criminal law. Becoming an attorney is not a guarantee of financial success. There are many "starving lawyers" who graduated from law school but did not have the business acumen to develop a successful practice. Many individuals who have law degrees go into other types of work where their education can be of some benefit. A criminal defense attorney must be able to find clients, administer his or her law firm, and be successful at winning cases and negotiating favorable plea bargains in order for the community to recognize his or her legal competence.

Question
Discuss why criminal defense work is not as lucrative as other types of law.

Check on Arbitrary or Excessive State Power

One of the Constitution's founding principles is that there should be a balance of power among the branches of government. Additionally, defendants should be protected from the arbitrary and capricious power of government officials. The Bill of Rights provides the basis for the protection of the individual from the state. The defense attorney plays a critical role in ensuring that defendants are treated in a just and fair manner [14].

As a member of the courtroom workgroup the defense attorney is sometimes considered the "odd man out." The rest of the courtroom workgroup, the prosecutor, law enforcement officials, bailiffs, and judges are committed to moving the docket in an efficient and effective manner and may sometimes overlook the central premise of the criminal court, that of determining guilt [15]. The defense attorney who objects to procedures and raises motions to dismiss cases works against the orderly processing of the courtroom workgroup and is subjected to informal pressures to be reasonable. In the adversarial court setting, it is the defense attorney who looks out for the rights of the accused [16].

The U.S. criminal justice system is designed to safeguard individuals against excessive government power, something that has not always been available in other criminal justice systems. For instance, in his acclaimed book, *The Gulag Archipelago*, Aleksandr Solzhenitsyn describes how the Soviet government arrested people and sent them to labor camps in Siberia with no due process [17]. In fact, citizens were picked upon the street and sent to the camps with no notification about the charges against them and no notice to their family that they had been arrested. The citizens simply disappeared, and the state was not accountable for providing any explanation of their activities nor the individual afforded any explanation or ability to contest their confinement.

Monitoring of Procedural Law

The defense attorney must ensure that clients receive several constitutional and statutory protections. This is the job of the defense attorney who must ensure the prosecution follows the procedural rules in presenting the case against the defendant. These procedural rules are derived from the Bill of Rights and from federal or state legislatures that have crafted laws dictating how the courts will handle criminal cases. These laws vary from state to state or from federal to state courts but outside of specialized courts, such as those found in the military, the procedures are similar. Some of the main concerns of the procedural law include:

- Limits on the discretionary power of the criminal justice system. The police have the discretionary power to investigate, arrest, and interrogate subjects based upon probable cause that a criminal offense has been committed. Police officers who violate defendants' rights during the performance of their duty may be held accountable, and the case may be deemed inadmissible. Additionally, prosecuting attorneys and judges have a wide range of discretion in selecting cases for prosecution and in the exercise of plea bargaining or trials. Again, this discretion is limited by protections derived mainly from the Bill of Rights [18].

- Jurisdiction. The defense attorney can challenge whether the client's case is being processed in the proper jurisdiction. The United States has a dual court system with both federal and state jurisdictions, and the court's jurisdictional authority must be established to ensure that it has a legal right to process the case. Often, these jurisdictions overlap or coincide, so one way to appeal convictions in state courts is to ask the federal court to consider whether there are basic constitutional issues at stake in the case [19].

- Questions of unreasonable search. The Fourth Amendment protects citizens from unreasonable search and seizure by the police and other governmental agencies. In effect, it asserts that a person's home, possessions, and communications are generally beyond the reach of government prying. The government must have a compelling reason to tread on Fourth Amendment rights and must convince a judge or magistrate to issue a search warrant. The defense attorney must challenge the prosecution's claim that there is sufficient information to convince a reasonably prudent person that evidence is likely to be found at the defendants' home. Also, there are contingencies in which the police may search a home if they believe evidence is likely to be destroyed before a warrant can be obtained. The defense attorney will challenge the case to ensure that any searches are reasonable and legal [20].

- Questions of unreasonable seizure. Police officers must have a warrant to arrest persons or seize property they believe are involved in a criminal offense. The warrant must specify who is to be arrested, the place that is to be searched, and the property or documents to be seized. The defense attorney must ensure that the defendant's legal rights are protected from improper use of police discretion in seizing property or arresting individuals without a warrant or probable cause [21].

- The right to a grand jury. In federal prosecutions and in several state courts, a grand jury must be impaneled to consider cases that may result in the death penalty or incarceration. The grand jury's purpose is to limit the government's power to maliciously prosecute citizens by requiring that the prosecutor to show enough evidence to indict the accused despite his/her reputation and good standing [22].
- Protection from double jeopardy. Once a person is acquitted or receives a conviction, that person cannot be tried again for the same offense. For instance, if someone is convicted of a burglary, the prosecution cannot come back later and try the convicted person for criminal trespass. Therefore, the prosecution must press all relevant charges of the case because no future case can be prosecuted once a disposition has been reached. This does not include cases in which the appellate court returns the case to the lower court or in cases which have a hung jury or the judge declares a **mistrial**. There are exceptions to the **double jeopardy** rule that includes cases in which the offense violates both federal and state criminal codes [23].
- Privilege against self-incrimination. The Fifth Amendment specifies that suspects are not required to present evidence that can be used against them in court. They have the right to not answer questions posed to them by the police, court, or other governmental powers, such as Congress. The right against self-incrimination is not absolute, however. Individuals cannot refuse to answer questions when subpoenaed if it would simply embarrass them, but not expose them to criminal sanctions. A person cannot refuse to testify if their testimony would incriminate others. Also, if someone takes the witness stand to defend themselves from the charges against them, they are subject to cross-examination from the prosecutor. Finally, someone who has been granted immunity cannot refuse to answer questions [24].
- The protection against self-incrimination cannot be reclaimed after voluntary disclosure of incriminating evidence by the defense. The defense attorney must be careful about exposing the client to incriminating evidence, and there are several vital concerns that have yet been not settled by the law regarding DNA tests, breathalyzer tests, and a wide range of records such as business and personal papers. The defense attorney is mandated to challenge the use of the prosecution's evidence when involuntary self-incrimination is at stake..
- *Miranda* rights. Defense attorneys carefully consider the procedures used during the arrest and questioning of suspects to determine if their

Miranda **rights** were violated. *Miranda* rights are procedural rules that protect suspects from incriminating themselves when in police custody. Suspects may voluntarily waive their *Miranda* rights but only after they have heard them. For instance, once formal questioning by police officers begins, they must advise the suspect that they have a right to not answer the questions and to have an attorney present. Furthermore, suspects must be advised that if they cannot afford an attorney, the court will appoint one to protect their due process rights. Suspects can invoke their *Miranda* rights any time during interrogation. Defense attorneys may either ask for the case to be thrown out altogether or request exclusion of incriminating evidence obtained by a deliberate disregard of *Miranda* rights [25].

- Right to a speedy trial. The defense attorney will challenge the prosecution if it appears they are dragging their feet and delaying the case. Because defendants are often incarcerated during the pretrial period, it is in their interest to quickly resolve the case. They can go through extreme mental anguish while in jail, and the defense of their case may be compromised by witnesses moving, dying, or forgetting what happened. The Speedy Trial Act of 1974 was passed to prevent such delays and require the federal government to initiate prosecutions within 100 days of arrest. Most states have enacted similar legislation. Although delays are sometimes inevitable, the defense can request that charges be dropped if the prosecution violates the speedy trial rule. If the defense attorney asks for continuances the speedy trial rule is waived.

- The right to be informed of charges and to confront accusers. In order to mount an effective defense, the defense attorney must know exactly what charges are pressing against the accused and under what statute the case is being prosecuted. However, this has not always been the case in the history of criminal law. Individuals could be held without specific charges, which made mounting an effective defense nearly impossible. The right to confront one's accusers is also an important part of the criminal defense. In the past, under the inquisitorial method of justice, people could anonymously accuse others. The English Magna Carta, issued in 1215, expressed the policy that "In the future no bailiff shall upon his own unsupported accusation put any man to trial without producing credible witnesses to the truth of the accusation" [26]. All 50 states have some provision allowing the defense to cross-examine hostile witnesses and to present witnesses on their own behalf. There are, however, some exceptions. Some **hearsay evidence** is admissible for certain types of concerns in which a witness cannot appear in court for cross-examination. Examples of this include dying declarations (when a witness makes an utterance on his or her deathbed), excited utterances (made in the heat of the moment during a traumatic event when there is little opportunity to fabricate a response), or scientific data compiled for reasons other than the trial [27]. Other examples of when hearsay evidence may be used without giving the defense an opportunity to cross-examine include cases of child molestation in which grilling the child about the offense may cause mental anguish [28].

- Bail. The Eighth Amendment states that "Excessive bail shall not be required, nor excessive fines imposed, nor cruel and unusual punishment inflicted." The defense attorney argues for the defendant in an effort to get him or her release from detention pending resolution of the case. The courts use various mechanisms to make this release decision. The most common type of pretrial release is **bail**. Bail decisions are made during the initial appearance and rest on the likelihood of the defendant returning for future court hearings. The judge must ensure that defendants have sufficient motivation to return, so requiring a financial transaction is deemed sufficient in most cases [29]. Defendants are required to put down cash as collateral guaranteeing their return to court. One problem with such a system is that not all defendants have enough cash on hand to make bail, so the bail bond industry was created to address this issue [30]. Typically, the defendant hires a bail bond agency by putting down 10 percent of the bail, and the bail bond agency guarantees the rest. The bail bond agency is insured against defendants not returning to court, but if they make too many faulty judgments, they may lose their insurance. Individuals who have their own financial resources can bail themselves out. Another mechanism for pretrial release is release-on-recognizance. Under this type of release, those who have established that they are not a flight risk can be released on their promise to return. These individuals usually have no criminal record, have good community ties, and a good personal reputation. These early release programs have advantages for both the state and the defendant. Jail crowding encourages judges to release as many individuals as permitted by the circumstances of their cases. The defendants benefit because it allows them to maintain their employment, retain their family ties, and prepare themselves for future court proceedings. It is the defense attorney's obligation to present an argument to the court as to why the client should be granted early release and to challenge the state when procedures are violated [31].
- Reasonable fines. These fines are usually imposed as a form of restitution for petty offenses such as shoplifting or traffic violations. Additionally, they can be imposed for **victimless crimes** such as illegal gambling or prostitution. Although the court has the authority to impose fines, the Eighth Amendment limits this power. It is implied that defendants who are able to pay fines should not have an advantage in how they're dealt with by the court. What constitutes a reasonable fine depends on the

defendant's resources; a steep fine for an impoverished (or even middle-class defendant) may pose no problem for a wealthy defendant. So, an ethically challenged court may impose large fines on the wealthy in order to pad the government's budget. Conversely, the impoverished may find themselves incarcerated because they cannot afford to buy their way out of trouble. The defense attorney is responsible for protecting the client by arguing that the fine can be so excessive that it is not reasonable to expect the client to produce such a sum [32].

Burden of Rebuttal

The most basic responsibility of the defense attorney is to challenge or rebut the prosecution's case against the client. The prosecution must prove beyond a reasonable doubt that the defendant is guilty of the offenses charged. The defense attorney does not "prove innocence," but merely establish that the prosecution has not proven guilt beyond a reasonable doubt. Therefore, the defense attorney attempts to discredit the prosecutor's evidence and poke holes in the case.

At several points during the case, the defense attorney will either directly or indirectly question the prosecutor's case. This is done in private conversations with the prosecutor and in open court. Much of it is accomplished within the setting of the courtroom workgroup where the defense attorney will challenge the quality of the charges and evidence. For instance, if a prosecutor is making a case based on a defendant's confession that was obtained under interrogation by a police officer who has a reputation for excessive force, abusing suspects, and lying on the witness stand, the defense attorney will use this to try to get the prosecutor to drop the case or plea bargain. The defendant may be guilty but it is the defense attorney's responsibility to find whatever angle is possible to rebut the prosecutor's evidence [33].

Although we will detail specific steps in defending a criminal case later in this chapter, here we seek to establish the philosophical responsibility of the defense attorney to act as an adversary to the prosecutor and as an advocate for the client. However, we must be aware of the fact that the defense attorney often has limited resources and almost always has limited understanding of what really happened in the case. Consequently, the defense attorney's ability to rebut the prosecution's evidence is often constrained by practical realities and does not measure up to the ideal illustrated in many textbooks or in the media. The political, social, and economic contingencies that many defense attorneys find in the criminal justice system affects their ability to challenge the prosecutor's case. This reality brings us to the importance of the type of defense attorney a client can afford.

THE RIGHT TO COUNSEL

The Sixth Amendment to the U.S. Constitution states that "In all criminal prosecutions, the accused shall enjoy the right to have the assistance of counsel for his defense." This basic protection means that someone trained in the law must be available to advocate for the accused and oppose the prosecution. (See Landmark Cases for *Gideon v. Wainwright* for the Supreme Court ruling on this.)

LANDMARK CASES

Gideon v. Wainwright (1963)
Indigent defendants have the right to court-appointed attorneys in felony cases.

In 1961, Clarence Gideon, an impoverished drifter, was charged with breaking and entering into a Panama City, Florida, pool hall and stealing money from the vending machines, a felony under Florida law. Gideon went to court without money or an attorney and asked the court to appoint counsel for him. The judge told him counsel was appointed only if the punishment for the offense involved the death penalty. The case went to a jury trial in which Gideon defended himself. He was found guilty and sentenced to 5 years in prison.

Gideon filed a petition for release from unjust imprisonment to the Florida Supreme Court, claiming that his conviction was unconstitutional because was tried without a defense attorney. The court denied his petition, and Gideon appealed to the U.S. Supreme Court, which reviewed the case in 1963. The Supreme Court overturned his conviction, ruling that the Sixth Amendment gives defendants charged with a serious offense the right to counsel in criminal trials. The Court also ruled that states must provide defense attorneys to any indigent criminal defendant charged with a felony.

The right to counsel is a relatively new protection. Under **English common law**, a person charged with a criminal offense was not usually accorded the privilege of representation. In the early American colonial period, although prosecutors were provided by the state, the general rule was that defense counsel was not allowed at all. One of the issues that most irked the colonists was that they were being tried by British courts in British colonies, but were not given the rights and protections of British citizens. The colonies individually sought to allow counsel for defendants and, after the Declaration of Independence, the states included such provisions in their constitutions. The ratification of the U.S. Constitution and its Bill of Rights solidified this protection [34].

In addition to Sixth Amendment protections, the issue of providing a defendant with counsel is also considered in the Fourteenth Amendment, which deals with the issue of due process. Under the Fourteenth Amendment, the courts have decided that the inability to pay for an attorney should not be a limiting factor in the due process provided in the criminal trial [35]. Simply permitting defendants to hire a defense attorney is not the same as providing them the protections of a defense attorney. Many people simply cannot afford to hire a defense attorney, and to try them without this basic protection violates the Fourteenth Amendment's due process clause. How defense attorneys are provided to criminal defendants is a matter of great debate and variation among the states. We now turn to the advantages and disadvantages of privately retained attorneys and public defenders.

Privately Retained Attorney

In a perfect world, defendants would have the best defense money could buy. Defendants would have a team of highly trained defense attorneys who had the resources to travel the country to interview witnesses, hire experts on how to select a jury, and have plenty of money to do independent laboratory testing of the physical evidence presented by the prosecution. Additionally, we would even have famous appellate lawyers examining the trial process to determine if there were improper procedures that could be used as grounds for appeal. For instance, during his trial for murder, O.J. Simpson had as part of his legal "dream team" famed Harvard criminal law professor Alan Dershowitz [36]. Unfortunately, economics prevents most defendants from affording this type of high-powered defense.

Hiring a private defense lawyer has its advantages. The first is that this person works for the defendant. If the attorney is experienced in criminal defense, it is possible that the money can be well worth it in terms either getting an acquittal or at least a good plea bargain. A private attorney is likely able to invest more time and resources in investigating possible defenses for the case and may therefore have a distinct advantage over a public defender who is limited by the money the state provides to their offices. Private attorneys can hire private investigators to interview witnesses and track down physical evidence the police may overlooked [37]. Private defense attorneys may spend a great deal of time preparing for a case and thus represent the client more effectively.

We should note, however, that not all private defense attorneys are equal. On one hand, they are not part of the normal courtroom workgroup and may not have relationships with the prosecutor that allows them to effectively plea bargain. On the other hand, this may be an advantage for the private defense attorney because he or she does not have to worry about working in that courtroom workgroup on a daily basis and in which relationships with the judge and the prosecutor are important not only to favorable outcomes for the case at hand but also other cases, as well.

Another disadvantage of the private defense attorney is that although some are general practitioners of law, they may not have the criminal trial experience to be effective. In fact, many private attorneys do not specialize in criminal defense work [38]. Many sole practitioners may practice criminal law as one of several specialties. Experience in divorces, wills, and real estate closings do not prepare someone to practice in the criminal court. For example, a father who hires the family attorney to defend his son who is in trouble for shoplifting may find out the hard way that the attorney has little experience or expertise in dealing with the criminal law or the courtroom workgroup.

It is difficult to disentangle the impact of being able to afford a private defense attorney from the other beneficial aspects of social class. If a defendant can afford a private defense attorney, it is probable the defendant enjoys many of the benefits of being able to demonstrate to the court that he or she is not a menace to society. A stable income, a nice home, a good education, and the support of a loving family all signal to the court that even if the defendant is not innocent, he or she is probably the type of person who can be placed on probation without endangering the community [39]. Some private attorneys will even hire ex-probation officers to do an alternative **presentence investigation** report in which they list programs that will look the most promising to the judge. For instance, they might place a driving under the influence (DUI) suspect in a private rehabilitation program prior to sentencing to show the judge that their client takes the offense seriously and is already on the path to correcting his or her behavior. By having a convincing treatment plan already in place before sentencing, the private defense attorney can make the client looks like someone for whom incarceration would be inappropriate and a waste of taxpayers' money.

Public Defenders

Part of the *Miranda* rights state that "if you cannot afford a lawyer one will be provided to you." This usually means a public defender. A public defender is employed by the government and is assigned to provide legal defense to those who cannot afford a private attorney. Some people are skeptical about the agenda of the public defender because they work for the state but defend those accused of criminal offenses. Public defenders are sometimes considered "double agents" whose allegiance is suspect because they, like the prosecutor, are paid by the state. For the most part, this suspicion is unwarranted. Public defenders in major urban jurisdictions work many hours and have extremely high caseloads. They are among the most experienced criminal defense lawyers because they are burdened with hundreds of clients (Photo 9.1).

Being represented by a public defender has advantages and disadvantages. The public defender is an integral part of the courtroom workgroup and has

PHOTO 9.1
Public defenders often are not paid large salaries. This Minnesota public defender sets up the bar for a wedding at one of her two side jobs that supplements her public defender salary.

a relationship with the judge and prosecutor that may span many years and hundreds of cases. This relationship allows the prosecutor and the public defender to size up the case and determine "the going rate," or more specifically, what has been the outcome of similar cases with similar circumstances over the years. The public defender has the experience to determine how "winnable" a case is and to advise the client on the best conditions that a plea bargain may obtain. Should the case go to trial it may be advantageous to have a public defender because he or she knows their way around the court and the criminal law [40].

The disadvantages of having a public defender revolve mainly around the resources available for any one case [41]. As a member of the courtroom workgroup, the public defender must work with the judge and the prosecutor to ensure that the all cases receive due regard. The public defender must decide which cases to expend time and resources on. Given that many defendants are guilty of the offense for which they have been charged, the public defender must make value judgments as to where to expend the office's limited resources. Once the public defender is satisfied that the defendant's rights are not being violated, he or she may decide that spending time interviewing police officers or witnesses would be fruitless and would not produce sufficient information upon which to rebut the prosecutor's case. In such cases, the public defender would advise the defendant to accept a plea bargain.

Often, defendants feel shortchanged by the public defender because it does not appear that the case is being taken seriously and is being neglected. Even when the defendant admits guilt, he or she may expect the public defender to leave no stone unturned in trying to find a hole in the prosecutor's case and obtain acquittal. However, the public defender must make value judgments about whether cases can be won, when the defendant is guilty, and how many resources and how much time should be expended.

Types of Indigent Defense Attorneys

All criminal defendants are entitled to a competent defense. The federal government and each state provide legal counsel for those who are indigent and cannot afford their own private defense counsel. However, this service is offered in a variety of ways depending upon the state or jurisdiction. Large metropolitan areas are more likely to have a public defender's office to serve the high volume of criminal cases. In sparsely populated rural areas where it is not cost-effective to have full-time public defenders, there are other ways of covering this requirement. There are four primary indigent defense systems: the public defender's office, contract systems, assigned counsel programs, and *pro bono publico*.

Public Defender's Office

Many jurisdictions elect or appoint public defenders. The state or county gives the public defender a budget and assigns him or her to provide legal defense for indigent defendants. The public defender then hires assistant public defenders who are the workhorses of the agency and defend most of the cases. The main public defender may occasionally represent a high-profile client. Usually, these cases are somewhat sensational, such as having a celebrity victim or defendant, or it may be a death penalty case.

The public defender's office, depending upon size, will have several divisions that specialize in certain types of criminal offenses [42]. For instance, in Palm Beach County, Florida, the public defender's office is divided into the following divisions: appellate, mental health, county court, felony, investigations, intake, juvenile, major crimes, and social services [43]. This allows the assistant public defenders to specialize in specific types of cases. For instance, the juvenile division works with the juvenile court and represents all juveniles in the jurisdiction who are accused of status offenses or delinquency and whose parents are indigent. The intake division is a service that operates at the Palm Beach County Jail to oversee intake of new clients. Additionally, the division handles the **first appearance** of some clients, which is the first court hearing before a judge and is required by law to take place within 24 hours of arrest.

The intake division represents clients at first appearance who are charged with misdemeanors or traffic offenses and misdemeanor and felony arraignments for clients in custody. Given the high volume of indigent defendants in Palm Beach County, it is necessary to have this type of fully staffed public defender office. Working as an assistant public defender can provide an attorney with a wealth of experience in the criminal law. This experience can later be translated into private practice where the attorney may make a lot more money. Consequently, public-defender offices have a high turnover rate as the large caseloads turn young, inexperienced attorneys into experienced attorneys.

Contract Systems

In some jurisdictions, the public defender is neither elected nor appointed. Rather a local law firm will contract with the court to provide indigent defense services. The firm is paid a certain amount based upon negotiations between the local government and the law firm. The basis for payment may be either a fixed fee for all indigent defense services or a fixed fee per case. Local governments preferred the fixed fee for all cases approach because it allows them to control their costs. Several firms may apply for this business, and the local government must consider not only cost but also the quality of services that will be provided based upon the reputation of the lead attorneys. Once a private firm secures this contract, they may have to hire additional attorneys or refer cases to other attorneys while remaining responsible for supervising the cases.

There are advantages for a law firm entering into this type of contractual obligation with local government. First, it guarantees a certain level of funding for each year of the contract. The law firm can cover its overhead in terms of office space and paralegal and secretarial help while doing other types of legal work to supplement the contract. Second, it gives the law firm high visibility. Should they decide not to renew the contract or lose it to another law firm, they have established themselves as defenders of those accused of crime and can expect some repeat business from those whom they have helped.

Assigned Counsel Programs

A third way of providing legal defense services for indigent defendants is the assigned counsel program, of which there are two types. The first is the ad hoc assigned counsel program in which attorneys are assigned to cases as needed, typically only one or two cases a year. For new attorneys, this represents an opportunity to practice criminal law and to establish themselves in the legal community. Experienced attorneys with thriving practices may consider this assignment as a real imposition and something to be avoided if possible. The court pays the attorneys by the hour—usually much less than they would charge as a private attorney— and attorneys must petition the court for legal expenses, such as expert witness fees or investigative services [44].

The ad hoc assigned counsel program has advantages and disadvantages for a defendant. On one hand, the indigent defendant may be assigned one of the jurisdiction's top legal counsels. The indigent defendant may find that the attorney the court assigns is one that he or she could never afford to hire. Many successful attorneys will spend their own time and resources to preserve their reputation for winning cases, and the indigent defendant will benefit from this luck of the draw. On the downside, the defendant's case may be costly to adequately prepare for and require a trial. Thus an attorney who is assigned to the case who does not wish to spend his or her own money will provide only the minimal defense and may be more likely to suggest a plea bargain that the prosecutor finds more attractive than does the defendant [45].

The other type of assigned counsel program is the coordinated assigned counsel system. Like the ad hoc system, this system pays the attorneys on an hourly or per case basis. Attorneys apply to be put on a rotational system. The court requires that the attorneys have some minimal qualifications to be accepted into the program, ensuring that the attorneys have some type of criminal defense experience. Additionally, more experienced attorneys may be assigned to the more complex and serious cases.

Pro Bono Publico

Finally, an indigent criminal defendant may find that his or her attorney is working *pro bono* (for no payment). Some attorneys consider it their ethical obligation to give back to the law profession by providing free services to defend indigent cases. An attorney cannot afford to do too many *pro bono* cases, but they can derive some satisfaction by providing their services to those most in need. There are also some additional advantages to attorneys who provide *pro bono* services. An attorney who desires a political career can point to his or her *pro bono* service. In this case, the defendant may find that the *pro bono* lawyer is one of the top legal players in the jurisdiction and can provide a quality defense. Some top legal attorneys will offer their service *pro bono* for high-profile cases as a way of advertising their services.

Jurisdictions meet their responsibilities to provide legal services to those who cannot afford them in a variety of ways. In times when the economy is suffering and tax revenues are down, jurisdictions are constantly looking for cheaper ways to fulfill this obligation. Providing legal help for accused "criminals" is not high on the wish list for local government officials, and they are constantly looking for ways to control these costs while fulfilling the minimal obligations of ensuring that everyone has a competent legal defense in spite of their inability to pay for one themselves. Consequently, the quality of indigent defense can vary widely between jurisdictions and within jurisdictions [46].

Which is Better? Private Attorney or Public Defender

There is considerable debate about the relative merits of appointed counsel and private counsel [47]. On one hand, it is commonly believed that money talks in the criminal justice system and that defendants who are able to afford their own attorneys have a better chance. On the other hand, the specialized public defender can be assumed to have an advantage over private counsel in effectively defending criminal defendants. There is probably no right answer in this debate. Much depends upon how effective representation is measured.

Attorneys who are paid by their clients tend to spend more time on the cases. This is due in part to the fact that public defenders have heavy caseloads and cannot spend an inordinate amount of time on any single case. A more cynical interpretation might suggest that the private attorney who charges by the hour (sometimes $300, $400, or $500 per hour) has a vested interest in working the case hard to pump up the final fee. Consequently, private attorneys tend to file more motions, attend more hearings, and meet with family members more often than do appointed counsel or public defenders. In effect, private attorneys must put on a show for their clients to demonstrate that they are worth the money they are being paid. This is not to suggest, however, that private attorneys do not provide quality representation, because many do. We do suggest, however, that the number of hours that go into a case may not be the best measure of whether private attorneys are more effective than public defenders or appointed counsel [48].

Research shows that there is a lack of consensus as to whether private attorneys provide better outcomes than public defenders [49]. According to several studies, there is little difference in the rate of case dismissals, convictions, and severity of sentences between defendants who are represented by a private attorney and those who are represented by an appointed counsel or a public defender. It is difficult to evaluate the effectiveness of attorneys because much of what they do is done in the corridors, elevators, and back rooms of the courthouse rather than in the courtroom. Although a private attorney may make a splash by arguing vigorously in open court, the public defender may be just as effective by quietly negotiating with the prosecutor over coffee in the courthouse cafeteria.

Working Within the Courtroom Workgroup

In working within the courtroom workgroup, the defense attorney interacts most extensively with the prosecutor. Because the prosecutor is responsible for moving the docket, he or she deals with several defense attorneys on individual cases. Some defense attorneys, such as the public defender, may have several cases before the court on any particular day, and the prosecutor and public defender may negotiate all these cases simultaneously. This is sometimes seen as "cattle call" justice because it appears that the merits of individual cases are devalued. Because the prosecutor must find suitable dispositions for all the cases, the defense attorney may have some leverage in arguing for a particular clients who are likely to be innocent or subject to a weak case by the prosecutor. Thus, the defense attorney can significantly influence the defendant's fate at several points in the court process [50].

Discovery

The **discovery** process favors the defense attorney. The prosecutor must lay out the evidence to the defense attorney so that an adequate defense can be constructed. This is an opportunity for the defense attorney to see how strong the prosecutor's case is. If the defense attorney senses weakness in the case, this can be pointed out during the discovery phase, and it will be suggested that the prosecutor drops the case because the evidence seems weak. On the other hand, the defense attorney may realize that not only is the defendant guilty but also that the prosecutor has such a solid case that there is little hope of winning the case at trial and that the prosecutor is unlikely to be amenable to a plea negotiation that is favorable to the defendant. Consequently, the discovery phase helps crystallize what is going to happen in the case [51].

The defense attorney has obligations during discovery that are similar to but not as extensive as those of the prosecution. For instance, if the defense plans to present an alibi or invoke an insanity defense, this is something that should be told to the prosecution during discovery. Names and contact information of potential witnesses who will testify on the defendant's behalf should also be exchanged. If the defense plans to call expert witnesses to refute the prosecution's expert witnesses, this information must be given to the prosecution. In such cases, the prosecutor and the defense should provide the curriculum vitae of their expert witnesses so that the other side can evaluate the witnesses' credentials. In short, the objective of discovery is to ensure that neither the prosecution nor the defense attorney is "ambushed" at trial with evidence or arguments that they have not had the opportunity to prepare for [52].

Many cases are resolved after the discovery portion of the court process. By "laying the cards on the table," both the prosecution and the defense can develop a realistic notion of the relative strengths of their cases. The defense attorney is obliged to closely examine the prosecutor's case and develop an argument that challenges the facts of the case, the use of the legal statute in terms of what offense the defendant is being charged with, and the quality of the prosecutor's evidence.

Plea Negotiations

The criminal defense attorney must ensure that the client is fully aware of the ramifications of a plea negotiation. There are several considerations the defense attorney will tell the client about when considering whether to "cop a plea" to the charges.

- Strength of the prosecutor's case. The defense attorney will advise against a plea negotiation if the prosecutor's case appears weak. Because the prosecutor has the burden of proof, the defense attorney can look for deficiencies in the evidence. Can the prosecutor establish motive, opportunity, and means? These are all questions that the defense attorney and the client will consider in determining whether to enter into plea negotiations [53].
- Strength of the defense case. Can the defense attorney and the client present contravening evidence to the prosecutor's case? If the defendant has an alibi, it is important to consider how convincing it will appear to the prosecutor and the jury. For instance if the defendant claims he was home in bed with his wife on the night in question, a reasonable person would expect that the wife would support the defendant even if she perjured herself. On the other hand, if the defendant claims that he was at a fund-raising event with the mayor and that there are pictures of him and the mayor in the newspaper and on the Internet, this alibi would present a much stronger case. The prosecutor may be convinced to either drop the case or greatly reduce the charges for fear of losing at trial [54].
- Severity of charges. The defense attorney and the client must consider the potential penalties if the prosecutor obtains a guilty verdict. When the client is looking at life in prison, or in some states, the death penalty, a plea bargain looks more attractive than when the potential penalties are less extreme [55].
- Actual guilt or innocence. We generally assume that anyone who enters into a plea bargain is guilty as charged. Why would an innocent person plead no contest or guilty to offenses that he or she did not commit? This is a complicated question. For instance, if you were involved in the robbery and your co-defendant shot and killed the store clerk, you would expect that you would be charged with armed robbery and not murder. However, suppose your co-defendant cooperated with the police and fingered you as pulling the trigger? Another possibility is that although you did not actually commit the murder, you are in a state that considers everyone involved in a robbery in which a murder occurs to be responsible for the murder. In such cases, the defense attorney may advise the client that a plea negotiation is for the best [56].
- An attractive deal. The defense attorney may advise the client to accept the plea negotiation if an attractive bargain can be reached. Part of a

good defense is limiting the client's exposure to severe penalties. Sometimes, when the client admits guilt to a defense attorney, the prosecution has a strong case, and the prosecutor presents a compelling plea negotiation, the defense attorney advises the client to take the deal. However, things do not always go as planned. For example, the defense attorney of football player Ray Lewis was criticized for a plea bargain he obtained to protect Lewis from a murder conviction (see Focus on Discretion) [57].

■ Enhanced penalties. In some cases, the defense attorney may advise a client to accept a plea bargain if enhanced penalties are attached to the charges. For instance, in states with a "three strikes and you're out" provision, a third conviction for even a minor offense can result in an extremely long incarceration. Although under normal circumstances, the defense attorney may advise a client to demand the right to a criminal trial or at least insist on a better plea bargain, such enhanced penalties change the equation of the plea negotiation and make some type of accommodation more attractive. Similarly, special status is often attached to sex offenses in which the convicted is declared a "sex offender," with enhanced penalties such as being required to register as such and being denied the choice of where to live or place of employment. In this case, a plea bargain might seem more reasonable [58].

The defense attorney sees plea bargaining as a way to protect the defendant from being found guilty by a jury. Some more practical issues may enter into the plea bargain recommendation. Because the prosecutor must ensure that the docket is dealt with not only effectively but also efficiently, the defense attorney can bargain harder with the prosecutor, although this can sometimes backfire. If other defense attorneys quickly reach accommodations with the prosecutor, then the prosecutor has more time and resources available to vigorously pursue the remaining defendants, and the defense attorney's client may find that the attractive deal is no longer on the table [59].

FOCUS ON DISCRETION

Questionable Plea Bargaining

Plea bargaining is always risky for the defendant. The defense attorney must consider the strength of the prosecution's case when advising the client to accept or reject a plea bargain. Sometimes, this is difficult to do. Even after discovery, the prosecution's case may appear strong, but weaknesses may be revealed once the testimony starts. Still, the defense attorney, who must look out for the client's best interests, could be tempted to enter into a plea bargain even though the prosecution's case seems to be falling apart.

One example of this dilemma occurred in the case of Ray Lewis, a linebacker for the Baltimore Ravens football team. On January 31, 2000, Lewis and several friends were attending a Super Bowl party at the Cobalt Lounge nightclub in the trendy Buckhead neighborhood in Atlanta, Georgia. Upon exiting the nightclub at 4:30 a.m., Lewis and his friends argued with another group of people, and a fight broke out. Two men, Jacinth Baker and Richard Lollar, were stabbed to death, and Lewis and two of his companions, Reginald Oakley and Joseph Sweeting, were charged with murder.

Four months later, the case went to trial, and the prosecution found that many of the witnesses failed to testify in a way consistent with statements they had made to the police at the time of the murders. The prosecution's case quickly crumbled as one witness after another surprised the court with their lack of eyewitness testimony that Lewis and his co-defendants had actually engaged in the murders.

Eventually, Ray Lewis turned state's evidence and testified against his co-defendants. In exchange for this, he was allowed to plea bargain to two misdemeanors for obstructing evidence and received 1 year probation [60]. At the time, this looked like a brilliant move on the part of Lewis's attorneys as they were able to protect him from possibly spending the rest of his life in prison. However, his two defendants were subsequently acquitted on all charges and set free. Later, Lewis reached a financial settlement with the families of the two victims.

It is a legitimate question to ask whether Lewis's defense team made a mistake in accepting a plea bargain near the end of the trial when it appeared that the prosecutor's case was so weak. Presumably, if they had waited for the jury's deliberations, Lewis might have been acquitted along with his co-defendants. It is impossible to know whether this plea bargain was a mistake. The jury may have decided that if Lewis was going to be charged with only two misdemeanor counts of obstruction of justice, that the case was so weak that it was not worth convicting his co-defendants. Ultimately, Ray Lewis escaped the full force of the charges and was able to keep his freedom.

Questions

Do you think that Ray Lewis's celebrity status influenced the case?

Was the defense attorney wise in making this plea bargain?

Voir Dire

The defense attorney is interested in selecting a jury that is partial to the defendant's case. The ideal of the U.S. criminal court system is an independent and objective jury: the defendant should be able to expect a "jury of peers." In reality, however, each jury has its own dynamics, and a competent defense attorney will attempt to ensure that those selected are, at the least, not hostile toward the defendant and, at best, sympathetic. *Voir dire* is the process in which the prosecutor and the defense attorney ask questions of members of the jury pool in an attempt to select a jury that would consider the case as objectively as possible [61]. For instance, if the defense attorneys' client is accused of rape, the attorney would not want anyone who had been a rape victim on the jury. Similarly, if the client is accused of embezzlement, the defense attorney would not want on the jury someone who works in a bank and understands how embezzlement works and has an occupational pride in their work. The defense attorney does not want someone who is an expert in the issues surrounding the case because that person may be harder to convince than someone who is not.

CASE STRATEGY AND PREPARATION

The defense attorney must craft an argument against the prosecutor's case. This argument typically takes one of two forms. The first type of argument asserts that the defendant did not commit the offense. The defense attorney may successfully argue several defenses that can cast doubt on the prosecutor's evidence. The second form of argument admits that the defendant committed the offense, but that extenuating circumstances absolve the client from all or much of the blame. Ideally, the defense attorney would like to mount a defense that argues that the defendant is innocent, but often it is more reasonable to admit the behavior and try to defuse or deflect the blame. Let's look in more detail at the types of reasoning a defense attorney may use to protect the defendant.

- I didn't do it (presumption of innocence). The prosecutor must prove that the defendant committed the offense. The defendant is granted a presumption of innocence which means that not only must the prosecutor convince the jury of the defendant's guilt but also the defendant need not say or do anything in his own defense. A defendant may remain silent, not present any witnesses, and argue that the prosecutor failed to prove his or her case.
- I didn't do it (reasonable doubt). The defense attorney may try to raise a reasonable doubt that the prosecutor failed to prove the charges. Here, the defense attorney may challenge the evidence, the timeframe of the alleged offense, or the veracity of the witnesses. The intent is not to prove that the defendant did not commit the offense but only to introduce reasonable doubt that the defendant did commit the offense.
- I didn't do it (alibi). The defense attorney presents evidence showing that the defendant could not have committed the offense because he or she was not at the location when the offense was committed.
- I did it but . . . (self-defense). The self-defense argument is used in cases of violence such as battery or homicide. The defendant claims that because of the victim's threatening actions, violence was necessary for self-protection or the protection of others. Issues that must be decided in this argument include why the defendant felt violence was necessary, whether the level of violence was reasonable, and whether there were alternatives, such as running away. This can be a tricky and difficult defense because the defendant is admitting that the client actually struck or killed someone, and the self-defense may be difficult to illustrate. For example, if a 220-pound man claims that he shot 110-pound woman first because she intimidated him, a jury might not believe that he acted in self-defense. An easier case to present to a jury would be if the woman shot the man because she felt threatened.
- I did it but . . . (I was insane). The insanity defense is another case where the defense attorney allows the defendant to admit that he or she committed the offense. This defense centers around the argument that the defendant did not fully appreciate the consequences of his or her

actions. In essence, the defendant is claiming that because of mental illness he or she could not tell right from wrong and was incapable of making logical choices. The insanity defense is not used often and it is difficult to argue because the defense attorney must also present evidence that the defendant had diminished capacity. By this we mean that there must be some type of evidence to show that the defendant was not acting rationally immediately before the offense occurred. Appearing to be insane at the time of the trial is not sufficient evidence to argue that the person was insane at the time of the offense. Both the prosecutor and the defense attorney may produce psychologists or psychiatrists to evaluate the defendant. It may come down to which of these mental health professionals the jury finds most credible. Acquittal on an insanity defense does not necessarily mean that the defendant will go free. An insane person who is capable of killing someone is still a threat to society, and the court may, and often will, determine that the defendant needs to be locked up in a secure mental health facility until it can be determined that he is no longer a threat to himself or others.

- I did it, but ... (I was under the influence). When a defendant commits an offense under the influence of drugs or alcohol, they may assert that their mental functioning was so impaired that they should not be held accountable. Voluntary intoxication does not excuse criminal conduct because the defendant knows, or should know, that drugs and alcohol affect mental functioning.

- I did it, but ... (It was entrapment). In entrapment cases, the defendant argues that the government enticed them to break the law. The argument is that if not for the government's actions, the defendant would not have broken the law. This is difficult to prove if one has a criminal record or has made threats. For instance, a government agent may infiltrate a terrorist organization and assist in obtaining weapons and selecting a target. Once an arrest is made, the defendant may claim that it was the government agent's idea to commit the offense and that the agent provided intelligence about the target and the weapon. However, if the defendant had made threats of physical violence against individuals or organizations, the entrapment defense would not hold because the government could argue that the defendant was predisposed to the violence and would have found other means without the aid of the government agent.

- I did it, but ... (It was consensual). The defendant claims that the alleged victim actually consented to the behavior. This defense is often used in cases of rape where it becomes a he said/she said argument about the circumstances of the event.

- I did it, but ... (Statute of limitations). Most offenses have a statute of limitations that specifies that charges must be brought within a specified time period. If the charges were brought after that time, the defense could argue that the court no longer has jurisdiction over the case because it was not considered in a timely fashion.

These are the most common examples of the types of defenses a defense attorney may employ. The factors that go into selecting the type of defense that will be used are many and varied. The defendant's guilt or innocence is a major criteria but not the determining criteria. Perhaps more important is the defense attorney's assessment of the nature and strength of the prosecutor's case. Depending upon the charge and the evidence identified during discovery, the defense attorney will make a reasoned decision as to the type of defense to put forth.

SUMMARY

1. List and explain the advantages and disadvantages of the position of defense attorney.
   - The advantage of being a defense attorney is a degree of freedom from the state. Disadvantages include the defense attorney's role as an entrepreneur, the necessity to bring in clients and money, and the task of maintaining a positive image
2. Discuss the obligations the defense attorney must fulfill to adequately represent a client.
   - The defense attorney must fulfill several obligations to the client. These include advising the defendant of his or her legal rights in the criminal prosecution; defending the client in court; examining the evidence against the client and contesting its credibility; ensuring the police follow due process; make proper and timely motions and objections during the trial; presenting evidence, alibis, and witnesses to testify on the client's behalf; advising the client about the advantages and disadvantages of plea bargain offers; bargaining with the prosecutor for reduced charges or sentences; preparing the case for appeal if the defendant is found guilty.
3. Explain how the defense attorney acts as a check on state power.
   - The defense attorney helps ensure that defendants are treated in a just and fair manner, in part by objecting to procedures and raising motions to dismiss cases. The defense attorney looks out for the rights of the accused in the adversarial court setting.
4. Describe the defense attorney's role in ensuring that procedural rules are followed.
   - The defense attorney must ensure that clients receive constitutional and statutory protections by making sure the prosecution follows

the procedural rules in presenting the case. These procedural rules are derived from the Bill of Rights and from federal or state legislatures.

5. Understand the most basic responsibility of the defense attorney.
   - The most basic responsibility of the defense attorney is to challenge or rebut the prosecution's case. The prosecution must prove beyond a reasonable doubt that the defendant is guilty of the offenses charged. The defense attorney establishes that the prosecution has not proven guilt beyond a reasonable doubt.

6. Compare and contrast private defense attorneys and public defenders.
   - Defense attorneys may be privately retained attorneys or public defenders.

7. List and explain the four primary indigent defense systems.
   - The four primary indigent defense systems are the public defender's office, contract systems, assigned counsel programs, and *pro bono publico*.

8. Discuss three points during the court process at which the defense attorney may influence the defendant's outcome.
   - The defense attorney may influence the defendant's outcome at three points in the court process, including discovery, plea negotiations, and during *voir dire*.

9. Detail the differences between the two main types of defense arguments.
   - The defense attorney's argument against the prosecutor's case typically takes one of two types: The first asserts that the defendant did not commit the offense, and the second admits that the defendant committed the offense, but that extenuating circumstances absolve the client from all or much of the blame.

Questions

1. What disadvantages of the defense attorney's occupation make it precarious?
2. What obligations must the defense attorney fulfill in order to adequately represent a client?
3. What are the first 10 amendments to the Constitution called and what do they do?
4. What is the defense attorney's most basic responsibility?
5. What does the Sixth Amendment to the U.S. Constitution state?
6. What are the advantages and disadvantages of a private defense attorney?
7. What are the advantages and disadvantages of public defenders?
8. What are the four primary indigent defense systems?
9. Which member of the courtroom workgroup does the defense attorney interact with the most?
10. What are the two basic forms of the defense attorney's argument?

REFERENCES

[1] Geis G. Revisiting Blumberg's 'The practice of law as a confidence game'. Crim Justice Ethics 2012;31(1):31−8.

[2] Kozin AV. Standing for the client: on the interactional becoming of the criminal defence attorney. Int J Legal Prof 2007;14(2):173−93.

[3] Shackelford DC, Quade v. A league of their own: treating civil rights law as a business. Human Rights 1994;21(2):8−21.

[4] Copley J. How to get paid a fair price for what you do. Elder Law Rep 2012;23(11):1−5.

[5] Trautner M. Tort reform and access to justice: how legal environments shape lawyers' case selection. Qual Soc 2011;34(4):523−38.

[6] Lawry RP. Images and aspirations: a call for a return to ethics for lawyers. San Diego Law Rev 2011;48(1):199−232.

[7] Asimow M, et al. Perceptions of lawyers—a transnational study of student views on the image of law and lawyers. Int J Legal Prof 2005;12(3):407−36. Bowen DM. Calling your bluff: how prosecutors and defense attorneys adapt plea bargaining strategies to increased formalization. JQ 2009;26(1):2−29.

[8] Gold RM. Promoting democracy in prosecution. Washington Law Rev 2011;86(1):69−124.

[9] Halldorsdottir I. Orientations to law, guidelines, and codes in lawyer−client interaction. Res Lang Soc Interact 2006;39(3):263−301.

[10] Barnhizer DR. The purposes and methods of American legal education. J Legal Prof 2011;36(1):1−76.

[11] Winston C. Are law schools and bar exams necessary? New York Times, October 25, 2011:1.

[12] Rampell C. Judges compete for clerks on lawless terrain. New York Times, September 24, 2011:1.

[13] Bureau of Labor Statistics, U.S. Department of Labor, Occupational Outlook Handbook, 2012−13 Edition, Lawyers. Available at <www.bls.gov/ooh/legal/lawyers.htm> [accessed December, 2012].

[14] Kamisar Y. How much does it really matter whether courts work within the 'clearly marked' provisions of the bill of rights or with the 'generalities' of the Fourteenth Amendment? J Contemp Legal Issues 2009;18(1):513−33.

[15] Haynes SH, Ruback B, Cusick GR. Courtroom workgroups and sentencing. Crime Delinquency 2010;56(1):126−61.

[16] Rudes D. Expanding courtroom workgroups: roles and interactions within federal problem-solving court teams. Conference Papers—Law and Society 2010 Annual Meeting: 1.

[17] Solzhenitsyn AI. The Gulag archipelago. New York, NY: Harper and Row; 1974.

[18] Mengyan Dai J, Frank, Sun I. Procedural justice during police−citizen encounters: the effects of process-based policing on citizen compliance and demeanor. J Crim Justice 2011;39(2):159−68.

[19] van der Wilt H. Equal standards? On the dialectics between national jurisdictions and the international criminal court. Int Crim Law Rev 2008;8(1/2):229−72.

[20] Chun BH. The unclearly established rule against unreasonable searches and seizures. J Crim Law Criminol 2000;90(3):799.

[21] McInnis T. The changing definition of search or seizure. Insights Law Soc 2011;11(2):10−28.

[22] Hall JW. A fairer and more democratic federal grand jury system. Fed Sentencing Rep 2008;20(5):334−6.

[23] Ibid.

[24] Cohen TA. Self-incrimination and separation of powers. Georgetown Law J 2012;100 (3):895−928.

[25] DeClue G. Oral *Miranda* warnings: a checklist and a model presentation. J Psychiatr Law 2007;35(4):421−41.

[26] Ostfeld G. Speedy justice and timeless delays: the validity of open-ended 'Ends-of-Justice' continuances. Univ Chicago Law Rev 1997 (Summer);1037.

[27] Liptak A. Jury can hear dying man's words, justices say. New York Times, March 14, 2011.

[28] Orenstein AA. Children as witnesses: a symposium on child competence and the accused's right to confront child witnesses. Indiana Law J 2007;82(4):909−15.

[29] Maruna S, Dabney D, Topalli V. Putting a price on prisoner release: the history of bail and a possible future of parole. Punishment Soc 2012;14(3):315−37.

[30] Tabarrok A. The bounty hunter's pursuit of justice. Wilson Q 2011;35(1):56−61.

[31] Wooldredge J. Distinguishing race effects on pre-trial release and sentencing decisions. JQ 2012;29(1):41−75.

[32] Waring EJ. Incorporating co-offending in sentencing models: an analysis of fines imposed on antitrust offenders. J Quant Criminol 1998;14(3):283.

[33] Orthwein J., et al. Filicide: gender bias in California defense attorneys' perception of motive and defense strategies. Psychiatr Psychol Law 2010;17(4):523−37.

[34] Fisher JL. Originalism as an anchor for the Sixth Amendment. Harvard J Law Public Policy 2011;34(1):53−62.

[35] Kamisar Y. How much does it really matter whether courts work within the 'clearly marked' provisions of the bill of rights or with the 'generalities' of the Fourteenth Amendment?

[36] Dershowitz A. After O.J.: changes in the courts. U.S. News World Rep 1995;119(25):83.

[37] Douglas F. An ultra-aggressive use of investigators and the courts. New York Times, March 9, 1997:31.

[38] For want of a good lawyer: injustice in murder cases. New York Times, December 25, 2011:14.

[39] Alarid LF, Montemayor CD. Attorney perspectives and decisions on the presentence investigation report: a research note. Crim Justice Policy Rev 2010;21(1):119−33.

[40] Hartley RD, Miller HV, Spohn C. Do you get what you pay for? Type of counsel and its effect on criminal court outcomes. J Crim Justice 2010;38(5):1063−70.

[41] Brummer BH. The banality of excessive defender workload: managing the systemic obstruction of justice. St Thomas Law Rev 2009;22(1):104−95.

[42] Abrams DS, Yoon AH. The luck of the draw: using random case assignment to investigate attorney ability. Univ Chicago Law Rev 2007;74(4):1145−77.

[43] Palm beach county office of the public defender, <www.pbcgov.com/opd/PD-15_Frameset-2.htm/> [accessed December, 2012].

[44] Winter B. See fee changes for assigned counsel. Am Bar Assoc J 1981;67(1):32.

[45] Bright SB. Legal representation for the poor: can society afford this much injustice? Missouri Law Rev 2010;75(3):683−714.

[46] Mcleay F. The legal profession's beautiful myth: surveying the justifications for the lawyer's obligation to perform *pro bono* work. Int J Legal Prof 2008;15(3):249−71.

[47] Cohen LJ, et al. Assigned counsel versus public defender systems in Virginia: a comparison of relative benefits. In: McDonald WF, editor. The defense counsel. Beverly Hills, California: Sage; 1983.

[48] Foster JE, Falcone V. Revisiting the standard attorneys' fee and cost provision. Florida Bar J 2011;85(8):48−51.

[49] ABA. Division for Legal Services Standing Committee on Legal Aid & Indigent Defense. Gideon's broken promise: America's continuing quest for equal justice. Chicago, IL: American Bar Association; 2004.

[50] Ulmer JT. Recent developments and new directions in sentencing research. JQ 2012;29 (1):1−40.

[51] Kohn AC. It's time to try your case. J Missouri Bar 2012;68(2):94−6.

[52] Mosteller RP. Discovery against the defense: tilting the adversarial balance. California Law Rev 1986;74(5):1567.

[53] Fisher T. The boundaries of plea bargaining: negotiating the standard of proof. J Crim Law Criminol 2007;97(4):943−1007.

[54] Kramer GM, Wolbransky M, Heilbrun K. Plea bargaining recommendations by criminal defense attorneys: evidence strength, potential sentence, and defendant preference. Behav Sci Law 2007;25(4):573−85.

[55] Piehl A, Bushway S. Measuring and explaining charge bargaining. J Quant Criminol 2007;23(2):105−25.

[56] Andrew Hessick III F, Saujani RM. Plea bargaining and convicting the innocent: the role of the prosecutor, the defense counsel, and the Judge. BYU J Public Law 2002;16(2):189.

[57] Pierson D. Lewis agrees to plea bargain. Chicago Tribune, <articles.chicagotribune.com/2000-06-06/sports/0006060066_1_duane-fassett-joseph-sweeting-reginald-oakley/> [accessed June 6, 2000].

[58] Kosman MAH. Falling through the crack: how courts have struggled to apply the crack amendment to 'nominal career' and 'plea bargain' defendants. Michigan Law Rev 2011;109 (5):785−812.

[59] Bowen DM. Calling your bluff: how prosecutors and defense attorneys adapt plea bargaining strategies to increased formalization. JQ 2009;26(1):2−29.

[60] CNNSI. Lewis murder charges dropped. <sportsillustrated.cnn.com/football/nfl/news/2000/06/04/lewis_agreement/>, [accessed June, 5, 2000].

[61] Bennett JMW. Unraveling the Gordian knot of implicit bias in jury selection: the problems of judge-dominated *voir dire*, the failed promise of batson, and proposed solutions. Harvard Law Policy Rev 2010;4(1):149−71.

The judge's role is to act as a disinterested evaluator of the prosecutor's case and to run the courtroom. Here, a judge talks with attorneys at the bench during a trial.

CHAPTER 10

The Criminal Trial Process: Judges, Bench Trials, Jury Deliberation, and Sentencing

KEY TERMS

best evidence rule
challenge for cause
circumstantial
evidence
demonstrative
evidence
eyewitness testimony

general deterrence
going rate
hedonistic calculus
jury nullification
lex talionis
peremptory challenge
preventive detention

sequester
social location
specific deterrence
venire
voir dire

Learning Objectives

After reading this chapter, you should be able to:

1. List and explain the three major types of trials.
2. Discuss the role of the judge.
3. List and explain the judge's pretrial duties.
4. Identify the duties and responsibilities of the judge during the trial.
5. Compare and contrast the characteristics of large juries and small juries.
6. Differentiate between *venire* and *voir dire*.
7. Evaluate the forms of jury verdicts.
8. Discuss the overriding philosophy of sentencing.
9. List and discuss the four philosophies of sentencing.
10. Understand why the idea of judicial discretion is contentious.

The most iconic or stereotypic perspective the public has about the role and function of the courts revolves around the criminal trial process. As we have demonstrated elsewhere in this text, U.S. courts, even criminal courts, encompass a wide range of activities aimed at dispensing justice. The criminal trial

341

is only a small part of what goes on in the court system but is important for at least two reasons.

First, we think of the criminal trial as the public face of the courts process. The trial is the subject of novels, television programs, and films where it is depicted as an intensely stressful drama where it's good versus evil, protectors of the victims versus criminals, and truth versus falsehoods. Although these popular views of the U.S. criminal trial are entertaining, they do not present a realistic and accurate picture of the work of the court or the courtroom workgroup [1].

The second reason the criminal trial is such an important part of the court system is that it is the process of last resort in resolving the case. After a case has failed to be resolved through mediation or plea bargaining the criminal trial is the final opportunity to come to some type of closure. Few cases proceed this far through the court process, and it is usually cases that are particularly serious where the defendant is looking at substantial periods of incarceration. Additionally, in cases in which the defendant is innocent, he or she will be much less likely to accept a plea bargain and demand a trial. In deciding whether to go to trial or not defendants and their attorneys will look to the history of the prosecutor success in obtaining guilty verdicts [2].

The government's success in litigating criminal cases directly affects the prosecutor's ability to negotiate a guilty plea and avoid going to trial in other cases. With the government prevailing in 70–80 percent of the cases that go to trial, the odds of conviction are great for the defendant whose case is tried. Doubtless, the high conviction rate in tried cases inspires many defendants to think seriously before insisting on a trial [3].

To some, the decision to go to trial may appear to be a game of calling the prosecutor's bluff. If the defendant and his or her attorney don't want to plea bargain, they will request a jury trial and force the prosecutor to decide whether to spend state resources on that particular case. Several factors go into this decision, and not all of them are legal factors. Despite the prosecutor's desire to pursue the case, he or she may have a packed docket, a limited number of assistant prosecutors to assist, a case that isn't as strong as other cases competing for docket time, or a host of other resource and logistical issues that may encourage the prosecutor to offer a better plea bargain. When all else fails, the prospect of a criminal trial takes on a whole new level of seriousness for both the state and the defendant. Prosecutors are usually successful in convicting those they take to trial primarily because they have weeded out the weaker cases. Defendants, on the other hand, have much to lose by insisting upon a trial because they can expect the prosecutor to recommend the maximum punishment [4].

TYPES OF TRIALS

The court uses three main types of adjudications. For example, a defendant may request a bench trial or a jury trial. Juvenile court proceedings are handled informally in a hearing rather than a trial. The distinction between these types of adjudications in criminal cases is significant.

- Bench trial. As you will recall from Chapter 4, the judge acts as both judge and jury in a bench trial. Bench trials are used most often in cases in which the issues may be of a highly technical nature, and the defendant will want to convince only one person (the judge) who presumably has more education and insight into the matter than a jury of individuals with a variety of educational backgrounds and political and social attitudes. Additionally, there may be cases of a highly sensitive nature, such as incest, in which the defendant wishes to limit the number of people who have input into the case [5].
- Jury trial. Most defendants request this type of trial. The idea here is that being judged by one's peers will result in a better chance of an acquittal. Ordinary citizens who make up the jury pool have a variety of backgrounds, and if one or two who are sympathetic to the defendant make it to the final jury, the defendant's chances of success are better. Because the U.S. criminal court process requires a unanimous decision, the presence of a jury increases the likelihood that one person can be convinced to side with the defendant. This, of course, is not always the case because once the jury starts their deliberations, individuals sympathetic to the defendant may change their minds. A complex, unpredictable dynamic operates in the jury room that may result in an acquittal, a conviction, or a hung jury [6].
- Juvenile court hearing. Although we will cover this type of hearing in greater detail in a later chapter, it is important to note here that the juvenile court holds a process similar to a trial. However, the juvenile hearing has distinct features that differentiate it from the criminal trial. The goal of the juvenile court hearing is not to adjudicate guilt or innocence, but rather to determine if the juvenile is in need of protection or intervention. Although the juvenile hearing is a nonadversarial process, it does not afford the child the same level of legal protections as the criminal trial [7].

Regardless of the type of judicial hearing, the criminal court process is bound by several laws, rules, and regulations that specify how the proceedings are to be conducted. Let's turn now to a discussion of some of the duties that are vested in the judge to ensure that hearings are conducted in an appropriate legal manner.

THE ROLE OF THE JUDGE

The judge's role is to act as a disinterested evaluator of the prosecutor's case. By "disinterested" we do not mean uninterested, but that the judge does not take sides. Instead, the judge acts as a neutral evaluator to ensure that the prosecution has presented a compelling case and that the defense attorney has had the opportunity for rebuttal. It is the judge's responsibility to ensure that a fair trial is conducted and that the defendant's legal rights are honored. To do this, the judge has a number of duties that require decisions to be made in light of the conflicting demands of the prosecutor's desire to fight crime and the defense attorney's responsibilities to protect the defendant from unreasonable state power [8].

Pretrial Duties

Several issues and concerns must be decided before a criminal trial can take place. These pretrial issues affect what the prosecutor will be allowed to present, so tension develops as the prosecutor and defense attorney try to position their cases in the most favorable light. Often, rulings on the pretrial issues are so important that one side or the other may be more inclined to plea bargain if the pretrial motions go against their best interests. Some of the important pretrial duties of the judge include:

- Issuing warrants. Long before the trial and even before the arrest, a judge may issue a warrant that allows law enforcement officers to gather evidence. The Fourth Amendment to the U.S. Constitution bars unreasonable searches and requires government agents to present evidence that the public interest is best served by a warrant to search someone's house or property. The judge is looking for probable cause that a criminal offense has been committed [9]. The issuing of this warrant is a function of the government's checks and balances system. The executive branch (law enforcement) must convince the judicial branch (judge) that evidence exists of a criminal offense, contraband, or items that are illegally possessed. Typically, the warrant is requested in the presence of the judge by a law enforcement officer who may be required to present the affidavit under oath. Alternatively, the warrant can be issued by telephone or other means of communication, but is subject to the same level of scrutiny. The warrant specifies a description of the person or property to be seized and is not used as a "fishing expedition" in which law enforcement officers are free to search areas not specified in the warrant. The warrant typically is time sensitive (usually 10 days) and, unless otherwise noted, is to be served during daylight hours (although this can vary by state). It is normal for law enforcement officers to alert the owner of the property that it has been searched if an owner is absent. This typically takes the form of a receipt that tells property owner the residence was inspected and what seizures of property were made. A major exception to this is the provisions under the U.S. Patriot Act which allows federal agents investigating terrorism suspects to conduct their searches without the owner's permission or knowledge [10].

- Ruling on motions. The judge must also rule on a number of motions brought by the defense attorney or the prosecutor. Typically, these motions are aimed at disallowing illegally obtained evidence from being presented to the jury and thus excluded from their considerations of the case [11]. Additionally, the prosecutor and the defense attorneys each want to see the other's evidence and so ask for discovery in which each side is obliged to show their cards. Another issue the judge will rule on during pretrial motions includes seizure of evidence. For instance, the defense attorney may wish to suppress the defendant's confession and not allow it to be presented to the jury. The defense attorney may argue that the confession was given without the defendant being made fully aware of his or her rights (*Miranda* rights) [12]. The prosecution must establish that the confession was voluntary and did not violate the defendant's privacy rights [13]. In addition to suppressing evidence and confessions, there may be motions to suppress the eyewitness testimony regarding a police lineup. Often, lineups (where an accused is presented along with several other individuals for viewing by a witness) are conducted days or weeks after the offense. A host of regulations dictate how lineups are to be conducted; for instance, if the witness said the perpetrator was a tall person it would be disingenuous of the police to produce the person they suspected in a lineup with four extremely short people [14].

- Conducting hearings. In addition to the trial, the judge conducts several different types of hearings. These hearings include the pretrial hearings we previously discussed, as well as other types of pretrial and posttrial hearings. This activity highlights an important feature of the judge's role: the judge is the supreme arbiter of the criminal justice court process. Although the prosecutor is the one that initiates cases, it is the judge who decides which cases are ultimately accepted into the criminal court system and when those cases will be considered. Although the jury may have its own agenda, all activity is conducted under the auspices of the judge. The judge has discretion in deciding which issues require a hearing and how those hearings are conducted. To efficiently move the court docket, this discretion is shared with other members of the courtroom workgroup. This means that the prosecutor and the defense attorney, as well as other members of the courtroom workgroup, such as bailiffs, court reporters, and court administrators have input into how and when hearings are conducted. Ultimately, however, it is the judge who has the authority to set the tone of the hearings [15].

■ Appointing counsel. Another important function of the judge is the appointment of counsel for indigent defendants. Although many defendants have the financial means to retain private attorneys, many do not, and it is up to the state to ensure that they are adequately represented by competent counsel to ensure that their due-process rights are respected. The manner in which the judge appoints government-supported attorneys to defendants who cannot afford private counsel varies by state and jurisdiction [16]. Although this issue is covered more extensively in Chapter 9, it is worth briefly reviewing here in order to appreciate the judge's role in determining whether a defendant is granted the state's support in contesting the prosecutor's charges. As previously noted, in jurisdictions with public defender system, the judge will determine if the defendant lacks the necessary financial resources to hire a private attorney and will appoint a public defender. Typically, the public defender works exclusively in the courtroom of a particular judge and therefore is an important and influential member of the courtroom workgroup. Sometimes, however, in smaller jurisdictions, a public defender may work in many judges' courtrooms and have varying degrees of influence depending on his or her relationship with the judge and the prosecution. In jurisdictions lacking a well-funded public defender's office, the judge will appoint one of the private attorneys who routinely practices in the court to represent an indigent defendant. Commonly, this is done on a rotating basis so that private attorneys are not unduly exploited for their legal expertise and have time to spend on their paying clients. Although the court will provide a fee to these attorneys, it is typically not adequate compensation in a case in which the attorney spends a good deal of time and resources. Finally, in jurisdictions that have little or no provisions for the representation of indigent defendants, the judge may require a private attorney to represent someone *pro bono* (essentially for free). One consideration the judge evaluates in appointing private counsel to represent indigent defendants is the attorney's reputation and competency. In order to protect against a successful appeal due to ineffective representation, the judge carefully considers the qualifications of a private attorney for each type of case. For instance, in some states, in order for a private attorney to be appointed as a defense attorney in a case that may result in capital punishment, that counsel must meet certain qualifications above and beyond the requirements to be a member of the state bar. Specifically, these requirements may include that the attorney has served as co-counsel in a previous death-penalty case.

When someone's life is on the line, it is important that the defense attorney has some experience with death-penalty cases.

■ Setting bail. The judge must make determinations on setting bail for those accused of criminal offenses. This is usually done in a hearing in which the prosecutor and the defense attorney present arguments for the bail decision. The judge is under a tremendous amount of pressure to set bail for every defendant who looks eligible. This is for two reasons. The first reason is the expense of keeping a defendant in jail prior to plea bargaining or trial. The types of defendants who are denied bail usually exhibit a danger to society or are at risk of attempted escape. The second reason the judge is encouraged to set bail is because of the criminal justice system's philosophy that the defendant is "innocent until proven guilty." Therefore, the prevailing wisdom is that those accused of breaking the law should be granted bail unless there is a compelling reason not to. Those who are out on bail are better able to aid their defense attorney in developing a credible case for defense, are able to stay employed, support their families, and pay taxes. In many jurisdictions, those who look like they are reliable and will return for future court hearings are granted release on recognizance, which is essentially their pledge that they will return to court. The judge will look for community ties such as employment, owning a house, and having family in the area as indications that the defendant will not flee. The setting of bail is an extremely important decision that affects not only individual defendants but also the criminal justice system. The tension between releasing defendants on bail so they can maintain community ties and the risk that they will commit future offenses (sometimes serious ones) is foremost in the judge's concerns [17].

■ Taking pleas. A final pretrial duty of the judge is the consideration of plea bargains made by the prosecutor and the defense attorney. As members of the courtroom workgroup, the prosecutor and the defense attorney (especially the public defender) are motivated to work together to efficiently manage the court docket. The agreements made by the prosecutor and the defense attorney are subject to the judge's approval. The judge's role in this process is to ensure that the plea bargains are fair and predictable. Each courtroom workgroup establishes a **going rate**, in cases that share characteristics are dealt with in a consistent manner. If a plea bargaining agreement is wildly out of step with the court's normal agreements, the judge may question why a particular case merits such a divergent outcome. For instance, if the case concerns the sale of large amounts of illegal drugs and the plea bargain calls for probation when other similar cases have resulted in long periods of incarceration, the judge will question the prosecutor and defense attorney as to why this case is exceptional. For example, the answer may be that the defendant has agreed to assist law enforcement in working their way up the drug distribution chain so that cases can be made against large-scale drug dealers. The judge must make a decision in such cases. Is the possibility of convicting large-scale drug dealers worth putting a mid-level drug dealer on probation? What does this say about justice? What message does it give to the general public? These are questions that cannot be addressed by the prosecutor and the defense attorney, but rather are the purview of the judge in determining how justice in the jurisdiction is meted out. Plea bargaining is extremely controversial activity in the U.S. criminal court system and it is the judge's responsibility to ensure not only that justice is served but also that there is a perception that justice is served [18].

Presiding at Trial

The judge has numerous duties and responsibilities during the trial. The responsibilities are crucial to ensuring that the defendant gets a fair trial in accordance with procedural law so that the verdict will not be overturned on appeal. Although the trial has predictable stages, the judge will have still to rule on a number of issues once it starts. Many of these issues will be standard, but some will be unique to the circumstances and individuals involved in the case [19].

During the trial phase, the judge exercises considerable discretion in granting motions or allowing evidence. It is because of this discretion that attorneys may build their cases in ways that (they hope) the judge will look upon favorably. It is this human element of the criminal courts process that makes the criminal trial a "roll of the dice" for the prosecutor, the defense attorney, and the defendant. The argument can be made that judges' personal and legal philosophies are important to the success of the prosecutor and the defense attorney [20].

As Finder of Fact

All evidence is not the same. Some evidence is more convincing than other evidence, and it is evaluated as to whether it is direct evidence or circumstantial evidence. Although direct evidence may seem more convincing, this is not always the case. Sometimes the judge and jurors are more convinced by circumstantial evidence. Many juries want scientific physical evidence because they think it has more weight than other types of evidence (see Courts in the Media for more on this phenomenon).

COURTS IN THE MEDIA

CSI Effect or Not?

It has been reported that a phenomenon, called the "CSI effect" after the CSI: Crime Scene Investigation television shows, has resulted in juries expecting prosecutors to produce compelling physical evidence. Apparently, prosecutors have despaired that because they could not present the latest and greatest scientific evidence, juries have been acquitting defendants who really should have been convicted.

However, Michigan Judge Donald Shelton doubted this and did his own study of more than 2000 potential jurors and their television habits. Shelton found that crime-related television shows had little to do with juror expectations of evidence. Instead, broader social forces, such as advances in personal technology, had a greater effect on whether jurors expected evidence to be gathered and presented with advanced scientific methods. Shelton's study produced three main findings:

- Jurors generally have high expectations that they will be shown scientific evidence.
- In all rape cases and other types of cases that rely on circumstantial evidence, jurors exhibit a high demand for scientific evidence as a condition of guilt.
- Jurors who watch CSI and those who do not showed no significant difference in their demand for scientific evidence as a condition of guilt [21].

Regardless, many criminal justice professionals believe television affects how jurors approach trials and evidence and that they expect scientific evidence that is not available. The reason it generally is not available, however, is not because the techniques do not exist to produce such evidence; it is because producing such evidence is expensive and time-consuming. In an era of shrinking government budgets, many state labs are overwhelmed with evidence to process, and it often just does not get processed.

For example, many medical examiner and coroner offices have stopped doing autopsies for some types of deaths. Some states do not autopsy suicides, people who die in car accidents, or people over the age of 60 unless the death is obviously violent [22]. In Detroit, 11,000 unprocessed rape kits were found in a police storage facility, many of them from the 1980s. A state criminal justice official said the state lab would process the kits as soon as possible but that the lab already takes in up to 2000 kits a year [23].

Unfortunately, backlogs only lead to more backlogs. According to a 2005 Bureau of Justice report, a typical public crime laboratory ended the year with a backlog of about 400 requests for forensic analysis. A typical laboratory performing DNA testing finished the year with 152 backlogged requests [24].

Questions

If you were on a jury in a murder trial, what standard of evidence would you expect?

Do you watch crime television shows? In your opinion, has it affected your expectations of the trial process and standards of evidence?

You will recall that direct evidence does not require the jury to make any inferences. For example, if the victim was thrown off the top of a building and landed with a thud that stopped the victims watch at 2:12 p.m., this could be considered direct evidence that the offense occurred at this specific time. In order to reason differently, one would have to assume that the victim's watch was broken before the fall. Few people walk around wearing broken watches, so a jury would likely be convinced that this direct evidence is valid.

Circumstantial evidence on the other hand requires one to "connect the dots" between the evidence and the offense. For instance, if the defendant's fingerprints were found on the broken lock of the victim's front door, one could argue that the defendant had been at the location. However, additional evidence would be needed to show that the defendant had broken into the home. For instance, the presence of stolen property from the home in the defendant's apartment could establish that the defendant committed the offense. The fingerprints alone, although important, are considered only circumstantial and not sufficient to warrant a conviction.

The judge must evaluate the evidence based upon the commonly accepted rules of evidence of the criminal trial process. Although there are some rules concerning discovery, the judge must also rule on how evidence is presented. Different judges may make different decisions about what is be admissible in court. In many cases, evidence that supports either conviction or acquittal may not be seen by the jury because the judge has ruled that the way the evidence was collected violated the procedural rules of evidence. For example, in the infamous O.J. Simpson murder trial, a police officer violated the chain of custody of physical evidence by taking a blood sample home overnight rather than entering it into the police forensic laboratory on the day it was collected. This raised doubt as to whether the evidence actually came from the crime scene and link the defendant to the murders [25].

Although evidence may be considered direct evidence, it may also be false or inaccurate. The best example of this is **eyewitness testimony**. We consider eyewitness testimony to be convincing and to have a high degree of credibility. However, it can be misleading when the eyewitness is mistaken or is committing perjury. Eyewitness testimony can be inaccurate simply due to mistakes or the fallible nature of human perception and memory. The eyewitness may have vision problems; may have been excited or hysterical during the commission of the offense; or may feel pressure from the police and prosecutors to testify to events that they did not actually see or really remember. In addition to mistakes, the eyewitness may be prejudiced in the case and present false information to either help or convict the defendant. Consequently, the eyewitness testimony of a defendant's wife may not be considered as reliable as a stranger's eyewitness testimony [26].

Other evidence may be considered **demonstrative evidence**. This type of evidence does not bear directly on the case but instead is used to provide context in evaluating other evidence [27]. For instance, in a hit-and-run accident case, the prosecutor may produce a chart showing the intersection where the accident occurred in order to orient the jury as to which car came from which direction. (See Court Procedures for more on how judges evaluate scientific evidence.)

COURT PROCEDURES

Before an expert witness can be allowed to testify, it first must be determined that the witness is competent to testify. A couple of standards are used to this end, both of which are aimed at excluding pseudoscience from the testimony. The Frye standard relies on the "general acceptance" of the expert and the methodology used. The Daubert standard is based in the scientific method, an investigative process by which phenomena are observed, ideas are tested, and conclusions are drawn. It is interesting, however, that one 2005 study found that a state's use of either Frye or Daubert did not affect how the judges handled scientific evidence [28].

The Frye Standard

Established in *Frye v. United States* (1923), this standard is used to determine the admissibility of an expert's scientific testimony. In applying the Frye standard, the court determines whether the method by which the evidence in question has been obtained is generally accepted by experts in the particular field to which it belonged. Although the Frye standard is still law in some states, over 30 states and the federal courts use the Daubert standard.

The Daubert Standard

The Daubert standard, established in *Daubert v. Merrell Dow Pharmaceuticals, Inc.* (1993), is more strict than the Frye standard. The Daubert standard is used to assess whether an expert's scientific testimony is based on scientifically valid reasoning or methodology and can properly be applied to the issue at hand. The factors that may be considered in determining whether a methodology is valid are:

1. Whether the theory or technique in question can be and has been tested.
2. Whether the methodology has been subjected to peer review and publication.
3. The known or potential error rate of the methodology.
4. The existence and maintenance of standards controlling the operation of the methodology.
5. Whether the methodology has attracted general acceptance within a relevant scientific community.

Question

In your opinion, which method of determining the validity of scientific evidence is more sound?

The judge uses several considerations to determine whether the evidence is adequate for conviction. The judge instructs the jury about what legal requirements the evidence must meet. The most important issue concerning the evidence is concerned with the prosecution's requirement to prove the case beyond a reasonable doubt. This requirement in criminal cases differs from civil cases in which one party needs only to present a "preponderance of evidence." This higher standard of evidence means that the prosecution must carry the burden of proof for all the elements of the offense (means, motive, opportunity), and the defense need only poke holes at any point in the case to raise a reasonable doubt. The judge has a great deal of discretion in deciding what evidence is admissible according to the law, and the appellate court will not reverse the trial judge's decision unless a clear abuse of discretion is demonstrated [29]. The judge's role in deciding what evidence to admit or exclude revolves around the consideration of the following issues:

- Competency of witnesses. The judge must determine whether the witnesses are competent to testify to the facts they allege and that the evidence presented meets the criteria of being relevant and material. In order for a witness to take the stand, he or she must take an oath (or a substitute if they are philosophically opposed for religious reasons), be able to remember facts, and be able to communicate to the court [30].
- Competency of evidence. Evidence is considered competent if it does not rely on mere surmise or conjecture and establishes the fact at issue. There are three reasons why evidence might be considered incompetent: evidence is wrongfully obtained (such as an illegal search or a forced confession), evidence is obtained in violation of a state or federal statute, and evidence violates a court-established rule such as allowing the judge or jury-member to testify [31].
- Best evidence rule. The **best evidence rule** refers to the documents used to support a case. The best evidence rule states that the original document should be used rather than a copy to establish authenticity [32].
- Expert witnesses. An expert witness is someone who has particular skills that the average person does not have. The expert witness may have education or experience sufficient to provide scientific, technical, or specialized opinion about the evidence or a particular fact in question. The judge and the jury may give extra weight to the opinion of the expert witness, and it is common for the defense or prosecution to call their own expert witnesses to testify. Expert witnesses need not be university-educated professionals, but rather need only to be considered experts in the question at hand. Plumbers, carpenters, electricians, and police officers may all be considered expert witnesses in their respective fields. The judge may reject the use of expert witnesses if he or she believes they do not meet the criteria to be impartial or do not have the necessary qualifications to be considered expert. Additionally, the judge may appoint expert witnesses of the court's own selection [33].
- Hearsay. Hearsay evidence is when someone repeats in court what he or she heard outside court. Because the person who originally made the statement is not in court to testify as to its veracity, the evidence may be considered inadmissible. Hearsay evidence is deemed unreliable because the person who originally made the statement is not under oath or available for cross-examination. The judge and jury have no way of determining the credibility or demeanor of the person who originally made the statement. There is no way to know if the statement was accurately repeated by the person testifying in court. Therefore, hearsay

evidence is usually excluded because the words might have been taken out of context or the witness may have a faulty memory of what was actually said, and there is no opportunity to challenge or cross-examine the original witness. There are exceptions to the prohibition of hearsay testimony, however. For instance, the "dying declaration" of someone who was aware that their death was imminent may make statements about who murdered them. Because this person is a victim of a criminal offense and is no longer able to testify, the dying declaration may be used as evidence [34].

- Privilege. The judge may rule that some witnesses do not have to testify because they enjoy a privilege of confidentiality based upon the law. Typically, these types of privileges are concerned with a husband-and-wife not being required to testify against each other, privilege accorded to clergy and members of their congregation, privilege between an attorney and client, and privilege between physicians and psychotherapists and their patients [35].

As Finder of Law

In addition to ruling on the admissibility of evidence, the judge must also determine whether the charges brought against the defendant are appropriate. The substantive law (law that specifies which behaviors constitute specific offenses) is something that law enforcement officers, prosecutors, and the judge must consider carefully to ensure that the charges brought against the defendant are consistent with the circumstances of the offense. For instance, there are distinct differences between capital murder, murder, manslaughter, and aggravated assault. Each offense has characteristics that differentiate them from each other, and they must be considered by the court to ensure that the appropriate charges are leveled. Prosecutors may overcharge a defendant in hopes of forcing a plea bargain to a less serious offense. Defense attorneys will argue that their clients deserve to be charged with more modest offenses than the prosecution alleges. The judge must make decisions upon exactly what offenses are going to be charged to ensure that the elements of the offense fit the charges.

Enforcing Procedural Law

The substantive law specifies what behaviors are subject to criminal penalty, and procedural law dictates how the government goes about prosecuting the case. Procedural laws essentially determine how law enforcement officers and the courts go about arresting and charging the suspect, and prosecuting the case. It is the judge's responsibility to ensure that procedural laws are adhered to so that the case cannot be successfully overturned on appeal because of irregularities in how the court allowed the case to proceed.

Instructing the Jury

Although we will talk about juries in greater detail later in this chapter, it is important to note here that the judge is responsible for ensuring that the jury is fully instructed as to not only their duties, but about certain important elements of the law. The judge is the person the jury turns to when they have questions about the case or the procedural process. The judge instructs the jury on matters such as the burden of proof and legal elements that must be established before the defendant can be convicted. Additionally, the judge will instruct the jury as to what lesser offenses can be considered as well as the procedures to be followed in the jury room. The judge's instructions are important because they can be a matter of appeal by the defense if the judge was not clear and accurate in instructing the jury as to their role and the law [36].

Ruling with Impartiality and Adhering to Precedent

The judge must also ensure that justice is served by being impartial in rulings and considering legal precedent. In a sense, the judge is responsible for ensuring fairness in the trial and that includes being mindful of his or her own biases and predilections. The judge may have a personal opinion as to whether the defendant is guilty or innocent but must strive to keep those opinions out of the judicial rulings. It is important that the judge not only be impartial but appear to be impartial in order for the trial participants and the public to have confidence that the process is fair [37].

The public perception of the role of the judge as demonstrated by "television judges" is flawed and does a disservice to the justice system. Television judges get ratings and develop their reputations by being controversial to the point that they often abuse the defendant [38]. This is a great contrast to how judges act in actual criminal trials where they take great pains to ensure that their demeanor and their proclamations are respectful and fair. Precedent is another consideration that the criminal trial judge must be mindful of. The judge cannot make up procedures or the law as the case progresses, but rather must conduct the hearings in ways that are consistent with how other judges have ruled in the past. It is through precedent that the body of law is at least partially constructed. Although the legislature provides the legal statutes that govern the criminal trial process, precedent reveals how the statutes have been interpreted by other judges and so influences the rulings of the judge [39].

Maintaining Decorum in the Courtroom

The judge is unquestionably the authority figure in the courtroom. Sitting on a bench that overlooks the courtroom and wearing a black robe, the judge directs how the criminal trial process will proceed. The judge controls the bailiffs, court reporter, court clerk, has indirect control over the attorneys. Individuals are allowed to speak in court when they obtain permission from the judge. Those who violate the courtroom equilibrium may be held in contempt, which could result in being removed from the courtroom, incarceration, or a fine. Although most individuals respect the courtroom's serious atmosphere, others either intentionally or unintentionally violate the judge's expectations of behavior. Individuals may interrupt the court proceedings with verbal outbursts when they disagree with how witnesses testify or how the judge rules. All criminal trials are open to the public, and the judge may decide that clearing the courtroom of all but those who are directly involved in the trial may be necessary to ensure that the defendant and the state are accorded the respect and fairness that the law commands [40].

Issuing Verdicts in Bench Trials

In bench trials, the judge is responsible for issuing the verdict and determining the sentence. Although bench trials are not as common as jury trials, they provide an alternative that many defendants wish to take advantage of. A defendant may believe that a single judge is easier to convince than a jury of 12 individuals. In some trials, the evidence can be extremely technical, and the defense attorney may believe that it would be easier to sway one judge who has a high level of education rather than a jury that varies widely in their ability to comprehend the evidence. In fulfilling this dual role of determining guilt and passing sentence, the judge can exercise a great deal more discretion than in a jury trial. In many ways, this expanded power can work to the defense attorney's advantage by allowing him or her to target the presentation of the case to the specific judge [41].

Sentencing

The sentencing hearing is conducted after conviction. Typically, the judge will delay the sentencing for 30 days to give the probation office a chance to conduct a presentence investigation (PSI). The PSI is a valuable resource for the judge in making a sentencing decision. The PSI outlines the circumstances of the case (seriousness of offense and prior record of the defendant), as well as the social circumstances of the defendant (employment history, education, living situation, and treatment plan). Although the probation office typically makes a recommendation concerning the sentence, it is the judge's responsibility to make the ultimate decision on what will happen to the defendant [42]. The judge is constrained in some ways by the statutory range permitted by law, and also has a good deal of discretion in determining whether the defendant is placed on probation or incarcerated. We will deal with sentencing in greater detail later in this chapter, but it is sufficient to say here that sentencing is an important function of the judge and is the most visible reflection of the philosophy and strictness of each individual judge [43].

Presiding over the Jury Trial

The right to a trial by jury has a long history. It can be traced to the Magna Carta of 1215 in which English noblemen were afforded the right to a trial by a jury of their peers. It was encoded in the U.S. Constitution and 1789 in Article III, Section 2, as well as in provisions of the Sixth and Seventh Amendments. Additionally, case law has greatly refined the conditions for a trial by jury over the history of the United States. The right to a jury trial is not extended to all offenses. For the most part, it covers those accused of serious offenses in which the possibility of incarceration for more than 6 months is authorized. However, in some states, a jury trial is available to anyone who is charged with a criminal offense. Jury trials are expensive and typically used only as a last resort when plea bargaining between the prosecutor and the defense attorney has failed [44].

THE ROLE OF THE JURY

Juries typically consist of 12 individuals plus one or two alternates. This varies greatly by state and by the type of charges. Some states require 12 jurors for felonies and fewer jurors for misdemeanors. There are advantages and disadvantages to large juries versus smaller ones. Typically, the smaller jury consists of six individuals, and it is believed that they have more time to deliberate because of their smaller size. Large juries make it more likely that racial and ethnic minorities, as well as women, are included. There is also a greater possibility of a hung jury when there are 12 jurors rather than six [45].

Most states require unanimous decisions with the idea that the verdict has a greater chance of being correct when all the jurors must vote to convict. The exceptions to this rule are Louisiana, Montana, Oregon, Oklahoma, and Texas. The requirement of a unanimous verdict affects how juries deliberate. In states that do not require a unanimous verdict, juries are more likely to vote early in the deliberation process to see if they can come up with the required number of votes to convict. In states that require a unanimous verdict, juries are much more likely to deliberate longer and discuss the evidence more thoroughly before they vote. Some observers wonder if a nonunanimous jury really establishes proof beyond reasonable doubt. If some jurors are unconvinced, then reasonable doubt may exist [46] (Photo 10.1).

Jury Selection

Jury selection is important part of the criminal trial process. Prosecutors and defense attorneys spend a great deal of time attempting to ensure that the

PHOTO 10.1
Juries in many jurisdictions now have computers to assist them in their duties.

jury is at best, favorable to their case and at least, impartial and unbiased. The court must go through three major steps to pick a jury.

The Master Jury List

A "jury of one's peers" means that the jury should be selected from members of that community who represent a cross-section of the racial, ethnic, and sex composition of the jurisdiction's population. Therefore, the first step in selecting a jury is to develop a list of eligible jurors who meet the qualifications of being community members. Typically, the master jury list is drawn from the voter registration rolls. However, to ensure a greater representation of poor people and minorities, this list may be supplemented by list of citizens with driver licenses, utility customers, or even listings in telephone directories. Those who draw the list must contend with duplications and with individuals who do not really live the community such as landlords [47].

Venire

At the beginning of any court session (courts typically run on a cycle of several months), the master jury list is used to construct a jury pool called a *venire*. This jury pool must be available for multiple cases heard during the court session. Jurors are sent a summons advising them that they are members of the jury pool and are instructed to show up at the courthouse on a certain date for jury duty. Jury duty is considered a responsibility of being a citizen, and those who fail to show up at their assigned time may be fined or imprisoned.

Several criteria can disqualify someone from the jury pool. Jurors must be U.S. citizens, of a certain age, and live in the jurisdiction. Additionally, they must be competent to understand the workings of the court which means they need a minimal understanding of English. Other individuals are exempt because of their occupation. Those who work in law enforcement or the medical community are typically statutorily exempted from jury duty. Historically, others, such as full-time students, have been statutorily exempt, but that is rare today. The court administrators want as large jury pool as possible, and only those who can reasonably be expected to have a conflict of interest (such as police officers) are excluded from the jury pool.

Individuals selected to be in the jury pool may request to be excused from jury duty because of hardship. The judge can grant hardship exemptions for various reasons. Medical conditions or critical job-related duties (military personnel, doctors, or teachers) may make it difficult for someone to serve on jury duty. These individuals may be excused, or more commonly, they have their jury duty delayed to a time that is more convenient for them. Convincing a judge that one has a unique hardship that should excuse them from jury duty can be difficult and precarious if the judge believes one is lying about their potential hardships [48].

Voir Dire

To ensure that the jury is as impartial as possible the process of *voir dire* is used to question the potential jurors about a wide range of issues that may influence their objectivity. The prosecutor, defense attorney, and judge will question potential jurors about their backgrounds, their knowledge of the case, potential relationships with defendants or attorneys, and willingness to consider the case impartially [49]. For example, if a potential juror was a victim of child abuse, he or she may be excused from a child-abuse trial because it would be believed that they could not be objective. It is difficult to ensure that potential jurors will be truthful during this process because they may wish to avoid being on a jury, or conversely, they may have a desire to "punish criminals." There may be questions during *voir dire* that they do not wish to answer because of embarrassment or because they believe they would be disqualified.

Excusing jurors. Another part of the *voir dire* process is allowing the defense attorney and the prosecutor to screen potential jurors from the proceedings. The defense attorney and the prosecutor can do this in one of two ways. The first is termed **challenge for cause**. Jurors who have a prior relationship with someone in the case (such as the defendant) may be challenged by the prosecutor because the potential juror can be suspected of not being able to give an unbiased consideration to the case. Challenges for cause are unlimited, but each is subject to the judge's ruling. The other method of excusing jurors is the **peremptory challenge** in which the prosecutor and the defense attorney can have a limited number of jurors excused. Peremptory challenges allow the attorneys and prosecutors to attempt to craft a jury that will be favorable to their side of the case [50]. The criteria they use for determining whether a potential juror is amenable to their arguments is more art than science. Attorneys may consult jury-selection experts but are more likely to base their decisions to excuse a juror based on their history with similar types of individuals, hunches, or outright prejudices. For instance, a defense attorney might believe that limiting the number of women on a child-abuse trial would give their defendant a better chance of a favorable outcome. This is a precarious tactic because recent court cases have prohibited excusing jurors based on their sex or race. If the judge suspects a pattern of excluding females or minorities, the attorney suspected of such behavior may have to explain the basis behind the challenges [51].

Jury Deliberations

As the jury's goal is to reach a consensus, its work can be frustrating. As we mentioned earlier, most states require a unanimous verdict. Getting everyone to agree, however, can be difficult. Sometimes it seems that the goal of determining the truth in a case is obscured by the legal process as jurors have a passive role in selecting the evidence, questioning witnesses, and challenging the attorneys' statements. To ensure that the defendant gets a fair trial, the process has evolved to the point that an abundance of legal requirements hamper any straightforward search for the truth. Procedural law dictates how cases are presented to the jury and the jury's ability to obtain more information [52].

Once the jury is selected, the case begins. The attorneys present their opening arguments; the prosecutor presents the case against the defendant, and the defense attorney cross-examines witnesses to demonstrate that the prosecution's case does not stand up to the requirements for a verdict. The defense then has an opportunity to present its evidence aimed at showing that the defendant did not commit the offense. The prosecutor can cross-examine the defense witnesses, and once the defense attorney rests his or her case, the attorney's present their closing arguments. During this time, the jury sits silently listening to and individually evaluating the evidence for both sides of the case. Jurors may be tempted to ask questions themselves, but the process does not allow this. Jurors can only hope that the attorneys cover all the important issues and ask the pertinent follow-up questions of witnesses.

A case may be over in one afternoon or may take several weeks or months depending on the complexity of the case. The jurors come to court each day and sit in the jury box while the case proceeds. In exceptional cases, the jury may be sequestered, that is, confined together in a location away from their homes, under the supervision of court authorities, throughout all or part of the trial. Because of the amount of publicity these cases entail, the judge may decide that jurors should not be allowed access to the media or their friends. They are checked into a hotel each night, eat their meals together, and are prohibited from watching television, reading newspapers, or accessing the Internet. The idea is to allow the jurors to decide on the case according to the evidence and testimony produced during the trial rather than listening to the opinions of media pundits and other observers. Jurors are instructed not to talk among themselves about the case until they can consider all the facts in the jury room.

Typically, the judge will instruct the jury before deliberations, discussing a number of issues that pertain the law concerning particular elements of the case. For instance, the judge will explain the legal principles behind the concepts of innocent until proven guilty, guilty beyond a reasonable doubt, or the insanity defense. Additionally, the judge will instruct the jury as to how they can find the defendant guilty of lesser included offenses. For instance, in a murder case, the evidence may not support a conviction of first-degree murder, and the jury could find for lesser included offenses such as second-degree murder or manslaughter.

These are highly technical legal issues that the judge must explain to the jury before they begin deliberations. The jury instructions include input from the prosecutor and the defense attorney each of whom may have suggestions as to how to instruct the jury. If the judge rejects the suggestions, the prosecutor or defense attorney may register an objection that can be put on the record and used during an appeal [53].

Jury instructions are important because any error can be grounds for appeal. Therefore, instructions are typically written out so that there is no confusion as to exactly what the judge has outlined as the responsibility of the jurors. During deliberations, the jury may ask specific questions of the judge pertaining to the law and the evidence. The judge is usually circumspect in answering these questions so as to not unnecessarily complicate the case. Most of the time, the requests are for clarification of the law or to have specific testimony or evidence reviewed. At times, jurors may disagree about what was actually said, and the judge can respond to their questions by having the testimony read to the jurors in open court [54].

What happens inside the jury room greatly depends on the nature of the case and the personalities of the individual jurors. Movies and television tend to make jury deliberations appear more dramatic and entertaining than they actually are. However, because each jury has its own "personality," there may be times when sincere and heated arguments ensue. Each juror has his or her own opinion about the case, and these change as the jury deliberates and each juror has an opportunity to specify what they think about the case.

Typically, everyone has an opportunity to have a say. A poll is then taken, and if the jurors are unanimous for either guilt or innocence after this first poll, their work is essentially done. Often, there is disagreement by one or more jurors. The jury must determine whether these disagreements are based upon errors in understanding the testimony or evidence or based upon a specific juror's understanding as to whether the evidence is beyond a reasonable doubt. A holdout juror is typically unable to convince all the other jurors to see things his or her way. More often the holdout is convinced by the others to go along with their determinations [55].

In some cases, the jurors simply fail to agree and cannot reach a unanimous decision. One juror may be holding out, or the split may involve several jurors, but the result is a hung jury. The prosecutor then has the option of trying the case again or letting the defendant go. Sometimes the prosecutor can identify the reason for a hung jury and address the concerns of those who voted for acquittal in the preparation for a new trial. Sometimes, the prosecutor has little or no idea as to why the jury split. Trials are expensive, so the prosecutor needs to have a solid plan for presenting the case in a new, more convincing way. Taking the case to a new trial is not done often, and the prosecutor may be accused of political motives.

Sometimes a funny thing happens in the jury room. Even though the jury understands the judge's instructions, they may disagree. Popular concepts of criminal justice will sometimes influence the jury to disregard the evidence and the law and acquit the defendant. This is especially true in cases in which racial discrimination may be a factor or in cases in which local customs are violated [56]. Even though the prosecution has presented a solid case, the jury may decide that, in their view, justice is not served by a guilty verdict. This results in **jury nullification**, which is the right of juries to refuse to apply the law in cases even though it is clear the defendant is guilty.

For example, in parts of northern California, marijuana is the basis for the local economy. Finding a jury that will convict someone who grows marijuana may be difficult. Even though the evidence may be overwhelming, the jurors may be sympathetic to the local attitude that marijuana is not a harmful drug and that its cultivation is crucial to the community's economic well-being. Therefore, regardless of the strength of the prosecution's case, the jury may simply disagree with the marijuana laws and acquit the defendant [57].

Verdicts

Jury verdicts can take one of three main forms.

1. Guilty. A guilty verdict is the worst thing that can happen to the defendant. It means the jury determined that there was a proof beyond a reasonable doubt that the defendant committed the offense. Essentially the jury believed the prosecutor's case and rejected the defense attorney's attempt to discredit the evidence or present contradictory evidence. In most cases, the defendant would have been better off with a plea bargain.
2. Not guilty. A not-guilty verdict is an acquittal of the case against the defendant. It means the jury did not find proof beyond reasonable doubt and that they do not have confidence in the prosecutor's case. However, it could also mean that they think the defendant is guilty but that, in good conscience, they did not believe that the prosecutor provided the legal justification for arriving at a guilty verdict. This is where a great deal of frustration enters into the public's judgment about the criminal justice system. Nevertheless, there are times when the defendant is actually innocent, and the jury concurs with the case presented by the defense attorney.
3. Guilty but insane. In this verdict, the jury determines that the defendant has committed the offense, but that he or she does not have the mental competency to understand the ramifications of his or her behavior. A guilty but insane verdict does not mean that the defendant will go free or go to prison. Most likely such defendants go to some type of mental health facility where they receive psychiatric treatment. It is assumed that defendants will not be released until they are deemed no longer a danger to themselves or others [58].

Critique of the Jury System

Even though the jury system has a long history in Western thought and is encoded in the U.S. Constitution, some critics believe the jury has lost its usefulness and credibility. These critics contend that the law has gotten much more complicated and that the application of the law to criminal cases ought to be done by trained professionals. The uncertainty that is introduced when 12 untrained citizens make such important decisions frustrates many people.

Although there may be attempts to reform the jury system from time to time, it is unlikely that it will ever be dismantled. Philosophically it protects citizens from abuses of state power. As we have previously discussed, the courtroom workgroup has agendas, motivations, and demands that emanate from the various criminal justice agencies that renders it suspect in terms of protecting citizens' rights. Those who advocate for the jury system contend that having regular people on juries introduces checks and balances against the bureaucratization of justice by state agencies. When the defendant looks in the jury box and sees his or her peers, that defendant can have some hope that the jury deliberations will include some "common sense" [59].

SENTENCING

When the jury arrives at a guilty verdict, the case reverts to the judge who must pass sentence. Sentencing is a controversial part of the criminal justice process. Each of us has our own ideas of how a defendant should be punished or treated, and we often find ourselves in disagreement [60]. Basically, however, the overriding philosophy is "let the punishment fit the crime." This attitude goes back to the ancient dictate of **lex talionis**, or "an eye for an eye and a tooth for tooth." Although many people think this is a justification for applying severe sentences to criminal defendants, it was actually a way of introducing a sense of proportionality into matters of justice. There are four basic philosophies of sentencing that compete for the primacy in the criminal justice system. Depending on one's **social location** and religious background, one or more these philosophies may seem more important than others.

Deterrence

Deterrence is one of the bedrocks of the criminal justice system. There are two types of deterrence: general and specific. **Specific deterrence** occurs when someone breaks the law, is punished for it, and desists from committing future offenses. Specific deterrence applies to the individual and has only a limited effect. More important to the criminal justice system is the concept of **general deterrence**. General deterrence occurs when we see other people punished for their offenses, and we desist from violating the law. Society would be chaotic if each of us had to be punished for breaking the law before we would desist [61].

Deterrence is based upon three principles: celerity of punishment, certainty of punishment, and severity of punishment. Celerity of punishment means that punishment occurs swiftly after the offense has been committed. In the U.S. criminal justice system, celerity can take a long time. In some death-penalty cases, the punishment may occur as long as 20 years after the offense was committed. Those who argue that delays in bringing defendants to trial and sending them to prison results in them not learning the deterrent lesson are relying on the celerity argument [62].

Certainty of punishment speaks to how likely someone will be punished for breaking the law. Obviously, many offenders are never caught, which to their way of thinking makes "crime pay." According to general deterrence theory, potential offenders do a **hedonistic calculus** in which they weigh the risk of getting caught against the potential benefits of successfully breaking the law. When the risks are higher than the potential benefits, they will choose not to break the law. Unfortunately, in many cases, offenders think the risks are worth taking. Those who sell illegal drugs see a great deal of profit to be made with little risk of apprehension. Even when caught, they factor in the potential prison sentence and calculate that incarceration is just part of the price of doing business [63].

The third principle of general deterrence is severity of punishment. The criminal code is based upon the idea that serious offenses merit severe punishment. Although the criminal justice system can do little to affect the swiftness and certainty of punishment, much has been done to influence the severity of punishment. For a number of offenses, state and federal legislatures have enacted laws that require mandatory minimum sentences that are aimed at deterring potential offenders because the severity of the punishment is so high [64].

One problem with the general deterrence philosophy is that it assumes individuals contemplating violating the law can accurately do the hedonistic calculus and make a rational decision to not commit the offense. Unfortunately, many of those contemplating an offense are unrealistic about their abilities and make bad decisions. Many will risk years in prison for robbing a convenience store just to acquire a small amount of money [65].

Retribution

The idea behind retribution is that convicted offenders should get what they deserve. Many people believe that bad behavior has consequences and that those who break the law deserve to be punished, suffer the loss of liberty, and bear other pains of imprisonment. The idea of retribution on the part of the criminal justice system is important because it prevents people from taking vengeance on offenders. Convicted offenders "get what they deserve" from the state, which satisfies the public's demand that the convicted get their "just desserts." Here, the idea of proportionality is also an important concept. The punishment should reflect the harm done to the victim [66].

Incapacitation

Incapacitation is concerned with protecting society from crime. It is a rather limited goal aimed at disabling an offender from committing more offenses.

This is typically done through incarceration in which the offender is taken off the street and put in a secure environment where he or she cannot harm others. Even once an offender is incarcerated, the institution may take further steps to incapacitate them by putting them in solitary confinement so they do not hurt fellow inmates or staff [67].

Historically, incapacitation also includes policies such as transportation into exile, which was practiced by England when it sent its convicts to the North American colonies and Australia. Some Islamic nations practice incapacitation by, for example, cutting off the hand of a thief, thus making it more difficult for him or her to steal. Incapacitation is sometimes used as a justification for **preventive detention**. Here, it is assumed that those who are likely to break the law can be prevented by being detained. This is a controversial idea because history shows us that we are not good at predicting exactly who is likely to commit further offenses. All kinds of compounding and discriminatory factors can enter into those predictions, including stereotypes about gender, race, and social class [68].

Rehabilitation

Rehabilitation is a main goal of the criminal justice system in dealing with offenders. The idea behind rehabilitation is to address offenders' social, educational, employment needs so they can become productive members of society. Some might argue that rehabilitation is a misleading term because many offenders never had the skills necessary to be socially and economically well-adjusted. They might argue that the term "habilitation" would be more accurate. Regardless, the criminal justice system's goal is to provide a wide range of services so that offenders need not resort to criminal behavior in order to meet their basic social and economic needs.

Additionally, some offenders may need only moral and ethical guidance and instruction in order to convince them that deviant behavior violates the social contract. Rehabilitative sentences may require offenders to seek more education, enter drug or counseling treatment programs, or pursue job training so they might become gainfully employed [69].

These four sentencing philosophies—deterrence, retribution, incapacitation, and rehabilitation—influence the sentence an offender receives from the judge. In many respects, it makes a big difference in terms of which judge is hearing the case or approving the plea bargain. Prosecutors and defense attorneys consider the judge's sentencing philosophy when preparing their cases. In most courts, judges have a tremendous amount of discretion in deciding specific sentences. However, judicial discretion has been subject to numerous efforts aimed at making it more predictable.

Judicial Discretion

The idea of judicial discretion is contentious because it is really an argument about the balance of our values. On one hand, it is believed that judges should be allowed broad discretion in deciding cases because of their knowledge of the particulars of each case. In an ideal world, the judge can craft individual sentences based upon knowledge of the case, the victim's attitude, and the degree of remorse shown by the offender. Presumably, the sentences have a greater chance of reflecting social values and the possibilities of successful rehabilitation of the offender [70].

On the other hand, however, the broad discretion afforded to judges can mean that there is wide disparity in sentences given to offenders with similar backgrounds and offenses. This can erode confidence in the criminal justice system when one offender is placed on probation by one judge, while another judge sentences another offender with an almost identical case to a long period of incarceration. This has led to some jurisdictions to develop policies to make sentencing patterns more consistent. These types of sentencing policies include indeterminate sentences, fixed or mandatory sentences, and presumptive sentences.

Indeterminate Sentences

Indeterminate sentences mean that the offender does not have a good idea of exactly how long the incarceration will be. At its extreme, an indeterminate sentence may specify that the offender will serve a minimum 1-year incarceration in and, at maximum, a life sentence. This 1-year to life sentence means that the discretion in determining exactly how long the sentence will be rests not with the judge but with the parole board. The parole board determines when the offender is successfully rehabilitated and is no longer a danger to society. This has led to a great deal of dissatisfaction with the criminal justice system when people believe that offenders lie to the parole board to convince them that they no longer need incarceration. Many believe that parole boards are no better at judging successful rehabilitation than a judge was at predicting it when making the sentence [71].

Additionally, the parole board may have other criteria pressuring it to make early-release decisions. Prison overcrowding is a serious concern in many prison systems, and as society sends more offenders to prison, the parole board is under pressure from the courts to relieve overcrowding and release other inmates. Indeterminate sentences would be a good idea if prisons did a good job of rehabilitating offenders, and parole boards could accurately measure rehabilitation. What actually happens, however, is that this type of unfettered discretion results in offenders serving vastly different sentences for similar offenses [72].

Mandatory Sentences

Mandatory sentencing practices shift the exercise of discretion from the judge and parole board to the legislature and the prosecutor. Lawmakers specify the exact amount of time of incarceration for each type of offense [73]. Once the offender is convicted of this offense, the judge has little discretion in altering it and the parole board little discretion in releasing offenders. At one level, this seems fair because offenders convicted of similar offenses serve the same amount of time behind bars. But a number of things make mandatory sentences problematic:

- Lack of planning for early release. Legislators are not good at predicting how these laws will affect the availability of prison beds. Typically, the types of sentences the legislators specify result in prison overcrowding. When this happens, other methods of early release are necessary. In order to satisfy court-ordered interventions into prison overcrowding, some states have had to release many offenders without the proper preparation that a parole board requires. Parole plans typically include residency and employment plans that are designed to ensure a smooth transition from incarceration to the free world. They also might include some type of transitional living arrangement such as a halfway house. When prisons are forced to release inmates because of overcrowding, little support and planning occurs, which can result in a greater likelihood of recidivism [74].
- Pressure for more prison construction. Increased demand for prison space often requires more prisons. Building more prisons is expensive for taxpayers and it can take money away from other priorities, such as transportation projects, education, and social welfare initiatives.
- Increased prosecutorial discretion. Mandatory sentences provide the prosecutor with a new tool for extracting plea bargains from offenders and defense attorneys. The prosecutor can charge the offender with the most serious offense that the evidence can support which exposes the offender to a severe sentence that cannot be altered by the judge. Consequently, there is pressure on the defense attorney and the offender to plea bargain to a lesser included offense that requires a less severe penalty. This takes discretion away from the judge and places it in the hands of the prosecutor and the legislature. This is especially true in states with "three strikes" sentencing policies in which a third felony conviction can result in a life sentence. If that third conviction is for a relatively minor offense for which a judge might want to sentence the offender to a short period of incarceration, the three-strikes policy prevents that and the common-sense discretion of a judge is blocked [75].

Although mandatory sentences appeal to those who wish to see offenders treated equally in the sentencing process, it does have some unintended consequences that limit the criminal justice system's flexibility. So, to take advantage of both the flexibility of indeterminate sentencing and the uniformity of mandatory sentencing, many states have reached a compromise called presumptive sentencing (Figure 10.1).

SENTENCING RANGE

NON DRUG OFFENSES

	A 3 + Person Felonies	B 2 Person Felonies	C 1 Person & 1 Nonperson Felonies	D 1 Person Felony	E 3 + Nonperson Felonies	F 2 Nonperson Felonies	G 1 Nonperson Felony	H 2 + Misdemeanor	I 1 Misd No Record	PROB	POST REL
1	653/620/592	618/586/554	285/272/258	267/253/240	246/234/221	226/214/203	203/195/184	186/176/166	165/155/147	36	36
2	493/467/442	460/438/416	216/205/194	200/190/181	184/174/165	168/160/152	154/146/138	138/131/123	123/117/109	36	36
3	247/233/221	228/216/206	107/102/96	100/94/89	92/88/82	83/79/74	77/72/68	71/66/61	61/59/55	36	36
4	172/162/154	162/154/144	75/71/68	69/66/62	64/60/57	59/56/52	52/50/47	48/45/42	43/41/38	36	36
5	136/130/122	128/120/114	60/57/53	55/52/50	51/49/46	47/44/41	43/41/38	38/36/34	34/32/31	36	24
6	46/43/40	41/39/37	38/36/34	36/34/32	32/30/28	29/27/25	26/24/22	21/20/19	19/18/17	24	24
7	34/32/30	31/29/27	29/27/25	26/24/22	23/21/19	19/18/17	17/16/15	14/13/12	13/12/11	24	12
8	23/21/19	20/19/18	19/18/17	17/16/15	15/14/13	13/12/11	11/10/9	11/10/9	9/8/7	18	12
9	17/16/15	15/14/13	13/12/11	13/12/11	11/10/9	10/9/8	9/8/7	8/7/6	7/6/5	12	12
10	13/12/11	12/11/10	11/10/9	10/9/8	9/8/7	8/7/6	7/6/5	7/6/5	7/6/5	12	12

Postrelease for felonies committed before 4/20/95 are:

24 months for felonies classified in Severity   Levels 1-6

12 months for felonies classified in Severity   Levels 7-10

Presumptive Imprisonment

Border Box

Presumptive Probation

DRUG OFFENSES

	A 3 + Person Felonies	B 2 Person Felonies	C 1 Person & 1 Nonperson Felonies	D 1 Person Felony	E 3 + Nonperson Felonies	F 2 Nonperson Felonies	G 1 Nonperson Felony	H 2 + Misd.	I 1 Misd. No Record	PROB	POST REL
1	204/194/185	196/186/176	187/178/169	179/170/161	170/162/154	167/158/150	162/154/146	161/150/142	154/146/138	36	36
2	83/78/74	77/73/68	72/68/65	68/64/60	62/59/55	59/56/52	57/54/51	54/51/49	51/49/46	36	36
3	51/49/46	47/44/41	42/40/37	36/34/32	32/30/28	26/24/23	23/22/20	19/18/17	16/15/14	18	24
4	42/40/37	36/34/32	32/30/28	26/24/23	22/20/18	18/17/16	16/15/14	14/13/12	12/11/10	12	12*

Probation Terms are:
*18 months (up to) for felonies classified in Severity Level 3 and, on and after July 1, 2009, felony cases sentenced pursuant to K.S.A. 21-4729 (SB 123)
Postrelease for felonies committed before 4/20/95 are:
24 months for felonies classified in Severity Levels 1-3
12 months for felonies classified in Severity Level 4
12 months for felonies classified in Severity Level 4 except for some K.S.A. 2009 Supp 21-36a06 offenses on and after 11/01/03.

"Good Time" Sentencing Reductions	Felony Fines	
Pre 4/20/95 – 20% reduction	Off Grid or DGSL1	$500,000
Post 4/19/95 – 15% reduction	SL1-SL5 or DGSL2-DGSL3	$300,000
Post 1/1/08 – 20% D3-4 or SL7-10	SL6-SL10 or DGSL4	$100,000

After 11/01/03 certain K.S.A. 2009 Supp 21-36a06 (K.S.A.65-4160 & 65-4162) offenses have no postrelease supervision time.

FIGURE 10.1

This is a typical presumptive sentencing chart. For example, if an offender is convicted of a first-time felony that is a level 1 in severity (see column D), the judge is directed to sentence that offender to 253 months of incarceration. If the offense has aggravating factors, the judge may increase the number of months served to 267. In the case of mitigating factors, the judge may lower the term to 240 months. Source: *Kansas Sentencing Commission, www.accesskansas.org/ksc/2010desk/2010_Nondrug_and_Drug_Grid_quick_reference.pdf.*

Presumptive Sentencing

Presumptive sentencing is an attempt to add some uniformity to sentencing patterns while allowing some discretionary room for a judge to consider the mitigating and aggravating factors of individual offenses. For instance, the presumptive sentence for a first-degree felony may be 20 years, but the judge may subtract 5 years or add 5 years depending on the nature of the offense. The presumptive sentence satisfies the requirement that judges treat similar cases equally and also respects the individual discretion of the judge to ensure that the particular features of the case are considered [76].

SUMMARY

1. List and explain the three major types of trials.
   - The criminal court uses a variety of trials: the bench trial, the jury trial, and the juvenile court hearing.
   - In a bench trial, the judge acts as judge and jury. Bench trials are used when a defendant does not want a jury.
   - Most defendants request jury trials, with the idea that being judged by one's peers will result in a better chance of an acquittal.
   - The juvenile hearing is different from the criminal trial. The goal of the juvenile court hearing is not to adjudicate guilt or innocence, but rather to determine if the juvenile is in need of protection or intervention. The juvenile hearing is nonadversarial process and does not afford the child the same level of legal protections as the criminal trial.

2. Discuss the role of the judge.
   - The judge acts as a disinterested evaluator of the prosecutor's case to ensure that the prosecution has presented a compelling case and that the defense attorney has had the opportunity for rebuttal.

3. List and explain the judge's pretrial duties.
   - Some of the important pretrial duties of the judge include issuing warrants, ruling on motions, conducting hearings, appointing counsel, setting bail, and taking pleas.

4. Identify the duties and responsibilities of the judge during the trial.
   - During the trial, the judge is the finder of fact, the finder of law, enforces procedural law, instructs the jury, rules with impartiality, adheres to precedent, maintains courtroom decorum, hands down sentences, and presides over the jury trial.

5. Compare and contrast the characteristics of large juries and small juries.
   - Juries typically consist of 12 individuals plus alternates. Some states require 12 jurors for felonies and fewer for misdemeanors. Small juries comprise six jurors: it is believed they have more time to

deliberate because of their size. Large juries make it more likely that racial and ethnic minorities, and women, are included. There is also a greater possibility of a hung jury.

6. Differentiate between *venire* and *voir dire*.
   - At the beginning of any court session, the master jury list is used to construct a jury pool called a *venire*. To ensure that the jury is as impartial as possible, *voir dire* is used to question the potential jurors about a wide range of issues that may influence their objectivity.

7. Evaluate the forms of jury verdicts.
   - Jury verdicts can take one of three major forms: guilty, not guilty, and guilty but insane. A guilty verdict means the jury determined that there was a proof beyond a reasonable doubt that the defendant committed the offense. A not-guilty verdict is an acquittal of the case against the defendant. It means the jury did not find proof beyond reasonable doubt. However, it could also mean that they think the defendant is guilty but did not believe that the prosecutor provided the legal justification for arriving at a guilty verdict. In the guilty but insane verdict, the jury determines that the defendant has committed the offense, but that he or she does not have the mental competency to understand the ramifications of his or her behavior.

8. Discuss the overriding philosophy of sentencing.
   - The overriding philosophy of sentencing is "let the punishment fit the crime." This attitude goes back to the ancient dictate of lex talionis, or "an eye for an eye and a tooth for tooth."

9. List and discuss the four philosophies of sentencing.
   - The four basic philosophies of sentencing are deterrence, retribution, incapacitation, and rehabilitation.
   - Deterrence is one of the bedrocks of the criminal justice system. Specific deterrence occurs when someone breaks the law, is punished for it, and desists from committing future offenses. General deterrence occurs when we see other people punished for their offenses, and we desist from violating the law.
   - The idea behind retribution is that convicted offenders should get what they deserve.
   - Incapacitation is concerned with protecting society from crime and is aimed at disabling an offender from committing more offenses.
   - The idea behind rehabilitation is to address offenders' social, educational, employment needs so they can become productive members of society.

10. Understand why the idea of judicial discretion is contentious.
   ▫ The idea of judicial discretion is contentious because it is an argument about the balance of values. On one hand, it is believed that judges should have broad discretion in deciding cases because of their knowledge of the particulars of each case. On the other hand, judges' broad discretion can mean there is wide disparity in sentences given to offenders with similar backgrounds and offenses.

Questions

1. What are the three major types of trials?
2. What is the role of the judge?
3. What are the judge's pretrial duties?
4. What are the duties and responsibilities of the judge during the trial?
5. Compare and contrast the characteristics of large juries and small juries.
6. What is the difference between *venire* and *voir dire*?
7. What are the forms of jury verdicts?
8. What is the overriding philosophy of sentencing?
9. What are the four philosophies of sentencing?
10. Why is the idea of judicial discretion contentious?

REFERENCES

[1] Muraskin R, Domash SF. Crime and the media: headlines vs. reality. Upper Saddle River, NJ: Pearson; 2007.

[2] Bushway S, Redlich A. Is plea bargaining in the "shadow of the trial" a mirage? J Quant Criminol 2012;28(3):437−54.

[3] Carlson RL. Criminal justice procedure. 7th ed. Cincinnati, OH: Anderson Publishing; 2005. p. 144.

[4] Douglass JG. Can prosecutors bluff? *Brady v. Maryland* and plea bargaining. Case Western Res Law Rev 2007;57(3):581−92.

[5] Ross DE. Special considerations in bench trials. Trial Pract 2011;25(1):13−23.

[6] Riordan K. Ten angry men: unanimous jury verdicts in criminal trials and incorporation after Mcdonald. J Crim Law Criminol 2011;101(4):1403−33.

[7] Yan J, Dannerbeck A. Exploring the relationship between gender, mental health needs, and treatment orders in a metropolitan juvenile court. J Child Family Stud 2011;20(1):9−22.

[8] Bell E. Reflecting on the judicial role: how valid is the analogy that "judges are like umpires"? Commonwealth Law Bull 2012;38(1):3−29.

[9] Jenkins J. The state of our trash in Florida: the use of evidence found in residential garbage to establish probable cause to search a citizen's home. Florida Bar J 2008;82(1): 30−3.

[10] Curbs placed on phone tapping. New Scientist 2006;191(2566):25.

[11] Fourth Amendment—exclusionary rule—California superior court holds that the knock-and-announce requirement is applicable when an absent third party has consented to search. Harvard Law Rev 2007;120(3):836—43.

[12] Rushin S. Rethinking Miranda: the post-arrest right to silence. California Law Rev 2011; 99(1):151—78.

[13] Carlson. Criminal justice procedure 155.

[14] Wogalter MS, Malpass RS, McQuiston DE. A National survey of U.S. Police on preparation and conduct of identification lineups. Psychol Crim Law 2004;10(1):69—82.

[15] Mack K, Anleu SR. Performing impartiality: judicial demeanor and legitimacy. Law Soc Inquiry 2010;35(1):137—73.

[16] Slonim S. NLADA: Ala. Counsel System is "Time Bomb." Am Bar Assoc J 1981;67(1):28.

[17] Handler MR. A law of passion, not of principle, nor even purpose: a call to repeal or revise the Adam Walsh act amendments to the bail reform act of 1984. J Crim Law Criminol 2011;101(1):279—308.

[18] Bibas S. Regulating the plea-bargaining market: from caveat emptor to consumer protection. California Law Rev 2011;99(4):1117—61.

[19] Weller S, Martin JA. Implications of *Padilla v. Kentucky* for the duties of the state court criminal judge. Judges J 2011;50(1):13—7.

[20] Lammon BD. What we talk about when we talk about ideology: judicial politics scholarship and naive legal realism. St John's Law Rev 2009;83(1):231—305.

[21] Shelton DE. Juror expectations for scientific evidence in criminal cases: perceptions and reality about the "CSI effect": myth. Thomas M Cooley Law Rev 2010;27(1):1—35.

[22] Bartlett S. Autopsy cutbacks reveal "gray homicides." NPR, <www.npr.org/2011/02/05/133476533/autopsy-cutbacks-reveal-gray-homicides?ps = rs>; 2011 [accessed February 5, 2011].

[23] Williams C. Old rape kits from Detroit crime lab could be tested. Associated Press/Detroit Free Press; 2012. <www.freep.com/article/20120216/NEWS01/202160576/Old-rape-kits-from-Detroit-crime-lab-could-be-tested>.

[24] Durose MR. Census of publicly funded forensic crime laboratories, 2005. U.S. department of justice office of justice programs bureau of justice statistics. Washington, D.C.: U.S. Government Printing Office; 2008:1-12: Online at <bjs.ojp.usdoj.gov/content/pub/pdf/cpffcl05.pdf>.

[25] Margolick D. Blood used in frame-up, Simpson lawyers assert. New York Times, May 5, 1995:16: Online at <www.nytimes.com/1995/05/05/us/blood-used-in-frame-up-simpson-lawyers-assert.html>.

[26] Kim YS, Barak G, Shelton DE. Examining the "CSI-effect" in the cases of circumstantial evidence and eyewitness testimony: multivariate and path analyses. J Crim Justice 2009;37(5):452—60.

[27] Cox T. Using demonstrative evidence to win. Proof 2010;18(2):8—12.

[28] Cheng EK, Yoon AH. Does Frye or Daubert matter? A study of scientific admissibility standards. Virginia Law Rev 2005;91:471—513: Online at <www.virginialawreview.org/content/pdfs/91/471.pdf>.

[29] Ingram JL. Criminal evidence. 11th ed. Boston, MA: Anderson Publishing; 2012. p. 135.

[30] McCarron AL, Ridgway S, Williams A. The truth and lie story: developing a tool for assessing child witnesses' ability to differentiate between truth and lies. Child Abuse Rev 2004;13(1):42—50.

[31] Yin W. Resolution to conflict of competency of evidence: the analysis based on legal culture and litigant system. Canadian Social Sci 2011;7(2):47−51.

[32] O'Leary EP. Satisfying the best evidence rule when the original document exists only as electronically stored information. 2009; Proof 18(1):3−15.

[33] Blalock CM. Professional designations: evaluating expert witness credentials. Am J Family Law 2012;26(1):31−7.

[34] Kainen JL, Tendler CA. The case for a constitutional definition of hearsay: requiring confrontation of testimonial, nonassertive conduct and statements admitted to explain an unchallenged investigation. Marquette Law Rev 2010;93:4.

[35] Stern CC. Don't tell mom the babysitter's dead: arguments for a federal parent−child privilege and a proposal to amend article V. Georgetown Law J 2011;99(2):605−49.

[36] Giel MM. Avoiding fundamentally erroneous jury instructions: pointers for counsel in criminal trials and appeals. Florida Bar J July 2007;81(7):61−5.

[37] Shepard RT. Electing judges and the impact on judicial independence. Tennessee Bar J 2006;42(6):22−36.

[38] Marder N. Judging judge judy and other television judges, Conference papers—law & society (2010 Annual Meeting): 1.

[39] Horty JF. Rules and reasons in the theory of precedent. Legal Theory 2011;17(1):1−33.

[40] Scharf MP. Chaos in the courtroom: controlling disruptive defendants and contumacious counsel in war crimes trials. Case Western Res J Int Law 2007;39(1/2):155−70.

[41] Bohlander M. Prosecution appeals against acquittals in bench trials—the criminal justice act 2003 and the government's fear of the dark. J Criminal Law 2005;69(4):326−9.

[42] Homant RJ, DeMercurio MA. Intermediate sanctions in probation officers' sentencing recommendations: consistency, net widening, and net repairing. Prison J 2009;89(4):426−39.

[43] Wooldredge J. Judges' unequal contributions to extralegal disparities in imprisonment. Criminology 2010;48(2):539−67.

[44] Frampton TW. The uneven bulwark: how (and why) criminal jury trial rates vary by state. California Law Rev 2012;100(1):183−222.

[45] Kaye D. And then there were twelve: statistical reasoning, the supreme court, and the size of the jury. California Law Rev 1980;68(5):1004.

[46] Zeisel H. The verdict of five out of six civil jurors: constitutional problems. Am Bar Found Res J 1982;:141−56. Smith A, Saks MJ. The case for overturning *William v. Florida* and the six-person jury: history, law, and empirical evidence. Florida Law Rev 2008;60:441−70.

[47] Fukurai H. Critical evaluations of Hispanic participation on the grand jury: key-man selection, jurymandering, language, and representative quotas. Texas Hispanic J Law Policy 2001;5(1):7.

[48] White T, Baik E. Venire reform-assessing the state and federal efforts to attain fair, cross-sectional representation in jury pools. J Social Sci 2010;6(1):113−8.

[49] Bennett JMW. Unraveling the Gordian knot of implicit bias in jury selection: the problems of judge-dominated *voir dire*, the failed promise of Batson, and proposed solutions. Harvard Law Policy Rev 2010;4(1):149−71.

[50] Futterman R. Playing the other side's hand: strategic *voir dire* technique. Jury Expert 2011;23 (2):29−32.

[51] Sommers SR, Norton MI. Race and jury selection psychological perspectives on the peremptory challenge debate. Am Psychol 2008;63(6):527−39.

[52] DeBarba K. Maintaining the adversarial system: the practice of allowing jurors to question witnesses during trial. Vanderbilt Law Rev 2002;55(5):1521.

[53] From JC. Avoiding not so harmless errors: the appropriate standards for appellate review of willful-blindness jury instructions. Iowa Law Rev 2011;97(1):275−301.

[54] Ibid.

[55] Curriden M. The holdout. ABA J 1996;82(7):54.

[56] Collins-Chobanian S. Analysis of Paul Butler's race-based jury nullification and his call to black jurors and the African American community. J Black Stud 2009;39(4):508−27.

[57] Cockburn A. The trials of Ed Rosenthal. Nation 2003;276(20):8.

[58] Liptak A. Younger of suspects in sniper shootings will claim insanity. New York Times, October 10, 2003:1.

[59] Liptak A. Ideas and trends: trial and error; facing a jury of (some of) one's peers. New York Times, July 20, 2003:12.

[60] Bronsteen J. Retribution's role. Indiana Law J 2009;84(4):1129−56.

[61] Thornton D, Gunningham NA, Kagan RA. General deterrence and corporate environmental behavior. Law Policy 2005;27(2):262−88.

[62] Yu J. Punishment celerity and severity: testing a specific deterrence model on drunk driving recidivism. J Crim Justice 1994;22(4):355.

[63] Paternoster R. How much do we really know about criminal deterrence? J Crim Law Criminol 2010;100(3):765−823.

[64] Kleck G, et al. The missing link in general deterrence research. Criminology 2005;43(3):623−60.

[65] Seipel C, Eifler S. Opportunities, rational choice, and self-control: on the interaction of person and situation in a general theory of crime. Crim Delinquency 2010;56(2): 167−97.

[66] Bradley GV. Retribution: the central aim of punishment. Harvard J Law Public Policy 2003;27(1):19−31.

[67] Bhati A. Estimating the number of crimes averted by incapacitation: an information theoretic approach. J Quantitative Criminol 2007;23(4):355−75.

[68] Auerhahn K. Selective incapacitation and the problem of prediction. Criminology 1999;37 (4):703−34.

[69] McNeill F. Four forms of "offender" rehabilitation: towards an interdisciplinary perspective. Legal Criminol Psychol 2012;17(1):18−36.

[70] Bushway SD, Piehl AM. Judging judicial discretion: legal factors and racial discrimination in sentencing. Law Soc Rev 2001;35(4):733.

[71] O'Hear MM. Beyond rehabilitation: a new theory of indeterminate sentencing. Am Crim Law Rev 2011;48(3):1247−92.

[72] Kelly WR, Ekland-Olson S. The response of the criminal justice system to prison overcrowding: recidivism patterns among four successive parolee cohorts. Law Soc Rev 1991;25(3):601−20.

[73] Mann R, Schlagenhauf D. Economic response to a crime deterrence program: mandatory sentencing for robbery with a firearm. Econ Inquiry 1984;22(4):550.

[74] Mayeux S. The origins of back-end sentencing in California: a dispatch from the archives. Stanford Law Policy Rev 2011;22(2):529−43.

[75] Ulmer JT, Kurlychek MC, Kramer JH. Prosecutorial discretion and the imposition of mandatory minimum sentences. J Res In Crim Delinquency 2007;44(4):427−58.

[76] Engen RL. Assessing determinate and presumptive sentencing—making research relevant. Criminol Public Policy 2009;8(2):323−36.

PART

Specialized Courts

OVERVIEW

Part 4 describes the courts that operate outside of the traditional trial court. Most people convicted in a trial have a right to one appeal. The appellate courts do not conduct retrials. They usually don't even ask whether the defendant is guilty or innocent. Their job instead is to review the procedures of the trial court. They examine questions such as, "Did the prosecutor conceal evidence from the defense?" and "Did the judge's jury instructions bias the jurors against the defendant?" In most appeals, appellate courts uphold the trial court procedures and rulings. When they find fault, they usually send the case back for a retrial or resentencing; much less often, they dismiss the case. Other courts have been crafted to address emerging problems. Some of the special courts have already developed an established position in our court system, and some have emerged recently and are still undergoing radical restructuring. The juvenile justice system is an example of a specialized court that, over the past century, has become well-established in every state. More recent courts deal with particular populations, such as those charged with drug crimes and veterans charged with crimes.

In the United States, justice is a process, which includes the right to appeal, sometimes all the way to the U.S. Supreme Court. This statue, "Authority of Law," sits at the Supreme Court's entrance.

CHAPTER 11

The Right to Appeal and the Appellate Process

KEY TERMS

affirm

appeal

appeal by right

appellant

appellant brief

appellee

avoidance canon

brief

certiorari appeals

collateral

collegial court

concurring opinion

direct-collateral categorization scheme

dismissal with prejudice

dismissal without prejudice

dismiss

dissent

distinguishing

en banc

error-correcting function

final-judgment rule

grant *certiorari*

habeas corpus

interlocutory appeal

intermediate court–high court–final court categorization scheme

judgment

judicial review

mandatory–discretionary categorization scheme

notice of appeal

opinion

per curiam opinion

petition

petitioner

plain error

pre-sentence–direct–post-conviction categorization scheme

preserve

procedural due-process challenges

reasoning by analogy

remand

reply brief

res judicata

respondent

response brief

reverse

rule of four

ruling

substantive due-process challenges

trial *de novo*

Warren Court

CONTENTS

379

Learning Objectives

After reading this chapter, you should be able to:

1. Define appeal and explain how it relates to the trial court.
2. Describe the functions of an appellate court.
3. Explain who has standing in an appeal.
4. Tell what it means to preserve an issue and whose responsibility it is.
5. Identify the parties in an appeal.
6. Describe the role of a petition in getting an appeal started and how a court may respond to it.
7. Define the types and functions of briefs.
8. Define what influences appellate decisions.
9. Summarize the effects of judicial law.
10. Explain the significance of the Warren Court.

Think back to your night in Boston described in Chapter 1. You and a friend are accused of conspiracy to commit terrorist acts. Imagine it takes a different turn: you are convicted in the trial instead of exonerated. What do you do? Appeal, of course. Appeal courts are in place precisely to serve as a self-correcting mechanism in the judicial system. When the trial court makes a mistake, the appeal court may fix it.

You think your conviction is obviously an error in need of correction. As it turns out, though, you may not be able to get to an appellate court. It is actually a popular misconception that all cases are or even can be appealed. There is neither automatic right to appeal if you are convicted in the United States nor do appellate courts provide a retrial, establish guilt or innocence, or issue new sentences. Rather, their business is to review the process of lower courts and to ask whether the rules were followed during the trial. So to get your case reviewed by an appeals court, you cannot just say that you are not guilty, that you didn't like the verdict, that the jurors were dumb, that or you want a retrial. You must argue that there is a legal basis for the appeal, namely, that the trial court made a material error in procedure that changed the outcome of the ruling.

If your attorney invoked a right, but the trial court did not recognize it, you may have grounds for an appeal. As it turns out, your attorney did invoke the 1963 *Brady v. Maryland* rule and asked for forensic evidence on the pipe bomb. The lab gave the prosecutor a couple of fingerprints, and neither was similar to your or your friend's prints. This is clearly exculpatory evidence that, by law, must be disclosed. However, the prosecutor never gave your defense attorney those prints, and the police lab technician did not mention them during cross-examination. They only came to light after the conviction, when a whistleblower in the prosecutor's office informed your attorney of their existence. Now you have what is called an issue of law: your rights were violated because the prosecutor did not follow proper procedure.

The appellate court will now likely hear your case if you file all the proper appeal paperwork. Keep in mind, though, that the appellate courts are different from trial courts. Even if they agree that your rights were violated, they probably will not declare you innocent but send the whole case back for a retrial. So appellate courts do protect your rights, but only if you can identify specific places where your rights were substantially violated, and even then, they have limited power of review.

SITUATING APPEALS COURTS WITHIN THE COURT SYSTEM

Trial courts alone handle the great majority of criminal case hearings, from first appearance to sentencing. They generally do not create precedent but rather focus on disputes about the facts: did the accused commit the crime? The trial court uses evidence to decide whose version of the facts to endorse. Thus, they are largely triers of fact.

In the United States, justice is a process. When reviewing the facts, the courts must follow procedural laws and assure that everyone involved, including the police, attorneys, and jurors, are following proper procedures. Appeal courts, which have taken many different forms over the years and across nations, were introduced centuries ago, in large part, to correct errors in the process. The United States uses the appellate courts—which include intermediate courts of appeal and high courts in both the state and federal systems—as a corrective mechanism within the judicial system. To correct errors in the other two branches, people and organizations lobby, protest, and often sue in the courts. However, within the courts, the principal method of correcting errors is internal: a party with standing argues that the lower court's actions were wrong and should be revoked or corrected. An **appeal**, therefore, is a formal request to have a higher court review and change a procedural step, verdict, or sentence of the trial court.

Appeals are a complicated level in the courts system. Just like the trial courts, they follow an elaborate set of rules and rituals. The legal reasoning used in both courts share many of the same basic principles. Yet, the jurisdiction of appellate courts are issues of law, which involve reviewing the criminal trial procedure or the constitutionality of the law, not the facts of the case as they relate to guilt or innocence. They are almost exclusively triers of law, not triers of fact. These courts do not deal with pretrial hearings, rulings on objections, giving jury instructions, matching the facts of the case to a substantive law, or issuing verdicts. They usually do not even look at new evidence or hear from witnesses. Usually the actual defendant is not even present. Rather, they review whether the trial court's actions adhered to the law or deviated so far from procedural law or due-process principles that they changed the outcome of the case. In making these decisions, appellate courts rely more explicitly on legal principles and precedent, or previous rulings, sometimes not even mentioning the substantive law or whether or not the accused violated it. They focus on upholding the integrity of the process itself [1].

The varied structure of appellate courts adds to this complexity. We will focus in this chapter on appeals from criminal courts and the typical procedures in the United States. It is useful to keep in mind that these courts deal with a wide range of issues, including appeals from all civil and original jurisdiction criminal courts, and the jurisdiction of appellate courts is regularly changed by legislation or the court's own rulings [2]. Plus, as a matter of dual sovereignty, appellate court structures vary considerably across states and the federal system. The federal courts and most states, but not all, have intermediate appellate courts between the trial courts of general jurisdiction and the highest court in the state. However, the jurisdiction of intermediate courts varies. Some, for instance, may choose the cases they hear, and others must hear the cases that come before them. Some must hear cases from state agencies dealing with administrative law, but in other states such cases are heard in separate courts. Similarly, variation exists in state high courts and the U.S. Supreme Court, and as we saw in Chapter 3, there are even differences in the names of each court.

Role of Appellate Courts

Regardless of the variation across appellate courts, we can identify the jurisdictional limits and core functions of both intermediate courts of appeals and high courts. Legal principles and jurisdiction greatly limit the power of appellate courts. Nonetheless, appellate courts protect the rights of people in the nation. They are considered "authoritative interpreters" of the Constitution and have as their central concern the constitutionality of government actions and laws. In short, they serve as a check on government power [3]. If courts did not uphold the rights stated in the Constitution, those rights would just be words on paper. This power of review is sometimes called the **error-correcting function** of the appellate courts.

Appellate courts protect rights in two broad ways, by reviewing the procedures in individual cases and by reviewing the constitutionality of laws and executive-branch policies. These are known as the powers of **judicial review**. Appellate courts, like trial courts, do not actively seek disputes to resolve and do not offer political opinions or advice. They remain passive until someone with standing, usually a defendant convicted in a trial, brings a case to them. All appeals, therefore, involve a particular case that must be dispensed. In most of these cases, the court reviews alleged errors and injustices in the lower court procedures. The ruling in such cases affects only the people involved in the case. For instance, does the person get a retrial with additional evidence included, or does the sentence stand and the defendant return to prison? Though these rulings are limited to one case, it is a structural deterrent against future abuses in the lower courts: they make judges and prosecutors more careful to avoid error because of fear of appeal [4].

Less often but with much wider effect, an appellate court, particularly a state high court or the Supreme Court, will not only rule on the case before them but will also include in their ruling a new legal doctrine that becomes precedent or a nullification of an existing law. This is the power of judicial lawmaking, which, at the federal level, is implied in Article III. It includes, though not often, declaring a law or part of a law unconstitutional and therefore unenforceable in the courts. For instance, the Supreme Court ruled that states could not ban burning of the U.S. flag because that is a form of protest and speech that is protected by the First Amendment [5]. In another case, *Furman v. Georgia* (1972), the Court suspended executions for 4 years and required states to revamp their death-penalty laws [6].

Judicial lawmaking also includes stating rights and clarifying past rulings or legal principles, such as what constitutes cruel and unusual punishment. This includes rights (penumbra rights) not stated in the Constitution but inferred from it, such as the right to privacy and the right to an appeal [7]. This is creating precedent: articulation or modification of legal principles that other courts must follow. When an appellate court creates or clarifies a right, it often ends up creating new rules for criminal justice system workers, such as having to provide defense counsel under the *Gideon v. Wainwright* (1963) ruling or having to disclose evidence under the *Brady* rule.

Such rulings on the rights of the people and duties of the government alter the legal principles themselves, rules of evidence, and other trial-court procedures. These changes almost always affect the government operations rather than creating new laws that regulate the general public. For instance, an appellate court will not criminalize a new drug such as bath salts, but they will require police to read *Miranda* rights when arresting and interrogating someone for suspected possession of illegal drugs. Finally, judicial lawmaking sometimes includes clarifying laws or their own previous rulings.

For example, in 1966, the Supreme Court ruled in *Miranda v. Arizona* (see Landmark Cases) that due-process rights protect people even outside of the courtroom, such as during police interrogations. If police or prosecutors do not inform people in custody of these rights prior to an interrogation, then the confessions cannot be admitted as evidence in a trial. Also, police must stop an interrogation when a suspect invokes one of the rights.

In *Edwards v. Arizona* (1981), a suspect stopped an interrogation by asking for an attorney. The police returned to his cell, read him *Miranda* again, and he confessed. The Court ruled that the confession was not admissible. If a suspect stops an interrogation, the police cannot return to his cell the next day and interrogate him without an attorney being present because he has not waived that right [8].

In 2010, however, the Court ruled that a 14-day noncustodial lapse between two interrogations (in contrast to a 1-day custodial lapse) "provides plenty of time for the suspect to get reacclimated to his normal life, to consult with friends and counsel, and to shake off any residual coercive effects of his prior custody." Therefore his refusal to talk at the first interrogation has effectively "expired," and police may interrogate him again [9]. That same year, the Court also ruled that police do not have to use the exact *Miranda* warning language as long as they basically communicate the rights [10].

Each of these rulings will need clarification in future cases. If there is not a "bright line" between acceptable and unacceptable *Miranda* warnings, the appellate courts will have to hear endless cases on what is a legitimate informing of rights.

LANDMARK CASES

Miranda v. Arizona (1966)

Prior to interrogation, police must notify individuals in custody of their right to counsel and their protection against self-incrimination.

In 1963, police arrested Ernesto Miranda at his Phoenix, Arizona, home and took him to a police station where he was identified by the complaining witness. Police interrogated Miranda without informing him of his rights. During the 2-hour interrogation, Miranda—who had not finished ninth grade and had a history of mental instability—produced a signed, written confession that he had committed rape, kidnapping, and robbery. Miranda had no attorney present and was charged with the offenses.

The case went to trial with Miranda's oral and written testimony as the prosecution's only evidence. Miranda was convicted of rape and kidnapping and sentenced to 20–30 years in prison on each count. He appealed to the state Supreme Court, claiming that his interrogation was unconstitutional. The court upheld the conviction. In 1966, the case went to the U.S. Supreme Court.

In a 5-4 decision written by Chief Justice Earl Warren, the Court ruled that the prosecution could not use Miranda's confession as evidence in a criminal trial because the police had not informed Miranda of his right to an attorney and his constitutional protection against self-incrimination. The Fifth Amendment gives a criminal suspect the right to refuse "to be a witness against himself." The Sixth Amendment guarantees criminal defendants the right to an attorney. Without these rights, the Court stated, "no statement obtained from the defendant can truly be the product of his free choice."

Some court observers note the changing nature of court interpretation and some critics argue that the court rulings generally benefit groups already in power [11]. Either way, the appellate courts play a critical role in tempering the power of the government, at least in some respects, which is likely the reason public opinion polls indicate that people respect the judicial branch more than other branches of government. Court Procedures 11.1 explains the case in which the Supreme Court first clarified its power of judicial review.

COURT PROCEDURES

The Origin of Judicial Review: The Constitution and the Supreme Court

Judicial review is the power of the U.S. Supreme Court and lesser appellate courts to review legislative and executive actions and declare them in line with the Constitution, and therefore permissible, or in violation of the Constitution and therefore unenforceable. This power to overturn congressional laws and to direct the activities of the executive branch is implied in Article III—"The judicial Power shall extend to all Cases, in Law and Equity, arising under this Constitution, the Laws of the United States, and Treaties made, or which shall be made, under their Authority"—and Article VI, which declares the Constitution the supreme law of the land.

Judicial review was firmly established in the 1803 Supreme Court ruling, *Marbury v. Madison*[12]. In this early case, the Court effectively gave itself the powers that were only implied in the Constitution. Namely, that if a law violates the Constitution it is not valid or enforceable, and it is the duty of the appellate courts to make this determination. Even if Congress passes a law and even if most people want the law passed, if it violates the foundational principles of the government—the Constitution—it necessarily must be invalid.

Question
What is the significance of *Marbury v. Madison* to judicial review?

Appellate Jurisdiction

Appellate court authority is limited not only by principles of precedent and judicial restraint but also by jurisdiction. Within the court hierarchy, appellate courts are the superior courts that review and correct legal errors of an inferior court. With this authority comes a sort of structural isolation: they generally cannot hear a case until it is first heard and disposed by the lower court. It must wait its turn. Even after the trial is over, it cannot hear a case unless a convicted defendant brings the case forward.

When cases do move up from the trial, the appellate courts have additional subject-matter limits. They generally do not even consider the verdict in the case. If a convicted person is upset only at the evidence and the ruling, the appellate court probably will not hear it because that case is considered *res judicata* (REAZ joo di KA ta)—a settled matter that cannot be judged again—and outside the court's subject-matter jurisdiction. Appellate courts, then, focus mainly on the process the trial court used to reach its ruling and usually only on one specific point in the process that is being contested. Sometimes, however, an appellate court will hear new evidence if it rules that there was substantial error or a "clearly erroneous ruling" at the trial level. In either situation, the case must be justiciable. It must have a reviewable question and be ripe. For a case to be justiciable at the appellate level, the person must have exhausted all other remedies at the lower level, such as going through an intermediate court of appeals before appealing to the high court.

Summary of Appellate Process

Appeal courts hear far fewer cases than do trial courts. In 2011, 55,000 cases were filed in federal appellate courts, 43,000 terminated, and 44,000 pending from 2010. Criminal case appeals made up 12,198 of the filed cases, and an additional 15,678 were prisoner petitions. About 50 percent, therefore, are cases related to criminal cases [13]. In a study of 14 states, the National Center for State Courts found that intermediate courts of appeals heard 43,000 cases in 2009, with a low of 83 in Indiana and high of over 20,000 in Florida. The average is about 3,000 appellate cases annually. Of these appeals, 50 percent, or 1,500, are from criminal trial courts. If we assume that average for all states, this is about 75,000 criminal appeals at the state level and approximately 103,000 at the combined state and federal level. State high courts hear an average of 220 cases per year, of which only 35 percent involve criminal cases [14]. The U.S. Supreme Court in 2010 heard 27 criminal or prisoner cases, or about 32 percent of the 84 cases they heard. None of these numbers are large considering the more than 1,000,000 annual felony convictions. Perhaps only a small percent of trial cases have a substantial error that threatens due-process rights, or perhaps the system is designed to minimize the use of appeals.

Fewer than 10 percent of those convicted or imprisoned have their case heard on appeal. Nonetheless, it is an important mechanism for reducing government abuse of power. Most appeals go to an intermediate court first. Of those, about 16 percent go to the next level of appeals, either the state high court or, for cases in the federal system, the U.S. Supreme Court. A few cases will be appealed from the state high court to the U.S. Supreme Court, the court of final opinion. Most appeals, about 70 percent, are for a sentence only—meaning they are not appealing the conviction, just the sentence—and the remainder are for a sentence and conviction [15]. Common due-process arguments in appeals are:

- ineffective counsel
- tainted evidence admitted or exculpatory evidence not disclosed
- flawed jury instructions
- coerced or nonvoluntary confession

The person who initiates an appeal is the **appellant** or **petitioner**. The appellant (usually someone just convicted) files a **notice of appeal**, a document that advises the court and the opposing party that the appellant is appealing the court's decision. If the appellate court accepts the case, the appellant then files a written argument, or **brief**, explaining how her or his rights were violated by the respondent or **appellee** (the party responding to or opposing an appeal). The respondent then submits a **response brief** arguing against the first brief. Sometimes, the appellant will submit a second brief. Often, the court will decide and rule on the case just based on this written record. If they decide to listen to oral arguments, they do so as a **collegial court**, which means that either a panel of three or so judges listen to the same case or all the judges in the jurisdiction sit *en banc* (as a "full bench") to hear the case (especially for major cases).

In approximately 75 percent of the cases, the appellate court **affirms** the lower court, which means it rules that there was no serious constitutional violation in the trial, and the conviction and sentence will remain in place [16]. Even when they reverse a case—set aside or overturn a trial-court conviction—it rarely leads to an immediate release. Usually it is remanded, or sent back to the lower court for a retrial, if the prosecutor chooses. Other times, it is remanded without a reversal, that is, the appellate court gives them instructions to re-do one part of the trial, such as sentencing. Occasionally, a defendant wins an appeal, has the case remanded, and receives a *harsher* sentence in the retrial. Winning an appeal is not necessarily a victory for the appellant [17].

INITIATING AND PREPARING FOR AN APPEAL

Someone or an organization must have standing to initiate an appeal. For a first appeal, this is usually the convicted person. Once the process begins, the parties in the criminal trial switch places: the person (or, in rare cases, the organization) who was prosecuted and convicted by the government files legal action against the state, which now becomes, in effect, the defendant. However, starting an appeal is not easy for someone convicted in the United States. Many filters and barriers prevent most cases from a first appeal. One of the filters is that if the defense attorney does not "preserve an issue for appeal" during the trial by filing a motion against or objecting it, then often that issue cannot be appealed.

Standing and the Right to Appeal
Standing is the right to initiate a legal action. For instance, the government has standing in trials: only a state or federal government can prosecute someone for a crime. In an appeal of a criminal trial, usually only the convicted person has standing to appeal. This is because if prosecution were to appeal

Table 11.1 Appellate Court Standing: Who Can Initiate the First Appeal and Subsequent Appeals?

First Appeal (usually an intermediate court of appeals, such as a Circuit Court on the federal level) →	Appeal to Second Level (usually either to a state high court or the U.S. Supreme Court) →	Appeal to Third Level, the U.S. Supreme Court (generally only when a case goes from a state high court to the U.S. Supreme Court)
If the defendant is convicted and sentenced at trial, the defendant has standing and a right to appeal, which is the most common criminal appeal.	The party who lost in the first appeal has standing to initiate a second-level appeal. This can be either the appellant (criminal trial defendant) or the respondent (the state).	The party who lost in the second-level appeal has standing to initiate a third-level appeal.
If the defendant is exonerated at the end of the trial, no one has standing and no appeal can be initiated.		

a not-guilty verdict, the person could be forced into a second trial, which is a violation of the Fifth Amendment prohibition of double jeopardy. The trial and final judgment "attach jeopardy" to the defendant [18]. Therefore, the defense files nearly all initial criminal appeals.

Defendant standing is the general rule, and it holds for most appeals. However, standing may shift depending at what stage of appeals one is considering. Usually only the defendant has standing for the first appeal, but after that whoever lost at the previous appeal has standing. Table 11.1 shows who has standing in various stages. Figure 11.1 shows how standing changes as a case moves from trial to the appeal and from the first appeal to the second.

Neither the Constitution nor the Supreme Court has declared the right to appeal a criminal conviction. Yet due process entails the right to challenge criminal justice actions. Most states and the federal government, then, consider at least the first appeal as a right and have established that in statutes. However, certain conditions must be met:

■ The case went to trial and was not settled in a plea bargain, as most pleas involve waiving a right to appeal.
■ The defendant was convicted and sentenced at trial, which is called the **final-judgment rule**.
■ The defense can allege an issue of law, namely that due-process rights were violated in either the conviction and/or the sentencing.

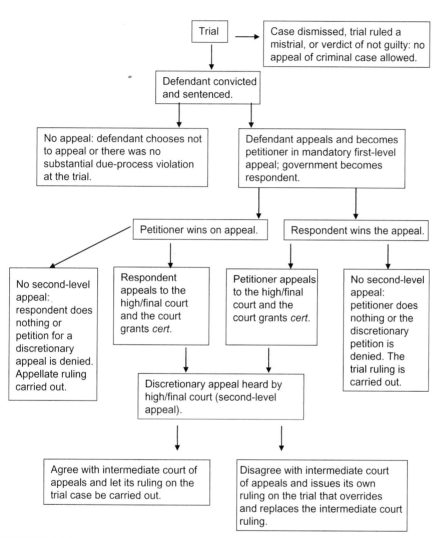

FIGURE 11.1

Appeals process.

Historically, appeals were available only to those who could afford them, "the doors of escape thrown open thereby to the rich and closed to the poor" [19]. The Supreme Court, however, has ruled that states that grant the right of appeal must make it available to everyone by providing counsel for the first appeal and providing free transcripts if defendants cannot afford them [20]. Because a defendant is granted only one **appeal by right**, or mandatory appeal, such cases often argue multiple points of law because this may be the only chance to have them reviewed. The Supreme Court, for instance, hears only about 1 percent of the 10,000 petitions it receives every year.

Defense Duties: Preserving for Appeal

Case assessment and preparation should include preparing a case for the eventuality of going to appeal, even though most cases are not appealed. If the defense attorney does not follow proper procedures at the pretrial and trial stages, a case may not be appealable. In other words, due-process violations go uncorrected when a defense attorney skips steps. With regard to preparing for appeal, the defense's main task is to preserve issues for appeal.

To **preserve** an issue for appeal means that the attorney must challenge during pretrial or trial the constitutionality of that part of the case. The two most common challenges are motions and objections, as discussed in Chapter 6. Let's say prosecution has evidence that a police officer obtained without a search warrant. The defense can motion to suppress that evidence even before the trial begins. If the judge denies that motion and allows the evidence, the issue of Fourth Amendment violation has been preserved for appeal. Similarly, if the prosecutor asks a burglary defendant, "Is it true that you engage in sex with prostitutes?", the defense can object or file a motion for a mistrial because the information is irrelevant to the charge of burglary and prejudices the jury against the defendant. If the trial continues and the defendant is convicted, that challenge preserves for appeal the legal issue of a violation of the Sixth Amendment right to an impartial jury. Without preserving an issue for appeal, the defendant often cannot appeal that issue. *Habeas corpus* appeals, however, do not require that the issue was preserved in trial, nor do some appeals that claim there was a **plain error**, or serious defect in the trial.

Parties in an Appeal: Appellant and Respondent

When a criminal defendant meets the criteria described above, he or she still must decide if an appeal is worth it. If a defendant decides to appeal, he or she will become the "appellant," or, depending on the jurisdiction, the "petitioner," "plaintiff," or "moving party." The appellant challenges the constitutionality of the procedures in the lower court or the law itself. The state or district jurisdiction is the appellee because it responds to the accusation in the appeal and defends the trial-court procedures and the constitutionality of the law. Focus on Discretion describes a situation in which a defendant must decide whether or not to appeal.

FOCUS ON DISCRETION

Deciding to Appeal

Imagine that you are a defense attorney. Your client, a 22-year-old male, was walking down a street in his neighborhood when the police stopped him, asked him to lift his arms, and frisked him. They found a gun in his pocket. They arrested him, and he was subsequently convicted of possessing an illegal firearm.

No one disputes any of the facts. No one disputes that your client was violating a criminal statute. First, you must decide if you even want to bother with an appeal. Let's say you are an ethical attorney and decide to appeal. What do you appeal? Your client was *Mirandized*, and you were even present during the questioning. You cannot appeal the evidence because those facts are not in dispute. The prosecutor disclosed everything you requested in discovery; the jury was given clear instructions; and the sentence was within the guidelines. The court procedure looks good.

However, did the police have justification for the initial stop? That will be a point that you hopefully argued in court and preserved for appeal, that the police did not have a right to do a stop-and-frisk. *Terry v. Ohio* (1968) allows stop-and-frisks only when the police have reasonable suspicion that a criminal offense occurred, and the suspect is carrying a weapon. In this case, police had no justification for the stop other than a routine check of people in the neighborhood. The police stopped your client on a hunch. You could argue that any evidence obtained from that illegal search should have been suppressed, and that is material because it would have changed the outcome of the case. Without the gun as evidence, conviction would have been much less likely, and the prosecutor would probably have dismissed the case.

Question

Two cases similar to this were reversed recently by a New York state court of appeals. In those two cases, as in this example case, why were the searches ruled unconstitutional?

Types of Appeals

Trial courts vary in design across jurisdictions, but their core function is always the same, to review the facts of a case and determine culpability. Appeals courts also have a core function—to review issues of law—but there is a much wider range of appeal court types and functions. Because of this variation, rules and outcomes differ depending on the type of appeal. There are five categories of appeal cases, but these are not mutually exclusive. Cases are always placed in at least three of the schemes.

- The **mandatory–discretionary** categorization scheme divides appeal cases based on the court's obligation and power to hear a case.
- The **direct–collateral (indirect)** scheme divides appeals into appeals that come directly from a trial court after sentencing and appeals that are removed from that, coming either before the end of a trial or after other appeals have been attempted.
- The **pre-sentence–direct–post-conviction** scheme identifies where on the chronological path the case falls. Some occur before the end of the trial. Direct appeals refer to the first appellate hearing of a case after conviction. Although the trial is over, a direct appeal is not considered a post-conviction hearing because the conviction is suspended and not final until

it has been affirmed on direct appeal. The phrase "post-conviction appeals" is used to refer to appeals that are filed farther down the line, such as an appeal from prison arguing that the confinement is illegal.

- The **intermediate court–high court–final court** scheme separates cases based on their location in the court hierarchy. Intermediate courts exist in the federal and most state systems. The high court refers to the top court in each respective system, either a state supreme court or the U.S. Supreme Court. However, a state court does not always have the final say. Sometimes the appeal moves to the federal system, in which case the Supreme Court is the final court. So, in the federal system, the Supreme Court is both the high and final court, but in the state system the high court is in the state and the final court is the Supreme Court.
- The **federal-state** scheme divides cases based on geographic jurisdiction. Each of these is broken into other jurisdictions within the federal system and each of the states.

Consider the case in the Focus on Discretion feature in which you are a defense attorney. If that was a California case, and you did appeal the evidence obtained through what you are alleging was an illegal search, that case would be a mandatory and direct appeal (both meanings of direct) that is heard in an intermediate state court. Say you win that appeal, but the state attorney wants to put your client away and wants to be sure police have the power to stop and frisk anyone they want. So the state appeals to the California Supreme Court. That case would be a discretionary appeal heard in a state high court. If it is appealable beyond that, it would go to the U.S. Supreme Court. A *habeas corpus* appeal, in which someone has already tried appeals but is still in prison, would be a discretionary collateral appeal heard in any federal court.

Mandatory and Discretionary Appeals: Appeal by Right, Interlocutory Appeal, and Writ of Certiorari

Appeals by right are all direct appeals, but the rules vary by jurisdiction. Some states, for instance, allow direct appeals of death penalty cases to bypass the intermediate appeal and go straight to the state high court. Pennsylvania is such a state. Mandatory appeals are usually guaranteed by statute but still have specific rules, such as having already been sentenced at trial.

Discretionary appeals require the court's permission to be heard. They include some direct appeals and also include pre-sentence and post-conviction appeals. The three most common are the interlocutory appeals, writ of *certiorari*, and writ of *habeas corpus*.

Prosecutors rarely have a right to appeal because jeopardy attaches once a trial begins, but one type of appeal that either a prosecutor or a defendant can use is an **interlocutory appeal** (in ter LOCK yuh tor ee), which is an appeal made before or during a trial that seeks to clarify an important issue that may affect the case-in-chief and cannot effectively be addressed after the trial. Also called original-proceeding appeals or pre-conviction relief, these are exceptions to the final-judgment rule and are made prior to sentencing, either before or during the trial. The subject of these appeals is an issue separate from the merits of the case-in-chief and would be effectively unreviewable after final judgment, such as whether the bail is excessive. They are considered to be indirect or **collateral appeals** because they do not appeal the main case but are too important to leave unresolved [21]. These are considerably constrained by state and federal law, such as federal courts denying appeals of illegal evidence because they have ruled that such evidence is not collateral but actually attached to the merits of the case [22]. Nonetheless, many examples of these can be identified, including:

- prosecutor appealing the suppression of evidence because that would make carrying out prosecution nearly impossible
- defense appealing the denial of a motion to suppress evidence (some states allow this)
- defense requesting disqualification of a prosecutor or judge who has a conflict of interest
- appeals regarding the other party not abiding by discovery orders
- defense appealing excessive bail
- appealing questioning of children or victims of violent offenses
- appealing either for or against a defendant's immunity from prosecution
- appealing for or against a stay, or postponement, of a trial [23]

Such an appeal is like hitting the pause button in a case. If the appeals court agrees to hear the appeal, the trial-court parties run to the appellate court to see if some technical rule has been violated, then return to continue the trial with the appellate court's directives. Sometimes this can take weeks. When successful, these appeals often have significant positive outcomes, including to save a great deal of time and money by avoiding a trial that will almost certainly be reversed anyway on appeal; assure that the trial proceedings are fair; avoid someone with a legitimate appeal having to wait till he or she is convicted and sentenced before appealing; and prevent harm created by the trial process itself [24]. Consider appeals to prevent a child victim or rape victim from having to testify, appeals about excessive bail, or appeals about immunity. If defendants cannot appeal until after the trial, the harm they are trying to avoid has already occurred. Or consider the denial to suppress evidence: the verdict may be determined by the suppression of that evidence, so why not decide the issue before trial rather than afterward? Nonetheless, people criticize interlocutory appeals because they interrupt and delay proceedings, and courts are hesitant to allow them because they clog case processing and undermine the final-judgment standard for appeals [25].

Most second appeals are discretionary direct appeals. This means that the issue in the petition flows directly from the trial itself: he first appeal did not satisfy one of the parties and they want a higher appellate court to review the same trial issue. These are *certiorari* **appeals**, which means "to make more certain." They ask a state high court or the Supreme Court to review a possible error of law in the trial court and the intermediate court's ruling on it. However, the courts are not obligated to hear these. It is a matter of discretion. If they agree to grant *cert.*, the high court sends a *writ of certiorari* to the lower courts asking them to send up the case transcripts [26].

Habeas Corpus *Appeal*

If all the direct appeals fail, there is one more option for those who are convicted or detained. Both the first court of appeals (usually intermediate courts) and the high courts adhere to the doctrine of *res judicata*, and are therefore reluctant to rule on matters that have already been judged. This is why even on direct mandatory appeals the court will not re-hear the facts of the case. The assumption is that the trial court did an adequate job of hearing the evidence and issuing a verdict. They instead limit most of their review to issues of law that were not ruled on or settled in the trial. Similarly, the high court or final court usually will not hear new evidence but just look at the same case to assure no errors occurred in the lower courts.

However, if the conviction and sentence have been affirmed on appeal and all other state options exhausted, the incarcerated person can still file a petition for *habeas corpus*, as long as there is a new legal issue that was not settled in the direct appeals and the federal court agrees to review it [27]. This is the only appeal identified and protected explicitly in the Constitution (Article I, Section 9), and is considered "the fundamental instrument for safeguarding individual freedom against arbitrary and lawless state [and federal] action" [28].

A *habeas* is a discretionary post-conviction collateral appeal heard by federal courts. It is an attempt to start a new case (technically a civil trial) to challenge the validity of the trial court's judgment, either the conviction itself or the length or nature of the sentence [29]. Like everything in law, it changes with statutes and precedent-setting rulings. Sometimes the right is expanded and sometimes more limits and rules are set which constrict the right [30]. Either way, this appeal is a significant part of the appeal system.

For instance, a single small state, Connecticut, has a division with more than 12 prosecutors working full time and numerous others spending a substantial portion of their workload on *habeas* litigation [31]. On the federal level, the District Courts have authority along with the Circuit Courts and Supreme Court to review *habeas* petitions, and about 4 percent of its civil caseload, or 10,000 cases, are *habeas* petitions, the majority of which involve people convicted for violent offenses. Sample research shows that over 90 percent of these are prisoners without legal counsel (*pro se*), and that most the others receive *in forma pauperis* counsel or representation from the American Civil Liberties Union (ACLU) [32]. Common due-process issues raised are ineffective assistance of counsel, discrimination in the jury selection, and other trial-court errors. Most petitions are denied for technical reasons (wrong paperwork) or legal reasons (failure to exhaust state remedies). In the small percent that are heard, few petitioners get relief from a *habeas* appeal. Those who do receive *habeas corpus* relief, get a new trial, a new sentence, or release from incarceration. Court Procedures 11.2 describes uses and constraints on *habeas corpus*.

COURT PROCEDURES

Habeas Corpus: Uses and Hurdles

Habeas corpus is mainly used as a postconviction remedy. In other words, someone has already been convicted and sentenced, and he or she sends in the petition from prison. However, other cases where the writ can be used include when people are facing:

- detention without bail or with a excessive bond
- prosecution by a court that does not have jurisdiction over the matter
- double jeopardy
- denial of a speedy trial
- institutionalization in a psychiatric facility
- extradition
- illegal detainment or deportation because of immigrant status
- military detentions
- denial of parole (conditional early release from prison)

The *habeas corpus* petition is a right all inmates and detainees have: anyone who has legitimate reason to think her or his incarceration or detention violates the law can petition the courts to review the case. In practice, however, many statutes and judicial rulings make filing a petition difficult. Some hurdles the petitioner must overcome include:

- Petitioner must be incarcerated.
- Petitioner must be able to read and write. The government is not required to help with filing. So, if no outside individual or organization is helping, the petitioner alone must read the many legal rules within the federal statute, then complete and submit the application. This is difficult for anyone, but when we consider that many inmates never graduated high school, are illiterate, have low cognitive development and intelligence, and have severe mental health problems that make them unable to deal with complex issues, we can see that this right is effectively out of reach of many people in prison, no matter how unjust their incarceration [33].
- Burden of proof is on the petitioner, and the evidentiary threshold is high. The person in custody must show that the state's actions are substantially contrary to federal law and violate her or his federal constitutional rights [34].

- Petitioner must have fulfilled "total exhaustion" of all state options before the federal courts will accept the petition [35]. For each claim in the petition, the person in custody has to have exhausted, or tried unsuccessfully, all possible state remedies, such as petitioning the state high court for relief.
- Petitioner must follow all state and federal procedures. The *habeas* petition may be dismissed on procedural grounds.
- Subject-matter limits. Generally prisoners and detainees cannot petition Fourth Amendment violations, and a claim of actual innocence based on newly discovered evidence is not necessarily a basis for *habeas corpus* relief.
- The number of petitions is limited. If the U.S. District Court dismisses or rejects the petition, the inmate can then appeal to the U.S. Circuit Court, and then to the Supreme Court [36]. However, the inmate generally is allowed only one chance at a *habeas corpus* petition to the Supreme Court. Any beyond the first are usually considered abusive or successive petitions and are rejected summarily. The Supreme Court has justified this limit by citing "scarce judicial resources" [37]. States vary in their limits.
- Petitioner must file the application within 1 year. This is one of several limits on petitions created by the 1996 Antiterrorism and Effective Death Penalty Act.

Question
Is access to a *habeas* petition fair or should it be modified?

Getting an Appeal Started: Filing a Petition to Appeal

If a party has standing to file an appeal, that does not necessarily mean the case will be heard. Even mandatory appeals, in which the defendant has a right to appeal and the appellate court must hear all legitimate cases, must meet many standards and can be filtered out. Many other appeals, however, are fully discretionary, which gives the court the option to hear and rule on a case or refuse to hear the case at all, in which case the previous court's ruling stands. This screening and filtering is sometimes described as "triage work" because the judges must try to tend to the cases with the most egregious violation of rights or most far-reaching effects, but leave untended many other cases with various due-process violations and injustices [38]. Describing this winnowing of cases, Justice Louis Brandeis once remarked, the "most important thing [the Court does] is not doing" [39].

Requesting an appeal by right is generally easier than requesting a writ of *certiorari*, because the first appeal is mandatory, has a clear checklist of requirements, and usually has an *in forma pauperis* lawyer provided for low-income petitioners [40]. Nonetheless, whether considering an appeal by right or discretion, the petitioner, either *pro se* or with the assistance of counsel, must convince the judges (or increasingly, their law clerks) that the trial had due-process violations that may have changed its outcome and violated the defendant's substantial rights [41].

This initial argument is presented to the appellate court in a petition that asks the court to accept the appeal and review the case. In some jurisdictions, the defendant wanting to file a direct appeal must first get permission from the trial court to appeal the case, which is known as "filing a notice to appeal" or "getting a leave to appeal." The petition requires a form of legal reasoning distinct from preparing for trial; an attorney must be a "law lawyer" rather than a "fact lawyer." Rather than argue that evidence supports guilt, innocence, enhanced sentences, or leniency, the petition must distill the trial case to its essential constitutional issues. The court can grant or reject a petition. Most cases, especially discretionary appeals, are filtered from the queue based on a court's read of this short document.

For a petition to succeed in getting an appeal, it usually must overcome appellate court reluctance to review other courts. The appellate court's general assumptions are that there was no error and that most errors are "harmless", or did not affect the verdict. This can be thought of as the "no harm, no foul" principle. "Yes," the court may reason, "one piece of evidence should have been suppressed, but plenty of other evidence proved guilt. Removing that one piece probably would not have changed the verdict." Therefore, to convince the judges that there was one or more legal errors and that they affected the verdict, the petitioner must overcome these assumptions. For instance, rather than just arguing that the appointed defense counsel was indifferent, it is better to point out that he showed up to court drunk and unprepared, which violated Sixth Amendment right to counsel.

Granting Certiorari

When a court accepts a discretionary petition, it is said to **grant** *certiorari*, which involves issuing a writ of *certiorari* ordering the lower court to send up the files. The process of reviewing petitions and deciding when to grant *cert.* varies across courts. In many courts, a judge never sees most petitions. Rather, the law clerks—attorneys who assist a judge or several judges—read the petitions, summarize and evaluate them in what are called memoranda, and filter out many. The final decision to accept a petition, however, rests on a judge or a panel of judges.

The Supreme Court uses the **rule of four**: if four of the nine justices vote to accept a petition, it is accepted. The 1988 Supreme Court Case Selections Act gave the Court full control over its own docket. Now all cases must go through the rule-of-four filter; as a result the number of cases it reviews has dropped from around 140 per term through the 1940s to 1980s to around 90 today [42].

The decrease in cases heard by the Supreme Court has corresponded with an increase in petitions. According to the Supreme Court's Web site, petitions increased from around 1,500 per year in the 1940s to over 10,000 today [43]. Diminished writs of *certiorari* may leave important cases and issues unaddressed, may concentrate the power of a smaller number of litigants, and may further isolate the Supreme Court justices from issues facing the rest of the judiciary and country and thereby diminish its integrity. However, since the 1960s the Court has shifted more of its attention to hearing cases involving criminal procedure and civil liberties [44].

Cues for the Acceptance of Discretionary Appeal

There are many explanations for why a court may accept or reject a petition, particularly a discretionary one [45]. Some researchers have attempted to find single cues, or stimuli, that have the most influence, such as research that found that federal circuit judges are more likely to grant *cert.* if the petitioner is of high status [46]. However, it is more useful to look at signs and cues as a collection of signals that lawyers and judges must combine and weigh in totality in order to carry out their duties [47].

The two fundamental focal concerns are the presence of a constitutional issue in the petition and evidence that it had a substantial effect on the case. These two issues allow them to filter out the frivolous petitions from the ones that are "cert-worthy." Yet increasingly, the courts and their clerks take into account if all the rules of submission were followed. Missing a submission date, for instance, will usually result in an appeal being rejected, regardless of the injustice it is intended to resolve. Beyond the fundamental and logistical issues, the following may increase the likelihood of some courts accepting a discretionary appeal petition and granting *certiorari*:

- The federal government is filing the petition.
- The case introduces a new question of law and has significant policy implications.
- Multiple *amicus briefs* are filed in support to *certiorari*.
- There are contradictory rulings in lower courts [48].

Other variables, many of them part of the internal ecology, that may influence discretionary decisions include the following:

- If the panel of judges or justices share ideological positions, they may be more likely to accept a greater number of petitions than a fractured court [49].
- The use of law clerks may suppress the number of appeals granted *cert* [50].
- The existence of a legal norm against issue creation may suppress certs.

THE APPELLATE PROCESS

A party with standing files a petition for an appeal and the appellate court issues a writ. This could be a writ of appeal on a direct appeal, a writ of *certiorari* on a discretionary appeal, or a writ of *habeas corpus* on a collateral appeal. In each of these hearings, the same procedures are followed. Interlocutory appeals, however, focus on only a narrow part of a case, are often pre-conviction, and are sometimes briefer than other appeals. For the sake of clarity, this section will focus on direct appeal by right and *habeas corpus* appeals because both involve the criminal defendant as the appellant who is initiating the appeal.

Appellate hearings are similar to trial-court hearings in that both are part of the administration of justice and are tethered to the law, the facts of the case, and legal principles. However, they resolve different issues and follow different rules. The trial court's purpose of determining legal guilt or innocence requires that it be laden with physical evidence, witness testimony, and prosecutor and defense attorney maneuvering. Appellate courts must resolve questions of law, or whether proper procedure was followed. These cases therefore revolve more around the judges themselves. Appellate courts do not review new facts or hear any witnesses; the defendant is often already serving her or his sentence unless the trial judge granted a motion for stay; and the attorneys do not negotiate any plea or other settlement among themselves. The attorneys present their arguments in written briefs and oral statements, the judges question the attorneys directly, and the judges then vote on a ruling and issue a single decision.

Briefs and Oral Arguments

A **brief** is a party's written description of the facts in the case, the law that applies, and the party's argument about the issues being appealed. The goal of briefs and oral arguments is not to provide objective summaries of the case but rather to persuade the court to either correct or sustain the trial court's work. The task is advocacy. An "appellate brief", or "merit brief" or simply "brief", is a written argument in an appeal. These are written position papers, in which both parties state the question under review and describe the legal principles, precedent, and arguments that support each party's position. The merits of the case are based on the "record", which includes a transcript of the trial and pre-trial hearings and sometimes original exhibits from the trial. Oral arguments occur when the attorney's summarize their briefs and answer questions from the judges. Both follow the same logic as used in the petitions: focus on alleged violations of constitutional rights and their effect on the verdict or sentence. They usually do not appeal the ruling *per se* but the process of reaching the decision.

The rules of appeals vary by state, but in all cases, each party must "sell" its position in the briefs and oral arguments using the tools of legal reasoning, which include:

1. identifying the alleged rights violation and a legal or constitutional question that allows the case to cross the "threshold" of the appeals court (threshold or sufficiency question)

2. summarizing or reciting the relevant parts of the case, especially the procedural turning points, that led to the appeal
3. arguing that one interpretation is more clearly supported by the rule of law than the other position (often considered the narrative section)
4. balancing the argument against the court's standards of review
5. advocating particular relief, or how the court should rule [51]

Usually, there are three layers of briefs. First, the **appellant brief** (or the opening or petitioner brief) raises legal concern about errors and constitutional violations at the trial that deprived the defendant of due process of law. Second, the response brief (or opposition brief), submitted by the state, counters these claims. Third, the petitioner can submit a **reply brief** that addresses objections raised by the respondent. These are not on-the-spot, rapid-fire legal arguments but usually take at least a couple of weeks between each brief and sometimes months between each [52].

During this process, attorneys on both sides will sometimes solicit or at least approve and manage *amici* briefs, or Brandeis, third-party, or friend-of-the-court briefs. These are legal, moral, social, or scientific arguments presented by people not involved in the case. When done well, these can increase the stature of one's position, bring in unique perspectives, and even increase the chances of having a discretionary appeal granted [53]. These are especially common in cases that have the potential to change law, and they come from a wide array of organizations [54]. In criminal cases, this includes organizations such as the ACLU, National Association for the Advancement of Colored People, National Rifle Association, the American Bar Association, Mexican American Legal Defense Fund, the American Medical Association, Corrections Corporation of America, the American Sociological Association, the American Psychological Association, and the Attorney General of the U.S. Justice Department [55].

Appellant Briefs and Precedent

The goal of the petitioner (when it is the criminal defendant) is to have the trial ruling vacated, reversed, or at least partially reconsidered, such as a re-trial with a competent attorney or a re-sentencing with mitigating information included. The petitioner argues that in the trial there was a violation of constitutional rights and that the violation was substantial, material, or prejudicial (called **procedural due-process challenges**) or that the law itself or one of its provisions, such as a certain punishment, is unconstitutional (called **substantive due-process challenges**). A daunting part of this job is that the lawyers are often working to protect the rights of people they know are factually guilty but who nonetheless had their rights violated.

Writing a brief is a difficult process. It requires copious legal research, significant legal decisions, and the citation of often hundreds of cases. Both parties rely on case citation, but precedent is a better tool for the petitioner, who will cite Supreme Court rulings, and also Circuit Court rulings, state court rulings, and sometimes even rulings from other nations [56]. The strategy is to link essential aspects of the case at hand (the "instant case") to precedent cases that had favorable outcomes for the defendant or provide good positioning for the defense. Through deduction, the rule of law found in the precedent case can be applied to the instant case [57]. This is the process of reasoning by analogy described in Chapter 5. Lawyers will change the legal issue of their case if they cannot find precedent that provides a strong fit for the instant case. The goal is to find a precedential case that is a good fit and addresses an important and similar issue [58].

For instance, if the defense attorney first wants to argue that police could not search a mobile home after an arrest without a warrant, but that turned up only weak analogies, the issue could be changed to police cannot search a mobile home without a warrant if the driver and owner were arrested for unpaid child support. As it turns out, this may yield a good analogy with *Arizona v. Gant* (2009), in which the Court ruled, in part, that arrest unrelated to the vehicle cannot lead to a warrantless search [59]. Sometimes, although much less often, an appellant (or respondent) will ask the court to overturn its own precedent on the grounds that it produces unjust outcomes.

Respondent Briefs and Distinguishing
The respondent both in first-level appeals to intermediate courts and in *habeas corpus* appeals is a state or the federal government, and they usually want the court to rule that the verdict and sentence should stand, or remain unchanged. They argue, depending on what is in the appellant brief, that proper procedure was followed and there was no violation of constitutional rights; that if some procedure was violated, it was incidental; or that the law itself is constitutional.

Often the person or team handling appeals for the state is a special appeals unit in the prosecutor's office. They will usually order all the cases cited in the appellant brief and the trial transcript. Just like defense, their handling of this information is framed by the legal principles and reasoning. Both parties rely on precedent in constructing their case theories. However, the defense tends more toward establishing links between the instant and precedent cases and arguing that precedent should be followed. The prosecution tends more toward breaking the link.

The tactic of arguing that the instant and precedent cases are too distinct to deduce a connection is called **distinguishing**, and though both attorneys use it, it is a favored tool of the respondent. Distinguishing is the second side of precedent. Rather than following precedent, it involves identifying the binding rule set forth in a precedent case but arguing that the two cases differ in facts or principles such that the precedent should not be carried forward to the new case [60]. It does not change the precedent rule but attempts to narrow it so as to exclude the instant case.

For example, if the precedent case involved due-process rights for adults, the respondent can argue that the instant case involves juveniles so the rule should not apply. This is exactly what happened in *McKeiver v. Pennsylvania* (1971), when the appellant argued that their juvenile clients were denied the right to a jury trial, but the state argued that the precedent that establishes right to a jury trial in state courts applies to adults and is therefore distinguishable from the instant case [61]. The Supreme Court agreed with the respondent, and defendants in the juvenile justice system have no right to a jury trial.

Distinguishing has advocates who say it allows judges to come to just rulings without disturbing precedent, and critics, who say it allows judges to selectively apply precedent in order to come to rulings that are in line with their ideology or personal preferences. Either way, it is part of U.S. legal reality.

Oral Arguments

Often the appellate panel will decide a case based on the briefs and record alone, which is called a "paper review." If the court wants to hear oral arguments, it schedules a hearing. The attorneys summarize their legal arguments and answer questions from the judges, who often interrupt. This is called a "hot court," not because anyone is angry but because they have already read the briefs and have particular questions they want to ask. These will often turn into what is best characterized as a conversation rather than a legal presentation. Rules vary across jurisdictions, and it used to be that some oral arguments would last 6 hours. The current Supreme Court usually allows 1 hour for oral arguments. These are generally only to clarify a few legal issues in the briefs. Michael Dreeben, who as the Solicitor General (Advocate) of the Department of Justice has argued many cases in front of the Supreme Court, stated in a Duke Law School lecture that briefs shape appeal outcomes more than do oral arguments [62].

Making the Appellate Decision: Judicial Restraint and Judicial Review

U.S. appellate courts are collegial courts, and thus review and decide on cases as a panel. Cases that get to the appeal stage tend to be more complex. This means that appellate judges generally have a greater scope in interpreting and applying the law. Two fundamental principles shape their decision-making, judicial restraint and judicial review.

Appeals in the United States is a conservative enterprise—not in a political sense, but in that the courts tend to "conserve" previous decisions. There is an institutional preference to avoid changing rulings. We often hear about cases being overturned, but these are the minority of cases. Right from the start, we see that appellate courts exercise what's called prudence. They do not actively investigate the lower courts, as a manager or quality-control officer may do in other organizations. Almost nothing in the lower courts is reviewed until a defendant petitions the courts for an appeal. Appellate courts actually put up barriers to reviewing lower court cases, such as the exhaustion requirement, specific paperwork, the discretion to refuse to review cases, and justiciability requirements to hear cases [63]. Several mutually enforcing presumptions create this conservation tendency.

- Presumption of constitutionality and legality of procedures. Appeals courts start with the assumption that proper procedures were followed in the lower court.
- Presumption of accuracy of lower court. Appeal courts assume the trial court accurately assessed the facts of the case.
- Presumption of competence of counsel. An appellant must prove that her or his defense was both deficient in performance and that it substantially prejudiced the outcome [64].
- Presumption of legitimacy of the conviction. As the flip side of presumption of innocence at the trial stage, appeals courts rely on the manifest weight standard that the lower-court decision will stand unless the appellant can show that the verdict was so clearly unreasonable, given the evidence, that it is unjust.
- Presumption of constitutionality of law. The appellate court's first preference is to defer to actions of congress and rule that the law is constitutional.

People often complain about judicial activism, but judicial restraint creates situations that may just as strongly offend people. The **avoidance canon**, related to the last presumption, compels courts to avoid hearing appeals that challenge the constitutionality of a law and when they do, to try to avoid ruling it unconstitutional. What this means in real terms is that the appellate courts leave in place laws that many people consider stupid or harmful [65]. This includes laws that criminalize marijuana possession or specify mandatory-minimum sentences. Or consider the presumptions related to the trial process. These collectively mean that even if the defense counsel was of questionable competence, the prosecution a touch unethical, or the conviction based on unreliable evidence, defendants are assumed to have received a fair trial and the convictions usually stand. When they do overturn a case, it is based on the principle of the "narrowest ruling," and therefore involves overturning only problematic parts of the case, not the whole ruling, if possible [66]. (This is unlike trial courts, which have a binary choice between guilt and innocence.)

The principle of judicial restraint, of course, does not paralyze the appellate court. The courts are an independent branch of government and review not only their own work but that of the other branches. They tend to adhere to the doctrine of *stare decisis* and carry precedent forward to new cases. If there is a substantial error in the trial proceedings, the courts are obligated to intervene. However, reviewing trial cases, sometimes a decade after the trial itself, is not a seamless process. Judges must consider the standards of review set out in precedent; they must determine if an error is harmless or prejudicial; and they must decide how to rule on the case. Also, they must contend with many other influences, such as *amici* briefs (which seem to influence over 80 percent of the Court's rulings); focal concerns and cues, such as cases dealing with national security; their ideological leanings; concerns about effects of a ruling; and organizational issues such as caseload and availability of law clerks [67]. Consider what is called the "panel effect": white, male, ideologically moderate judges, when sitting on a panel with a black or female judge, tend to shift their rulings toward favoring the litigants in affirmative action or sexual harassment cases [68].

Appellate Rulings, Opinions, and Dissents

After briefs have been reviewed and oral hearings held, the court must decide how to rule on the case, which is called a **ruling** or **judgment**. The court's decision is constrained by standards of review, precedent, and other legal mechanisms, but they retain the power to issue a range of rulings. (This section deals only with error-correcting rulings, not constitutionality-of-law rulings.) Most appellate cases are affirmed, which means the court "lets stand" the ruling in the lower court. On the federal level, the affirmance rate for most years since 1995 has been between 75 and 80 percent. State courts generally fall in that same range [69]. Although there is significant variation across jurisdictions, the courts clearly tend toward conservation and prudence in affirming lower court decisions. When a case is affirmed at the first level of appeal or *habeas corpus*, the trial-court verdict and sentence go into effect, unless the losing party appeals to the next level (when possible). Courts will affirm if no error was found or if the error was determined to be harmless.

If the court finds substantial error in the trial, it can reverse the decision and/or remand the case. **Reverse** means the superior court annuls, cancels, vacates, or sets aside the decision of the lower court. The court can "reverse in full" and vacate the entire trial-court decision or "reverse in part" and cancel only part of the trial court's conclusions. Sometimes an appellate court will combine a reversal with a change in the sentence. Most times, though, a reversal is accompanied by a remand. "Reverse and remand" decisions take many forms. Sometimes the appellate court will determine that the error was so substantial that it tainted the whole trial.

For instance, imagine that a trial judge allowed a coerced confession into evidence. In such cases the remand may order a **trial** *de novo*, or a whole new trial excluding the illegal evidence. This does not violate double jeopardy because it is, according to precedent and legal reality, an extension of the first trial. Many of these cases will be dismissed by the trial prosecutor because the suppression of key evidence weakens the case, but about half of the remanded cases result in a conviction in the second trial, though sometimes to lesser charges [70].

More often, the remand will be partial, which instructs the trial court to re-evaluate part of the case with certain evidence suppressed or included, new counsel, or some other change. This is often the case with orders to re-sentence the defendant.

At the highest level of appellate intervention, a court can **dismiss** a case, which means to terminate a case without further legal action. Just like a prosecutor or judge can dismiss a case before trial begins, an appellate court can dismiss a case after the defendant has been convicted and sentenced (or before the trial, in an interlocutory appeal). A **dismissal with prejudice** is permanent. It means the appellate court is tossing out the case and prohibiting the state from taking action on the issue again. There is no retrial. A case may be dismissed with prejudice, for example, the government violated the Sixth Amendment right to a speedy trial; brought a case that was frivolous or in bad faith; engaged in prosecutorial vindictiveness (elevated charges or sentence in response to a defendant exerting constitutional rights); or committed another gross violation of rights. [71]. Also, if the appellate court finds the trial court's guilty verdict "clearly erroneous," it may dismiss the case with prejudice and set the accused free. Less common is **dismissal without prejudice**, in which the appellate court terminates the case but leaves open the option for the state to bring the same charges against the defendant. Unlike a remanded re-trial, this does not order the lower court to have another trial, but the option is there.

The appellate courts can express their decision in several ways. After a case is orally argued or otherwise presented for judgment, the appeals-court judges will meet to discuss the case. They usually do not have a simple yes/no vote. Rather, one judge, often assigned by the chief justice, will write a draft opinion, often with input from the other judges. They then discuss, debate, and revise the draft, often for weeks and sometimes months, until a majority agrees with it. That becomes the **opinion**, which is the controlling opinion and states the court's ruling and explains the legal reasoning behind it such that others trained in law will understand it [72].

Sometimes, especially in the intermediate courts of appeals, the courts will issue a *per curiam* (per KYOOR-ee-am) **opinion**. These "by the court" decisions are usually brief. They do not identify a judge as the author of the opinion; generally deal with issues that the court does not view as controversial because they have been settled in earlier cases; and sometimes do not even involve briefs or oral arguments—but the judges simply reviewing the trial transcript [73].

The majority opinion is then reported in the law books and on the Internet. The *ratio decidendi* is the part of the opinion that becomes, as a result of the ruling, a settled point of law, or the *res judicata*. The *obiter dicta*, or simply *dicta*, are the examples, moral statements, warnings, predictions, and so on that provide context for the decision but are not within the domain of legal reasoning and are generally not considered legally relevant.

Sometimes, a judge or justice will agree with the outcome of the majority decision but not the logic expressed in the opinion. They may then write a **concurring opinion**, which allows them to be counted with the majority but still express their own legal interpretation of the case. However, if a justice disagrees with the decision, he or she can **dissent**, which is a disagreement by one or more judges with the majority decision on a case. This can be done by simply being registered as a dissenter at the end of the majority opinion or by writing a dissenting opinion. Written dissenting opinions are more common in the U.S. Supreme Court than in intermediate appellate courts or state supreme courts. Dissenting opinions do not change the outcome in the case in which they are written, but they may provide guidance for others who have similar cases before the court in the future.

EFFECTS OF SUPREME COURT RULINGS

All appellate hearings and decisions are bound by precedent, but not all create precedent. Some cases only resolve the case at hand, but others change the operations of the criminal justice system, sometimes even retroactively. All appellate courts have this ability, but the court with the greatest power to make judicial law is the U.S. Supreme Court. After it has reached a decision, there is no other court to appeal to. Although judicial law is less precise than statutory law, it does provide guidelines on what the government should do to avoid the violation of rights, such as provide some type of defense counsel or inform suspects of their rights [74].

The effect of judicial law is immense. Supreme Court decisions alter what laws are permissible, how police and trial courts perform their duties, how lawyers prepare cases, and what happens on appeal [75]. Their decisions alter the lives of millions of people accused of crime and the massive prison system into which hundreds of thousands are sent every year. Consider four cases in which the Supreme Court ruled that mandatory minimums do not violate the Eighth Amendment prohibition of cruel and unusual punishment and thus upheld these lengthy sentences for non-violent repeat offenders.

- *Rummel v. Estelle*, 445 U.S. 263 (1980). Life sentence with the possibility of parole for a felony fraud crime amounting to $120.75
- *Harmelin v. Michigan*, 501 U.S. 957 (1991). Life sentence without the possibility of parole for the possession of 672 grams of cocaine
- *Lockyer v. Andrade*, 538 U.S. 63 (2003). Fifty years for petty theft of $150 worth of toys from K-mart
- *Ewing v. California*, 538 U.S. 11 (2003). Twenty-five years for theft of three golf clubs worth a total of $1,200

The United States pays billions of dollars annually for the incarceration of people sentenced under these laws. A single change in precedent—that lengthy sentences for non-violent crimes are so disproportional as to be cruel and unusual—would have, for better or worse, altered the budgets of every state and the federal government.

An interesting case that may be revisited as attitudes toward technology change is *District Attorney's Office v. Osborne* (2009), in which the Supreme Court ruled that suspects do not have a due-process right to DNA testing regarding their guilt or innocence, even if samples are available and the defendant or convicted person is willing to pay for the testing [76]. The Court acknowledges that DNA testing may often conclusively prove guilt or innocence but has allowed states to withhold that option at will. Sometimes the Court's rulings even change cases that have been settled, such as when they ruled that mandatory life sentence without parole for juveniles violates the Constitution's prohibition of cruel and unusual punishment [77].

Rights for people accused of crime were greatly expanded during the **Warren Court** (1953–1969), when Chief Justice Earl Warren led what is often called the due-process revolution. Since that time, rights for the accused have not vanished, but the Burger Court, Rehnquist Court, and current Roberts Court have all tended to restrict the rights of people accused of crime.

Just like a few decisions could have greatly altered the U.S. prison system, it is quite possible that, were it not for the Warren Court, states would still be allowed to have separate schools for racial groups (prohibited by the 1954 *Brown v. Board of Education* case); low-income defendants could be denied access to counsel (counsel became required in the 1963 *Gideon v. Wainwright* case); and evidence could be admitted from illegal police

PHOTO 11.1
Supreme Court Chief Justice Earl Warren.

searches (prohibited in 1961 in *Mapp v. Ohio*). Thirty years ago, an insightful legal scholar wrote, "Convicts not only have no right to vote but also are not a very respectable constituency for any legislator or executive. Yet they have played an important role in creating safeguards in criminal law that protect all members of society" [78].

SUMMARY

1. Define appeal and explain how it relates to the trial court.
   - An appeal is a formal request to have a higher court review and change a procedural step, verdict, or sentence of the trial court.
   - Trial courts hear cases for the first time, and handle most criminal cases, from first appearance to sentencing. They do not create precedent but rather focus on disputes about the facts. Trial courts are largely triers of fact. The United States uses the appellate courts as a corrective mechanism within the judicial system.
2. Describe the functions or roles of an appellate court.
   - Appellate courts protect the rights of people in the nation. They have the powers of judicial review, judicial lawmaking, and the error-correcting function.

3. Explain who has standing in an appeal.
   - Standing is the right to initiate a legal action. Usually only the defendant has standing for the first appeal, but after that whoever lost at the previous appeal has standing.
4. Tell what it means to preserve an issue and whose responsibility it is.
   - To preserve an issue for appeal means that the attorney must challenge during pre-trial or trial the constitutionality of that part of the case. With regard to preparing for appeal, the defense's main task is to preserve issues for appeal.
5. Identify the parties in an appeal.
   - If a defendant decides to appeal, he or she will become the "appellant," "petitioner," "plaintiff," or "moving party." The state or district jurisdiction is the "respondent" or "appellee," because it responds to the accusation in the appeal and defends the trial-court procedures and the constitutionality of the law.
6. Describe the role of a petition in getting an appeal started and how a court may respond to it.
   - This initial argument is presented to the appellate court in a written petition, which asks the court to accept the appeal and review the case. The petition must distill the trial case to its essential constitutional issues. The court can grant or reject a petition.
7. Define the types and functions of briefs.
   - A brief is a party's written description of the facts in the case, the law that applies, and the party's argument about the issues being appealed. The goal of briefs and oral arguments is to persuade the court to either correct or sustain the trial court's work. Usually, there are three layers of briefs: the appellant brief, the response brief, and the reply brief.
8. Define what influences appellate decisions.
   - Two fundamental principles shape appellate court decision-making, judicial restraint and judicial review. The court tends to "conserve" previous decisions. There is an institutional preference to avoid changing rulings. Regarding judicial restraint, the avoidance canon compels courts to avoid hearing appeals that challenge the constitutionality of a law and when they do, to try to avoid ruling the law unconstitutional.
9. Summarize the effects of judicial law.
   - The effect of judicial law is immense. Supreme Court decisions alter what laws are permissible, how police and trial courts perform their duties, how lawyers prepare cases, and what happens on appeal. Their decisions alter the lives of millions of people accused of crime and the prison system into which hundreds of thousands are sent every year.

10. Explain the significance of the Warren Court.
   - Rights for people accused of crime were greatly expanded during the Warren Court (1953–1969), when Chief Justice Earl Warren led what is commonly called the due-process revolution.

Questions

1. What is an appeal? How does it relate to the trial court?
2. What are the functions or roles of the appellate court?
3. Who has standing in an appeal?
4. What does it mean to preserve an issue? Whose responsibility is this?
5. Who are the parties in an appeal?
6. What is the role of a petition in getting an appeal started? How may a court respond to it?
7. What are the types and functions of briefs?
8. What influences appellate decisions?
9. What are the effects of judicial law?
10. What is the significance of the Warren Court?

REFERENCES

[1] Peyser M. Foote D. Strike three, you're not out Newsweek August 29, 1994: 53.

[2] Marks Jr TC. Jurisdiction creep and the Florida Supreme Court. Albany Law Rev 2006;69 (2):543–9.

[3] Jacobs H. Justice in America: courts, lawyers, and the judicial process. 4th ed. Boston, MA: Little, Brown and Company; 1984. p. 4.

[4] Smyth NA. The limitation of the right of appeal in criminal cases. Harvard Law Rev 1904;17(5):317–30.

[5] *Texas v. Johnson*, 491 U.S. 397 (1989).

[6] *Furman v. Georgia*, 408 U.S. 238, 240 (1972).

[7] Milovanovic D. A primer in the sociology of law. New York, NY: Harrow and Heston; 1988. p. 134–6.

[8] *Edwards v. Arizona*, 451 U.S. 477 (1981).

[9] *Maryland v. Shatzer*, No. 08–680 (2010).

[10] *Florida v. Powell*, 559 U.S. ____ (2010).

[11] Kammen M. A machine that would go of itself: the constitution in American culture. New York, NY: Alfred A. Knopf; 1987. Balbus ID. The dialectics of legal repression: black rebels before the American criminal courts. New York, NY: Russell Sage Foundation; 1973.

[12] *Marbury v. Madison*, 5 U.S. 137 (1803).

[13] Hogan TF, Judicial business of the United States Courts, The statistics division, office of judges programs, administrative office of the United States Courts, <www.uscourts.gov/uscourts/Statistics/JudicialBusiness/2011/JudicialBusiness2011.pdf/>; 2011. United States Courts, caseload statistics 2011, 2012, <www.uscourts.gov/Statistics/FederalJudicialCaseloadStatistics/FederalJudicialCaseloadStatistics2011.aspx/>.

[14] Court Statistics Project. Criminal matters are half of appeal by right caseloads in intermediate appellate courts. Examining the work of state courts: an analysis of 2009 state court caseloads; 2009.

[15] Heise M. Federal criminal appeals: a brief empirical perspective. Marquette Law Rev 2009;93(2):825–43.

[16] Ibid.

[17] *North Carolina v. Pearce*, 395 U.S. 711 (1969); Ruled that the trial court cannot have "vindictiveness" when resentencing someone on remand, but otherwise the sentence can be harsher. See for instance, *United States v. McFalls*, No. 10–6238 (2012).

[18] In the civil court system either the defendant or the plaintiff can appeal.

[19] Smyth, The limitation of the right of appeal in criminal cases, p. 318.

[20] *Douglas v. California*, 372 U.S. 353 (1963); *Griffin v. Illinois*, 351 U.S. 12 (1956).

[21] *Cohen v. Beneficial Industrial Loan Corp.*, 337 U.S. 541 (1949); Fed 28 USC, section 1291.

[22] *Parr v. United States*, 369 U.S. 121 (82S.Ct. 654, 7L.Ed.2d 614). *Mario di Bella, Petitioner v. United States of America. United States of America, Petitioner v. Daniel J. Koenig* (1962).

[23] *Stack v. Boyle*, 342 U.S. 1 (1951).

[24] Gellhorn E, Larsen PB. Interlocutory appeal procedures in administrative hearings. Michigan Law Rev 1971;70:109.

[25] *Parr v. United States*, 369 U.S. 121 (82S.Ct. 654, 7L.Ed.2d 614). *Mario di Bella, Petitioner v. United States of America. United States of America, Petitioner v. Daniel J. Koenig* (1962).

[26] Abraham HJ. The judiciary: the Supreme Court in the governmental process. 6th ed. Boston, MA: Allyn and Bacon; 1983. p. 24–7.

[27] *Stowers v. State*, 657N.E.2d 194 (1995).

[28] *Harris v. Nelson*, 394 U.S. 286, 290–91 (1969).

[29] Hanson RA, Daley HWK. Federal habeas corpus review: challenging state court criminal convictions. Washington DC: Bureau of Justice Statistics; 1995. Cornell University Law School, Legal Information Institute, 28 USC § 2254–State Custody; Remedies in Federal Courts, <www.law.cornell.edu/uscode/text/28/2254/>.

[30] Robbins IP, Sanders JE. Judicial integrity, the appearance of justice, and the great writ of *habeas corpus*: how to kill two thirds (or more) with one stone. Am Crim Law Rev 1977;15(1):63–86. *Sanders v. United States*, 373 U.S. 1 (1963); *Cullen v. Pinholster*, 131S.Ct. 1388 (2011); *Brecht v. Abrahamson*, 507 U.S. 619 (1993); Cornell University Law School, Legal Information Institute, Antiterrorism and Effective Death Penalty Act of 1996, <www.law.cornell.edu/wex/antiterrorism_and_effective_death_penalty_act_of_1996_aedpa/> [accessed October, 2012].

[31] State of Connecticut, division of criminal justice, testimony of the division of criminal justice, <www.ct.gov/csao/cwp/view.asp?A = 1802&Q = 474904/>.

[32] Hanson and Daley, Federal *Habeas Corpus* review.

[33] For a case study of the complexity of this process, see Todd Maybrown, Federal *Habeas Corpus* review, Findlaw, <library.findlaw.com/1999/Jan/1/241464.html/>; March, 2008 [accessed January 1, 1999].

[34] Cornell University Law School, Legal Information Institute, 28 USC § 2254–State Custody; Remedies in Federal Courts.

[35] *Rose v. Lundy*, 455 U.S. 509, 520 (1982).

[36] Cornel University Law School, Legal Information Institute, 28 USC § 2241–Power to grant writ, < www.law.cornell.edu/uscode/28/usc_sec_28_00002241——000-.html/> [accessed October, 2012].

[37] *McCleskey v. Zant*, 499 U.S. 467 (1991).

[38] Wasby SL, Martha HG. Triage in appellate courts: cross-level comparison. Judicature 2005;88(5):216−24.

[39] Caldeira GA. The United States Supreme Court and criminal cases, 1935−1976: alternative models of agenda building. Br J Pol Sci 1981;11(4):449−70.

[40] Watson WL. The U.S. Supreme Courts *in forma pauperis* docket: a descriptive analysis. Justice Syst J 2006;27(1):47-VI.

[41] *Olano v. United States*, 507 U.S. 725 (1993).

[42] Owens RJ, Simon DA. Explaining the Supreme Court's shrinking docket. William Mary Law Rev 2012;53(4):1219−85: Online at <scholarship.law.wm.edu/wmlr/vol53/iss4/4/>.

[43] United States Supreme Court, <www.supremecourt.gov/> [accessed October, 2012].

[44] Owens, Simon, Explaining the Supreme Court's shrinking docket.

[45] Brenner S. Granting *certiorari* by the United States Supreme Court: an overview of the social science studies. Law Libr J 2000;92(17):193−201.

[46] Baum L. Policy goals in judicial gatekeeping: a proximity model of discretionary jurisdiction. Am J Pol Sci 1977;21(1):13−35. Songer DR. Concern for policy outputs as a cue for Supreme Court decisions on *certiorari*. J Pol 1979;41(4):1185−94. Herman Pritchett C. Divisions of opinion among justices of the U.S. Supreme Court. Am Pol Sci Rev 1941;35:890−8. Murphy WF, Tanenhaus J. The study of public law. New York, NY: Random House; 1972. Songer DR. Concern for policy outputs as a cue for Supreme Court decisions on *certiorari*. J Pol 1979;41(4):1185−94.

[47] Provine DM. Case selection in the United States Supreme Court. Chicago, IL: University of Chicago Press; 1980. p. 174. Perry HW. Deciding to decide: agenda setting in the United States Supreme Court. Cambridge, MA: Harvard University Press; 1994. p. 116−25.

[48] Murphy, Tanenhaus, The study of public law. Sidney Ulmer S, Hintze W, Kirklosky L. The decision to grant or deny *certiorari*: further consideration of cue theory. Law Soc Rev 1972;6 (4):637−44. Caldeira GA, Wright JR. Organized interests and agenda setting in the U.S. Supreme Court. Am Pol Sci Rev 1988;82(4):1109−27.

[49] Owens, Simon, Explaining the Supreme Court's shrinking docket.

[50] Ibid.

[51] *Herrera v. Collins*, 506 U.S. 390 (1993).

[52] Ciano K. A briefreader's guide to briefwriting. Fed Lawyer 2012;59(1):42−5.

[53] Caldeira, Wright, Organized interests and agenda setting in the U.S. Supreme Court. McGuire KT, Caldeira GA. Lawyers, organized interests, and the Law of obscenity: agenda setting in the Supreme Court. Am Pol Sci Rev 1993;87(3):715−26.

[54] For a summary of the *Brown* case *amici* see Susan D. Carle, Race, class, and legal ethics in the early NAACP (1910−1920), *Law and History Review* 2002;20(1):122. *Webster v. Reproductive Health Services* (1989). For instance, had 78 *amicus curiae* briefs attached. Caldeira and Wright, Organized interests and agenda setting in the U.S. Supreme Court. For a wide sampling of *amicus* briefs, go to <www.lawsource.com/also/usa.cgi?usb/>.

[55] American Bar Association, *Amicus curiae* briefs, <www.americanbar.org/groups/committees/amicus.html/> [accessed October, 2012]; American Sociological Association, <www.asanet.org/about/amicus_briefs.cfm/> [accessed October 2012]; American Psychological Association, <www.apa.org/> [accessed October, 2012].

[56] Posner EA, Sunstein CR. The law of other states. Stanford Law Rev 2006;59(1):131−79.

[57] Levi EH. An introduction to legal reasoning. Chicago, IL: University of Chicago Press; 1949. Lamond G, Precedent and analogy in legal reasoning, Stanford encyclopedia of philosophy. Zalta EN, editor, <plato.stanford.edu/archives/fall2008/entries/legal-reas-prec/>; Fall 2008.

[58] Alexander L, Sherwin E. Demystifying legal reasoning. Cambridge, UK: Cambridge University Press; 2008. p. 68−9.

[59] *Arizona v. Gant*, 556 U.S. 332 (2009).

[60] Lamond G. Precedent and analogy in legal reasoning.

[61] *McKeiver v. Pennsylvania*, 403 U.S. 528 (1971).

[62] Lecture with Michael Dreeben, criminal deputy solicitor general at the U.S. department of justice, challenges and rewards of representing the Government in the Supreme Court, <www.youtube.com/watch?v = EmeHI4TryIw/>.

[63] *Friends of the Earth, Inc. v. Laidlaw Environmental Services (TOC), Inc.*, 528 U.S. 167, 212 (2000).

[64] See *Harvard Law Review* 2006;121(1); For a discussion of this principle; and John Capone; Facilitating fairness: the Judge's role in the sixth amendment right to effective counsel, *J Crim Law Criminol* 2003;93(4):881−912; For a discussion of related cases.

[65] Dickson, J. 2010. "Interpretation and coherence in legal reasoning." In: Zalta EN, editor. The stanford encyclopedia of philosophy, < http://plato.stanford.edu/archives/spr2010/entries/legal-reas-interpret/ > [accessed August 10, 2010].

[66] *Youngstown Sheet Tube Co. v. Sawyer* 343 U.S. 579, 635 (1952).

[67] Corbally SF, Bross DC, Flango VE. Filing of *amicus curiae* briefs in State Courts of last resort: 1960−2000. Justice Syst J 2004;25(1):39−56. Songer, Concern for policy outputs as a cue for Supreme Court decisions on *certiorari*. See Brenner, Granting *certiorari* by the United States Supreme Court; for an overview. Cox AB, Miles TJ. Judging the voting rights act. Columbia Law Rev 2008;108. Sunstein CR, Schkade D, Ellman LM. Ideological voting on federal courts of appeals: a preliminary investigation. Univ Chic Law Econ, Olin Work Pap 2003;198. Nelson RL, Bright lines and no lines in Criminal Law: balancing the rule of Law on the scales of justice. Paper prepared for presentation at the annual meeting of the Academy of Criminal Justice Sciences, New York, New York March 13−17, 2012. Owens, Simon, Explaining the Supreme Court's shrinking docket.

[68] Boyd CL, Epstein L, Martin AD. Untangling the causal effects of sex on judging. Am J Pol Sci 2010;54(2):389−411.

[69] Heise, Federal criminal appeals: a brief empirical perspective.

[70] Roper R, Melone A. Does procedural due process make a difference? A study of second trials. Judicature 1983;65:136−41.

[71] The Federal Congress wrote a similar provision into law with U.S. Code Title 18,3006A; Barbara Schwartz, The limits of prosecutorial vindictiveness, 69 Iowa Law Review 127 (1983−1984). John Patrick Krimmel, Prosecutorial vindictiveness, University of Tennessee Honors Thesis Projects, 1994, <trace.tennessee.edu/utk_chanhonoproj/39/>.

[72] Dworkin R. Philosophy and critique of law. In: Wolff RP, editor. The rule of law. New York, NY: Simon and Schuster; 1971. p. 152.

[73] Garner BA, editor. 9th ed. St. Paul, MN: Thomson Reuters; 2009.

[74] Recent years can be viewed at YouTube, Supreme Court: The term in review 2009−2010. Part 2 of 2, <www.youtube.com/watch?v = becvvGzk9Xo/> and YouTube, Supreme Court Review—Criminal, <www.youtube.com/watch?v = 8AqQgYbJ8xI&feature = relmfu/> [accessed October, 2012].

[75] Jordan SD. Have we come full circle? Judicial sentencing discretion revived in Booker and fanfan. Pepperdine Law Rev 2006;33:615−38.

[76] District Attorney's office for the third judicial district, et al. *v.* Osborne. 557 U.S. ___ (2009).

[77] *Miller v. Alabama*, 567 U.S. ___ (2012); *Graham v. Florida*, 130S. Ct. (2011).

[78] Jacobs, Justice in America, p. 45.

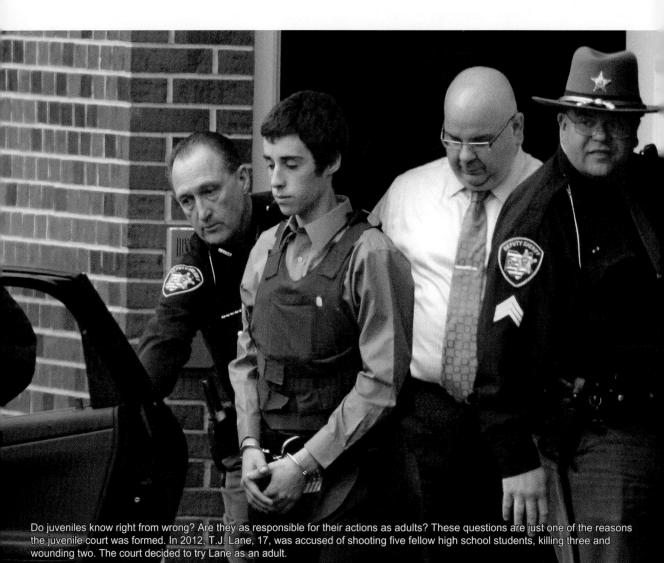

Do juveniles know right from wrong? Are they as responsible for their actions as adults? These questions are just one of the reasons the juvenile court was formed. In 2012, T.J. Lane, 17, was accused of shooting five fellow high school students, killing three and wounding two. The court decided to try Lane as an adult.

Juvenile Courts

KEY TERMS

adjudicate

broken-windows

child savers

concurrent jurisdiction

dark figure of crime

dependent

disposition

judicial waiver

labeling

parens patriae

recidivism

status offense

statutory exclusion

Learning Objectives

After reading this chapter, you should be able to:

1. Understand the relationship between youths and *mens rea.*
2. Tell why youths are considered to be more amenable to rehabilitation than adults.
3. Discuss the reasons that the juvenile court hands down dispositions rather than punishment.
4. Describe the role of the child savers and *parens patriae* in the forming of the juvenile court.
5. List and discuss the four eras of the juvenile court.
6. Briefly explain how the modern juvenile court works.
7. Differentiate juvenile delinquency from status offending.
8. Discuss the history and current role of due process in the juvenile court.
9. Criticize and then defend the concept of net-widening.

Youths and adults have separate legal systems. The juvenile court was established to ensure that children and teenagers are given the opportunity to turn their lives around. The philosophy is that by intervening early into the lives of troubled youths, treatment rather than punishment can provide the necessary support to compensate for an inadequate education, faulty parenting, or negative peer groups.

In the United States, we conceive of juveniles as still developing intellectually and psychologically, so the juvenile system is supposed to be focused more on rehabilitation and less on punishment. This system has been shown to have both positive features and several drawbacks. Does the juvenile court help children turn their lives around or "let them get away with murder"? One of the ideas behind the systematic separation of juveniles and adults is to allow juveniles the chance to become productive adults. In most cases, punishing a youth for the rest of his or her life for an offense committed at a young age, when the child was still developing, is counterproductive to society's goals of nurturing productive, healthy adults.

The juvenile court does not act in isolation. It is part of a broader process that includes the efforts of law enforcement, juvenile facilities, and a broad array of community services aimed at addressing the problems of troubled youths. One of the central themes of this chapter is that as well-meaning as the juvenile court may be, many jurisdictions simply do not have the necessary treatment facilities or the variety of sentencing options available to be effective. Consequently, the power of the state is often wielded disproportionately against youths because the juvenile justice system does not provide them with the constitutional legal protections that adults have. This chapter covers:

- how and why we conceive of juveniles as different from adults;
- the history of the juvenile court;
- the development and workings of the modern court;
- some of the issues associated with the modern court.

Finally, let's clarify some of the terminology used in this chapter. Juvenile delinquents are young people, typically under the age of 18 in most states, who have committed actions that would be considered criminal offenses if committed by an adult. Youths may also be status offenders in that they have broken laws that only apply to youths. The "adult" criminal court will be referred to as criminal court, and the juvenile court will be referred to as such.

ASSUMPTIONS ABOUT YOUTHS

We know some things for sure about youths: their brains and bodies are immature; they require adult supervision and guidance to develop properly; they endure a difficult time at puberty; and they grow quickly, with physical development typically outpacing mental development. Society also makes several assumptions about youths, many of which we are still learning about. One of these assumptions concerns cognitive development.

Almost every parent has a story (or several) about their child in which, in complete frustration, the parent asks the child, "Why did you do that?" and the child responds, "I don't know." Further conversation between parent and child reveals the assumptions that adults have about the abilities of children to make decisions based not only on current knowledge but also on foresight and hindsight. Some parents will insist the child *did* know, but simply chose not to follow the rules. Some parents will explain to the child (one more time) why what he or she did was ridiculous, unreasonable, or just plain wrong. Finally, some parents will consider the idea that the child really did not know, despite repeated warnings, lectures, and past punishments. It is this last possibility that is the most controversial: at what age does deep understanding of right and wrong, of the consequences of breaking rules, and of risky behavior really develop?

The field of juvenile neuroscience is still developing, but, according to some research, the adult ability to use empathy and planning to chart the correct behavioral course is not fully developed until young adulthood [1]. This use of empathy to guide behavior is a result of the interaction of several areas of the brain and points to the difference between *knowing* what is right and wrong and *understanding* it. For instance, a 15-year-old hears his father tell him that stealing is bad and that if he is caught, he will be punished. But how capable is that 15-year-old of understanding not only what punishment means but also the likelihood of getting caught and the severity of the punishment? It is unlikely that a teenager understands these things the same way that a 45-year-old adult does. This depth of understanding as related to age is what neurological research is currently looking into.

Because of the cognitive differences between juveniles and adults, the juvenile justice process operates on three principles:

1. youths are assumed to have less appreciation and control of their actions;
2. youths are more amenable to rehabilitation and have more time than adults to change their behavior [2];
3. dispositions imposed on youths who have broken the law should be proportional to the offense, but should not be as severe as the punishment imposed on adults.

Let's look at these principles in detail.

Youths and *Mens Rea*

The law requires two conditions for a criminal offense to be defined as such: *mens rea* and *actus reus*. As you will recall from Chapter 4, *mens rea* is the "guilty mind" or criminal intent, and *actus reus* is the "guilty act." Adults and older juveniles are considered to be capable of both. Young children are not.

Just as state juvenile courts have upper age limits, such as 16, 17, or 18, many also have lower age limits, such as 10.

In the criminal law, judgment of *mens rea* focuses on cognitive ability and the ability to make choices and does not consider goals, values, emotions, or psychological development that affect an individual's choices. Anyone who is able to choose one act over another is considered to be able to form criminal intent. To establish *mens rea*, the common law typically uses the knowing-right-from-wrong standard. That is, if it can be established that an individual knows right from wrong, then he or she is considered capable of forming criminal intent.

This low threshold introduces a bit of a paradox when considering the age requirements of *mens rea* formation. Nearly any parent will affirm that children younger than age 10 and older than age 2 are perfectly capable of choosing to perform an act that they know their parents have told them is wrong [3]. Whether that intent may actually be criminal is fodder for another hypothetical discussion and stands as one of the reasons for the existence of the juvenile court, which uses a slightly different philosophy and terminology to deal with its clients (which we will discuss later).

In short, because the juvenile court is focused on rehabilitation rather than incarceration or punishment, and is supposed to work for "the good of the youth," juveniles are not "proven guilty" of "crimes." However, they are held responsible for delinquent acts or **status offenses**, or the breaking of a law that only applies to juveniles. The standards for establishing responsibility are not as strict as the standards for proving guilt in criminal court. Therefore, concepts such as *mens rea* and *actus reus* are less important as neither must be established for a juvenile to be found responsible for a given act. This issue does become more of a concern, however, when a juvenile is believed to have committed an act grave enough to be sent to criminal court. It is then that the juvenile becomes subject to the strict establishment of criminal intent.

Youths and Rehabilitation

Juveniles are largely considered to be more amenable to rehabilitation than adults. Most adults believe that teenagers and children are still growing and that their bad habits, rebelliousness, or criminal tendencies (if any) are not firmly set. Depending on the philosophy of the adults in charge of rehabilitation, youths can be put on the right track with therapy, education, good role models, discipline, medication, punishment, hard work, opportunity, or just a good scare, such as a run-in with police officers.

Unfortunately, the last three decades have seen the juvenile justice system stray from its rehabilitative focus and turn to more punitive dispositions for delinquents and status offenders, although research indicates that this track is unproductive. A recent study has revealed that longer participation in community-based reentry programs decreases the likelihood of **recidivism**, or repeat offending. That is, the longer a youth participated in the rehabilitative program, the less likely he or she was to return to the juvenile court [4]. Other research has found that long terms in institutional facilities are not effective in reducing recidivism for serious delinquents [5]. A long stay outside the community in an incarceration-style environment that is more punitive than rehabilitative does little to prevent further delinquency [6].

One issue affecting the susceptibility of a juvenile to rehabilitation is mental health and learning abilities. Delinquents tend to have higher rates of learning disabilities and mental health disorders as compared to nondelinquent youths [7]. However, the juvenile justice system is notoriously short of resources when it comes to such rehabilitative efforts as education, job training, and psychological and substance-abuse services. One long-term study followed 449 delinquents ages 13−17 in Los Angeles, California. These youths had been referred to group homes between February 1999 and May 2000. Seven years later, researchers found the following:

- 12 respondents had died, seven of them from gunshots;
- 36 percent reported recent hard drug use;
- 66 percent reported committing an illegal activity within the previous year;
- 37 percent reported being arrested within the previous year;
- 25 percent reported being incarcerated every day for the previous 90 days;
- 58 percent completed high school or obtained a GED;
- 63 percent reported having a job in the previous year [8].

Clearly, not enough had been done to help many of these youths. Despite the weak commitment of the juvenile justice system to rehabilitation, the public appears to still believe that "bad kids can be made good." A survey of adults in Pennsylvania found "broad consensus in support of juvenile rehabilitation and an abiding optimism that youthful offenders can be reformed deep into the teenage years if not well beyond" [9].

Youths and Dispositions

Because of its rehabilitative focus, the juvenile court hands down **dispositions**, which is the final determination of treatment for a juvenile found responsible for delinquency or status offense, rather than punishments. Youths found to be responsible for a status offense or delinquency are supposed to receive a disposition aimed at rehabilitation. However, the dispositions for serious delinquency look much like punishments, such as several years in a reformatory, training school, or other secure confinement.

Prior to the 1980s, the philosophy of the juvenile justice system was more focused on treatment and rehabilitation. However, rising juvenile delinquency in the 1980s led to calls to "get tough" on youths with "zero tolerance" for the breaking of rules and laws. So, although rehabilitation and treatment is still available for delinquents and status offenders, the dispositions have become more punitive. For example, although waiver to criminal court has always been available in the juvenile justice system, it was relatively uncommon prior to the modern era [10]. Currently, about 1 percent of cases sent to juvenile court are waived to criminal court. However, many more are waived nonjudicially. That is, they are subject to automatic waiver laws and sent directly to criminal court and never get as far as the juvenile court [11]. With the drop in delinquency over the past decade (Figure 12.1), the juvenile justice system has edged back a bit more toward the rehabilitative ideal.

For status offenders, the federal government has tried to make juvenile court less punitive. The Juvenile Justice and Delinquency Prevention Act (JJDPA) of 1974 (which we will discuss in greater detail later) offered states federal funds if they kept status offenders out of detention. Prior to this, status offenders—for example a 14-year-old caught drinking a beer—were regularly

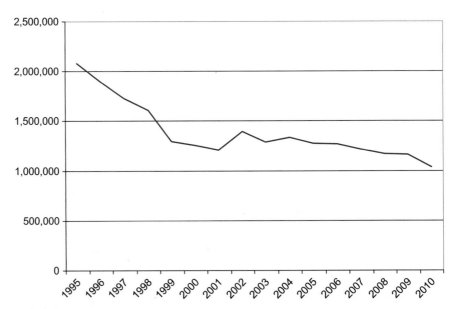

FIGURE 12.1

Number of Youths Arrested Under Age 18. The arrests of youths under 18 have followed a fairly steady downward trend since 1995, which is related to a general decrease in juvenile delinquency. Source: *Federal Bureau of Investigation, Uniform Crime Reports: Crime in the United States, 1995–2010, www.fbi.gov/about-us/cjis/ucr.*

held in lockups with serious delinquents. The idea was not only to soften punitive treatment for status offenders but also to keep them from being influenced by more hardened delinquents. This is also the reasoning behind keeping delinquents separate from adult suspects and offenders. Incarceration facilities are places not only where the older and stronger prey on the younger and weaker but also where young inmates may learn more effective ways to break the law.

HISTORY OF THE JUVENILE COURT

To appreciate the differences between the juvenile court and the criminal court, we must know more about the history of how youths have been treated in the justice system. From a legal perspective throughout history, youths have not always been considered different from adults and harsh sentences for youths who broke the law were not uncommon [12]. However, courts had special provisions for young children as of the early 1800s. For example, in Illinois in 1817, a child under age 7 was not considered responsible for a criminal act. A new law in 1827 raised the age to 10, and by 1831, youths under 18 could not be sent to the state penitentiary. Typical legal punishments for children included corporal punishment, fines, and short jail sentences. However, the idea of youths as being **dependent**, or needing the support of parents or the state, and requiring special treatment under the law did not take root in the United States until the child-saving movement of the late nineteenth century [13].

The Child Savers and *Parens Patriae*

The philosophical foundation of the modern juvenile justice system is based on *parens patriae* and the nineteenth-century child-savers movement. *Parens patriae*—a concept that derives from the ancient English consideration that the Crown is responsible for the well-being of its subjects—is the philosophy that the government has the duty to act as guardian of people who cannot effectively take care of themselves. Although *parens patriae* may be extended to the mentally ill, the intellectually disabled, and the elderly, the government's *parens patriae* authority is most often invoked in connection with juveniles.

The major proponents of *parens patriae* in the early days of the juvenile court were the **child savers**. The child savers were a group of social reformers who sought to change the justice system to provide better treatment for children. To be fair, their assessment of society at the time was not far off the mark. Children still labored in factories and coal mines for low wages; many did not go to school and even fewer went to high school (as of 1900, fewer than 7 percent of 17-year-olds graduated from high school); and youths accused of breaking the law were regularly locked up with adult suspects and offenders [14].

This was also a time of intense social upheaval in the United States with the influx of immigrants from various nations, as well as people from the nation's rural areas. Many of the families who gravitated to large, prosperous cities struggled to overcome impoverishment, unemployment, racism, language differences, and the challenge of raising children in an unfamiliar culture. There is another point of view of this era, however. According to criminologist Anthony Platt, the child-saving movement—and the ensuing juvenile court—was little more than an effort by the wealthy and middle class to enforce their version of order and correct living (see Focus on Discretion).

FOCUS ON DISCRETION

Platt v. The Juvenile Court

The traditional view of the juvenile court is that it revolutionized the justice system's treatment of young offenders. Before the twentieth century, children and adolescents who had broken the law were either turned over to their parents or tried and sentenced in criminal court. In a rural, nonindustrialized nation, this seemed to be enough. However, late nineteenth-century immigration, urbanization, and industrialization caused a panic amongst the middle and upper classes, who despised the chaos, pollution, and unrest. According to sociologist Anthony Platt, the upper classes believed the lower classes of workers, immigrants, and people of color had to be controlled, especially their children, who appeared to run wild in the streets, truant from school and breaking the law at will.

The child savers, according to Platt, were not the progressive heroes who sought to reform a punitive, unfair system for the good of children, but instead were a tool of the wealthy, upper classes who wanted to return order to society. The new classification of "juvenile delinquent" and a punitive, controlling juvenile court free from the restrictions of due process were just the remedy. According to Platt, if the idea of a juvenile court had been truly radical, the wealthy philanthropists of the era would have had little use for it.

In *The child savers: the invention of delinquency*, Platt makes the case that pre-twentieth century courts took pains to consider the immaturity of young lawbreakers during trials. In his study of 14 major cases between 1806 and 1882, 10 children were acquitted; one child went to state prison for 3 years; and

two children, both of them black slaves, were executed. (Platt notes that if those two boys had been white, their lives might have been spared.) The juvenile court, then, was not necessarily an improvement over a criminal court that tried children with full due-process rights. It merely provided a new means of social control by creating a new underclass defined by age. It also served as a means to reinforce middle- and upper-class rural, white, Protestant values.

This is a harsh indictment of the juvenile court, but the twentieth century provides plenty of evidence to support Platt's point. Youths in the juvenile court enjoyed little to no due process until the late 1960s. Although the juvenile justice system flirted with rehabilitative ideals in the 1970s, the 1980s until the present day has seen the justice system continue to crack down on children and adolescents with zero-tolerance policies, incarceration, and sporadic rehabilitative efforts. Juveniles were not exempt from capital punishment until 2005 (*Roper v. Simmons*), and juvenile Miranda rights were not firmly established until 2011 (*JDB. v. North Carolina*). It is unlikely that the juvenile court will experience any sweeping revolutions, but perhaps it can be made to work better for children.

Question

According to Platt, what was the aim of the child savers? What was the true purpose of the juvenile court?

Source: Platt AM, The child savers: the invention of delinquency. Chicago, IL: University of Chicago Press; 1969.

The first model juvenile court statute was passed in Illinois in 1899. The intent was to create a separate court system for youths who had broken the criminal law, as well as institute special programs for neglected and dependent children. The early juvenile court had three themes related to *parens patriae*:

1. Youths must be controlled and supervised.
2. The government must intervene in families that inadequately care for and control their children.
3. All children are dependent. When a youth is delinquent or at risk of delinquency, it is the government's duty to decide what is best for the youth [15].

The Four Eras of the Juvenile Court

Ten years after the institution of the Illinois juvenile court, similar courts were established in 22 states. By 1925, 46 of the 48 states had juvenile courts. The juvenile court of today is not the juvenile court of 1900, however. It has changed quite a bit over the last century with four distinct periods.

1. Refuge Period (1824–1898)
2. Juvenile Court Period (1899–1960)
3. Juvenile Rights Period (1961–1980)
4. Crime Control Period (1981–present) [16]

Let's take a look at each of these periods.

Refuge Period (1824–1898)

The study of crime began in earnest during this period. Scholars and reformers began to look at the causes of crime from a scientific rather than philosophical point of view. Rather than believing that crime was caused by the free will of offenders who chose to break the law (the classical view), some thinkers adopted a positivist view that considered crime as originating from elements outside the human decision-making process, such as environment, peers, family, social class, and the body. It is this positivism that led to the child savers' belief that if a youth's environment could be changed, then that youth could be set on a moral, crime-free course.

The "refuge" of this period is a reference to the efforts to provide, literally, refuges for delinquent and dependent children. Wealthy philanthropists set up houses of refuge in large cities such as New York, Philadelphia, and Boston to provide a safe environment where youths could be trained in a trade. From 1850 to the early 1900s, some children from eastern cities were even sent out west on "orphan trains" to work on farms and ranches. This practice removed impoverished children from the cities, where jobs were scarce, and provided labor to western landowners. Although the ideal situation was that the children would learn useful skills while receiving food, shelter, and an education, many of the adults who took in the orphans used them purely for labor.

Finally, in Chicago, toward the latter part of the nineteenth century, some states began setting up reform schools, which emphasized indeterminate sentencing (sentences that do not have a predetermined duration), moral training, religion, and labor. When these reformatories turned out to be little more than penitentiaries for children, many critics suggested instead "the cottage plan," or home-like cottages in rural areas located near the wholesome soil and away from the temptations of urban life. It was not long until the ideas of separate refuges for children led to the idea of the creation of a separate justice system [17].

Juvenile Court Period (1899–1960)

The creation of the Illinois juvenile court in 1899 marked the beginning of the juvenile court period. It was during this period, perhaps, that juveniles had the fewest rights. Because the stated purpose of the juvenile court was to help and rehabilitate youths, youths were not considered to have, or require, due-process rights. In the criminal court, due-process rights exist, in part, because the defendant is in danger of losing his or her freedom, or at least having it abbreviated with parole or another alternative sentence. However, as the juvenile court saw it, delinquents were sent to reformatories or training schools for their own good, and not for punishment. The youth was not losing freedom, but gaining assistance. That many reformatories were as punitive as adult penitentiaries, and the juveniles sent to them certainly felt punished by the experience was beside the point.

The other benchmark of this period was the blossoming of scholarly research into crime and delinquency. The 1920s "Chicago School" of sociologists— so-called because they were based at the University of Chicago—carried out some of the most sophisticated early efforts to measure and understand delinquency. This positivist research looked for clear patterns in delinquent behavior. As such, the medical model, or the idea that law-breaking represented an "illness" and that a "cure" is possible, dominated the thinking about crime and delinquency. Some scholars believed that if they could only pinpoint the cause of delinquency, then delinquents could be cured of their undesirable and antisocial behavior [18].

Juvenile Rights Period (1961–1980)

Cultural shifts strongly influenced delinquency theory and policy during the juvenile rights period. During the 1960s, civil unrest and legal advances in civil rights put the rights of youths under intense scrutiny. Social and cultural influences on delinquency also gained prominence partly due to initiatives during the presidency of Lyndon Johnson, such as the war on poverty and the Great Society programs that sought to alleviate racial injustice and improve education, job training, and skills training.

This period is also known for the amount and rigor of its court activity. Supreme Court decisions during the 1960s implied that youths deserved the same constitutional protections that adults had, including due-process rights. Such due-process cases, such as *In re Gault,* led to a more adversarial justice process, and the focus of juvenile delinquency shifted away from the causes of delinquency to how the court and corrections system dealt with delinquents. Some scholars asserted that the juvenile justice system was more deeply concerned with ideological views, political dynamics, and social control than with helping delinquent and dependent children [19].

Crime Control Period (1981–present)

The rate of juvenile delinquency began to rise during the mid-1980s (Figure 12.2). The rehabilitative efforts and positivist perspective of the 1960s and 1970s were all but abandoned in favor of a more punitive approach and a return to the classical criminological philosophy that considered lawbreakers, both juvenile and adult, as rational people who chose their actions and were accountable for them. The juvenile court focused more closely on offenses

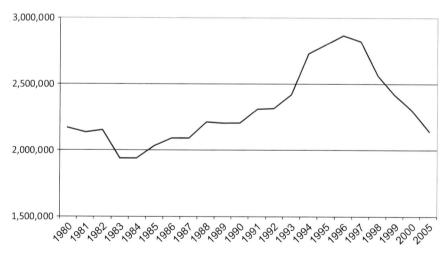

FIGURE 12.2

Number of Youths Arrested Under Age 18, 1980–2005. The arrests of youths under age 18 rose steadily from the mid-1980s to the mid-1990s. Since then arrests have followed a steady downward trend, although the arrest rate didn't return to 1980 levels until 2005. Source: *Bureau of Justice Statistics, Arrest Data Analysis Tool, Arrests by Age in the United Sates, www.bjs.gov/index.cfm? ty = datool&surl = /arrests/index.cfm.*

and imposing sanctions matched to the seriousness of the delinquency. As the justice system continued its crackdown on delinquents, the courts began to waive more youths to criminal court.

This period has also seen the institution of "zero-tolerance policies," in which any infraction of public rules or regulations, such as school rules, are dealt with harshly and without consideration for the youth's age, intent, or the context of the infraction. Zero-tolerance policies have also helped renew the focus on status offending. Today, many status offenses receive dispositions of probation and referrals to prevention and diversion programs [20].

THE MODERN JUVENILE COURT

The modern juvenile court is a specialized court within the criminal court system. Juvenile courts handle only youths, and each state sets its own age requirements for juvenile court. State juvenile courts handled about 1.7 million delinquency cases in 2008 [21].

Only states and local jurisdictions have juvenile courts. The federal government does not prosecute juveniles because it has no true juvenile court or juvenile correctional system. The structure and title of juvenile courts varies by state and even by jurisdiction. Some states place most of their delinquency services at the state level, whereas others distribute their services among the state and local levels. These courts may be called "juvenile courts," but some jurisdictions refer to them as "family courts" or "magistrate courts." Some states use a juvenile court for serious delinquency and a limited-jurisdiction juvenile court for minor delinquency. Cases involving status offenses, dependency, and neglect may go to probate court. In populous jurisdictions, the juvenile court is part of a juvenile justice system that works with other youth agencies. In other areas, the juvenile court is a specialized court that operates in a courthouse with other courts.

Although the federal government has no juvenile court, it specifies some of the rules and laws that apply to juvenile courts. The federal government becomes involved in juvenile cases only if "substantial federal interest" is met; the state has no jurisdiction or refuses jurisdiction; the state with jurisdiction does not have adequate juvenile programs or services; or the offense is a violent felony, drug trafficking or importation offense, or firearm offense. If the juvenile must be incarcerated, the government will send the youth to a state juvenile correctional facility [22]. Before we move on to the juvenile court process, let's first address one of the key idiosyncrasies of the juvenile justice system: the status offense.

The Status Offense

As mentioned earlier, a status offense is the breaking of a law that only applies to juveniles. Running away, drinking alcohol, using tobacco, curfew violations, and being truant from school are all examples of status offenses. The status-offender category was invented in 1961 to separate juvenile delinquents, or those who had committed offenses that would be considered criminal offenses for adults, from juveniles who had broken laws that apply only to youths. Another intent of status-offender laws was to minimize the stigmatization of status offenders by distinguishing them from delinquents. California was the first state to create the status-offender category, but other states soon followed [23].

Status-offense laws also protect youths from behaviors that society believes are especially harmful to them. For example, although many adults use alcohol too much, youths are considered to be especially prone to using alcohol irresponsibly, such as binge-drinking, driving under the influence, and drinking until blackout. Too much alcohol is also thought to damage the juvenile brain [24]. Along with liquor-law violations, the Federal Bureau of Investigation Uniform Crime Reporting Program collects data on runaways and curfew violations.

The juvenile court receives more delinquents than status offenders. In 2008, juvenile courts handled about 1,653,300 delinquency cases as opposed to 156,300 status-offense cases [25]. However, in keeping with the trend of more punitive treatment of juveniles, the juvenile court increased its handling of status offenders 34 percent between 1995 and 2008. As of 2008, the most common status offense sent to the juvenile court was truancy [26]. Status-offense cases can be referred to the court by law enforcement agencies, schools, relatives, social service agencies, probation officers, and victims [27].

The JJDPA generally prohibits the use of secure detention or confinement for status offenders, so a common practice is for states to divert status offenders from the juvenile justice system and place them in rehabilitative service- and community-based programs. In many jurisdictions, a variety of agencies, such as family-crisis units, county attorneys, and social service agencies, take status-offense cases [28]. The most common status offense to receive detention in 2008 was liquor-law violations [29] (Photo 12.1).

Status offenses tend to increase with age, and the type of status offense committed generally depends on age. For example, curfew and liquor-law

PHOTO 12.1
The State of Georgia is at risk of losing $2 million in federal funds for violating the JJDPA with the repeated detention of status offenders.

violations increase steadily until age 17, whereas cases involving running away, truancy, and ungovernability drop off after peaking at age 15 [30]. The youth's sex is also a factor: in 2008, males accounted for 58 percent of total petitioned status-offense cases. However, females accounted for 59 percent of runaway cases, the only category in which females represented a larger proportion of cases [31]. In 2008, most of the status-offense cases referred to the juvenile court resulted in the youth being **adjudicated** a status offender and given probation (Figure 12.3). It is interesting, however, to note that of the 41 percent of youths not adjudicated a status offender, the cases of most were dismissed [32].

A common idea today is that breaking the law, any law, as a youth serves as a "gateway" to serious delinquency and adult offending. However, although many status offenders are also serious delinquents, there appears to be little hard evidence that status offending is a sure path to adult criminality. It is true that many serious delinquents are adjudicated of or self-report status offending. However, this is a chicken-and-egg issue: did those youths' status offending lead step-by-step to serious delinquency, or were they

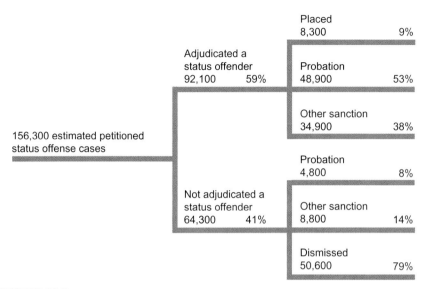

FIGURE 12.3
Status Offenders. Source: *Data from [25].*

delinquent-prone to begin with and committed status offenses in the course of general delinquent behavior? A 16-year-old who has no compunction about robbing a liquor store probably does not give a second thought to smoking a cigarette.

One thing we know for sure about most delinquents—both status offenders and serious delinquents—is that they outgrow delinquency. As they grow older, they commit less delinquency and crime which continues to taper off throughout adulthood (Figure 12.4). Also, the **dark figure of crime** (or delinquency, in this case)—the idea that the actual amount of crime and delinquency cannot be known because some offenses are not counted in the official crime statistics and may even occur without anyone's knowledge—must be considered. Many serious delinquents, and likely many more status offenders, are never caught. Almost any adult who is honest will remember parties they attended as teens in which most of the teenagers there drank alcohol and smoked cigarettes, or even marijuana. All of those teenagers were status offenders, and chances are, most never set foot in a courtroom. It is just as likely that practically none of those teens went on to become adult criminals. They drank alcohol and smoked to test boundaries and look like adults, then grew up and went on with their lives. So the idea that status offenses are necessarily a gateway to criminality is questionable simply because we cannot know the true amount of status offending.

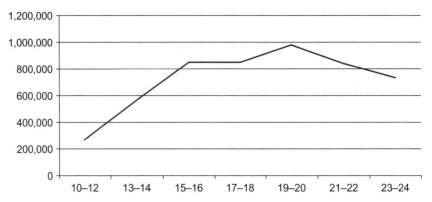

FIGURE 12.4

Peak Arrest Age. Arrests peak during young adulthood, then drop throughout adulthood. Source: *Federal Bureau of Investigation, Uniform Crime Reports: Crime in the United States, Table 38: Arrests by Age, 2010, www.fbi.gov/about-us/cjis/ucr/crime-in-the-u.s/2010/crime-in-the-u.s.-2010/tables/10tbl38.xls.*

The Juvenile Court Process

The criminal court is adversarial: the prosecutor tries to prove the defendant guilty, and the defense attorney tries to introduce reasonable doubt into the prosecution's case. Because the juvenile court is not adversarial, it follows a slightly different course than the criminal court. In the criminal court, most cases are plea bargained and do not go to trial. Regardless of the proceedings, the focus of the trial is not the defendant's rehabilitation but whether the defendant has broken the law. The juvenile court, on the other hand, is concerned with the youth's rehabilitation, and any outcome is supposed to be for the youth's good.

The first item we must address before moving on to the process itself is the terminology of the juvenile court. In order to avoid **labeling** juveniles as "criminal,"—that is, applying a tag that may affect the juvenile's self-perception and behavior—a different set of terms and definitions applies to the treatment of their cases. Although the less severe terms of the juvenile court are used to limit the negative connotations of the proceedings, each action in the juvenile court has an analog in the criminal court (Table 12.1).

Jurisdiction

Juvenile courts have two areas of jurisdiction: age and subject matter. In the case of juvenile courts, these two jurisdictions are quite similar. Let's look at age jurisdiction first.

Juvenile courts have upper age limits and, depending on the state, lower age limits. For example, juvenile courts in the state of Colorado have an upper

Table 12.1 Terminology in the Criminal Court and Juvenile Court

Criminal Court	Juvenile Court
An adult is arrested.	A juvenile is taken into custody.
An adult is charged or indicted.	A juvenile is petitioned.
An adult stands trial.	A juvenile attends a hearing.
An adult is convicted of a crime.	A juvenile is adjudicated delinquent.
An adult is sentenced.	A juvenile receives a disposition.
A convicted adult is an offender.	A juvenile adjudicated of delinquency is a juvenile delinquent.

age limit of 17—meaning that a suspect age 18 or older is sent to criminal court—and a lower age of 10, meaning that the state only has jurisdiction on youths between those ages [33]. Some states have no lower age limits and young children may face juvenile or criminal charges. The state of Kentucky, for example, has no lower age limit. In recent years, a 5-year-old child was charged with abuse of a teacher, and a 7-year-old child was charged with criminal assault [34].

The other jurisdiction is subject-matter jurisdiction. This is the court's jurisdiction over a specific subject matter: in this case, juvenile delinquents and status offenders. So, in most instances, the case of a 14-year-old who commits arson would be sent to a juvenile court because the child's delinquency places the case within the juvenile court's subject-matter jurisdiction. The same would go for a youth caught consuming alcohol because of the status offense.

Custody and Detention

The juvenile court process begins when the police take a juvenile into custody (the most common type of referral), or an authority, such as a parent or teacher, refers the child to the court. Custody is not necessarily arrest. The juvenile may be suspected of committing delinquency, a status offense, or simply be neglected, abused, or dependent, in which case the youth is under the state's control for his or her own protection. In this and the following sections, our discussion of the court process will focus on the handling of suspected delinquents and status offenders.

Depending on the activities the youth is suspected of, the police or other juvenile authority may place the youth in detention. Detention practices vary amongst jurisdictions, and the court may place a youth in a detention facility at different points as a case progresses through the juvenile justice system. Federal regulations discourage holding youths in adult jails and detention areas. If a youth must be held in secure custody for a short time, regulations require that the youth be detained for no longer than six hours and out of sight or sound of adult inmates [35].

Intake

After referral, an intake department—typically within the juvenile probation department or the prosecutor's office—screens the cases. The intake department may dismiss the case because the evidence is not sufficient, decide to handle the case informally (diversion), or decide to handle the case formally with a petition to the court.

The likelihood of formal processing increased between 1985 and 2008, when juvenile courts petitioned 56 percent of all delinquency cases [36]. In 2008, 18 percent of delinquency cases were dismissed at intake, and 25 percent were handled informally [37]. Informal cases may be referred to a social service agency, receive informal probation, or be ordered to pay fines or voluntary restitution. Petitioned cases are sent to court for a hearing. The intake department may also decide that a case should be handled in criminal court instead of juvenile court.

Diversion

Youths diverted from the juvenile court rarely escape the system completely. Most of the time, they are referred to a community agency or treatment program, given probation, or both. The reason for diversion, which is reserved for minor delinquency and status offenses, is to prevent **recidivism** and avoid labeling while still holding youths accountable for their actions. Diversion is also a more economical alternative to juvenile court processing and official sanctions. During the current Crime Control period, alternative programs have focused more on work programs, skills-training programs, and providing restitution. Some states and jurisdictions provide family therapy and parent support programs.

A popular form of diversion is the teen or youth court. In these programs, youths sentence other youths for minor delinquency and status offenses. As of 2012, more than 1400 youth-court diversion programs were in operation. Typical youth-court clients are first-time offenders between the ages of 11 and 17 who have been charged with misdemeanor or status offenses such as theft, vandalism, disorderly conduct, assault, and marijuana possession. Youth courts may also be used to handle school disciplinary issues, as well as cases of drinking alcohol and possessing tobacco.

A criticism of diversion programs is that they maintain social control of youths who, in the past, simply would have been released into the community under the supervision of their parents or guardians. Because the youth is still involved in the system, critics argue that any efforts at de-stigmatization or preventing recidivism are wasted.

Petitioning and Adjudication

For cases that are to be handled formally, a petition is filed with the juvenile court, and the case is placed on the court docket for an adjudicatory hearing. Adjudicatory hearings establish responsibility for a delinquent act. Adjudicating a juvenile as delinquent is like convicting an adult in criminal court, and hearings are like criminal trials. One of the differences is that there is no jury, and the judge decides the issue of whether the juvenile is responsible for the delinquent act or status offense. In 2008, juveniles were adjudicated delinquent in 61 percent of petitioned cases.

A few petitions are usually dismissed before the hearing, and more—just over 25 percent in 2008, for example—are dismissed after the hearing. In cases of dismissal after the hearing, the court may recommend that the youth do something prior to the final adjudication decision, such as pay restitution or attend drug counseling.

In adjudicatory hearings, the issue of guilt or innocence is not as important as it is in the criminal court. For example, a youth may not have committed the delinquent act in question, but if a judge decides the youth is in danger of becoming delinquent, he or she may still receive a disposition that includes probation, further detention, attending a rehabilitative program, or some combination of these. In deciding what is in the juvenile's best interests, the judge will apply one of two standards of proof:

1. Status-offense cases. The judge will look for a preponderance of evidence, a low standard that allows the judge to determine if the youth probably committed the offense or just needs supervision.
2. Delinquency cases. The standard of proof is beyond a reasonable doubt in delinquency cases. This standard ensures that there is convincing evidence that the youth committed the action. The youth may admit or deny the charges, and the youth's lawyer (if she or he has one) may plea bargain for a reduced disposition [38].

Disposition

If the juvenile is adjudicated delinquent, the judge orders a predispositional report—a report with information about the youth, the youth's legal and personal history, and sometimes a dispositional recommendation—prepared by the probation officer to help the judge create a disposition. The court will then hold a disposition hearing to decide what action is best for the juvenile. An interesting note on this practice is that at this, and at other points during the process, judges will often disregard the predispositional report and decide what to do with youths based on their own intuition about whether the youth is likely to recidivate and whether he or she would be amenable to treatment [39].

Many cases result in complex dispositions, most involving probation supervision. In 2008, formal probation was the most severe disposition ordered in 57 percent of the cases in which the juvenile was adjudicated delinquent. Of the rest of the cases adjudicated delinquent, 28 percent were ordered to residential placement and 15 percent received some other disposition [40].

Options other than probation typically include commitment to an institution; placement in a group home or residential facility; foster home placement; referral to an outside agency, treatment, or mental health program; or imposition of a fine, community service, or restitution. The court monitors the youth's progress with review hearings and may modify the dispositions. The likelihood of a harsh disposition or one that removes the youth from the home is affected by several factors, including detention before adjudication. Youths detained prior to adjudication were more likely to be petitioned, less likely to have petitions dismissed, and more likely to be removed from the home at disposition [41].

Waiver to Criminal Court

Most states have provisions to waive certain juvenile cases to criminal court so the youth can be tried as an adult. In 2008, 1 percent of delinquency cases were waived to criminal court. Half were person offenses; 29 percent were property offenses; 12 percent were drug offenses; and 10 percent were public order offenses [42]. Most cases involved males aged 16 or older [43]. Transferred juveniles, particularly those convicted of violent offenses, usually receive longer sentences than youths sentenced in juvenile court for similar offenses. However, many transferred juveniles serve time in adult facilities for no longer than they would have served in juvenile facilities, with 78 percent being released before turning 21 [44].

Depending on the state, delinquency cases may be waived to criminal court in three ways. The first, **concurrent jurisdiction** (sometimes called "direct filing"), allows prosecutors the discretion to file cases in either juvenile or criminal court. The legislature makes concurrent jurisdiction laws, and the decision about where to file the case is up to the prosecutor and out of the purview of the juvenile court. The second method of waiver, **statutory exclusion**, requires certain delinquency cases—usually those that are particularly heinous, such as murder—to be waived automatically.

Finally, **judicial waiver** laws either authorize or require juvenile court judges to waive certain types of cases. The three categories of judicial waiver are discretionary, presumptive, and mandatory.

- The discretionary waiver provisions of 45 states give juvenile court judges the discretion to waive jurisdiction over individual cases.
- Fifteen states allow presumptive waiver, which defines a category of acts that *should* be sent to criminal court. Therefore, if a juvenile who meets the age, offense, or other legal criteria does not present a convincing argument against waiver, the juvenile court must send the case to criminal court.
- Fifteen states have mandatory waiver laws in which the juvenile court's only duty is to confirm that the statutory requirements for mandatory waiver are met—such as age or type of offense—before the case is sent to criminal court.

Due Process and the Court

Until the 1960s, rehabilitation was the driving force of the juvenile court. Juveniles were not considered to require the due-process protections of the criminal court because the court was acting for the benefit of the youth. Why would children need to be protected from something that was good for them and aimed at improving their lives? In the late 1960s, however, the Supreme Court heard three cases that would challenge these ideas: *Kent v. United States* (1966), *In re Gault* (1967), and *In re Winship* (1970) (see Landmark Due Process Cases for details on these cases).

LANDMARK CASES

Kent v. United States (1966)

The Supreme Court ruled that waiving a juvenile case to criminal court without a formal hearing violates the juvenile's due-process rights.

In 1961, in the District of Columbia, 16-year-old Morris Kent was charged with entering a woman's apartment, then robbing and raping her. Kent had been adjudicated delinquent in 1959 after a series of housebreakings and attempted purse-snatchings. Kent admitted to the robbery and rape, and the juvenile court judge waived Kent to criminal court. The case went to the U.S. district court for the District of Columbia where Kent was convicted of several counts of housebreaking and robbery, but not the rape "by reason of insanity."

The Supreme Court reversed Kent's conviction, objecting to the way juvenile cases were waived to criminal court and the broad discretion of judges. The Court held that a hearing must be held for a juvenile case to be waived to criminal court, with the youth having access to counsel. Also, the youth and/or their attorney must have access to the youth's records on which the waiver decision is based, and the judge must state the reasons for waiver in writing. The Court ruled that Kent's right to due process was denied when he was not allowed a formal hearing on the waiver.

In re Gault (1967)

The Supreme Court held that juvenile proceedings had to comply with the Fourteenth Amendment. The requirements include adequate notice of charges, notification to both the parents and the youth of the youth's right to counsel, the opportunity to confront and cross-examine witnesses at the hearings, and safeguards against self-incrimination.

On June 8, 1964, Gerald Gault, aged 15, was accused of making an obscene telephone call to a female neighbor. At the time, Gault was on probation for 6 months because he had been in the company of another boy who had stolen a wallet. Gault was taken into custody without the knowledge of his parents, who were both at work, and taken to a youth detention home.

On June 9, Gerald, his mother, his older brother, and two probation officers appeared before the juvenile judge in chambers. The female neighbor who made the complaint was not there, and no one was sworn at the hearing. The judge questioned Gault about the telephone call. Gault was then returned to detention and held until June 11 or 12, then released to his parents. After a second hearing on June 15, the probation officers filed "referral report" with the court, unknown to Gerald or his parents. At the hearing, the judge committed Gault as a juvenile delinquent to the State Industrial School until age 21.

Gault was never advised of his rights, never allowed to cross-examine his accuser, who was never present, and never allowed to testify in his own behalf. No appeal was permitted in juvenile cases in Arizona at that time. In 1967, the Supreme Court reversed the decision on appeal and established that juveniles have a right to an attorney, as well the right to confront accusers, and protection from self-incrimination.

In re Winship (1970)

A case against a juvenile must be proven beyond a reasonable doubt if the juvenile is charged with an offense that would be considered a criminal offense for an adult.

In 1967 in New York City, 12-year-old Samuel Winship was accused of breaking into a locker and stealing $112 from a woman's purse. He was charged as a juvenile delinquent because, according to the New York Family Court Act, if the theft had been committed by an adult, it would have constituted larceny. The act defined a juvenile delinquent as "a person over 7 and less than 16 years of age who does any act, which if done by an adult, would constitute a crime." The act also specified that determinations of youth's guilt be based on a preponderance of the evidence. A family court found Winship guilty but acknowledged that the evidence did not establish his guilt beyond a reasonable doubt. The judge rejected Winship's contention that the Fourteenth Amendment required such proof.

Winship was adjudicated a juvenile delinquent and ordered to a training school for at least 18 months up to a maximum of 6 years, until he reached his eighteenth birthday. The Supreme Court reversed the ruling as the reasonable-doubt standard had not been considered in a case in which the defendant was subject to loss of freedom.

In re Gault is considered to be the most pivotal case. Prior to 1967, juvenile and criminal courts were considered to be vastly different: the criminal court was adversarial, and the juvenile court was not. Up to this point, youths had no say in what the juvenile court prescribed. In theory, at least, *Gault* provided juveniles some minimum due-process protections (see Court Procedures for another view). In his dissent to *Gault*, Justice John Harlan argued that allowing juveniles due process would make the court more adversarial and jeopardize the juvenile court's rehabilitative mission. However, the *Gault* decision states that due-process protections and rehabilitative aims do not necessarily conflict. The *Gault* decision did suggest that juvenile and criminal courts were actually more alike than the juvenile court's founders intended; that is, the juvenile court was more punitive than anyone was willing to admit. In short, although the adults in a juvenile court could justify that sending a boy to a reformatory was for his own good, to the boy, it just felt like incarceration.

COURT PROCEDURES

The Worst of Both Worlds

When the Supreme Court decided in *In re Gault* (1967), many juvenile court observers hailed it as a landmark decision that would reform the court. Instead, over the next 40 years the juvenile justice system became increasingly punitive, and possibly even less observant of juvenile rights than before *Gault* (several states had begun reforming their juvenile courts prior to 1967) [45]. In his dissent to *Gault*, Justice Harlan argued that allowing due process in the juvenile court would only make it more like criminal court and interfere with the juvenile court's rehabilitative focus. In a way, he was right. What happened?

A 1969 study found that many state and local courts were not complying with *Gault* [46]. Many judges thought the case was not binding as long as the disposition did not call for the youth's incarceration. Some judges were unfamiliar with the specifics of the case. Finally, some local officials would not observe Supreme Court rulings because they did not consider the Court as being able to enforce them. The result was that the juvenile court became more punitive and more like criminal court while leaving behind the due-process requirements of both *Gault* and the criminal court [47].

Part of the problem was that no one was willing or able to make the necessary changes. No institution external to juvenile courts sought to enforce *Gault*, and inside the courts, juvenile defense attorneys often neglected their adversarial role to act as mediators [48]. Judges, still committed to the rehabilitative ideal, were concerned with protecting their powers of discretion [49]. Meanwhile, individuals outside the court were in no position to demand compliance as juvenile court hearings are typically closed to the public [50].

Increasing rates of delinquency, as well as the commission of some heinous acts by youths, did not help matters. During the early 1990s, some scholars anticipated the rise of "superpredators," a particularly vicious species of juvenile delinquent. In 1994, critics of rehabilitation howled when Jesse Rankins, aged 10, and Tykeece Johnson, aged 11, who dropped a 5-year-old boy out of a high-rise window, were not tried as adults for the murder [51]. This incident, and others like them, led to the expansion of juvenile waiver laws despite the fact that superpredators never materialized.

Although youths tried as adults receive the criminal court's full due-process rights, they are still at a disadvantage. Several studies have shown that youths tried as adults receive little or no rehabilitation or treatment [52]. Even in juvenile court, youths represented by attorneys receive tougher dispositions than youths with no representation, and there is evidence that juvenile justice system involvement increases recidivism as well as the chances that youths will grow up to become adult offenders [53].

Questions

Why did the juvenile justice system become more punitive?

Why did the *Gault* decision fail to reform the juvenile court in the best interests of youths?

Prior to Gault, *Kent v. United States* addressed waiver to criminal court. Although waiver laws gained prominence in the late 1980s and 1990s, when so many of them were written or expanded, youths have always been subject to transfer to criminal court under specific conditions [54]. Prior to *Kent*, the juvenile court could waive jurisdiction without stating a reason. The *Kent* decision established that juveniles facing waiver in the juvenile court are entitled to representation by counsel, access to social services records, and a written statement of the reasons for waiver.

It is important to understand that *Kent* does not apply to concurrent jurisdiction or statutory exclusion. To get a waiver hearing, the case must already be filed in juvenile court. In states with concurrent jurisdiction and other types of automatic transfer laws, the case is transferred *before* it gets to juvenile court, thus circumventing the *Kent* hearing requirement. The reasoning is that at least in criminal court, the juvenile will receive full due-process rights, as well as any advantages of the adversarial system.

Critics point out that the stated purpose of the juvenile system is rehabilitation, and that although youths do not receive full due process in the juvenile system, the disposition will be rehabilitative. Sentencing in criminal court is punitive. This recalls Justice Harlan's objection in *Gault* that full due process in the juvenile court is at odds with that court's rehabilitative mission and belongs solely in an adversarial court. That is, if due process, and not rehabilitation, is the key concern, then why have separate courts? Why not just do away with the juvenile court, allow juveniles full due-process rights, and send all juvenile cases to criminal court? One answer to this is that automatic waiver is typically reserved for the most heinous offenses and the most intractable young recidivists. It is for juveniles whom the court believes are not amenable to rehabilitation; thus, by going to criminal court, they will at least have due process.

After *Gault*, the Supreme Court addressed standards of proof in *In re Winship*. In *Winship*, the court extended to juveniles the same protections that adults have in criminal court in that every element of a delinquency case must be proven beyond a reasonable doubt. It was also the first time the Court explicitly noted the reasonable-doubt standard as a requirement of due process for all defendants [55]. The Court did this for three broad reasons:

1. Through the reasonable-doubt standard, juries are reminded that the defendant, whether juvenile or adult, must be convicted of a criminal offense, not just being a bad person.
2. The jury is reminded of the social consequences of convicting an innocent person. The problems may be that much more acute in the case of a juvenile conviction if a lighter standard of proof is used. Society may be even more harmed by incarcerating youths for offenses they did not commit than by incarcerating adults under the same circumstances.
3. The reasonable-doubt standard compensates defendants for the state's power. Again, this issue may be that much more acute for juveniles, who are not only at the mercy of a powerful state, but of every adult and institution in their lives [56].

The Juvenile Justice and Delinquency Prevention Act

The Juvenile Justice and Delinquency Prevention Act (JJDPA) addresses the treatment and institutionalization of status offenders and juvenile delinquents. Congress reauthorized the current version of the JJDPA in 2002. The first JJDPA was passed in 1974 in response to a growing concern that the juvenile court's status-offense system often failed to act in the best interests of youths. Central to the JJDPA is the deinstitutionalization of status offenders, who were increasingly being incarcerated with delinquent youths. The JJDPA asked states to develop programs and alternative sentences for status offenders and to end the practice of sending them to secure detention facilities [57].

Today, the JJDPA offers federal funding to states that adopt its four mandates:

1. deinstitutionalize status offenders;
2. remove juveniles from adult jails and lockups;
3. separate juvenile inmates from sight and sound of adult inmates;
4. assess and address disproportionate minority contact at various points within the juvenile justice system.

States that do not comply with these requirements must implement a corrective plan or have their funding cut. For each core requirement the state fails, the state's federal funding is reduced by 25 percent [58]. In 1980, the act was amended to allow the secure detention of status offenders "who are charged with or who have committed a violation of a valid court order" [59].

Net-Widening

Net-widening in the context of the juvenile justice system refers to activities by the system to increase the numbers of youths involved in the system and to increase the involvement of those already in the system. Although this sounds like an odd goal for an overburdened, publicly funded institution, there are at least two reasons that some people would like to see more youths become involved in the juvenile justice system.

The first reason is related to the philosophy that drawing more youths into the juvenile justice system, even for minor acts, deters them from more serious delinquency and leads to less crime in the community [60]. This is sort of an extension of the **broken-windows** idea that legal consequences for every infraction of the law, no matter how minor, prevents more serious crime. For example, a youth who is arrested and processed through the juvenile justice system for spray-painting graffiti on the school sidewalk may be at risk for more serious delinquency later, such as burglary. This philosophy is also aimed at specific deterrence or discouraging the individual who is being punished from breaking the law again. Exposing the youth to treatment and counseling now and showing him that his actions have consequences may make him think twice about getting into trouble again. The criticism of this idea is that it leads to harmful labeling and shaming and actually causes more delinquency and crime through recidivism than it prevents.

The second reason for net-widening is that some youth diversion programs draw more youths into the system in order to continue their own existence and provide jobs for those who work in the program. Most diversion programs are funded by state and federal grants, so in applying and reapplying for grants, the program must make the case that it is actually processing delinquents and at-risk youths through the program. A program with few or no clients will not be awarded grant money. Therefore, youths who are guilty of little more than age-appropriate, mischievous behavior are gathered into the program via ever-widening legal nets.

This is a cynical view of youth diversion programs, but a couple of studies have found that such net-widening activities do occur. Although the programs in the studies processed a lot of youths, their offenses were minor and better explained by immature behavior that was likely to evaporate with maturity than any deep, criminal tendencies that needed to be nipped in the bud. The studies also found that the programs did not target youths who had committed more serious delinquencies, such as burglary, motor vehicle theft, theft of more than $100, arson, and drug trafficking. Some diversion programs, then, only processed the "easy" cases—cases that would probably be best excluded from the system entirely and instead handled by parents or teachers—and left the more difficult ones for other arms of the juvenile justice system [61].

SUMMARY

1. Understand the relationship between youths and *mens rea*.
    - One of the assumptions about youths concerns cognitive development and their understanding of right and wrong. Adults and older youths are considered to be capable of *mens rea*. Young children are not. To establish *mens rea*, the common law typically uses the knowing-right-from-wrong standard.
2. Tell why youths are considered to be more amenable to rehabilitation than adults.
    - Most adults believe that teenagers and children are still growing and that any delinquent or criminal tendencies are not set. One important issue affecting the susceptibility of a youth to rehabilitation is mental health and learning abilities.

3. Discuss the reasons that the juvenile court hands down dispositions rather than punishment.
   - The juvenile court hands down dispositions rather than punishments because of its rehabilitative focus. Youths found to be responsible for a status offense or delinquency are supposed to receive a disposition aimed at rehabilitation.

4. Describe the role of the child savers and *parens patriae* in the forming of the juvenile court.
   - The philosophical foundation of the modern juvenile justice system is based on *parens patriae* and the nineteenth-century child-savers movement. *Parens patriae* is the philosophy that the government must act as guardian of people who cannot effectively take care of themselves.
   - The major proponents of *parens patriae* during the early juvenile court were the child savers. The child savers were a group of late nineteenth-century social reformers who sought to change the justice system to provide better treatment for children.

5. List and discuss the four eras of the juvenile court.
   - During the Refuge Period (1824–1898), scholars and reformers began to look at the causes of crime from a scientific point of view. During the Juvenile Court Period (1899–1960), the Illinois juvenile court was created and scholarly research into crime and delinquency began. During the Juvenile Rights Period (1961–1980), cultural shifts influenced delinquency theory and policy. This period is also known for the amount and rigor of its court activity. During the Crime Control Period (1981–present), the rate of juvenile delinquency began to rise, and the juvenile court focused more closely on offenses and imposing sanctions matched to the seriousness of the delinquency.

6. Briefly explain how the modern juvenile court works.
   - The modern juvenile court is a specialized court within the criminal court system. Each state sets its own age requirements for juvenile court. Only states and local jurisdictions have juvenile courts. The federal government has no true juvenile court or juvenile correctional system.

7. Differentiate juvenile delinquency from status offending.
   - A status offense is the breaking of a law that only applies to youths. Juvenile delinquency is the commission of an offense that would be considered criminal for an adult.

8. Discuss the history and current role of due process in the juvenile court.
   - Three cases redefined due process in the juvenile court. In *Kent v. United States*, the Supreme Court ruled that waiving a juvenile case to criminal court without a formal hearing violates the youth's due-process rights. In *In re Gault*, the Supreme Court held

that juvenile proceedings had to comply with the Fourteenth Amendment, including adequate notice of charges, notification of the youth's right to counsel, the opportunity to confront and cross-examine witnesses at the hearings, and safeguards against self-incrimination. *In re Winship* set forth that a case against a youth must be proven beyond a reasonable doubt if the youth is charged with an offense that would be considered criminal for an adult.

9. Criticize and then defend the concept of net-widening.
   - One reason for net-widening is related to the philosophy that drawing more youths into the juvenile justice system deters them from more serious delinquency. The second reason is that some youth diversion programs draw more youths into the system in order to continue their own existence.

Questions

1. How do children form *mens rea*? Adolescents?
2. Why are youths considered to be more amenable to rehabilitation than adults?
3. Why does the juvenile court use dispositions rather than punishments?
4. What is *parens patriae*?
5. What are the four eras of the juvenile court?
6. How does the modern juvenile court work?
7. What is a status offense?
8. What is the role of due process in the juvenile court?
9. What is net-widening?

REFERENCES

[1] Jennings JC. Juvenile justice, Sullivan and Graham: how the supreme court's decision will change the neuroscience debate. Duke Law Technol Rev no.6, May 18 2010, p. 1–10: Dobbs D. Beautiful brains. Natl Geogr October 2011. p. 37–59.

[2] Myers DL. Boys among men: trying and sentencing juveniles as adults. Westport, CT: Praeger; 2005. p. 34.

[3] Feld BC. Abolish the juvenile court: youthfulness, criminal responsibility, and sentencing policy. J Crim Law Criminol 1997;88(1):68–136.

[4] Franke TM, Abrams LS, Terry D. Community-based juvenile reentry services: the effects of service dosage on juvenile and adult recidivism. J Offender Rehabil 2011;50(8):492–510.

[5] Thomas A, Loughran, et al. Estimating a dose–response relationship between length of stay and future recidivism in serious juvenile offenders. Criminology 2009;47(3):699–740.

[6] Fagan J. The contradictions of juvenile crime & punishment. Daedalus 2010;139(3):43–61.

[7] Cruise KR, Evans LJ, Pickens IB. Integrating mental health and special education needs into comprehensive service planning for juvenile offenders in long-term custody settings. Learn Individ Differ 2011;21(1):30–40.

[8] Ramchand R, Morral AR, Becker K. Seven-year life outcomes of adolescent offenders in Los Angeles. Am J Public Health 2009;99(5):863–70.

[9] Piquero AR, et al. Never too late. Punishment Soc 2010;12(2):187–207.

[10] Myers DL. Boys among men: trying and sentencing juveniles as adults. Westport, CT: Praeger; 2005. p. 33.

[11] Adams B, Addie S. Delinquency cases waived to criminal court, 2008. Washington, DC: U.S. Department of Justice Office of Justice Programs Office of Juvenile Justice and Delinquency Prevention; 2011: Online at <www.ojjdp.gov/pubs/236481.pdf>.

[12] Myers. Boys among men: trying and sentencing juveniles as adults [Chapter 2].

[13] Platt AM. The child savers: the invention of delinquency. Chicago, IL: University of Chicago Press; 1973. p. 101–102.

[14] Youth: transition to adulthood, report of the panel on youth of the president's science advisory committee. Washington DC: Government Printing Office; 1973.

[15] Platt AM. The child savers: the invention of delinquency. Chicago, IL: University of Chicago Press; 1973. p. 134. Zimring FE. American juvenile justice. New York, NY: Oxford University Press; 2005. p. 6.

[16] Harris PW, Welsh WN, Butler F. A century of juvenile justice. In: LaFree G, editor. The nature of crime: continuity and change, vol. 1 of criminal justice 2000. Rockville, MD: National Institute of Justice/NCJRS; 2000. p. 366: Online at <www.ncjrs.gov/criminal_justice2000/vol_1/02h.pdf>.

[17] Platt. The child savers: the invention of delinquency [Chapter 3].

[18] Butler HW. A century of juvenile justice.

[19] Ibid.

[20] Ibid.

[21] These are the most recent statistics available. Knoll C, Sickmund M. Delinquency cases in juvenile court, 2008. Washington, DC: U.S. Department of Justice Office of Justice Programs Office of Juvenile Justice and Delinquency Prevention; 2011: Online at <www.ojjdp.gov/pubs/236479.pdf>.

[22] Fuller JR. Juvenile delinquency: mainstream and crosscurrents. 2nd ed. New York, NY: Oxford University Press; 2013. p. 422–25.

[23] Shubik C, Kendall J. Rethinking juvenile status offense laws: considerations for congressional review of the Juvenile Justice and Delinquency Prevention Act. Family Court Rev 2007;45(3):384–98.

[24] Giovannini M, et al. Effect of alcohol consumption in prenatal life, childhood, and adolescence on child development. Nutr Rev 2011;69(11):642–59. Tapert SF, et al. Adolescent binge drinking linked to abnormal spatial working memory brain activation: differential gender effects. Alcohol Clin Exp Res 2011;35(10):1831–41.

[25] Puzzanchera C, Adams B, Sickmund M. Juvenile court statistics 2008. Pittsburgh, PA: National Center for Juvenile Justice; 2011: Online at <www.ncjj.org/pdf/jcsreports/jcs2008.pdf>.

[26] Ibid.

[27] Ibid.

[28] Ibid.

[29] Ibid.

[30] Ibid.

[31] Ibid.

[32] Ibid.

[33] National center for juvenile justice, <www.ncjj.org/State/Colorado.aspx> [accessed December, 2012].

[34] Spears VH. Kentucky kids age 10 and younger routinely face criminal charges, <Kentucky.com>, <www.kentucky.com/2011/08/14/1845047/kentucky-kids-age-10-and-younger.html> [accessed August 24, 2011].

[35] Snyder HN, Sickmund M. Juvenile offenders and victims: 2006 national report. Washington, DC: U.S. Department of Justice, Office of Justice Programs, Office of Juvenile Justice and Delinquency Prevention; 2006: Online at <www.ojjdp.ncjrs.org/ojstatbb/nr2006/downloads/NR2006.pdf>.

[36] Puzzanchera A, Sickmund. Juvenile court statistics 2008. p. 36–7.

[37] Knoll, Sickmund. Delinquency cases in juvenile court 2008. p. 3.

[38] Fuller. Juvenile delinquency: mainstream and crosscurrents [Chapter 13].

[39] Mulvey EP, Iselin A-MR. Improving professional judgments of risk and amenability in juvenile justice. Future Child 2008;18(2):35–57.

[40] Knoll, Sickmund. Delinquency cases in juvenile court 2008. p. 3.

[41] Rodriguez N. The cumulative effect of race and ethnicity in juvenile court outcomes and why preadjudication detention matters. J Res Crime Delinq 2010;47(3):391–413.

[42] Knoll, Sickmund. Delinquency cases in juvenile court 2008. p. 3.

[43] Adams B, Addie S. Delinquency cases waived to criminal court, 2008. Washington, DC: U.S. Department of Justice Office of Justice Programs Office of Juvenile Justice and Delinquency Prevention; 2011: Online at <www.ojjdp.gov/pubs/236481.pdf>.

[44] Redding RE. Juvenile transfer laws: an effective deterrent to delinquency? Washington, DC: U.S. Department of Justice Office of Justice Programs Office of Juvenile Justice and Delinquency Prevention; 2010: Online at <www.ncjrs.gov/pdffiles1/ojjdp/220595.pdf>.

[45] Norman Lefstein VS, Teitelbaum L. In search of juvenile justice: Gault and its implementation. Law Soc Rev 1969;3(4):491–562.

[46] Ibid.

[47] Birckhead TR. Juvenile justice reform 2.0. J Law Policy 2011;20(1):15–62.

[48] Horowitz DL. The courts and social policy. Washington, DC: The Brookings Institution; 1977. p. 174, 177–78 Birckhead TR. Toward a theory of procedural justice for juveniles, conference papers—Law & Society (2009 Annual Meeting). p. 1.

[49] Horowitz. The courts and social policy. p. 188–91. Rosenberg GN. The hollow hope: can courts bring about social change? Chicago, IL: University of Chicago Press; 1993. p. 315–6.

[50] Birckhead. Juvenile justice reform 2.0.

[51] Marx G. 5-year-old Eric Morse's killers: growing up behind bars. Chicago Tribune, <www.chicagotribune.com/news/local/chi-eric-morse-killersmar24,0,2304592,full.story> 2009, [accessed March 24, 2009].

[52] Birckhead. Juvenile justice reform 2.0.

[53] Armstrong GS, Kim B. Juvenile penalties for "lawyering up": the role of counsel and extralegal case characteristics. Crime Delinq 2011;57(6):827–48 Birckhead. Juvenile justice reform 2.0.

[54] Mack JW. The juvenile court. Harvard Law Rev 1909;23(2):104–22.

[55] Winship on rough waters: the erosion of the reasonable doubt standard. Harvard Law Rev 1993;106(5):1093–110.

[56] Ibid.

[57] Shubik, Kendall. Rethinking juvenile status offense laws: considerations for congressional review of the Juvenile Justice and Delinquency Prevention Act.

[58] Gaudio CM. A call to congress to give back the future: end the "war on drugs" and encourage states to reconstruct the juvenile justice system. Family Court Rev 2010;48(1):212−27.

[59] Shubik, Kendall. Rethinking juvenile status offense laws: considerations for congressional review of the Juvenile Justice and Delinquency Prevention Act.

[60] Mears DP. Sentencing guidelines and the transformation of juvenile justice into the 21st century. J Contemp Crim Just 2002;18:6−19.

[61] Béchard S, et al. Arbitrary arbitration: diverting juveniles into the justice system— a reexamination after 22 years. Int J Offender Ther Comp Criminol 2011;55(4):605−25 Berg B. Arbitrary arbitration: diverting juveniles into the justice system. Juvenile Fam 1986;37:31−41.

In Ketchikan Youth Court in Alaska, youth ages 11 to 18 begin youth court work by completing a 10-week training course.

Specialized Courts

KEY TERMS

domestic violence court

drug court

mental health courts

specialized courts

veterans' treatment courts

victimless crime

youth courts

Learning Objectives

After reading this chapter, you should be able to:

1. Define specialized courts.
2. Discuss the goals of youth courts.
3. Talk about the distinguishing features of youth courts.
4. Understand the two ways that domestic violence cases can reach the court.
5. Discuss the court's challenges in dealing with mentally ill defendants and offenders.
6. List and discuss the 10 essential elements of the ideal mental health court.
7. Explain the relationship of drug courts to the war on drugs.
8. List some criticisms of drug courts.
9. Examine the role of veterans' treatment courts.
10. Compare and contrast veterans' treatment courts with other specialized courts.

The criminal court in the United States is a limited resource [1]. As we have seen in previous chapters, the court uses plea-bargaining to manage its vast caseload. Prosecutors and defense attorneys make deals that compromise their desires to see their vision of justice enacted, and the courtroom workgroup must process cases in a routinized way just to move the docket.

Is there another way to manage the criminal court system so cases can get the attention justice requires? One solution to this problem is specialized

447

courts [2]. Specialized courts are sometimes called problem-solving courts, alternative courts, or boutique courts [3]. The main idea behind specialized courts is that they are able to handle similar cases that are confined to a particular offense or social problem. Specialization allows the justice system to deal with cases in a more uniform manner and affect their outcomes in a way that prevents recidivism [4].

The juvenile court can be considered a specialized court. Chapter 14 demonstrated how the juvenile court developed its own procedures and philosophies to deal with the offenses and behavior of young people. As you will recall, this type of specialized court is not without its own problems of overcrowding and due-process concerns. Nevertheless, the juvenile court is considered a positive alternative to processing delinquents through the criminal court. To do so would not only overload the criminal court, but would also fail to address the special needs of young lawbreakers.

Some of the specialized courts in this chapter enjoy widespread popularity whereas others are limited to only a few jurisdictions. What they have in common is that they are considered problem-solving courts where judges actively try to solve problems and to change the behavior of offenders [5]. In Chapter 15, we will address procedures that can be considered "alternatives *to* the court." These include mediation and restorative justice programs, as well as special procedures to deal with terrorists. It is important to understand the distinction between alternative courts and alternatives to the court in order to appreciate how defendants are treated.

TYPES OF SPECIALIZED COURTS

Specialized courts are branches of the criminal court that deal with specific segments of the offender population who may respond better to treatment than to punishment. These limited-jurisdiction courts, which seek to solve specific problems of the criminal court system, relieve the criminal court of cases that not only clog up the system but also require a more focused expertise (Figure 13.1). In many ways, specialized courts can be accused of expanding the court's role into areas that are traditionally the responsibilities of the correctional system.

Judges in specialized courts are concerned with more than imposing a sentence. The judges are also concerned with how effective the sentences are in changing the behavior of those who appear before the court. (For a look at how judges may go too far in this mission, see Focus on Discretion) To this end, specialized courts have treatment and enforcement mechanisms via diversion programs or probation officers who strive to ensure that defendants receive the help they need, pay any restitution that has been ordered, or

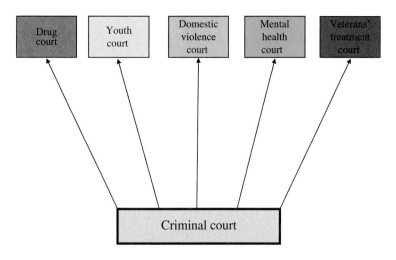

Advantages
1. Specialized courts are less costly than typical criminal court processes.
2. Specialized courts target specific demographics.
3. Specialized courts are treatment-oriented.
4. Participation relieves system overcrowding.

Disadvantages
1. Due process is diminished.
2. Defendants may feel coerced to participate.
3. The public may consider specialized courts as too lenient.

FIGURE 13.1
Specialized criminal courts.

perform community service [6]. Another important thing to understand about specialized courts is that they do not adjudicate guilt. The participants are there voluntarily and have already admitted culpability in the offenses they are accused of. The purpose of these courts is to provide a less costly and more efficient way of dealing with offenders that bypasses the typical adversarial criminal court process of plea-bargaining, trials, and incarceration.

FOCUS ON DISCRETION

The Role of a Judge

J., a juvenile drug-user, had been in trouble with the court for a while. Since J.'s mother had died, he had been caught using cocaine, marijuana, Oxycontin, and alcohol. After repeatedly violating probation and failing to show up for his rehabilitation program, J. overdosed. After another round in family court, Judge Andrew G. Tarantino, Jr., ordered J. to receive grief counseling. A few days later, J. overdosed again. At a subsequent court appearance, he told the court he was "miserable."

During a meeting with his treatment manager, J. asked to speak with Judge Tarantino. The judge agreed, and during a court recess, he drove J. in his car to a nearby park. There, the judge spoke with J. about his substance abuse, his mother's death, and getting grief counseling. After about 20 minutes, they returned to the courthouse. Later, a complaint was filed against Tarantino, and he was formally reprimanded. The commission determined that Tarantino "showed a serious misunderstanding of the role of a judge," by having an informal, out-of-court meeting with a defendant without the knowledge of the youth's attorney or treatment court team [7].

What is the role of a judge in a specialized court? Although specialized courts have been around for a few years, they still represent new territory for the courtroom workgroup, especially the judge. The role of the courtroom workgroup changes, as well. Instead of acting as adversaries, the courtroom workgroup acts as a team to assist the offender in getting help with his or her particular problem. If the offender is in a drug court, the courtroom workgroup will work toward options for rehabilitation and counseling for the offender. A mental health court will be concerned with getting the offender treatment and a stable living situation (if needed).

This altered dynamic presents special issues for the judge. The judge's traditional role requires dignity, objectivity, discipline, and a personal distance from the proceedings. The judge must conduct the court in a fair and impartial manner. Specialized courts require a slightly different role from judges, however, in that they must become "involved adjudicators," and observe more fluid boundaries according to the demands of their particular specialized court. For example, judges in some courts may celebrate defendants' successes with hugs, cheers, or applause. This behavior would never occur in a traditional court, but it may be beneficial in a specialized court [8]. Judges must be careful, however, as they still tread a fine line between propriety and impropriety. Because specialized courts are so new, this role is still being worked out.

Questions

What challenges do judges face when presiding over specialized courts?

What is the courtroom workgroup's role in a specialized court?

The origins of specialized courts can be traced back to initiatives in policing such as the problem-oriented policing scholarship of Herman Goldstein and the policy implications of the "broken windows" idea of James Q. Wilson and George Kelling [9]. These scholars essentially argued that small offenses can turn into large ones if they are not effectively addressed. By addressing minor offenses such as vandalism, graffiti, loitering, minor drug use, public drunkenness, and panhandling, the police can affect the culture of the street and demonstrate that society cares about public spaces. If those who commit minor offenses are arrested and sanctioned, they will be less likely to engage in more serious offenses. Additionally, when minor offenses are dealt with consistently and effectively, potential offenders will be less likely to break the law themselves [10]. But how do we deal with minor offenses effectively?

The police have a limited capacity to affect street culture. Although they can arrest minor drug offenders, chase panhandlers off the corner, and enforce curfew laws for juveniles, their efforts are labor-intensive and short-lived. The problem isn't discovering and arresting those who commit minor offenses, but deciding what to do with them afterward. The criminal court is simply too overloaded to deal effectively with all the minor offenses that are committed every day. Therefore, the specialized courts movement has developed to address these minor concerns in a way that solves the problems a more comprehensive manner. Specialized courts operate differently than criminal courts in several ways. The New York Center for Court Intervention provides the following six principles of specialized justice [11].

- Enhanced information. Ideally, each specialized court is staffed by people with the education and training to handle specific types of problems. Judges can become educated on the issues that surround concerns such as DUI, drug-use, domestic violence, or juvenile delinquency. Additionally, probation officers and other court personnel can devote their time to dealing with only one or a few types of cases. This allows them to develop a greater appreciation for the causes of these offenses and possible treatment options.
- Community engagement. By enlisting community resources, specialized courts can better develop not only specialized programs but also funding for addressing specific problems. For instance, organizations such as the Boys and Girls Club help recruit members for youth courts. Also Mothers against Drunk Driving can work with DUI courts to educate those convicted of driving under the influence.
- Collaboration. Criminal justice officials and those who provide social services can specifically target problem populations. Drug courts can work with drug-treatment programs to ensure that treatment slots are allocated to those sentenced to drug treatment. Additionally, some jurisdictions have developed programs to assist veterans suffering posttraumatic stress syndrome. These programs can work with the Veterans Administration to help veterans take advantage of their benefits to receive medical treatment or education.
- Individualized justice. Specialized courts can ensure that offenders are provided sanctions and treatments directed at the underlying problems that cause their behavior. For instance, those convicted of domestic violence can be directed to anger-management classes. In this case, traditional punishment, such as incarceration, might be counterproductive for someone with anger issues, and the specialized court can better discover and address the problem.
- Accountability. The specialized court can better ensure that offenders fulfill their sanctions and treatment obligations. Offenders are less likely to fall through the cracks when specialized personnel are reporting to the judge about whether they are attending their treatment programs, performing the community service they were sentenced to, or paying restitution. These are all issues that the criminal court would like to ensure, but cannot because of limited resources and expertise.
- Outcomes. The specialized court enables the judge to follow up on cases and make sure that offenders receive the prescribed punishment and/or treatment. The judge can focus on whether the programs actually work rather than just on whether the case was processed correctly. Just as the

specialized court wants to hold the individual accountable for fulfilling his or her sentence, it is also important to ensure that the court is held accountable for developing adequate programs and or effective collaborations with other service providers. The focus on outcomes allows the court to evaluate its effectiveness and modify its programs.

There is a wide variety of specialized courts. Each of these courts is aimed at a different demographic population and utilizes different modalities to affect offenders' behavior. For instance, the drug court may use drug-testing to monitor an offender who is supposed to stop using drugs. Because of the differences in philosophy, methodology, and target populations, it is impossible to lump all specialized courts together when assessing their efficacy. However, specialized courts generally have five common features:

1. close and ongoing judicial monitoring;
2. a multidisciplinary or team-oriented approach;
3. a therapeutic or treatment orientation;
4. the altering of traditional roles in the adjudication process; and
5. an emphasis on solving the problems of individual offenders [12].

Now let's look at several of these types of specialized courts individually.

Drug Courts

Drug courts are a branch of the criminal court that specializes in assisting low-level drug offenders and drug-users. In drug courts, offenders are handled in a more comprehensive and timely manner and their drug-use problems are treated rather than just punished [13]. As of December 2011, more than 2600 drug courts, which are the most common specialized courts, were operating in the United States [14]. More than half processed adults, whereas others were even more specialized: juvenile drug courts, family drug courts, tribal drug courts, designated DUI courts, campus drug courts, reentry drug courts, veterans' drug courts, and cooccurring disorder courts.

The U.S. drug war has been long and costly (see Figure 13.2 for a look at drug arrests). In the early 1970s, President Richard Nixon declared a "war on drugs" [15]. Today, each presidential administration appoints a "drug czar" to oversee the nation's efforts to deal with drug use and abuse in a comprehensive manner [16]. The war on drugs has affected the criminal justice system to such an extent that courts and the correctional system spend a disproportionate amount of time dealing with what some individuals consider a **victimless crime**, or a criminal offense that does not directly harm people or property but offends the social mores and norms of a large segment of society.

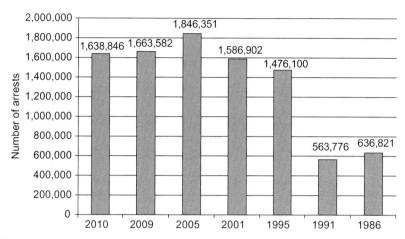

FIGURE 13.2

Arrests for drug-abuse violations more than doubled between 1991 and 1995 and have remained high relative to 1980s arrest rates. Drug courts help the criminal court deal with the increased number of cases. Source: *Federal Bureau of Investigation,* Crime in the United States, *table 29 and table 32, various years. Online at www.fbi.gov/stats-services/crimestats.*

Many drug-users question whether the government should intervene in a personal habit. However, others argue that drug-use is not a victimless crime in that those who use drugs may steal and rob in order to support their drug habits, commit offenses while under the influence of drugs, and victimize their families. We will not engage in this debate here but simply point out that there is a considerable difference of opinion as to how society should respond to drugs [17]. Regardless of one's opinion about drug-use, it is clear that the war on drugs has been a failure. Several indications support this statement:

- The supply of illegal drugs has not been curtailed to any significant degree. Those who want drugs can find them. In fact, a lucrative underground economy has evolved to supply illegal drugs to those who seek them [18].
- The cost of illegal drugs has risen to the point that those who are addicted must constantly seek the money necessary to purchase them. Today, a large percentage of street crime is drug-related.
- The criminal justice system is overwhelmed with drug-related cases. Many of these cases are minor offenses, such as possession of a small amount of marijuana. This diverts resources from more serious types offenses. Some question the efficacy of using the criminal justice system to deal with drug-users, advocating a medical, rather than a legal, approach [19].

Often, offenders are given the choice to participate in the drug court rather than go through the traditional criminal justice system. Most programs exclude serious offenders who are high-volume drug traffickers, used weapons in their offenses, or have extensive criminal records. Drug courts are generally based on a model that involves offender assessment, judicial interaction, monitoring (drug-testing) and supervision, graduated sanctions and incentives, and treatment services [20].

The procedure of the drug court is to have the judge instead of the parole officer supervise offenders' treatment programs. The judge negotiates the treatment plan with the offender, bypassing treatment proposals developed by a probation officer. The plan is subject to the prosecutor and defense counsel's arguments over whether it will do the offender any good. Experts point out that this concentrates more power in the office of the judge, who not only helps develop and implement treatment, but also may incarcerate the participant if the plan does not work out [21]. This relaxing of due process is what the participant agrees to, however, when he or she chooses drug court over criminal court.

The Drug Court Standards Committee of the National Association of Drug Court Professionals has developed 10 key components for designing drug courts [22]. These components are as follows:

1. Drug courts should integrate alcohol and other drug treatment services with justice system case processing. This usually entails a multiphase treatment process that is divided into a stabilization phase, intensive treatment phase, and a transition phase. The intensive treatment phase usually involves counseling individuals or groups, and the transition phase emphasizes reintegration, employment and education, housing services, and other aftercare activities.

2. Using a nonadversarial approach, prosecution and defense counsel promote public safety while protecting participants' due-process rights. Rather than focusing on the merits of the case, the prosecutor and defense attorney work as a team to facilitate the individual's progress in treatment.

3. Eligible participants are identified early and promptly placed in the drug-court program. Immediately after arrest, or after booking, the individual is provided an opportunity to enter the drug-court program. This "crisis situation" is a traumatic event for the offender's and an opportune time to provide them with the alternative of drug treatment.

4. Drug courts provide access to a continuum of alcohol, drug, and other related treatment and rehabilitation services. Although the drug court is primarily concerned with drug abuse, other problems cooccur, such as mental illness, sexually transmitted disease, homelessness, unemployment, and family problems.

5. Abstinence is monitored by frequent alcohol and drug-testing. This is done to monitor the offender's compliance in the treatment program.

6. A coordinated strategy governs drug-court responses to participants' compliance. Although abstinence is the ultimate goal, the drug court recognizes that relapses often occur. Incremental successes such as showing up at all required court appearances, regularly arriving at the treatment program on time, and fully participating in the treatment sessions are rewarded as ways to bolster the confidence and inspire the offender to continue the program.

7. Ongoing judicial interaction with each drug-court participant is essential. Judges are encouraged to step beyond their traditional independent and objective roles and develop new expertise.

8. Monitoring and evaluation measure the achievement of program goals and gauge effectiveness. In addition to monitoring the success of individuals in fulfilling their treatment plans, the drug court must also monitor its own processes and outcomes. This keeps the program focused on its mission, identifies developing problems, and allows for procedural changes.

9. Continuing interdisciplinary education promotes effective drug-court planning, implementation, and operations. Drug-court personnel must be continually educated about the changing nature of drug treatment. Additionally, they should be constantly reminded of the spirit of commitment and collaboration that is required to be effective in dealing with those who have drug addictions.

10. Forging partnerships among drug courts, public agencies, and community-based organizations generates local support and enhances drug-court program effectiveness. Community partnerships are essential to ensuring that all the resources available within the jurisdiction are afforded to the offenders in the program.

This list provides a firm idea as to the structure and motivations that underlie this alternative court process. All programs may not fully comply with this list of components because of lack of resources.

Those selected to participate in the drug court do so voluntarily. The voluntary nature of their participation is problematic, however. The offenders are not freely seeking drug treatment, but rather attempting to escape the full punishment afforded by the law [23]. It is this aspect of coercion that gives the drug courts leverage over its participants. If offenders relapse and are kicked out of the program, or quit because they do not wish to be subjected to drug-testing, they can be returned to the court and receive a traditional and, most likely, a more punitive sentence [24]. Part of the drug-court philosophy is that this coercion is necessary to deal with those who have drug problems and lack the motivation to quit drugs on their

PHOTO 13.1

Drug court professionals rally in Washington, DC, during the seventeenth annual Drug Court Training Conference. Proponents of drug courts say the courts are less expensive than traditional criminal court processing.

own. However, there is another aspect to this coercion. As an alternative to traditional processing that involves punishment, the drug court must satisfy policymakers and the public that it is not only effective, but also at least somewhat punitive (Photo 13.1).

The drug court was established to ease some of the criminal courts' caseload and to ensure that those with drug problems did not escape all major decisions but rather are dealt with in a firm and accountable manner [25]. The constant monitoring (including drug-testing) is designed to intervene in the offenders' life to such an extent that radical lifestyle changes occur. Those participating in drug-court programs are expected to address the reasons they use drugs [26]. They may be required to change where they live, their friends, what they do for fun, and even the music they listen to [27].

This comprehensive approach to dealing with drug offenders may have some unintended consequences. Placing all of their activities, not just their drug use, under constant surveillance increases the likelihood they will be caught in some kind of violation of the program's rules. Although this is certainly part of the design of the drug-court program, this type of surveillance is akin to "stacking the deck" against the offender. Researchers have observed that instead of diverting offenders from the system, some diversion programs, with a multitude of conditions and requirements, pull offenders into a deeper quagmire of legal entanglements [28]. (For more criticism of drug courts see Court Procedures 13.1.)

COURT PROCEDURES

Drug Courts: Just Another Net?

The first drug court was instituted in Dade County, Florida, in 1989. Since then, the model has taken off, inspiring other drug courts and other types of specialized courts. Although the model is popular, critics question whether the courts relieve offenders of dependence on drugs and alcohol and reduce recidivism, or whether they are just another funnel to the corrections system.

Scholars note that U.S. drug courts operate on a different philosophy than those in England, Scotland, Ireland, Australia, and Canada. The drug courts in those nations focus on a harm-reduction approach rather than complete abstinence. For example, for heroin users other nations may offer services such as needle-exchange programs, clinics that prescribe heroin, and safe places to use the drug. The idea is not to make the heroin user stop using heroin—as it is in the United States—but to help him or her use heroin in a manner that is safer for both the user and the society. This difference in philosophy is important because it keeps more drug-users out of prison. In the United States, a drug-user who is unsuccessful in court-prescribed treatment—the object of which is quitting drugs completely—may be incarcerated. In other nations, the user continues using, but stays out of jail. In this way, it is possible for the user to continue to function in society and maintain family and community ties [12].

This philosophical difference is the basis of one of the main criticisms of drug courts: that they represent a criminal justice solution to a health problem. The Justice Policy Institute and the Drug Policy Alliance have criticized drug courts as not only being used inappropriately but also overused. These organizations, as well as other critics, point out that drug courts have a net-widening function in that they draw people into the system who otherwise would not be there at all. Low-level users processed by the regular criminal court may have received probation, a fine, or even dismissal. However, because of the drug court's ability to incarcerate defendants who "fail" treatment, these low-level users may end up in jail. One report found that 33–75 percent of drug-court participants are kicked out of the program and receive a sentence that is often more harsh than the one they would have received if they had not gone to drug court in the first place [29].

One scholar has stated that the popularity of drug courts is a result of Americans' contradictory desire to both punish and treat drug-users [30]. This attitude may be an indicator of the nature of justice in a heterogeneous culture, in which different segments of society try to get what they want from the system, as well as the political struggles between factions that advocate treatment versus those that advocate punishment. The shift to drug courts, however, may be a sign that the criminal justice system is admitting the wisdom of moving from a punishment model to a treatment model.

Questions

How does the philosophy of U.S. drug courts differ from those in some other nations?
What may be contradictory about Americans' attitudes toward dealing with drug-users?

Another aspect of the drug courts that some scholars find problematic is the over-representation of minorities and the impoverished [31]. Also, as a mechanism for social control, drug courts attempt to meld treatment with accountability. This approach appeals to those who consider drug-use as a medical problem that should be treated and those who consider drug-use as a social choice that should be discouraged and deterred. The use of drug courts presents us with a new paradigm that is not only more politically feasible but also keeps the responsibility for dealing with the social problem of drug use firmly in the hands of the criminal justice system [32].

Finally, is the judge the best evaluator of the efficacy of drug-court treatment modalities? In the traditional criminal court, the judge acts as a neutral arbiter who makes judgments on the legal circumstances of the case. In the drug-court program, the judge is much more therapeutically involved or heavy-handed depending on your point of view. Here, the judge follows up on the treatment of offenders and can modify the sentence based upon successes and relapses. Although there is a treatment team who advises the judge, it is within his or her discretion to continue treatment or sentence the offender to incarceration. This gives judges greater latitude in deciding what to do with offenders. Judges report that they prefer this type of discretion and believe that they are more effective in dealing with those experiencing drug addiction [33].

Youth Courts

Youth courts are informal courts composed of youths who handle the minor offenses of other youths. These courts attempt to divert young lawbreakers from the juvenile justice system. Youth courts work within the auspices of the juvenile court to provide an alternative to the traditional processing of juveniles. Some states exclude gang-related offenses because of the dangers of allowing young people to make decisions on sentences for those involved in gang activity. Typically, the cases that end up before youth court are status offenses and minor delinquency. Offenses such as alcohol or marijuana possession, vandalism, disorderly conduct, minor assault, weapons possession, minor traffic violations, and truancy make up the bulk of teen-court cases [34]. As of 2010, more than 1000 youth court programs were operating throughout the nation [35].

Youth courts are not adjudicatory. This means that matters of guilt have been decided before the case goes to court. If the youth disputes the charges, the case will go to the traditional juvenile justice system. This is done to ensure that defendants are afforded their legal rights, that they are represented by competent attorneys, and that an experienced judge determines the outcome. The deliberations of the youth court, then, are not concerned with the issue of guilt, but with mitigating or aggravating circumstances. The goal is to understand the motivations that led the youth to break the law and to craft dispositions that address those problems. In many minor cases, it is clear to all, especially other youths, what the problems are and what a common-sense solution would be.

The distinguishing feature of youth courts is that young people are not only defendants but also serve on the jury, act as prosecutors, and in some cases serve as the judge [36]. The youth court's philosophy is that peer pressure can have a major and positive influence on the behavior of young people. Youth courts produce several benefits for those who participate.

- Defendants. Those who come before the youth court are not exposed to the stigmatization of the juvenile court. Also, having peers handle these youths' cases may make them more likely to modify their behavior. The idea behind this philosophy is that young people dismiss the advice and judgment of older people because they do not see them as significant arbiters. This is, of course, a difficult theory to evaluate, and it remains an open question as to whether teenagers are more or less alienated by this process than by the traditional juvenile court system.
- Juries. Although only minor offenses come before the youth court, those who serve on the jury must develop the sentence. The experience of listening to the particulars of the case and deciding upon the sentence is thought to help jury members develop good judgment. This form of shared governance is designed to exert peer pressure on the offender, as well as solidify the commitment to good behavior on the part of those on the jury. Often, jury members include youths who have been defendants. This allows them to see both sides of the process and gives the jury a bit of extra credibility.
- Prosecutors and judges. Depending on the jurisdiction, these roles may be performed by adults. Sometimes they are performed by local attorneys who act as role models and ensure that a modicum of legal procedures are followed and that the defendants are afforded a degree of fairness. In other jurisdictions, these roles may be performed by youths. As with the jury, the young people who fulfill the roles of prosecutor or judge are deemed to benefit from the experience.

The sentences imposed by the youth court vary widely. Depending on the instructions given to the judge and the jury, the disposition may be punitive or rehabilitative. Also, many dispositions involve a degree of reintegrative shaming which is aimed at allowing offenders to claim responsibility for their guilt and express remorse. Many of these processes are derived from the restorative justice movement (discussed in greater detail in Chapter 14) in which the goal is to repair the harm done to relationships. For instance, one requirement may be that the offender apologize to the victims and to his or her own family members for the harm he or she caused by the offense. The youth may also be required to perform community service.

How should youth courts be evaluated? On the one hand, the most accurate way of measuring the effectiveness of any court is the recidivism rate of those who come before it [37]. This can be problematic for a youth court because of how cases are selected and how dispositions are imposed. For instance, one of the goals of a youth court is to divert minor offenders from the traditional juvenile justice system. But there is a real question whether this type of processing is actually a diversion. The youth court selects minor offenders for processing. If the youth court did not exist, it is possible that many, if not most, of these youngsters would not encounter the juvenile justice system at all. Labeling theory suggests that exposure to the juvenile justice system, even youth court, not only stigmatizes the youth, but also affects their self-concept and self-esteem to the point where they consider themselves to be "bad" [38]. It may actually be better for everyone involved to exclude these youths from the justice system altogether.

This propensity to target minor offenders makes evaluation of youth courts difficult [39]. Most evaluations of youth courts have compared those who have been processed through the youth court with those who have been processed through the juvenile court. This is an unfair comparison that is weighted toward demonstrating that the youth court is effective. A more realistic evaluation would be to compare youths processed by the youth court with youths who have been released would only a warning. The second evaluation would reveal whether youth court is more effective in reducing recidivism for a target population of minor offenders [40].

An additional issue we must consider when thinking about evaluating youth courts has to do with the philosophy that the youth court is multifunctional in nature. If we evaluate youth courts only on recidivism, we are missing some of the other, possibly more important, benefits of the court. Although reducing crime is certainly a goal of the juvenile justice system and the youth court, other positive benefits can accrue from such a quasi-legal process. For example, youth courts have been evaluated as to whether they increased the positive attitude of offenders toward the legal system. Other evaluations include accountability, restoration, and offender reengagement in the community. One study found that the more offenders were involved with the youth court after completing their sentences—that is, returning as jurors, bailiffs, advocates, and clerks—the less likely they were to reoffend [41]. Another study found that although those who completed their sentences were half as likely to recidivate as those who did not, increased sanctions resulted in earlier reoffending [42].

If we consider youth courts according to traditional concepts of justice, we can see that they are problematic. Although offenders are selected after admitting guilt, they are still vulnerable to being taken advantage of by the court and losing their legal rights. Although they may be represented by an attorney, in youth court this attorney is often another teen. To suggest that this sort of legal representation is competent is unrealistic. Another issue that has not been evaluated has to do with the idea of the courtroom workgroup as applied to the youth court. In the criminal and juvenile courts, the courtroom work-group consists of professionals who have worked together for years. In the youth court, the courtroom workgroup consists of youngsters with no legal training who are almost randomly assigned to their roles of judge, prosecutor, or juror and are subject to the same peer pressure that they are attempting to focus upon the offender. We can only guess at the complex interpersonal dynamics that operate in such a quasi-legal setting [36].

Domestic Violence Courts

Domestic violence courts are a branch of the criminal court that specializes in dealing with abusive and violent behavior that emerges from the home. In the past, what happened in the home was not under the purview of the criminal court. After all, "a man's home is his castle" meant that men were relative kings in their domicile and that their wives and children were under their protection and dominance. Men were expected to exercise discipline and keep women and children "in their place." Although the law has changed in this regard, this paternalistic philosophy is still alive and well in many families. The incidence of child abuse and spousal abuse continues at a high rate and has prompted the justice system to consider alternative ways of addressing this harm.

Cases of domestic violence can reach the court in one of two ways [43]. The case can come to the criminal court after an arrest. Typically, these cases involve violence inside the home that is heard by the neighbors who call the police. Should there be physical evidence of the battery, the perpetrator will be arrested and charged accordingly. Sometimes, the victim does not have the bruises and bleeding that will serve as obvious evidence, and police officers must decide what to do based upon the cooperation of the victim. Changes in the law have limited the discretion that police officers can exercise when dealing with reports of domestic violence. Mandatory arrest laws in many jurisdictions state that police officers must make an arrest once they have determined that domestic violence has occurred [44]. This is a result of many high-profile cases in which police have been called to a residence repeatedly, failed to intervene effectively, and the domestic violence escalated into a fatality. Mandatory arrest laws have made it necessary to develop court-processing procedures to deal with the increase of this type of caseload [45].

The second way a case of domestic violence may reach the specialized court is through civil court. In this case, the victim can petition the court for a restraining order for protection. These restraining orders legally (but not always physically) prevent the perpetrator from entering the home or coming within so many feet of the victim. This is often a high-risk strategy on the part of the victim in that it may further enrage the perpetrator and result in more violence. However, this civil procedure allows the victim to initiate the legal response to domestic violence and does not require the initial intervention by police. Often, the case appears in both courts after an incident in which police make an arrest, and the victim files a restraining order. If the subject of the restraining order violates the order, then that person may be arrested and the case may go to criminal court.

This dual response to domestic violence has both negative and positive consequences. On the one hand, the victim may initiate legal proceedings in a civil court and there enjoys a certain flexibility that is absent in the criminal court. However, the criminal court traditionally has jurisdiction over the case and this can delay civil court proceedings that deal with concerns such as child custody [46]. The important thing to remember here, however, is that specialized domestic violence courts can alleviate this problem by dedicating specific resources to adjudicating cases in a timely and effective manner.

The Violence against Women Act of 1974 provided the impetus to develop domestic violence courts [47]. Hundreds of courts nationwide give special attention to domestic violence cases and coordinate with social service agencies to provide services to domestic violence victims. Perhaps the most distinguishing feature of domestic violence courts is that they focus on the victim's safety more than the offender's rehabilitation. Although the domestic violence court holds the offender accountable, the courts primarily consider the needs of the victims and families.

As of 2009, there were 208 domestic violence courts in the United States [48]. The components of a domestic violence court vary according to jurisdiction. For an example of the elements of domestic violence courts in New York, see Court Procedures 13.2.

COURT PROCEDURES

New York's Domestic Violence Courts

New York's Domestic Violence Courts include the following key elements:

- A dedicated judge
  presides over cases from arraignment through disposition
  monitors offenders and their compliance with orders of protection
  promotes consistent and efficient case handling.

■ Resource coordinator
  prepares offender and victim information for the judge
  holds agencies accountable for accurate and prompt reporting
  identifies any problems that challenge court components
  screens and refers offenders to court-mandated programs
  coordinates information with the police, defense counsel, prosecutors and others.
■ On-site victim advocate
  serves as primary contact to victims, creates safety plans, and coordinates housing
    counseling, as well as other social services
  provides victims with information about criminal proceedings, and special conditions
    within their orders of protection.
■ Research and evaluation
  provides feedback about project performance
  examines success of intervention programs
  studies offender compliance with court mandates and analyzes recidivism.

Question

How does the New York Domestic Court differ from a traditional courtroom?

Source: New York State Division of Criminal Justice Services, www.criminaljustice.ny.gov/ofpa/domviolcrtfactsheet.htm. Accessed June 2012.

Several questions must be addressed in order to determine the efficacy of domestic violence courts. These questions range from concerns about the services provided to victims and offenders to concerns about how the domestic violence court affects arrest rates and its place in the overall court system of the jurisdiction. For example, legitimate questions to ponder would be:

1. Does a domestic violence court increase or decrease the domestic violence arrest rate in a jurisdiction?
2. Do victims express a greater satisfaction with the justice system because of their interaction with a domestic violence court?
3. Are domestic violence cases processed in a more timely manner in domestic violence courts than in the traditional court system?
4. Do those accused of domestic violence receive more rehabilitative services through the domestic violence court than through the traditional criminal justice system?
5. Are defendants who are processed through a domestic violence court less likely to be arrested again?
6. Is the community more aware of domestic violence and does it develop programs and agencies to address it?

These questions reflect the range of goals that domestic violence courts strive to achieve. To date, there have been several evaluations of domestic violence courts but it is difficult to answer these questions in a definitive manner. However, some of these questions have been at least partially answered. For instance, an evaluation in Lexington, South Carolina, found that domestic violence courts had increased police responsiveness to domestic violence, and the arrest rate for domestic violence increased by 10 percent over the monthly average of traditional domestic violence arrests. Additionally, offenders who were processed by the domestic violence court had lower recidivism rates than those who had gone through the traditional court system. These findings underscore the benefits of having a dedicated and coordinated system of law enforcement, court, and social services agencies responding to the problem of domestic violence [49].

Domestic violence courts may be effective in ways that have not been measured. Although the direct effects of such a court, such as recidivism rates and arrest rates, are certainly important issues to consider, these courts may also have indirect influences that would be difficult to measure, but still important to con-sider [50]. For instance, if a domestic violence court intervenes in a family in which a battering father is arrested and the mother is provided social services that include the opportunity to separate from the abuser, how does this affect their children? Several factors must be considered. Children whose parents are processed by this type of court may have a much better opportunity to develop healthy self-concepts and compete in the classroom. Mothers who are not physically abused will be able to provide better parenting. Offenders who receive rehabilitative services, such as anger-management training, may become more confident parents [51]. Although difficult to measure, the indirect benefits of domestic violence courts should be considered when judging the overall benefits to victims, offenders, and the community.

Mental Health Courts

Mental health courts are a branch of the criminal court that specializes in finding treatment for and assisting mentally ill offenders. The criminal justice system is ill-equipped to deal with those who have difficulty understanding the differences between right and wrong. Police officers have few resources to employ when dealing with troublesome individuals who have mental health problems. The police must often arrest mentally ill people who appear to be breaking the law, but the local jail is the worst place to send them. They may pose threats to jail staff and other inmates, as well as become victims them-selves. It is not unusual for mentally ill suspects to be convicted of offenses they do not understand and for which they lack criminal intent. If they are sent to prison, or even if they receive probation, the criminal justice system is not equipped to provide mentally ill offenders with treatment. Therefore, some communities have established alternative ways of processing those with mental health problems. About 150 mental health courts are currently in operation in the United States [52].

The first nationally recognized mental health court was established in Broward County, Florida, where more than 100 courts were developed to provide an alternative to traditional court processing of those with mental health problems. In 2000, President Clinton signed a bill allocating $7 million to the development of mental health courts. Therapeutic jurisprudence has become an approach that will help courts more effectively deal with those who commit minor offenses because of their mental problems.

The U.S. Department of Justice has developed a list of 10 essential elements of the ideal mental health court:

1. Planning and administration. When establishing a mental health court, it is essential that the planning include all those who have a stake in its outcomes. This means that policymakers such as county commissioners and city mayors, as well as prosecutors and judges, be included in the planning process. Additionally, community members and mental health practitioners must have a voice in how the program functions.

2. Eligibility criteria. Not everyone who is mentally ill is a good candidate for mental health court. The eligibility criteria must be specified in terms of type of offense (misdemeanor versus felony, violent versus nonviolent), and social support system (local friends or family that can assist in postconviction outcomes).

3. Timely processing. The hearings should be conducted in such a way that addresses the problems in a timely manner. This means identifying those who meet the eligibility criteria shortly after they are placed in jail and determining appropriate treatment options.

4. Terms of participation. Participation should not expose the offender to excessive court intervention. The sentence should not extend beyond what would be expected in a traditional court. Mental health treatment should not be an indeterminate sentence in which the offender must prove he or she is sane before being released from court supervision. Unless offenders are clearly a threat to themselves or others, they should not receive more severe sanctions than those not experiencing mental health problems.

5. Informed choice. Potential participants in the mental health court should be able to make an informed choice about their voluntary participation in this type of case processing. The terms and regulations must be clearly spelled out to the participants and they must be provided counsel to aid them in making an informed choice.

6. Treatment supports and services. Treatment supports and services should be comprehensive and individualized. Offenders should be provided with treatment that speaks to their specific needs and not

lumped into various treatment programs simply because these programs have vacancies.

7. Confidentiality. Information about these offenders should be limited to only that which is necessary for the treatment staff to provide services.

8. Trained staff. There should be a collaborative effort between criminal justice personnel and treatment staff. Staff should be trained so that each staff member understands the others' roles and responsibilities. Criminal justice personnel and treatment staff should be able to agree upon the goals of the program and individual treatment plans.

9. Monitored treatment plan. Both treatment staff and the court should monitor individual treatment plans. It is essential that the treatment plan be modified as the offender's needs change.

10. Program evaluation. In addition to monitoring the participants' progress through the program, the program itself should be fully evaluated to ascertain if it is meeting its objectives. Program evaluations should be done not only on the outcomes of individual participants, but also on the court processes. Questions regarding the effectiveness of court staff, relationships with other mental health institutions and law enforcement agencies, and the satisfaction of the community should constantly be asked [53].

These elements of an ideal mental health court provide an ambitious agenda for those who wish to establish this alternative to traditional criminal justice processing. A recent evaluation of a large metropolitan mental health court found that these elements were only partially accomplished. The study's authors concluded that the court's challenges included being unable to advance from only hearing municipal cases to hearing state misdemeanors and felonies; having no resources to expand program capacity for municipal cases; and participants being unable to consistently access mental health treatment, rehabilitation, and support services [54]. Consequently, many defendants with mental health issues who were brought before the court did not receive attention from the mental health court. Additionally, even those who did experience the benefits of the mental health court did not always get the range of treatment and rehabilitation services suggested by court personnel. As can be expected, this has to do with funding and the resources available within the community [55].

Those who work within the mental health court may feel the strain between doing what is best for the offender and fulfilling the demands of their decision-making position. Caseworkers act as "double agents" who sometimes advocate for the client, and sometimes suggest punitive sanctions that are the agreed-upon norms of the courtroom workgroup [56]. For instance, in one ethnographic study of the dynamics of the courtroom workgroup the author provided the following analysis:

> ... the centrality of case managers in court obligated them to market their treatment authority to the other team members and clientele cautiously for fear of alienating either party. As [one case manager] said, "I am pretty assertive and will play the clinical card if I feel the court is making a bad decision.... I don't play it often for fear of overplaying it."

This quotation suggests that case managers have a vested interest in softening the appearance of taking sides, which could threaten the therapeutic relationship with the client as well as their standing as collaborative team members of the mental health court [57]. We can see how alternative courts operate with different philosophies, objectives, and motivations than the traditional criminal court system. The goals of mental health courts are to protect society and address the needs of the mentally ill offender. What sometimes gets lost in this process is the protection of the offender's legal rights as the court attempts to deal with the mental health issues. The potential for abuse here is significant, and the constant monitoring not only of the offenders' treatment plans but also the process issues of the court are necessary in order to ensure that those with mental health issues are handled consistently.

Veterans' Treatment Courts

Veterans' treatment courts are a branch of the criminal court that specializes in assisting veterans who have broken the law. The first veterans treatment court was founded by Judge Robert Russell in Buffalo, New York, in 2008 after he noticed an increase in the number of veterans appearing in his drug court and mental health court. As of 2012, 95 veteran treatment courts were operating in the United States, many in conjunction with drug courts and mental health courts [58].

Combat service has affected the mental health of veterans in every war. For example, after World War I, soldiers returning from stressful trench warfare were referred to as "lost soldiers." After the war in Vietnam, the American Psychological Association recognized the unique mental health problems of returning veterans and developed the diagnosis "posttraumatic stress disorder" (PTSD) to refer to the unique problems of those affected by combat experience. PTSD was added to the Diagnostic and Statistical Manual of Mental Disorders in 1980. PTSD problems include sleeplessness, alienation, a proclivity for drug and alcohol abuse, blackouts, uncontrollable rage, and depression. Up to 26 percent of those returning from Iraq and Afghanistan may be suffering from PTSD [59].

Returning veterans may also suffer from drug and alcohol abuse as they attempt to adjust to civilian life. They may also engage in violent crime, especially domestic violence. This is a counterintuitive finding because those who apply for military service are screened for mental health issues. However, military experience, especially combat, socializes, trains, and rewards soldiers for violent behavior. For many soldiers, turning off the instinct to use violence when they return to civilian society can be difficult. Veterans of the wars in Iraq and Afghanistan face additional problems. Because these wars have gone on for so long and because there is no national draft to replenish the number of combat soldiers needed to prosecute these wars, many veterans have been sent on multiple tours in combat zones. This has led to a problem of increased suicide by veterans, as well as other mental health issues, and veterans who have been caught up in the criminal justice system have not been amenable to treatment through traditional programs [60]. Veterans who are experiencing PTSD may not seek mental health services for a number of reasons.

> By far the biggest barrier to treatment is stigma. The fear of being labeled as weak or cowardly for seeking mental health treatment has been a persistent problem in military culture. Of those surveyed… who declined to seek treatment, a reason generally cited was a fear about treatment not remaining confidential or harming the soldier's career [61].

Veteran treatment courts differ from other specialized courts in significant ways. These differences cast another light upon the stigma associated with criminal activity.

1. Veterans' courts explicitly project the attitude that participants should be honored for their service, and that they are being diverted from traditional sentencing because the government is grateful for their sacrifice.
2. Specialized courts allow the judge, prosecutors, and public defenders to develop expertise on veterans' issues and to connect participants with service providers who are also familiar with the military experience.
3. Veterans who are gathered on the same docket and are present in the same courtroom support each other. Seeing other defendants who have similar experiences and problems helps to break down the stigma associated with treatment. A program filled with veterans in some ways replicates the camaraderie of the military [62].
4. Most veterans' courts have a mentoring program that pairs each participant with a volunteer mentor from a similar background. The mentoring program is the most direct response to the observation that veterans respond better to treatment when they work with other veterans [63].

In some ways, the treatment of veterans in these courts is similar to other specialized courts. Referrals to drug and alcohol-abuse programs, employment services, family counseling programs, and educational institutions are typically the types of help that veterans require [64]. Veterans' courts can also develop good relationships with the veterans' administration to help offenders receive the benefits that their service has entitled them to. This is one of the primary benefits of an established veterans' court. Court personnel can help veterans take advantage of federal benefits and spare the local community the cost of treatment.

There is some criticism of veterans' courts, however. Some believe that veterans should not be singled out for special courts because it seems as if their offenses are more excusable than those of nonveteran offenders. Veterans should not receive a "get out of jail free card" simply because they have served in the military. Another criticism is that there are many types of veterans. Not all veterans served in combat and are victims of PTSD. Some veterans simply have drug problems like many other offenders and should not be treated any differently. Other critics contend that having a special veterans treatment court perpetuates the stereotype of the "wacko veteran" who could fly off the handle at any moment and commit mass murder with an automatic weapon [63].

SPECIALIZED COURTS AND GOALS OF THE CRIMINAL JUSTICE SYSTEM

Are offenders better off going to the traditional criminal justice system or being diverted into treatment programs through specialized courts? Is the public better served by specialized courts or should all offenders be treated equally by being processed in the criminal court? These questions strike to the heart of the debate over the goals of the criminal justice system. If one believes that the primary goal of criminal justice system is retribution, then offenders should be processed by the criminal court and get their "just desserts." However, if one believes that rehabilitating offenders is more desirable, then specialized courts provide better results.

Regardless of one's philosophy of what the court should do, there is an additional question of due process. In specialized courts, offenders waive many of their due-process rights. Entering into diversion programs through specialized courts allows offenders to escape potential incarceration. But this "deal with the devil" has two sides. If offenders do not successfully complete the treatment specified by these courts, they are vulnerable to the original charges. This means that their escape from possible punishment is conditional. Another important question is just how voluntary the offenders' decisions are, especially when they are faced with incarceration.

Regardless, specialized courts are probably good for the criminal justice system. They relieve overcrowded court dockets by diverting minor offenses to the specialized courts. The selection criteria for most of these specialized courts involve the selection of nonviolent offenders who probably would not have been sent to prison anyway because of the lack of prison space. The diversion of these cases allows the court to impose a variety of intermediate sanctions that relieve the criminal justice system of expensive incarceration while trying to provide effective rehabilitation strategies.

SUMMARY

1. Define and talk about specialized courts.
   - Specialized courts are branches of the criminal court that deal with specific segments of the offender population who may respond better to treatment than to punishment.
   - Specialized courts have treatment and enforcement mechanisms to ensure that defendants receive the help they need, pay any ordered restitution, or perform community service.
   - Specialized courts do not adjudicate guilt. The participants are there voluntarily and have already admitted culpability in their offenses. Specialized courts provide a less costly and more efficient way of dealing with offenders than the typical criminal court process.
2. Discuss the goals of youth courts.
   - Youth court cases are usually status offenses and minor delinquency, such as alcohol or marijuana possession, vandalism, disorderly conduct, minor assault, weapons possession, minor traffic violations, and truancy. The goal of youth courts is to understand the motivations that led the youth to break the law and to craft dispositions that address those problems.
3. Talk about the distinguishing features of youth courts.
   - In youth courts, young people are not only defendants but also serve on the jury, act as prosecutors, and sometimes serve as the judge. The court's philosophy is that peer pressure can have a major and positive influence on young people's behavior.
4. Understand the two ways that domestic violence cases can reach the court.
   - A domestic violence case can come to the criminal court after an arrest. Laws in many jurisdictions state that police officers must make an arrest once they have determined that domestic violence has occurred.
   - A domestic violence case can come to the criminal court through civil court. In this case, the victim petitions the court for a

restraining order. The case may appear in both courts after an incident in which police make an arrest, and the victim files a restraining order. If the subject of the order violates the order, that person may be arrested, and the case will go to criminal court.

5. Discuss the court's challenges in dealing with mentally ill defendants and offenders.

   - In local jails, mentally ill arrestees may pose threats to jail staff and other inmates, as well as become victims themselves. Sometimes mentally ill suspects are convicted of offenses they do not understand and for which they lack criminal intent. The criminal justice system is not equipped to provide mentally ill offenders with treatment.

6. List and discuss the 10 essential elements of the ideal mental health court.

   - (1) The planning of mental health courts must include all those who have a stake in its outcomes. (2) Not everyone who is mentally ill is a good candidate for mental health court. (3) The hearings should be conducted in a way that addresses the problems in a timely manner. (4) Participation should not expose the offender to excessive court intervention. (5) Potential participants should be able to make an informed choice about their voluntary participation. (6) Treatment and services should be comprehensive and individualized. (7) Information about offenders should be limited to only that which is necessary for the treatment staff to provide services. (8) There should be a collaborative effort between criminal justice personnel and treatment staff. (9) Both treatment staff and the court should monitor treatment plans. (10) Programs should be evaluated to ascertain if it is meeting its objectives.

7. Explain the relationship of drug courts to the war on drugs.

   - The criminal justice system is overwhelmed with drug-related cases. Drug courts were established to ease some of the criminal courts' caseload and to ensure that those with drug problems did not escape all major decisions, but rather are dealt with in a firm and accountable manner.

8. List some criticisms of drug courts.

   - Offenders relapse who do not make it through the program can be returned to the court and may receive a more punitive sentence. Placing all of participants' activities under constant surveillance increases the likelihood they will be caught in a violation of the program's rules. Minorities and the impoverished also tend to be over-represented in drug courts.

9. Examine the role of veterans' treatment courts.
   - Veterans' treatment courts restrict their clientele to veterans and those in military service. Returning veterans may suffer from drug and alcohol abuse as they attempt to adjust to civilian life, and may also engage in violent crime. Military experience socializes, trains, and rewards soldiers for violent behavior. Some soldiers have trouble turning off this instinct when returning to civilian society.

10. Compare and contrast veterans' treatment courts with other specialized courts.
   - Veterans' courts project the attitude that participants should be honored for their service. The courts allow the courtroom workgroup to develop expertise on veterans' issues. Veterans on the same docket and present in the same courtroom support each other. Most veterans' courts have a mentoring program that pairs each participant with a mentor from a similar background.
   - The treatment of veterans in veterans' courts is often similar to other specialized courts. Veterans may be referred to drug and alcohol-abuse programs, employment services, family counseling programs, and educational institutions. Court personnel can help veterans take advantage of federal benefits and spare the community the cost of treatment.

Questions

1. What is a specialized court?
2. What are the goals of youth courts?
3. What are the distinguishing features of youth courts?
4. How do domestic violence cases reach court?
5. What are the court's challenges in dealing with mentally ill defendants and offenders?
6. What are the essential elements of the ideal mental health court?
7. What is the relationship of drug courts to the war on drugs?
8. What are some criticisms of drug courts?
9. What is the role of veterans' treatment courts?
10. How do veterans' treatment courts operate in contrast with other specialized courts?

REFERENCES

[1] O'Scannlain DF. Striking a devil's bargain: the federal courts and expanding caseloads in the twenty-first century. Lewis Clark Law Rev 2009;13(2):473–83.

[2] Hannah-Moffat K, Maurutto P. Shifting and targeted forms of penal governance: bail, punishment and specialized courts. Theor Criminol 2012;16(2):201–19.

[3] Spohn C, Hemmens C. Courts: a text/reader. Los Angeles: Sage; 2009. p. 507−8.

[4] Martinson DJ. One case−one specialized judge: why courts have an obligation to manage alienation and other high-conflict cases. Family Court Rev 2010;48(1):180−9.

[5] Office of Juvenile Justice and Delinquency Prevention, Gun Courts, <www.ojjdp.gov/mpg/progTypesGunCourt.aspx/> [accessed June, 20 2012].

[6] Wolf RV. Breaking with tradition: introducing problem solving in conventional courts. Int Rev Law Comput Technol 2008;22(1/2):77−93.

[7] Determination, State of New York Commission on Judicial Conduct, In the Matter of the Proceeding Pursuant to Section 44, subdivision 4, of the Judiciary Law in Relation to Andrew G. Tarantino, Jr., a Judge of the Family Court, Suffolk County: Online at <www.scjc.state.ny.us/Determinations/T/Tarantino.pdf/> [accessed June, 20 2012].

[8] Greenstein MN. Creative judging: ethics issues in problem-solving courts. Judges' J 2012;51 (2):40.

[9] Parks RB. Broken windows and broken windows policing. Criminol Publ Policy 2008;7 (2):159−61.

[10] Galea S, et al. Race/ethnic-specific homicide rates in New York city: evaluating the impact of broken windows policing and crack cocaine markets. Homicide Stud 2011;15(3):268−90.

[11] Harper JA, Finkle MJ. Judicial leadership and effective court intervention. Judges' J 2012;51 (2):4−8.

[12] Nolan Jr JL. Harm reduction and the American difference: drug treatment and problem-solving courts in comparative perspective. J Health Care Law Policy 2010;13(31):31−47.

[13] Koob J, Brocato J, Kleinpeter C. Enhancing residential treatment for drug court participants. J Offender Rehabil 2011;50(5):252−71.

[14] National Institute of Justice, Drug Courts, <www.nij.gov/nij/topics/courts/drug-courts/welcome.htm/> [accessed June, 20 2012].

[15] Scherlen R. Why can't the U.S. end this war? Explaining the persistence of the war on drugs. Conf Pap—South Pol Sci Assoc 2010 Annual Meeting:1.

[16] G. Fields White house Czar calls for end to "War on Drugs." Wall St J May 14, 2009: A3.

[17] T. Rogers New voice in drug-war debate: businessmen who are feeling the pinch Christian Sci Monit, February 26, 2012.

[18] N.D. Kristof Drugs won the war N Y Times, June 14, 2009.

[19] Sweet RW. Will money talk? The case for a comprehensive cost−benefit analysis of the war on drugs. Stanford Law Policy Rev 2009;20(2):229−56.

[20] Ibid.

[21] Miller EJ. Drugs, courts, and the new penology. Stanford Law Policy Rev 2009;20(2):417−61.

[22] National Association of Drug Court Professionals. Defining drug courts: the key components. Washington, DC: U.S. Department of Justice Office of Justice Programs Bureau of Justice Assistance; 2004. Available from <www.ncjrs.gov/pdffiles1/bja/205621.pdf/>.

[23] Brown R. Associations with substance abuse treatment completion among drug court participants. Subst Use Misuse 2010;45(12):1874−91.

[24] Satel SL. Drug treatment: the case for coercion. Nat Drug Court Inst Rev 2000;3:1−23.

[25] Snavely KR. The critical need for jail as a sanction in the drug court model. Drug court practitioner fact sheet. Alexandria, VA: National Drug Court Institute; 2000.

[26] Cooper CS. Drug courts—just the beginning: getting other areas of public policy in sync. Subst Use Misuse 2007;42(2−3):243−56.

[27] Tiger R. Drug courts and the logic of coerced treatment. Sociol Forum 2011;26(1):169−82.

[28] Blomberg TG, Lucken K. Stacking the deck by piling up sanctions: is intermediate punishment destined to fail. Howard J Crim Justice 1994;33(1):62−80.

[29] Alcoholism & Drug Abuse Weekly, Two reports criticize drug courts; NADCP pushes back. 2011;23(13): 1−3.

[30] Murphy J. The continuing expansion of drug courts: is that all there is? Deviant Behav 2012;33(7):582−8.

[31] Tiger R, Drug courts and the logic of coerced treatment. 181−182.

[32] Stinchcomb JB. Drug courts: conceptual foundation, empirical findings, and policy implications. Drugs Educ Prev Policy 2010;17(2):148−67.

[33] Chase D, Hora PF. The best seat in the house: the court assignment and judicial satisfaction. Family Court Rev 2009;47(2):209−38.

[34] Jane Irons E, Jones R. Youth court: an effective intervention for youth at risk of interpersonal violence and substance abuse. J Correctional Educ 2001;52(4):149−51.

[35] National Association of Youth Courts, Facts and Stats, <www.youthcourt.net/?page_id = 24/> [accessed June, 2012].

[36] Smith S, Chonody JM. Peer-driven justice: development and validation of the youth court peer influence scale. Res Social Work Pract 2010;20(3):283−92.

[37] Forgays DK, Demilio L. Is youth court effective for repeat offenders? A test of the restorative justice approach. Int J Offender Ther Comp Criminol 2005;49(1):107−18.

[38] Wilson DM, Gottfredson DC, Povitsky Stickle W. Gender differences in effects of youth courts on delinquency: a theory-guided evaluation. J Crim Justice 2009;37(1):21−7.

[39] Minor KI, Wells JB. Sentence completion and recidivism among juveniles referred to youth courts. Crime Delinquency 1999;45(4):467.

[40] Smith KS, Blackburn AG. Is youth court the best fit? Assessing the predictive validity of the youth court peer influence scale. J Crim Justice 2011;39(2):198−204.

[41] Forgays DK. Three years of youth court offender outcomes. Adolescence 2008;43 (171):473−84.

[42] Norris M, Twill S, Kim C. Smells like teen spirit: evaluating a midwestern youth court. Crime Delinquency 2011;57(2):199−221.

[43] MacDowell EL. When courts collide: integrated domestic violence courts and court pluralism. Tex J Women Law 2011;20(2):95−130.

[44] Hirschel D, Buzawa E, Pattavina A, Faggiani D. Domestic violence and mandatory arrest laws: to what extent do they influence police arrest decisions? J Crim Law Criminol 2007;98(1):255−98.

[45] White MD, Goldkamp JS, Campbell SP. Beyond mandatory arrest: developing a comprehensive response to domestic violence. Police Pract Res 2005;6(3):261−78.

[46] Bolotin L. When parents fight: Alaska's presumption against awarding custody to perpetrators of domestic violence. Alaska Law Rev 2008;25(2):263−301.

[47] Violence Against Women Act. Congressional Digest 2012; 91(1):15.

[48] Labriola M, et al. A national portrait of domestic violence courts, iv. New York, NY: Center for Court Innovation 2010. Available from <www.ncjrs.gov/pdffiles1/nij/grants/229659.pdf/>.

[49] Gover AR, MacDonald JM, Alpert GP. Combating domestic violence: findings from an evaluation of a local domestic violence court. Criminol Publ Policy 2003;3(1):109−32.

[50] Haas SM, Bauer-Leffler S, Turley E. Evaluation of cross-disciplinary training on the co-occurrence of domestic violence and child victimization: overcoming barriers to collaboration. J Health Human Serv Adm 2011;34(3):352−86.

[51] Hall JE, Walters ML, Basile KC. Intimate partner violence perpetration by court-ordered men: distinctions among subtypes of physical violence, sexual violence, psychological abuse, and stalking. J Interpersonal Violence 2012;27(7):1374−95.

[52] Bureau of Justice Assistance, Mental Health Courts Program, <www.bja.gov/ProgramDetails.aspx?Program_ID = 68/> [accessed June, 20 2012].

[53] Thompson M, Osher F, Tomasini-Joshi D. Improving responses to people with mental illnesses: the essential elements of a mental health court. Washington, DC: Bureau of Justice Assistance Office of Justice Programs U.S. Department of Justice; 2008. Available from <www.nationaltasc.org/PDF/MHC_Essential_Elements.pdf/>.

[54] Linhorst D, et al. Implementing the essential elements of a mental health court: the experiences of a large multijurisdictional suburban county. J Behav Health Serv Res 2010;37 (4):427−42.

[55] Ibid, 440.

[56] Castellano U. Courting compliance: case managers as "double agents" in the mental health court. Law Social Inquiry 2011;36(2):484−514.

[57] Ibid, 509. Vance LM. The other unconstitutional war. N Am 2011;27(21):20−4.

[58] Justice for Vets. The History, <www.justiceforvets.org/vtc-history/>.

[59] Jaycox L, Tanielian T, editors. Invisible wounds of war. Santa Monica, CA: Rand Corporation; 2008. . p. xix.

[60] CMHS National GAINS Center's Forum on Combat Veterans, Trauma, and the Justice System, Responding to the Needs of Justice-Involved Combat Veterans with Service-Related Trauma and Mental Health Conditions, <www.gainscenter.samhsa.gov/pdfs/veterans/CVTJS_Report.pdf/> [accessed August 2008].

[61] Cartwright T. "To care for him who shall have borne the battle": the recent development of veterans' treatment courts in America. Stanford Law Policy Rev 2011;22(1):295−316.

[62] W.H. McMichael The battle on the home front: special courts turn to vets to help other vets ABA J, <www.abajournal.com/magazine/article/the_battle_on_the_home_front_special_-courts_turn_to_vets_to_help_other_vets/> [accessed November 2011].

[63] Cartwright T. To care for him who shall have borne the battle, Stanford Law Policy Rev.

[64] Mikkelson K. Veterans' courts offer hope and treatment. Publ Lawyer 2010;18(1):2−5.

Frontiers of Justice

OVERVIEW

Part 5 considers controversies and adaptations that are starting to take shape. The U.S. criminal justice system in general is criticized for producing injustice rather than pursuing justice. Individuals are stigmatized for life, often for crimes like drug possession that do not victimize anyone. From searches to convictions, the criminal justice system falls more heavily on minorities. Families and communities are damaged by severe sentences. States are facing budget shortfalls and even bankruptcy, yet the prison system continues to grow. Given these and other problems, people are starting to look for other avenues to justice. As the old monopoly of adversarial justice within the criminal courts gives way to new forms of justice, the very notion of justice has become blurred. One example is that courts across the nation are beginning to adopt forms of restorative justice that do not establish guilt but strive to improve the community by increasing the understanding between offenders and victims. More changes can be seen on the horizon of the U.S. courts, such as increasing controversy around elections and partisan judges.

The terrorist events of September 11, 2001, resulted in the creation of military commissions to deal with enemy combatants. Here, U.S. military personnel transport a detainee at the Guantánamo Bay U.S. Naval Base.

Fuzzy Justice: Alternatives to Court

KEY TERMS

military commission	rendition
ombud	restorative justice

Learning Objectives

After reading this chapter, you should be able to:

1. Discuss restorative justice as an alternative to formal court processing.
2. Give the advantages and disadvantages in bringing victims and offenders together.
3. Tell how reconciliation can be accomplished in a restorative justice framework.
4. Define ombud.
5. List and discuss the four principles upon which ombud standards of practice are based.
6. Describe the activities that ombuds participate in.
7. Define military commissions.
8. Discuss reasons that military commissions are appropriate for dealing with terrorism. Discuss reasons that they are inappropriate for this task.

The criminal court is not always the best place to address every dispute [1]. The court is an arena where the state can bring charges against and prosecute suspects, and sentence those who are convicted of breaking the law. But the criminal court is often overworked. In this chapter, we looked at some alternative courts that relieve some of the extremely heavy caseload of criminal courts because those courts can devote resources that deal more specifically with certain types of issues.

A step beyond using alternative courts is to bypass the court system altogether. There are times when the legal machinations of the court system are not

American Criminal Courts.
© 2014 Elsevier Inc. All rights reserved.

necessary or are even counterproductive [2]. Sometimes it is preferable to let individuals work out their differences in a structured environment without resorting to the often expensive resources of the criminal or even the civil court. Alternative dispute resolution mechanisms can not only save a great deal of money, but relationships between disputants can be preserved and more satisfactory outcomes can be achieved [3].

In this chapter, we will look at restorative justice programs, ombud programs, and military commissions. These programs, which are used by the communities, private companies, and the government, are often successful in diverting cases from the court system. Although alternative programs offer some benefits, going outside the court system also has some disadvantages. For example, participants may forfeit some legal protections and due process in exchange for the greater efficiency of alternative processes. Granted, participants often voluntarily waive these protections, but sometimes they do not [4]. A prime example is the military commissions the government uses to deal with terrorism suspects. These quasi-court mechanisms were invented to give the appearance of legitimate legal processing. This is a disputed and controversial practice that requires serious consideration. Without taking a position on the legality and morality of such hearings, this chapter will present arguments from both perspectives as to their efficacy [5].

The term "fuzzy justice" suggests that alternative court processes can be both beneficial and problematic to the goals of ensuring that both individuals and the state are afforded an equal opportunity to achieve justice. Fuzzy justice mechanisms will find adherents and detractors. As we explore these alternatives to formal court processing, we will be especially attuned to the power of the state to control the process and to the range of protections afforded to participants in quasi-legal courts and dispute resolution programs.

RESTORATIVE JUSTICE

One promising and popular alternative to formal court processing is a program called **restorative justice**. Restorative justice is an informal method of resolving disputes between individuals that acts to preserve their relationships [6]. By forgoing the adversarial processes of the traditional court system, restorative justice programs seek a less formal way to allow people to resolve their conflicts in a manner that allows for mutually agreed-upon compromises. Each party must feel that not only has justice been done, but also that they have not been declared a loser by the court system.

Many, if not most, of the cases brought to criminal court involve people who have prior relationships. It may be a dispute between neighbors, a fight between members of rival gangs, a case of domestic violence, or a larceny of a store by a regular customer. In each of these cases, not only have the disputants had a prior relationship, they are also likely to have an ongoing relationship in the future. Restorative justice programs seek to solve the present dispute and address the underlying issues so the parties feel that they have settled their present issue fairly and have obtained new tools for resolving future problems. In this way, restorative justice programs can be more effective than traditional criminal-court programs in solving problems of the present and the future [7].

Restorative justice practices require that we rethink what justice means [8]. At the heart of the theories behind restorative justice is the concept of "victim." Traditionally, the victim of a criminal offense has always been the party that suffered the offense. In ancient times, the victim or the victim's family was enti- tled to seek revenge or retribution from the offender and/or the offender's family. This is true of many cultures from ancient times and was encoded into the ancient Code of Hammurabi and several other Middle Eastern codes. Additionally, both Roman and Germanic tribal laws, as well as those in England, required restitution to victims and their families [9]. The crucial distinction here is that the victim and the victim's family were the ones entitled to justice, not the state.

Things are different today, and victims have been pushed farther toward the periphery of the justice process. The government prosecutes criminal suspects and demands that the legal outcome be focused on punishment or rehabili- tation rather than restitution, thus taking the case away from the victim. Norwegian criminologist Nils Christie compares these conflicts to property [10]. The conflict has become the responsibility of the prosecutor who determines charges, engages in plea bargaining, and works with other members of the court to achieve justice for the state. What is missing in the modern court is a place for the victim and the offender to reconcile their differences, and the victim is often left with the feeling that he or she is superfluous to the case [11].

To understand restorative justice, we must look at it through a different lens [12]. Instead of considering the offense as a violation of the law, restorative justice looks at the way the injury has affected the victim and the community. Instead of limiting the concerned parties to the offender and the government, restorative justice includes the community and the victim. The goal of restorative justice is to repair the damage done to relationships rather than simply sentence offenders to punishment or treatment in the hope that this will deter future crime. But how is this done? Ron Claassen at Fresno Pacific University has developed a list of fundamental principles of restorative justice (see Focus on Discretion). From this list of principles, it is easy to see how restorative justice principles differ from those of the criminal court. Although there are a variety of restorative justice programs, each with its own methods and practices of implementing restorative justice principles, some of the core values of restorative justice find their way into programs in one manner or another.

FOCUS ON DISCRETION

1. Crime is primarily an offense against human relationships and secondarily a violation of law since laws are written to protect safety and fairness in human relationships.

2. Restorative justice recognizes that crime (the violation of persons and relationships) is wrong and should not occur. It also recognizes that there are dangers and opportunities after crime does occur. The danger is that the community, victim(s), and/or offender emerge from the response further alienated, more damaged, disrespected, disempowered, feeling less safe, and less cooperative with society. The opportunity is that injustice is recognized, equity is restored, and the future is clarified so that participants are safer, more respectful, more empowered, and cooperative with each other and society.

3. Restorative justice is a process to "make things as right as possible" which includes attending to needs created by the offense such as safety and repair of injuries to relationships and physical damage resulting from the offense; and attending to needs related to the cause of the offense, such as addictions, lack of social or employment skills or resources, lack of moral or ethical base, and so on.

4. The primary victim(s) of a crime is/are the one(s) most affected by the offense. The secondary victims are others affected by the offense and may include family members, friends, witnesses, criminal justice officials, and the community.

5. As soon as immediate victim, community, and offender safety concerns are satisfied, restorative justice views the situation as a teachable moment for the offender, and an opportunity to encourage the offender to learn new ways of behaving in the community.

6. Restorative justice prefers responding to the offense at the earliest point possible and with the maximum amount of voluntary cooperation and minimum coercion, since healing in relationships and new learning are voluntary and cooperative processes.

7. Restorative justice prefers that most offenses are handled using a cooperative structure, including those affected by the offense, as a community to provide support and accountability.

This might include primary and secondary victims and family (or substitutes if they choose not to participate), the offender and family, community representatives, government representatives, faith community representatives, school representatives, and so on.

8. Restorative justice recognizes that not all offenders will choose to be cooperative. Therefore, outside authority must make decisions for uncooperative offenders. The actions of the authorities and the consequences imposed should be tested to confirm that they are reasonable, restorative, and respectful to the victim(s), offender, and community.

9. Restorative justice prefers that offenders who pose significant safety risks and are not yet cooperative be placed in settings where the emphasis is on safety, values, ethics, responsibility, accountability, and civility. They should be exposed to the effects of their offenses on victims, invited to learn empathy, and offered learning opportunities to become better equipped with skills to be a productive member of society. They should continually be invited, not coerced, to become cooperative with the community and be given the opportunity to demonstrate this in appropriate settings as soon as possible.

10. Restorative justice requires follow-up and accountability structures utilizing the natural community as much as possible, since keeping agreements is the key to building a trusting community.

11. Restorative justice recognizes and encourages the role of community institutions, including the religious/faith community, in teaching and establishing the moral and ethical standards which build up the community.

Question

How does restorative justice differ from our traditional concepts of justice based upon retribution?

Source: *Ron Claassen, Restorative Justice—Fundamental Principles, Center for Peacemaking and Conflict Studies, Fresno Pacific College, peace.fresno.edu/docs/rjprinc.html.*

Bringing Victims and Offenders Together

Many victims do not want contact with those who have harmed them. This is particularly true in cases of violence [13]. However, in other cases, it is appropriate to bring victims and offenders together in order to attempt to repair the harm done to their relationship. Bringing victims and offenders together works best when it is done under the auspices of a well-run restorative justice program.

In a regular courtroom, there is limited opportunity for the victim to address the offender. Recently, courts have recognized that crime victims get little or no opportunity to participate in the cases other than being witnesses and have allowed victims to provide victim impact statements for the judge to use during the sentencing phase. Victim impact statements typically express the victims' outrage and detail the emotional and physical injuries that were sustained. The intent is to convince the judge to prescribe a severe punishment. Although this may assuage the victims to some extent, it does little to repair the damage to the relationship or bring closure to the victim [14].

Several types of restorative justice programs allow encounters between victims and offenders. Let's take a look at some of these, including mediation, conferencing, circles, and impact panels.

Mediation

Mediation programs involve bringing the offender and victim together along with a trained mediator who helps guide the interaction [15]. Although reconciliation might be a primary goal in some victim–offender mediation programs, it is not always a realistic one. Often, the victim and offender were strangers before their conflict and have little likelihood of seeing each other again. Repairing the harm done by the offense in cases such as this is not something that is vigorously pursued by either party, but it may still occur. More important, the goal of resolving the conflict revolves around the issues of identifying the injustice that has been done, discussing how to make things right, then developing a plan.

Mediation helps the offender comprehend the harm that has been done to the victim and to ascertain his or her responsibility. It also allows victims to "have a voice" in which they may confront the offender and tell their side of the story. Mediation programs allow the victim and offender to negotiate a resolution to their conflict that can be satisfying to each.

There are some obstacles, however, to reaching a satisfying resolution, such as a power differential between the victim and the offender [16]. The offender may be the victim's boss, spouse, or landlord. A truly successful mediation ends up with the offender committing to an agreement and making restitution or providing an apology (Photo 14.1).

PHOTO 14.1 Mediation.
Mediators must often undergo several hours of training. Here, a student covers his face while laughing during an exercise at a New York Department of Education mediation training session. The exercise involved the participants treating one another in the manner suggested on their headbands.

Conferencing

Conferencing is another way of bringing offenders and victims together to craft solutions to their conflicts. The primary distinction between conferencing and mediation is that conferencing involves many more parties. Besides the offender and the victim, members of each family, the arresting officer, representatives from the criminal justice or juvenile justice system, and concerned members from the community who have input into the circumstances of the case (or an interest in the result) are present [17]. It is not unusual to have a dozen or more people present at the conference. Rather than being mediated, conferences are guided by a trained facilitator who ensures that the discussion stays on topic and does not wander into unproductive and argumentative territory.

The conference begins with the person thought to be responsible for the harm explaining what happened. Then, beginning with the victim, the other conference participants ask questions, make suggestions, or detail their experiences and feelings about the event. The conference then moves on to the task of developing a plan to resolve the problem. The goal of the conference is to repair the harm brought about by the act. By allowing all concerned parties to have a hand in developing the resolution plan, it has been shown that not only does recidivism decrease, but that there is a higher level of victim satisfaction than with normal court processing [18].

Conferencing was first developed in New Zealand and Australia. Today, most conferencing is performed with young lawbreakers and their families. Although there are distinct differences between various models of conferencing, the overall structure remains consistent. The goal of repairing the harm done to the relationship between the offender and the victim, as well as other affected parties, remains primary [19]. The challenge for the conference facilitator is to maintain a positive atmosphere without resorting to dominating the proceedings. The idea is to let the participants express their perspectives and feelings and craft their own resolution plan. In this way, everyone becomes more committed to making the process work because, rather than have it dictated to them, they actually develop it themselves [20].

Circles

Restorative justice circles share many of the qualities of conferencing. There are, however, several distinct differences. This technique was first developed by American Indians and focuses on the harmony of the community as much as it does on the offender and the victim [21].

The circle includes a wide range of participants including not only the offender and the victim but also friends and families, community members, and justice system representatives. The primary distinction between conferencing and circles is that circles do not focus exclusively on the offense and do not limit their solutions to repairing the harm between the victim and the offender. Rather, circles consider the situation that has caused the conflict in a more holistic manner. The advantage of this process is that it allows the community to look at the underlying problems that may produce conflict. For instance, if groups of young people are fighting over limited recreational facilities, such as a basketball court, the solution may be for the community to build more basketball courts. This is a solution that cannot be affected by the traditional court system, mediation, or even conferencing programs. It requires the input of community stakeholders who have the authority and resources to solve the underlying problem of limited recreational facilities.

The restorative justice circle can be cumbersome and time-consuming. Often, the issues cannot be resolved in a single meeting; circles typically require multiple sessions in which new participants continuously enter the process. In this way, systemic change can be accomplished, the initial conflict between offender and victim is addressed, and a wider solution that affects the entire community is developed [22].

Impact Panels

Impact panels differ significantly from the types of restorative justice practices that we have discussed. In impact panels, offenders and victims exchange viewpoints, but not with those involved in their particular offense. That is, the offender does not meet the victim, but rather victims of offenses similar to the one he or she committed [23].

In a particularly traumatic offense, a victim does not want to meet with their actual offender. However, victims often desire to tell their story to other offenders. For instance, those who have lost loved ones in a drunk-driving accident will address a group of those convicted of driving under the influence and impress upon them the distress they experience because of the accident. The hope is that by listening to the victims of a similar incident, drunk-driving offenders will appreciate how their behavior has affected their victims [24].

Impact panels are not the give-and-take discussion that allows offenders to talk about their actions, and not all offenders are suitable for this type of encounter. Offenders who participate in impact panels need to have shown some type of remorse for their offense and a willingness to listen respectfully to their victim's story. Not all victims are suitable for impact panels, either. The idea is not to demean or humiliate the offenders, but rather to allow them to listen and try to appreciate the harm they have done. For example, it is been shown that those convicted of burglary begin to understand how it is not necessarily the loss of property that has most upset the victim, but rather the fact that a stranger has entered their house and violated their sense of security [25].

Making Amends

As can be seen from the above examples of restorative justice encounter sessions, bringing together offenders and victims and other interested parties can promote healing for everyone. At first blush, this may seem counterintuitive, but reconciliation can be accomplished by giving offenders and victims an opportunity to understand the effects of the offense [26]. Furthermore, by including community members in some sessions, some of the underlying conditions that led to the offense can be addressed.

What does this have to do with justice? Rather than the offender answering to the state by being sentenced to incarceration or required to pay financial restitution, the offender answers to the victim or victims of the offense and is able to express remorse, ask forgiveness, and begin the journey toward repentance. For the victim, the experience allows them to "have voice" by telling their story to their offender, or in cases of impact panels, to those who have committed similar offenses.

For a victim/offender encounter to be successful, the offender must make amends to the victim. These amends include three distinct characteristics [27]:

- Apology. The offender must apologize to the victim. In this apology, the offender must take responsibility for his or her actions by acknowledging the offending behavior and admitting it was wrong. Second, the offender should express regret. When the victim witnesses this regret, he or she may be better able to forgive the offender. Finally, the offender must make this apology without offering excuses [28]. The key is that offenders do not try to cast themselves as a victim of circumstances or try to excuse their behavior [29].
- Change of behavior. An apology falls flat if the offender continues to commit the offense. By changing behavior, the offender can show as well as tell. For instance, a man who makes inappropriate sexual innuendos at work must stop this type of behavior so that females feel comfortable in his presence. By saying he is sorry, but still engaging in inappropriate behavior, the apology is a hollow platitude.
- Restitution. A third step in making amends is for the offender to pay restitution to the victim or the community. Restitution is an important step to repairing the harm done to not only the relationship between the offender and the victim, but also as a way for the offender to develop the feelings of "paying his dues." Restitution can take many forms: a financial payment to the victim, performing direct services for the victim, or engaging in community service. Depending upon the situation, the victim may desire no further contact with the offender but this does not mean the offender cannot engage in activities that mitigate the harm [30].

The elements of restorative justice can be considered as efforts to make the justice system more responsive to the needs of victims and offenders. They allow for the reintegration of offenders into the community and for victims into the normal routines of their life before the offense. Crime is a traumatic event for its victims, and the criminal justice system process can be traumatic for the offender.

What is the role of restorative justice programs in the criminal justice system? The answer depends upon the ability of restorative justice professionals to convince traditional criminal justice practitioners that restorative justice is not only a viable alternative to normal criminal justice processing but also that it advances the goals of justice. This can be a difficult case to make. For many people, justice implies retribution, punishment, and incapacitation. They have a difficult time understanding the idea that victims and offenders can negotiate a fair outcome of the case. There are a number of conceptual and practical objections to restorative justice programs, including:

- Multiple parties cannot pursue multiple goals and achieve a single purpose.
- Not all offenses can be identified, and of those that are, not all are of equal importance.

- Government and community will not be able to share responsibility for public safety in the way anticipated by restorative justice theory.
- Restorative justice will diminish due-process protections.
- Victims cannot receive adequate attention in any model that simultaneously considers offender rehabilitation.
- Restorative justice will cause unacceptable disparity of sanctions.
- Coercion will be necessary, and coercion is antithetical to a restorative model.
- Restorative justice will not work with dangerous offenders.
- Most victims and offenders are never identified.
- Large-scale use of restorative justice will lead to its depersonalization.
- Individualistic and pluralistic cultures will keep restorative justice from working.
- Restorative justice may work for minor offenses, but certainly not for rape or murder [31].

Many of these objections are substantial and require a good deal of reflection and explanation. Let's highlight a couple of these objections and discuss how they affect crucial criminal justice system issues.

One of the important objections that highlights the theme of our discussion of the criminal justice system is the allegation that due-process protections will be reduced. As discussed in previous chapters, the development of due-process protections has been difficult and contentious in the history of the criminal court [32]. Anything that reduces these protections may be considered a threat. So how do restorative justice practices affect due process? The answer is "it depends." It depends upon the training of the restorative justice personnel and the structure of the program. The argument can be made that because restorative justice requires voluntary participation from offenders, they waive some of their due-process rights. However, most of the offenders who participate in restorative justice are willing to admit their guilt and are interested in resolving the conflict in a harmonious manner. Those who believe they are completely innocent of any wrongdoing are unlikely to choose a restorative justice process.

Another commonly expressed objection to restorative justice is that it will not work with serious offenses. However, when one closely examines a large percentage of the types of murders committed in the United States, it becomes clear that murder may be one of the offenses that is most amenable to restorative justice (see Courts in the Media). In many cases of homicide, the victim and offender know each other or may even be related. Those who have ongoing relationships can benefit from programs that help them ease some of the harm that has been done [33]. A man who murders his wife will continue, in some fashion, to be a parent to his children. It may be possible for the family to come to terms with the tragedy and find ways of mitigating the harm done to the relationship between father and children. It is important to note that not all cases can be successfully resolved through restorative justice practices. History has shown us, however, that some of the most unlikely cases have been successfully brought to closure.

COURTS IN THE MEDIA

Forgiveness

A criticism of restorative justice is that it can only be used for minor offenses. Setting up a meeting between a victim and offender and attempting to reintegrate the offender into the community may serve well for an offense like vandalism, shoplifting, or even burglary, but not for serious offenses such as rape and murder. How can healing and forgiveness occur after such a destructive offense? Even if the victim or the victim's family did forgive the offender, what good does it do? After all, the breaking of a law is an offense against the state, and the state punishes offenders, in part, to set an example to others who may be considering breaking the law.

Although the restorative justice model has not been used extensively enough in serious offenses for any reliable data to be gathered, some individuals have been successful in applying restorative justice processes and ideals in their own lives to recover from tragedy. In the cases below, victims' families embarked on their own restorative justice plans; these were not processes suggested or required by the state. However, the positive effects of forgiveness and reconciliation in these instances are unmistakable.

- In 1973, Marietta Jaeger Lane, her husband, and five children were on a camping trip in Montana. During the first night, David Meirhoffer cut through the family's tent and kidnapped 7-year-old Susie. The child was never found, although police continued to search for the kidnapper. Lane says she "was just ravaged with hatred and a desire for revenge," but drew on her religious faith for guidance. A year later, when Meirhoffer phoned Lane to taunt her about the kidnapping, Lane spoke to him with compassion and asked what she could do to help. Meirhoffer broke down in tears, and their hour-long conversation helped police find Meirhoffer. In court, Meirhoffer admitted to the rape, strangulation, and

dismemberment of Susie, along with three other murders. He plead guilty when offered, at Lane's request, mandatory life imprisonment without parole. Just hours after confessing, Meirhoffer killed himself [34].

- In 1987, Mike Carlucci, a career offender and drug addict, shot 24-year-old Scott Everett in the head outside an apartment complex after mistaking him for a burglar. Everett's father, Walt, a pastor, struggled with feelings of rage and hate for a year after the murder, especially when he learned Carlucci was only sentenced to 5 years in prison. After Everett gave his victim impact statement, Carlucci apologized. Later, Everett wrote Carlucci a letter explaining that he forgave Carlucci for murdering his son. Carlucci thanked Everett for his forgiveness, and the two began a correspondence. In 1991, Everett went to the parole board in support of Carlucci's freedom, and Carlucci left prison after serving 3 years. Today, the two men are good friends and together give talks about their experiences [35].

- In 1993, 16-year-old Oshea Israel shot and killed Laramiun Byrd, 20, at a party. Israel served 16 years in prison. Byrd's mother, Mary Johnson, admitted that when she saw the 16-year-old Israel in court, she had wanted to "go over and hurt" him. However, after 12 years of anger, she began visiting Israel in prison and telling him about her son. It was then that "he became human to me," Israel says. Today, the two live next door to each other in Minneapolis. Israel visits Johnson and runs errands for her, and Johnson treats Israel as a son. "It motivates me to make sure that I stay on the right path," Israel says [36].

Question

Can you identify the restorative justice principles at work in each case?

Ombud

An **ombud** serves as a neutral party within an organization and provides conflict resolution and problem-solving services. Ombud programs have been around for many years and are used as alternative methods of settling disputes before they reach the courts. The cases heard by ombud programs are not criminal cases. At least not yet. If the ombud is successful, he or she resolves the conflict between the parties before it reaches formal grievance procedures, lawsuits, or violence. As a form of dispute resolution program, ombud programs actively involve the contesting parties in the resolution of the case. Because individuals get to participate in the solution, they have a greater sense that justice has been served. This means that the resolutions are more likely to last a long time. By opening lines of communication between the disputing parties and teaching them how to negotiate in a civil manner, ombud programs empower the participants to deal with future conflicts. In this manner, ombud programs can help change the culture of an organization so that it becomes more cooperative [37]. (See Careers in the Court for more on the occupation of ombud.)

CAREERS IN THE COURT

Ombud

An ombud serves as a neutral party within an organization and provides conflict resolution and problem-solving services. An internal ombud serves members of the organization, and an external ombuds serves the organization's clients and customers. Of course, a single ombud may do both jobs. Some organizations split the job along different lines. For example, a university may employ an ombud for faculty and students and another ombud for staff. Any sector of the workforce may employ ombuds, including corporate, academic, governmental, and nonprofit sectors.

Because the job of ombud is so new, there is no established path to the position, nor any specific training or certification required. However, an ombud must be at good at both listening and talking, be able to communicate with a diverse range of people, be discreet, be creative, and able to analyze and solve problems.

Typically, ombuds have a high school diploma or equivalent, and a college degree. Some ombuds have worked as lawyers and professors. A prospective or newly hired ombud may be required to complete training in conflict resolution, negotiation, or conflict management. Many ombuds have held other jobs within their organizations, such as positions in customer service, human resources, or administration. An academic ombud may have a degree in law, criminology, criminal justice, sociology, social work, and may have held a previous administrative position. Organization that does not hire an ombud from within may use independent or freelance ombud who contract their services.

Ombuds are most likely to find work in large metropolitan areas that have many corporations or government agencies. The salary ranges depend on the employer, the field, the geographic location, and the size of the organization. The average salary is about $65,000, although some small government agencies may pay as little as $25,000. Some ombuds in medical fields earn over $90,000.

Question

What skills should an ombuds possess in order to resolve conflicts?

Four Principles of Ombud Programs

The International Ombudsman Association has established standards of practice that dictate how member organizations should implement ombud programs. These standards of practice revolve around the four following principles: independence, neutrality and impartiality, confidentiality, and informality [38].

Independence

The ombud who works within an organization should be independent from other entities within the organization. The ombud should not hold any other position in the organization that could compromise neutrality. However, this separation is typically difficult to achieve, and only large organizations have the resources to employ a dedicated ombud. In smaller organizations, the ombud holds other duties and performs the ombud's activities on a part-time basis. Nevertheless, the ombud's office should conscientiously pursue independence.

In maintaining independence, a few concerns must be considered. First, the ombud should report directly to the head of the organization. The ombud's reports should be general in nature and not disclose any circumstances of any cases. Additionally, the ombud should have sole authority to hire staff for the office and manage the budget. The ombud's office should not be part of human resources or personnel because the policies of these offices, and the actions of their employees, are often the subjects of dispute. The ombud should be organizationally located outside of these offices. The ombud should have access to all the organization's records and be able to view them without being required to explain anything about any cases that are currently under consideration. Additionally, the ombud should have the discretion to open any case based upon any complaint or upon his or her direct observation.

Neutrality and Impartiality

The ombud should be neutral. The ombud should not advocate for the organization or for any of the participants in the dispute and have no personal or organizational interests in the outcome. The ombud's role is to help the participants find common ground to resolve their disputes. The ombud does not act as prosecutor or judge, but simply as a facilitator who helps the participants to identify ways of resolving their differences.

This impartiality can sometimes be difficult to achieve. In many cases, one of the participants may have acted illegally, unethically, or against the organization's best interests. The ombud must hold in abeyance his or her moral judgment on the case and assist the participants in identifying the issues, developing options, and choosing the best resolution. These judgments must be made by the disputing parties and not the ombud. However, the ombud has an opportunity and the responsibility to ensure that the legitimate concerns of the participants are fully addressed.

Confidentiality

The ombud must pledge confidentiality to all those who seek help from the office. By contacting the ombud's office, complaining parties should not be required to press the case forward, defend their concerns, or be worried that administrators or supervisors will learn that they have contacted the ombud. Participants should feel that their conversations are confidential and that the ombud office will not "run away with their case."

The ombud pledges confidentiality and in trying to resolve the case, always asks permission from each party about what can and cannot be shared with the opposing party. The information provided in the ombud's office is considered privileged and others cannot waive this. For instance, if the president of the organization wanted to know who had concerns with a particular policy, the ombud would not reveal this even though instructed to by the president. The idea behind the privilege of the ombud's office is that it serves a higher goal of truth and trust rather than the organization's immediate concerns. The idea is that the organization is healthier when individuals have confidence that what they tell the ombud will not be shared with others in the organization without their permission.

The ombud does not testify in court or in formal grievance procedures should the case not be satisfactorily resolved. Although it may be tempting for some attorneys to use the ombud's proceedings as a form of discovery, the principles of the International Ombud Association specifically guard against this. Any notes concerning the meeting should be destroyed once the case is completed. Additionally, any appointment books, calendars, or other materials that are directly or indirectly related to the case should be kept secure from observations by others and destroyed once the case is concluded.

Informality

Informality means that conflicts may be addressed without leaving a paper trail or putting individuals on the record as having difficulties within the organization. The ombud's office is not a place where notice to an organization can be registered. This means that some activities, such as sexual assault, require members of the organization to record and report allegations even if the victim desires otherwise. The ombud is not required to report such cases and in fact is prohibited from doing so by the standards of practice. What the ombud does do is provide the victim with the information about how and where to register notice of the activity. This allows the victim to decide whether to make the report. If the ombud's office was required to make reports in such cases, then individuals would be reluctant to talk to the ombud for fear that the case would be "taken away from them" and reported to his or her supervisors. The informal nature of the ombud's office helps to provide disputants with an arena to explore the conflicts they are having with others and an opportunity to participate in crafting solutions.

How Ombud's Offices Work?

Ombud's offices engage in several activities, including mediation. One variant of mediation that ombud's offices use frequently is "shuttle diplomacy." Many cases can be resolved without sitting the disputants down in a room and having them air their grievances to each other. Sometimes this type of mediation can be counterproductive because it increases the tension between the parties. By using shuttle diplomacy, the ombud, armed with permission from each party, negotiates a resolution without the parties ever meeting.

In these third-party negotiations, the ombud will go from one party to the other and try to distinguish what the core principles of the dispute are. Within the parameters of the permission, the ombud has been given to share information, the ombud will attempt to find a resolution to the problem by demonstrating how one party may have a legal or morally superior position, by showing how both parties may benefit from a compromise, or by establishing that the dispute is so trivial that the disputants are spending unnecessary time and resources to address it.

Often, the ombud does not have a clear picture of exactly what the dispute is until he or she is well into the case. The disputants may not have a clear idea either until the ombud shares the concerns of the other party. This process can happen quickly or it could drag on for weeks. Sometimes the resolution calls for a direct face-to-face mediation, and sometimes it can be resolved with a verbal agreement. By using ascertainable criteria, such as the employee handbook, the ombud can often demonstrate to the disputants that policies are already in place that dictate how the case should be decided. It is remarkable how often employees (as well as employers) are not familiar with their organization's policy documents.

In addition to shuttle diplomacy, the ombud can help complaining disputants identify options. Often, individuals simply do not understand the policies and procedures of the organization or how to deal with their problems. After talking with the ombud, they can gather valuable information about the organization's policies and ascertain whether they have actually been disadvantaged. Once this has been decided, the ombud can help them appreciate the options that are available to them and to select one that best satisfies their sense of justice. At no time does the ombud make decisions on the part of the individual or the organization. The role of the ombud is simply to provide an arena where people can gather the necessary information to make informed decisions themselves.

Although the ombud does not participate in policy development, he or she may be called upon to help the organization evaluate problematic trends. As long as confidentiality is not compromised, the ombud may give advice on a wide range of issues. It is up to the traditional structures of the organization to implement any recommended changes. The ombud's goal is to make sure that the concerns of all involved are carefully considered in evaluating policy changes.

Several concerns can be raised about the practice of ombud offices. Sometimes the process fails to protect the rights of the individuals in conflict. The International Ombud Association has gone to great lengths to develop a code of ethics and standards of practice that address these concerns. Still, a few issues continue to be of interest to those that question the efficacy of the ombud's office.

■   Confidentiality. Although the ombud makes it a point to assure confidentiality to all those who come in contact with the office, the ombud may not be able to fulfill that promise in all cases. Once a case escalates to the level of a lawsuit or trial, the ombud may be compelled to provide the information the office has gathered. To protect against this, ombud's offices purposefully destroy their records once cases have been resolved or move on to more formal proceedings. However, a court can instruct ombud's office not to destroy records [39].

■   Power differentials. There are times when the disputants have a vastly different status with the organization. This difference between a secretary and a boss, a maintenance worker and a faculty member, or a manager and a CEO may make it difficult for the subordinate to feel comfortable in providing information about the case. It is always possible that the conflict will reappear in a different form later and that the subordinate will suffer from challenging the organization. Even if a satisfactory resolution is created, the subordinate may still fear not having adequate legal protection against thinly guised reprisals. Subordinates may also be uncomfortable in arguing their case in the presence of a boss who they deem to be a bully [40].

- Due-process protections. Most organizations have a well-articulated grievance procedure that defines the protections afforded each party. At minimum, each disputant should have the opportunity to present his or her side of the story, question hostile evidence and witnesses, and be provided written notice of the charges against them. In the ombud's process, these due-process procedures are often considered unnecessary. Because the participants voluntarily engage in the ombud's process, they are not so concerned with the details of their due-process rights as long as they feel they are being treated fairly. Individuals are much more likely to share their feelings, suggest options for mutual gain, and commit to solutions when they are released from worrying about all the legal issues that may arise in the case [41].

The effect of restorative justice programs and ombud offices on the number of cases in the criminal court is difficult to measure. Because the goal of these types of programs is to address the dispute at the lowest level possible, there is really no way to measure how many of these cases have been diverted from the criminal court and how many never would have made it there anyway.

Nevertheless, these processes engender a type of fuzzy justice that is difficult to evaluate. There is no question that these programs have become popular ways of resolving disputes that have saved courts a great deal in terms of time and resources but, it can be argued, some of the cases handled this way would have been better served had they been sent to criminal court.

The central theme of this chapter is concerned with the efficacy of using these alternatives to the criminal-court programs. It can be argued that individuals feel more empowered by using these programs even though they utilize quasi-legal processes that bypass the normal protections of court procedures. But what happens when individuals do not voluntarily give up their due-process rights, but rather are deprived of them?

MILITARY COMMISSIONS

The terrorist events of September 11, 2001, were a turning point in how the United States utilizes its criminal justice system and military. To deal with those who attacked the United States as part of al Qaeda, the government created **military commissions**, or courts that try violations of the laws of war and other offenses.

Military Commissions Versus the Criminal Court

The criminal-court system is designed to achieve two goals. First, it seeks to assign guilt and sentence those who have broken the criminal law. Second, it attempts to do this within the rule of law. This means that U.S. citizens are protected by a variety of legal devices designed to ensure that the power of the state does not overwhelm their individual rights and liberties. The Constitution, particularly the Bill of Rights, state constitutions, federal and state statutes, and court precedent all make the functions of the criminal court not only transparent and ascertainable but also fair in its application of justice. The phrase "a nation of laws, not of men" is often used to describe how the rule of law drives criminal-court processes.

Foreign nationals who break the law in the United States are also protected by the rule of law, and well-designed legal processes handle issues such as immigration and deportation, extradition, and transnational crime [42]. Those suspected of criminal offenses enjoy many of the same privileges as citizens in terms of access to attorneys and the right to confront hostile witnesses. For individuals from many nations around the world, the legal rights provided in a U.S. court far exceed those of their native lands. There are, however, some notable exceptions, as well as some legal trends that make the phrase "rule of law" a matter of much contention.

The Military Commissions Act of 2006 (MCA) is currently the statutory basis for military commissions (some improvements were made in the MCA of 2009). Congress enacted the MCA in direct response to the Supreme Court's decision in *Hamdan v. Rumsfeld* (see Landmark Cases). The military commission's jurisdiction is "alien unprivileged enemy belligerents for violations of the law of war and other offenses triable by military commission" [43].

The commission is a group of at least five commissioned armed forces officers who are appointed by the secretary of defense or the secretary's designee. Military attorneys serve as defense and prosecution, and a military judge presides over the proceedings. The commission only hears some of the evidence because classified information remains protected. After the arguments, the commission deliberates in private, votes by secret paper ballot, and may convict a defendant by a two-thirds majority. The standard of proof required by the commission is proof beyond a reasonable doubt. If the death penalty is possible, then conviction and sentencing requires a unanimous vote [44].

LANDMARK CASES

Hamdan v. Rumsfeld (2006)

The military commissions set up in the wake of September 11 do not have the power to try Guantánamo Bay detainees because they violate the Geneva Convention and the Uniform Code of Military Justice.

In 2001, Afghani forces captured Yemeni national Salim Ahmed Hamdan, Osama bin Laden's former chauffeur, and the U.S. military incarcerated him in Guantánamo Bay. Over a year later, President Bush deemed Hamdan eligible for trial by military commission. Hamdan challenged his detention by filing writ of habeas corpus in federal district court. Before the district court ruled, Hamdan was designated an enemy combatant in a military commission hearing.

The district court granted Hamdan's petition a few months later, ruling that he must first receive a hearing to determine whether he was a prisoner of war under the Geneva Convention before a military commission could try him. The Circuit Court of Appeals for the District of Columbia reversed the decision, finding that federal court could not enforce the Geneva Convention and that Congress had authorized the establishment of military commissions.

The Supreme Court held that the military commission used in this case was unauthorized by either Congress or the Executive branch. The military commission had to comply with U.S. law and the laws of war, including the Geneva Conventions and the statutory Uniform Code of Military Justice. The defendant's exclusion from parts of his own trial that the military commission considered classified violated the Geneva Conventions and the Uniform Code of Military Justice. The trial was therefore illegal.

If a defendant is found guilty, that finding is subject to automatic review by a panel of appellate military judges. The convicted may appeal the decisions of both the commission and the appellate panel to the U.S. Court of Appeals for the DC Circuit, and the Supreme Court may review the decision. The president must approve death sentences [45].

Despite the existence of the military commission, those accused of terrorist activities can be held indefinitely, in secret, without access to attorneys, without charges, and with no opportunity to defend themselves against allegations [46]. For an example of why this situation has developed, we will look at a hypo-thetical case of a Saudi Arabian citizen who has been captured on a battlefield in Afghanistan.

- *Saudi Arabia*. Even though this man is a citizen of Saudi Arabia, the behavior for which he is being incarcerated occurred in Afghanistan. Therefore, the legal protections that Saudi Arabia has for its citizens are not available to this man. This is a well-established legal principle. When visiting another nation, you are subject to that nation's laws.
- *Afghanistan*. The laws of Afghanistan do not apply to this Saudi citizen because Afghanistan is not prosecuting him. Therefore, instead of being subject to the laws of Afghanistan, one would expect this individual be subject to the Geneva Conventions, which, in part, sets forth the international standards for the humanitarian treatment of prisoners of war.

- *The United States.* After capturing this man in Afghanistan, the United States transports him to a U.S. military base in Cuba. Even though this man was captured on a battlefield, he is not designated a "prisoner of war" but rather an "enemy combatant," a designation invented to describe alleged terrorists. Because this man was not part of a regulated army, but was rather a volunteer to the al Qaeda movement, the United States asserts that he is not actually a soldier, but an uncommitted resistance fighter or terrorist. Because he lacks a uniform, is not subject to a hierarchical chain of command in his combat unit, is free to leave the battlefield and go home whenever he wants, and is not subject to a specified military discipline system, it is reasoned that this man lacks the circumstances of a soldier and so is not entitled to be considered a prisoner of war. Additionally, because this man is not a U.S. citizen, he is not protected by the Constitution. Furthermore, this man is not part of the United States military, so he is not covered by the Uniform Code of Military Justice. In effect then, no system of law provides any protection to a man who is accused of terrorism under these circumstances.
- *Cuba.* The U.S. military base at Guantánamo Bay, Cuba, is not subject to Cuban law. Instead, the U.S. military under the auspices of the Department of Justice has developed its own legal mechanism for dealing with those alleged to have committed terrorist acts. Because they are enemy combatants rather than prisoners of war, they are not protected by any national or international legal convention.

This method of combating terrorism has been defended in a number of ways. It can be argued that terrorism is somewhat similar to war, but is so different that extraordinary measures are required to deal with it. Typically trials for war crimes, such as the Nuremberg trials after World War II, occur after hostilities have ceased. Germany was defeated, and any evidence or testimony that was revealed by these trials could not affect a war that was already over [47]. By contrast, the war on terrorism is an ongoing endeavor with no end in sight. Any trials or military commissions that seek to assign culpability for terrorism risk providing intelligence to the enemy. Revealing how evidence was obtained (electronic surveillance, covert operators, al Qaeda informants) could compromise human assets and shut off productive streams of intelligence. There are good reasons to protect sensitive information that should not be made public because of the ongoing nature of the war on terror.

The United States a history of using military commissions during war. It was used as a tool of the legal system in the Mexican-American war, the Civil War, and World War II. A military commission tried those implicated in the 1865 assassination of President Abraham Lincoln and the attempts on Vice President Andrew Johnson, Secretary of State William Seward, and General Ulysses

Grant. This commission, called the Hunter Commission, was a commission composed of nine officers in which more than 350 witnesses testified. Given the condition of Washington, DC, after the Civil War and assassination, it is unlikely that a fair and impartial civilian trial would have been possible [48].

Military Commissions and Fuzzy Justice

Although there may be good reasons to refer to military commissions to deal with international terrorists, this method of justice has drawn a great deal of criticism. One fundamental problem is concerned with how terrorism is defined.

> One of the central problems with the presidential order is that its definition of terrorism is so broad that it could include almost any behavior ... Further confounding the definition of terrorist is that the President, through the Attorney General, has discretion to determine who fits the definition. This unreviewable decision places tremendous powers of life and death into the administration's hands. Moreover, the definition of terrorist is vague and indefinite, providing the Attorney General, vis-à-vis the authority of the Executive, wide latitude in determining who is subject to a commission. It is this open-ended latitude to place U.S. persons in commissions that is an affront to our U.S. cultural and legal identity [49].

In addition to this concern about the shift of power from the criminal justice system to the executive branch of the government, the use of military commissions for the prosecution of terrorist suspects is problematic for other reasons. For instance, why are al Qaeda fighters not afforded Geneva Conventions protections? They fight as military units and have been captured on battlefields. One reason given for the lack of Geneva Conventions protections is that the conventions do not cover "unlawful actors." Al Qaeda fighters do not follow the rules of war; therefore they lose the right to be considered soldiers [50].

The process the commission uses to gather evidence against the alleged terrorists has also been criticized. Several tactics have used the war on terror to circumvent the principles of due process.

- Rendition. **Rendition** is the process of sending a criminal suspect to another country to be interrogated or detained. The Central Intelligence Agency (CIA) purportedly renditions terrorism suspects to nations that have different standards from the United States on what constitutes torture. By using the CIA's aviation fleet to deliver prisoners to nations such as Egypt, Syria, and Iraq, the CIA is able to allow officials from these nations to torture prisoners for information on terrorist activities [51]. Although CIA officials do not participate in the torture themselves, they are present when suspects are tortured. This gives the CIA "plausible deniability" that they did not perform the torture themselves. Although the argument can be made that rendition might save lives, they undermine the credibility of the United States as a nation that adheres to the rule of law [52].

- Torture. The United States has engaged in a wide range of what they term "enhanced interrogation techniques." These include physical and psychological tactics aimed at breaking down suspected terrorists. The most controversial of these techniques is waterboarding. Waterboarding, or simulated drowning, typically consists of forcing the victim to lie supine, then force water into his or her mouth. This type of torture has several advantages. First, it can be done frequently. Suspects recover quickly and can be subjected to it many times the same day or over many weeks or months. Second, it does not leave marks or scars. Waterboarding produces acute temporary discomfort, but no long-term physical damage. At issue is the value of the information obtained by this method. Because these prisoners have been held in custody for such a long time, it is suggested that whatever interrogation techniques elicited the information that is being used against the detainees is still considered by the detainees as being produced by the threat of torture.

- Indefinite detention. Some of the detainees at the Guantánamo Bay detention camp have been there for many years, held without charges, without a formal hearing, and without an opportunity to challenge their confinement. Under most established legal systems, they would have been either charged with criminal offenses or released a long time ago. It is unclear how the prisoners can receive a fair trial when they have been incarcerated for such a long time. The offenses they are accused of occurred on the battlefields of Afghanistan, and the prisoners do not have access to interviewing witnesses or accusers. After such a long incarceration, it is highly unlikely that detainees can produce a credible defense against any charges [53].

- Access to attorneys. Although these detainees are being held in various prisons around the world, including Guantánamo Bay, they have been denied access to attorneys. When attorneys are provided to some of these detainees, the usual attorney–client privilege is suspended. Attorneys are not allowed to meet their clients privately, and any information the detainees give their attorneys is considered "contraband information" [54]. The government has instructed the attorneys that there are certain topics, including torture, that they are not to discuss with their clients. One attorney who served as a defense counsel with the Office of

Military Commissions observed that, contrary to popular belief, it is the prosecuting attorneys who had the most difficulty with the proceedings because they were "... more likely to find that the prosecution of detainees in the Military Commissions was incompatible with their oath to defend the Constitution." On the other hand, the defense attorneys, "... were highly motivated, quite vigorous, and indisputably effective in this role because challenging the fundamentally flawed military commissions and the inexcusable treatment of detainees presented no conflict of interest to military counsel dedicated to core American values of due process, humane treatment, justice, and the rule of law" [55].

These are but a few of the more serious concerns about the efficacy of military commissions to deal with terrorism suspects. From a due-process perspective, the military commissions have failed to accord even the most elementary legal protections to the detainees. What is the justification? Several lines of reasoning are used to justify these types of quasi-legal maneuverings. One of the first is that the war on terror requires extreme measures. International terrorists are not typical offenders and should not expect the privileges and protections of the U.S. Constitution when they attack U.S. citizens. As international terrorists, they do not enjoy the protections of other sovereign states that have treaties with the United States. In fact, the detainees are stateless individuals because they reject by their actions all the conventions of orderly society.

Another argument is that military commissions are the appropriate place to try international terrorists because their actions are more like military campaigns than traditional street crime. The traditional components of crime such as motive, means, and opportunity are not as crucial to adjudicating acts of terrorism as are concerns such as political ideology, membership in terrorist organizations, and evidence of conspiracy.

Finally it can be argued that military commissions are appropriate because sensitive information vital to national security can be protected from the transparent nature of the criminal court. Because terrorism is an ongoing threat to the United States, information that comes out in the commissions must be censored so that enemies of the United States do not benefit from the evidence that is presented. In the hearings dealing with terrorism suspects in Cuba, the alleged mastermind of the September 11 attacks, Khalid Sheikh Mohammed, protested the nature of that captivity. The observers allowed to witness the hearings over closed-circuit television found that:

> When he [Mohammed] said the word torture, all anyone heard was white noise. The military commissions pipe white noise into the

viewing rooms whenever there is a concern that classified information is being revealed. Because the sound coming out of the courtroom is on a 40-second delay and outsiders are behind soundproof glass or watching on monitors, censors have time to block out classified information with static [56].

FUZZY JUSTICE AND THE CRIMINAL COURT

In some ways it can be argued that all justice in the criminal court is fuzzy justice. This is because justice is a contested and negotiated commodity. Although individuals have rights within the U.S. court system, these rights must be asserted with the aid of counsel. In an adversarial system, it is necessary to be vigilant of the state's obligations to protect society by prosecuting crime and the potential abuses of the government as it delivers justice. A vast body of procedural law has developed to constrain law enforcement and court officials. "Fuzzy justice" alternatives to the court raise several issues and concerns regarding the voluntary and involuntary waiver of traditional legal rights.

There may be good reasons to forgo the due-process requirements of the traditional court system. As we have seen, many conflicts are better handled by informal processes that allow individuals to work out their difficulties with each other under the guidance of a trained mediator or ombuds. Disputants can come away with a higher degree of satisfaction when they have the opportunity to provide input into how their cases are decided, are able to confront those they are in conflict with directly, and have their arguments taken seriously. These alternatives to the court that increase victim participation and satisfaction may also be considered as efficient and cost-effective ways of resolving disputes. However, we must remain vigilant about the potentials for frustrating justice when legal rights are held subservient to goals of efficiency and convenience.

SUMMARY

1. Discuss restorative justice as an alternative to formal court processing.
    - Restorative justice is an informal method of resolving disputes that seeks to preserve relationships. Restorative justice programs forgo the adversarial processes of the traditional court system in favor of a less formal way to allow people to resolve conflicts. Restorative justice

programs seek to solve the present dispute and address underlying issues.

2. Give the advantages and disadvantages in bringing victims and offenders together.
   - The advantages of restorative justice processes are that they attempt to repair the harm done to relationships and give the victim the opportunity to address the offender. The disadvantages of restorative justice processes are that victims often do not want contact with those who have harmed them, particularly in cases of violence, and that restorative justice processes do not necessarily guarantee due-process rights.

3. Tell how reconciliation can be accomplished in a restorative justice framework.
   - Bringing offenders, victims, and other interested parties together can give everyone an opportunity to understand the effects of the offense. By including community members, some of the underlying conditions that lead to offending can be addressed.

4. Define ombud.
   - An ombud serves as a neutral party within an organization and provides conflict resolution and problem-solving services.

5. List and discuss the four principles upon which ombud standards of practice are based.
   - Ombud program standards of practice revolve around four principles. These are independence (the ombud should be independent from other entities within the organization); neutrality and impartiality (the ombud should not advocate for the organization or for any of the participants in the dispute and have no interests in the outcome); confidentiality (participants should feel that their conversations are confidential); and informality (conflicts may be addressed without putting individuals on the record).

6. Describe the activities that ombuds participate in.
   - Ombud's offices engage in mediation, help disputants identify options for resolution, and help the organization evaluate problematic trends.

7. Define military commissions.
   - Military commissions are courts used to try violations of the laws of war and other offenses.

8. Discuss reasons that military commissions are appropriate for dealing with terrorism. Discuss reasons that they are inappropriate for this task.
   - Some reasons that military commissions are appropriate for dealing with terrorism are they protect sensitive information; the United

States has a history of using military commissions during war; al Qaeda fighters do not follow the rules of war, so they lose the right to be considered soldiers; and terrorist activities are not like traditional street crime.

▪ Some reasons that military commissions are inappropriate for dealing with terrorism are that the definition of terrorism is so broad that it could include almost any behavior; military commissions circumvent the principles of due process; terrorism is enough like war that fighters should be accorded Geneva Conventions protections; military commissions flout constitutional values.

Questions

1. How is restorative justice an alternative to formal court processing?
2. What are the advantages and disadvantages in bringing victims and offenders together.
3. How can restorative justice achieve reconciliation?
4. What is an ombud?
5. What are the four principles that inform ombud program standards of practice?
6. What do ombud offices do?
7. What is a military commission?
8. What are the advantages and disadvantages of military commissions?

REFERENCES

[1] Shapiro M. Courts: a comparative and political analysis. Chicago, IL: University of Chicago Press; 1981.

[2] Harris DA. Justice rationed in the pursuit of efficiency: *de novo* trials in the criminal courts. In: Larry Mays G, Gregware PR, editors. Courts and justice: a reader. 3rd ed. Long Grove, IL: Waveland Press; 2004. p. 94−121.

[3] Dorne CK. Restorative justice in the United States. Upper Saddle River, NJ: Pearson; 2008.

[4] Schiff M, Bazemore G. Dangers and opportunities of restorative community justice: a response to critics. In: Bazemore G, Schiff M, editors. Restorative community justice. Cincinnati, OH: Anderson Publishing; 2001. p. 309−32.

[5] New York Times, Delaying justice at Guantánamo, May 8, 2012<www.nytimes.com/2012/05/09/opinion/delaying-justice-at-guantanamo-bay-cuba.html>.

[6] Sullivan D, Tift L. Restorative justice: healing the foundations of our everyday lives. Monsey, NY: Willow Tress Press; 2001.

[7] Braswell M, Wells K. Correctional treatment and the human spirit: the context of relationship. In: Polizzi David, Braswell M, editors. Transforming corrections: humanistic approaches to corrections and offender treatment. Durham, NC: Carolina Academic Press; 2009. p. 173−96.

[8] Van Ness DW, Strong KH. Restoring justice, 4. Cincinnati, OH: Anderson Publishing; 2002.

[9] Ibid., 8.

[10] Christie N. Conflicts and property. Br J Criminol 1977;17(1):1–15.

[11] Kaster J. The voices of victims: debating the appropriate role of fraud victim allocution under the crime victims' rights act. Minn Law Rev 2010;94(5):1682–705.

[12] Zehr H. Changing lenses: a new focus for crime and justice. Scottdale, PA: Herald Press; 1990.

[13] Woods L, Porter L. Examining the relationship between sexual offenders and their victims: interpersonal differences between stranger and non-stranger sexual offenses. J Sex Aggression 2008;14(1):61–75.

[14] Paternoster R, Deise J. A heavy thumb on the scale: the effect of victim impact evidence on capital decision making. Criminology 2012;49(1):129–61.

[15] Beckwith SS. District court mediation programs: a view from the bench. Ohio State J Dispute Resolut 2011;26(2/3):357–61.

[16] Beck CJA, Raghavon C. Intimate partner abuse screening in custody mediation: the importance of assessing coercive control. Fam Court Rev 2012;48(3):555–65.

[17] Olsen KB. Family group conferencing and child protection mediation: essential tools for prioritizing family engagement in child welfare cases. Fam Court Rev 2009;47(1):53–68.

[18] Calhoun A, Pelech W. Responding to young people responsible for harm: a comparative study of restorative and conventional approaches. Contemp Justice Rev 2010;13(3):287–306.

[19] Ibid., 8.

[20] Abrams L, Umbreit M, Gordon A. Young offenders speak about meeting their victims: implications for future programs. Crim Justice Rev 2006;9(3):243–56.

[21] Coates RB, Umbreit M, Vos B. Restorative justice circles: an exploratory study. Contemp Justice Rev 2003;6(3):265–78.

[22] Ibid., 8.

[23] Fulkerson A. The use of victim impact panels in domestic violence cases: a restorative justice approach. Contemp Justice Rev 2001;4(3/4):355–68.

[24] Rojek DG, Coverdill JE, Fors SW. The effect of victim impact panels on dui rearrest rates: a five-year follow-up. Criminology 2003;41(4):1319–40.

[25] Ibid., 8.

[26] Badovinac K. The effects of victim impact panels on attitudes and intentions regarding impaired driving. J Alcohol Drug Educ 1994;39(3):113–8.

[27] Ibid., 8.

[28] Choi JJ, Severson M. What kind of apology is this? The nature of apology in victim offender mediation. Child Youth Serv Rev 2009;31(7):813–20.

[29] Blecker NJ. Sorry justice: apology in Australian family group conferencing. Psychiatr Psychol Law 2011;18(1):95–116.

[30] Ruback BR, Ruth GR, Shaffer JW. Assessing the impact of statutory change: a statewide multilevel analysis of restitution orders in Pennsylvania. Crime Delinq 2005;51(3):318–42.

[31] Ibid., 8.

[32] Aviram H. Packer in context: formalism and fairness in the due process model. Law Soc Inq 2011;36(1):237–61.

[33] Khamisa A. A father's journey from murder to forgiveness. Reclaiming Child Youth 2006;15(1):15–8.

[34] Jaeger-Lane M, Burton L. The night I forgave my daughter's killer, YES! Magazine, May 27, 2011<www.yesmagazine.org/issues/beyond-prisons/the-night-i-forgave-my-daughters-killer?icl = yesemail_may11&ica = titleNightIForgave>. ABCNEWS, Forgiving her daughter's murderer, January 6, 2006 <abcnews.go.com/2020/story?id = 124051&page = 1>. Montana Abolition Coalition, Testimony of Marietta Jaeger lane on behalf of murder victims' families for human rights and journey of hope, February 7, 2007. Senate Judiciary Committee Hearing, <www.mtabolitionco.org/news/Lane%20Testimony.pdf>. Phillips C, Jaeger Lane M. <www.clairephillips.com/Marietta%20Jaeger%20Lane.htm>.

[35] Solotaroff P. Forgiving the murderer, June 24, 2004. United Methodist Church, reprinted from Rolling Stone, <archives.umc.org/interior.asp?mid = 5379>.

[36] National Public Radio, Forgiving her son's killer: not an easy thing, <www.npr.org/2011/05/20/136463363/forgiving-her-sons-killer-not-an-easy-thing>.

[37] Morris J. Tackling systemic incivility problems: the ombud as change agent. J Int Ombud Assoc 2010;3(2):34–8.

[38] International Ombud Association Standards of Practice, <www.ombudsassociation.org/sites/default/files/IOA_Standards_of_Practice_Oct09.pdf>.

[39] Howard CL. The organizational Ombud: origins, roles, and operations, a legal guide. Chicago, IL: ABA; 2010.

[40] Loraleigh K. A researcher speaks to ombud about workplace bullying. J Int Ombud Assoc 2010;3(2):10–23.

[41] Hill LB. Bureaucratic injustice, reform, and the Ombud. Conference Papers Am Polit Sci Assoc August 28, 2003:1–26.

[42] Das A. The immigration penalties of criminal convictions: resurrecting categorical analysis in immigration law. NY Univ Law Rev 2011;86(6):1669–760.

[43] Military Commissions, The Military Commissions Act of 2009, <www.mc.mil/Portals/0/MCA20Pub20Law200920.pdf>.

[44] Aronson O. Out of many: military commissions, religious tribunals, and the democratic virtues of court specialization. VA J Int Law 2010;51(2):231–98.

[45] Ibid.

[46] Meek J. People that law forgot. Guardian, December 3, 2003.

[47] Linfield S. War crimes trials, now and then. Dissent 2002;49(1):125–30.

[48] Crank JP, Gregor PE. Counter-Terrorism after 9/11, 190. Cincinnati, OH: Lexis Nexis; 2005.

[49] Ibid., 193–194.

[50] Petty KA. Are you there, Geneva? It's me, Guantánamo. Case West Reserve J Int Law 2010;42(1/2):171–86.

[51] Warrick J. Ten years later, CIA "Rendition" Program still divides N.C. Town. Washington Post February 9, 2012: <www.washingtonpost.com/world/national-security/ten-years-later-cia-rendition-program-still-divides-nc-town/2012/01/23/gIQAwrAU2Q_story.html>.

[52] Grey S. Ghost plane: the true story of the CIA torture program. New York, NY: St. Martin's Press; 2006.

[53] Green D, Rasmussen A, Rosenfeld B. Defining torture: a review of 40 years of health science research. J Trauma Stress 2010;23(4):528–31.

[54] Amnesty International, Guantanamo, Bagram and illegal U.S. detentions, <www.amnestyusa.org/our-work/issues/security-and-human-rights/guantanamo> [accessed December, 2012].

[55] Frakt DJR. The myth of divided loyalties: defending detainees and the constitution in the Guantánamo Military Commissions. Case West Reserve J Int Law 2011;43 (3):545–64.

[56] Temple-Raston D. Sept. 11 Defendants focus on torture during hearing, NPR, <www.npr.org/2012/05/07/152171198/sept-11-defendants-make-torture-focus-of-hearing> 2012 [accessed May 7, 2012].

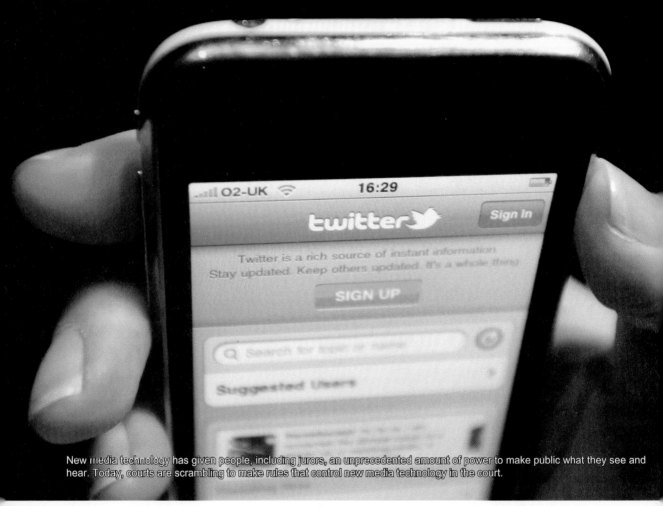

New media technology has given people, including jurors, an unprecedented amount of power to make public what they see and hear. Today, courts are scrambling to make rules that control new media technology in the court.

Courts in the Future

KEY TERMS

judicial accountability

judicial activism

judicial independence

judicial restraint

prior restraint

recusal

Learning Objectives

After reading this chapter, you should be able to:

1. Compare and contrast the judicial branch of the government with the executive and legislative branches.
2. List and discuss the three major methods of judicial selection.
3. Compare judicial restraint with judicial activism. Compare judicial independence with judicial accountability.
4. Give reasons that the court's work is confidential and secret.
5. Talk about the opposing aims of the media and the courts.
6. Understand the disadvantages of the new media in terms of reporter's privilege.
7. Discuss the court's difficulties with social media and how social media may benefit the legal process.
8. Evaluate the advantages of sophisticated communications technology in the courts.
9. Explain the need for security in the courthouse.

The criminal courts face challenges as they move into the future, most of which are beyond their control. These challenges include the politicization of the court, finding the proper relationship between the media and privacy concerns, and the evolving role of technology. Each of these issues is undergoing transformation and promises to introduce considerable controversy as they get resolved, if they are resolved, in the future. Although the courts are always in some stage of transition, these issues present some fundamental concerns that have the potential to reshape the criminal court as an institution in the United States.

POLITICS AND THE COURT

Anyone who has taken a high school civics class knows that the three branches of the U.S. government are the legislative, the executive, and the judicial. It was the intent of the framers of the Constitution that the legislative and the executive branches do the work of running the nation, while the judicial branch interpreted its laws. The judicial branch is supposed to be both the weakest and the most impartial branch of the government [1].

Recently, many scholars and critics are calling attention to what they say is increased judicial politicization, which refers to the presence of partisan politics in the judicial process. Court justices, from the lowest jurisdictional court up to the U.S. Supreme Court, are to avoid siding with any political party. Observers may point to decisions as leaning "right" or "left" or appearing to be "liberal" or "conservative," but these decisions are ideally interpretations and applications of the law and should not reflect the opinions of the judges. One highly criticized phenomenon is called "judicial activism" or "activist judges," interchangeable terms used to describe judges who appear to be using decisions to affect political or social issues.

Because the court is part of political life and has a role in running the nation, it cannot avoid interpretations of the law that have a political effect. Two examples are *Brown v. Board of Education* (1954), in which the Supreme Court declared state laws enforcing separate public schools for black and white students to be unconstitutional, and *Miranda v. Arizona* (1966), which affirmed that arrestees had to be informed of their right to consult with an attorney and their protection against self-incrimination prior to police interrogation. Both decisions touched on sensitive social issues during their eras, that of racial segregation and the rights of citizens under arrest. Both political parties had definite positions on each of these issues, but the court's job was to interpret the issues in accordance with the Constitution. Most observers would say that the Court did its job correctly. Today, however, with political polarization increasing, many observers are accusing judges of using their positions to shape society according to their political views.

This chapter will examine the effects of politics on the courts in recent years. Politics may affect the courts in two major ways: through the selection of judges (judicial selection) and the decisions those judges make (judicial decisions). One may be assumed to be related to another—a judge chosen or elected for his or her political philosophies may be expected to produce decisions that reflect those philosophies—but not always. Also, keep in mind that ideal judges do not make decisions that reflect personal politics, but decisions that reflect the law. Lawmakers and the voting public often either do not know of this ideal, lose sight of it, or, worse yet, ignore it.

Judicial Selection

Judges may be appointed by a legislator, selected by a nominating committee, elected by citizens, or achieve office by some combination of these. In all cases, partisan politics usually affects the selection of the judge. Nonpartisan elections and merit selection—the use of nominating committees to help select a judge (we will discuss this in greater detail later)—seek to reduce partisanship, but this is not always possible. A legislator may be likely to nominate or appoint a judge whose ideas appear to be in line with his or her own political party. In an election, citizens will usually vote for a judge from their own party affiliation if the judge's party affiliation is known. That is, a Republican voter is likely to vote for a Republican judge.

The most controversial issue of party affiliation rests with the judge up for appointment or election. Should the presumptive judge let his or her party affiliation, ideology, or politics be known? During Supreme Court confirmation hearings, nominees go out of their way to reassure legislators and the public that politics will not affect their decisions. In her confirmation hearing, U.S. Supreme Court Justice Sonia Sotomayor ... stated, "[t]he task of a judge is not to make the law—it is to apply the law" [2]. However, in state and local judicial elections, knowledge of the candidate's party affiliation is becoming increasingly important.

The U.S. Supreme Court and Federal Courts

U.S. Supreme Court justices, federal court of appeals judges, and federal district court judges are nominated by the president and confirmed by the Senate. Potential nominees may be recommended by senators or House members from the president's political party. The senate judiciary committee conducts confirmation hearings for nominees, who are appointed for life.

Because nominees for the Supreme Court and federal courts are chosen by the president and legislators, it can be expected that these nominations are politically motivated in nature. Supreme Court confirmation hearings are interesting when the president is from one party and the Senate is controlled by the other party. Sometimes, nominees are even voted down.

A good example is the failed nomination of Judge Robert Bork in 1987. Nominated by President Ronald Reagan, Bork, then a federal appeals court judge, was Republican. With Justice Lewis Powell, stepping down, the court would have been divided between justices who favored Republican issues and those who favored Democrat issues. The Democrats, who controlled the

Senate, feared that Bork would swing the court in a Republican direction. Many critics accuse the Democrats of taking their campaign to reject Bork too far, "demonizing" Bork as a "right-wing loony" [3]. When the Senate voted in October, the vote was 58 to 42 in favor of rejection, with only two Democrats favoring nomination and six Republicans siding with the Democratic majority. Republicans were furious, and many point to Bork's failed nomination as the day when extreme partisanship began to affect the government [4].

Although no one expects the nomination process to be completely free of politics, many observers may agree that too many nasty partisan fights are generally not good for the nation, who watches these proceedings and how they are conducted. The Court must continue to try to do its job in spite of politics. However, politicized altercations may charge the process, and possibly even the justices, with even more partisanship, beyond any views the individual justices may hold. According to judicial politicization theory, the greater the politicization of the court, the more likely its judges will vote according to ideology [5].

Some studies have found that voting according to ideology or attitude is most likely to occur only in certain areas, such as civil liberties cases and in non-unanimous cases [6]. For example, in 2012 the current Supreme Court, which is widely considered to be politicized, affirmed that the federal government had the right to require citizens to purchase health care. This ruling supported a law enacted by President Barack Obama, a Democrat. The swing vote on this issue, however, came from a judge who had been a Republican nominee, Chief Justice John Roberts. Many observers, especially Republicans, were shocked by this decision. Others say Justice Roberts simply did his job: he applied the law.

Others scholars assert that the idea of judges doing their jobs completely unaffected by ideology is unrealistic. According to one scholar, "[F]ederal judges (especially justices) are picked through a highly politicized process that often borders on theatre of the absurd. All of the prominent models of judicial decision-making tell us to expect the judges' ideological preferences to affect outcomes...." [7].

The best solution to judicial politicization may be one that already exists: divided government in which the executive office is held by one party and Congress by another. Although the confirmation hearings are often more contentious under these conditions, some scholars have found that a significant predictor of moderation in rulings concerning civil rights and liberties is judicial appointment under divided government [8].

There are good reasons that divided government makes for a more moderate court. Although federal appeals and district court nominees must often wrest their appointments from a hostile Senate, the nominees are recommended to the president by legislators from his own party. At this stage, patronage and politics are important factors in the process [9]. For instance, California Senators Barbara Boxer and Dianne Feinstein have established a committee that screens and interviews potential nominees for the judicial vacancies in their state. Similar federal nominating commissions have been established in several states. These commissions submit lists of candidates to U.S. senators, who may then pass those names on to the president for possible nomination.

Once a judge is nominated, the Senate sends his or her name to the judiciary committee which conducts a confirmation hearing. Senators from a nominee's home state participate in the process by approving movement of the nominee through the committee process (although this is not a commitment to vote for the nominee in the hearing). The American Bar Association's Standing Committee on the Federal Judiciary then evaluates the nominee's professional qualifications, such as integrity, competence, and judicial temperament.

Politics enters the process when nominees answer questions from the Judiciary Committee. An interesting note here is that any political or ideological values that attracted the initial attention of the state nominating commissions and senators may be the very values that cause the most friction during the hearing process. For example, a nominee known for values consistent with those of the Republican senators from his or her state may have a difficult time during questioning from Democrat members of the judiciary committee. On the other hand, sometimes, a nominee's values may have little effect on the process which may be stalled instead by other political posturing. For instance, in 2012, Republican senators were accused of stalling the confirmation of nominees to federal courts for reasons that had little to do with the nominees themselves, leaving the heavily burdened district courts in need of judges [10].

State and Local Courts

Judicial selection for state and local courts often follow an even more politically charged path than that of federal courts. First, let's review how state and local judges are selected. The three basic models for selecting judges are appointment, merit selection, and election. However, these models have as many variations as there are states. See Table 15.1 for a detailed look at how each state selects its judges.

- Appointment. During the early years of the United States, most judges were selected by a state's governor or legislature. However, this system was considered to be corrupt, and many states turned to the electoral system [11]. Appointment usually occurs when a governor must choose a judge to fill a midterm vacancy. In these cases, the judges

Table 15.1 Methods of Judicial Selection in the States

State	Election	Appointment	Merit Selection	Details
Alabama	Partisan			Judges in Alabama are chosen in partisan elections. Between elections, the governor appoints judges to seats when judicial vacancies occur. Appointments in some counties are made from a list of names provided by a judicial nominating commission.
Alaska			x	Alaska is one of only two states that has always used a merit selection system to choose its judges.
Arizona	Nonpartisan		x	Appellate judges and superior court judges in Maricopa and Pima Counties are chosen through merit selection. The judges run for retention after 2 years. Superior court judges in small counties are chosen in nonpartisan elections.
Arkansas	Nonpartisan			Judges are selected in nonpartisan elections.
California	Nonpartisan	x		The governor nominates supreme court and appeals courts judges who must be confirmed by an appointment commission. Appellate judges run for retention. Superior court judges run in nonpartisan elections, and the governor fills vacancies by appointment.
Colorado	Retention		x	The governor appoints judges from a list of nominees submitted by a judicial nominating commission. Judges run for retention at least 2 years after appointment.
Connecticut			x	A judicial selection commission recommends candidates to the governor for nomination. The nominee must then be appointed by the general assembly. Judges serve 8-year terms and must be renominated and reappointed.
Delaware			x	The governor appoints and reappoints judges with the consent of the senate. Delaware requires a partisan balance within its judiciary.
District of Columbia			x	Judges of the appeals court and the superior court are appointed to 15-year terms by the president with senate confirmation. The president appoints the judges from lists submitted by the judicial nomination commission. Judges seeking reappointment are evaluated by a commission. Judges rated "well qualified" are automatically reappointed. Judges rated as "qualified" may be appointed by the president subject to senate confirmation.
Florida	Nonpartisan		x	Appellate judges are chosen through merit selection and retention. Trial judges are chosen in nonpartisan elections. The governor fills trial court from candidates recommended by a judicial nominating commission.

(Continued)

Table 15.1 Methods of Judicial Selection in the States *Continued*

State	Election	Appointment	Merit Selection	Details
Georgia	Nonpartisan		x	Judges run in nonpartisan elections, and the governor fills midterm vacancies. Nominating commissions recommend candidates to fill the vacancies. Most judges are appointed and run in elections to retain their seats.
Hawaii			x	The governor appoints appellate court and the circuit court judges from a list submitted by the judicial selection commission. The chief justice appoints district and family court judges from a commission list. The senate confirms appointees. At the end of their terms, judges may be retained by a majority vote of the judicial selection commission.
Idaho	Nonpartisan		x	Judges are chosen in nonpartisan elections. The governor fills midterm vacancies from a list of names submitted by the Idaho Judicial Council.
Illinois	Partisan, nonpartisan			Illinois judges run in partisan elections. Judges run in nonpartisan retention elections for additional terms.
Indiana	Partisan	x	x	The governor appoints appellate court judges from a list submitted by the nominating commission. Circuit court judges are elected in partisan elections. The governor fills midterm vacancies through appointment.
Iowa	x		x	Iowa judges are chosen through merit selection. After a year in office, and then at regular intervals, judges run in retention elections.
Kansas	Partisan		x	Appellate court judges are chosen through merit selection. Each district chooses district court judges through either merit selection or partisan election. Most districts use merit selection.
Kentucky	Nonpartisan		x	Judges are chosen through nonpartisan elections. The governor fills midterm vacancies from a list submitted by a judicial nominating commission.
Louisiana	Partisan			Judicial candidates initially run in a "blanket primary," in which candidates of both parties appear on the same ballot. The winners run in the general election.
Maine		Nominated by the governor		Judges are nominated by the governor and confirmed by the senate.
Maryland	Nonpartisan		x	Nominating commissions recommend candidates for appointment to the governor. However, circuit court judges run in contested, nonpartisan elections. Appellate judges run in retention elections.

(Continued)

Table 15.1 Methods of Judicial Selection in the States *Continued*

State	Election	Appointment	Merit Selection	Details
Massachusetts		x	x	Massachusetts governors have created nominating commissions by executive order to advise them in making judicial appointments.
Michigan	Nonpartisan, partisan			Judges run in nonpartisan elections. Supreme court candidates may be nominated at political party conventions or by nominating petition.
Minnesota	Nonpartisan	x		According to the constitution, judges are chosen in nonpartisan elections, but many judges resign before their terms end, allowing the governor to appoint their replacements.
Mississippi	Nonpartisan			Judges run in nonpartisan judicial elections.
Missouri			x	In 1940, Missouri became the first state to use merit selection.
Montana	Nonpartisan		x	Supreme court and district court judges run in nonpartisan elections. The governor fills midterm vacancies from a list submitted by the nominating commission. Appointees must be confirmed by the senate.
Nebraska	x		x	The governor appoints judges from a list submitted by the nominating commission. Judges run for retention in the next general election more than 3 years after their appointment, and every 6 years thereafter.
Nevada	Nonpartisan			Judges are chosen in nonpartisan elections.
New Hampshire			x	The governor nominates judges, who must then be confirmed by the executive council.
New Jersey	x	x		The governor, with the approval of the senate, chooses all judges in New Jersey. Judges run for reappointment after 7 years. Once reappointed, they serve until age 70.
New Mexico	Partisan, retention		x	Judicial candidates run in contested partisan elections during general elections. The winner runs in retention elections thereafter. The governor fills vacant seats by appointing a judge from a list provided by a nominating commission.
New York	Partisan			Most trial court judges run in partisan elections. Candidates compete in primaries to determine who will represent the party in the general election. Supreme court candidates are chosen through a party convention system, in which primary voters elect delegates who choose candidates for the judgeships.
North Carolina	Nonpartisan			Judges are chosen in nonpartisan elections.
North Dakota	Nonpartisan		x	Court of appeals judges are chosen from among active and retired district court judges, retired supreme court justices, and attorneys. Supreme court and district court judges are chosen in

(Continued)

Table 15.1 Methods of Judicial Selection in the States *Continued*

State	Election	Appointment	Merit Selection	Details
				nonpartisan elections. Midterm vacancies are filled by special election or by the governor, who fills midterm vacancies from a list submitted by nominating commission.
Ohio	Nonpartisan			Judges are selected in nonpartisan elections. Candidates are nominated in partisan primaries and endorsed by political parties.
Oklahoma	Nonpartisan		x	Oklahoma has a bifurcated system of judicial selection. Appellate court judges are chosen through merit selection, and trial court judges are chosen in nonpartisan elections.
Oregon	x	x		The governor appoints judges to fill midterm vacancies, and the appointee runs for election at the next general election.
Pennsylvania	Partisan			Judges are chosen in partisan elections.
Rhode Island			x	Rhode Island adopted merit selection in 1994.
South Carolina		x		South Carolina is one of only two states whose legislature selects judges.
South Dakota	Nonpartisan		x	The governor appoints supreme court justices from a list submitted by the nominating commission. Circuit court judges are chosen in nonpartisan elections.
Tennessee	Partisan		x	Some judges are chosen through merit selection and others run in partisan elections. Appellate court judges are chosen through merit selection and run in retention elections.
Texas	Partisan			Judges run in partisan elections.
Utah			x	Except for justice court judges, Utah's judges are chosen through merit selection. The governor fills all judicial vacancies from a list submitted by a nominating commission. The appointee must be confirmed by the senate.
Vermont			x	The governor appoints candidates from a list submitted by the nominating commission. Judges serve 6 years then must be retained by a majority vote of the general assembly.
Virginia			x	The legislature is responsible for selecting judges.
Washington	Nonpartisan			Judges run in nonpartisan elections.
West Virginia	Partisan			Judges run in partisan elections.
Wyoming	Retention		x	Judges of the supreme, district, and circuit courts are chosen through merit selection. After at least 1 year in office, the judge runs for retention. If retained, supreme court justices serve 8 years; district court judges serve 6 years; and circuit court judges serve 4 years.

Each state has its own method of choosing judges, with most using some combination of merit selection and election.
Source: *American Judicature Society, Methods of Judicial Selection, www.judicialselection.us/judicial_selection/methods/selection_of_judges.cfm.*

usually run for election during the next election cycle. Legislatures appoint judges in only two states, South Carolina and Virginia.

- Merit selection. Generally, an appointed committee reviews applicants for open judgeships, then the best-qualified applicants are chosen to fill the positions. Every state that practices merit selection does so in its own way. For example, under the Missouri Plan—so-named because Missouri was the first state to adopt this system in 1940—the committee reviews applicants and compiles a list of those most qualified for the position. The governor then chooses one of those nominees. After serving a term, and for every term thereafter, the judge must then run in a retention election in which citizens vote on whether the judge remains in the job. As for the committee members themselves, they are typically appointed by the governor, although bar associations and attorneys make the appointments in some states [12].

- Election. The United States is almost the only nation that elects judges (some judges in small Swiss jurisdictions are elected, and Japan has retention elections for high court judges) [13]. Several jurisdictions and states hold partisan and nonpartisan elections for judges. A partisan election is one in which the candidates run as part of a political party, with the party listed on the ballot. In nonpartisan elections, candidates may not be nominated or endorsed by a political party, appear on a party ticket, or list a party affiliation on the ballot. Some states used to limit the political speech of candidates in nonpartisan elections, but the Supreme Court ruled that this was unconstitutional (see Landmark Cases 15.1). Many states combine these elections with merit selection and appointment in some fashion. Some states use partisan elections for the initial election of judges and nonpartisan elections for retention. Most elections are for trial judges. The fewest states hold elections at the level of state supreme court. Legal scholars criticize elections for valuing accountability to popular opinion over independence, whereas citizens and politicians praise it for the very same reason [14].

LANDMARK CASES 15.1

***Republican Party of Minnesota v. White* (2001)**
States cannot restrict the speech of judges running for election.

Judges in the State of Minnesota run for their seats in nonpartisan elections. The Minnesota Supreme Court's canon of judicial conduct prohibited candidates from discussing their views on disputed legal or political issues. In 1998, Gregory Wersal, who was running for associate justice of the Minnesota Supreme Court, filed suit on grounds that the "announce clause" violated

the First Amendment. The state district court found that the clause did not violate the First Amendment, and the state court of appeals affirmed.

The Supreme Court disagreed, holding that the clause violates the First Amendment. The Court stated that the clause prohibits speech about the qualifications of candidates for public office, speech that is specifically at the core of the First Amendment. The Court also concluded that the clause did not preserve the state judiciary's impartiality.

States tend to be attached to their methods of judicial selection. No state that has adopted merit selection has chosen replace it with elections. However, when given a choice, the citizens of most states vote to keep their judicial election systems, although merit selection promises a less politicized process [15]. The arguments against merit selection are:

1. It deprives citizens of their right to vote.
2. It does not truly liberate judicial selection from politics.
3. The members of nominating commissions in merit-selection states are not drawn from all segments of society and thus do not represent the population.
4. Judges are rarely removed in retention elections and thus serve life terms.
5. Elections educate the public and allow them to participate in the democratic process, whereas merit selection does not [16].

The arguments in favor of merit selection are:

1. Elections often rely on stirring citizens' emotions to get votes.
2. The public is not always attentive to the issues and well-informed about the candidates.
3. Many voters may make their decisions based on ethnic name recognition.
4. Elections usually have low voter turnout. Most incumbents win reelection easily and often run unopposed.
5. Elections may discourage well-qualified judicial candidates from seeking office [17].

Some scholars assert that no judicial selection method is completely free from politics. Merit selection shifts political discretion from the voters to the governor or legislators who choose the commission members. Politics are present in any sort of election, be it partisan or nonpartisan [18]. Competitive retention elections are relatively rare, but they may become more common as the nation becomes more politically divided.

Campaign spending is a particularly controversial issue. For example, in Michigan, independent groups who fund candidates in judicial elections do not have to disclose who they are. Between 2000 and 2012, the average spending by all candidates for Supreme Court seats had reached $3.5 million, with half the total spending, 20.8 million, coming from undisclosed sources. Not knowing the sources of these funds can be problematic for litigants because they cannot find out if their case involves a party that financed the justice's campaign [19]. One study found that elections and campaign donations do affect the decisions judges make. Groups, such as pro-business groups, that donated money to a judge's campaign tended to have more decisions go their way. Judges facing reelection from a Republican citizenry decided cases in accord with Republican policy, being more likely to make decisions for businesses over individuals, for employers in labor disputes, and against those convicted of criminal offenses in appeals cases. The same principle held true for judges up for reelection in Democratic jurisdictions [20].

Another problem with judicial campaign spending is that the money can come from anywhere, even from groups out of state. That means people who do not even live in the state where the elections are held can affect the elections. In 2010, Iowa voters ousted three state Supreme Court judges after an expensive and powerful campaign that came after a unanimous ruling legalizing same-sex unions. The supreme court judges in Iowa's retention elections run unopposed, so the vote is simply up-or-down on whether they keep their seats. Conservative groups inside and outside the state spent about $700,000 on the campaign targeting the judges, causing concern among legal scholars that the judges were punished for an unpopular interpretation of the law [21].

Although the Iowa justices undoubtedly knew a storm was brewing, none of them formed committees to raise money and campaign on their behalf. On the other hand, in Illinois in 2010, Thomas Kilbride, the chief justice of

PHOTO 15.1

It is not unusual for judges who make unpopular decisions to be accused of judicial activism. Here, the three Iowa judges who were ousted after their ruling concerning same-sex unions receive the 2012 John F. Kennedy Profile in Courage Award. From left are Michael Streit, former Iowa Supreme Court Justice; Marsha Ternus, former Iowa Supreme Court Chief Justice; and David Baker, former Iowa Supreme Court Justice.

the Illinois Supreme Court, raised $2.8 million for his retention vote, which was more money that every judge in every state raised for every retention election from 2000 to 2009. Unlike the Iowa justices, Kilbride won [22].

The near future of judicial elections will probably look much like the present. The states that have elections will keep them, and states that use merit selection will retain that process. For example, in 2012, weeks after the indictment of a state supreme court justice on campaign-finance law violations, the Pennsylvania legislature attempted to replace its system of electing appellate judges with merit selection. The measure died in the legislature, however, with supporters of the election system claiming it prevents the institution of a potentially elitist and unaccountable judiciary [23].

Judicial Decisions

Politics affects the courts through the decisions judges make. Judges are encouraged to practice **judicial restraint**, or to limit the exercise of their own power and defer to written law as long as it is constitutional. At the other end of the spectrum is **judicial activism**, which is sometimes applied to judicial decisions that appear to contradict voters' desires or are suspected of being based on the judge's personal or political preferences rather than on law. For example, the judges in the Iowa elections case we discussed earlier could be, and probably were, accused of judicial activism. Judicial activism is a controversial topic because judges are much like referees: they interpret the law; they do not make or change the law [24].

Judicial independence is the idea that the judiciary should not be affected by other branches of government, or private or partisan interests. **Judicial accountability** is the idea that judges should defer to the wishes and opinions of the electorate. Given the controversy over judicial selection, it is easy to understand how judicial independence is difficult to maintain. Let's look at both of these concerns in more detail.

Judicial Independence vs. Judicial Accountability

Judicial independence is composed of two concepts: decisional independence and institutional independence. Decisional independence refers to a judge's ability to make decisions based on the facts and the law free from political or popular influence. Institutional independence refers to the separation of the judicial branch from the executive and legislative branches of government [25]. Scholars believe judges should have decisional and institutional independence because such independence results in a better quality of justice [26]. According to legal scholar Charles Geyh, "It is thought that if judges are independent—if they are insulated from political and other controls that could undermine their impartial judgment—they will be better able to uphold the rule of law, preserve the separation of powers, and promote due process of law" [27].

However, as discussed earlier, proponents of judicial elections, especially political scientists, consider elections as the only way to assure that judges remain accountable to popular opinion [28]. Some scholars assert that this can be achieved by having a transparent judicial nomination commission system, stronger standards for **recusal**, and increasing the use of judicial performance evaluations [29]. However, it is important to remember that almost all judges, except for supreme court judges, are accountable.

> [T]rial judges' rulings are subject to at least two levels of appellate review. Intermediate appellate judges act in panels of three or more, so the judgment of two colleagues may rein in the excess of another. Next are the canons of ethics, judicial conduct committees, and grievance procedures. Recusal motions (and self-recusal) exist as a mechanism to exclude a judge from hearing cases in which he or she may have a financial interest or bias [30].

Independence and accountability are closely tied to the way judges are selected. Imagine a continuum that ranges from independence to accountability (Figure 15.1). Appointed judges are considered to be more independent, and judges elected in partisan elections are the most accountable to the public. An important observation is that judicial elections were instituted in the nineteenth century as a way to liberate judges from the influence of governors and legislators; that is, elections were intended to increase independence from government influence. This tactic may have worked, although not quite as planned, as appointment and merit selection (which involves legislators) are now considered the most independent methods of judicial selection versus elections, which moved the accountability of judges away from legislators and toward the public [31].

It is important to understand that the concepts of independence and accountability are not absolute, regardless of selection process. Judges are human, and no judge is completely free from all influence. A judge may be influenced by

Independence   Accountability

Appointment   Merit selection   Nonpartisan election   Partisan election

FIGURE 15.1

Appointment of judges is considered to be most conducive to judicial independence and partisan elections the most conducive to judicial accountability. Source: *Champagne A. Judicial selection from a political science perspective. Arkansas Law Rev 2011;64(1):221–47.*

legislators, the public, campaign contributors, other judges, and sometimes his or her own politics, beliefs, and morals. Neither is any judge completely free from accountability. A judge is accountable to legislators, the public, campaign contributors, other judges, and sometimes his or her own politics, beliefs, and morals. There is no perfect system that will place all judges precisely in the middle of the continuum. Ultimately, it is the judge, through his or her decisions, who determines his or her place on the continuum.

Here is a good way to consider this line of thinking. Recall that most elections are held at the trial-judge level and the fewest at the supreme court level. Trial judges are held accountable through appellate review, and appellate judges are accountable to their panel members. So why is accountability to voters so important when the judges they are most likely to vote for are already held accountable in various ways? The answer that is probably closest to the truth is that trial judges are the judges voters are most likely to interact with in misdemeanors, low-level felonies, traffic citations, divorces, and civil cases. Many voters want to be able to choose the judge they may meet in court [32]. So, the issue is not simply that judges are independent or accountable, it is *who* they are independent from and accountable to.

Many legal scholars, especially those critical of judicial elections, consider judicial independence to be under attack. Although interpretation of the law is important in a society, the judiciary is considered to be the weakest branch. As Alexander Hamilton stated:

> [T]he judiciary is beyond comparison the weakest of the three departments of power; that it can never attack with success either of the other two; and that all possible care is requisite to enable it to defend itself against their attacks. [33]

For example, some scholars believe judges are not independent enough from legislators. One study has pointed to federal sentencing guidelines and mandatory minimum sentences as incursions on judicial independence. If all cases and all defendants are different, what is the point of having a judge if he or she is restrained from using discretion during sentencing? [34] According to the American Judicature Society, congressional limits on or curtailment of jurisdiction is only one threat to judicial independence. Others include:

- threats of impeachment prompted by unpopular decisions;
- political threats intended to influence a judge's decision in a case;
- elections leading to potential conflicts of interest regarding campaign contributions;
- underfunding and workload [35].

Note that the first three items are related to elections and accountability. The last one, underfunding and workload, may come as a bit of a surprise. The court needs funding to do the work of the criminal and civil justice systems despite being relatively inexpensive, with budgets accounting for a small percentage of a state's budget, sometimes less than 2 percent [36]. In the face of political battles, however, some legislators see cutting funds as a way to "punish" judges and courts. For example, in 2011, former presidential candidate Newt Gingrich suggested that executives and legislatures should respond to court rulings with which they disagree by cutting court budgets, eliminating judges' law clerks, and not paying the court's electric bills [37]. Although funding cuts may sound like a way to guarantee accountability, it results in weakened justice. For example, from 2009 to 2011:

- Twenty-six states delayed filling judicial vacancies; 31 delayed judicial support positions; and 34 delayed filling vacancies in clerks' offices.
- The salaries of judges or staff were frozen or reduced in 31 states.
- Clerical staff were furloughed in 16 states and laid off in 14 states.
- Some courts had to reduce the number of hours and days they were open.

Reduced staff and hours means that disputes over the custody of children may be delayed for years. Suspects and defendants spend longer times in jail waiting for a court date, and some criminal defendants who have been preventively detained may be released because the court cannot meet the requirements for a speedy trial [38].

It is likely that the judicial independence vs. accountability debate will continue into the future, even as the states cling to their various methods of choosing judges. The once-sleepy retention elections, nonpartisan elections, and midterm appointments will probably lose their casual atmosphere, however, as voters and legislators continue on the partisan path, and political parties turn issues that were once considered settled, or not even issues at all, into points of contention.

Judicial Activism vs. Judicial Restraint

The terms "judicial activist" or "judicial activism" are derogatory terms used to describe judges who appear to be making decisions based on their own ideology or decisions that run contrary to popular opinion. These ideas are commonly considered to be the opposites of judicial restraint, which refers to making decisions in strict accordance with the written law and Constitution.

Although "judicial activism" is heard more often in recent years, it is not a new term. The term "judicial activist" first appeared in 1947 in a *Fortune* magazine article about Supreme Court justices [39]. The author, Arthur M. Schlesinger, Jr., was ambiguous about the term's meaning, but it has since arrived at its current derogatory connotations. The terminology has its critics who state that not only does it have no place in scholarly legal discussions, but that it is also actually a myth. Although judges may make decisions according to ideology, they believe they are making the correct decisions according to the law [40]. A study that attempted to measure how activist judges actually are found "no evidence of any statistically significant connection between judicial activism and political party." That is, regardless of party affiliation, judges from one party were no more activist than judges from another [41].

A final note about both "judicial activism" and "judicial restraint" is that the terms are most used to describe what an individual prefers. That is, a ruling that you disagree with is judicial activism, whereas one that you like is the model of judicial restraint. The debate, then, is not so much about what the terms mean, but about the fact that these terms exist and are being used with greater frequency in everyday discussions about the activities of our courts. As the voting public becomes more partisan and more divided along social, class, racial, religious, and moral lines, it is likely that discussions about a particularly "activist" judge or a judge who showed admirable "restraint" are going to become more common.

THE MEDIA AND THE COURT

Media, both old and new, are a challenge for the court. Much of the court's work depends on confidentiality and secrecy. Jurors are not supposed to talk about cases they are hearing, even with each other, until deliberation. Sometimes, juries are even sequestered so they will not be influenced by factors external to the court. Many courts do not allow cameras in their courtrooms, which is why when some cases are covered by the news media, they are accompanied by artist's drawings rather than photographs or video. The work of grand juries is so secret that targets of their investigations often do not even know they are being investigated. Much of this confidentiality is to avoid prejudicing potential or current jurors, who, ideally, should know as little as possible about the case they are hearing.

Given a choice between providing a defendant a fair trial and providing the news media with unlimited access, the courts have chosen the fair trial. This means the court's work is somewhat of a paradox in a democracy, which demands transparency. Although individuals prefer openness from their institutions, they wish privacy for themselves in legal matters and as fair a trial as possible. It is this desire for individual privacy and justice that the courts are trying to protect, and requirements of transparency in a democracy that the media are trying to pursue.

The general guidelines for the traditional media in courtrooms were settled long ago, although there are exceptions in individual jurisdictions. However, Internet-based and social media is providing a new challenge, and new rules and etiquette must be created for jurors, court-watchers, bloggers, and others who wish to integrate social media and the Internet into coverage of the courts, as well as into the court's work.

Old Media

The courts and the traditional media—newspapers, magazines, and television—have always been at odds over how court cases are reported. The court is interested in conducting a fair trial and protecting the rights of both the defendant and victims. The media is interested in the public's "right to know."

The level of coverage tolerated by the court is up to the individual court. For example, cameras are not allowed in the Supreme Court, although the idea is occasionally discussed. In particularly controversial cases—such as those concerning President Barack Obama's health care mandate or the 2000 presidential clash between George W. Bush and Al Gore—the Supreme Court will release audio of its decision [42]. On a local level, the news media sometimes has trouble accessing court records, such as search warrants, in high-profile or especially heinous cases, but these controversies rarely travel beyond their localities [43].

Prior restraint is the prohibition by the government of documents or speech before publication or broadcast. This is a sticky issue where the courts and the media—both old and new—are concerned. Sometimes a judge will seek to prohibit a news organization or blogger from reporting on or publishing documents pertaining to a specific case. There is no law prohibiting all instances of prior restraint, so the courts and media must negotiate it all over again every time the issue comes up [44]. The issue was settled, somewhat, in the Supreme Court case *Near v. Minnesota* (see Landmark Cases 15.2) in which officials sought to use state law to prevent the publication of a newspaper. The Court ruled that such statutes violated the First Amendment and that, generally, the government should not practice prior restraint. However, this did not close the issue completely, leaving some exceptions in which prior restraint may be used such as when a defendant's right to a fair trial may be endangered or national security secrets revealed. The decision also did not preclude the possibility of punishment for a news organization that violated an order not to publish [45].

LANDMARK CASES 15.2

Near v. Minnesota (1931)

The government cannot censor or prohibit a publication in advance of its publication.

Jay Near published a newspaper in Minneapolis, Minnesota, in which he accused local officials of being associated with gangsters. State officials obtained an injunction in accordance with state law to prevent Near from publishing his newspaper. The law provided that anyone who regularly published or circulated a "malicious, scandalous, and defamatory"

newspaper or periodical was guilty of a nuisance, and could be stopped from committing or maintaining the nuisance.

The case went to the Supreme Court, which held that the law authorizing the injunction was unconstitutional. The Court held that the law constituted a prior restraint and thus violated the First Amendment. This ruling established the doctrine that, with some exceptions, the government could not censor or prohibit a publication in advance, even though the communication might be punishable after publication.

The desire and right to withhold information can cut both ways. Sometimes, under "reporter's privilege" reporters will refuse to release information to the court. This usually occurs when the reporter is trying to protect a source of information. In this case, the reporter—much like the court when it seeks to embargo information—is trying to protect an individual at the expense of the public's right to know.

One reason reporters give for withholding sources is that failing to do so will cripple his or her effectiveness as a reporter. "No source will ever talk to me again," is a common explanation. Reporters also appeal on the basis of the First Amendment, which includes the clause: "Congress shall make no law ... abridging the freedom of speech, or of the press. ..." In this case, the protection of a source enables the free flow of news. If sources think they are endangering their freedom by speaking to reporters, they may choose not to do so, which would be detrimental to reporters' ability to gather information important to the workings of democracy. Secrecy, in this case, obscures some information so that more important, relevant information can reach the public.

Like prior restraint, the issue is decided on an individual basis, but such controversies only occasionally reach the national stage. The last major dustup occurred in 2004–2005, when *Washington Post* journalist Judith Miller refused to reveal the source of a name of an undercover CIA officer. Miller eventually released the source's identity, I. Lewis "Scooter" Libby, Jr., assistant to the president and chief of staff to Vice President Dick Cheney, after Libby gave her permission to do so [46]. Libby, who resigned in 2005, was later convicted obstruction of justice, perjury, and making false statements, and sentenced to 30 months in prison [47].

Although reporters are firm in their insistence that unrestricted coverage of the courts is supported by the First Amendment and strengthens democracy, some legal scholars and critics believe the media should have even less access than it does now. Here are some arguments against allowing the media free access to the courts.

1. Media coverage often undermines the values underlying the right to free speech: human dignity, the state's duty to secure equal respect for everyone's basic rights, and the right to a fair trial.
2. Media coverage affects the fairness of trials. The publication of facts, such as inadmissible evidence, damages the defendant's presumption of innocence. One attorney said, "I have tried cases where material was excluded from evidence because it was too prejudicial for the jury to hear, only to have the same material broadcast and printed so often that the jurors later actually thought it was presented as evidence."
3. Attempts to counter the effects of media coverage on jurors are ineffective. Judges are too confident in the ability of jury instructions to neutralize prejudice resulting from media coverage. Sequestration, which has no effect on pretrial publicity, is rare because it is expensive for the state and troublesome for jurors. Delaying the trial offends the Sixth Amendment guarantee of a prompt trial and becomes less effective as witnesses begin to forget the relevant events. Change of venue does little good as the mass media and the Internet have made all events local. As for asking jurors about their level of prejudice, research has found that jurors do not reliably report their levels of prejudice or may not tell the truth when asked about it. Gag orders—a judge's order restricting anyone from the court from releasing information—do little to prevent anonymous leaks to the press, which, through reporter's privilege, often successfully defends disclosure of its sources [48].

This debate is likely to continue as long as there are courts and a media to cover them. Given the success of court-related programming on television, it is clear that the public likes to hear about high-profile cases. Much of the coverage is sensational, and it is doubtless that much of the public's interest has less to do with the First Amendment and the foundations of democracy than it does with selling exciting details for advertising dollars. Still, the news media argues that with the bad comes the good: keeping a close eye on the court process and the workings of justice in American society.

New Media

New media consists of any form of reportage that is Internet-based, including blogs, and postings to sites like Facebook and Twitter. Like old media reporters, many people who use new media want access to the courts, to be able to report on their processes, and to be able to protect their sources, if necessary. One interesting difference is that the new media lacks the institutional nature of the old media. Newspapers, magazines, and television stations are businesses that employ hundreds of people. Many, if not most, have editorial boards, corporate directors and officers, owners, and stockholders. These outlets also have deep pockets and lawyers and can challenge the courts and support reporters in their quests for information.

Much of the new media has none of this, at least not in the way that old media does. Media outlets on the Internet that do have such institutional advantages are often just old media outlets that went online, so they always had these advantages. However, new media outlets act mainly as conduits for information; unlike new media outlets, they do not research and report information. Therefore, the new media's relationship to its users is different from the old media's relationship with its reporters. For example, a newspaper produces what it prints. A blog host, however, does not produce blogs. It just provides a place for the blogger to post. The blog host, then, does not have a real interest in a court blogger's access to the courts or the blogger's desire for reporter's privilege. The blog host or social media outlet may be interested in protecting its users in general, but only because not to do so—by, for instance, giving out identities or passwords to law enforcement—may damage its business by scaring off potential users. This is not the same as a newspaper siding with a reporter who wants to protect a source or fight a gag order.

New media technology—personal computers and portable devices such as laptop computers and mobile phones—has given individuals an unprecedented amount of power to make public what they see and hear. Social media has opened a new dimension of access to the courts, and now jurors, bloggers, freelance journalists, and court-watchers are testing the court's ability to adapt its nineteenth-century methods to twenty-first-century communications. The court, then, must deal with the activities of two emerging subsets of people. The first group, mainly composed of jurors, are people party to court processes who may release information about those processes. The second group, mainly composed of bloggers unaffiliated with old media, want court access and reporter's privilege but do not work for an acknowledged media outlet. The court is currently developing policy on these two groups, but several anecdotes point to the direction in which the court appears to be headed.

- In 2011, an Arkansas judge overturned Erickson Dimas-Martinez's murder conviction because, despite the judge's instructions, a juror posted to the social media site Twitter during the trial. Although some of what the juror posted was of a personal nature ("The coffee sucks here"), he posted "It's over." less than an hour before the jury announced its verdict [49].
- In 2009, a woman sitting on the jury of an Illinois wrongful death case regularly posted to her blog describing the discussions in the jury room.

The defense attorneys discovered the posts after the plaintiff won a $4.75 million verdict, but the trial court refused to hold a hearing to determine if juror misconduct had occurred. As of 2012, the case had gone to the Illinois Supreme Court to determine whether the blogging affected the case [50].

- In a type of incident that has become more common, a Maryland appeals court voided the 2009 murder conviction of Allan Jake Clarke when it was discovered that a juror had looked up scientific terms on Wikipedia. The appeals court held that an "adverse influence on a single juror compromises the impartiality of the entire jury panel" [51].

- In 2010, the owner of a Dallas, Texas, bar subpoenaed neighborhood blogger Avi Adelman to testify in a deposition about the names of anonymous sources quoted in a post about a shooting near the bar. Adelman refused to reveal the sources' identities, citing Texas reporter's privilege law. The bar owner's attorney pointed out that the law requires that journalists be paid to be covered by the law [52]. Although the bar's case was later dismissed, the issue of whether freelance bloggers count as journalists, at least in this case, was never settled [53].

- In 2011, a judge allowed reporters to e-mail, text, and tweet updates from a hearing for former Pennsylvania State University football coach Jerry Sandusky. The judge overturned a ruling barring electronic communication from the courtroom, saying, "Permitting tweeting will enhance the news-gathering capabilities of reporters, which is in the public interest" [54].

The court's reaction to jurors using social media to share information and the Internet to learn information is largely predictable: these activities interfere with the fairness of trials, and jurors should engage in neither. However, the debate about who qualifies as a journalist for the purposes of receiving reporter's privilege is likely to remain open, just as the debate about when to extend reporter's privilege to reporters has remained open. It is likely that these incidents will be decided on a case-by-case basis within the states.

Social media is also giving the legal system and law enforcement expanded access to individuals. In a Pennsylvania civil case involving a 2009 auto accident, Facebook accounts became evidence. Timothy Lesko had claimed he was not driving the car that struck another vehicle, killing Jessica Trail and injuring her brother Michael and two of their friends, one of whom died 6 months later. The Trails' attorney asked the judge for permission to see Lesko's full Facebook profile for a possible admission of guilt. Meanwhile, Lesko's attorneys wanted to see Trail's profile to determine whether his injuries were as severe as he had said. The judge denied both requests stating that discovery into a person's Facebook profile when that person is not "friends" with those seeking access violates the state's Rules of Civil Procedure [55].

Individual courts approach these cases differently, however. In New York, a judge ordered the texts and Facebook posts of four teenage boys to be released for use against them in a rape case [56]. In a 2012 case, a New York judge ruled that Twitter had to release the posts of an Occupy Wall Street protester. Twitter refused to hand over the posts, citing First Amendment privacy protections. The judge replied that Twitter posts were about as private as screaming from a window. In this case, Twitter's lawyers are fighting the order not only on behalf of the site's user but also the site itself [57].

Social media has become a goldmine for law enforcement because it seems nothing is off-limits for some users who feel free to post information about criminal offenses they have committed. If the general public begins to understand that everything posted on a social media site is subject to use in civil or criminal cases, it could affect the number of users, which is the profit center for social media sites. Although these cases are relatively small, they pose big questions about the applicability of the First Amendment to speech that is conducted on a public forum by people who expect their utterances to be treated as if private.

TECHNOLOGY AND THE COURT

Technology is having a revolutionary effect on all aspects of society. Advances in communications technology have changed our lives in ways never imagined. As more people connect to social media and almost any information becomes available instantaneously to all who desire, the laws concerning privacy and security are constantly being revisited as newer and more intrusive technologies arrive. Although these issues have opened new areas of dispute for the courts to arbitrate, technology has also offered the courts new tools to deal with burgeoning caseloads. The use of technology in the criminal court has changed the way it handles cases, but it also presents several challenges that must be addressed so that efficiency does not intrude upon the goals of providing justice [58].

New courtroom technology includes advances in both video and audio. In support of the technologies that judges and attorneys bring, such as cell phones, tablets, and laptop computers, the courtroom will have wireless technology to allow these devices to connect to the Internet. Additionally, monitors will allow jurors to see displays presented by the judge and the attorneys. This can be especially useful when dealing with complicated evidence and can overcome many of the problems associated with poor acoustics in the courtroom or unsophisticated evidence displays by the attorneys [59].

Another advantage of courtroom technology is that it can use video monitors to display instructions and orders by the judge to defendants, ensuring that each defendant can understand the process. Routine orders and judge's instructions can be translated into various languages so that non-English-speaking defendants may understand what is happening in the courtroom.

Small microphones worn by the attorneys can provide them with the freedom to walk around the room and still be confident that their words are being clearly communicated to the judge, jurors, and opposing attorneys. Sophisticated audio equipment also allows the judge to speak confidentially to the attorneys standing before the bench by turning on a "white noise" sound that masks what is being said. This allows the judge to ask questions and give instructions to attorneys without having to dismiss the jury from the courtroom. The use of cordless microphones allows digital recorders to accurately record everything that is said in the courtroom.

The amount and quality of information that the judge can convey to defendants is unlimited. By using a computer on the bench, the judge can display on monitors vast amounts of sophisticated information that would take a long time to explain and about which there is a real risk of misunderstanding [60]. For instance:

> [A] judge might display records of payment from the court's management system if the defendant asks what happened to all of the money he or she has already paid to the court. Or run an amortization schedule to show how long it would take to pay a judgment accumulating interest at a particular rate, and then show how additional payments could reduce the amount of time required to pay off the debt. Or find a bird's-eye view of a location [on the Internet]. The photographs come with a mileage scale. The image of any intersection or scene of an accident can be sent to the monitors and facilitate discussion about the location, direction, and so forth of the vehicles. The court no longer has to rely on out-of-scale diagrams drawn by the litigants [61].

It is easy to see how such technology could greatly enhance not only the effectiveness of courtroom interactions but also the quality. The judge may use a computer to prepare a complicated sentencing statement, then display the sentencing statement to the convicted party while reading it. This allows the convicted party to read as well as hear the terms of the sentence. Often, convicted parties are interested only in the possibility of incarceration and do not hear or comprehend the often complicated terms of probation. By allowing the convicted party to read the sentence along with the judge, the defendant is more likely to understand what is happening. This written record also allows the court reporter and the clerk of the court to maintain accurate records of the judge's declaration.

Another technological innovation is videoconferencing. Videoconferencing allows judges to hold arraignments from the courtroom without requiring the defendants to leave the jail. The defendant's physical presence in the courtroom is not always required for such routine activities. Typically, the agreement consists of the judge reading the charges to the defendant and the defendant entering a routine plea of not guilty. The case is then rescheduled for a later time so the prosecutors can do a more thorough evaluation of the charges and consult with the defense attorneys or the public defender. Videoconferencing hearings have two major advantages [62].

1. Cost. Transporting dozens of defendants from the jail to the court each day is expensive. Prisoners must be moved from their cells to vans, driven to the courthouse, secured in a holding cell, transferred to the courtroom, and controlled while in the courtroom. Holding a hearing via videoconferencing eliminates these expenses, and law enforcement personnel are freed up for other duties.
2. Security. The possibility of the defendant escaping or assaulting correctional officers or courtroom personnel is always present (see Court Procedures 15.1). Defendants held in jail prior to their legal proceedings are potential security risks. Even though a defendant's present charge may be for a minor offense, there is no way to know which defendants have the potential for violent behavior. Therefore, each defendant must be carefully guarded to ensure that courtroom personnel and the public are not at risk.

In addition to using videoconferencing to communicate with incarcerated defendants, this technology can also be used to elicit testimony from witnesses and experts who cannot be in the courtroom. Busy attorneys who must use several courtrooms on the same day can participate in videoconferencing during routine pretrial procedures while reserving their physical presence for important jury trials. Additionally, witnesses and experts who live out of state can provide testimony without incurring the expenses of traveling to the courtroom.

COURT PROCEDURES

The Atlanta Courthouse Shootings

The courthouse is the only place (apart from crime scenes) in which the general public comes in contact with known violent criminal offenders. With the exception of police officers who provide security, the courthouse staff, court observers, and jurors are all civilians who must deal with these violent offenders. Therefore, it is imperative that the courthouse be a safe place for courthouse staff and jurors to do their work. The best way to maintain courthouse security is a subject for debate. Some courthouses allow police and security officers to carry firearms; others do not [63]. Each courthouse has its own procedures to provide security, and the sophistication of security depends on the courthouse. Sometimes security procedures fail, however, with tragic results.

In 2005, Bryan Nichols, who was on trial for rape, was being held in a lockup at the Fulton County Courthouse in Atlanta, Georgia. Nichols, 33, attacked his guard after convincing her to remove his handcuffs so he could change clothes before appearing in court. Leaving her unconscious, Nichols removed her gun, went to the judge's chambers, and took several hostages. He then disarmed a sheriff's deputy who entered the chambers, but the deputy pretended to have a heart attack so he could press an alarm. Nichols locked the deputy in a restroom, then entered the courtroom and shot and killed Judge Rowland Barnes, court reporter Julie Ann Brandau, and another deputy, Sgt. Hoyt Teasley. Nichols then fled the courthouse, killing David Wilhelm, an off-duty federal agent, several hours later. Police finally caught Nichols in an Atlanta apartment where he was holding a woman hostage [64].

Nichols's defense team argued that he was not guilty by reason of insanity. The jury found Nichols guilty on all 54 counts against him, which included murder, assault, battery, kidnaping, and carjacking. The cost of defending Nichols approached $2 million and came close to financially ruining the state of Georgia's public defense system [65]. Although the city of Atlanta tightened courthouse security after the murders, another inmate escaped 8 months later, leaving the sheriff's department and city police department to blame each other for poor security procedures [66].

Question

Describe technology that may have prevented Nichols's escape.

The use of technology allows the court to be both efficient and protect the integrity of legal processes. For example, evidence must often be considered by the judge and the attorneys before being considered by the jury. Having a system that allows this privacy and permits everyone to view the evidence simultaneously offers a tremendous advantage.

> In the high-tech courtroom, the exhibit is placed under a document camera or shown from the attorney's computer. The witness, the opposing counsel, and the judge can observe the document at the same time. Upon admission, it can be published to the jury. As the witness comments, everyone can look at the exhibit. The witness, the attorney, and the judge also can highlight certain portions of the exhibit with an annotation system, better known as the John Madden telestrator, and the annotated image can be saved and printed out for the record [67].

Without sacrificing the integrity of the process, the judge can ensure that vital information is made available to those who need it. Additionally, accurate records can be kept of the proceedings. This is not to say that the use of technology in the modern courtroom does not have disadvantages. Efficiency should not come at the cost of justice.

There are concerns that the increasing use of technology could disrupt traditional notions of the trial, specifically the idea of space and physical boundaries. Some observers believe that the gathering of the judge, attorneys, jury, defendant, prosecution, and witnesses in one space is critical to the efforts of justice. For example, a defendant has the right to face his or her accuser. If the accuser is not physically present, but instead appears on a screen from a location hundreds of miles away, is the defendant really getting a chance at facing the accuser? Is a virtual presence the same as a physical presence in terms of courtroom proceedings? [68] In *Maryland v. Craig*, the Supreme Court set forth that one-way video testimony did not violate Sixth Amendment confrontation requirements "in certain narrow circumstances." In *Craig's* case, these circumstances concerned the testimony of a young child against a defendant accused of sexual abuse [69]. As of 2011, only one federal circuit had found two-way video testimony compatible with the Sixth Amendment [70].

There is also the more basic problem of technology "getting in the way" of courtroom procedure. In some advice to attorneys who wish to use technology in their presentations, one judge stated the following:

- Make sure the technology adds to the presentation and does not distract from key points by allowing the attorney to present an argument in a way that could not otherwise be presented.
- Tell the client about the use of technology. Clients do not like surprises and want to know how information will be presented in a trial.
- Understand the environment of the court. Sometimes, simple things can ruin a brilliant technological presentation, such as the angle of the sun coming through the window and washing out a computer screen. The attorney should ensure that any device he or she brings into the court will interface with the devices the court may provide, should as projectors. Power supply is also important. A depleted battery on a laptop or a lack of available electrical outlets can halt the most persuasive presentation [71].

The courtroom of the future will doubtless boast more devices and a legal expansion in the ways that those devices may be used. For example, it may one day be decided that two-way video testimony does not violate the Sixth Amendment. The Supreme Court may eventually allow its proceedings to be broadcast on the Web (although we do not suggest holding your breath waiting for that development), and both reporters and bloggers may be allowed to post regular updates on trials via social media. These changes will almost certainly occur slowly, much more so than the pace of technological development. It is unlikely that the customs of the court will ever catch up to capabilities of society's electronic devices and the expectations of the society that uses them.

SUMMARY

1. Compare and contrast the judicial branch of the government with the executive and legislative branches.
   - The legislative and the executive branches run the nation, while the judicial branch interpret its laws. The judicial branch is supposed to be both the weakest and the most impartial branch of the government.

2. List and discuss the three major methods of judicial selection.
   - Judges may be appointed by a legislator, selected by a nominating committee (merit selection), elected by citizens, or achieve office by a combination of these methods.
   - Appointment usually occurs when a governor must choose a judge to fill a midterm vacancy. In merit selection, an appointed committee reviews applicants for open judgeships, then the best-qualified applicants are chosen to fill the positions. Several jurisdictions and states hold partisan and nonpartisan elections for judges. A partisan election is one in which the candidates run as part of a political party, with the party listed on the ballot. In nonpartisan elections, candidates may not be nominated or endorsed by a political party, appear on a party ticket, or list a party affiliation on the ballot.

3. Compare judicial restraint with judicial activism. Compare judicial independence with judicial accountability.
   - Judges are encouraged to practice judicial restraint, or to limit the exercise of their own power and defer to written law as long as it is constitutional. The term "judicial activism" is sometimes applied to judicial decisions that appear to contradict voters' desires or are suspected of being based on the judge's personal or political preferences rather than on law.
   - Judicial independence is the idea that the judiciary should not be affected by other branches of government, or private or partisan interests. Judicial accountability is the idea that judges should defer to the wishes and opinions of the electorate.

4. Give reasons that the court's work is confidential and secret.
   - The court use confidentiality to help guarantee the defendant a fair trial. Jurors are not supposed to talk about cases they are hearing until deliberation in order to avoid prejudicing potential or current jurors who should know as little as possible about the case.

5. Talk about the opposing aims of the media and the courts.
   - The court is interested in conducting a fair trial and protecting the rights of both the defendant and victims. The media is interested in the public's "right to know" and encouraging the flow of

information, which helps to encourage transparency and the health of democracy.

6. Understand the disadvantages of the new media in terms of reporter's privilege.
   - The new media lacks the institutional nature of the old media. Old media outlets have the ability to challenge the courts and support reporters. New media outlets act mainly as conduits for information and do not research and report information. Bloggers have little to fall back on when protecting a source or requesting access to information.

7. Discuss the court's difficulties with social media and how social media may benefit the legal process.
   - New media technology has given individuals power to make public what they see and hear. The court must deal with the activities of jurors who use social media to disseminate information about a case and bloggers who want court access and reporter's privilege.

8. Evaluate the advantages of sophisticated communications technology in the courts.
   - Judges may use computers and monitors to display information to the courtroom, defendants, and convicted parties regarding the case and sentencing. Videoconferencing allows judges to hold arraignments from the courtroom without requiring the defendants to leave the jail, thus strengthening court security. Witnesses may also use videoconferencing to testify from remote locations.

9. Explain the need for security in the courthouse.
   - The general public often comes into contact with known violent offenders at the courthouse. With the exception of police officers who provide security, the courthouse staff, court observers, and jurors are all civilians who must deal with these violent offenders. Therefore, the courthouse must be a safe place for courthouse staff and jurors to do their work.

Questions

1. How powerful is the judicial branch of the government as compared to the executive and legislative branches?
2. What are the three major methods of judicial selection?
3. What is judicial restraint? What is judicial activism? Define judicial independence and judicial accountability.
4. Why does the court try to keep its work confidential and secret?
5. Why do the media and the courts tend to be at odds?
6. In terms of reporter's privilege, how are bloggers at a disadvantage to reporters?

7. What trouble has the court had with social media? How can social media benefit the legal process?

8. How may sophisticated communications technology improve the court process?

9. Why are courthouses secure?

REFERENCES

[1] Chandonnet BH. The increasing politicization of the American judiciary: Republican Party of *Minnesota v. White* and its effects on future judicial selection in state courts. William Mary Bill Rights J 2004;12(2):577−604: Online at <scholarship.law.wm.edu/wmborj/vol12/iss2/9>.

[2] de Vogue A, Greenburg JC. Sotomayor's pledges "fidelity" to the law. ABC News, <abcnews.go.com/Politics/SoniaSotomayor/story?id = 8065546> [accessed July 13, 2009].

[3] J. Nocera The ugliness started with Bork New York Times October October 22, 2011 17: Online at <www.nytimes.com/2011/10/22/opinion/nocera-the-ugliness-all-started-with-bork.html>.

[4] Ibid.

[5] Weiden DL. Judicial politicization, ideology, and activism at the high courts of the United States, Canada, and Australia. Polit Res Quart 2011;64(2):335−47.

[6] Ibid.

[7] Shapiro SA, Murphy R. Politicized judicial review in administrative law: three improbable responses. George Mason Law Rev 2012;19(2):319−62.

[8] Richardson Jr. LE, Scheb II JM. Divided government and the Supreme Court. Am Polit Quart 1993;21(4):458.

[9] Kingsbury A. The long road to remaking the courts. U.S. News World Rep 2009;146(5):54.

[10] Welna D. Senate democrats battle over court nominees NPR, < www.npr.org/2012/03/13/148536630/senate-democrats-battle-over-court-nominees>2012, [accessed March 13, 2012]. C. Savage Obama nominates two for federal appeals court. New York Times, <www.nytimes.com/2012/06/12/us/politics/obama-nominates-halligan-and-srinivasan-to-dc-appeals-court.html> [accessed June 11, 2012] Canham M. Lee ready to deal on his judicial protest Salt Lake Tribune, <www.sltrib.com/sltrib/politics/54388966-90/lee-nominees-court-rule.html.csp>. [accessed June 11, 2012]

[11] Shepherd JM. Money, politics, and impartial justice. Duke Law J 2009;58(4):623−85.

[12] Rachel Paine Caufield. Inside merit selection: a national survey of judicial nominating commissioners. Des Moines, IA: American Judicature Society; 2012: Online at <scholarship.law.duke.edu/cgi/viewcontent.cgi?article = 1386&context = dlj>; <w2.georgiacourts.gov/journal/files/AJS_JNC_Survey_Report_FINAL_March20_18A7EF17126C1.pdf>.

[13] Brandenburg B, Schotland RA. Justice in peril: the endangered balance between impartial courts and judicial election campaigns. Georgetown J Legal Ethics 2008;21(4):1229−58.

[14] Chertoff. Trends in judicial selection in the states.

[15] Chertoff Meryl J. Trends in judicial selection in the states. McGeorge Law Rev 2011;42 (1):47−64. Rotunda RD. Constitutionalizing judicial ethics: judicial elections after *Republican Party of Minnesota v. White, Caperton,* and *citizens united.* Arkansas Law Rev 2011;64(1):1−70.

[16] Goldschmidt J. Merit selection: current status, procedures, and issues. Univ Miami Law Rev 1994;1(4). Excerpt available online at <www.pbs.org/wgbh/pages/frontline/shows/justice/howshould/merit.html>.

[17] Ibid.

[18] Foster JC. Rethinking politics and judicial selection during contentious times. Albany Law Rev 2004;67(3):821–8.

[19] Fairer ways to choose judges. New York Times, May 23, 2012: Online at <http://www.nytimes.com/2012/05/23/opinion/fairer-ways-to-choose-judges.html>.

[20] Shepherd JM. Money, politics, and impartial justice. Duke Law J 2009;58(4):623–85.

[21] Thompson K. Gay marriage fight targeted Iowa judges, politicizing rulings on issue Washington Post, November 3 2010 <www.washingtonpost.com/wp-dyn/content/article/2010/11/03/AR2010110307058.html>.

[22] J. Goodman Conservative activists take aim at Florida justices Kansas City Star, June 25, 2012 <www.kansascity.com/2012/06/25/3674502/conservative-activists-take-aim.html>.

[23] Mondics C. Trial lawyers, anti-abortion group stymie judicial-selection bill, The Inquirer (Philadelphia), June 16, 2012, <articles.philly.com/2012-06-16/business/32255575_1_merit-selection-appellate-judges-anti-abortion-group>.

[24] Shapiro C. The context of ideology: law, politics, and empirical legal scholarship. 75. Mo. L. Rev. 2010;79(81): (quoting Nomination of Judge John G. Roberts, Jr. to Be Chief Justice of the Supreme Court: Panel One of a Hearing of the S. Judiciary Comm., 104th Cong. (2005)).

[25] American Judicature Society, what is judicial independence, <www.ajs.org/cji/cji_whatisji.asp> [accessed July, 2012].

[26] Buhlmann M, Kunz R. Confidence in the judiciary: comparing the independence and legitimacy of judicial systems. West Eur Polit 2011;34(2):317–45.

[27] Geyh CG. The endless judicial selection debate and why it matters for judicial independence. Georgetown J Legal Ethics 2008;21(4):1259–81.

[28] Champagne A. Judicial selection from a political science perspective. Arkansas Law Rev 2011;64(1):221–47.

[29] Chertoff. Trends in judicial selection in the states.

[30] Chertoff. Trends in judicial selection in the states.

[31] Champagne. Judicial selection from a political science perspective.

[32] Chertoff. Trends in judicial selection in the states.

[33] Hamilton A. The federalist 78, 1788, <www.constitution.org/fed/federa78.htm>.

[34] Murphy SM. Reflections on judicial independence in the criminal justice system. Human Rights 2009;36(1):14–25.

[35] American Judicature Society, what is judicial independence.

[36] Dixon Jr. JHB. The real danger of inadequate court funding. Judges J 2012;51(1):1–43.

[37] Associated Press, Washington Post, October 23, 2011, <www.washingtonpost.com/politics/gop-candidates-would-cut-federal-judges-power/2011/10/23/gIQA5u4Z9L_story.html>.Dixon. The real danger of inadequate court funding.

[38] Dixon. The real danger of inadequate court funding.

[39] Yung CR. Flexing judicial muscle: an empirical study of judicial activism in the federal courts. Northwestern Univ Law Rev 2011;105(1):1–60.

[40] Kohn AC. A legal essay: the judicial activism myth. J Missouri Bar 2011;67(2):106–12.

[41] Yung. Flexing judicial muscle: an empirical study of judicial activism in the federal courts.

[42] de Vogue A. Cameras in the Supreme Court: why the justices are skeptical. ABC News, March 16, 2012, <abcnews.go.com/blogs/politics/2012/03/cameras-in-the-supreme-court-why-the-justices-are-skeptical/>.

[43] E. Knott Local news media battle DA in court for public access San Diego Reader, June 21 2012l;   <http://www.sandiegoreader.com/weblogs/news-ticker/2012/jun/21/local-news-media-battle-da-in-court-for-public-acc/>.

[44] Green DD. Is the 'most extraordinary remedy' becoming more common? News Media Law 2010;34(4):24−6.

[45] Judge fines reporters despite unlawful prior restraint. News Media Law 2002;26(3) 5.

[46] Sourcewatch, Miller J. <www.sourcewatch.org/index.php?title = Judith_Miller> [accessed June 3, 2010].

[47] Fitzgerald P. Bush commutes Libby's prison sentence. CNN, July 2, 2007.

[48] Phillipson G. Trial by media: the betrayal of the First Amendment's purpose. Law Contemp Probl 2008;71(4):15−29.

[49] Nuss J. Death row inmate gets new trial after juror tweet. U.S.A Today, December 8, 2012, <www.usatoday.com/tech/news/story/2011-12-08/juror-tweet-death-row/51741370/1>.

[50] Ecker K. Juror use of social media, blogs compromise cases, Lawyers.com, December 2, 2011,<blogs.lawyers.com/2011/12/juror-use-of-social-media-blogs-compromises-cases/>.

[51] Siegel AF. Judges confounded by jury's access to cyberspace. Baltimore Sun, December 13, 2009,   <articles.baltimoresun.com/2009-12-13/news/bal-md.ar.tmi13dec13_1_deliberations-period-florida-drug-case-jurors>.

[52] Texas Legislature Online, HB 670, <www.legis.state.tx.us/tlodocs/81R/billtext/pdf/HB00670F.pdf> [accessed January, 2013].

[53] Reporter's Committee for Freedom of the Press, Andrea Papagianis, April 30, 2012, <http://www.rcfp.org/browse-media-law-resources/news/dallas-judge-dismisses-defamation-case-against-neighborhood-blogger>.

[54] Auerbach N. Judge OKs tweets, texts for hearing, U.S.A Today, December 13, 2011.

[55] Present B. Motions for Facebook discovery denied, Post-Gazette.com, July 23, 2012, <www.post-gazette.com/stories/business/legal/motions-for-facebook-discovery-denied-645792>. Brandolph A. Social media postings may be fodder in court. TribLive, July 20, 2012, < triblive.com/news/2222925-74/lesko-social-media-discovery-evidence-profile-attorney-attorneys-facebook-trails > .

[56] Lieberman S. Chestnut ridge sex-abuse case: judge seeks text, Facebook records, Lohud.com, June 29, 2012, <www.lohud.com/article/20120629/NEWS03/306290071/Chestnut-Ridge-sex-abuse-case-Judge-seeks-text-Facebook-records>.

[57] Morphy E. Twitter may face Sisyphean challenge in protected speech battle. TechNewsWorld, July 20, 2012, <www.technewsworld.com/story/75687.html>.

[58] Quigley ML. Courtroom technology and legal ethics: considerations for the ABA commission on ethics 20/20. Prof Lawyer 2010;20(3):18−21.

[59] Antweil B, Grosdidier P, Dexter R. Using technology to meet jurors' expectations. Verdict 2011;25(1):10−2.

[60] Kiefer JS. Using technology in the courtroom: a subjective evaluation of the benefits of visual presentation of evidence. Reporter 2008;35(2):17−21.

[61] Kelly WG. The promise of a high-tech courtroom. Judges' J 2011;50(1):28−31.

[62] Diamond SS, et al. Efficiency and cost: the impact of videoconferenced hearings on bail decisions. J Crim Law Crim 2010;100(3):869−902.

[63] Feige D. Put down your gun New York Times, March 19, 2005 <www.nytimes.com/2005/03/19/opinion/19feige.html>.

[64] Dewan S. Report details fatal minutes in courthouse New York Times, April 8, 2005 <www.nytimes.com/2005/04/08/national/08courthouse.html>.

[65] Brown R. Man guilty in murders at Atlanta courthouse New York Times, November 7, 2008 <www.nytimes.com/2008/11/08/us/08nichols.html>.

[66] B. Goodman Prisoner flees custody in Atlanta but is caught New York Times, November 11, 2005 <www.nytimes.com/2005/11/11/national/11escape.html>.

[67] Kelly. The promise of a high-tech courtroom.

[68] Mulcahy L. An unbearable lightness of being: shifts toward the virtual trial, Conference Papers—Law and Society (Annual Meeting 2010). p. 1.

[69] Montell ND. A new test for two-way video testimony: bringing *Maryland v. Craig* into the technological era. Univ Louisville Law Rev 2011;50(2):361−82.

[70] Ibid.

[71] Thumma JSA. The trials and tribulations—and benefits—of technology. Judges' J 2010;49 (3):15−7.

Appendix A: The Constitution of the United States

PREAMBLE

We the People of the United States, in Order to form a more perfect Union, establish Justice, insure domestic Tranquility, provide for the common defence, promote the general Welfare, and secure the Blessings of Liberty to ourselves and our Posterity, do ordain and establish this Constitution for the United States of America.

ARTICLE I – THE LEGISLATIVE BRANCH

Section 1 – The Legislature
All legislative Powers herein granted shall be vested in a Congress of the United States, which shall consist of a Senate and House of Representatives.

Section 2 – The House
The House of Representatives shall be composed of Members chosen every second Year by the People of the several States, and the Electors in each State shall have the Qualifications requisite for Electors of the most numerous Branch of the State Legislature.

No Person shall be a Representative who shall not have attained to the Age of twenty five Years, and been seven Years a Citizen of the United States, and who shall not, when elected, be an Inhabitant of that State in which he shall be chosen.

(*Representatives and direct Taxes shall be apportioned among the several States which may be included within this Union, according to their respective Numbers, which shall be determined by adding to the whole Number of free Persons, including those bound to Service for a Term of Years, and excluding Indians not taxed, three fifths of all other Persons.*) **(The previous sentence in parentheses was modified by the 14th Amendment, Section 2.)**

The actual Enumeration shall be made within three Years after the first Meeting of the Congress of the United States, and within every subsequent Term of ten Years, in such Manner as they shall by Law direct. The Number of Representatives shall not exceed one for every thirty Thousand, but each State shall have at Least one Representative; and until such enumeration shall be made, the State of New Hampshire shall be entitled to chuse three, Massachusetts eight, Rhode Island and Providence Plantations one, Connecticut five, New York six, New Jersey four, Pennsylvania eight, Delaware one, Maryland six, Virginia ten, North Carolina five, South Carolina five and Georgia three.

When vacancies happen in the Representation from any State, the Executive Authority thereof shall issue Writs of Election to fill such Vacancies.

The House of Representatives shall chuse their Speaker and other Officers; and shall have the sole Power of Impeachment.

Section 3—The Senate
The Senate of the United States shall be composed of two Senators from each State, (*chosen by the Legislature thereof,*) (**The preceding words in parentheses superseded by 17th Amendment, Section 1.**) for six Years; and each Senator shall have one Vote. Immediately after they shall be assembled in Consequence of the first Election, they shall be divided as equally as may be into three Classes. The Seats of the Senators of the first Class shall be vacated at the Expiration of the second Year, of the second Class at the Expiration of the fourth Year, and of the third Class at the Expiration of the sixth Year, so that one third may be chosen every second Year; (*and if Vacancies happen by Resignation, or otherwise, during the Recess of the Legislature of any State, the Executive thereof may make temporary Appointments until the next Meeting of the Legislature, which shall then fill such Vacancies.*) (**The preceding words in parentheses were superseded by the 17th Amendment, Section 2.**)

No person shall be a Senator who shall not have attained to the Age of thirty Years, and been nine Years a Citizen of the United States, and who shall not, when elected, be an Inhabitant of that State for which he shall be chosen.

The Vice President of the United States shall be President of the Senate, but shall have no Vote, unless they be equally divided.

The Senate shall chuse their other Officers, and also a President pro tempore, in the absence of the Vice President, or when he shall exercise the Office of President of the United States.

The Senate shall have the sole Power to try all Impeachments. When sitting for that Purpose, they shall be on Oath or Affirmation. When the President of the United States is tried, the Chief Justice shall preside: And no Person shall be convicted without the Concurrence of two thirds of the Members present.

Judgment in Cases of Impeachment shall not extend further than to removal from Office, and disqualification to hold and enjoy any Office of honor, Trust or Profit under the United States: but the Party convicted shall nevertheless be liable and subject to Indictment, Trial, Judgment and Punishment, according to Law.

Section 4–Elections, Meetings

The Times, Places and Manner of holding Elections for Senators and Representatives, shall be prescribed in each State by the Legislature thereof; but the Congress may at any time by Law make or alter such Regulations, except as to the Place of Chusing Senators. The Congress shall assemble at least once in every Year, and such Meeting shall (*be on the first Monday in December,*) (**The preceding words in parentheses were superseded by the 20th Amendment, Section 2.**) unless they shall by Law appoint a different Day.

Section 5–Membership, Rules, Journals, Adjournment

Each House shall be the Judge of the Elections, Returns and Qualifications of its own Members, and a Majority of each shall constitute a Quorum to do Business; but a smaller number may adjourn from day to day, and may be authorized to compel the Attendance of absent Members, in such Manner, and under such Penalties as each House may provide.

Each House may determine the Rules of its Proceedings, punish its Members for disorderly Behavior, and, with the Concurrence of two-thirds, expel a Member.

Each House shall keep a Journal of its Proceedings, and from time to time publish the same, excepting such Parts as may in their Judgment require Secrecy; and the Yeas and Nays of the Members of either House on any question shall, at the Desire of one fifth of those Present, be entered on the Journal.

Neither House, during the Session of Congress, shall, without the Consent of the other, adjourn for more than three days, nor to any other Place than that in which the two Houses shall be sitting.

Section 6–Compensation

(*The Senators and Representatives shall receive a Compensation for their Services, to be ascertained by Law, and paid out of the Treasury of the United States.*)

(The preceding words in parentheses were modified by the 27th Amendment.) They shall in all Cases, except Treason, Felony and Breach of the Peace, be privileged from Arrest during their Attendance at the Session of their respective Houses, and in going to and returning from the same; and for any Speech or Debate in either House, they shall not be questioned in any other Place.

No Senator or Representative shall, during the Time for which he was elected, be appointed to any civil Office under the Authority of the United States which shall have been created, or the Emoluments whereof shall have been increased during such time; and no Person holding any Office under the United States, shall be a Member of either House during his Continuance in Office.

Section 7–Revenue Bills, Legislative Process, Presidential Veto

All bills for raising Revenue shall originate in the House of Representatives; but the Senate may propose or concur with Amendments as on other Bills. Every Bill which shall have passed the House of Representatives and the Senate, shall, before it become a Law, be presented to the President of the United States; If he approve he shall sign it, but if not he shall return it, with his Objections to that House in which it shall have originated, who shall enter the Objections at large on their Journal, and proceed to reconsider it. If after such Reconsideration two thirds of that House shall agree to pass the Bill, it shall be sent, together with the Objections, to the other House, by which it shall likewise be reconsidered, and if approved by two thirds of that House, it shall become a Law. But in all such Cases the Votes of both Houses shall be determined by Yeas and Nays, and the Names of the Persons voting for and against the Bill shall be entered on the Journal of each House respectively. If any Bill shall not be returned by the President within ten Days (Sundays excepted) after it shall have been presented to him, the Same shall be a Law, in like Manner as if he had signed it, unless the Congress by their Adjournment prevent its Return, in which Case it shall not be a Law.

Every Order, Resolution, or Vote to which the Concurrence of the Senate and House of Representatives may be necessary (except on a question of Adjournment) shall be presented to the President of the United States; and before the Same shall take Effect, shall be approved by him, or being disapproved by him, shall be repassed by two thirds of the Senate and House of Representatives, according to the Rules and Limitations prescribed in the Case of a Bill.

Section 8–Powers of Congress

The Congress shall have Power To lay and collect Taxes, Duties, Imposts and Excises, to pay the Debts and provide for the common Defence and general Welfare of the United States; but all Duties, Imposts and Excises shall be uniform throughout the United States; To borrow money on the credit of the United States; To regulate Commerce with foreign Nations, and among the several States, and with the Indian Tribes; To establish a uniform Rule of Naturalization, and uniform Laws on the subject of Bankruptcies throughout the United States; To coin Money, regulate the Value thereof, and of foreign Coin, and fix the Standard of Weights and Measures; To provide for the Punishment of counterfeiting the Securities and current Coin of the United States; To establish Post Offices and Post Roads; To promote the Progress of Science and useful Arts, by securing for limited Times to Authors and Inventors the exclusive Right to their respective Writings and Discoveries; To constitute Tribunals inferior to the supreme Court; To define and punish Piracies and Felonies committed on the high Seas, and Offenses against the Law of Nations; To declare War, grant Letters of Marque and Reprisal, and make Rules concerning Captures on Land and Water; To raise and support Armies, but no Appropriation of Money to that Use shall be for a longer Term than two Years; To provide and maintain a Navy; To make Rules for the Government and Regulation of the land and naval Forces; To provide for calling forth the Militia to execute the Laws of the Union, suppress Insurrections and repel Invasions; To provide for organizing, arming, and disciplining the Militia, and for governing such Part of them as may be employed in the Service of the United States, reserving to the States respectively, the Appointment of the Officers, and the Authority of training the Militia according to the discipline prescribed by Congress; To exercise exclusive Legislation in all Cases whatsoever, over such District (not exceeding ten Miles square) as may, by Cession of particular States, and the acceptance of Congress, become the Seat of the Government of the United States, and to exercise like Authority over all Places purchased by the Consent of the Legislature of the State in which the Same shall be, for the Erection of Forts, Magazines, Arsenals, dock-Yards, and other needful Buildings; And To make all Laws which shall be necessary and proper for carrying into Execution the foregoing Powers, and all other Powers vested by this Constitution in the Government of the United States, or in any Department or Officer thereof.

Section 9–Limits on Congress

The Migration or Importation of such Persons as any of the States now existing shall think proper to admit, shall not be prohibited by the Congress prior to the Year one thousand eight hundred and eight, but a tax or duty may be imposed on such Importation, not exceeding ten dollars for each Person.

The privilege of the Writ of Habeas Corpus shall not be suspended, unless when in Cases of Rebellion or Invasion the public Safety may require it.

No Bill of Attainder or ex post facto Law shall be passed.

(*No capitation, or other direct, Tax shall be laid, unless in Proportion to the Census or Enumeration herein before directed to be taken.*) (**Section in parentheses clarified by the 16th Amendment.**)

No Tax or Duty shall be laid on Articles exported from any State.

No Preference shall be given by any Regulation of Commerce or Revenue to the Ports of one State over those of another: nor shall Vessels bound to, or from, one State, be obliged to enter, clear, or pay Duties in another.

No Money shall be drawn from the Treasury, but in Consequence of Appropriations made by Law; and a regular Statement and Account of the Receipts and Expenditures of all public Money shall be published from time to time.

No Title of Nobility shall be granted by the United States: And no Person holding any Office of Profit or Trust under them, shall, without the Consent of the Congress, accept of any present, Emolument, Office, or Title, of any kind whatever, from any King, Prince or foreign State.

Section 10—Powers Prohibited of States

No State shall enter into any Treaty, Alliance, or Confederation; grant Letters of Marque and Reprisal; coin Money; emit Bills of Credit; make any Thing but gold and silver Coin a Tender in Payment of Debts; pass any Bill of Attainder, ex post facto Law, or Law impairing the Obligation of Contracts, or grant any Title of Nobility.

No State shall, without the Consent of the Congress, lay any Imposts or Duties on Imports or Exports, except what may be absolutely necessary for executing it's inspection Laws: and the net Produce of all Duties and Imposts, laid by any State on Imports or Exports, shall be for the Use of the Treasury of the United States; and all such Laws shall be subject to the Revision and Control of the Congress.

No State shall, without the Consent of Congress, lay any duty of Tonnage, keep Troops, or Ships of War in time of Peace, enter into any Agreement or Compact with another State, or with a foreign Power, or engage in War, unless actually invaded, or in such imminent Danger as will not admit of delay.

ARTICLE II – THE EXECUTIVE BRANCH

Section 1 – The President

The executive Power shall be vested in a President of the United States of America. He shall hold his Office during the Term of four Years, and, together with the Vice-President chosen for the same Term, be elected, as follows:

Each State shall appoint, in such Manner as the Legislature thereof may direct, a Number of Electors, equal to the whole Number of Senators and Representatives to which the State may be entitled in the Congress: but no Senator or Representative, or Person holding an Office of Trust or Profit under the United States, shall be appointed an Elector.

(*The Electors shall meet in their respective States, and vote by Ballot for two persons, of whom one at least shall not lie an Inhabitant of the same State with themselves. And they shall make a List of all the Persons voted for, and of the Number of Votes for each; which List they shall sign and certify, and transmit sealed to the Seat of the Government of the United States, directed to the President of the Senate. The President of the Senate shall, in the Presence of the Senate and House of Representatives, open all the Certificates, and the Votes shall then be counted. The Person having the greatest Number of Votes shall be the President, if such Number be a Majority of the whole Number of Electors appointed; and if there be more than one who have such Majority, and have an equal Number of Votes, then the House of Representatives shall immediately chuse by Ballot one of them for President; and if no Person have a Majority, then from the five highest on the List the said House shall in like Manner chuse the President. But in chusing the President, the Votes shall be taken by States, the Representation from each State having one Vote; a quorum for this Purpose shall consist of a Member or Members from two-thirds of the States, and a Majority of all the States shall be necessary to a Choice. In every Case, after the Choice of the President, the Person having the greatest Number of Votes of the Electors shall be the Vice President. But if there should remain two or more who have equal Votes, the Senate shall chuse from them by Ballot the Vice-President.*)* **(This clause in parentheses was superseded by the 12th Amendment.)**

The Congress may determine the Time of chusing the Electors, and the Day on which they shall give their Votes; which Day shall be the same through-out the United States.

No person except a natural born Citizen, or a Citizen of the United States, at the time of the Adoption of this Constitution, shall be eligible to the Office of President; neither shall any Person be eligible to that Office who shall not have attained to the Age of thirty-five Years, and been fourteen Years a Resident within the United States.

(*In Case of the Removal of the President from Office, or of his Death, Resignation, or Inability to discharge the Powers and Duties of the said Office, the same shall devolve on the Vice President, and the Congress may by Law provide for the Case of Removal, Death, Resignation or Inability, both of the President and Vice President, declaring what Officer shall then act as President, and such Officer shall act accordingly, until the Disability be removed, or a President shall be elected.)* **(This clause in parentheses has been modified by the 20th and 25th Amendments.)**

The President shall, at stated Times, receive for his Services, a Compensation, which shall neither be increased nor diminished during the Period for which he shall have been elected, and he shall not receive within that Period any other Emolument from the United States, or any of them.

Before he enter on the Execution of his Office, he shall take the following Oath or Affirmation: "I do solemnly swear (or affirm) that I will faithfully execute the Office of President of the United States, and will to the best of my Ability, preserve, protect and defend the Constitution of the United States."

Section 2–Civilian Power over Military, Cabinet, Pardon Power, Appointments

The President shall be Commander in Chief of the Army and Navy of the United States, and of the Militia of the several States, when called into the actual Service of the United States; he may require the Opinion, in writing, of the principal Officer in each of the executive Departments, upon any subject relating to the Duties of their respective Offices, and he shall have Power to Grant Reprieves and Pardons for Offenses against the United States, except in Cases of Impeachment.

He shall have Power, by and with the Advice and Consent of the Senate, to make Treaties, provided two thirds of the Senators present concur; and he shall nominate, and by and with the Advice and Consent of the Senate, shall appoint Ambassadors, other public Ministers and Consuls, Judges of the supreme Court, and all other Officers of the United States, whose Appointments are not herein otherwise provided for, and which shall be established by Law: but the Congress may by Law vest the Appointment of such inferior Officers, as they think proper, in the President alone, in the Courts of Law, or in the Heads of Departments.

The President shall have Power to fill up all Vacancies that may happen during the Recess of the Senate, by granting Commissions which shall expire at the End of their next Session.

Section 3–State of the Union, Convening Congress

He shall from time to time give to the Congress Information of the State of the Union, and recommend to their Consideration such Measures as he shall judge necessary and expedient; he may, on extraordinary Occasions, convene both Houses, or either of them, and in Case of Disagreement between them, with Respect to the Time of Adjournment, he may adjourn them to such Time as he shall think proper; he shall receive Ambassadors and other public Ministers; he shall take Care that the Laws be faithfully executed, and shall Commission all the Officers of the United States.

Section 4–Disqualification

The President, Vice President and all civil Officers of the United States, shall be removed from Office on Impeachment for, and Conviction of, Treason, Bribery, or other high Crimes and Misdemeanors.

ARTICLE III–THE JUDICIAL BRANCH

Section 1–Judicial powers

The judicial Power of the United States, shall be vested in one supreme Court, and in such inferior Courts as the Congress may from time to time ordain and establish. The Judges, both of the supreme and inferior Courts, shall hold their Offices during good Behavior, and shall, at stated Times, receive for their Services a Compensation which shall not be diminished during their Continuance in Office.

Section 2–Trial by Jury, Original Jurisdiction, Jury Trials

(*The judicial Power shall extend to all Cases, in Law and Equity, arising under this Constitution, the Laws of the United States, and Treaties made, or which shall be made, under their Authority; to all Cases affecting Ambassadors, other public Ministers and Consuls; to all Cases of admiralty and maritime Jurisdiction; to Controversies to which the United States shall be a Party; to Controversies between two or more States; between a State and Citizens of another State; between Citizens of different States; between Citizens of the same State claiming Lands under Grants of different States, and between a State, or the Citizens thereof, and foreign States, Citizens or Subjects.*) **(This section in parentheses is modified by the 11th Amendment.)**

In all Cases affecting Ambassadors, other public Ministers and Consuls, and those in which a State shall be Party, the supreme Court shall have original Jurisdiction. In all the other Cases before mentioned, the supreme Court shall have appellate Jurisdiction, both as to Law and Fact, with such Exceptions, and under such Regulations as the Congress shall make.

The Trial of all Crimes, except in Cases of Impeachment, shall be by Jury; and such Trial shall be held in the State where the said Crimes shall have been committed; but when not committed within any State, the Trial shall be at such Place or Places as the Congress may by Law have directed.

Section 3—Treason

Treason against the United States, shall consist only in levying War against them, or in adhering to their Enemies, giving them Aid and Comfort. No Person shall be convicted of Treason unless on the Testimony of two Witnesses to the same overt Act, or on Confession in open Court.

The Congress shall have power to declare the Punishment of Treason, but no Attainder of Treason shall work Corruption of Blood, or Forfeiture except during the Life of the Person attainted.

ARTICLE IV—THE STATES

Section 1—Each State to Honor all others

Full Faith and Credit shall be given in each State to the public Acts, Records, and judicial Proceedings of every other State. And the Congress may by general Laws prescribe the Manner in which such Acts, Records and Proceedings shall be proved, and the Effect thereof.

Section 2—State Citizens, Extradition

The Citizens of each State shall be entitled to all Privileges and Immunities of Citizens in the several States.

A Person charged in any State with Treason, Felony, or other Crime, who shall flee from Justice, and be found in another State, shall on demand of the executive Authority of the State from which he fled, be delivered up, to be removed to the State having Jurisdiction of the Crime.

(*No Person held to Service or Labourin one State, under the Laws thereof, escaping into another, shall, in Consequence of any Law or Regulation therein, be discharged from such Service or Labour, But shall be delivered upon Claim of the Party to whom such Service or Labour may be due.*) (**This clause in parentheses is superseded by the 13th Amendment.**)

Section 3—New States

New States may be admitted by the Congress into this Union; but no new States shall be formed or erected within the Jurisdiction of any other State; nor any State be formed by the Junction of two or more States, or parts of States, without the Consent of the Legislatures of the States concerned as well as of the Congress.

The Congress shall have Power to dispose of and make all needful Rules and Regulations respecting the Territory or other Property belonging to the United States; and nothing in this Constitution shall be so construed as to Prejudice any Claims of the United States, or of any particular State.

Section 4—Republican Government

The United States shall guarantee to every State in this Union a Republican Form of Government, and shall protect each of them against Invasion; and on Application of the Legislature, or of the Executive (when the Legislature cannot be convened) against domestic Violence.

ARTICLE V—AMENDMENT

The Congress, whenever two thirds of both Houses shall deem it necessary, shall propose Amendments to this Constitution, or, on the Application of the Legislatures of two thirds of the several States, shall call a Convention for proposing Amendments, which, in either Case, shall be valid to all Intents and Purposes, as part of this Constitution, when ratified by the Legislatures of three fourths of the several States, or by Conventions in three fourths thereof, as the one or the other Mode of Ratification may be proposed by the Congress; Provided that no Amendment which may be made prior to the Year One thousand eight hundred and eight shall in any Manner affect the first and fourth Clauses in the Ninth Section of the first Article; and that no State, without its Consent, shall be deprived of its equal Suffrage in the Senate.

ARTICLE VI—DEBTS, SUPREMACY, OATHS

All Debts contracted and Engagements entered into, before the Adoption of this Constitution, shall be as valid against the United States under this Constitution, as under the Confederation.

This Constitution, and the Laws of the United States which shall be made in Pursuance thereof; and all Treaties made, or which shall be made, under the Authority of the United States, shall be the supreme Law of the Land; and the Judges in every State shall be bound thereby, any Thing in the Constitution or Laws of any State to the Contrary notwithstanding.

The Senators and Representatives before mentioned, and the Members of the several State Legislatures, and all executive and judicial Officers, both of the United States and of the several States, shall be bound by Oath or Affirmation, to support this Constitution; but no religious Test shall ever be required as a Qualification to any Office or public Trust under the United States.

ARTICLE VII—RATIFICATION

The Ratification of the Conventions of nine States, shall be sufficient for the Establishment of this Constitution between the States so ratifying the Same. Done in Convention by the Unanimous Consent of the States present the Seventeenth Day of September in the Year of our Lord one thousand seven hundred and Eighty seven and of the Independence of the United States of America the Twelfth. In Witness whereof We have hereunto subscribed our Names.

Go Washington—President and deputy from Virginia
New Hampshire—John Langdon, Nicholas Gilman
Massachusetts—Nathaniel Gorham, Rufus King
Connecticut—Wm Saml Johnson, Roger Sherman
New York—Alexander Hamilton
New Jersey—Wil Livingston, David Brearley, Wm Paterson, Jona. Dayton
Pennsylvania—B Franklin, Thomas Mifflin, Robt Morris, Geo. Clymer, Thos FitzSimons,
Jared Ingersoll, James Wilson, Gouv Morris
Delaware—Geo. Read, Gunning Bedford jun, John Dickinson, Richard Bassett, Jaco.Broom
Maryland—James McHenry, Dan of St Tho Jenifer, Danl Carroll
Virginia—John Blair, James Madison Jr.
North Carolina—Wm Blount, Richd Dobbs Spaight, Hu Williamson
South Carolina—J. Rutledge, Charles Cotesworth Pinckney, Charles Pinckney, Pierce Butler
Georgia—William Few, Abr Baldwin
Attest: William Jackson, Secretary

THE AMENDMENTS

The following are the Amendments to the Constitution. The first ten Amendments collectively are commonly known as the Bill of Rights.

Amendment 1—Freedom of Religion, Press, Expression. Ratified 12/15/1791.

Congress shall make no law respecting an establishment of religion, or prohibiting the free exercise thereof; or abridging the freedom of speech, or of the press; or the right of the people peaceably to assemble, and to petition the Government for a redress of grievances.

Amendment 2—Right to Bear Arms. Ratified 12/15/1791.

A well regulated Militia, being necessary to the security of a free State, the right of the people to keep and bear Arms, shall not be infringed.

Amendment 3—Quartering of Soldiers. Ratified 12/15/1791.

No Soldier shall, in time of peace be quartered in any house, without the consent of the Owner, nor in time of war, but in a manner to be prescribed by law.

Amendment 4—Search and Seizure. Ratified 12/15/1791.

The right of the people to be secure in their persons, houses, papers, and effects, against unreasonable searches and seizures, shall not be violated, and no Warrants shall issue, but upon probable cause, supported by Oath or affirmation, and particularly describing the place to be searched, and the persons or things to be seized.

Amendment 5—Trial and Punishment, Compensation for Takings. Ratified 12/15/1791.

No person shall be held to answer for a capital, or otherwise infamous crime, unless on a presentment or indictment of a Grand Jury, except in cases arising in the land or naval forces, or in the Militia, when in actual service in time of War or public danger; nor shall any person be subject for the same offense to be twice put in jeopardy of life or limb; nor shall be compelled in any criminal case to be a witness against himself, nor be deprived of life, liberty, or property, without due process of law; nor shall private property be taken for public use, without just compensation.

Amendment 6—Right to Speedy Trial, Confrontation of Witnesses. Ratified 12/15/1791.

In all criminal prosecutions, the accused shall enjoy the right to a speedy and public trial, by an impartial jury of the State and district wherein the crime shall have been committed, which district shall have been previously ascertained by law, and to be informed of the nature and cause of the accusation; to be confronted with the witnesses against him; to have compulsory process for obtaining witnesses in his favor, and to have the Assistance of Counsel for his defence.

Amendment 7—Trial by Jury in Civil Cases. Ratified 12/15/1791.

In Suits at common law, where the value in controversy shall exceed twenty dollars, the right of trial by jury shall be preserved, and no fact tried by a jury, shall be otherwise reexamined in any Court of the United States, than according to the rules of the common law.

Amendment 8—Cruel and Unusual Punishment. Ratified 12/15/1791.

Excessive bail shall not be required, nor excessive fines imposed, nor cruel and unusual punishments inflicted.

Amendment 9—Construction of Constitution. Ratified 12/15/1791.

The enumeration in the Constitution, of certain rights, shall not be construed to deny or disparage others retained by the people.

Amendment 10—Powers of the States and People. Ratified 12/15/1791.

The powers not delegated to the United States by the Constitution, nor prohibited by it to the States, are reserved to the States respectively, or to the people.

Amendment 11—Judicial Limits. Ratified 2/7/1795.

The Judicial power of the United States shall not be construed to extend to any suit in law or equity, commenced or prosecuted against one of the United States by Citizens of another State, or by Citizens or Subjects of any Foreign State.

Amendment 12—Choosing the President, Vice-President. Ratified 6/15/1804.

The Electors shall meet in their respective states, and vote by ballot for President and Vice-President, one of whom, at least, shall not be an inhabitant of the same state with themselves; they shall name in their ballots the person voted for as President, and in distinct ballots the person voted for as Vice-President, and they shall make distinct lists of all persons voted for as President, and of all persons voted for as Vice-President and of the number of votes for each, which lists they shall sign and certify, and transmit sealed to the seat of the government of the United States, directed to the President of the Senate; The President of the Senate shall, in the presence of the Senate and House of Representatives, open all the certificates and the votes shall then be counted; The person having the greatest Number of votes for President, shall be the President, if such number be a majority of the whole number of Electors appointed; and if no person have such majority, then from the persons having the highest numbers not exceeding three on the list of those voted for as President, the House of Representatives shall choose immediately, by ballot, the President. But in choosing the President, the votes shall be taken by states, the representation from each state having one vote; a quorum for this purpose shall consist of a member or members from two-thirds of the states, and a majority of all the states shall be necessary to a choice. And if the House of Representatives shall not choose a President whenever the right of choice shall devolve upon them, before the fourth day of March next following, then the Vice-President shall act as President, as in the case of the death or other constitutional disability of the President.

The person having the greatest number of votes as Vice-President, shall be the Vice- President, if such number be a majority of the whole number of Electors appointed, and if no person have a majority, then from the two highest numbers on the list, the Senate shall choose the Vice-President; a quorum for the purpose shall consist of two-thirds of the whole number of Senators, and a majority of the whole number shall be necessary to a choice. But no person constitutionally ineligible to the office of President shall be eligible to that of Vice-President of the United States.

Amendment 13—Slavery Abolished. Ratified 12/6/1865.

1. Neither slavery nor involuntary servitude, except as a punishment for crime whereof the party shall have been duly convicted, shall exist within the United States, or any place subject to their jurisdiction.
2. Congress shall have power to enforce this article by appropriate legislation.

Amendment 14—Citizenship Rights. Ratified 7/9/1868.

1. All persons born or naturalized in the United States, and subject to the jurisdiction thereof, are citizens of the United States and of the State wherein they reside. No State shall make or enforce any law which shall abridge the privileges or immunities of citizens of the United States; nor shall any State deprive any person of life, liberty, or property, without due process of law; nor deny to any person within its jurisdiction the equal protection of the laws.
2. Representatives shall be apportioned among the several States according to their respective numbers, counting the whole number of persons in each State, excluding Indians not taxed. But when the right to vote at any election for the choice of electors for President and Vice-President of the United States, Representatives in Congress, the Executive and Judicial officers of a State, or the members of the Legislature thereof, is denied to any of the male inhabitants of such State, being twenty-one years of age, and citizens of the United States, or in any way abridged, except for participation in rebellion, or other crime, the basis of representation therein shall be reduced in the proportion which the number of such male citizens shall bear to the whole number of male citizens twenty-one years of age in such State.
3. No person shall be a Senator or Representative in Congress, or elector of President and Vice-President, or hold any office, civil or military, under the United States, or under any State, who, having previously taken an oath, as a member of Congress, or as an officer of the United States, or as a member of any State legislature, or as an executive or judicial officer of any State, to support the Constitution of the United States, shall have engaged in insurrection or rebellion against the same, or given aid or comfort to the enemies thereof. But Congress may by a vote of two-thirds of each House, remove such disability.
4. The validity of the public debt of the United States, authorized by law, including debts incurred for payment of pensions and bounties for services in suppressing insurrection or rebellion, shall not be questioned. But neither the United States nor any State shall assume or pay any debt or obligation incurred in aid of insurrection or rebellion against the United States, or any claim for the loss or emancipation of any slave; but all such debts, obligations and claims shall be held illegal and void.

5. The Congress shall have power to enforce, by appropriate legislation, the provisions of this article.

Amendment 15—Race No Bar to Vote. Ratified 2/3/1870.

1. The right of citizens of the United States to vote shall not be denied or abridged by the United States or by any State on account of race, color, or previous condition of servitude.
2. The Congress shall have power to enforce this article by appropriate legislation.

Amendment 16—Status of Income Tax Clarified. Ratified 2/3/1913.

The Congress shall have power to lay and collect taxes on incomes, from whatever source derived, without apportionment among the several States, and without regard to any census or enumeration.

Amendment 17—Senators Elected by Popular Vote. Ratified 4/8/1913.

The Senate of the United States shall be composed of two Senators from each State, elected by the people thereof, for six years; and each Senator shall have one vote. The electors in each State shall have the qualifications requisite for electors of the most numerous branch of the State legislatures.

When vacancies happen in the representation of any State in the Senate, the executive authority of such State shall issue writs of election to fill such vacancies: Provided, That the legislature of any State may empower the executive thereof to make temporary appointments until the people fill the vacancies by election as the legislature may direct.

This amendment shall not be so construed as to affect the election or term of any Senator chosen before it becomes valid as part of the Constitution.

Amendment 18—Liquor Abolished. Ratified 1/16/1919. Repealed by Amendment 21, 12/5/1933.

1. After one year from the ratification of this article the manufacture, sale, or transportation of intoxicating liquors within, the importation thereof into, or the exportation thereof from the United States and all territory subject to the jurisdiction thereof for beverage purposes is hereby prohibited.
2. The Congress and the several States shall have concurrent power to enforce this article by appropriate legislation.
3. This article shall be inoperative unless it shall have been ratified as an amendment to the Constitution by the legislatures of the several States, as provided in the Constitution, within seven years from the date of the submission hereof to the States by the Congress.

Amendment 19—Women's Suffrage. Ratified 8/18/1920.

The right of citizens of the United States to vote shall not be denied or abridged by the United States or by any State on account of sex.

Congress shall have power to enforce this article by appropriate legislation.

Amendment 20—Presidential, Congressional Terms. Ratified 1/23/1933.

1. The terms of the President and Vice President shall end at noon on the 20th day of January, and the terms of Senators and Representatives at noon on the 3rd day of January, of the years in which such terms would have ended if this article had not been ratified; and the terms of their successors shall then begin.
2. The Congress shall assemble at least once in every year, and such meeting shall begin at noon on the 3d day of January, unless they shall by law appoint a different day.
3. If, at the time fixed for the beginning of the term of the President, the President elect shall have died, the Vice President elect shall become President. If a President shall not have been chosen before the time fixed for the beginning of his term, or if the President elect shall have failed to qualify, then the Vice President elect shall act as President until a President shall have qualified; and the Congress may by law provide for the case wherein neither a President elect nor a Vice President elect shall have qualified, declaring who shall then act as President, or the manner in which one who is to act shall be selected, and such person shall act accordingly until a President or Vice President shall have qualified.
4. The Congress may by law provide for the case of the death of any of the persons from whom the House of Representatives may choose a President whenever the right of choice shall have devolved upon them, and for the case of the death of any of the persons from whom the Senate may choose a Vice President whenever the right of choice shall have devolved upon them.
5. Sections 1 and 2 shall take effect on the 15th day of October following the ratification of this article.
6. This article shall be inoperative unless it shall have been ratified as an amendment to the Constitution by the legislatures of three-fourths of the several States within seven years from the date of its submission.

Amendment 21—Amendment 18 Repealed. Ratified 12/5/1933.

1. The eighteenth article of amendment to the Constitution of the United States is hereby repealed.
2. The transportation or importation into any State, Territory, or possession of the United States for delivery or use therein of intoxicating liquors, in violation of the laws thereof, is hereby prohibited.

3. The article shall be inoperative unless it shall have been ratified as an amendment to the Constitution by conventions in the several States, as provided in the Constitution, within seven years from the date of the submission hereof to the States by the Congress.

Amendment 22–Presidential Term Limits. Ratified 2/27/1951.

1. No person shall be elected to the office of the President more than twice, and no person who has held the office of President, or acted as President, for more than two years of a term to which some other person was elected President shall be elected to the office of the President more than once. But this Article shall not apply to any person holding the office of President, when this Article was proposed by the Congress, and shall not prevent any person who may be holding the office of President, or acting as President, during the term within which this Article becomes operative from holding the office of President or acting as President during the remainder of such term.
2. This article shall be inoperative unless it shall have been ratified as an amendment to the Constitution by the legislatures of three-fourths of the several States within seven years from the date of its submission to the States by the Congress.

Amendment 23–Presidential Vote for District of Columbia. Ratified 3/29/1961.

1. The District constituting the seat of Government of the United States shall appoint in such manner as the Congress may direct: A number of electors of President and Vice President equal to the whole number of Senators and Representatives in Congress to which the District would be entitled if it were a State, but in no event more than the least populous State; they shall be in addition to those appointed by the States, but they shall be considered, for the purposes of the election of President and Vice President, to be electors appointed by a State; and they shall meet in the District and perform such duties as provided by the twelfth article of amendment.
2. The Congress shall have power to enforce this article by appropriate legislation.

Amendment 24–Poll Tax Barred. Ratified 1/23/1964.

1. The right of citizens of the United States to vote in any primary or other election for President or Vice President, for electors for President or Vice President, or for Senator or Representative in Congress, shall not be denied or abridged by the United States or any State by reason of failure to pay any poll tax or other tax.

2. The Congress shall have power to enforce this article by appropriate legislation.

Amendment 25—Presidential Disability and Succession. Ratified 2/10/1967.

1. In case of the removal of the President from office or of his death or resignation, the Vice President shall become President.
2. Whenever there is a vacancy in the office of the Vice President, the President shall nominate a Vice President who shall take office upon confirmation by a majority vote of both Houses of Congress.
3. Whenever the President transmits to the President pro tempore of the Senate and the Speaker of the House of Representatives his written declaration that he is unable to discharge the powers and duties of his office, and until he transmits to them a written declaration to the contrary, such powers and duties shall be discharged by the Vice President as Acting President.
4. Whenever the Vice President and a majority of either the principal officers of the executive departments or of such other body as Congress may by law provide, transmit to the President pro tempore of the Senate and the Speaker of the House of Representatives their written declaration that the President is unable to discharge the powers and duties of his office, the Vice President shall immediately assume the powers and duties of the office as Acting President.

Thereafter, when the President transmits to the President pro tempore of the Senate and the Speaker of the House of Representatives his written declaration that no inability exists, he shall resume the powers and duties of his office unless the Vice President and a majority of either the principal officers of the executive department or of such other body as Congress may by law provide, transmit within four days to the President pro tempore of the Senate and the Speaker of the House of Representatives their written declaration that the President is unable to discharge the powers and duties of his office. Thereupon Congress shall decide the issue, assembling within forty eight hours for that purpose if not in session. If the Congress, within twenty one days after receipt of the latter written declaration, or, if Congress is not in session, within twenty one days after Congress is required to assemble, determines by two thirds vote of both Houses that the President is unable to discharge the powers and duties of his office, the Vice President shall continue to discharge the same as Acting President; otherwise, the President shall resume the powers and duties of his office.

Amendment 26—Voting Age Set to 18 Years. Ratified 7/1/1971.

1. The right of citizens of the United States, who are eighteen years of age or older, to vote shall not be denied or abridged by the United States or by any State on account of age.

2. The Congress shall have power to enforce this article by appropriate legislation.

Amendment 27—Limiting Congressional Pay Increases. Ratified 5/7/1992.

No law, varying the compensation for the services of the Senators and Representatives, shall take effect, until an election of Representatives shall have intervened. This file was prepared by USConstitution.net. Find us on the web at http://www.usconstitution.net.

Glossary

actus reus A voluntary act that causes legally prohibited harm. "Reality of the act."

adjudicate In the case of the juvenile court, to hear a case involving a juvenile and hand down a disposition.

adjudication system A system for reviewing and applying laws.

administrative laws Laws written and enforced by executive branch agencies.

adversarial system A framework in which the prosecutor and defense attorney have competing goals of conviction and exoneration.

affirm The court rules that there was no serious constitutional violation in the trial and the conviction and sentence will remain in place.

affirmative defense A response to charges that does not deny the allegations against the defendant but gives a reason why the defendant should not be held responsible.

age of empires The period between 1000 BCE and the nineteenth century CE when most people around the world were controlled by empires.

Age of Enlightenment The 18th-century era during which intellectuals advanced science and reason as ways to improve the human condition, increase human knowledge, and advance the ideals of individual rights and justice.

agents of the state People who work for the state and exert the state's power when enforcing the law.

Alford plea A plea of guilty in which a defendant does not admit guilt.

appeal A formal request to have a higher court review and change a procedural step, verdict, or sentence of the trial court.

appeal by right Mandatory appeals.

appellant The person who initiates an appeal.

appellant brief A document that raises legal concern about errors and constitutional violations at the trial that deprived the defendant of due process of law.

appellee The party responding to or opposing an appeal.

arraignment A defendant's first appearance before a judge.

arrest The deprivation of the liberty of an individual by a legal authority.

Article III The third article of the U.S. Constitution, which creates the federal courts as an independent branch of the government and broadly outlines their jurisdiction and limitations.

Article IV The fourth article of the U.S. Constitution, which gives states independent power to handle affairs within their borders.

Articles of Confederation and Perpetual Union The 1781 constitution of the provisional government of the 13 original states during the Revolutionary War.

Assimilative Crimes Act A federal statute that allows state law to apply to nonfederal criminal offenses committed on property that has been reserved or acquired by the federal government.

565

avoidance canon A practice in which courts avoid hearing appeals that challenge the constitutionality of a law.

avoidance-of-stigma plea An agreement with the prosecutor that allows a defendant to avoid a negative label.

B

bail The money or bond offered to release from detention a person who has been charged with a criminal offense.

bail-bond agent A person who is hired to promise to pay the accused's bail if he or she doesn't show up for court. Sometimes called a surety.

bench trial A trial in which the judge decides the case and there is no jury.

best evidence rule The original copy of a piece of evidence such as a writing, recording, or photograph must be provided unless the original is lost, destroyed, or unobtainable.

beyond a reasonable doubt The standard of proof used to find a defendant guilty in criminal trials.

bill of indictment A document that specifies the charges against the defendant.

Bill of Rights The first 10 amendments to the U.S. Constitution.

bond A bail-bond agent's promise to pay the full bail of a defendant who doesn't appear in court.

bracketing The process of channeling the way people think about and deal with a task.

brief A written argument.

broken windows The idea that minor criminal offenses lead to larger offenses and that a community that allows minor offenses will eventually be plagued by more serious crime.

burden of persuasion The prosecutor's responsibility of persuading the judge or jury that the fact at issue is true.

burden of producing evidence The prosecutor's responsibility of providing evidence that a fact exists.

burden of production The prosecutor's task of producing the *corpus delicti* to establish that an act occurred that violated a criminal statute.

burden of proof The prosecutor's task of convincing a decision maker that a given version of the facts is true.

bureaucracies Organizations with specific goals, an explicit hierarchy of authority, specialization, and standardization of many tasks.

C

case-in-chief The main body of a case, not including rebuttals or opening statements.

case law A judgment that becomes a law for all cases; judicial law.

Case or controversy clause The constitutional requirement that the claims of individuals must be brought before a court for resolution for the court to exercise its jurisdiction.

certiorari **appeals** Appeals that ask a state high court or the U.S. Supreme Court to review an alleged error of law in the trial court and the intermediate court's ruling on it.

challenge for cause The opposition by an attorney against the inclusion of a prospective juror on a jury based on a specific cause or reason.

charge The specification of an alleged crime, the elements of the alleged crime based on the criminal statute, the person(s) alleged to have committed it, her or his intention, and the date, time, and location of the alleged crime.

charging document A statement that specifies the law that has been broken and the date and location of the offense.

checks and balances The right of each branch of a government to amend or void acts of another that fall within its purview.

child savers A group of late nineteenth century social reformers who sought to change the justice system to provide better treatment for children.

circumstantial evidence Proof of a factual matter by proving the existence of other events or circumstances from which the occurrence of the matter at issue can be inferred.

civil commitment The court-ordered institutionalization of a person suffering from a condition, such as mental illness, on the grounds that the person is dangerous.

civil courts Courts that have subject-matter jurisdiction over noncriminal cases involving one party suing another for damages or injunctions.

civil law Law that defines and regulates obligations between private parties.

clear and convincing evidence Evidence that shows a high probability of truth; the plaintiff's standard of proof in some civil cases and the state's standard of proof for civil commitment.

collateral appeal Indirect appeals that do not involve the main case but nonetheless seek to clarify an important issue in the trial process or review the legality of incarceration.

collegial court A panel of about three judges who listen to the same case.

colonial court system A judicial system designed within the political and cultural conditions of a colony but were subject to the colonizing government.

common law Law that emanates from judges and early English systems.

community policing A law enforcement style that uses input from the community to address the conditions that cause crime.

community prosecution A legal initiative in which the prosecutor's office seeks to prevent and address crime with the help of the community.

compartmentalized prosecution When a case is handled by a different attorney at each stage.

complaint A document filed with the court by a victim or police officer that describes a criminal offense and that sets the criminal court process in motion.

concurrence The intention to produce harm that occurs at the same time as the criminal act and harm.

concurrent jurisdiction A form of juvenile waiver that allows prosecutors the discretion to file cases in either juvenile or criminal court.

concurring opinion An opinion that allows a judge to be counted with the majority but still express their own legal interpretation of a case.

conforming cases The type of case the court handles most regularly.

constitution A document created to describe the structure of a government and delegate authority among its branches.

constitutional courts Courts that create the core of the federal judiciary and hear federal criminal trials and appeals. Article III courts.

constitutional law Obligations and powers specified in the government's charter.

corpus delicti The evidence of the crime. "Body of the crime."

courtroom workgroup The judge, attorneys, police officers, bail-bond agents, and others who do the work of the court.

crime An intentional act or omission committed without justification or defense, which is in violation of criminal law and punishable by the state.

criminal law A type of public law that defines certain behaviors as harms against the community, rather than harms against the victim alone, and authorizes the government to prosecute offenders and punish offenders; also called "penal law."

criminal procedure The process by which a case is handled.

criminal statute see "criminal law"

culpability Sufficient responsibility for criminal offenses to be at fault and liable for the conduct.

D

dark figure of crime The idea that the actual amount of crime and delinquency cannot be known because some offenses are not counted in the official crime statistics and may even occur without anyone's knowledge.

demonstrative evidence Evidence in the form of objects that illustrate and clarify the factual matter at issue.

dependent The state of requiring the support of another party, such as a parent or the state.

deposition A sworn statement.

direct-collateral categorization scheme A practice that divides appeals into ones that come directly from a trial court after sentencing and ones that come either before the end of a trial or after the appeals have been attempted.

direct evidence Evidence that, on its own, proves an issue.

directed verdict A ruling awarding the decision to the defense because the prosecutor has not presented sufficient evidence.

discovery Methods used to obtain information relevant to the action held by the opposing party.

discretion The capacity to choose from a range of permissible options that exist within the organizational and institutional constraints.

dismiss To terminate a case without further legal action.

dismissal without prejudice When the appellate court terminates the case but leaves open the option for the state to bring the same charges against the defendant.

dismissal with prejudice When the appellate court tosses out the case and prohibits the state from taking action on the issue again.

disposition The juvenile court's final determination of treatment for a juvenile found responsible for delinquency or status offense.

dissent Disagreement by one or more judges with the majority decision on a case.

distinguishing The tactic of arguing that the instant and precedent cases are too distinct to deduce a connection.

diversion The removal of a case from the courts to another form of legal dispensation.

docket The schedule of cases a court must hear.

domestic violence court A branch of the criminal court that specializes in dealing with abusive and violent behavior that emerges from the home.

double jeopardy A rule from the Fifth Amendment that prohibits the court from trying a criminal defendant twice for the same offense.

drug court A branch of the criminal court that specializes in assisting low-level drug offenders and drug users.

dual sovereignty The federalist system.

due process The central legal principle in the court system that states that a person's rights must be protected during government proceedings and that arbitrary and excessive government power must be inhibited.

due-process provisions Legal principles, laws, and system rules that protect the rights of individuals who are being processed by the government and that constrain the arbitrary or excessive power of the government.

due-process revolution A period from the 1950s to the early 1970s in which due-process protection was rapidly expanded.

E

empires Societies that use military dominance to gain economic and political control over other societies.

en banc When all the judges in the jurisdiction hear a case.

English common law The traditional, customary, unwritten law of England, which began to develop over a 1000 years before U.S. law.

Equal Protection clause Part of the Fourteenth Amendment that prohibits states from denying any person within their jurisdictions equal protection of the law.

error-correcting function The appellate courts' power of review.

Establishment clause A section of the First Amendment that prohibits the government from favoring or endorsing one religion over another.

evidence Items or testimony presented for the purpose of proving or refuting an issue.

exceptional cases Cases that do not conform to definitions of a normal case.

exclusionary rule A court rule stating that evidence secured by illegal means cannot be introduced in a criminal trial.

executive orders Rules declared by the executive branch that have the force of law.

external ecology Pressures on the courts from cultures, people, and organizations outside the court.

extradite The process in which one state surrenders a criminal suspect or offender to another state.

Extradition clause The Interstate Rendition clause.

eyewitness testimony An account given by a person of an event he or she has witnessed.

F

federalist system A system of government in which the national government shares power with the states; also called dual sovereignty.

federal-state scheme The categorization of appeal cases based on geographic jurisdiction.

federal supremacy The requirement that if a state law conflicts with a federal law, the state law must be changed, abolished, or overridden by federal enforcement.

felony A criminal offense that carries a possible sentence ranging from over a year incarceration in a prison to execution.

final-judgment rule A rule that states that appeals can be made only after a defendant is convicted and sentenced at trial.

finder of fact The entity that applies substantive law to the charges and evidence presented against the defendant.

first appearance The initial hearing in which a defendant is advised of his or her rights and the procedure the court will follow.

formal sanctions Responses to a violation of a codified rule by an agent of an official organization designated to enforce that rule.

formal social control Efforts by official agencies, acting in their designated capacity, to constrain and direct the conduct of people.

Full Faith and Credit clause The constitutional requirement that states respect the laws of other states.

G

Gemeinschaft Small tribes in which everyone shares the same ethnicity and culture.

general deterrence The idea that a punishment applied to one person will influence the judgment of others to obey the law.

geographic jurisdiction The authority of a court to hear a case as determined by the location of the offense.

Gesellschaft Large, heterogeneous, complex societies.

going rate The common understanding that prosecutors and defense attorneys have as to the most likely sentence given for a specific offense.

good-faith exception Refers to an exception made to the exclusionary rule when the court believes that a law enforcement officer isn't trying to be deceptive and is doing the job as he or she understands the law.

grand jury A panel of citizens who are convened to review the prosecutor's bill of indictment.

grant *certiorari* The practice of issuing a writ of *certiorari* ordering the lower court to send up the files.

H

habeas corpus An order to bring a party before the court.

hearsay evidence Evidence in which the witness tells what others have said instead of telling what he or she knows.

hedonistic calculus An idea that an offender makes a decision to break the law based on the potential rewards of the offense, the risk of getting caught, and the severity of the punishment.

hierarchical jurisdiction The authority of a court to hear a case as determined by the court's function.

higher courts Courts that do not hear trials but instead have appellate jurisdiction.

horizontal plea An agreement with the prosecutor in which the prosecutor dismisses several charges in return for a guilty plea on one of them.

hung jury A jury that cannot agree on a verdict of guilty or not guilty.

I

indictment A charge of felony voted by a grand jury based upon a proposed charge presented by the prosecutor. Sometimes called a "true bill."

indirect evidence Evidence that does not directly connect the defendant to the offense and requires some reasoning to be used as proof.

information A criminal charge brought by the prosecutor without a grand jury indictment.

initial appearance The first time a defendant appears in front of a judge.

interlocutory appeal An appeal made before or during a trial that seeks to clarify an important issue that may affect the case-in-chief and cannot effectively be addressed after the trial.

intermediate court–high court–final court scheme The categorization of appeal cases based on their location in the court hierarchy.

intermediate courts of appeals The circuit courts of appeals within the nine federal appellate circuits of the United States.

internal ecology The characteristics within the court that frames the decisions, actions, and motivations of the individuals participating in it.

Interstate Rendition clause Constitutional requirement that a state return a criminal suspect to the state in which the offense occurred if that state requests it. Often called the Extradition clause.

J

Jim Crow laws Laws in the southern United States that enforced racial segregation.

judgment See ruling.

judicial accountability The idea that judges should defer to the wishes and opinions of the electorate.

judicial activism A term applied to judicial decisions that appear to contradict voters' desires or are suspected of being based on the judge's personal or political preferences rather than on law.

judicial independence The idea that the judiciary should not be affected by other branches of government, or private or partisan interests.

judicial restraint A judge's choice to limit the exercise of his or her own power and defer to written law as long as it is constitutional.

judicial review The power of the court to review the procedures in individual cases and the constitutionality of laws and executive branch policies.

judicial waiver A form of juvenile transfer that either authorizes or requires juvenile court judges to waive certain types of cases.

judiciary The court system.

jurisdiction The legal authority of a court to hear and rule on a particular case.

jury nullification The jury's acquittal of a defendant in disregard of the judge's instructions and contrary to the jury's findings of fact.

justice A judge.

justiciability Whether or not a case can be heard by a court.

justiciability doctrines Legal principles that identify what issues can and cannot be heard in a court of law.

L

labeling Applying a tag to a person that can affect self-perception and behavior.

law According to Max Weber: "Codified rules of conduct that are established by the government, that the people within the jurisdiction must follow, and that agents of the government can enforce with the use or threat of punishment."

leading question A query that suggests a preferred answer.

legal logic The capacity to understand and engage power, disputes, and resolutions in terms of legal principles and rules.

legal merits The facts of the case, substantive law, and precedent that serve as the legal basis of attorney decision-making and judicial rulings.

legal principles The ideals and imperatives that serve as the basis for legal thinking and guide legal decision-making.

legal procedures The rules that specify how lawyers and judges are to proceed when enforcing substantive criminal law.

legal reality The priorities, social relationships, hierarchies, values, and processes that are established and maintained by the legal system.

legal reasoning The logic, evidence, laws, principles, language, and strategies lawyers and judges use in deciding if the facts of the case match the law.

legal rules The specific laws and procedures derived from foundational legal principles.

legal–rational authority The idea that the creation and enforcement of law is based on stable principles and rules.

lex talionis The ancient law of retribution, best represented by the statement "an eye for an eye."

M

mandatory–discretionary categorization scheme The categorization of appeal cases based on the court's responsibility and power to hear a case.

mandatory minimum laws Statutes that mandate sentence lengths based on the type of offense.

mens rea The intent of the accused to commit the offense and/or produce the resultant harm. "Guilty mind."

mental health courts A branch of the criminal court that specializes in finding treatment for and assisting mentally ill offenders.

military commission Courts used to try violations of the laws of war and other offenses.

Miranda **rights** A rule set forth by the U.S. Supreme Court in *Miranda v. Arizona* (1966) that states that prior to the arrest and any interrogation of suspects, they must be told they have the right to remain silent, the right to legal counsel, and the right to be told that anything they say can be used against them in court.

misdemeanor A lesser offense than a felony with a maximum sentence that may include jail time, fines, community service hours, probation, and other forms of community corrections.

mistrial The ending of a trial before its regular conclusion because of procedural errors, the prejudicing of a jury, jury deadlock, or failure to complete the trial within a specified time limit.

N

negotiated order Informal routines among the workers that emerge over time as the workers themselves negotiate (or interact) with the court's formal structure, each other, and external organizations and conditions.

net-widening Activities undertaken by a legal system to increase the number of people involved in the system and to increase the involvement of those already in the system.

no bill A notice from a grand jury that it has failed to find probable cause to prosecute.

no-contest plea A defendant's agreement with the prosecutor that he or she will not contest the charge.

nolle prosequi The declaration by the prosecutor that the charges against the accused are being dropped.

nolo contendere Latin for "I will not contest." Allows defendants to neither admit nor deny responsibility for the charges, but still accept punishment.

notice of appeal A document that advises the court and the opposing party that the appellant is appealing the court's decision.

O

officer of the court Any court worker who has an obligation to promote justice and effective operation of the judicial system.

ombud A neutral party within an organization who provides conflict resolution and problem-solving services.

opinion A statement that states the court's ruling and explains the legal reasoning behind it.

P

parens patriae The principle that the government has the duty to act as guardian of people who cannot effectively take care of themselves.

parole The release of inmate early for good behavior or a demonstration of rehabilitative success and as long as he or she abides by conditions of the early release.

Peace of Westphalia A set of treaties in 1648 that ended the Thirty Years War in Europe.

per curiam opinion Decisions that generally deal with issues that the court does not view as controversial because they have been settled in earlier cases.

peremptory challenge An attorney's opposition of including a prospective juror on a jury that does not require a stated cause or reason.

petition To submit a written request to a court.

petitioner See appellant.

petit jury A jury that sits on a trial.

plain error A serious defect in a trial.

plea bargain A negotiation between the defense and prosecution in which the defendant agrees to plead guilty or no contest to some offenses in return for reduction or dismissal of some charges or a reduced sentence.

precedent A legal decision that is cited as a rule to resolve similar legal questions in later cases.

preliminary hearing A court proceeding to determine if a suspect charged with a felony should be tried based on probable cause that he or she committed the offense.

preponderance of the evidence The standard of proof for plaintiffs in civil cases and the prosecutor's standard in establishing exceptions to the exclusionary rule. A less severe standard than beyond a reasonable doubt.

presentence–direct–postconviction categorization scheme The categorization of appeal cases based on its chronology.

presentence investigation The report prepared to assist a judge in sentencing, which usually contains information about the offender's arrests, convictions, work history, and family.

preserve When an attorney challenges during pretrial or trial the constitutionality of a part of the case he or she may wish to appeal.

pretrial motions Arguments made before a trial about how the trial is to be conducted.

preventive detention The detention of a defendant awaiting trial in order to prevent further criminal offending or to protect an individual or society.

principle of legality A principle that mandates that the courts enforce only positive laws; that the laws apply equally to all members of the society; and that law adhere to corollary principles. Also called the rule of law.

prior restraint The prohibition by the government of documents or speech before publication or broadcast.

Privileges and Immunities clause The constitutional requirement that a state treats its residents and residents of other states equally.

probable cause Sufficient reason to believe a criminal offense has been committed. Required for police to make an arrest, conduct a search, or seize evidence, and for prosecutors during preliminary hearings.

probation A sentence in which a convicted person stays in the community as long as he or she follows court-ordered conditions.

procedural due process Government agents must adhere to the lawful procedures when processing a case.

procedural due-process challenges When attorneys argue that there was a violation of constitutional rights and that the violation was substantial, material, or prejudicial.

procedural justice The expectation of fairness in legal proceedings.

procedural law Statutes that constrain and direct the conduct of the agents of the state when they are processing a case.

professionalization The professional training and certification of workers.

public law Law that defines and regulates the relationship, which individuals and organizations have with the state.

public policy Government efforts to achieve social goals.

R

real evidence Concrete objects that link a defendant to a criminal charge.

recidivism Repeat offending.

recidivism rates The percentage of ex-convicts who are convicted of new offenses after being released from prison.

recusal The disqualification of a judge or jury for reasons of prejudice or conflict of interest.

reduced-sentence plea An agreement with the prosecutor in which the defendant serves less than the maximum sentence in exchange for a guilty plea.

rehabilitation and reentry programs Plans that aim to improve offenders and prepare them for self-sufficient and law-abiding lives.

release-on-recognizance The release of a defendant without bail based on the defendant's promise to return to court.

religion-based court systems Courts that have elements of common law precedent and civil law statutes that add a religious component to their proceedings.

remand When a judge sends a case back to the trial court for further action.

reply brief A document that addresses objections raised by the respondent.

rendition The process of sending a criminal suspect to another country to be interrogated or detained.

res judicata A settled matter that cannot be judged again.

respondent See appellee.

response brief A document submitted by the appellee addressing the appellant's initial brief.

restorative justice An informal method of resolving disputes between individuals that acts to preserve their relationships.

reverse When a superior court annuls, cancels, vacates, or sets aside the decision of the lower court.

rules of evidence The definitions of what constitutes evidence and how it is introduced in court.

rule of four When four of nine U.S. Supreme Court justices vote to accept a petition.

ruling The court's decision.

S

sequester To confine jurors together in a location away from their homes, under the supervision of court authorities, throughout all or part of a trial.

Shari'a Law derived from the Koran.

social control A concerted effort or process that constrains and directs the conduct of people by inducing conformity and preventing nonconformity.

social engineering Intentional efforts by the government to change a population's beliefs, attitudes, and behavioral patterns.

socialization The process of learning a group's norms and habits.

social location The status, disadvantages, and privileges one enjoys based upon their social class, sex, age, and race.

social order A society's ability to operate in predictable patterns.

sociological variables Attributes that place people into social categories, such as race, social class, sex, and employment status.

specialized courts Branches of the criminal court that deal with specific segments of the offender population who may respond better to treatment than to punishment.

specific deterrence The idea that a punishment applied to one person influences the judgment of that person not to break the law again.

stare decisis The principle that a trial court is bound by appellate court decisions. Short for *stare decisis et non quieta movere*, which means "to stand by decisions and not disturb settled points."

status offense The breaking of a law that only applies to juveniles.

statutes Laws written by the legislature.

statutory exclusion A form of juvenile waiver that requires certain delinquency cases to be waived automatically.

statutory law Laws enacted by national and state legislatures.

street crime Felonies and misdemeanors, usually low level, that involve offenses against the person and some types of property crime.

subject-matter jurisdiction The authority of a court to hear a case as determined by the type of offense.

substantive due process The constitutional principle that people have basic rights that the government cannot violate without clear justification.

substantive due-process challenges An assertion that the law itself or one of its provisions is unconstitutional.

substantive law Statutes that establish the rights and obligations of individuals in society and define criminal offenses and punishments.

Supremacy clause The constitutional requirement that contradictions between state and federal law shall be resolved in favor of the federal law.

systemic agency Imperatives set on the workers not by a single boss but by the legal system itself.

systemic imperatives What a person or organization must do in order to survive and flourish within a system.

T

test cases Strategies that involve having someone violate a law, be convicted in a trial, and then appeal the case on the grounds that the law is unconstitutional.

testimonial evidence Declarations from witnesses that link a defendant to a criminal charge.

three-strikes laws Statutes that mandate a lengthy sentence on the third offense.

traditional authority According to Weber, societies that have no stand-alone government to write and enforce rules because the rules and leaders are respected and followed as a matter of culture and traditions.

trial by battle An ancient method of establishing guilt or innocence in which two opponents would fight each other until submission or death, with the winner being declared the legal victor.

trial by compurgation An ancient method of establishing guilt or innocence in which a defendant would establish innocence by asking or paying others to testify to the accused's innocence.

trial by ordeal An ancient method of establishing guilt or innocence in which the accused would be physically tortured with the belief that an innocent person would be delivered from the ordeal by divine intervention.

trial *de novo* A whole new trial excluding illegal evidence.

trier of law The judge in his or her role of assuring due process of law and protecting the rights of the accused.

true bill A notice from a grand jury that it has found probable cause to prosecute.

U

urbanization A process in which people move from rural areas to urban areas.

V

venire The list from which a jury is selected.

venue The particular court that hears a case.

vertical plea An agreement with the prosecutor in which a defendant pleads guilty or no contest to a charge less serious than the one with which he or she was originally charged.

vertical prosecution When a single attorney handles a case from the initial screening all the way to dismissal, acquittal, or sentencing.

veterans' treatment courts A branch of the criminal court that specializes in assisting veterans who have broken the law.

victimless crime A criminal offense that does not directly harm people or property but offends the social mores and norms of a large segment of society.

voir dire The process used to question the potential jurors about a wide range of issues that may influence their objectivity.

W

Warren Court The U.S. Supreme Court from 1953 to 1969 when Chief Justice Earl Warren led the due-process revolution.

wergeld The monetary value of a person's life paid as compensation by the family of an accused murderer to the family of the deceased in order to prevent a blood feud.

writ of *certiorari* An order to the intermediate court of appeals, district court, special federal court, and/or state high court to send their trial transcripts to the Supreme Court for review.

Y

youth court An informal court composed of youths who handle the minor offenses of other youths.

Case Index

577

Subject Index

Note: Page numbers followed by *"f" "b"* and *"t"* refer to figures, boxes and tables, respectively.

579